THIRD EDITION

COMMUNITY PSYCHOLOGY

KAREN GROVER DUFFY

State University of New York at Geneseo

FRANK Y. WONG

George Washington University
School of Public Health and Health Services

Boston ■ New York ■ San Francisco
Mexico City ■ Montreal ■ Toronto ■ London ■ Madrid ■ Munich ■ Paris
Hong Kong ■ Singapore ■ Tokyo ■ Cape Town ■ Sydney

For PJD

Executive Editor: *Carolyn O. Merrill*
Editorial Assistant: *Jonathan Bender*
Marketing Manager: *Wendy Gordon*
Editorial-Production Administrator: *Annette Joseph*
Editorial-Production Coordinator: *Holly Crawford*
Editorial-Production Service: *Lynda Griffiths, TKM Productions*
Composition Buyer: *Linda Cox*
Electronic Composition: *TKM Productions*
Manufacturing Buyer: *JoAnne Sweeney*
Cover Administrator: *Kristina Mose-Libon*
Cover Designer: *Joel Gendron*

For related titles and support materials, visit our online catalog at www.ablongman.com

Between the time Website information is gathered and then published, it is not unusual for some sites to have closed. Also, the transcription of URLs can result in unintended typographical errors. The publisher would appreciate notification where these occur so that they may be corrected in subsequent editions.

Library of Congress Cataloging-in-Publication Data

Duffy, Karen Grover.
  Community psychology / Karen Grover Duffy, Frank Y. Wong.--3rd ed.
    p. cm.
  Includes bibliographical references and indexes.
  ISBN 0-205-35026-7
    1. Community psychology. I. Wong, Frank Y.

  RA790.55 .D84 2003
  362.2--dc21

                              2002019620

Printed in the United States of America

10 9 8 7 6 5   RRD-IN   07 06

BRIEF CONTENTS

CONTENTS

CHAPTER 4

Creating and Sustaining Social Change   72

PART III COMMUNITY MENTAL HEALTH

PART IV   COMMUNITY PSYCHOLOGY IN OTHER SETTINGS

CHAPTER 7

Social and Human Services in the Community   138

CHAPTER 10

Health Care   218

CHAPTER 11

Community Health and Preventive Medicine   229

CHAPTER 12

Community Organizational Psychology   256

PREFACE

Welcome to the field of community psychology. We trust that you will find our book to be a scholarly, complete, yet engaging and interesting introduction to community psychology. This text presents a general overview of the concepts, theories, and research in the field of community psychology. The extensive scope of this book showcases more than community mental health issues. We believe that the field of community psychology has long outgrown its mental health image and is ready for a new text that goes beyond that focus.

Using our book, you, the reader, will develop an appreciation for community psychology. This text will foster an understanding of and a respect for the values of community psychology that often go beyond those of traditional psychology to which most of you have already been exposed. Although *Community Psychology* is designed for upper-division psychology students, it is suitable for all perceptive students who have a rudimentary background in psychology. We hope the book promotes in you a respect for the cultural diversity of this country's communities. Wherever we can, we highlight research on cultural diversity.

This third edition of *Community Psychology* is comprised of five parts and 13 chapters. The first 2 chapters (Part I) are introductory and will educate you about the purpose, history, philosophy, and research methods in community psychology. Part II pertains to social change. In the first chapter of Part II, you will discover what social change is, why it is important, and how change is implemented in the community.

The chapters that follow systematically examine various community settings, interventions, and populations of interest to community psychologists. We examine in each chapter a few of the traditional approaches to serving the affected groups and settings and then review some of the alternative approaches as developed within community psychology. We do so first for the classic area in community psychology—mental health. Two chapters (Chapters 5 and 6) are dedicated to mental health because it is still a prominent theme in the field. These two chapters constitute Part III.

Part IV features areas into which community psychology has expanded since its inception. Chapters 7 through 12 focus on social and human services, schools and education, law and society, health care, preventive medicine, and community organizations. Again, in each of these chapters, we first explore past approaches to relevant issues and then discuss alternatives offered by community psychologists. Finally, we conclude the text with Chapter 13, which summarizes the field and forecasts future trends for community psychology (Part V).

Every chapter contains special interest features that we believe will engage you, our student readers. The Cases in Point are designed to make the issue or topic practical and to stimulate critical thinking. In the typical Case in Point, a topic such as homelessness or community conflict is discussed in two ways: The issues related to the topic are examined and/or the relevant research is reviewed.

The chapters also contain several pedagogical aids. Each chapter begins with a chapter outline and an opening vignette. The vignettes are alluded to throughout the chapters and are used to crystallize the material at various points in your reading. We have done something with these vignettes that might be highly controversial for some adopters. The vignettes start with a case history, a very clinical and therefore a debatable approach. We did so in recognition of the fact that more than half of the graduate community psychology programs are clinical-community programs. For instructors trained in this tradition, the opening vignettes will assist them in moving their students from a clinical point of reference (in which the individual in each vignette is the "figure") to a community (or "ecological") orientation by the end of the chapter. For those instructors oriented exclusively to community psychology, the Cases in Point are constructed to be more purely based on community psychology. Instructors will want to emphasize the approach and pedagogical aid that best suits their needs. In addition, key terms that are important in the field of community psychology are boldfaced in all chapters. Each chapter then concludes with a summary.

By critically examining the field, its issues, and its research, we hope that you will be inspired to become involved in your community in meaningful ways, such as in community volunteer work, research, or political activism. We also hope that you will think about pursuing a career in the exciting field of community psychology.

ACKNOWLEDGMENTS

We would be remiss if we did not thank the many people involved in this project. We owe sincere gratitude to the individuals who encouraged us in this undertaking and whose remarks on earlier drafts were extremely helpful. We also wish to thank our reviewers, whose critical appraisals of the book often helped us reframe issues and add material that resulted in a better product. The reviewers of this edition include Stephen Couch, Pennsylvania State University; Jean Ann Linney, University of South Carolina; and Paul A. Toro, Wayne State University.

We are grateful to the many individuals at Allyn and Bacon for their patience, gentle prodding, and insights. Our thanks also go to our families, friends, and colleagues who also demonstrated immense kindness and patience while we pounded away on our computers and spent long hours in library stacks searching for materials. Special gratitude is extended to Karen Duffy's students who graciously consented to having their contributions included and to her many students who studied from and stumbled through earlier rough drafts, pencil marks and all. Our sincerest thanks to everyone.

K. G. D.
F. Y. W.

ABOUT THE AUTHORS

Karen Grover Duffy received her Bachelor of Science degree in psychology with honors from St. Lawrence University and her doctoral degree in social/personality psychology from Michigan State University in 1973. Since then, she has been a professor of psychology at the State University of New York (SUNY) at Geneseo, where she teaches general, community, organizational, social, and personality psychology. While at SUNY Geneseo, she also developed the community internship program for psychology students.

Duffy serves on the advisory board for the Center for Dispute Settlement, one of the oldest community mediation programs in the country, and has served at various times on other community agency boards. She won the Gold Mediator award for her service as a certified community and family mediator. Recently, she won the Community Service for Peace Award for her work in conflict resolution.

In 1995 and 2000, Duffy also won Fulbright Fellowships to teach community psychology and community mediation at St. Petersburg University, St. Petersburg, Russia. She has also returned to Russia to teach and to work with various community agencies, including AIDS International and Partnership for Children. Duffy became a distinguished Service Professor within the SUNY system for her community work and also was the recipient of the New York United Teachers Community Service Award as well as the Harry Van Arsdale Community Service Award from the AFL-CIO of New York State.

Frank Y. Wong, Ph.D., is an Associate Research Professor at the Prevention and Community Health Department and a Senior Research Staff Scientist at the Center of Health Services Research and Policy, both of the George Washington University School of Public Health and Health Services. Dr. Wong has ongoing national and international research programs on HIV and substance abuse targeting vulnerable and underserved populations. He has served as a consultant to various national, state, regional, and local agencies on health-related prevention and intervention efforts (including health policy).

INTRODUCTION TO COMMUNITY PSYCHOLOGY

*Social progress makes the well-being of all more and more the business of each; it binds
all closer and closer together in bonds from which none escape.*
—Henry George, 1884

Dory was born Doreen Snyder. While her mother was pregnant, Dory's father abandoned them. Dory's mother did not want to go on public assistance, so she worked two
different jobs. From 7 A.M. to 4 P.M., Mrs. Snyder worked at a budget hotel as a house-
keeper. From 6 P.M. to 11 P.M., she worked as a short-order cook in a local bar. Dory's
mother was just able to make enough to pay for the rent, food, and Dory's child care with
an older woman who also cared for four other children. The truth is that the Snyders lived
in poverty.

When Dory was 3 years old, her caregiver remarked to Mrs. Snyder that Dory was "odd" compared to the other children. By odd, the woman meant that Dory did not laugh and giggle or play with the other children. When Dory entered school, her mother was very proud and also relieved, since the child-care cost would be reduced. However, Mrs. Snyder was soon confronted with the same news about Dory's strange behavior. Dory did not interact with the other children and seemed aloof when the teacher tried to engage her in conversation or in the learning process.

The school recommended an evaluation, which showed that Dory did have some "personality problems," as the psychologist called them, and that Dory's speech was delayed. The psychologist suggested a special class for Dory. Dory seemed to do well in this special class until the school was faced with declining enrollments, at which point the school closed. Dory was transferred to a bigger school where she seemed to get lost in the shuffle. She did not make much progress in her learning or her social skills from then on.

One day when Dory was about 16 years old, her mother received a call from the school saying that Dory had been truant for several days. When her mother confronted Dory about this, Dory flew into a rage, ran out the door, and disappeared onto the streets of the city. At first, Dory's mother searched for her and filed a missing person's report. After several days, when her mother had given up hope of finding her runaway daughter, Dory returned home.

The cycle of Mrs. Snyder's confronting Dory about attending school or obtaining a job and Dory fleeing in anger was to be repeated several times. Each time Dory left her mother's small, dingy apartment, her disappearance grew longer and longer. When Dory was about 19 years old, she disappeared onto the streets for the final time. She became one of America's homeless.

On the streets, Dory eventually established a small territory that she considered hers in which she routinely wandered and foraged each day. She knew that Mrs. Fisher at the bakery would give her day-old cookies late each afternoon. She also visited Randy's Diner late at night for whatever was left over. Sundays were particularly hard on Dory, as neither the diner nor the bakery was open. At night, Dory slept in an alley under her big coat, which she had been given by a local shelter for the homeless. Dory often frequented this same shelter in inclement weather. Dory had no other relatives in the big, cold city who could take her in.

Dory knew she was a bit odd and could feel other people's discomfort in her presence, so she became a loner. This is probably why no one missed her for several days. Mrs. Fisher at the bakery finally became concerned that Dory had not appeared for several afternoons. The weather had been particularly harsh, too, with temperatures below zero. Mrs. Fisher called the shelter she knew Dory frequented, only to find that the shelter manager had not seen Dory either. Mrs. Fisher's worst fears were realized when she heard from another homeless person that Dory's body had been found under some newspapers in an alley not far from the bakery. Dory had frozen to death.

Pressing community problems such as acquired immune deficiency syndrome (AIDS), homelessness, school failure, teenage pregnancy, chemical dependency, violent crime, and the "isms" (ageism, racism, and sexism) require interdependent and long-lasting interventions. Unfortunately, single approaches to intervention usually seem to dominate in our society (Kelly, 1990). Which discipline asserts that addressing these problems in a multifocused fashion is its goal? *Community psychology*—the focus of this book.

This chapter will examine the history and growth, philosophy and goals, and current status of community psychology. This background should provide you with ample knowledge as well as encouragement to explore the rest of this book.

BRIEF HISTORICAL BACKGROUND

In colonial times, the United States was not without social problems. However, the close-knit, agrarian communities that existed often cared for needy individuals, and such care was generally provided without special places to house these individuals (Rappaport, 1977). As cities grew and became industrialized, a trend developed to institutionalize various populations: people who were mentally ill, indigent, and otherwise powerless. Perhaps from an abnormal psychology or other class, you know what these early institutions were like. They were often dank, crowded places where treatment ranged from restraint to cruel punishment.

It was not until the 1700s that Philip Pinel, followed somewhat later by Dorothea Dix and others, attempted to reform institutions by removing the restraints and establishing more positive attempts at changing behavior. However, these more "moral" treatments were sometimes limited to people of financial means (Rappaport, 1977). Nonetheless, institutions, especially the public ones, continued to grow and to house lower-class as well as powerless and other less privileged members of society. As waves of early immigrants entered the United States, many were often mistakenly diagnosed as mentally incompetent and found themselves in the same overpopulated institutions.

In the late 1800s, Sigmund Freud developed a keen interest in mental illness and its then current treatment. You are probably already familiar with his method of treatment, **psychoanalysis,** and his other contributions to psychology and psychiatry. Freud's basic premise was that emotional disturbance was due to intrapsychic forces within the individual and caused by past experiences. These disturbances could be treated by individual therapy and by attention to the unconscious. Freud gave us a legacy of intervention aimed at the individual (rather than the societal) level. Likewise, Freud conferred on the profession the strong tendency to divest individuals of the power to heal themselves; the physician, or expert, knew more about psychic healing than did the patient. Freud also oriented professional healers to examine an individual's past rather than current circumstances as the cause of disturbance and to view anxiety and underlying disturbance as endemic to everyday life. Freud certainly concentrated on an individual's weaknesses rather than strengths.

With regard to Dory Snyder, the young woman you met in the chapter opening, Freud probably would have maintained that her so-called personality problem stemmed from her father's absence and her mother's passing her off to another caregiver. He would have focused on Dory's problems rather than on any competencies she might have. Many other forms of therapy today are based on the assumption that individuals can be treated out of context—that is, without regard to their situation—and that professionals possess the most expert knowledge and therefore ought to design the treatment. Such philosophies fly in the face of community psychology.

World War II commenced around the time of Freud's death. Because of the war, there was an influx of immigrants to the United States. At the same time, large numbers of civilians with emotional problems were also being turned away from the armed services. These situations, in part, fostered the growth of professional psychology as society sought more healers for its disturbed masses.

At about the same time, President Franklin Roosevelt proclaimed his New Deal era. Specifically, heeding the lessons of the Great Depression of the 1920s and 1930s, he proposed a two-pronged approach for attacking poverty: income transfers and employment programs. Both led to the development of the social security system, unemployment and disability benefits, and a variety of work relief programs. President Roosevelt's programs seemed more employment based than anything; at the time, there were no broad-based programs to attack poverty (Gottschalk & Gottschalk, 1988). For example, many women did not work. They could not benefit from these programs, however, even though they may have been living in poverty. On the other hand, the idea that poverty (at least as caused by unemployment) can be rectified with social programs had been planted in the American psyche.

Another important point in the history of the development of community psychology occurred in 1946 when Congress passed the National Mental Health Act. This act gave the United States Public Health Service broad authority to combat mental illness and to promote mental health. With the passage of this act and the interest in mental illness generated by the war, clinical psychology began to thrive. Shortly thereafter, the National Institute of Mental Health was established; this organization made significant federal funds available for research and training in mental health issues (Strother, 1987).

At the time, clinical psychologists were battling with psychiatrists to expand their domain from testing, which had been their primary thrust, to psychotherapy (Walsh, 1987). Today, **clinical psychology** is the field within psychology that deals with the diagnosis, measurement, and treatment of mental illness. It differs from **psychiatry,** in part, in that psychiatrists have a medical degree and can prescribe medication. Psychiatrists, then, might have medicated Dory Snyder so that she would have fit into her school environment better. On the other hand, clinical psychologists hold doctorates or Ph.D.s in psychology, which are considered to be research degrees. The battle between the two fields continues today, as some psychologists seek the right to administer and prescribe medications and to obtain privileges at the balance of the hospitals that do not yet allow them to practice (Sammons, Gorny, Zinner, & Allen, 2000). Case in Point 1.1 discusses another issue, the identity crisis that community psychology continues to experience both within and outside of the field.

Another aspect of history related to both world wars is that when formerly healthy veterans of the wars returned home, some returned as psychiatric casualties (Rappaport, 1977; Strother, 1987). What had intervened to change the soldiers' mental status? The wars. The terror of war forced psychologists to recognize the role the environment plays in an individual's mental health. Consider Dory, for instance. Perhaps Dory's placement in a large, less caring school or her family's poverty rather than something inherent in Dory's

■ ■ ■ ■ ■

CASE IN POINT 1.1
CLINICAL PSYCHOLOGY, COMMUNITY PSYCHOLOGY: WHAT'S THE DIFFERENCE?

Is community psychology experiencing growing pains? Perhaps the field of community psychology is mimicking the field of psychology as a whole. Just as psychologists have labored to distinguish themselves and their work from psychiatry, so, too, have community psychologists attempted to differentiate themselves from clinical psychology—but not without debate.

Few community psychologists would argue that clinical psychology and community psychology are exactly the same. On the other hand, some community psychologists appear unsure where the boundaries between the two subfields really are.

Dana Wardlaw (2000) attempted to research just how well defined the field of community psychology is. Using *The Community Psychologist* (the newsletter of the Society for Community Research and Action), Wardlaw found that many community psychologists have voiced their concern about "community psychology [as] a discipline seeking to establish its own identity within the realms of academic and community activism" (p. 17).

Surely, clinical psychology differs from community psychology in that clinical psychology is reactive (applying treatments after the fact) while community psychology is proactive (seeking to actually alleviate risk and promote health within communities). Wardlaw's research revealed that on this point some community psychologists feel that the field is "all talk and no action" while others feel the field is already too activist oriented.

In the same issue of the newsletter, results of a survey of community psychologists disclosed again that the field may well have a mixed identity (Solarz, 2000). Many survey respondents acknowledged that they work in academia (nearly 70 percent), not in the field or the community; we therefore might question whether academics indeed have their finger on the pulse of community life. And, while the discipline propones the celebration of diversity, most community psychologists are White (over 80 percent). Just how sensitive, then, are community psychologists to the diversity found in U.S. communities?

character or in her family background promoted further decline in her learning and social skills.

In 1949, the United States Public Health Service sponsored a conference in Boulder, Colorado. At this conference, the participants fashioned a model for the training of clinical psychologists that would guide training for years to come (Rappaport, 1977). The model emphasized education in science *and* in the practice of testing and therapy. Psychologists sometimes credit this event with the ability of psychology to further divorce itself from psychiatry, or the field of human medicine.

The 1950s brought significant change to the treatment of mental illness. One of the most influential developments was the discovery of pharmacologic agents that could be used to treat psychosis and other forms of mental illness. Various antipsychotics, tranquilizers, antidepressants, and other medications created extensive change in the institutions, the major change being that patients became more tractable, or docile. The use of these drugs proliferated despite their major side effects.

In 1952, a pioneering article was published. Hans Eysenck, Sr., a renowned British scientist, launched an attack on the practice of psychotherapy (Eysenck, 1952, 1961). By reviewing the literature on psychotherapy, Eysenck was able to demonstrate that no treatment—in fact, the mere passage of time—was often as effective as professional treatment. Other mental health professionals followed suit and leveled criticisms at other psychological practices, such as psychological testing (Meehl, 1954, 1960), and the whole concept, or "myth," of mental illness (Elvin, 2000; Szasz, 1961). These criticisms, of course, have not gone unrebutted; we will review these issues further in the chapters on mental illness. If intervention were not useful, as Eysenck maintained, individuals like Dory Snyder would be left to roam the streets because they would be given little hope by the helping professions, especially if communities and helping systems remained uncaring.

The 1960s witnessed further, sometimes sweeping, reforms. The Civil Rights movement of the 1950s carried over to the 1960s. Minorities, women, and other less privileged members of society cried out for equal rights. At the same time, foreign economic competition, the threat of nuclear confrontation with the former Soviet Union, and the space race forced U.S. citizens to adopt more outward-looking viewpoints. Psychologists were therefore encouraged to "do something to participate in society as psychologists" (Walsh, 1987, p. 524). Those issues, coupled with the increasing moral outrage over the Vietnam War, fueled excitement about citizen involvement in social reform and generated understanding about the interdependence of social movements (Kelly, 1990).

With the election of John Kennedy as president came an invigorated concern about institutionalization, mental health, and the general availability of human services. Kennedy's own sister with mental retardation may have augmented his interest in these issues. Kennedy also was elected on his platform of social change. Social conditions and poverty, he reasoned, were responsible in large part for negative psychological conditions (Heller, Price, Reinharz, Riger, & Wandersman, 1984). Kennedy helped secure the passage of the Community Mental Health Centers Act of 1963, which authorized funds for *local* mental health centers. The centers were to provide outpatient, emergency, and educational services, among others. Although not without problems and not necessarily revolutionary, this act recognized the need for immediate, local intervention in the form of emergency services as well as the need for prevention through education. Such centers meant that individuals like Dory Snyder could seek immediate assistance right in their own neighborhoods.

After Kennedy's assassination, President Lyndon Johnson appeared to be moving the country toward "the Great Society." For the first time, a president issued a blueprint for the War on Poverty in his State of the Union address. The 1964 annual report of the President's Council of Economic Advisors stated:

> Conquest of poverty is well within our power. About $11 billion a year would bring all poor families up to the $3,000 income level we have taken to be the minimum for a decent life. The majority of the Nation could simply tax themselves enough to provide the necessary income supplements to their less fortunate citizens.... But this "solution" would have untouched most of the roots of poverty. Americans want to earn the American standard of living by their own efforts and contributions. It will be far better, even if more difficult, to equip and to permit the poor of the Nation to produce and to earn the additional $11 billion, and more.

These statements strongly indicate that President Johnson and his advisors wanted to find ways or mechanisms that could empower people who were less fortunate, to assist them to become productive citizens. Programs such as **Head Start** (addressed in Chapter 8) and other federally funded early childhood enhancement programs for the disadvantaged were conceived within this ideology. Also, many of the prototypes of social and human services were developed around this time. (The social history of the United States will be discussed in other parts of this book.)

Although less important to social history, very important to the history of community psychology was a conference held in Swampscott, Massachusetts, in May of 1965. This conference is usually cited as the official birth date of community psychology (Heller et al., 1984; Hersch, 1969; Rappaport, 1977). This first conference was attended by clinical psychologists concerned with the inadequacies of their field and oriented to creating social and political change. As a result of their small-group discussions, the Swampscott participants agreed to move from treatment to prevention and to the inclusion of an ecological perspective (loosely, a person-environment fit) in their work (Bennett et al., 1966). This perspective is from Kurt Lewin (1951), the father of social psychology, another area of psychology much akin to community psychology.

The Swampscott Conference was followed by other conferences. Today, research conferences are planned nearly every year. Community psychology is a recognized division of the American Psychological Association (Division 27). Several journals (the *Journal of Community Psychology,* the *American Journal of Community Psychology,* the *Journal of Rural Community Psychology,* the *Journal of Community and Applied Social Psychology,* the *Journal of Primary Prevention,* and the J*ournal of Prevention and Intervention in the Community*) represent the field, along with many other related journals on social change, community mental health, and other relevant areas (Kelly, 1990).

Contemporary community psychologists have long enjoyed intellectual and research exchanges with colleagues in other academic disciplines such as political science, anthropology, and sociology, as well as other areas of psychology such as social psychology (Altman, 1987). Some are calling for renewed interdisciplinary efforts (Linney, 1990; Wardlaw, 2000) with other community professionals, too, such as substance-abuse counselors, enforcement agencies, school psychologists, and human services professionals, among others.

Given this legacy of reform and expansion within and outside the field of psychology, what are the current goals and values of community psychology today?

PHILOSOPHY AND GOALS OF COMMMUNITY PSYCHOLOGY

Before beginning this section, the definition of *community psychology* is in order. Singular agreement on a definition for the field does not exist, but the following are among popular definitions:

> Community psychology . . . has evolved to study the effects of social and environmental factors on behavior as it occurs at individual, group, organizational, and societal levels. (Heller et al., 1984, p. 18)

> Community psychology is, in part, an attempt to find other alternatives for dealing with deviance from societal-based norms. . . . Community psychology viewed in this way is an attempt to support every person's right to be different without risk of suffering material and psychological sanctions. (Rappaport, 1977, p. 1)

> Community psychology is regarded as an approach to human behavior problems that emphasizes contributions to their development made by environmental forces as well as the potential contributions to be made toward their alleviation by the use of such forces. (Zax & Specter, 1974, p. 3)

These definitions from earlier books in the field are all useful and capture the thrust of community psychology. Our definition will complement and embellish on these to reflect changes in the field. **Community psychology** focuses on social issues, social institutions, and other settings that influence groups and organizations (and therefore the individuals in them). The goal is to optimize the well-being of communities and individuals with innovative and alternate interventions designed in collaboration with affected community members and with other related disciplines inside and outside of psychology.

With that definition in mind, discussion will turn to more specific goals and philosophies that have guided the field over the years. Remember that community psychology today is not what it was at the Swampscott Conference when participants had a decided interest in community mental health. Community psychology has shed its "mental health only" image. Also keep in mind that the community psychology you read about today will probably not be the community psychology of the next decade as the field outgrows its adolescence and matures. Each of the themes presented next is elaborated upon in depth with research and examples in other chapters. Here, the intent is merely to introduce you to each concept.

Prevention Rather than Treatment

The philosophy of **prevention** rather than treatment was inspired at the Swampscott Conference and more broadly by the public health movement (Caplan, 1964; Heller et al., 1984; Kelly, 1990) and is an important, pivotal concept in the field. The underlying theme is that treatment comes too late in the intervention process; it is usually provided long after the individual has developed the problem, so is often ineffective. Noted psychologist Emory Cowen (1980) stated, "We became increasingly, indeed alarmingly, aware of (a) the frustration and pessimism of trying to undo psychological damage once it had passed a certain critical point; (b) the costly, time-consuming, culture-bound nature of mental health's basic approaches, and their unavailability to, and effectiveness with, large segments of society in great need" (p. 259).

On the other hand, prevention might counter any trauma before it begins, thus saving the individual and perhaps the whole community from developing a problem. In this regard as stated earlier, community psychology takes a proactive rather than reactive role. For example, community psychologists believe it is possible that sex education *before* adolescence, teamed with new social policy, can reduce the teenage pregnancy rate. In the following chapters, you will read about a variety of techniques in prevention: education, altering the environment, development of alternate interventions, public policy changes, and so on (Long, 1992).

In community psychology, distinctions are made between levels of preventive intervention. **Primary prevention** attempts to prevent a problem from occurring altogether or at the earliest possible moment (Heller, Wyman, & Allen, 2000). Levine (1998) likened primary prevention to an inoculation. Just as a vaccination protects against a targeted disease, so, too, can other primary preventive strategies help an individual fend off other problems. Primary prevention refers most generally to activities that can be undertaken with a healthy population to maintain or enhance its health, physical and emotional (Bloom & Hodges, 1988), in other words "keeping healthy people healthy" (Scileppi, Teed, & Torres, 2000, p. 58). Primary prevention can also mean working with populations who are at risk for developing dysfunction and preventing the dysfunction from ever occurring (Cowen, 1997a, 1997b). Which preventive strategies are best (or are they equally efficacious) is part of the current debate in community psychology (Albee, 1998).

Cowen (1996) argued that the following criteria must be met for a program to be considered truly *primary* preventive:

- The program must be mass or group oriented.
- It must occur *before* the maladjustment.
- It must be intentional in the sense of having a primary focus on strengthening adjustment of the as yet unaffected.

Levine (1998, 1999) added further characteristics. Primary prevention interventions should include the following:

- Evaluate and promote synergistic effects and consider how to modify countervailing forces.
- Be structured to affect complex social structures, including redundant messages. They should be continued over time.
- Examine institutional and societal issues, not just individual factors.
- Recognize that whatever the program, it is but one part of a much larger cultural effort.
- Acknowledge that because high-risk behaviors tend to co-occur, several behaviors should be targeted.

On the other hand, **secondary prevention** attempts to treat a problem at the earliest possible moment before it become severe or persistent. In other words, at-risk individuals are already manifesting some symptoms or problems. For example, youths at a particular high school might already have experimented with drugs and alcohol. Secondary preventive efforts would be directed at preventing them from becoming habitual users.

Tertiary prevention, which is not the primary focus in this book, attempts to reduce the severity of a problem once it has persistently occurred, so is perceived as similar to therapy (Heller, Wyman, & Allen, 2000). In other words, at-risk individuals are already manifesting some symptoms or problematic behaviors. An example of tertiary prevention would be designing a program to help hospitalized persons with mental disorders return to the community as soon as possible (Scileppi, Teed, & Torres, 2000).

The case of Dory Snyder can be used to illustrate these concepts. In the case of Dory, early psychological testing or early knowledge of her family's poverty may have determined that she was at risk for running away. Had an intervention occurred early and prevented her homelessness, it would be an example of primary prevention. When Dory was first truant from school, had assistance been provided to her mother in dealing with her daughter, her mother would have been provided with secondary prevention. Finally, once Dory was on the streets, attempts to change her situation would have provided tertiary prevention. As you can well imagine, primary prevention is the most desirable of the preventive levels. Case in Point 1.2 discusses two different reviews of the literature that examined the efficacy of primary prevention programs. Both came to the same conclusion: Yes, primary prevention works.

■ ■ ■ ■ ■

CASE IN POINT 1.2
DOES PRIMARY PREVENTION WORK?

Community psychologists respect prevention efforts, especially those aimed at primary prevention. Can one demonstrate, however, that primary prevention works? Primary prevention programs have been around a long time. Some have been individually evaluated, but not until the 1990s did researchers set out to determine whether, overall, primary prevention works. Fortunately, two major statistical reviews of the literature, called **meta-analyses,** were performed. Each set of researchers came to the same conclusion. Primary prevention *does* work. It is helpful to understand why the converging conclusions of both studies are rather astonishing.

In the early 1990s, at the request of the U.S. Congress, the Institute of Medicine (1994) performed a statistical review of the mental health literature. Using "reduction of new cases of mental disorder" (p. 9) as its definition of *primary prevention,* the Institute of Medicine generated 1,900 journal citations on primary prevention of mental health problems. Overall, the institute found that primary prevention, as previously defined, does work. A quote from the final report divulges their conclusions: "With regard to preventive interven cases of mental disorder" (p. 9) as its definition of *primary prevention,* the Institute of Medicine generated 1,900 journal citations on primary pre-

vention of mental health problems. Overall, the institute found that primary prevention, as previously defined, does work. A quote from the final report divulges their conclusions: "With regard to preventive intervention research . . . the past decade has brought encouraging progress. At present there are many intervention programs that rest on sound conceptual and empirical foundations, and a substantial number are rigorously designed and evaluated" (p. 215).

Shortly thereafter, Durlak and Wells (1997) also completed a statistical review of the literature on primary prevention of mental health disorders. In this instance, the researchers examined programs only for children and adolescents. Using 177 programs designed to prevent behavioral and social problems such as depressive reaction to parental divorce, they, too, found empirical support for primary prevention. For example, the average participant in the primary prevention programs surpassed the performance of between 59 and 82 percent of children in control groups, depending on the study. A quote from their journal article summarizing their findings again lends support to the notion that primary prevention, at least of mental disorders, is effective: "Outcome data indicate that most categories of primary prevention programs for most categories of primary prevention programs for children and adolescents produce significant effects. These findings provide empirical support for further research and practice in primary prevention" (p. 142).

Psychologist Emory Cowen (1997) compared both of these statistical literature reviews and concluded that, although there was amazingly little overlap in the citations each set of researchers utilized, the concept of primary prevention is a sound one. One other point that Cowen made is that each meta-analysis used a different definition of *primary prevention*. Recall that the Institute of Medicine's study definition was "reduction of new cases of mental disorder." Durlak and Wells defined *primary prevention* as reducing potential for mental health problems (like the Institute of Medicine) *as well as* increasing the competencies (or well-being) of the prevention program participants. After his comparison, Cowen concluded that research on primary prevention programs is both positive and encouraging for the future.

Throughout this book, you will read about the utilities and failures of preventive programs in various settings in which psychologists work, whether they be industrial settings, law enforcement agencies, mental health agencies, or sports programs in communities. It is incumbent on psychologists, no matter where they work, to be knowledgeable about appropriate ameliorative interventions and appropriate prevention techniques (Price, Cowen, Lorion, & Ramos-McKay, 1988).

Emphasis on Strengths and Competencies

Related closely to the idea of prevention is the notion of wellness or competence. The field of psychology has historically focused on individuals' weaknesses and problems. Freud planted the seed that was cultivated by later clinicians. However, in 1959, Robert White wrote about **competence,** by which he meant a sense of mastery when interacting with the environment; competence is a basic desire to feel capable. White's notion offered a conceptual change for psychologists concerned that clinical psychology was mired in negative human behavior.

As individuals, none of us likes to feel incompetent; we like instead to feel a sense of strength that comes from mastering some part of our environment. Perhaps you recall your joy when you first passed your driver's test or your exhilaration when speaking a newly learned foreign language for the first time to a native speaker. The joy of mastery is the result of competence.

The concept of competence was quickly embraced by early community psychologists. First, it had ecological, or environmental, implications. Ecological settings could be altered to maximize an individual's competence in them, for example, placing Dory in a smaller school. Second, competence aligned nicely with the concept of prevention. If strengths were enhanced early in life, problems might be avoided more easily in the future.

Importance of the Ecological Perspective

Ecological settings can be altered; for this and other reasons, settings are important to community psychology. More correctly stated, **person-environment fit** (Pargament, 1986) is important in community psychology. Exactly what does this mean? Rappaport (1977) explained this term well. The **ecological perspective** means an examination of the relationship between persons and their environments (both social and physical) and establishment of the optimal match between the person and the setting. In other words, controlling the environment to control the individuals in it is not useful. Labeling the person who does not fit the setting as a "misfit" is also not productive. Rather, the ecological perspective recognizes the transactional nature that people and environments have. Individuals influence the settings in which they find themselves; settings influence the individuals in them (Kuo, Sullivan, Coley, & Brunson, 1998; Peterson, 1998; Seidman, 1990). If something is awry with the individual or the environment, *both* can be examined and perhaps changed in a symbiotic fashion.

A specific example of the importance of the person-environment transaction might help. Dory Snyder's earliest teachers reported to her mother that Dory seemed to have problems attending to educational and social stimuli. However, in the special class at the smaller school, Dory seemed to fare quite well. Sent to another school, with similarly trained teachers, Dory nonetheless did not flourish. The second school was larger, and for some reason Dory did not thrive there. For Dory, the smaller school seemed better. Another student with learning problems similar to Dory's but more socially engaging than Dory might have felt more comfortable in the large school and smothered in the small school. Individuals are unique and so are settings. Finding the right combination is one of the goals of community psychology.

Respect for Diversity

Dory's schools probably wished all their students were alike. How much easier the schools' jobs would be if students were homogeneous! Each individual, though, is unique. People come in all shapes and sizes, from different ethnic backgrounds, with different likes and dislikes, and with various attitudes and prejudices. Individual differences emerge by virtue of each person's unique developmental history. As people mature, they diversify; thus, people merely mimic as individuals what occurs in their communities. Often, as communities mature, they, too, diversify. The world is a more interesting place because of diversity, but it is a more complex world, too.

There is an appreciation for diversity in community psychology. People have the right to be *different,* and different does not mean *inferior.* If difference is accepted as a fact of life, then resources ought to be equitably distributed to all of these different people. These beliefs are not just noble rhetoric. From a belief in the diversity of people also comes a recognition of the distinctive styles of living, worldviews, and social arrangements that are not part of mainstream society but that characterize our society's diversity. Moreover, a recognition of these distinctions results in the ability to avoid comparing diverse populations with mainstream cultural standards and therefore labeling these different others as "deficient" or "deviant" (Snowden, 1987), as well as the ability to design interventions that are culturally appropriate (e.g., Dumas, Rollock, Prinz, Hops, & Blechman, 1999; Marin, 1993).

In an early examination of the community psychology literature, the reviewers found that about 11 percent of the articles in community psychology journals pertain to people from ethnic minorities. The authors concluded that progress toward understanding the diverse population is being made but that more needs to be done (Loo, Fong, & Iwamasca, 1988). A second early examination of the literature suggests that community psychology has had some success in improving mental health services to minorities (Snowden, 1987). However, other authors have decried the fact that there is no general framework for relating significant social-psychological markers such as gender and race to theory, research, and action in community psychology. It is hoped such a framework is emerging (Watts, 1992). Another and somewhat disappointing study indicated that community psychologists do not always practice what they preach about diversity. Suarez-Balcazar, Durlak, and Smith (1994) surveyed directors of 56 community psychology graduate programs to assess multicultural training practices and attitudes. Although most program directors agreed that cultural diversity was a major goal for training community psychologists, fewer than half of the programs required students to take any such coursework. Moreover, only half of the programs surveyed had any faculty who were members of an ethnic minority group.

A newer study (Cherniss, 1999) found that many graduate programs in community psychology have now found multiple avenues for introducing their students to diversity—for example, via the formal curriculum, research projects in minority communities, workshops on diversity, committees that develop ways to infuse the graduate program with diversity experiences, and so forth. Some in the field of community psychology still believe that certain marginalized groups continue to be ignored or underserved—for example, gays, individuals with disabilities, and women (Bond, Hill, Mulvey, & Terenzio, 2000).

Empowerment

If people recognize that everyone is unique and that individuals differ from one another, it would be presumptuous to think that one individual is more expert at designing environments for others. A crucial concept in community psychology is **empowerment,** the process of enhancing the possibility that people can more actively control their own lives (Rappaport, 1981). Empowerment is a process by which individuals not only gain control and mastery over their own lives but over democratic participation in their community, as well (Zimmerman & Rappaport, 1988). Julian Rappaport (1987), a leading proponent of empowerment, wrote that empowerment conveys a sense of personal control or influence and involves an individual's determination over his or her own life. Zimmerman (1995) described empowerment this way: "Empowerment is a construct that links individual strength and competencies, natural helping systems, and proactive behaviors to social policy and social changes. Empowerment theory, research, and intervention link individual well-being with the larger social and political environment" (p. 569).

Foster-Fishman, Salem, Chibnall, Legler, and Yapchai (1998), using interviews and observations, found that there are multiple pathways to empowerment in community organizations. One pathway is through job autonomy, where employees have control and influence on their jobs. A second pathway is through gaining job-relevant knowledge; the greater an employee's knowledge, the more influence that organizational member can have on the job. Other pathways to empowerment include feeling trusted and respected in the organization and having the freedom to be creative on the job. A fifth pathway to empowerment is the perception of job fulfillment or job satisfaction. Satisfied employees discern that they have more influence and control than dissatisfied employees. Of course, the converse is true, too; employees who have authority and direction over their jobs feel more satisfied with their jobs. One final pathway to empowerment is participatory decision making in the organization.

Empowerment, then, means *doing* (Swift & Levin, 1987); however, it does not mean that community psychologists do things for others. Rather, community psychologists, in the roles of researchers-reporters, collaborators-educators, or advocates-activists, empower others so that they can *do* for themselves.

The concept of empowerment has not gone without criticism. Riger (1993) argued that empowerment often leads to individualism and therefore competition and conflict. Similarly, she criticized the construct for being traditionally masculine, in that it involves power and control, rather than feminine, which concerns communion and cooperation. Riger issued a challenge to community psychologists to develop a vision that incorporates both empowerment and community, despite what she construed as the paradoxical nature of the two phenomena. Sprague and Hayes (2000) agreed that the notion of empowerment can indeed backfire, while Porter (2001b) added that the construct is vague and lacking in concrete ways to implement it.

There is a growing interest in empowerment as a research topic. From 1974 to 1986, there were 94 articles on the topic of empowerment. From 1987 to 1993, the number increased to 686 articles and 283 book chapters. Other disciplines have also recognized the importance of empowerment. For example, the number of articles on the topic in the educational literature rose from 66 between 1966 and 1981 to 2,261 articles from 1982 to early 1994 (Perkins & Zimmerman, 1995). In just seven short years between 1995 and 2001, over 1,000 other citations were added, an indication that interest in the concept of empowerment certainly is not waning (PsychInfo, 2002).

Related to empowerment is citizen participation in researching community problems, developing solutions, and evaluating the outcomes of community change. Also, citizen self-help and mutual support groups such as Alcoholics Anonymous empower individuals in the community to assist each other without benefit of professional help. These topics are addressed in detail in Chapter 4.

Choice among Alternatives

Given a respect for the uniqueness of each individual, respect should lead to an understanding that a single human services setting is not optimal for everyone. Enhancing the access of marginalized groups to various community resources is central to social change and to vibrant communities (Maton, 2000). Furthermore, a variety of alternative community settings and services would best serve the community's diverse population. Likewise, individuals need the power to participate in the design of the services and then select the one best suited to them (Salem, 1990). Providing *choices* in community services is a revered value of community psychology. In several chapters in this book, you will read about the variety of innovative services that community psychologists have promoted or designed as alternatives to traditional ones. Perhaps if a variety of services rather than only one overcrowded shelter had been available to Dory, she would have survived.

Another important aspect of choice among services is accessibility. *Accessibility* means that services should be taken to the people. People should not have to travel long distances for services, especially if access is difficult. For example, if mental health services are in the suburbs but people in the inner city most need them, the services will probably be underutilized by those most in need.

Action Research

If a variety of services are optimal for both individual and community well-being and the fit between the individual and the service is crucial, then the best way to ascertain which services and which individuals match is by means of science. Science can also help community psychologists evaluate which preventive efforts work best for whom, when, and why. Research grounded in theory and directed toward resolving social problems is called **action research.**

A strong, explicit value in community psychology is that research should promote social change (Hill, Bond, Mulvey, & Terenzio, 2000). And, in community psychology, most action research is *participatory*; affected individuals are not merely "subjects" in a study but rather active participants in shaping the research agenda (Nelson, Ochocka, Griffin, & Lord, 1998; Rappaport, 2000). An active partnership between researcher and participants is therefore the norm (Hill, Bond, Mulvey, & Terenzio, 2000). In other words, where research is concerned, community psychologists embrace the philosophy of "nothing about me, without me" (Nelson, Ochocka, Griffin, & Lord, 1990).

The next chapter discusses in detail how action research is conducted. At this point, it is important to remember that social problems are difficult to resolve, research or not, and that research in community settings is complex. For instance, if one wanted to change a human services agency so that it better addresses community needs, one would probably have to research the whole agency plus the people involved, including clients, staff, and their subgroups, as well as all of their interrelationships and processes within the agency. Community research is indeed complex.

Social Change

Armed with research, one of the goals of community psychology is to induce social change. Planned social change is such an important part of community psychology that two chapters in this book are dedicated to it. Here, the term will be defined and differentiated from unplanned change. **Unplanned social change** occurs spontaneously. No one plans it; the change just happens. An example of this is the influx of the homeless, such as Dory, onto our city streets. No one purposely decided that we should have more homeless people! On the other hand, **planned social change** is defined as intentionally created social change. In planned change, what is to be changed is targeted in advance, is directed toward enhancing the community, and provides for a role in the design of change by those affected by the change. In community psychology, planned change is often very innovative, too.

Collaboration with and Integration of Other Disciplines

Creating social change is a monumental task. Community psychologists would have to be quite audacious to suggest that they can create change by themselves. Collaboration with sister disciplines is a means of producing more sweeping and well-reasoned change (Maton, 2000; Strother, 1987). In fact, given recent and unfortunate trends in U.S. society, social change agents need, more than ever, to confer with other professionals. Kelly (1990) suggested that **collaboration** with others gives new awareness of how other disciplines experience a phenomenon. A benefit of consultation with others such as historians, economists, environmentalists, biologists, sociologists, anthropologists, and policy scientists is that perspectives can be expanded and new perspectives adopted. Case in Point 1.3 demonstrates integration of social and community psychology.

A Sense of Community

Because this concept, a sense of community, comes last does not mean it is less significant than the preceding concepts. In fact, the sense of community is one of the most important concepts for community psychology (Sarason, 1974). The topic was saved until last because here it best fits our scheme for unfolding the philosophy of community psychology.

　　If environments and individuals are well matched, a more optimal community as well as a community with a sense of spirit and a sense of "we-ness" can be created. Research has demonstrated that a sense of community, or what is sometimes called *community spirit* or

---

CASE IN POINT 1.3

SOCIAL PSYCHOLOGY, COMMUNITY PSYCHOLOGY, AND HOMELESSNESS

You have learned in this chapter that community psychologists have issued a clarion call for collaboration with other disciplines both within and outside of psychology. In response to that, the authors agree that community psychologists and social psychologists have much that they can learn from each other (Serrano-Garcia, Lopez, & Rivera-Medena, 1987).

　　Social psychologists, psychologists who study social phenomena as they affect an individual, may have the answer as to why the media, the public, and other psychologists blame an individual's homelessness on the individual (i.e., usually either the person's mental illness or alcoholism). Social psychologists have developed **attribution theory,** which explains how people infer causes of or make attributions about other's behaviors (Kelly, 1973). Research on attribution has clearly demonstrated that people are likely to place emphasis on characteristics of the individual or use trait explanations for another's shortcomings (Jones &

Nisbett, 1971). That is, when explaining the behavior of others—especially other's problems—people are less likely to attend to the situation and more likely to make person-centered attributions.

　　Does this theory apply to homelessness? Can this theory explain why the media and the public often blame the victim, the homeless person, for his or her problem? *Victim blaming* is a term that describes the tendency to attribute the cause of an individual's problems to that individual rather than to the situation the person is in. In other words, the victim is blamed for what happened to him or her. Social psychologists believe that blaming the victim is a means of self-defense (e.g., if a bad thing can happen to her, then it can happen to me). In the case of Dory, did her personality create her homeless situation? Did something in Dory's environment contribute to it? The average person who blames the victim would blame Dory for contributing to her homelessness.

Shinn, a prominent community psychologist, reviewed research on homelessness and conducted a monumental and well-designed study on the issue (Shinn & Gillespie, 1993). She concluded that person-centered explanations of homelessness, although popular, are not as valid as situational and structural explanations of homelessness. Specifically, Shinn suggested that the researched explanations for homelessness are bifurcated—that is, person centered and environmental. She reviewed the literature on each and concluded that person-centered or deficit explanations for homelessness are less appropriate than environmental or situational explanations.

Shinn found studies that suggest that structural problems offer some of the most plausible explanations of homelessness. For example, Rossi (1989) found that between 1969 and 1987, the number of single adults (some with children) with incomes under $4,000 a year increased from 3.1 to 7.2 million. Similarly, Leonard, Dolbeare, and Lazere (1989) found that for the 5.4 million low-income renters, there were only 2.1 million units of affordable housing according to the Department of Housing and Urban Development standards. Poverty and lack of affordable housing seem to be far better explanations for today's homelessness than person-centered explanations. Solarz and Bogat (1990) would add to these environmental explanations of homelessness the lack of social support by friends and family of the homeless.

What is important about Shinn's review is not so much that it illustrates that the public and the media may indeed suffer from **fundamental attribution error**—the tendency to blame the person and not the situation—but rather that Shinn offers these data so community psychologists can act on them. Public policy makers need to understand that situations and structural problems produce homelessness. Psychologists and community leaders need to be convinced that providing temporary solutions such as soup kitchens are merely bandages on the gaping wound of the homeless. Furthermore, shelter managers and others have to understand that moving the homeless from one shelter to another does little for them. Families and children, not just the stereotypical old alcoholic men, are part of today's homeless (Rossi, 1990). Being in different shelters and therefore different school systems has negative effects on children's academic performance and self-esteem (Rafferty & Shinn, 1991); homeless children lose their childhoods to homelessness (Landers, 1989).

Something must be done about the permanent housing situation in this country. On this point, both community and social psychologists would concur.

---

sense of belonging in the community, is positively related to the subjective sense of well-being (Davidson & Cotter, 1991). In an optimal community, members probably will be more open to changes that will further improve their community.

On the other hand, social disintegration of a community or neighborhood often results in high fear of crime and vandalism (Ross & Jang, 2000) as well as declines in children's mental health (Caspi, Taylor, Moffitt, & Plomin, 2000) and increases in school problems (Hadley-Ives, Stiffman, Elze, Johnson, & Dore, 2000), loneliness (Prezza, Amici, Tiziana, & Tedeschi, 2001), and a myriad of other problems. Community disorder may intensify both the benefits of personal resources (such as connections to neighbors) and the detrimental effects of personal risk factors (Cutrona, Russell, Hessling, Brown, & Murry, 2000).

Interestingly, research has demonstrated that happiness and the sense of satisfaction with one's community is not found exclusively in the suburbs. People living in the suburbs are no more likely to express satisfaction with their neighborhoods than people living in the city (Adams, 1992) or small towns (Prezza, Amici, Tiziana, & Tedeschi, 2001). Many lay-people and psychologists believe that residents of the inner city are at risk for a myriad of problems. However, research has found that some very resilient individuals are located in the most stressful parts of our cities (Work, Cowen, Parker, & Wyman, 1990).

Community has traditionally meant a locality or place such as a neighborhood. It has also come to mean a relational interaction or social ties that draw people together (Heller, 1989b). To these definitions could be added the one of community as a collective political power.

If those are the definitions for *community,* what is the sense of community? **Sense of community** is the feeling of the relationship an individual holds for his or her community (Heller et al., 1984) or the personal knowledge that one has about belonging to a collective of others (Newbrough & Chavis, 1986). More specifically, it is "the perception of similarity to others, an acknowledged interdependence with others, a willingness to maintain this interdependence by giving to or doing for others what one expects from them, the feeling that one is part of a larger dependable and stable structure" (Sarason, 1974, p. 157). If people sense community in their neighborhood, they then feel that they belong to or fit into the neighborhood. Community members sense that they can influence what happens in the community, share the values of the neighborhood, and feel emotionally connected to it (Heller et al., 1984).

A sense of community is specifically thought to include four elements: membership, influence, integration, and a sense of emotional connection (McMillan & Chavis, 1986).

1. *Membership* means that people experience feelings of belonging in their community.
2. *Influence* signifies that people feel they can make a difference in their community.
3. *Integration,* or fulfillment of needs, suggests that members of the community believe that their needs will be met by resources available in the community.
4. *Emotional connection* implies that community members have and will share history, time, places, and experiences.

A concept related to sense of community is **neighboring,** which is a person's emotional, cognitive, and social attachment to a neighborhood that makes him or her more likely to participate in neighborhood organizations (Unger & Wandersman, 1985a). and is therefore a different or distinct concept from sense of community (Prezza, Amici, Tiziana, & Tedeschi, 2001). **Neighborhoods** might be defined as local communities that are bounded together spatially where residents feel a sense of social cohesion and interaction, homogeneity, as well as place identity (Coulton, Korbin, & Su, 1996). Research has demonstrated the utility of conceptualizing "sense of community" separately from "neighborhoods" (Prezza, Amici, Tiziana, & Tedeschi, 2001). A sense of community need not be experienced only in a whole community. People can develop a sense of community in a group, an organization, or for almost any other aggregate of individuals. A promising scale has been developed to measure the sense of community (Buckner, 1988). This scale, which is designed to measure neighborhood cohesion or fellowship, seems psychometrically sound and asks reactions to statements such as, "I believe my neighbors would help me in an emergency."

COMMUNITY PSYCHOLOGY TODAY:
PROGRESS IN THE FIELD

Where is the field of community psychology today? Has it achieved some of its lofty goals? Fortunately, there is research assessing historical changes in the field to determine whether community psychology is making any progress.

Some in the field feel the ardor, zeal, optimism, and commitment that once character-ized community psychology have faded (Linney, 1990). Do data bear out that community psychology is progressing or backsliding? The authors hope to provide a lengthy answer throughout this book. Another way to look more briefly at this question is to compare early and later research in the field. A historical overview will help you to understand changes in the discipline.

Speer, Dey, Griggs, Gibson, Lubin, and Hughey (1992) examined the topics, the pop-ulations studied, and the sophistication of the measures and methodologies utilized in com-munity psychology research. Fortunately for them, previous research conducted by Lounsbury, Leader, Meares, and Cook (1980) from approximately a decade earlier was available for comparison purposes. Speer and colleagues reviewed 235 *empirical* studies (defined as reporting the results of research investigations) in the top two journals of com-munity psychology from 1984 to 1988 and compared their findings to those of Lounsbury and associates. Here is what they found.

In community psychology, the number of **experiments** where variables were actively manipulated decreased over the decade, whereas the number of **field studies** where no vari-ables were actively manipulated increased. The use of **control groups** or comparison groups also decreased as one might expect because experimental manipulations had decreased. Hence, there is a recognition today that experiments may not be feasible or appropriate for community research (Casswell, 2000).

Participants with identified psychological problems were less likely to appear in the more recent studies than the older studies. Over the years, the reporting of participant gender and ethnic origin increased. Articles categorized as dealing with mental health services decreased with time, but the number of articles categorized by the authors as problem spe-cific increased, particularly in the areas of social support and prevention.

What conclusions can be made about the direction of community psychology from this archival review? First, these researchers suggest that just because there was a shift from experimental research to correlational research does not mean the field is less sophisticated.

Second, there are now fewer studies of people who are chronically mentally ill. Instead, examination of larger portions of participants from the community at large demon-strates that recent research is being conducted in settings *as* and *where* social problems occur, which is one of the goals of community psychology. Likewise, the data indicate that the field is acquiring more information about diverse populations in more recent studies— another of its goals.

The disappointing news is that many of the recent dependent measures still focus on the individual level of analysis. Although it is true that today there are more studies on per-son-environment variables such as **social support** (where individuals assist one another with coping), the literature still very much retains an individual-based, adjustment orientation. Based on this literature analysis, the authors tentatively agree that community psychology is on its way toward fulfilling the goals outlined earlier.

COMMUNITY PSYCHOLOGY TODAY: WHAT'S IN IT FOR YOU?

Undergraduate Education

Many psychology departments now offer community psychology courses. Others offer courses in community mental health or clinical psychology, where the professor prefers to adopt a community orientation. However, the training offered to undergraduates may only be a course or two. Another way undergraduates can learn more about the community is to become involved in the local college community or the students' hometowns. Thousands of community agencies solicit volunteers, but, of course, many of these agencies do not adopt a community psychology orientation. For example, many supply treatment and therefore do not focus on prevention. Volunteers are the lifeblood of many community agencies that run on limited budgets. College personnel may be able to give you the names and phone numbers of local agencies. If you do choose to volunteer, try to determine whether the agency promotes the goals of community psychology and if not, why not.

Students often volunteer in the community as part of their course experience, and many continue the experience after the community psychology course ends. Volunteers are indeed special people in terms of their commitment and identification with the organizations for which they work (Clary & Snyder, 1999). Likewise, by working for someone else's benefit rather than for self-interest, volunteers show selflessness. Research on volunteerism demonstrates that volunteers report significantly greater satisfaction than stress from volunteering, despite whether their volunteer work is mandatory or fully voluntary (Ferrari, Billows, Jason, & Grill, 1997; Ferrari et al., in press; Ferrari & Jason, 1996). Research also confirms that volunteering gives coursework more meaning and students more awareness of social issues as well as increased appreciation for diversity (Primavera, 1999). However, there is research that demonstrates *requiring* service can actually reduce intentions to volunteer in the future. The most important aspect of volunteering appears to be the match between the motives of the volunteer and the actual volunteer situation (Clary & Snyder, 1999). Here are comments from some student volunteers:

> When I began volunteering I wasn't sure how much of an impact I would have, if any. I have come to realize that it is not the impact of me on members at [my volunteer site] but their combined effect on me. Each time I give my time for them, they truly appreciate it. My "problems" seem so superficial when I am at [my volunteer site]. I can compare myself to them and realize how fortunate I am for the life I live. Volunteering is one way that I can show how thankful I am for all I have. I plan to continue my volunteering through graduation. I know that the time I sacrifice is going to a good cause.
>
> —Sue Strom, Class of 1999

Admittedly, people lead very busy lives. However, when we say we do not have time, we often mean that we do not have time for others, not realizing the personal fulfillment that volunteering can bring. To volunteer is to not only make time for others but to make time for yourself and your community.... As I was getting ready to leave [my volunteer site at a developmental center for clients with mental disabilities] to go to class one morning, I made a point of walking over to Stephen to say goodbye. He and I had spent some time together that morning stenciling a rose and coloring it in. When I walked over to him and told him I was leaving, he gently grabbed my hand. He then reached for my other hand and held them both firmly. I smiled, and after a few seconds gradually pulled my hands loose. Stephen then raised his arms and reached for my neck. Although [he] is a very passive man, I do not know if he has mood swings or if there is a more aggressive side to his personality. Therefore, I was taken aback at first and pulled away. However, when I did so, Stephen looked a little puzzled and tried to pull me closer. Reluctantly, I decided to give him the benefit of the doubt and allowed him to put his hands around my neck. When he did so, he pulled me toward him and gave me a kiss on the cheek. He then gently let go and smiled.

I left that morning with a greater sense of personal satisfaction than I have felt in a long time. Stephen told me that he appreciated the time I spent with him. He taught me that a little time and patience go a long way.

—Susan Ehrhard, Class of 2000

Figure 1.1 provides some interesting facts about volunteering.

Another opportunity for involvement is to join the Society for Community Research and Action (SCRA), Division 27 of the American Psychological Association. Information about the society can be accessed on the American Psychological Association's web page by using *APA* as the keyword in your search. The SCRA is devoted to advancing theory, research, and social action to promote positive well-being, increase empowerment, and prevent the development of problems of communities, groups, and individuals. The society is divided into several interest groups based on the varied areas of expertise of the SCRA members.

Internships and service learning are another vehicle by which undergraduate and graduate students can experience and assist in their communities. Internships often provide students with opportunities to learn about program planning, networking, constraints on service delivery and funding, and other factors that affect community agencies. In addition, internships provide a better gateway for undergraduates hoping to enter programs in com-

FIGURE 1.1   Facts about Volunteering

- 70% of all American households volunteer
- 55.5% of American adults volunteer
- 89.5% of Americans asked to volunteer, do so
- Volunteers and contributors include both sexes and all races
- Volunteering in America has increased over the last decade
- Americans volunteered 109.4 million hours, with the average being 4 hours per week

Source: 1999 Independent Sector Biennial National Survey; available at http://www.independentsector.org

munity psychology, offset the influence of traditional psychology programs that seem to create students determined to help people only on a one-to-one basis (Elias, 1987) and result in positive academic and personal outcomes (McKenna & Rizzo, 1999). Volunteer experiences and internships at the undergraduate level can often help students find postgraduation employment in human services.

Advanced Training in Community Psychology

Concentrated training programs in community psychology tend to be master's or Ph.D. programs. The discipline is still rather new compared to other areas of psychology, but some research does exist on graduate training in community psychology. Sandler and Keller (1984), in a review of graduate programs in community psychology, found that most programs utilize a *scientific practitioner* model. The students are trained to conduct research but also to act on the research or to practice the discipline based on its scientific foundations. Some community psychology programs are freestanding; others are clinical-community programs (combinations of clinical and community psychology). Courses generally include program evaluation, a community psychology seminar, and interdisciplinary courses.

Clinical-community programs emphasize intellectual ability in selecting student applicants and are more likely to place students at child-family services, hospitals, and community mental health centers. On the other hand, freestanding community psychology programs emphasize a commitment to action in student applicants and place students at human services and advocacy organizations (Maton, Meissen, & O'Connor, 1993). Courses at the graduate level generally include program evaluation, a community psychology seminar, and interdisciplinary courses. The content relates to several areas of community psychology, including, but not limited to, systems change, individual change, prevention, and the psychology of particular settings.

Walfish, Polifka, and Stenmark (1986) conducted a survey of job-search outcomes recent doctoral students in community psychology. The doctoral students had little difficulty finding positions; in fact, 84 percent reported that it was easy or very easy to find a job. Some 83 percent reported obtaining the job at their *first-choice* agency. The major employment settings for the doctoral graduates were universities, community mental health centers, medical schools, research and consulting firms, and health care facilities. To our knowledge, no recent studies have been conducted on job prospects for community psychology graduates. Use caution, therefore, in applying these 1986 results to today's job market. Figure 1.2 lists sample universities with doctoral programs in community psychology.

PLAN OF THE BOOK

Now that you are on your way to understanding community psychology, you probably would like to know what the rest of your journey will be like. The remainder of Part I, which is the introductory portion of the book, will introduce you to theory and research in community settings. Researchers in community psychology employ some of the venerated methods

FIGURE 1.2   Sample Graduate Programs

Freestanding Community Psychology Programs (Doctoral)
    Georgia State University
    Michigan State University
    New York University
    University of Illinois at Chicago
    University of Illinois at Urbana–Champaign
    University of Virginia
    University of Waikato
Community/Clinical Programs (Doctoral)
    Arizona State University
    Bowling Green State University
    DePaul University
    George Washington University
    Rutgers University
    University of California–Berkeley
    University of South Carolina
Community Psychology/Interdisciplinary (Doctoral)
    Claremont Graduate University
    Iowa State University
    Penn State University
    University of Minnesota
    University of Nebraska
    Wayne State University
Community Psychology (Master's)
    Central Connecticut State University
    Mansfield University
    The Sage College
    University of Massachusetts at Lowell
    University of New Haven
    University of North Carolina–Charlotte

used by other psychologists as well as some techniques that are fairly unique to community psychology or interdisciplinary research.

You will next move to Part II, which consists of two chapters on social change. The first chapter outlines why social change is important yet so difficult. The second chapter discusses strategies for creating and maintaining social change.

The third part of the book focuses on the mental health foundations of community psychology. Mental health issues will be discussed first for a very good reason. Although community psychology is shedding its mental health image, mental health still represents one of the largest portions of the published literature.

Part IV will examine settings into which community psychology has expanded. From mental health settings and issues, community psychologists easily moved into social and human services, school systems, criminal justice, health care, and community organizational settings and issues. Part V, the final chapter of the book, looks ahead at what the future holds for the field of community psychology.

Each chapter will provide one or more Cases in Point to engage you more actively with the material or to exemplify or illucidate a particular point. Unlike the chapter opening vignettes, which will be somewhat clinical in nature, as explained in the Preface, the Cases in Point will be more purely oriented to community psychology.

SUMMARY

Community psychology's early history closely parallels the history of clinical psychology and psychiatry. Sigmund Freud's legacy of treating the individual rather than the setting and focusing on the expertise of the professional is intertwined with traditional treatment plans in clinical psychology and psychiatry. Both world wars assisted psychologists in realizing the effect the environment plays in people's behavior. The 1950s brought the development of psychoactive drugs and landmark research that questioned the traditions of psychology, including psychotherapy.

Both the Civil Rights movement of the 1960s and the Swampscott Conference spawned the birth of community psychology. The rights movement focused psychologists on empowerment, whereas the conference shifted psychologists' attention from individuals to settings and from treatment to prevention.

The goals of community psychology are interrelated and include prevention and empowerment as well as an emphasis on competencies and ecology, respect for diversity, choice among community settings, action research, planned social change, interdisciplinary efforts, and a sense of community. Research indicates that community psychology is making some headway on its goals. Literature reviews demonstrate the recent emphasis on diverse populations and on refocusing efforts away from mental health.

Students of community psychology, particularly undergraduates, are encouraged to serve in their communities to develop a better understanding of the community. Graduate programs, especially doctoral programs, have great success in placing their graduates who, when placed, report that they are usually employed in their first-choice settings.

SCIENTIFIC RESEARCH METHODS

The connection between cause and effect has no beginning and can have no end.
—Leo Tolstoy, *War and Peace*

Edisak, his wife, and his two young sons came to the United States as refugees in the early 1990s from a war-torn Southeast Asian country. Their application was sponsored by Catholic Charities. Soon after their arrival, there were signs of domestic problems. His wife and two young children moved into a shelter for a brief period of time. The family was subsequently united. Edisak started working as a full-time clerk in a grocery store and his wife worked part time as part of a cleaning crew in a local hospital. Caseworkers continued to work with the family in their adjustment to the new culture and environment, among other psychosocial issues.

In the mid-1990s, Edisak began one of his frequent trips back to his home country. It was unclear about the purpose of these trips; his wife did not question his motives, however. Edisak came back from his latest trip seriously ill. Subsequently, he tested positive for HIV. His wife also tested positive; she was pregnant with their third child. Edisak insisted he did not know how he contracted HIV; he denied any extramarital activities and drug abuse.

Without a vaccine, prevention is the only weapon for halting the further spread of the disease. There are many strategies of HIV prevention (see Chapter 11). A highly controversial prevention strategy is the use of legal means (i.e., health-related policy as prevention) to gauge the pandemic. The U.S. government requires all potential immigrants and refugees to undergo HIV testing before settling in the United States. Only those who test HIV-negative are allowed to enter the country; a waiver is available for refugees that requires them to be seen and have follow-up visits by medical and health professionals once they are admitted into the United States. But this legal mechanism has little recourse in preventing people (including those born in the United States) who are already HIV-positive or living with AIDS in the United States from traveling back and forth overseas. In the case of Edisak, he probably got infected during one of those trips to Asia. Because HIV and AIDS carry tremendous social stigma, verbal inquiry of people's HIV status may not be an effective prevention strategy. Meanwhile, testing as a prevention strategy is only effective when people are willing to be tested and understand the consequences and responsibilities when they test positive. What strategies or scientific methods should be used with a mobile population? What strategies should be used with HIV-positive pregnant women?

THE ESSENCE OF SCIENTIFIC RESEARCH

The preceding section presents a scenario all too familiar to community psychologists. The two scientific research techniques (HIV blood testing and self-report measures) *have not produced the same results.* Furthermore, some scientific research techniques are insensitive or inappropriate to investigate certain issues, especially those that may jeopardize the well-being of the participants. It should come as no surprise that many people do not disclose their HIV status because of its stigma as well as the general AIDS phobia and homophobia (despite the fact that it is not a disease afflicting only homosexuals) of the general U.S. public. Although the U.S. Supreme Court ruled that HIV falls within the general purview of the American Disability Act, disclosure is about more than legal rights and protection—it's about being socially ostracized.

This example also intimates that research in the field of community psychology is often conducted with a sense of urgency not seen in other fields of psychology. That is, the issues examined by community psychologists are often important, pressing social issues of the day. Before discussing some of the issues (e.g., confidentiality and cultural sensitivity) related to this urgency, the authors will present some definitions and the reasons for engaging in scientific research. The discussion will be followed with a review of the various types of scientific research methods utilized by community psychologists—both traditional and nontraditional psychological research methods.

Why Do Scientific Research?

As you may recall from Chapter 1, a major principle of the field of community psychology is to create or engage in some form of social change so that individuals and communities may benefit. In order to distinguish the effective from the less effective changes, psychologists need a way to help understand and assess these changes. Scientific research provides that mechanism.

For example, how can researchers be sure that decreases in risky behaviors such as unprotected sex or sharing needles when injecting drugs are solely due to people's participation in some form of prevention programs? If Edisak and his wife had the opportunity to participate in such a program, how could someone determine whether their participation reduced their likelihood of unprotected sex rather than other factors, such as sharing needles when injecting drugs? Although one might find that women who enroll in such programs (a social change) are less likely to engage in unprotected sex compared to those who do not, a further analysis of the data might indicate that it is those women with spouses who are willing to use condoms who benefit from the programs. That is, for many women, such as Edisak's wife, enrollment in a prevention program is not sufficient to reduce unprotected sex *unless* they can go back to a home environment or community with some support (the ecological perspective)—the differential power between the genders often work to the disadvantage of the women in negotiating safer sex. However, the validity of this assumption can be verified using some form of scientific research.

What Is Scientific Research?

On a daily basis, people observe and make attributions about many things. For example, you might have some hunches as to why men do or do not use condoms, or why people abuse alcohol and drugs. However, to scientists, research is more than hunches. In other words, when scientists conduct research, they utilize a set of related assumptions and activities. Figure 2.1 depicts the process of scientific research.

Theory and theory-based research are an integral part of all scientific disciplines (Kuhn, 1970), and the field of community psychology is no exception. Before discussing theory, however, the authors would like to explain three theoretical terms that often confuse scientists and laypersons alike.

At one time or another, you probably have heard some people use the terms *theory, model,* and *paradigm.* The terms are often used interchangeably, but they are not quite synonymous. A **theory** is a systematic attempt to explain observable or measurable events relating to an issue such as homelessness or alcoholism. More exactly, a theory is a "set of interrelated constructs (concepts), definitions, and propositions that present a systematic view of phenomena by specifying relations among variables, with the purpose of explaining

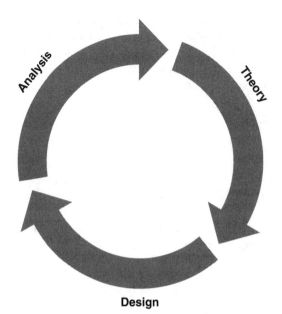

Design

FIGURE 2.1   The Process of Scientific Research

or predicting the phenomena" (Kerlinger, 1973, p. 9). The goal of a theory is to allow researchers to describe, predict, and control for *why* and *how* a variable or variables relate to observable or measurable events pertaining to an issue. For example, did Edisak's numerous trips to Asia predict his HIV status? During one of his trips, did he engage in risky behaviors promoting the contraction of HIV—injecting drugs (sharing needles) or having unprotected sex with someone other than his wife?

Bear in mind that social science theories best serve as guideposts for studying observable or measurable events. In other words, description and prediction of, as well as control for, these events are based on suggested *rules* rather than *absolute laws* such as what is more often found in the physical sciences (Kuhn, 1970).

On the other hand, a **model** is a working blueprint of a theory. A **paradigm** is a yet smaller framework that guides researchers to conceptualize events in a consistent fashion. Figure 2.2 depicts these relationships.

A theory may consist of more than one model or blueprint. These models guide the understanding of the different observable events pertaining to an issue. A well-developed theory is likely to be made up of two or more compatible models, which are likely to be conceptualized using similar paradigms or frameworks. In the case of an undeveloped theory, different paradigms may lead to the formulation of different models. It is plausible, then, for observable or measurable events relating to an issue to be explained by more than one theory.

A more concrete example will help you understand these terms. For decades, researchers investigating alcoholism or alcohol abuse (*the issue*) have conceptualized excessive drinking (*the observable or measurable event*) as a consequence of a genetic pre-

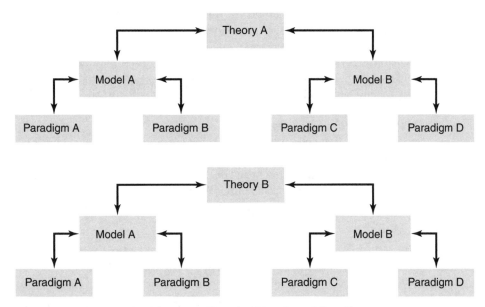

FIGURE 2.2   The Relationship among Theories, Models, and Paradigms

disposition—a medical explanation of alcoholism as a disease (*the theoretical perspective*). This theory helped shape the development of various models about alcohol abuse. For example, one model promoted the identification of the gene or genes responsible for the disease of alcoholism. Another model allowed for the comparison of alcohol use in identical twins versus genetically unrelated individuals.

In recent years, some researchers have begun to challenge the genetic disease theory of alcoholism. Instead, they argue that some aspects of excessive alcohol use (again, *the observable or measurable event*) may be a consequence of something in the environment, such as stress from losing one's home, a difficult life on the streets, prolonged unemployment, or some other traumatic life event. Thus, a new theory emerges—the distress or disorder theory of alcoholism. This *paradigm shift* or refocusing of thinking or conceptualizing from genetics to environment again leads to the development of models. One model specifies that socioeconomic status influences alcoholism. Another model suggests that the stress of minority ethnic status plays a role in alcoholism. In other words, this theory allows for the description and prediction of differential alcohol use for individuals with different environmental stressors. On the other hand, the first theory—the disease theory—offers description and prediction of individual differences based on genetics.

These two examples illustrate the dynamic nature or ever-evolving aspect of the development of scientific theories. Kuhn (1970) argued that major scientific development is not linear, not a step-by-step accumulation of fact. Such is the case of theory and research in the field of community psychology. Within a scientific discipline, a crisis may cause a shift in thinking; this paradigm shift may shape the development of a new theory. You will recall that just such a crisis (discouragement with traditional methods of treatment of mental illness) gave birth to the field of community psychology, which developed new methods and theories about community problems. Kuhn argued that a paradigm serves as a *guide* rather than an absolute theoretical standard for scientific interpretation.

Theories, models, and paradigms in the field of community psychology serve this function as guides. When a theory does not work, it needs fine-tuning or abandonment. You will read about many of the current theories, models, and paradigms in the field of community psychology in other chapters of this text. You will also be introduced to the research related to each theory; it is through research that one makes judgments about theories. Case in Point 2.1 introduces an integrated theory of drug abuse.

A special category of theory in the field of community psychology is systems theory. **Systems theories** are theories that presume that systems underlie the process, behavior, or issue being discussed. A **system** can be thought of as objects that relate together. More precisely, a system is an organized, unified whole that is made up of parts, components, or subsystems that are interdependent such that the whole is recognizable as a whole.

■ ■ ■ ■ ■

CASE IN POINT 2.1

A THEORY OF SUBSTANCE ABUSE AND HIV/STDS THAT INCORPORATES THE PRINCIPLES OF COMMUNITY PSYCHOLOGY

There are over 40 theories for studying drug abuse (cf. Lettieri, Sayers, & Pearson, 1984). Some of these theories are person centered, such as the medical or genetic theory of alcoholism; other theories are environmental, such as the stress or disorder theory.

Flay and Petraitis (1991) identified a number of determinants of drug abuse on the basis of 24 studies. They concluded that the determinants of abuse are some combination of the social environment; social bonding of the individual to the family, peers, and community organizations such as schools; social learning and learning from others; intrapsychic factors such as self-esteem; and the individual's own knowledge of, attitudes toward, and behaviors related to alcohol and drugs. Flay and Petraitis argued that a majority of these heories address only one of these domains. For the field to advance, an effort needs to be made to integrate more of these domains into one coherent theory. Community psychologists would heartily agree.

Responding to this challenge, Wong and Bouey (2001) proposed an integrated theory for studying substance abuse as well as HIV/STDs

(sexually transmitted diseases) among American Indian/Alaska Natives (AI/ANs). This population was singled out because, compared to other racial/ethnic groups in the United States, many AI/ANs have a more serious substance abuse problem (National Household Survey on Drug Abuse, 1999), which places them at risk for STDs—including HIV (CDC/IHS National Epidemiology Program, 2001; Howard, Bouey, Greenwood, & Duran, 2001).

Most substance abuse and HIV prevention and intervention programs have enlisted psychosocial models of individual behavior. These models, however, tend to isolate individuals and assume all individuals follow regular and rational decision-making processes (e.g., DiClemente & Peterson, 1994; Leviton, 1989; Valdiserri, West, Moore, Darrow, & Hinman, 1992), a position consistent with the reasoning of the dominant medical model in health-related programs (Singer, Flores, Davison et al., 1990). While individuals are undeniably the key component of such programs, "individual behavior" occurs in a complex social and cultural context, and analysis that removes that behavior from its broader setting ignores essential determinants (Auerbach, Wypijewska, & Brodie, 1994). Individuals may, in fact, behave "rationally," but they do so within the confines of their own sociocultural milieus. Attempts to address this breadth of factors result in the recognition that responses to typical knowledge, attitude, and behavior measures are constructions by individual actors situated within the interplay of (a) *political*, (b) *economic*, (c) *social*, and (d) *cultural* realms (Bouey, Duran, Hendrickson et al., 1997; Nemoto, Wong, Ching et al., 1998; see Figure 2.3). These forces create opportunities and obstacles for individuals, and define the parameters within which they function (Conners & McGrath, 1997). Bouey and others (1997) and Nemoto and others (1998) asserted that it is also necessary to recognize that although these domains are frequently isolated as conceptually distinct entities, these realms possess multiple dimensions and each overlaps those of the others. If one is to understand and address solutions to drug-HIV risks, one has to perceive clients as participants in these systemic contexts. These contexts, too, are anything but static. They and their constituent elements are very dynamic, evolving rapidly within themselves and within their encompassing milieus. Historical processes, consequently, are of great significance if one is to comprehend choices made by individuals. In brief, it is useful to understand substance use/abuse, sexual risk practices,

and HIV/STDs among AI/ANs as outputs of a *process* that involves or moves through at least *five domains*.

Within this theoretical setting, all populations are subject to factors associated with the distribution of power and resources (Conners & McGrath, 1997). This applies to all individuals in the larger scale of political-economic systems, as well as to those same persons in smaller-scale personal relationships (Conners & McGrath, 1997). Marginalized, inner-city populations provide the extreme examples of these relationships. Unemployment, homelessness, substandard nutrition, violence, substance abuse, health care access, stress, class, race, gender relations, family, community organization, support networks, sex-partner networks, and culture among other features of inner-city life contribute to this imbalance (Conners & McGrath, 1997; Singer et al., 1990; Singer, 1994a; Weeks, Schensul, Williams, Singer, & Grier, 1995).

As a consequence of these extremes, inner-city conditions represent one example of international manifestation of AIDS as a disease of poverty, wherein AIDS is just one of a host of community problems (Singer & Weeks, 1996). These circumstances also exhibit tremendous structural variability, supporting the notion that the AIDS pandemic is more adequately described as thousands of separate epidemics (Mann, Tarantola, & Netter, 1992). Exploratory models need to

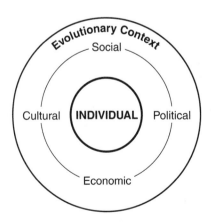

FIGURE 2.3   A Conceptual Model on Health-Related Prevention

(continued)

address individuals and communities through these unique circumstances, and these models have to possess the capacity to adjust to each "micro-epidemic and its particular route(s) of transmission, sub-population at risk, and socio-behavioral context" (Singer & Weeks, 1996, p. 490; also see Singer, 1994b).

Inner-city populations also constitute one class of "hidden populations" (Lambert, 1990; Watters & Biernacki, 1989), groups that are out of the mainstream and little known to those outside its boundaries. These communities are a particular challenge for research and program development, since they can be hard to define, difficult to understand, and especially complex. The initial step toward project goals is to engage the communities in the process, opening a dialogue to define their needs and priorities (Wallerstein & Bernstein, 1998; Weeks, Singer, Grier, Hunte-Marrow, & Haughton, 1991). It is through this form of participation, for example, that we can delineate how people assign meaning to their encompassing networks and communities, how they perceive risk and vulnerability, how they behave in particular ways, and how they are most likely to respond to prevention and intervention efforts. These models also must reflect the "micro-epidemics" and must be culturally competent in the manner by which they utilize cultural information (Singer & Borrero, 1984: Trotter, 1995; Weeks, 1990).

While it is clear that context has a tremendous influence on each individual, context alone does not account for all relevant aspects of the model. *Individuals* themselves play an important role, not only in the perpetuation of risky behaviors but also in constructing the parameters of those behaviors as well as their resolutions. Various psychosocial learning and behavior theories apply to these circumstances, and although their specific labels and categories might differ, they share the same basic components. For example, the Health Belief Model (e.g., Becker, 1974; Becker & Maiman, 1980; Janz & Becker, 1984) and the Theory of Planned Behavior (e.g., Ajzen, 1985, 1991; Ajzen & Fishbein,

1980) both incorporate aspects of an individual perspective, of a societal or normative perspective, of an individual's desire to behave in a particular manner, and of an individual's actual behavior. Versions of both models also integrate self-efficacy (Bandura, 1986, 1994) or "perceived control" (Ajzen, 1985; also see Jemmott & Jemmott, 1994) as key elements, and both identify nonspecific "external" factors as having some influence on any segment of the central, "individual" section of the model.

These learning/behavior models have been successfully used for decades and continue to be instrumental in contemporary efforts to describe, explain, and alter health-related behaviors. Wong and Bouey (2001) incorporated the Theory of Planned Behavior (TPB) into a more inclusive political-economic model with the intent of obtaining an improved understanding of substance use/abuse, sexual risk practices, and HIV/STDs (see Figure 2.4). The Theory of Planned Behavior holds that HIV/ STD infections are determined by behavior, which in turn is predicted by intentions. The latter are a product of individual attitudes and subjective norms, both results of more inclusive individual perceptions of social group expectations and of behavioral consequences. This particular model has been selected because of its long history of development and because of its successful use in prevention and intervention efforts pertaining to general health, sexual risk behaviors, and substance abuse. For interventions focusing on individuals, this model directs attention to specific attitudinal and normative components that are salient to certain behaviors. Simultaneously, with the expanded scope of our political-economic model, one can isolate those contextual and structural factors that predict beliefs/attitudes and norms related to behaviors. Individuals integrate these inputs, in addition to those they carry with their personal histories, and construct their perceptions of behavior and norms. Attitudes and subjective norms are derived from these exchanges, ultimately defining intentions with commensurate behavioral correlates. This framework is directly applicable to substance use/abuse, sexual risk practices, and HIV/STDs, facilitating the identification of linkages surrounding and coupling those behaviors and HIV/STDs.

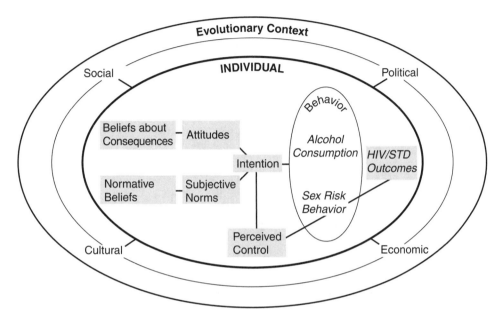

FIGURE 2.4   A Conceptual Model on HIV/STD Prevention

Another concrete example might be useful. A school is a system. It is comprised of its various rooms: the classrooms, cafeteria, gymnasium, and administrative offices. However, to be a system, in the sense that community psychologists use the term, the people, their roles, their interpersonal relationships, the informal and formal rules by which they operate, and other less tangible aspects must also be taken into account because all of these are interdependent on each other. Systems theories in the field of community psychology help capture the complexities of the world as well as the transactional nature between settings and the individuals in them so as to better understand them.

Given the fact that a theory is a global conceptualization of a set of related features pertaining to an issue, to measure or test features, or to do both, one must be specific. That is, one must first operationally define some features of the theory. An **operational definition** specifies how a construct will be measured, describing specifically the operations or steps that will be conducted to obtain the measurement. For example, Wong and Bouey (2001) postulated that some individual characteristics (e.g., coping skills) may be related to success (abstinence or recovery) or failure (relapse or recidivism) of individuals in primary and secondary drug-abuse prevention and treatment programs. Coping skills can be operationalized using the Drinking Profile, a scale designed to measure the circumstances under which people consume alcohol (Marlatt & Gordon, 1985).

Not all operational definitions share the same function. Some are meant to be used as independent variables; others are meant to be used as dependent variables. An **independent variable** is a presumed cause of an effect known as the **dependent variable.** Again, a concrete example is needed. Suppose you wanted to determine whether school climate in a drug or alcohol user's life influences or causes an individual to begin consuming drugs. In your study, the absence or presence of a positive school climate (i.e., an ecological factor) would be the independent variable. Consumption of drugs by your target individuals or study participants would be the dependent variable.

The decision of which operational definition of an independent or dependent variable to use is often dictated by the theory under study. For example, using Wong and Bouey's (2001) theory of drug abuse, independent variables might include levels of coping skills, self-esteem, tribal identity, urban- versus rural- (or reservation) dwelling status of study participants. Those who have a strong tribal identity might be presumed to use or abuse drugs less than those who do not. Upon testing the theory, you cannot ethnically manipulate or control AI/AN's tribal identity, but you might be able to correlate degree of tribal identification with treatment outcome or effectiveness. Two dependent variables that could be specified are the number of days of sobriety and the number of Alcoholics Anonymous or other support group meetings attended.

Having decided on some operational definitions for a particular theory, one begins to engage in activities pertaining to design and measurement. A **design** is a systematic plan to test out a hypothesis, including the quantification, or **measurement,** of the independent and dependent variables. For example, using Wong and Bouey's (2000) theory of drug abuse, you might interview nonpregnant AI/AN and pregnant AI/AN women concerning their substance use. To achieve this, some form of sampling strategies needs to be used. **Sampling strategies** are the procedures used to select participants in a study. You may want to be sure that all pregnant women have an equal statistical opportunity, or are drawn from a random sample to participate in the study. A **random sample** is a sample in which every member of a population has an equal chance of being selected. On the other hand, a **convenience sample** is one chosen for no other reason than that it is available. College students often represent a convenience sample in much psychological research, as the students are readily available to participate in research conducted in psychology departments in colleges and universities. A **purposive sample** is one chosen for a specific reason. In a test of drug use among pregnant women, only pregnant women would be chosen to be assessed; therefore, they would represent a purposive sample. Random samples are the revered form of sampling in psychology. However, a true random sample is not always possible, as in the case of a design where the independent variable can be totally manipulated or controlled. In such cases, it is important to determine that participants are **randomly assigned** to different conditions so that all in the sample are equally likely to be exposed to any condition.

As just mentioned, random sampling and random assignment are not possible for all designs. For example, using Wong and Bouey's (2001) theory of drug abuse, one may think there is a random sample of nonpregnant AI/AN and pregnant AI/AN substance abusers participating in some form of primary and secondary substance-abuse prevention or treatment program, but research indicates that substance abusers are likely to have come from economically disadvantaged backgrounds (e.g., homeless). Thus, a random sample does not exist because the groups differ in their economic backgrounds. However, even when a random sample of the two groups is secured, one cannot always randomly assign some participants to primary and secondary substance-abuse prevention or treatment programs that promise to be more effective than others, because federal guidelines dictate that no individual should be denied access to the best possible program. Ethical guidelines stand in the way.

All of these related assumptions and activities are implemented by way of a process known as **hypothesis testing.** For example, using Wong and Bouey's (2001) theory of drug abuse, one could postulate that there are no statistical differences (the null hypothesis) in substance use/abuse, as measured by self-reported drug use (dependent variable), between nonpregnant AI/AN and pregnant AI/AN women (independent variable). Psychologists do not usually predict the null hypothesis, however. They generally predict the **alternative hypothesis** or hypothesize differences between groups. When results indicate that there *are* statistical differences between the groups, the alternative hypothesis is confirmed. In other words, the use of hypothesis testing in science means that one can only *disprove* certain features (e.g., null hypothesis or no statistical differences between nonpregnant and pregnant women in substance abuse) not pertaining to a theory. Rarely can one *prove* features (the alternative hypothesis or statistical differences between the two groups) pertaining to the theory (cf. Popper, 1968).

Having implemented some form of hypothesis testing using our research design, we are ready for **analysis.** There are various levels of analysis (e.g., choice of statistics) but all must match the theory. Wong and Bouey's (2001) theory of drug abuse will once again be used as an example. If the hypothesis is that client characteristics (e.g., pregnancy status) are related to success (abstinence and recovery) or failure (relapse and recidivism) of individuals in primary and secondary drug-abuse prevention or treatment programs, the unit of analysis should be the individual. The individual level of analysis is not the primary one community psychologists hope to achieve. If the hypothesis is that program characteristics (e.g., infrastructure of an organization or type of treatment program) are important, the unit of analysis should be the programs. Communities could also be used as the level of analysis when research is conducted on how various communities differ.

Taken together, the three sets of defining features of scientific research (theory, design, and analysis) are multidimensional in nature. That is, theoretically speaking, there is an infinite number of operational definitions, independent and dependent variables, designs, levels of measurement, and so forth. Pragmatically, only a small fragment of a theory can be investigated. It is possible that two different types of measurement (e.g., umbilical cord blood specimens and self-reported drug abuse) investigating the same dependent variable (e.g., drug abuse during pregnancy) lead to two different conclusions. Even in the case when the **null hypothesis** is rejected (meaning that there *is* a statistical difference in the observations), there still exists an infinite number of other plausible or possible alternative hypotheses.

The Fidelity of Scientific Research

Reliability, internal validity, and external validity are the three sets of related issues that speak to the fidelity of research. Each of these needs to be examined in more detail.

Reliability refers to the extent that concrete or measurable features, or both, of a theory are replicable. For example, using Wong and Bouey's (2001) theory of drug abuse, pregnancy status (an individual characteristic or the independent variable) is said to be reliable if it consistently predicts the number of days of sobriety and the number of Alcoholics Anonymous meetings attended (the results or dependent variable) of women participating in primary and secondary substance-abuse prevention or treatment programs.

Internal validity refers to the degree to which an independent variable is responsible for any observed changes in a dependent variable. In other words, research is said to have high internal validity when confounding effects are at a minimum. **Confounding effects,** or variables, are extraneous variables that influence the dependent variable or results and invalidate the conclusions drawn from the research. For example, using Wong and Bouey's (2001) theory of drug abuse, pregnancy status (an individual characteristic) is said to have high internal validity if it is related to the number of days of sobriety (the results) of women participating in primary and secondary substance-abuse prevention or treatment programs. On the other hand, pregnancy status might not be related to sobriety, because some other factor (e.g., brain size or the presence of friends who use drugs) is. Researchers would then acknowledge that pregnancy status is not internally valid.

External validity refers to the generalizability of results from one study to other studies or to settings other than the researched one. Again, using Wong and Bouey's (2001) theory of drug abuse, one may find that women in New York City (urban dwelling) who enroll in primary and secondary substance-abuse prevention or treatment programs are less likely to abuse drugs during pregnancy compared to those in Long Island (suburban or rural dwelling) who do not. Until these results are replicated with similar samples in other cities or settings, the results must be interpreted as norms only for New York City women.

A number of factors may also influence the fidelity of research. If it is important for a study to have a random sample, one must be certain that there is no **selection bias.** That is, all potential participants should have a statistically equal opportunity to be selected into a study. For example, using Wong and Bouey's (2001) theory of drug abuse, one could investigate people's reactions to two different primary and secondary substance-abuse prevention and treatment programs, although those who are not selected to participate in the program that they desire may work harder, or **compensate,** for their participation in the program where they belong. Even when compensation (not to be confused with a monetary reward) is at a minimum, it is possible that those who enroll in different programs communicate with each other.

A consequence is **diffusion of treatment,** meaning that it would be difficult to draw definitive conclusions about the respective efficiency and effectiveness of each program because neither program is now pure. The effects of one treatment have spilled over into the other. Participants of such programs are also likely to have other problems (e.g., homelessness) in addition to substance abuse, which make them vulnerable to discontinued participation. When participants drop out, it is known as **experimental mortality.** Enrollment in such programs is no guarantee that participants' subsequent abstinence or recovery is solely due to some components of the programs. It is possible that certain client characteristics (e.g., less physical tolerance of the drug) lead to abstinence or recovery naturally over time. In other words, it is due to some form of **maturation.** Certain historical events (e.g., Nancy Reagan's campaign to "Just Say No" to drugs) may intentionally or inadvertently encourage participants' enthusiasm about such programs.

Community Researchers as Consultants

When community psychologists conduct research, they often do so in the role of consultant. A **consultant** is someone who engages in collaborative problem solving with one or more persons (the **consultees**) who are often responsible for providing some form of assistance to another third individual (the **client;** Mowbray, 1979). Because consultants *collaborate with* the consultees, those who participate in the research, including the consultees and their clients, are not called *subjects,* as they are in other psychological research, but rather are called *participants.*

Consultants work in a variety of community settings: educational, industrial, human services (especially related to mental health), governmental, and others. Some consultants conduct research for the government. A number of universities have developed or are developing public policy research laboratories to assist in public and private sector research. Other consultants evaluate programs or conduct needs assessments, and still others lend their expertise to solving social problems by designing preventive education programs or by helping to change aspects of agencies and communities. In other words, consultants appear in many different settings and work on a variety of problems, most of them related to research.

Many of you may perhaps dream of being a highly paid consultant, but the life of a consultant is not always easy. A variety of complex issues face most community consultants. Consultants often enter a situation not knowing what the real problem is that they are being asked to help solve. In a business setting, for instance, a consultant might be hired by management because productivity is low. However, the real underlying problem might be that the management style is so unwelcomed that employee productivity has declined. Would you want to be the consultant who delivers the news to the management team who hired you that management is the problem? Given the nature of the problems for which they are asked to intervene, community psychologists acting as consultants need to weigh the ethical considerations of to whom they are responsible and for what (O'Neill, 1989).

A consultant is also faced with what methods of investigation and change to utilize (Heller, 1990). For instance, the consultant might recommend educational or research services. Similarly, he or she might choose some mix of **outcome** or **process measures.** Outcome measures address what happens *after* the change occurred (i.e., did the change work?). Process research addresses the transactions or processes that took place *during* the change (Kazden, 1980). Processes often underlie outcome. An example of an outcome measure might be that there are fewer pregnant drug users in a community after instituting a prevention program for them. Higher self-esteem and satisfaction with their pregnancies would be processes that underlie the success of the prevention program.

Consultants also need to ask, Are the methods and research affordable, workable, and understandable for this set of clients? Furthermore, ethical consultants work *with* not *for* those who hire them (Benviente, 1989; Christensen & Robinson, 1989). In fact, all consultants need to ensure **constituent validity,** which means that those participating in the research or change are not considered subjects to be acted upon, but rather participants whose perspectives *must* be taken into account in planning and other related activities in order for the activities to be valid (Keys & Frank, 1987). Consultants need to *empower* the population with whom they are working to create and sustain the change initiated by the presence of the consultant. This means that the consultant needs to find a good way to "wean" the clients or participants, lest they become too dependent on the expert consultant.

Professional change agents or consultants also need to assess the prevailing culture as well as the trust and the respect held for them in a particular setting. Such assessment will help consultants determine how visible they should be. Consultants also need to evaluate their own personal values and communicate them openly *before* the consultation or research begins in order to avoid ethical dilemmas after the collaboration process has commenced (Heller, 1989a). Finally, consultants must evaluate their work with their clients; they need to ask the question, Did I improve the community by my presence? It is through research that this question can best be answered. Without evaluation, how would a change agent know if the change worked and whether it ought to be repeated?

TRADITIONAL SCIENTIFIC RESEARCH METHODS

There are research designs that all psychologists, including community psychologists, utilize. These include correlational and experimental methodologies. These research designs will be reviewed and then some specific methods will be given that are more likely to be utilized by community psychologists than most other types of psychologists (e.g., social psychologists).

Correlational Research

Traditional scientific research methods can be roughly classified into three broad types. Table 2.1 is a summary of their characteristics. **Correlational methods** include a class of designs (e.g., surveys) and measurement procedures, as well as techniques (e.g., self-report), that allow one to examine the associations or relationships between two or more variables in their natural environments. In other words, correlational methods do not contain active manipulations of the variables under study; rather, they are usually descriptive in nature. For example, using Wong and Bouey's (2001) theory of drug abuse, one might want to investigate the relationship between the number of months pregnant and the severity of substance abuse; these variables are not manipulated. The fact that one has no control over them means that the distinction of independent from dependent variables may be arbitrary, albeit dictated by a theory.

Also, causation cannot be determined, because intervening or other unstudied variables could easily have produced the effects noted. Associations are said to be **spurious** when intervening or confounding variables are thought to be responsible for the relationships. In experimental research, intervening variables are controlled for through randomly assigning participants to groups, holding conditions constant, and manipulating the independent variable. In correlational research, these criteria are seldom, if ever, met.

In its simple form, the associations between two or more variables are quantified using a statistic known as the **Pearson Correlation Coefficient,** which ranges from +1.00 to − 1.00. The sign (+ or −) indicates the direction of the association. For example, if the sign is positive (+), both variables move in the same direction, or as one gets smaller, so does the other. A positive correlation can also mean that as one variable increases, so does the other. A negative or inverse correlation means that the variables move in opposite directions. For

TABLE 2.1   Characteristics of Three Broad Types of Scientific Research Methods

	CORRELATION	QUASI-EXPERIMENTAL	EXPERIMENTAL
Type of question	Are the variables of interest related to each other?	Does an independent variable that the researcher does not completely control affect the dependent variable or the research result?	Is there a realtionship between independent and dependent variables that addresses the cause?
When used	Researcher is unable to manipulate an independent variable. Sometimes used in explanatory research.	Researcher wants to assess the impact of real-life intervention in the community or elsewhere.	Researcher has control over the independent variable and can minimize the number of confounding variables in the research.
Advantages	Convience of data collection. May avoid certain ethical and/or practical problems.	Provides some information about cause-effect relationships. Permits assessment of more real-world interventions.	Ability to demonstrate cause-effect relationship. Permit control over confounding variables and the ruling of alternative explanations.
Disadvantages	Cannot establish a cause-effect relationship.	Lack of control over confunding variable. Strong casual inference cannot be made.	Some questions cannot be studied experimentally for either practical or ethical reason. May lead to artificial procedures.

Source: Adapted from "Techniques and Pitfalls of Applied Behavioral Science Research: The Case of Community of Meditation" by F. Y. Wong, C. H. Blakely, & S. L. Worsham, in *Community Mediation: A Handbook for Practitioners and Researchers* (pp. 35–41) by K. G. Duffy, J. W. Grosch, & P. V. Olczak (Eds.), 1991, New York: Guilford. Copyright 1991 by Guilford Press. Used by permission.

example, as one variable increases, the other decreases. The number (e.g., .35) indicates the magnitude or intensity of the relationship, with 1.00 being the largest correlation and 0.00 indicating little or no relationship.

Using Wong and Bouey's (2001) theory of drug abuse, a Pearson Correlation Coefficient of −.80 between the number of months pregnant and substance abuse means that women who are at more advanced stages of pregnancy are less likely to abuse drugs (a strong negative association). However, one *cannot* conclude that advanced stages of pregnancy *cause* decreases in substance abuse. Also, this association may be spurious when there is reason to suspect that pregnant women's perceived support from their spouses later in pregnancy is largely responsible for decreases in substance abuse rather than due to the pregnancy itself.

Experimental Research

The **experimental method** includes a class of designs (e.g., between-groups designs where no two groups receive the same treatment) and measurement procedures, as well as techniques (e.g., umbilical cord blood specimens), that allow one to manipulate independent and dependent variables. A common design is the **pretest-posttest control group design,** which involves the assessment of an effect or effects both *prior to* and *following* an experimental manipulation in one group (the experimental group) but not another (no-manipulation group or control group). That is, one group of participants is exposed to an independent variable and another group is not. In addition, assignment to the experimental or control group is random; thus, participants have an equal chance of being assigned to either the experimental or control group.

If the experimental manipulation is functioning as predicted by a theory, the dependent variable should ideally be observable as a change from premanipulation to postmanipulation scores within the experimental *but not* the control group. In other words, the pretest-posttest observations of participants in the control group should remain relatively constant over time, unless some natural maturation occurs or the initial pretest sensitizes all participants to the nature of the assessment being conducted. For example, using Wong and Bouey's (2001) theory of drug abuse, pregnant substance abusers who participate in primary and secondary prevention or treatment programs should report an increase in days of sobriety from pretreatment to posttreatment compared to those who do not. Community experimentation is a fairly new idea in the history of psychology.

Quasi-Experimental Research

Many variables (e.g., school climate) studied in the field of community psychology cannot be experimentally manipulated for practical and ethical reasons. Similarly, subjects cannot always be randomly assigned to groups. For example, if a participant is pregnant, it is not possible to randomly assign her to the nonpregnant group. In studies of pregnancy, one would probably end up using intact groups. Thus, a compromise is the use of the **quasi-experimental method.** A common quasi-experimental design is the **nonequivalent pretest-posttest control design,** which involves the comparison of a group before and after some experimental manipulation with another group that has not been exposed to the manipulation or treatment. As mentioned earlier, this design differs from the pretest-posttest design previously discussed in that *participants are not randomly assigned* to experimental or control conditions.

Experimental manipulation is often restricted by practical or ethical reasons. Although this allows for a more natural or realistic research design, initial differences between experimental and comparison groups may not be balanced. For example, using Wong and Bouey's (2001) theory of drug abuse, pregnant women who voluntarily participate in primary and secondary prevention or treatment programs may be more educated than those in the comparison group, which may include women who are high school dropouts. Thus, differences already exist between the two groups before the study begins. Care must be taken in drawing conclusions about causal differences between the two groups, as the two groups already differ at the onset of the research.

At this point, some clarification about the terms *correlation, experimental methods,* and *field research* is necessary. **Field research** refers to the investigation of a set of related phenomena pertaining to an issue (or issues) *in natural settings.* Either correlational or experimental methods or both may be used in the field. Following is a brief review of three types of research methods or approaches frequently employed in field research—research that is far more typical in community psychology than in many other areas of psychology.

OTHER RESEARCH METHODS USED IN
COMMUNITY PSYCHOLOGY

Ethnography

Due to the urgency of the issues in the field of community psychology, diverse methods or approaches are often employed. One such research method is **ethnography,** which refers to a broad class of designs (e.g., semi-structured interviews) and measurement procedures and techniques (e.g., behavioral ratings) that allow one to conduct social interactions with participants of the study. The primary purpose of ethnography is to allow one to gain an understanding of *how* people view their own experiences.

Ethnography should allow an individual to describe his or her *own* experiences without having to translate them into the words of the researchers. In other words, the informants or participants should use their own language to describe their own experiences. An ethnographic interviewer should probably also provide an explanation of *why* he or she is asking particular questions so as to be more fully understood by the informants. Similarly, in contrast to the more traditional scientific definitions of objectivity or neutrality, in ethnography, the value systems of the researcher may influence the social interactions between the researcher and the informants and thus influence the course of the research. Hence, a researcher is better off taking a stance of ignorance about the experiences of the informants than making predetermined judgments (Heller, Price, Reinharz, Riger, & Wandersman, 1984). Of course, no scientific research method is truly objective, because how one conceptualizes an issue logically dictates the course of its action.

Compared to cultural anthropologists and sociologists who first developed this technique, community psychologists use ethnography at a lower rate. However, as research issues become more socially oriented, these methods (which are correlational in nature) are more likely to be employed than experimental methods (Speer, Dey, Griggs, Gibson, Lubin, & Hughey, 1992). Ethnography is perhaps most informative when research questions asked do not have a strong theoretical framework. Thus, *qualitative* information that is likely to be gleaned from ethnographic studies can inform the researcher about future directions of study, some of which may include field experiments where variables are actively manipulated.

Participant observation is a popular and special type of ethnographic technique. Although the researcher often assumes the role of an observer (i.e., systematic observation with neutrality) in participant observation and ethnography, a prototypical study using participant observation often involves ongoing dialogues between the researcher and participants. For example, a researcher who is interested in the study of teenage gangs often needs to "hang out" with the gangs for a period of time. Also, the researcher needs to acquire the language used by the gangs to facilitate his or her investigation of the gangs' social network characteristics as well as to establish trust. Meanwhile, the constant social interactions between the researcher and gang members may affect their perceptions of and relationships with each other. A consequence can be role ambiguity, where it becomes unclear to gang members what role the researcher is adopting. Is the researcher a member of the gang, a researcher, or both?

With difficult-to-reach or hidden populations, or when working with limited empirical databases, **network analysis** as a methodology has the advantage of informing researchers about key issues pertaining to these populations (i.e., formative research), thus allowing preparation for subsequent large-scale or population-based studies. Friedman and colleagues (1997) argued, "Social networks are relationships that can influence ideas, norms, and behaviors. Risk networks are behaviors and materials . . . that can transmit HIV from person to person. Social and risk networks often overlap. Recent evidence indicates that both kinds of networks have major consequences for HIV epidemiology and behavior" (p. 95). Case in Point 2.2 shows the utility of network analysis.

The two major types of network methodology are egocentric and sociometric. **Egocentric** methodology refers to the relationships and shared behaviors *between* an individual and his or her peers. **Sociometric** methodology refers to relationships and shared behaviors *among* individuals. In both types, the objective is to identity and delineate patterns of relationships and shared behaviors. Other methodological criteria (e.g., definitions for types of relationships and shared behaviors) are contingent on theoretical framework(s) or research question(s). For example, one variant of the sociometric network study on injection drug use and HIV is to ask participants to provide information about up to 10 individuals with whom

■ ■ ■ ■ ■

CASE IN POINT 2.2
CRACKING NETWORK

Gillespie and Murty (1994) used network analysis to determine potential "cracks" in a postdisaster service delivery system. Network analysis allows a community consultant to partition community organizations into equivalent, peripheral, isolated, or central organizations. In this manner, interrelationships among organizations can be examined to determine where the weak linkages, or cracks, are in a service system.

To avoid the problem of having to wait for an actual disaster to occur, Gillespie and Murty used a vignette with participants from various organizations (e.g., the American Red Cross) that respond to large-scale community disasters. The participants were asked to respond as if it were 18 hours after

the initial impact of an earthquake. In their research, Gillespie and Murty identified nine groups or clusters of organizations in the postdisaster network. One group had no interorganizational relations to the rest of the network. In other words, this group represented a serious crack in the network because it had not established any way to coordinate its services with organizations outside its origin. The researchers suggested that community planning councils, after using network analysis, target peripheral and isolated organizations and encourage them to initiate contacts with more central organizations such that service delivery can be improved.

they have injected drugs and had unprotected sex during the past 30 days. Analytic procedures for both types of network methodology can be quite elaborate and involved, as well as technical.

Conceptually, network analysis as a methodology should appeal to community-based researchers. However, the use of the methodology is not immune from cultural barriers or other social obstacles. Thus, to reap the benefit of this type of methodology, researchers must have a good grasp of the targeted populations. Trust is the foundation for the methodology.

Epidemiology

A second set of methods or approaches used more by community psychologists than other psychologists is **epidemiology,** which is "the study of the occurrence and distribution of diseases and other health-related conditions in populations" (Kelsey, Thompson, & Evans, 1986, p. 3). This includes a broad class of designs (e.g., prospective or, loosely, "futuristic" studies and retrospective or, loosely, "historical" studies) and measurement procedures and techniques (e.g., random telephone dialing).

These methods allow for the establishment of two phenomena: prevalence and incidence. The **prevalence** of a disease or health-related condition is the total number of people within a given population who have it. The **incidence** refers to the number of people within a given population who have acquired the condition *within a specific time period,* usually a year. Incidence rates can be established using a **prospective design** or investigation of new cases. Prevalence rates can be established using a **retrospective design** or investigation of known cases. In their purest forms, neither the examination of prevalence rates nor incidence rates should disturb or change the behavior of the community. There are differences between the two, however, beyond the difference in their definitions. Prevalence rate is a more inclusive measure than incidence rate and is easier to calculate. However, the disadvantage of prevalence rates is that they are difficult to interpret, as they indicate both the incidence and duration of a disorder.

Depending on the objectives of the epidemiological investigation, measurement procedures as well as techniques used in the design can range from household interviews to random telephone digit dialing. Others include the use of birth certificates, death certificates, census records, or all of these.

Having defined these concepts, an example is in order of how epidemiology is used. HIV is thought to be responsible for AIDS, one of the deadliest, incurable diseases of our time. Epidemiological surveys (mostly retrospective studies) conducted by the Centers for Disease Control and Prevention (CDC) in the early 1980s called attention to the onset of this epidemic in the United States. Subsequent investigations (including prospective studies) documented that in the United States, groups at high risk of contracting HIV included homosexual and bisexual individuals, as well as intravenous drug users. Epidemiologists, then, would say that these groups are *high risk* or *at risk.* Recent investigations illustrate that children (via birth) and women (via partners who are bisexual or intravenous drug users or both) are the fastest growing groups at risk of contracting HIV.

Once the prevalence and/or incidence rates for a disorder have been determined, epidemiologists can attempt to isolate variables that seem to have caused the disorder. For example, once the CDC had an understanding of who was at risk for HIV, the CDC could next search for the cause of the disease, which was discovered (the exchange of blood or other body fluids from an infected individual to another).

Needs Assessment and Program Evaluation

Community psychologists are beginning to realize the benefits of the use of epidemiological methods in the development and refinement of activities related to prevention, intervention, and treatment. However, for these activities to be effective and efficient, it is important to understand the significant issues and needs of the individuals involved. **Needs assessment** refers to a set of methods or approaches that elucidate the magnitude of an issue or examine a set of issues in relation to the available resources for addressing the issues. In other words, it is a way of determining if there is a need for a certain program or intervention because the need is not yet well addressed.

For example, given that the incubation period of AIDS is about 10 years—much longer than the nine-month gestation period for Edisak's baby—it is important to estimate the needs for health care and services of individuals who are at various stages of HIV. Individuals who are newly diagnosed may need social support, whereas individuals who are in the late stages of AIDS may need intensive medical and hospice care. Also, in the absence of a cure or vaccine for HIV, needs assessment should emphasize the development or refinement of prevention and intervention strategies, including the practice of safe sex by using condoms and implementing needle exchange programs.

Needs assessments can be conducted via ethnographic interviews, surveys, and other observational or descriptive techniques, each of which has its own advantages and disadvantages. For example, in ethnographic interviews, individuals might be reluctant to reveal face to face that they are unmarried and pregnant or are HIV-positive. They might be more likely to disclose this information in an anonymous survey. On the other hand, during an interview, the interviewer (or the informant, for that matter) can change the direction of the interview and thus reveal information not discovered on written surveys, which are less easily modified on the spot.

Having developed or refined a program to address needs related to a particular issue, whether it be AIDS or teen pregnancy, the effectiveness or efficiency of the program should be evaluated; this process is called program evaluation. **Program evaluation** refers to a broad class of designs (e.g., survey) as well as measurement procedures and techniques (e.g., birth certificate) that allow one to examine "social programs . . . , and the policies that spawn and justify them, [and] aim to improve the welfare of individuals, organizations, and society" (Shadish, Cook, & Leviton, 1991, p. 19). Given unstable economies worldwide, there is an increasing trend to hold social programs "accountable" for their performance, so program evaluation is becoming more and more important.

It is beyond the scope of this chapter to conduct an extensive discussion of the processes involved in the evaluation of a typical social program. Suffice it to say that an adequate evaluation consists of at least four related components: (1) the goals, (2) the objectives, (3) the activities, and (4) the milestones. The **goal** refers to the aim of the evaluation. A good evaluation is likely to be driven by theory. That is, the concept of goal addresses the question,

What does the evaluation hope to achieve? (or, *Why* should an evaluation be conducted?). The construct of an **objective** refers to the plan. That is, objectives address the question, *How* does one go about achieving the goal? The concept of **activity** refers to the specific task. That is, activity addresses the question, *What* does the plan consists of? **Milestone** refers to the outcome; that is, Does the evaluation *achieve* its intended goal?

Using Wong and Bouey's (2001) theory of drug abuse, one might want to investigate the differential effectiveness of mainstream versus native-focused prevention and treatment programs for AI/AN adults (the *goal*) Therefore, one reviews records and interviews clients and staff of the two types of programs (the *objective* or design). Given the voluminous records and possible number of informants or interviewees, only a randomized stratified sample will be used (the *activity,* including analysis). It might be reasonable to hypothesize that a higher enrollment rate will be observed in the native-focused programs than programs in the mainstream because of cultural competent services. However, the two types of programs may not differ in dropout rates, because, as you know by now, intervention outcomes are often contingent on a host of factors other than program type (the *milestones*).

This example no doubt is a very simplistic picture of program evaluation. Although program evaluation may seem more objective as a scientific research method than ethnography, role ambiguity is still possible. Role ambiguity is most likely to occur with internal evaluation. That is, an evaluator who is also on the staff of the agency assumes not only the role of evaluator but also is someone interested in using data derived from the evaluation for future program development or refinement. To guard against this problem, agencies usually establish an advisory panel so that program development or refinement is executed by the panel rather than a single, internal evaluator. Another solution is to employ an external evaluator such as a community consultant. The U.S. General Accounting Office, a research arm of the U.S. Congress, conducts a fair amount of evaluation of publicly funded social programs. Private firms such as Abt Associates, the Rand Corporation, and Stanford Research International also assume a large share of program evaluations in the United States.

In addition to methodological concerns (e.g., competing theories about a social issue and different operational definitions for a feature of the theory), social dynamics are crucial in evaluating any social program. That is, people do not like to be judged, especially when potentially negative consequences exist. Given the fact that not-for-profit social programs are more sensitive to funding issues and public scrutiny, if these programs have been demonstrated to be less than effective, they are likely to be eliminated. Even when they are effective but less than efficient (i.e., expensive to maintain), they may still be eliminated.

These tensions between program evaluators and practitioners often exist when a traditional evaluation paradigm is used, that is, only "objective" assessment or feedback (no active or direct engagement from program staff) should inform program development, refinement, and improvement. However, Wandersman, Morrissey, Davino and others (1998) argued that "there has been a growing discussion of new and evolving roles for evaluators. . . . Unlike traditional evaluation approaches, empowerment evaluators collaborate with community members . . . to determine program goals and implementation strategies, serve as facilitators . . . not outside experts . . . in ongoing program improvement" (p. 4). Ultimately, it is about program accountability. To that end, eight questions (their corresponding strategies) serve as guides for program accountability. They are as follows:

1. Needs for program (needs assessment)
2. Use of scientific knowledge or best practices for program (consult scientific literature and promising practice programs)
3. Congruence between new program(s) with existing programs (feedback on comprehensive and fit of program)
4. How to implement program (planning)
5. Effectiveness in implementation (process evaluation)
6. Effectiveness of program (outcome and impact evaluation)
7. How to improve program (lesson learned)
8. How to institutionalize effective program (replication or spin off)

THE URGENCY OF RESEARCH IN COMMUNITY PSYCHOLOGY AND RELATED PITFALLS

As mentioned earlier, research in the field of community psychology is often conducted with a sense of urgency not often seen in other areas of psychology. Some aspects of this urgency were demonstrated by using the example of drug abuse among pregnant women. Other related issues deserve some brief comment.

The Politics of Science and the Science of Politics

Up to this point, you have been "implicitly" introduced to the idea that sound policy (e.g., substance-abuse prevention targeting pregnant women) should be based and grounded in scientific evidence. That is, systematic and vigorous examination of an issue using scientific principles would result in the most desirable outcome(s) or impact(s). A close examination reveals that the impact of science on policy and the distinction between science and politics may be less than ideal and clear-cut. Two examples will illustrate these observations.

Research has consistently demonstrated that needle exchange programs could slow the spread of HIV. Yet, the U.S. Congress has steadfastly refused (based on "moral" grounds) to heed the scientific evidence. Meanwhile, some argue that "politics is dominant . . . with AIDS" (Moss, 2000, p. 1385). However, Collins and Coates (2000) argued that

> the real concern is not that AIDS is a charged political issue but that the debate around national AIDS policy is often motivated by narrow political agendas rather than legitimate disagreements about how best to fight the epidemic. "Politics" gave us the Ryan White CARE Act that has served hundreds of thousands of people living with HIV and AIDS. "Politics" has helped boost basic research funding at the National Institutes of Health, giving us unprecedented scientific breakthroughs in AIDS. The point is not that "politics" has been dominant in AIDS but rather that, too often, AIDS politics has been uninformed by scientific knowledge. (p. 1389)

In other words, research does not occur in a vacuum. All research (including research based on scientific principles) implicitly or explicitly promotes cultural, social, or political agendas. Collins and Coates rightly stated that

If advocacy affects research, the converse is also true. Research findings do not always carry the day, but often frame the context in which issues are discussed. The real question is how research can be better integrated into national health policy debates. The challenge to do this in AIDS policy is as immediate as ever. (p. 1390)

This complex relationship between science and politics is even more pronounced when the issue at hand is about racial relationships in the United States. Although the U.S. Census Bureau has collected information on race since the first census in 1790, racial and ethnic classifications have undergone many changes in the last two centuries. The idea of racial and ethnic classifications is a relatively recent phenomenon. For example, people with heritage from the Indian subcontinent were once classified as "White," now they are grouped into the umbrella category known as "Asian and Pacific Islander" (API), making up more than 40 culturally distinct groups with over 100 languages and dialects. This term only came to national attention and consciousness in the 1970s.

The prototype of the system used today was developed by the Office of Management and Budget in the 1970s—often known as "Directive 15" (see *Public Health Report, 109,* 1994; http://whitehouse.gov/omb/fedreg/ombdir15/html). The system is intended for census tracking. However, over time politicians have used it for resource allocations and distributions (including congressional redistricting). Researchers (including behavioral and social scientists) have used the various racial and ethnic categories to infer differences ranging from biological to genetic to psychological to social attributes. For example, as a country we are still engaging in the "one-drop blood" practice. Yet, it is not difficult to conclude that these classifications are social constructs. Although such classifications may serve as crude proxy indicators of "group-level" differences, the causal mechanisms of such difference are less than clear. Specifically, Directive 15 notes the absence of "scientific or anthropological" foundations in its formulations. Some disciplines, such as anthropology, are critical of this paradigm (see www.aaa.org on *American Anthropological Association Response to OMB Directive 15: Race and ethnic standards for federal statistics and administrative reporting*). However, given that the system is so intertwined in our daily life, it is not likely to be discontinued from the scientific fields any time soon. In other words, one needs to be mindful that scientific research has its cultural, social, and political biases.

Ethics: Cultural Relativism or Universal Human Rights?

A major principle of scientific research is that the well-being of research participants must be ensured (American Psychological Association, 1985). In other words, participation in research should not endanger people in any physical, psychological, or social way. All participants must be informed about the purpose of the research as much as possible (without jeopardizing the integrity of the research) and the use of deception must be minimized. It is **ethically** undesirable to do otherwise (cf. Christensen, 1988). In many research institutions and universities, before research can be initiated, approval from an **institutional review** board must first be secured, demonstrating that all ethical guidelines (e.g., participants must be fully debriefed about the purpose of the study) have been met.

These general principles and premises seem straightforward and objective (i.e., research is neutral). To the 399 African American men in the Tuskegee Syphilis Study (conducted by the U.S. government from 1932 to 1972) who were deliberately denied effective treatment for syphilis in order to document its natural history, the study at best reeked of *racist* overtones and at worst demonstrated *genocide*. Decades later, President Clinton expressed his regrets on May 16, 1997: "The legacy of the study at Tuskegee has reached far and deep, in ways that hurt our progress and divide our nation. We cannot be one America when a whole segment of our nation has no trust in America." However, to many African Americans, as well as other racial and ethnic minorities, such injustices (e.g., forced sterilization of the so-called mentally feeble) continue to prevail—they have just become more covert (in the name of science). These outrages and debates have also assumed new dimensions, guises, and significance in the AIDS pandemic (see *American Journal of Public Health*, 88, 1998)—extending the boundaries to international scientific research. These are extremely complex issues, so two related sets of ideas will be examined: informed consent and experimental-control (placebo) design.

Informed consent, a major principle of scientific research, is ensuring that a clear and articulated procedure and process is in place so that participants understand the nature of the research, including the right to refuse participation without any repercussions. In other words, the process of informed consent has two key components: comprehension of materials and voluntary participation. In an HIV testing study conducted in a South African hospital, Karim, Karim, Coovadia, and Susser (1998) found that although participants understood the process of informed consent (i.e., comprehension of materials), many participants felt that they had little choice in refusing enrollment in the study (i.e., voluntary participation) due to the fact that participation in the study was the only opportunity for receiving needed medical care or services. Karim and colleagues concluded that "subtle and unexpected elements of coercion can reside in the perceptions (real or imagined) held by patients being recruited into a research project in a medical care setting. . . . Ethicists and institutional review boards should certainly explore the issue further" (p. 640).

Once participants consent to enroll in a study, they may be assigned to an experimental or control (or comparison) group. A *true* control group (most scientifically rigorous) is one that does not receive any intervention or treatment (or receives a placebo). Without any other known efficacious intervention or treatment, a true experimental design is the preferred way to ascertain the efficacy of an intervention or treatment. However, what should researchers do when they know that, without any intervention or treatment, the participants in the control group will likely be in jeopardy? Alternatively, should researchers provide a known efficacious intervention or treatment (e.g., condoms) simultaneously when testing an intervention or treatment with unknown efficacy (i.e., vaginal microbicides)? This procedure might compromise the integrity of the scientific conclusions.

Based on findings of a trial in Thailand, the CDC, together with the National Institutes of Health (NIH) and the Joint United Nations Program on Acquired Immunodeficiency Syndrome (UNAIDS), announced that placebos should not be used in vertical HIV transmission clinical trials (maternal-fetal transmission, or the 076 Study). The Thailand study found that vertical HIV transmission was reduced by half, even in an abbreviated treatment (10 percent of the standard U.S. regimen). These issues have quickly prompted some researchers to advocate the use of *equivalency trials* (i.e., a new treatment versus a standard treatment). However, the CDC acknowledged that the efficacy of the newly found treatment could not have been achieved without the use of a placebo. Thus, Dr. Varmus (then director of NIH) and Dr. Satcher (then director of CDC) continued to favor placebo-controlled trials. Subsequently, the CDC and NIH, together with several European governments, funded a series of trials in Africa. Both Drs. Varmus and Satcher justified their position by quoting the chair of the AIDS Research Committee of the Uganda Cancer Institute: "These are Ugandan studies conducted by Ugandan investigators on Ugandans.... It is not NIH conducting the studies in Uganda, but Ugandans conducting their study on their people for the good of their people" (Varmus & Satcher, 1997). Nonetheless, it is not difficult to appreciate the controversy of the issue.

For some researchers, such as George Annas and Michael Grodin (cofounders of the Global Lawyers and Physicians), as well as the late Jonathan Mann (former director of WHO Global Programme on AIDS and a well-known advocate for human rights in the context of public health practice), the issue is about universal human rights. Annas and Grodin (1998) argued that "unless the interventions being tested will actually be made available to the improvised populations that are being used as subjects, developed countries are simply exploiting them in order to quickly use the knowledge gained from the clinical trials for the developed trials" (p. 561). In addition, Annas and Grodin raised similar concerns as Karim and associates (1998) did on informed consent. It is virtually certain that for many of the participants in these Third World countries, enrollment in such trials guarantees them access to minimal medical or health care. The argument of cultural sovereignty may be nebulous at best—for example, those authorities making the decision in the Third World countries are unlikely to be the ones to be enrolled in the trials or subjected to the experimentation. Moreover, many of these policy makers have economic ties to an increasing global economy (e.g., the pharmaceutical industry).

Does these mean we should not conduct any studies in such countries? There are no easy answers. These debates demonstrate the interdependence between the integrity of scientific research and societal forces (e.g., cultural norms, economy, racism, sexism, classism, etc.). Bayer (1998) stated:

> The tragedy of the recent trials is that they bear a profound moral taint, not of a malevolent research design but, rather, of a world economic order that makes effective prophylaxis for the interruption of maternal-fetal HIV transmission available but unaffordable for many— this is true, as well, for a host of treatment for AIDS and other diseases. In a just world, this would not be the case and the research under attack would be unnecessary. It is the social context of maldistribution of wealth and resources that both mandates these studies, and at the same time, renders them so troubling. (p. 570)

The Continuum of Research: The Value of Multiple Measures

As you may recall from Chapter 1, Speer and associates (1992) indicated that there has been a shift in the field of community psychology. This shift has been toward the use of correlational designs and away from experimentation, because topics of investigation often relate to major social issues. Even in those cases where quasi-experimental or experimental designs can be used, one may have to face a multitude of methodological issues or dilemmas. One class of issues or dilemmas concerns the logistics of implementing a research program. For example, how do researchers locate drug-using pregnant women to investigate drug use? Not only are they hard to access, especially if they do not seek medical attention, but they may also be homeless or change addresses often.

Also, how do researchers increase the probability that pregnant teens will tell the truth when using self-report measures? Another way to further validate self-reported alcohol use would be to count the number of empty alcohol beverage containers that pregnant women have discarded. A nonreactive measure such as this, where people are not contacted face to face, is called an **unobtrusive measure.** Unobtrusive measures are ethically questionable, as participant consent is often not obtained. Likewise, unobtrusive measures do not speak to *why* a certain behavior occurs, only that it does occur.

When working with complex social issues such as teen pregnancy, one should always make an attempt to use **multiple methods.** For example, self-reports, nonreactive or unobtrusive measures, as well as umbilical blood samples could be obtained to determine whether, indeed, pregnant women are using drugs or alcohol. However, multiple methods take more time than single methods and may generate different conclusions for the same issue. Although it is hoped that a theory is solid enough to guide the interpretation of results,

---

■ ■ ■ ■ ■

CASE IN POINT 2.3

CREATING A UNIFORM DATA SET FOR RACIAL AND ETHNIC MINORITY HEALTH IN THE UNITED STATES: SOME GUIDING PRINCIPLES

The Office of Minority Health (OMH) within the U.S. Department of Health and Human Services (DHHS) is mandated by Congress to coordinate federal agency efforts to improve racial and ethnic minority health status and reduce disparities in health, health care, and access to health care for these populations. Most (though not all) OMH program funding is directed to racial and ethnic minority community-based organizations, and most of these programs involve a mixture of health promotion, screening, access to services and treatment, training and education, materials development, case management, capacity-building, development of community linkages, and other such activities. These projects are funded by a range of grants and cooperative agreement programs, including (a) minority health coalitions, (b) bilingual/bicultural access to care grants, (c) managed care–related grants, (d) HIV/AIDS technical assistance grants, (e) coalition and state-level grants, and (f) cooperative agreements with hospitals and universities

related to health promotion, screening, and family/ community violence prevention. Along with the implementation of data collection processes at the project level, OMH is required to report on program effectiveness and impact to the Congress.

Working with OMH, one of the authors (Wong) of this book has been engaging in multiyear efforts to develop such a system. Developing a UDS (Uniform Data System) is not only an important accountability and performance monitoring for OMH, but also a significant attempt to develop a data collection system that is meaningful for OMH-funded community-based organizations and the racial and ethnic minority populations they serve. This knowledge can be applied to the general issues of evaluating community-based health programs and to identifying/assessing the nature of progress with respect to racial and ethnic health, beyond its direct application to OMH projects (cf. Wells & Conviser, 1998). It is important to recognize the enterprising and ground level work these programs carry out to improve the health status of diverse racial and ethnic minority populations. A great deal of their work is unique and often not adequately accounted for via traditional performance indicators. While guidelines to evaluating community-based programs (United Way, 1996) often argue against measuring such programs using uniform measures—a position well-understood by the author (Wong) and colleagues—it becomes necessary to find some way to do so for federal programs as required by Congress. Therefore, one important aspect of the UDS is to attempt to capture some of these unique elements in a standardized system.

Because of the range of barriers to health care for many racial and ethnic populations (e.g., language, cultural differences, socioeconomic status), programs intervening at points A (mobilization), B (knowledge change), and C (system change) may be necessary for outcomes at points D (behavior and utilization) and E (health outcome change). Office of Minority Health programs primarily target points A, B, and C—sometimes D—on the continuum. See Figure 2.5.

Because OMH programs intervene primarily at Points A, B, and C (and sometimes D), they are measurable by their commensurable data type:

■ Point A—Mobilization: Primarily *process* measures such as the formation of coalitions,

coalition activities and membership, training of community and health provider staff, as well as implementation of awareness activities.

■ Point B—Changes in Knowledge and Awareness: Primarily determined through *short-term assessments of changes in attitude and knowledge*, among project clients; health providers, who receive training; and community members, who participate in outreach/education activities or who receive informational messages/materials. In addition, *counts* of materials developed/disseminated, training and educational activities held and attendance at those activities, and *process records* of activities conducted.

■ Point C—System Changes: Primarily assessed through *process* measures, identifying actual changes in specific health systems, policies developed, committees formed, and so forth.

■ Point D—Behavior and Utilization Changes: Primarily determined through *survey or questionnaires* concerning self-reported behavior change, and potentially through *counts* of screenings conducted, referrals made, or services utilized by the target population—where such data are available.

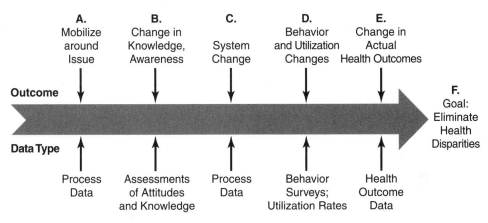

FIGURE 2.5   Data Types and the Public Health Continuum

one would need to reexamine the theory and research if different methods produce different outcomes.

The Importance of Cultural Sensitivity

Another class of methodological issues or dilemmas concerns **cultural sensitivity,** or awareness and appreciation of intragroup and intergroup differences. The authors have chosen to define cultural sensitivity in a very *liberal* sense. People belong to many categories and have multiple expectations or identities. For example, a person can be an African American (racial or ethnic identity) who is also a college graduate (educational background) and a white-collar worker (socioeconomic status). This individual may have more in common with White college graduates (of similar educational background) who are also white-collar workers (similar socioeconomic status) than other African Americans who are high school dropouts (different educational background) or living on welfare (different socioeconomic status).

In other words, cultural sensitivity underscores the importance of the issue of person-environment fit. For example, White researchers and consultants might encounter resistance from African American research participants or program clients. Similarly, male researchers who study pregnant women who are in drug treatment may encounter resistance not only from the women but also from the program staff. Neither the women nor the staff share the same goal or vision as the male researcher (i.e., effective treatment based on scientific knowledge). Rather, both the women and staff perceive the researcher as intrusive. In other words, there is a poor person-environment fit between the researcher and the pregnant women as well as between the researcher and staff. Ecologically valid research hinges on cultural sensitivity. The methodology used needs to enhance or at least take into account the person-environment fit.

Even when one is able to circumvent the preceding two classes of methodological dilemmas, there may be ethical dilemmas with which to contend. For example, when drug abuse among pregnant women is investigated, not only does one need to maintain the integrity of the study (including confidentiality) but one must also have a clear sense of ethical and legal responsibility. In other words, should one report to a legal authority those pregnant women one thinks are endangering themselves, their unborn children, and perhaps their other children? There are no simple answers. Although research in community psychology is crucial to a better society, the research is not easy to conduct.

SUMMARY

A major principle of the field of community psychology is to create or engage in some form of social change so that individuals may benefit. In order to sort the beneficial from the useless changes, psychologists need a way to help assess change. Scientific research provides that mechanism. Positive social changes are more likely than not to be driven by theory and evaluated with scientific research.

When scientists conduct research, they utilize a set of related assumptions and activities. Most scientific disciplines (especially the mature ones) are guided by theory. Within a theory, there may be more than one model (or blueprint) and paradigm (or framework). Thus, scientific research can be conducted with more than one design as well as various levels of measurement and analysis. These components are the defining features of scientific research.

A special category of theory often found in the literature of community psychology is systems theory. Systems theories presume that systems underlie the processes, behaviors, or issues being discussed. A system can be thought of as a set of objects that relate to each other. More precisely, a system is an organized, unified whole that is made up of parts, components, or subsystems that are interdependent, such that the whole is recognizable as a whole. An example of a system is a school.

The first set of steps in scientific research involves the translation of some related conceptual features of a theory into more concrete or measurable aspects, using the process of *operationalization.* The outcome of operationalization is some form of independent variable (the manipulated variable or cause) and dependent variable (the result or effect). The next two sets of steps involve some form of sampling strategy (e.g., random samples, convenience samples, purposive samples, and random assignment), followed by hypothesis testing (the null hypothesis versus the alternative hypothesis) and analysis.

The fidelity of scientific research is a function of such things as ethics (which are examined by an institute review board), reliability, internal validity, and confounding effects. Reliability is the extent to which concrete or measurable features of a theory can be replicated. Internal validity refers to the degree to which an independent variable is responsible for changes in the dependent variable. External validity is the generalizability of results from one study to another or to other settings. Confounding effects are those variables other than the independent variable that could also account for the research results.

Scientific research can be conducted using the correlational method (which produces a statistic known as the Pearson Correlation Coefficient), the experimental method (e.g., pretest-posttest control group design), or the quasi-experimental method (e.g., nonequivalent pretest-posttest control design), or all three. Ethnography (e.g., participant observation), epidemiology, and needs assessment, as well as program evaluation (including the processes of goal, objective, activity, and milestone), are descriptive types of methods frequently employed in field research. Each type of method has its advantages and disadvantages. Each is perhaps more likely to be utilized by community psychologists than any other type of psychologist.

Research in the field of community psychology is often conducted with a sense of urgency. This urgency is best achieved when multiple methods are used and cultural sensitivity is taken into account.

■ ■ ■ ■ ■

THE IMPORTANCE OF SOCIAL CHANGE

If a free society cannot help the many who are poor,
it cannot save the few who are rich.
—John F. Kennedy

What a beautiful day July 1, 1899, was! The sun was shining; there wasn't a cloud in the sky as the day stretched into night. The Hayden family, all eight of them, sat down for a hearty meal to celebrate the harvest. As soon as the first forkfuls were in their mouths, the family dog, outside in the yard, started barking frantically. Joe Hayden, the father and owner of the farm, yelled for the dog to stop. When the dog continued its intrusive barking, Joe went to the back door to find the barn in flames.

All family members, children included, ran to the well and set up a bucket brigade. Not only were their efforts futile as the freshly cut hay continued to burn, but the fire quickly spread to their old wood-frame house. Late that night, the neighbors consoled the Haydens. Although they did not lose any livestock in the fire, the Haydens lost their home and its contents, as well as the barn and their crop.

Some of the neighbor women took two or three of the children home with them; the men told Joe that they would help him rebuild his house and barn. Within four months, the Haydens had a new house and barn, which the neighbors helped them build on the same piece of property. Some community members also donated feed for the livestock, and the Haydens were soon reunited again.

In those days, if you were sick, disabled, or old, it was no business of the government (Sarason, 1976a). Neighbors helped neighbors; social support seemed commonplace.

The preceding vignette illustrates several important dimensions that have changed in U.S. society in the last 100 years. Compared to when the Haydens lived, today the United States is no longer an agrarian, rural society. Rather, this nation is an urbanized, industrialized society. Americans do not appear to be the neighborly, helping society we once were. Instead, people today tend to be less self-reliant and less cooperative with one another and more dependent on community services and government assistance, the latter perhaps an invitation to disaster according to some community psychologists (Morris, 2000; Sarason, 1976a). The turning point in U.S. history, turning from helping each other to dependence on external agencies, probably arrived with the Great Depression (Wilcox, 1983).

In 1971, psychologist Leigh Marlowe wrote that the rate of social change was accelerating. Change, some planned and some unplanned, continues today at a breakneck pace. In fact, change seems to be a pervasive condition of modern times (Christensen & Robinson, 1989). As you learned in Chapter 1, actively participating in and fashioning social change is a fundamental value of community psychology (Jason, 1991; Maton, 2000).

Questions regarding social change for community psychologists are complex and interrelated. Social scientists want to know what causes change; how to predict change; how best to cope with change; and, most of all, how to fashion or direct change that improves the living conditions of community members.

This chapter will look at what creates social change, whether planned or not (as in the Haydens' fire), particularly today. The discussion will draw from all areas within psychology, as well as anthropology, medicine, public health, political science, sociology, and other disciplines (Wandersman, Hallman, & Berman, 1989). In fact, a multidisciplinary approach for examining and intervening in social change is often desirable (Maton, 2000; Seidman, 1983), especially if the diversity and challenges of our vast population are to be appreciated (Freedman, 1989; Maton, 2000; Salazar, 1988).

What are some of the phenomena that induce change in society? Factors such as diverse populations, declining resources, demands for accountability, expanding knowledge and/or changing technologies (Kettner, Daley, & Nichols, 1985), economic changes, community conflict (Christensen & Robinson, 1989), dissatisfaction with traditional approaches to social problems, the desire for choices and the need for diversity of solutions to social problems (Heller, Price, Reinharz, Riger, & Wandersman, 1984), and other issues lead the list of reasons for social change. Although the list is not exhaustive, some of these forces need to be looked at in more detail to help you comprehend their roles in shaping social change.

REASONS FOR SOCIAL CHANGE

Diverse Populations

During the Middle Ages, no one expected a long life. Today, life expectancies in the United States are ever increasing as depicted in Figure 3.1. The increasing elderly population, as well as pregnant teens, victims of violence, the bereaved, the disabled, the unemployed, and other groups create dramatic social changes and the need for new community interventions. The Haydens would have experienced some of these problems in the early 1900s, such as the death of a family member, but they were less likely to experience violence, teen pregnancy, and drug problems than are families today.

A concrete example of how the needs of diverse groups are often not met but can be met in the community would be worthwhile. For a variety of reasons, some Americans do not vote. The Haydens could vote even though they lost their home. For example, the homeless are often denied the right to vote because they do not have fixed street addresses. Many with disabilities also do not vote due to transportation costs and other factors (Schur & Kruse, 2000). This situation creates the added problem that those individuals who most ought to voice their political opinions on nutrition, health care, housing, and other programs do not go to the polls. Finding a means for the disabled to have transportation to the polls on election day or furnishing them with alternate means of voting may provide them with a greater voice in issues directly concerning them. Taking the service to the people who most need it empowers them to participate in social change.

Special populations (Fairweather & Davidson, 1986) cause changes in society and, in turn, create more social change by virtue of either their swelling ranks or special situations. In fact, never underestimate the importance of population trends in social change (Light & Keller, 1985). If formal, established institutions are insensitive to the special issues of diverse populations, these groups, themselves, can and will create change (Kettner et al.,

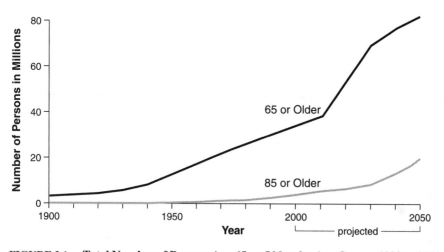

FIGURE 3.1   **Total Number of Persons Age 65 or Older, by Age Group, 1900 to 2050**

1985; Maton, 2000). Self-help or grass-roots efforts to create or deal with social change will be discussed in the next chapter.

Another example, related to the opening vignette, is that as farmers mechanized their production in the early 1900s, many could not afford the expensive equipment. Knowing that the equipment would require less labor, cooperatives of farmers formed in which owners of one piece of equipment, such as a tractor, traded equipment and labor with owners of other pieces of equipment, such as a hay baler and a hay wagon.

Declining Resources

Since few community service programs are self-supporting, most are highly dependent on external funding (Kettner et al., 1985), and most attempts to create social change are limited by lack of funding and other resources (Maton, 2000). External funding for community services generally comes in the form of legislated or government-sponsored funds as well as grants from public or private endowments or foundations. Both types of funds are likely to be awarded for experimental programs or services, which after some specified period must seek other sources of funding. New programs therefore compete with older programs for limited pools of money (Sarason, 1972; Levine & Perkins, 1987). Likewise, these "demonstration" programs are deemed insufficient because the time lag for them to be documented and disseminated to other communities is too long (Chavis, Florin, & Felix, 1992). Also, both the federal government and local governments have provided less and less funding for human services than in the past, thereby creating a sort of "Robin Hood in reverse" effect (Delgado, 1986).

Because government funding for community services is decreasing, there is more pressure on other granting institutions such as private foundations. Examples of such granting foundations for community services include the Ford Foundation, the Charles Stewart Mott Foundation, the Henry J. Kaiser Foundation, the Robert Wood Johnson Foundation, the McArthur Foundation, the Carnegie Foundation, and others (Chavis et al., 1992). More programs and human services agencies are applying for these limited funds; hence, the competition for both government and foundation monies is often fierce.

Although some agencies charge fees to clients for services, many are reluctant to become dependent on client fees, as such fees also fluctuate depending on caseload and other factors. Even those agencies that charge clients on a **sliding scale,** where fees are tied to income and/or number of dependents, are reluctant to increase charges to their most financially needy clients. A feeling exists that there has already been a trend for allocating resources away from the poor (Delgado, 1986). When funding issues become severe, and even when they are not so severe, clients and service administrators demand reform or social change. However, these groups are often answered just as vociferously by taxpayers angered that taxes will be raised again. All of these groups demand and/or create social change in response to already occurring social change.

One other source of funding for community service agencies is voluntary or charitable contributions from the public. Such contributions also vary as a function of the economy and other uncontrollable factors. Community service directors are therefore reluctant to become too dependent on charitable contributions. Funding issues for community services have been and will continue to be delicate and volatile for years to come (Frumkin, 2000).

Case in Point 3.1 discusses in more detail some of the funding dilemmas that nonprofit agencies face.

Accountability

Accountability and its sister term *cost effectiveness* seem to be the buzzwords of today. **Accountability** is the obligation to account for or be responsible for various transactions, monetary or otherwise. In times of scarce funding, it is especially fair and reasonable to ask for accountability of both new and continuing community programs (Wandersman, Morris-

---

CASE IN POINT 3.1

FUNDING DILEMMAS FOR NONPROFIT ORGANIZATIONS

The number of nonprofit or charitable organizations and the number of foundations willing to make philanthropic donations to them has grown in the last few decades. But are they keeping pace with each other? In other words, are funding opportunities shrinking?

In the 1950s, foundation start-ups grew by approximately 195 new funders a year. By the 1980s, the average number of new funders had increased to 348 per year. Other statistics also reveal that the number of philanthropic foundations has grown. Between 1980 and 1995, the number of foundations in the United States nearly doubled, from 22,088 to 40,140 (Siska, 1998). Indeed, the number of private funding sources is growing.

What about the number of nonprofit human services organizations that tap into or are dependent on grants from these foundations? Have their ranks grown? There are more than one million groups recognized by the Internal Revenue Service as nonprofit organizations. Some have receipts under $5,000; others have receipts of millions of dollars. Overall, between 1989 and 1994, the number of public charities, for example, grew from 120,300 to 161,700—a rate of growth of 34 percent (DeVita, 1997). On the surface, then, it appears that the growth in the number of foundations has outpaced the growth in the number of nonprofit agencies.

These statistics can be deceptive, though because of economic and other changes (The Center on Philanthropy, 2001). Closer examination shows that money is not evenly distributed among all nonprofit organizations. DeVita's 1997 study shows that although most nonprofit groups are quite small, the largest organizations obtain the bulk of the finances. More specifically, small organizations with expenses of less than $100,000 accounted for 42 percent of the organizations, whereas organizations with total expenses of over $10 million accounted for only 4 percent of charities. The smaller charities received only 3 percent of the support dollars, whereas the larger organizations received half of all support dollars. This same study demonstrated that a disproportionate share of monies ends up in nonprofit organizations related to educational or health issues. Additionally, organizations in northeastern United States receive the lion's share of support dollars. One-fourth of U.S. charities are located in the Northeast, yet they devour one-third of the support dollars.

The answer to the opening question, Are funding opportunities shrinking? is likely to be both *yes* and *no*—yes in that the number of foundations pouring dollars into nonprofit agencies is keeping pace with agency growth, and no in that the support dollars are not distributed equitably and fairly.

sey, Davino, Seybolt, Crusto, Nation, Goodman, & Imm, 1998). Table 3.1 provides a list of questions important to planning and evaluation as they relate to accountability.

Cost effectiveness means that money should be spent wisely; that is, there should be some return or profit on money expended. Cost effectiveness often refers to money; accountability can also refer to matters such as time expended, quality of decisions made, and so forth.

In the 1800s, citizens such as the Haydens were not bombarded by the media about the government and spending, legal or not. Spending has always been an important issue, but it is more likely to be historically in the forefront of the minds of today's citizens than it was in the past.

Who requests accountability? Almost anyone today: clients, staff, administrators, taxpayers, elected officials, licensing bureaus, and others. Any of these constituencies is likely to want to know the answers to such questions as: Where was my money spent? Did the targeted population benefit? Were goals accomplished, and if not, why not?

When answers to these questions are not forthcoming, are not the expected ones, or are not the best or most productive, the parties leveling the query are likely to demand change. Some individuals may want new administrators; others might want new spending guidelines. The list of demanded changes can be so exhaustive that the end result is the demise of any organization not readily accountable to its constituents. Again, the final outcome is likely to be some kind of ongoing change.

Knowledge-Based and Technological Change

In their day, the Haydens may have used some very innovative farm machinery that today would be called antiques. The Haydens probably felt timid and perhaps threatened the first time they used these machines. To give you some perspective, do you recall the first time you sat at a computer? You probably experienced trepidation and later felt the embarrassment caused by thinking a machine could get the better of you. **Technological changes** in the form of computer services and speedier communication systems have, in turn, created new demands on workforces in business as well as in human services. Some organizations

TABLE 3.1   Planning and Evaluation Strategies That Address Accountability

1. *Why* is the intervention needed?
2. *How* does the program include science and "best practices"?
3. *How* will this new program fit with other existing programs?
4. *How* will the program be carried out?
5. *How* well was the program carried out?
6. *How* well does the program work?
7. *How* can the program be improved?
8. *What* can be done to "spin off" or institutionalize the program?

Source: Adapted from A. Wandersman, E. Morrissey, K. Davino, D. Seybolt, C. Crusto, M. Nation, R. Goodman, and P. Imm (1998). Comprehensive quality programming and accountability: Eight essential strategies for implementing successful prevention programs. *The Journal of Primary Prevention, 19,* 3–30.

and individuals adapt well to technological advances. Others—for a multitude of reasons such as reluctance to utilize new technologies or lack of funds—do not adapt well or quickly.

People today may think that they are undergoing rapid and extreme technological changes more than ever before. Imagine, though, what adjustments the Hayden family would have undergone if they had changed from horse-driven equipment to gasoline-powered agricultural equipment in the early 1900s. What would they do with their teams of horses? Where would they get gasoline for their new tractors? Technological changes, whenever they occur, obligate further changes (Frank, 1983; Kling, 2000). Consider, for example, how your first experience with a computer changed you. Today, you probably complete your term papers, balance your checkbook, keep track of appointments, and perhaps pass your idle time browsing the Internet with your computer. The computer has therefore changed the methods of conducting business, completing your work, and socializing.

If these "galloping technological changes" (Frank, 1983) are not enough, mainstream U.S. society is also experiencing a knowledge explosion. New methods for practicing anything from psychotherapy to landscape architecture, new guidelines for human resources management, additional legislation controlling all parts of people's lives, as well as other innovations and applications all requiring new understanding and new skills can overwhelm society's members, create additional change, and perhaps at the same time stimulate much anxiety.

Pilisuk and Acredolo (1988) surveyed nearly 500 residents of California and found a high level of expressed fear of technology. The fear of technology has been called **technophobia** in the psychological literature. A specific fear of computers has also been identified and is known as computerphobia (Hudiburg, 1990; Hudiburg & Necessary, 1996). The surveyed subjects reported fears that technology would contaminate drinking water, cause cancer and nuclear accidents, pollute the air, and make food and transportation dangerous. The researchers were also interested in who held the most fear. They found that women, minority group members, and less-educated persons were the most fearful. In other words, those with the least commerce with technology were probably most afraid of it. Similar research has found computer anxiety in older adults (Laguna & Babcock, 1997). Perhaps as technological changes advance, the more these same individuals will continue to fear it. Few traditional community systems (such as the Department of Health) provide help in coping with technical disasters (Webb, 1989)—a situation that does not help to allay fears. One possible way to address these concerns is via education and information dissemination. These strategies are discussed in the next chapter on creating social change.

On the upside, Wittig and Schmitz (1996) and Kreisler, Snider, and Kiernan (1997) found that community organizing can now be done electronically. Such technological organizing seems to obscure social boundaries, alter perceptions regarding stigmatized groups, enhance participation of previous nonparticipants in civil life, and empower activism.

Community Conflict

The family in the opening vignette was fortunate to have neighbors who were so cooperative and caring. This is not always the case in communities, though. Some communities experience the strife of conflict. Conflict, however, does not always produce negative changes (Worchel & Lundgren, 1991). Sometimes a positive outcome of community conflict is social change. **Community conflict** involves two or more parties with incompatible goals that usually have specific values (positive and negative) attached to them. Because of the strongly held values, power struggles, and varying interest levels of the parties, conflict in the community can be difficult to resolve or manage (Christensen & Robinson, 1989). However, such conflict, whether resolved or unresolved, often results in social change, because goodwill alone does not always resolve or dissipate conflict (Fairweather & Tornatzky, 1977).

When diverse groups come together in any situation, there may be conflict. An example of change resulting from conflict within a diverse group occurred in the professional psychological community (Fowler, 1990). Within the large national organization for psychologists (the American Psychological Association, or APA), research psychologists grew increasingly dissatisfied with the perceived trend for the APA to cater more to the needs of practitioners than researchers. Such rifts between researchers and practitioners are sometimes viewed as counterproductive (Duffy, Grosch, & Olczak, 1991). However, from the APA criticism grew a new psychological society—the American Psychological Society. The APS has a different mission than the APA, and its membership is heavily comprised of scientists. For another example of change resulting from community conflict, see Case in Point 3.2.

Dissatisfaction with Traditional Services

Probably no other cause has fostered social change more than consumer dissatisfaction with existing community services, especially external expert-dominated approaches (Maton, 2000). In fact, you will recall from Chapter 1 that such dissatisfaction with traditional mental health services spawned the birth and growth of community psychology itself when psychologists at the Swampscott Conference expressed dismay with traditional forms of mental health treatment.

One example of dissatisfaction creating community change relates to this chapter's opening vignette. The Haydens lost their house because the bucket brigade they set up just was not fast enough to keep up with the damage from the fire. The Haydens might have asked for a town meeting to discuss with other citizens the formation of a fire district and fire department so that equipment such as a water wagon could be bought for everyone to use.

It is important to look at another, more modern example, though, of how dissatisfaction with services leads to change. As you may already know from your training in psychology and related disciplines, one of the earliest forms of psychotherapy (or "the talking cure") was psychoanalysis as designed by Sigmund Freud. Freud's own protégés, such as Carl Jung and Alfred Adler, became disenchanted with this brand of therapy and modified psychoanalysis as they knew it (Phares & Chaplin, 1997). Contemporary therapists, disgruntled with such concepts as pansexuality and the unconscious from Freudian theory have also developed a vast array of therapies exemplified by behavior modification, cognitive behavioral therapy, and humanistic counseling, to name a few. Today, the mental health client has a long menu of therapies from which to choose. In future chapters, you will read more about the history of the treatment of mental illness and why traditional therapies are a last resort for community psychologists.

CASE IN POINT 3.2

COMMUNITY CONFLICT: ADVERSITY TURNS TO OPPORTUNITY

In the 1960s, an unfortunate but interesting instance of community conflict occurred in Rochester, New York. Surprisingly, from this adversity grew opportunity. An African American neighborhood decided to hold a neighborhood party. The party occurred on a hot summer night with many young adults showing up for the festivities. Halfway through the night, a group of White youths came to the party and were seen as intruders. One brusque remark led to another, which eventually erupted in violence. Rochester, New York, like many cities, quickly exploded in racial conflict.

Several community groups, concerned that such violence not repeat itself, came together in an attempt to find a solution to the city's problems. As a result, the American Arbitration Association was asked to consult on the design of a community program for handling many types of conflict. The **community mediation** program was born. This program (showcased in Chapter 9) manages community disputes between individuals or groups in a peaceful fashion by assigning a neutral third party—a **mediator**—to facilitate discussion and problem solving between the disputants (Duffy et al., 1991). The program also monitors community agency elections as well as urban renewal housing lotteries, "lemon law" (automobile owner/manufacturer) arbitration, and other community projects where a neutral is needed. The initial community conflict, racial tension, was probably a part of the larger national civil rights movement—a movement that created sweeping social changes, which are not yet complete.

From the Rochester conflict, however, came more social change in the form of the Community Dispute Resolutions Centers Act (Christian, 1986). This legislation established in every county in New York a mediation center modeled after the one in Rochester. With New York as the pioneer state, other states followed. Today, there are hundreds of functioning mediation or neighborhood justice centers in the United States. Some are adjuncts to the courts; others are run by religious and other charities (McGillis, 1997). All hope to inspire the peaceful resolution of conflict. Community conflict, then, creates snowballing social reform and social change, of which the Rochester experience is only one example.

Desire for Diversity of Solutions

Walk into any store in the United States and the display of goods available is overwhelming. Americans are used to choices between brands X, Y, and Z. Americans do not just want diversity among goods, however; they also expect diversity and choice among services. Individuals seeking psychotherapy want to know that they have options in the training of the therapist, the type of therapy, the payment plan, and the length of treatment. Similarly, Americans want to be able to choose between private and public educational institutions for their children and between law firms and lawyers when they want to recover damages or close a real estate deal. Americans have come a long way since the 1800s when families had one doctor, one school, and one pharmacy in their towns. When individuals find that agencies are insensitive or that there are few options from which to choose, and sometimes this is coupled with dissatisfaction with those existing options, the individuals often demand and create change.

Here is an example from the justice system of how the desire for more options creates change. Anyone who has watched one of the several televised courtroom judges hand down a verdict knows that the courts often leave complainants and defendants alike disgruntled. Sometimes even the "winner" does not feel as if he or she has won. One answer to handling this dissatisfaction and to providing more diversity for users of the court system is to develop a **multidoor approach,** as is found in Washington, DC (Ostermeyer, 1991). This is a coordinated system of assisting citizens involved in the justice system to find the most appropriate option for them: various courts (small claims, city, state, and federal); mediation and arbitration programs; legal aid offices; public, private, and volunteer attorneys; and other agencies such as those assisting with mental health. The multidoor approach helps citizens and agencies avoid the frustration of multiple and overlapping referrals and lessens the perception that the justice system is a confusing maze of bureaucracies (Ostermeyer, 1991).

The preceding catalog of reasons for social change, which is not exhaustive, is summarized in Table 3.2. It will familiarize you with some of the causes for social changes. Next is the examination of some ways in which change occurs, whether planned or unplanned.

TYPES OF SOCIAL CHANGE

Forecasting social trends and social changes can be tricky but also very useful in designing prevention programs. For example, the U.S. Census Bureau expected the 2000 census to show demographic changes as well as population increases. The Census Bureau is able to

TABLE 3.2   Reasons for and Examples of Social Change

REASON FOR CHANGE	EXAMPLE OF SOCIAL CHANGE
Special population	AIDS patients desire emotional support from a group of other AIDS patients, and their families get together and form a support group.
Declining resources	The national economy is depressed; less grant money is available from private foundations.
Accountability	A taxpayer group attends a public hearing and demands to know how a tax increase will improve community services.
Technological advances	A corporation buys new software for midlevel managers who now require training.
Community conflict	An agency seeks a halfway house in a residential neighborhood not zoned for multiple-family dwellings; two residents groups, one in support and one against, conflict at a public meeting.
Dissatisfaction with traditional services	An area's private practice psychologists charge high fees not covered by insurance, so citizens inquire about funding possibilities for a mental health clinic that will charge on a sliding scale.
Desire for diversity of solutions	A multidoor courthouse program offers a variety of options for solutions to neighbors fighting in the neighborhood.

forecast some changes. Projected changes, though, do not always come true and are sometimes more or less dramatic than anticipated. If the 2000 census figures are correct, the population growth of 32.7 million people represents the largest census growth in U.S. history. For example, educators riding the tide of the baby boom built schools and school annexes in the suburbs until the number of schools had soared. Today, these same schools are witnessing a wave of violence from alienated youth. Community activists have much that they can learn from demographers and other forecasters about where change will occur next, particularly spontaneous or unplanned change.

Spontaneous or Unplanned Social Change

Naturally occurring change is called **unplanned** or **spontaneous change.** Most disasters are not planned. For instance, no one planned the fire at the Hayden farm, and, more recently, few predicted the epidemic of school violence.

Natural disasters result in much distress as well as social change (Ginexi, Weihs, Simmens, & Hoyt, 2000). Droughts, earthquakes, floods, fires, and other natural events displace community members from their homes and their jobs. Although these disasters are not necessarily always distressing (Bravo, Rubio-Stipec, Canino, Woodbury, & Ribera, 1990; Prince-Embury & Rooney, 1995), they typically result in some large-scale change.

Unplanned, major shifts in the population also cause social change and, in fact, much social dissatisfaction and divisiveness (Katz, 1983). For example, as the swell of baby boomers moves through time, their needs change. Baby boomers are now middle-aged and many are caring for their elderly parents (Naisbitt & Aburdene, 1990). They often find a dearth of community services that provide elder care, and this creates much stress in the boomers' lives. Some baby boomers also have young children who require day care, which can be in short supply. The stress of caring for both the younger and older generations in their lives has resulted in such adults being labeled the **sandwich generation** (Spillman & Pezzin, 2000).

Similarly, other demographic shifts create other social changes. Today, for instance, there is an increase in the number of two-career families (Winkler, 1998, see Table 3.3) that need day care for their young children (Naisbitt & Aburdene, 1990).

Behavioral changes in the population over time are often unplanned. A realistic example of these changes would be increases in crime, especially violent crimes. Although high

TABLE 3.3 Growth in Dual-Career Families

INDEX	1966	1994
Percent of married women in the workforce	35%	61%
Percent of married women with children under 3 years in the workforce	21%	60%

Source: From "Earnings of Husbands and Wives in Dual-Earner Families" by A. E. Winkler, April 1998, *Monthly Labor Review,* 42–48.

crime rates do not always result in fear (Taylor & Shumaker, 1990), individuals who live in areas where they do fear the high crime rate may desire special community programs, such as neighborhood watches or escort services for the elderly. One interesting study did establish that those who have been crime victims are not always the most afraid of crime. Rather, this research demonstrated that those most fearful of crime live in neighborhoods with abandoned buildings, vandalism, idle teens, and other signs of deterioration that indicate concomitant declines in social control within the community (Baba & Austin, 1989). These results have more recently been replicated by Ross and Jang (2000).

What makes unplanned or unintentional change stressful is that, although it is rare, it is often serious and uncontrollable, much as the Hayden's fire was. Research (Rodin, Timko, & Harris, 1986) has shown that uncontrollable events are quite stressful. In other words, when individuals feel they control their fates, they experience less stress; when they feel they have lost control, they experience distress (Boggiano & Katz, 1991; Duffy & Atwater, 2001; Taylor, Helgeson, Reed, & Skokan, 1991). Also, unplanned change is often confined to particular ecological situations in which individuals may unwittingly be placed. For example, crime and natural disasters are generally confined to particular environments (Taylor & Shumaker, 1990), so when individuals find themselves in those environments, they may experience stress.

Besides assisting in the design and development of community services, community psychologists can also assist with coping for unplanned change by playing a role in forecasting it. Remember that one of the tenets of community psychology is prevention. This does not mean that community psychologists can prevent these changes—certainly psychologists cannot prevent floods—but learning how to predict unplanned changes can enable the community to prepare for the changes as they occur or even before they occur. Such preparation can prevent the change from being as severe and distressing as it otherwise might be.

The science of prediction is complex, but there are scientists who specialize in prediction and forecasting. In *Megatrends 2000,* content analyses of the print media were utilized to forecast coming trends (Naisbitt & Aburdene, 1990). Census data can also help forecast population changes. For instance, as the baby boomers age, they will represent the largest group of elderly the United States has ever had, so if elder care is in short supply now, it may be in even shorter supply in two decades if no one prepares for it. **Social indicators** are measures of some aspect of society based on combined, corrected, and refined social statistics (Johnston, 1980) and can be used in social forecasting. By utilizing techniques such as extrapolative forecasting, network analysis, latent curve analysis, environmental prediction, and others, social trends can be forecasted and preventive measures can be prepared (Kellam, Koretz, & Mosciki, 1999a, 1999b). Indeed, the use of "future studies" can do much for prevention in communities (Sundberg, 1985), but not without some limitations. Lorion (1991), for example, raised the issue of the **base rate problem.** This issue pertains to the fact that although many individuals seem to have the antecedents of diagnosable disorders, for example, few may really actually develop the disorder.

Planned Social Change

Suppose people do not want to wait for change to happen, as in unplanned or unintended change (McGrath, 1983); instead, they want intentionally to create change, called **planned**

change or **induced change** (Glidewell, 1976). How could people go about this seemingly monumental task? There are some venerated strategies suggested in the community psychology literature: self-help, including grass-roots activism; networking of services and social support; the use of external change agents or consultants; educational and informational programs; and involvement in public policy processes. All of these issues are detailed in the next chapter. None of these approaches is easy, and each has its advantages and disadvantages. With planned change, however, the desired effects are more likely to be obtained than with unplanned or spontaneous change.

Exactly what is planned change? Kettner and associates (1985) wrote a good working definition. *Planned change* is an intentional or deliberate intervention to change a situation—or for the present discussion, a part of or a whole community. Planned change is distinguished from unplanned change by four characteristics. First, planned change is *limited in scope;* that is, in planned change, what is to be changed is targeted or earmarked in advance. Second, planned change is directed toward *enhancing the quality of life* of the community members. This is the primary purpose of planned change in communities. Planned change should enhance, not inhibit, community life. Third, planned change usually *provides a role* for those affected by change. Community psychologists should not impose change on community members. Rather, their role is to inform citizens of the viable options, assist them in the selection of appropriate options, and then participate with them in the design and implementation of change. Finally, planned change is often but not always *guided by a person who acts as a change agent.* **Change agents** (Lippett, Watson, & Westley, 1958; Oskamp, 1984) are often trained professionals but can also be advocates for or from client groups, political activists, educational experts, or others interested in inducing change. Psychologists often act as consultants or change agents. The role of consultants is detailed in the next chapter.

Issues Related to Planned Change

A major issue regarding planned change is *who* decides change will occur and *when, how,* and *what* changes will take place. Suppose the Haydens had called a town meeting to discuss how the community should manage fire disasters. Who should decide what the town should do? All voters? Only taxpayers? Only those who owned farms where hay could combust? Did they need to discuss temporary housing issues for fire victims? Should they ask an outside agency such as the Red Cross?

Some change experts argue that administrators and managers are responsible for initiating change; others argue that the bottom of the organization (e.g., staff, clients, or other laypersons) should create change (Bauman, 2000; Kettner et al., 1985). Many in the field of community development agree that almost anyone and everyone involved in the changes is the appropriate person (Christensen & Robinson, 1989; Heller et al., 1984; Kettner et al., 1985; Levine & Perkins, 1987).

In community psychology, the concept of *collaboration* is embraced (Bond, 1990; Fawcett, 1990; Maton, 2000; Oskamp, 1984; Rappaport, 1990; Rappaport et al., 1985; Serrano-Garcia, 1990). The idea of collaboration—of social scientists and clients coming together to examine and create solutions for social problems—is a major tradition in community psychology (Rappaport, 1990). Collaboration is also called **participatory decision making** or **collaborative problem solving** (Chavis et al., 1992) and has already been discussed in Chapter 1 as a process important to community psychology (Kelly, 1986a). As Christensen and Robinson (1989) suggested, self-determination has practical problem-solving utility in that those who live with the problem can best solve it. Acceptance is therefore higher than in imposed changes. Moreover, collaborative decision making helps build a stronger sense of community and avoids client-consultant conflict and duplication of effort because collaboration is a mutual influence process. The key to collaboration is empowerment, which enhances the possibility of self-determination.

Anyone embarking on planned social change needs to prepare carefully for the changes (Maton, 2000). Ongoing, carefully planned change requires hard work and a substantial investment of time, talent, money, and other resources that might otherwise be useful elsewhere (Kettner et al., 1985). The change agents should also prepare participants for change to take a long time (Fairweather & Davidson, 1986; Seidman, 1990), as it is likely to be resisted. Likewise, the more important the problem, the more difficult it will probably be to solve (Shadish, 1990), and the more numerous the necessary levels of intervention (Maton, 2000).

Planners also need to consider whether change is really possible (e.g., Will all involved parties cooperate? Are funds available? etc.) and whether, in the end, the desired results can be realistically achieved. For example, although thousands of community programs and organizations exist across the country, many fail (Florin, 1989). Prestby and Wandersman (1985) found that 50 percent of voluntary neighborhood associations, many of which are designed to create and support social change, become inactive after only one year. Such organizations, therefore, seem particularly vulnerable to demise or failure (Chavis et al., 1992).

Fairweather and Davidson (1986) have explained that a single attack on a social problem will not create substantial change. A multipronged and continual approach is generally more successful. A once-and-for-all solution probably will not be effective, either (Levine & Perkins, 1987). Fairweather and Davidson have also cautioned that although some old practices might work well, any useless approaches should be discarded. It is worthwhile to remember, too, that *complete* change might not always be necessary.

Besides the preceding dimensions, planners also need to consider the other parameters of beneficial change (Fairweather & Davidson, 1986). Change must be humane—that is, it must be socially responsible and represent humanitarian values that emphasize enhancing human potential. Change techniques should also be problem oriented—in other words, they should be aimed at solutions of problems rather than merely be idealistic. Similarly, change strategies should focus on multiple social levels rather than on specific individuals. The techniques may need to be creative and innovative. Old, stale methods may not work; creativity is the constant companion of community activists. The change plans also need to be feasible in terms of dissemination to other groups or situations. Not all techniques fit all groups, but there are some communities that can adopt tried methods from other communities.

Change agents should plan globally or holistically so as to see the whole picture rather than disjointed pieces of problems. Pluralistic (Freedman, 1989) or multilevel planning

(Maton, 2000) is likely to ensure success because the context or environment within which the change will occur will be more likely to have been considered.

As mentioned earlier, context or environment is a concept important to the ecological tradition of community psychology. In working with the Hayden family, a community psychologist would take into account the family's agrarian lifestyle as well as the social climate in the town they frequented. A contemporary example would perhaps prove more useful. Prince-Embury and Rooney (1995) examined psychological adaptation in a sample of residents who remained in the vicinity of Three Mile Island, the site of a nuclear disaster. Prince-Embury and Rooney found that the very same experts enlisted to assuage the fears of the residents when the nuclear generator was restarted were not trusted despite their high level of expertise and their worthwhile intentions. In some other environment or situation, experts might well be effective and more trusted. Taking into account the needs and attitudes of affected parties, the context or ecology, and the type of intervention is essential in community psychology.

Change agents also need to value social experimentation and action research. In this regard, planners cannot be timid about innovation—neither can they be afraid to evaluate their innovations. Social experimentation and evaluation go hand in hand (Fairweather & Davidson, 1986). Any interventions and programs developed to create community change need to be honestly evaluated, modified based on the evaluation, evaluated again, and so on. Then and only then do change agents and communities know that they have the best possible ideas in place.

Finally, planners or change agents need to be realists, particularly with regard to the prevailing political climate (Light & Keller, 1985). Change always makes something different that otherwise would not be changed (Benviente, 1989). Some individuals will like the change; others will not. Hence, the power struggles related to change are likely to commence as soon as change is suggested.

WHY CHANGE PLANS FAIL

Why do programs that are designed to create social change or provide alternative services fail? Why do the most well-intentioned efforts sometimes go awry? What if the Hayden family had called a town meeting to discuss what should or could happen when a family loses a home to a fire and no one came to the meeting? Or what if the citizens were divided as to what they should do? A multitude of reasons exist but only a few will be mentioned here. One of the most important reasons for failure of planned change is *resistance* (Glidewell, 1976; Levine & Perkins, 1987), which can come from a variety of sources, including administrators, practitioners, clients, or any other community member.

Why does resistance occur? Societies tend to have built-in resistance to change (Bagby, 1981); members of groups seem trained to follow their own ways—the old ways—which they regard as safe or superior (Glidewell, 1976). Groups feel their existence is threatened by new groups or new ideas. Psychologists have long documented the effects of in-groups and out-groups in which people favor their own groups (the **in-group**) and stereotype or denigrate outsiders (the **out-group**). In the community, for instance, for-profit businesses, especially big private sector corporations, often resist social change instituted by small nonprofit businesses or by new government policies because the for-profit enterprises think their revenues will be affected.

Change is often seen as unwelcome, not just by groups but by individuals, as well (Kettner et al., 1985). Social psychologists know that individuals are also resistant to change, one of the causes of which is mere cognitive laziness or the desire not to have to think too hard. Most humans are **cognitive misers** who take the path of least effort in terms of decision making and thinking. Other individuals are also closed-minded or **dogmatic** (Rokeach, 1960); they conserve their old ways and shun new ideas because of rigidity in their thinking. Individuals resist change for the same reasons as groups—because they feel that change threatens their reputation, job security, or well-being.

Other factors also create the failure of planned change. When a social movement is seen as promoting only a single cause or a cause alien to a large number of people, change is often slow or does not occur at all. For example, if the Haydens had proposed a temporary shelter for farm families only to the exclusion of townspeople, the Haydens might have failed. More contemporarily, had the March of Dimes, for example, stuck with the single issue of the defeat of polio, the organization would have assured its own demise. Refocusing on the elimination of *all* birth defects has ensured the health of that organization for a long time.

When those attempting to create change disregard others in the community or disregard other community problems, failure can also take place. A solution to avoiding isolated change is **networking.** A network is an interconnected and interactive social relationship among various individuals or organizations in which reciprocity of information, resources, and other support between individuals or organizations is maintained (Chavis et al., 1992). The next chapter contains more information on networking.

Often, agents of change and their programs fail because their tactics are unwelcome or negative. Alinsky (1971), Kettner and associates (1985), and Wolff (1987) see risk taking, including the risk that change will be unwelcome, as part and parcel of all change. However, the reality is that if those people planning change receive only negative exposure (by the media, for example) or fail to suggest their own solutions to the problems they are protesting, their protests are perceived as hollow or disruptive rather than productive. Agitation, protest, and confrontation do not always work, and published research supports this contention (Oskamp, 1984). If a community activist chooses a radical or confrontational route to change, Saul Alinsky's work will be of interest. Table 3.4 summarizes some of his approaches.

Collective planning for change is construed as good, but this is only true within limits. If the organization or individuals planning change are too loosely structured, if solid leadership does not exist, or if the decision makers show no discipline in their plans, then they, too, can fail. Often, as the planners begin to fail, conflict breaks out in the ranks (Levine & Perkins, 1987). Delgado (1986) reviewed several organizations that had good intent but that evaporated because of the inadequacy of their own organizational infrastructures. Due to the concern over the survival of community organizations, work on infrastructures and phenotypes of organizations is under way (Luke, Rappaport, & Seidman, 1991; Maton, 1988; Schubert & Borkman, 1991; Zimmerman et al., 1991). Maton, for example, using three different support groups within the community, found that the groups with higher role differentiation, greater order and organization, and capable leaders reported more positive well-

TABLE 3.4   Ten Rules for Radicals*

1. Use whatever you've got to get attention.
2. Don't go outside the experience of your people.
3. But whenever possible, go outside the experience of the enemy.
4. Make the enemy live up to its own rules.
5. Ridicule is a potent weapon, and it makes the opposition react to your advantage.
6. A good tactic is one that your people enjoy—if they don't enjoy it, there is something wrong.
7. A tactic that drags on too long becomes a drag.
8. The threat is usually more terrifying than the thing itself.
9. Power is what you have and what the enemy thinks you have.
10. Keep the pressure on.

*These are general guidelines. According to Saul Alinsky, they should be adapted to the uniquenesses of each situation.

Source: Adapted from *Rules for Radicals: A Practical Primer for Realistic Radicals* by S. Alinsky, 1971, New York: Random House.

being and more positive group appraisal. Chapter 12 will take a closer look at community psychology and community organizations.

One of the best solutions to prevent failure—and prevention is a critical part of all of community psychology—is to lay a good foundation for change by conducting research. Community psychologists regard research and practice as interdependent on one another (Kelly, 1986b). **Action research,** as you have already read, is scientific work grounded in theory but directed toward resolving problems (Lewin, 1948; Deutsch & Hornstein, 1975; Oskamp, 1984). Action research in the community is not without its problems (Price, 1990; Tolan, Keys, Chertak, & Jason, 1990). Problems include the lack of trust in the researcher by community members, breakdowns in negotiating with program and community administrators, the inability to randomly assign subjects to conditions, the selection of appropriate and adequate measures, and so on (Fairweather & Davidson, 1986). Research should not be done just at the front end of community change. Once an intervention has been implemented, it needs ongoing assessment (Wandersman et al., 1998). For example, one method for assessing interventions is program evaluation, as already reviewed in Chapter 2.

SUMMARY

Social change is a pervasive condition of today's world. There are many reasons change occurs. Diverse populations, such as the growing number of elderly, have issues that must be addressed but for which society may not be prepared. Another reason for change is declining resources, which include money, space, and commodities such as food. On the other hand, galloping technological advances also necessitate change on the part of individuals as well as society. One technology that has caused all sorts of modification in our daily lives and in methods of conducting business is the addition of computers. On the other hand, many people fear the advance of technology (technophobia), and traditional community services do little to help individuals cope with the fear.

Demands for accountability also create change. People expect that funds will be expended wisely, and they grow concerned when spending is not accounted for. Related to accountability is cost effectiveness, which refers to how wisely money is spent (i.e., Is there a profit?).

Community conflict is yet another reason for change. Groups in communities experience ethnic strife, conflict over resources such as land use, and so on to create change. A growing sentiment against traditional methods for dealing with today's problems—for instance, the treatment of the mentally ill—as well as a desire for choices or diversity among solutions to problems also prompt change.

There are two types of change: planned (or induced) change and unplanned (or spontaneous) change. Planned change occurs when changes are intentional or deliberate. Planned change is limited by its scope, usually enhances the quality of life for community members, provides for a role for affected groups, and is often guided by a professional change agent or consultant. In unplanned or spontaneous change, change is unexpected, sometimes disastrous (as in a natural disaster such as a flood), and often of a large magnitude (such as when a segment of the population experiences growth, as in the baby boom generation).

■ ■ ■ ■ ■

CREATING AND SUSTAINING SOCIAL CHANGE

You can't say that civilization don't advance,
for in every war they kill you a new way.
—Will Rogers

It was December 31, and the Marvin family—Melba, Harold, and their three young children—had just settled down to their New Year's Eve dinner. They were happy to be sharing a meal with each other. Their busy schedules often prohibited them from dining together. Harold's head suddenly snapped up as he asked what the popping sound was. Melba and the children giggled; they accused Harold of hearing noisemakers before midnight. They continued to eat, and this time they all heard the popping noise. Harold ran into the hall to find dense smoke pouring out of an upstairs bedroom.

Harold and Melba collected the children and ran into the street. Melba took the youngest child and ran in one direction while Harold ran in the opposite direction with the other two to find a neighbor at home who could call 911. By the time they found someone home down the street, the neighbor's house on the left of theirs was on fire. The police responded first to the call. After what seemed like an eternity but which was only about 20 minutes, the fire department arrived. By this time, several other of the old wooden homes had also caught fire. Gawking families from the rest of the neighborhood ran out into the street when they heard the sirens. Everyone, including the dismayed Marvin family, stared in wonder as the burning houses shot flames like fireworks high into the New Year's sky.

Four of the houses were decimated by the fire; a few others had water and smoke damage. The Red Cross, having arrived when the police called them, gave the Marvins and the other displaced families temporary shelter and also found used clothing for the families.

Harold and Melba were surprised when they started negotiating with their insurance company. Neither the house nor the contents were fully covered; their insurance policy had failed to keep pace with inflation. The Marvins felt a deep sense of depression but vowed to find a new, albeit smaller, home in the same school district if possible. Both Harold and Melba worried about the prospect of finding another home, given that they both worked full time. They knew the other families would probably be looking in the same neighborhood, too, so competition might be fierce. At least, the Marvins reasoned, they were all safe and together, even if their New Year's celebration had been ruined.

This opening vignette exemplifies the busy, daily life led by many working-class families in the United States. Both parents often work; young children are farmed out to caregivers, and the family rarely enjoys quality time together. Major tragedies upset the existence of the whole family, and in contrast to the opening story in the previous chapter, this situation is worsened by the fact that there is often little social and material support available to these families to help them cope.

Consider also how much more difficult daily life is for families who do not have the comforts of a two-parent income, a home in a secure neighborhood, good jobs, and healthy children. Finding food and clothing, seeking a safe shelter for the night, and caring for other basic needs are monumental, all-consuming daily chores.

CREATING PLANNED CHANGE

Some would argue society has not needed changing more than it does today. Multiple reports and commissions have concluded that we are a nation at risk with regard to many social indicators such as alcohol, drug use, teen pregnancy, and violence (Wandersman et al., 1998). Creating and sustaining social change is not an easy task, but community psychologists are at the forefront of researching the best ways to create and maintain positive societal change. Participating in social change is a fundamental value in community psychology (Jason, 1991; Maton, 2000) as well as a basic property of social reality (Keys & Frank, 1987). This chapter will examine established methods for fashioning both small- and large-scale social change. For each technique, its use, its advantages and disadvantages, and related research will be discussed. When change is intentional and planned in advance, it is termed **planned change.**

CITIZEN PARTICIPATION

Melba and Harold Marvin, the contemporary homeowners in the opening vignette, could have banded together with other homeowners who found that their insurance did not cover their losses. The homeowners' group could have approached the insurance companies and demanded an accounting of why coverage of losses is not keeping pace with replacement costs. The homeowners could also have presented their solutions to the problem and asked that a committee be formed of community citizens and insurance carriers to address which proposed solution is best. Or a citizens' group could have asked the fire department why they did not respond faster to the blaze, or the group could have formed a neighborhood watch so that when fires start in homes where no one is home, the fire still gets noticed and reported. Had the families taken any of these actions, they would have been citizens actively participating in social change.

Perhaps no other method of creating social change has received as much attention as participant-induced change, and interest in this type of change is mounting (Linney, 1990). Various authors have given different labels to this type of change, including *citizen participation* (Levi & Litwin, 1986; Wandersman & Florin, 2000), *empowerment* (Rappaport, Swift, & Hess, 1984), *grass-roots activism* (Alinsky, 1971), and *self-help* (Christensen & Robinson, 1989), among other terms. **Citizen participation** can be broadly defined as involvement in any organized activity in which the individual participates without pay in order to achieve a common goal (Zimmerman & Rappaport, 1988). At the root of this mechanism of change is the premise that people can, and should collaborate to solve common problems (Joseph & Ogletree, 1998). In fact, some hold self-help as the most promising mechanism for changing society (Florin & Wandersman, 1990). An example of citizen participation is **grass-roots activism,** which occurs when individuals define their own issues and press for social change to address these issues and work in a bottom-up rather than top-down fashion. For example, when citizens who are tired of lives being senselessly taken on our highways urge policy makers to pass laws with stiffer penalties against drunk driving, the citizens are practicing grass-roots activism. Case in Point 4.1 discusses further citizen involvement in community change by introducing the Community Development Society.

Another example of this type of change but at a more personal level is **self-help groups** (Levy, 2000), such as Alcoholics Anonymous, where individuals with common issues come together to assist and emotionally support one another. Because self-help groups are often overseen by professionals, some psychologists prefer the term **mutual assistance groups** for groups comprised solely of laypeople (Levine, 1988). Shepherd and associates (1999) pointed out, however, that the dichotomy between professionally led and peer-led groups is artificial because the extent of professional involvement in such groups

■ ■ ■ ■ ■

CASE IN POINT 4.1

THE COMMUNITY DEVELOPMENT SOCIETY

Community change and citizen participation have become an accepted—in fact, expected—part of daily life in the United States. For this reason and others, the Community Development Society (CDS) was established. CDS recognizes citizens' capacity to build and take democratic action as keys to success in a complex and ever-changing world. Community development is a process designed to create conditions of economic and social progress with the active participation of the whole community and with the fullest possible reliance on the community's initiatives (Bradshaw, 1999; Rothman, 1974; Levine & Perkins, 1997).

CDS members are multidisciplinary and come from the fields of education, health care, social services, government, and citizen groups, to mention just a few and believe that community is the basic building block of society (Bradshaw, 1999). In addition, members realize that communities can be complex, that growth and development are part of the human condition, and that development of each community can be promoted through improvement of the individual, organizational skills, and problem-solving knowledge. CDS members fervently believe that good practice can lead to sound community development and social change.

In response to these beliefs, the Community Development Society has developed several principles of good practice for community development specialists, whether they be citizens or professionals:

- Citizen participation needs to be promoted so that community members can influence the decisions that affect their lives.
- Citizens should be engaged in problem diagnosis so that affected individuals can understand the causes of the situation.
- Community leaders need to understand the economic, social, political, and psychological impact associated with various solutions related to community problems and issues.
- Community members should design and implement their own plans to solve consensually agreed-upon problems (even though some expert assistance might be needed). Further, shared leadership and active participation are necessary to this process.
- Finally, community leaders need the skills, confidence, and motivation to be influential in the community.

According to Maton (2000), these strategies for good practice result in *capacity-building* or *assets-based* change. Do these various principles sound familiar? Many of them are embraced by community psychologists. The significant point here is that there are many community citizens and leaders who adopt community psychology principles and goals without ever having studied community psychology.

varies on a continuum of minimal to extensive. Often, individuals in these groups learn coping strategies from each other. At a personal level, community members—such as friends, family, and neighbors—can assist in supporting each other through difficult times by providing **social support** (Barrera, 2000). Social support is an exchange of resources (such as emotional comfort or material goods) between two individuals where the provider intends the resources to enhance the well-being of the recipient (Shumaker & Brownell, 1984, 1985). Social support can be another means by which social change occurs. All of these methods are discussed elsewhere in the book in some detail.

The usual settings for citizen participation are work settings, health care programs, architectural environments, neighborhood associations, public policy arenas, education programs, and situations applying science (especially social science) and technology. This type of participation can occur by electoral participation (voting or working for a particular candidate or issue), grass-roots efforts (when citizens start a group and define its goals and methods), or government-mandated citizen participation in which citizens are appointed to watchdog committees or attend public hearings. Table 4.1 provides more examples of mechanisms for citizen participation, which vary in terms of effort expended and commitment.

Issues Related to Citizen Participation

Not everyone wants to participate in social change nor believes that he or she can be effective in fashioning social change, which is known as *helplessness* (Zimmerman, Ramírez-Valles, & Maton, 1999). Research by O'Neill, Duffy, Enman, Blackmer, and Goodwin (1988) examined what types of individuals are active in trying to produce social change. The researchers administered a modified *I-E Scale* and an Injustice Scale to introductory psychology students and single mothers (both of whom were considered nonactivist groups), board members of a day-care center (a moderately activist group), and board members of a transition house for victims of domestic violence (the high activist group). The *I-E Scale* (Rotter, 1966) measures **internal** versus **external locus of control.** Individuals with an

TABLE 4.1   **Examples of Citizen Participation**

Voting

Signing a petition

Donating money or time to a cause

Reading media articles on community needs or change

Boycotting environmentally unsound products

Being interviewed for a community survey

Joining a self-help group

Participating in a question-answer session or a debate

Serving on an ad hoc committee or task force

Participating in sit-ins and marches

Leading a grass-roots activist group in the community

Doing volunteer work in the community

Conducting fund-raising for a community service

Offering consultation services

Serving in public office or supporting a particular candidate internal locus of control believe that they control their own reinforcers; individuals with an external locus of control believe that other people or perhaps fate (something external to the individual) controls reinforcers. The researchers modified Rotter's scale to measure personal power or the sense that a person is in control of his or her fate. The *Injustice Scale* measures individuals' perceptions about whether the world is just (for example, do the courts let the guilty go free and convict innocent people). O'Neill and associates found that neither construct alone, personal power nor a sense of injustice, is sufficient to predict who will be a social activist. Both a sense of personal power *and* a belief in the injustices of society combine to produce social activism. Figure 4.1 reproduces these results in graphic form.

Kelly and Breinlinger (1996) suggested that community activists identify with the group with which they are associated. They also proposed that individuals need a self-image of themselves as activists in order to engage in social change projects. And, finally, Perkins, Brown, and Taylor (1996) found that community-focused cognitions (such as a sense of civic responsibility or a perception of community attachments) as well as relevant behaviors (such as volunteer work in the community) were consistently and positively predictive of participation in social activism. And, finally, Zimmerman, Ramírez-Valles, and Maton

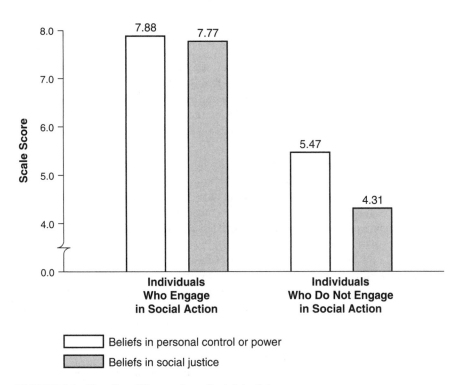

FIGURE 4.1   Results of Research on Social Activism

Note: Citizens who believe in personal control (or power) and social injustice are likely to be social activists.

Source: Data compiled from "Cognition and Citizen Participation in Social Action" by P. O'Neill, C. Duffy, M. Enman, E. Blackman, and J. Goodwin, 1988, *Journal of Applied Sociology, 18,* pp. 1067–1083.

(1999) found that for African American youths, high levels of sociopolitical control limited negative consequences of **helplessness** (feelings of no or low control) on mental health. **Sociopolitical control** may be defined as beliefs that actions in social and political realms can lead to desired outcomes. Zimmerman and associates believe that sociopolitical control contributes to self-esteem and self-confidence, making it more likely that individuals with such control will take action against challenges in other spheres of their lives.

Measuring the impact of citizen participation is difficult but necessary if one is to understand the process and to determine whether it works (Kelly, 1986b). The citizens—the stakeholders, so to speak—might want hard evidence that their efforts were worthwhile, but such direct evidence is often difficult to obtain. Involved individuals might also disagree about what is solid evidence: cost savings, increased profits, higher client satisfaction, less stress, improved community relations, and so forth.

Some citizens may want to participate but lack the appropriate skills; few laypeople, for example, know how to lobby for policy change or how to conduct meaningful and scientific research. Chavis, Florin, and Felix (1992) and Levi and Litwin (1986) noted that citizen groups might also need their group dynamics skills sharpened. Their leaders might need leadership development in the form of training in negotiations or incentive management (Prestby, Wandersman, Florin, Rich, & Chavis, 1990) or in strategic planning.

Citizens might also not understand the cycle of change. Speer and Hughey (1995) have identified the importance of the reciprocal relationship between development of power for community organizations and individual empowerment for organization members. In other words, the organization and its members both need to be empowered to change but in a transactional or dynamic way. Specifically, Speer and Hughey have identified four inter-related phases for community organizing or change. First is the process of *assessment,* through which crucial issues affecting the community are identified by its members and its organizations. This allows the organization, community, and its members to focus on the other three phases.

A second phase is labeled *research.* In this phase, participants examine causes and correlates of issues identified in the assessment phase. In other words, information about the nature of the issues and their potential influences and solutions is gathered. One important piece of information that needs to be gathered in the research phase is the ways in which community resources are allocated and how key players exercise social power around a particular issue.

A third stage, *action,* represents a collective attempt to exercise social power. Actions include public events that demonstrate organizational or citizen power and that perhaps attract attention from outside the organization or community. Finally, *reflection* from community or organizational members is important. Effectiveness of action strategies, discussion of lessons learned, consideration of how power was demonstrated, and development of future plans are explored. The process can then start over again with assessment of other related critical issues for the community.

Obtaining funding for citizen-initiated programs can be problematic, but when is funding not problematic? Citizens often do not know where or how to access funds. For example, how many of you know how to write or have written successful grants large enough to support a community program?

Advantages and Disadvantages of Citizen Participation

Active participation in change efforts usually is highly motivational (Chavis et al., 1992; Yates & Youniss, 1998). That is, people are more likely to accept change that they, themselves, have generated (Duffy, 1991). Involved individuals are also likely to know the problems that need addressing because they have lived with the problems. For that same reason, this type of community participation often helps build a sense of community (Levi & Litwin, 1986) or social consensus and cohesiveness (Heller, Price, Reinharz, Riger, & Wandersman, 1984). Conversely, feeling a sense of community also increases participation in grassroots efforts (Chavis & Wandersman, 1990).

Another advantage of citizen participation is that the average citizen often participates in change efforts for little pay but often with enthusiasm and a sense of responsibility (Selznick, 2000). For example, it is no secret that many community organizations are dependent on volunteers. The Beacon Hill Institute for Public Policy Research (1997) conducted a survey of executive directors of private charitable organizations and found the following results:

- Ninety percent of the directors say that volunteers are crucial to efficiency because they save the organization money.
- Seventy-three percent said that the time and money spent on training volunteers was well worth the effort.
- Seventy-seven percent said they can depend on their volunteers.

As desirable as this type of participation is, it is not without its pitfalls (Barrera, 2000; Oskamp, 1984). Christensen and Robinson (1989) reported that not every citizen wants to participate. Although it is easy to level a charge of apathy against nonparticipants, the rights of those who prefer not to be involved need to be respected.

With this type of social change, results can be long in coming. The delay may cause some early and inspired individuals to run out of steam before their efforts show results. Studies in human services settings suggest that burnout is high (Maslach & Jackson, 1981; Ross, Altmaier, & Russell, 1989) and that those with the highest dedication often burn out first (Schultz & Schultz, 1990).

Finally, because they often are not comprised of all members of a community but rather comprised of a select few, citizen groups can fail. If these individuals are not representative of the affected groups or the population at large, the solutions might not be viable or acceptable for everyone. Furthermore, if this small group of activists is not representative of the larger constituency, then the large group might distrust or reject the smaller group (Worchel, Cooper, & Goethals, 1991), which also causes failure. Participants in community intervention need to recognize the politics of the conflicting goals and interests of the various involved parties (Riger, 1989). Similarly, if activity in the efforts costs more than any benefits that accrue, individuals are likely to become inactive (Prestby et al., 1990; Wandersman & Florin, 2000).

Likewise, citizens hoping to be involved in or expand self-help organizations would be well served by an article by Zimmerman and colleagues (1991) in which they describe the successful expansion of a typical organization. Such an organization needs to mobilize resources from a variety of sources, display flexibility in securing resources, be creative in defining organizational roles, and encourage individual involvement.

For more radical rules for participation, you might want to see Alinksy's (1971) *Rules for Radicals* (mentioned in the previous chapter); however, be aware that Alinsky has been rebuked by others for his abrasiveness and lack of ideology (Delgado, 1986). Case in Point 4.2 discusses a case about the success of activism on a college campus.

NETWORKING

If Harold and Melba Marvin had formed their angry homeowners' group, they might have encountered trouble keeping the group organized and motivated. By joining a statewide coalition of homeowners for adequate insurance and insurance reform or an umbrella organization dedicated to overseeing local fire departments, the success of the Marvins' group might be greater. The formation of such coalitions is the focus of this section.

One means for fostering community development or community change is to develop enabling systems (Chavis et al., 1992). **Enabling systems** are vehicles whereby multiple community initiatives can be simultaneously mobilized, supported, and sustained in an efficient and effective manner by developing specified links among the social actors (Chavis et al., 1992). Chavis (1993) has offered a good example of enabling. He has empowered many community groups and organizations to conduct their own program evaluations by teaching them to design, conduct, and analyze research. He has therefore made them independent of the need for reliance on professionals in the future for their research needs.

Networks (Chavis et al., 1992; Fischer, Jackson, Stueve, Gerson, & McAllister-Jones, 1977; Sarason, Carroll, Maton, Cohen, & Lorentz, 1977) are confederations or alliances of related community organizations or individuals. Members of networks regularly share funding sources, information, and ideas with one another. Thus, their futures are more secure by networking their information and sometimes their clients. Another advantage is that clients are less likely to fall through the cracks in the service system. **Umbrella organizations** are usually overarching organizations that oversee the health of member organizations. Again, they act as clearinghouses for information that members can share. A concrete example might prove useful. United Way of America is perhaps one of the best-known umbrella organizations in the United States. United Way, through charitable contributions, is known for its financial support of community agencies that might otherwise flounder. In addition, it provides community service agencies with office supplies, furniture, and other desperately needed tangible provisions. However, United Way also offers expert consultation on fund-raising, staff training, development of publications, and other issues crucial for community agency survival.

Community development corporations (Vidal, Howitt, & Foster, 1986) and **neighborhood associations** (Speigel, 1987) are citizens' groups of communities and neighborhoods that have come together to conquer a community social problem or to ensure that the community develops in a healthy, planned fashion.

CASE IN POINT 4.2

GRASS-ROOTS ACTIVISM ON A COLLEGE CAMPUS

It seems inconceivable in this day and age that a college campus would be without gynecological and reproductive services for its students. Just a few short years ago, a medium-sized public college in the Northeast had no such services for male or female students. The student government president, an avant-garde young man undaunted by controversy, approached the college president to ask for a clinic. "No" was the answer he received repeatedly.

He next approached psychologists on his campus who recommended contacting sister schools with a survey to determine whether they housed gynecological services. Out of 21 campuses contacted, only 2 did not have such services. The results of the survey did not impress the college administrators, who exclaimed that the other college presidents must be violating policy.

The student government president next contacted the local family planning center, which reported being overwhelmed with student appointments. They needed to make room for other community members. Yes, the center would support him if only by way of moral support.

Without administrative support or funding, the student president knew he would have to look elsewhere. He examined the student government budget, which the elected student leaders controlled. He would have to spend student money, which was in short supply. With the help of a psychologist, he surveyed the student body and found that students indeed were desperate for the service. The money would be well spent, so the student leaders made allowance in their budget for gynecological and reproductive services through creative financial planning. Even then, college administrators would not let him establish the clinic on campus.

A subcommittee formed by the student president contacted local doctors to see whether they would provide the services to students for reasonable fees. One physician agreed. The student government used its van to transport students to the extra evening appointments the doctor had set aside just for them.

It occurred to the psychologists, however, that merely providing preventive and diagnostic services seemed inadequate. The student leaders concurred that educational programs were also needed. The subcommittee and the doctor agreed that his nurse practitioner (for slightly higher fees) would give sex education lectures in the dormitories. After all, they were all aware that sex education does not foster an increase in promiscuous behavior but rather causes a shift to more tolerant attitudes (Kilmann, 1984).

After the off-campus clinic had been in existence for several years, the college administration was replaced and a new college president came on board. The attitude of the campus administration changed, too. An on-campus gynecological and reproductive service was now more acceptable. However, there was no funding in the then current budget. The student government agreed to continue funding the clinic, to find the doctors and nurses, and to provide peer training to student counselors. In exchange, the campus administration agreed to house the clinic, still held in the evening, in the regular college health center where important student health records would be more accessible. In the end, both groups (students and administrators) won, but change was a long time in coming.

This case illustrates that a variety of appeals for change can be successfully used—in this case, a survey of other campuses, opinion polls, and support from another community agency. It also documents that sometimes compromise between two conflicting community groups is the most "winning" solution.

Issues Related to Networks

Networks and umbrella associations offer ongoing support to participants, use reciprocity in the sharing of ideas and resources, use role modeling for each other, and provide accessible resources to participants (Sarason et al., 1977). For instance, these systems allow small community agencies to share information about grants, staff-training opportunities, and resource libraries; to exchange successful publicity ideas; to refer clients to each other's services; to build lobbying coalitions; and so forth. Thus, the health and success of each smaller service is assisted or enabled. Research has documented the effectiveness of these networking systems for acquired immune deficiency syndrome (AIDS) services (Madera, 1986) and unemployed and deinstitutionalized populations (Wolff, 1987), among others.

A somewhat similar notion is that of a **clearinghouse.** Clearinghouses are typically umbrella organizations that individuals seeking self-help groups can contact for assistance in finding self-help. Of course, the clearinghouse concept means that the self-help groups, themselves, are loosely networked. These clearinghouses are reported to result in high consumer satisfaction and good community receptivity (Maton, Levanthal, Madera, & Julien, 1989; Wollert, 1987).

Enabling systems and networks represent a form of social change because they build on existing resources and develop more productive and creative relationships between already existing services. In other words, such systems reweave the social fabric of what might otherwise be a more tattered and frayed community and its services and thus ensure survival and continued growth of the services.

Advantages and Disadvantages of Networks

Besides enhancing the viability of many services, networks are advantageous because they assure that important systems come to know each other better, find effective ways to work together, and learn to plan or advocate for change in a collaborative rather than competitive manner (Wolff, 1987). Likewise, enabling systems better ensure that resources are equitably distributed (Biegel, 1984), help reduce community conflict (Christensen & Robinson, 1989), and focus collective pressure on public policy makers and other decision makers (Delgado, 1986; Seekins & Fawcett, 1987). Networks also enable related services to detect cracks in the service system. **Cracks** are defined as structural gaps in the service systems and are exemplified by missing or inaccessible services and missing information (Tausig, 1987).

Few authors have addressed the disadvantages of umbrella organizations, even though several disadvantages exist. For one, private sector businesses might feel threatened by and perhaps launch a successful attack against the collective power of activist community organizations (Delgado, 1986). Similarly, when umbrella organizations grow large, they develop their own set of problems in terms of sheer bureaucracy, conflict, and expense.

Another disadvantage is that when the umbrella organization, rather than being a loosely knit resource and support network, becomes a controlling, parental organization, member agencies can become dissatisfied. The authors know, for instance, of one rural domestic violence program that broke from a strong countywide coalition of churches over staffing and funding issues despite the domestic violence program's already precarious existence. The bad feelings between the smaller domestic violence program and the larger parent organization resulted in the establishment of a second, redundant domestic violence program in the same geographic region.

Another possible disadvantage of community coalitions is that different community services as well as the whole community may be in different stages of development or readiness for change (Edwards, Jumper-Thurman, Plested, Oetting, & Swanson, 2001). The new ones need staff training; the older ones may be seeking to expand their client bases. Coordinating the different developmental needs of member organizations can be difficult for the parent organization. Finally, if the tentacles of the association grow beyond one particular community's boundaries because member organizations have satellites in other geographic areas, existing associations in neighboring communities may feel threatened and subvert each other's purpose.

PROFESSIONAL CHANGE AGENTS: CONSULTANTS

Harold, Melba, and the other homeowners from this chapter's vignette might find that, despite their numbers, they collectively know little about confronting insurance or fire companies. Melba might therefore suggest finding a consultant who would collaborate with them in an effort to successfully guide the group through the process of obtaining fairer insurance coverage or in researching fire departments in other communities or neighborhood watch systems.

Professional change agents or expert consultants seek to create social change through modification, renewal, and improvement. A **consultant** or **professional change agent** is someone who engages in collaborative problem solving with one or more persons (the **consultees**) who are often responsible for providing some form of assistance to another third individual (the **client**) (Mowbray, 1979). As you read in Chapter 2, consultants are often professionals well versed in scientific research. They are typically called on to conduct program evaluations and needs assessments for community organizations.

Community psychologists seem uniquely qualified to be community consultants because they possess skills in community needs assessment, community organizing, group problem solving, and action research. The community psychologist is also likely to focus on the social systems and institutions within a community rather than on individuals (Weed, 1990). Weed suggested that community psychologists offer a community a cohesive perspective, which is, of course, one of the values cherished by community development specialists.

Issues Related to Consultants

An important issue related to the expense of consultants is whether they really do help the client. One general study of the use of consultants was conducted by Medway and Updyke (1985), who reviewed the literature on outcome of consultations. In the better-designed studies, the researchers found that, compared to control groups, both consultees and clients in the intervention groups (where consultants were utilized) made gains in solving their problems or promoting change as measured by such things as attitude scales, observed behaviors, and standardized scores. In the control groups (in which no consultants were used), there were fewer of these improvements. This literature review therefore offers clear statistical evidence for the value of consultants.

Weed (1990) identified several steps for community psychologists acting as consultants to primary prevention programs that are adaptable for almost all change agents—expert or not. The steps include, first, defining the goals to be accomplished. The second step is to raise the awareness of the individuals in the setting under consultation and then to introduce the new program or research. At this point, other related organizations or communities can be networked for collaboration, support, and learning about new techniques and funding sources. Consultants also need to collaborate on effective methods for evaluating changes. Favorable evaluation justifies the money, time, and effort expended. Evaluation also leads to modification and fine-tuning, should that be necessary. Unfortunately, evaluation is a step sometimes forgotten in many change situations. Without evaluation, how would people know if the change worked and whether it ought to be repeated?

Bishop and Drew (1998) stated that another issue related to consultation is that of trust. It takes time before the professional achieves the trust required to act in the role of consultant. The researchers discussed several projects for which years and years passed before consultants were let into the process and trusted.

Serrano-Garcia (1994) has explained that there are often unequal power relationships between community members and outside professionals, with the professional often having more power because of specialized knowledge and other resources. She has issued a challenge to professionals who act as community consultants to "establish more equitable professional-client relationships" (p. 17) by means of collaboration and empowerment.

Advantages and Disadvantages of Consultants

There are several advantages to expert consultation. The first is obvious; the professional is expert at what he or she does. The professional change agent has been specially trained and has the knowledge base upon which to make wise decisions. Another not so apparent advantage is that the consultant is a neutral person. Because the consultant is not embroiled in the presenting problems and should have no vested interest in the community or organization, the consultant can make unencumbered, unbiased judgments and recommendations.

Consultants also generally take a long-term approach to problem solving. Individuals in the community or organization often focus on short-term issues because they are living with them day to day. However, for the continued health of the community or organization, a long-term approach might be best. As stated earlier, too many community groups fail quickly and easily; quick fixes may be one of the reasons.

Finally, if a consultant is experienced, she or he comes with a vast array of ideas, past successes, and relevant ideas because of experiences with past but similar situations. Consultants should not betray nor create a conflict of interest with past clients, but previous experiences can help them find common ground that might be useful to other similar communities or organizations.

Despite these somewhat apparent advantages, professional change agents are not without disadvantages (Maton, 2000); one is high cost. Cost can be a major factor and can thwart the best-laid plans of any community or organization needing expert assistance. Ideally, some community psychologists acting as change agents would consider *pro bono* or voluntary consultations. The national psychological association, the American Psychological Association, encourages *pro bono* work by psychologists.

Developing cooperation from all involved in the consultation can also be problematic. Outside consultants sometimes inspire fear (of job loss or criticism), defensiveness, and resistance to change. Consultants might want to consider utilizing less direct or nondirective techniques to avoid these problems (Heller et al., 1984).

Consultants' contacts with their clients are often time limited. They need to quickly assess the issues, assist in the development of solutions and their implementation, and foster maintenance strategies in a short period of time. Often, the issues on which they are asked to consult are complex compared to the amount of available resources, including time. For example, many communities and their organizations grew haphazardly rather than in a planned fashion. Redesign can be difficult, if not impossible. Some problems defy solutions; they are essentially insoluble (Sarason, 1978). Many of these issues can be short-circuited if consultants carefully match their skills and expertise to client situations.

Finally, clients sometimes hold high and unrealistic expectations of what a consultant can do. Other clients may "use" the consultant for their own misleading purposes, especially when there are conflicting views about what ought to be done. In these situations, the ethical consultant will probably leave clients feeling disappointed. Again, careful intake by a consultant to ensure that his or her expertise fits the clients' issues can help.

THE USE OF EDUCATION AND INFORMATION DISSEMINATION TO PRODUCE SOCIAL CHANGE

Harold and Melba Marvin, in dismay at the fact that they could no longer afford a home as comfortable as their former one, could take their story to the newspapers. The papers, by disseminating the Marvin's story to researchers, insurance companies, other homeowners, and elected officials, would be assisting in agenda setting and education of the community regarding the plight of underinsured homeowners. This shared information could be the beginning of an insurance reform movement.

The dissemination of information and the education of community members has perhaps received less attention in the community psychology literature than any other aspect of change (Blakely et al., 1987), yet information dissemination remains a vital part of social change efforts. In fact, some community psychologists have challenged their colleagues to renew efforts to disseminate useful information and innovative programs as a method of addressing social problems (Linney, 1990).

Just what is meant by **information dissemination** (Mayer & Davidson, 2000) or **education** in community psychology? As you now know, community psychologists seek to prevent, intercede in, and treat, if necessary, community problems with what are typically innovative programs. If innovative or experimental programs are researched and found to be successful but the results are never shared with other communities or adopted by others, the results are of limited use (Fairweather, 1986). Dissemination of information can save change agents and social activists working with similar populations or in similar settings much time, money, and effort. Thus, dissemination of innovation is crucial.

However, there has been much debate in the literature about how programs can be efficaciously transferred to other settings. Adopters of innovations from community psychology need to be careful in their translation efforts. Adopters should be faithful to the original change model, especially to the mechanism that caused change, but adopters may also need to do some reinventing to a limited extent given that not all settings will be the same (Blakely et al., 1987; Bowman, Stein, & Ireys, 1991).

Whenever information from community psychology is shared with community members, its main purpose should be to improve the community, to promote prevention in favor of treatment, and to empower community members to shape their own destiny (Fairweather & Davidson, 1986). Information for educational purposes can also be used to shape ideology and to direct action in a community as well as to inform those in a position of power (the **gatekeepers**) to understand others in the community better (Levine & Perkins, 1987).With advances in technology—for example, distance learning—diverse and geographically distant communities can be educated and empowered, and information can be disseminated more easily than in the past (Kreisler, Snider, & Kiernan, 1997).

Issues Related to Information Dissemination

Several important issues need to be carefully considered by community psychologists hoping to educate community members about research results or innovative programs (Mayer & Davidson, 2000). First, it is important to remember that not all individuals will be receptive nor will they be receptive at the same time to the information and ideas. Despite great enthusiasm, some individuals will be slow but will eventually adopt what you wish to share, while some will never adopt what you have to offer (Rogers, 1982). Why will adoption be slow and somewhat diffuse? Fairweather and Davidson (1986) suggested that at least two phenomena will interfere: personal characteristics of adopters and the social context in which adopters find themselves. For instance, some individuals are close-minded or **dogmatic** (Rokeach, 1960). They will not accept new ideas readily; in fact, they might not accept the ideas at all. Other individuals may find themselves in a social situation or social context where the suggested change is unacceptable, so they conform with the group's wishes and do not adopt an idea, no matter how good it is.

Second, measuring whether the information dissemination is useful will be problematic. A variety of measures could be utilized, including number of adoptions, replication of previous results in the imitative program, and so on. Selecting several measures will result in better understanding of whether the shared information was successfully adopted. For example, Seitz, Apfel, and Rosenbaum (1991) used several measures—such as dropping out of school, failing grades, enrolling in vocational or alternate school programs, and grade-point average—to measure efficacy of an intervention program for pregnant teens. They found that on several different measures, the adolescents experiencing the special intervention were more likely to succeed in school. Had the researchers used only one measure, their results might have indicated otherwise.

Disseminators of information, especially those sharing information on new programs, should also be mindful that only some pieces of the program might be useful to adopters and that disseminators are collaborators rather than dictators about how the shared information should be utilized. Fairweather and Davidson (1986) suggested that anyone trying to diffuse innovation in a community needs to learn to be a graceful loser at times!

A final issue related to the use of education as a social change mechanism is that it must be culturally sensitive. What works for one ethnic group might not work in another. Snowden (1993); Snowden, Martinez, & Morris, 2000) also commented that ethnic minority groups are often high users of public sector community services. Even though innovations taking place are well intentioned and promising, equal benefits for minorities and equal avoidance of harm cannot be taken for granted. Researchers, policy makers, and advocates must give special attention to the impact of their interventions on the well-being of ethnic minority citizens.

An example might prove useful. Marin, Marin, Perez-Stable, Sabogal, and Otero-Sabogal (1990) tested a seven-month, media-based community intervention designed to increase levels of information on the damaging effects of cigarette smoking and on the availability of culturally appropriate cessation services. Knowing from their previous work (Marin et al., 1990) what messages best discriminated between Hispanics who quit versus those who continued to smoke assisted them in designing their campaign. The campaign was successful, especially given that change in knowledge occurred most in the less acculturated Hispanics. **Acculturation** generally means that the people in a minority group adopt as their own the norms, values, and behavior patterns of the dominant society but still are not admitted to more intimate social groups in that society (Hess, Markson, & Stein, 1991). In other words, in the study by Marin and colleagues (1990), those Hispanics least familiar with Anglo smoking cessation campaigns were most changed by the information dissemination *designed especially for them.*

Figure 4.2 provides a second example. This figure demonstrates what education and information dissemination can perhaps accomplish for the population in the United States. The graph depicts life expectancy (at age 65) by education, race, and sex. The important thing to notice is that individuals with the least education always have shorter life expectancies (regardless of race and sex) than those with more education.

Note also that there are other differences, for example between Blacks and Whites and between males and females. Sex differences might be accounted for by physiological differences between men and women or by occupational hazards faced by the types of jobs men and women stereotypically hold. The race differences might be accounted for by income level; those with higher incomes (the majority of whom are White) typically have better access to quality health care. In fact, income level and occupational status both correlate highly with education, so they, too, might account for the life expectancy differences between men and women and between Blacks and Whites. The secondary point here, then, is that education might not be the sole basis for life expectancy and other health differences.

Advantages and Disadvantages of Educational Change

Advantages of educational change are several. First, a wide audience can often be reached with these change efforts because a multiplex approach to disseminate ideas, especially by mass media such as television and newspapers, can be used (McAlister, 2000). Second, education as a whole is generally revered in the United States, so the average community citizen

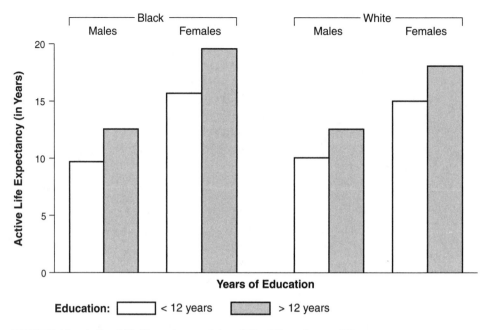

FIGURE 4.2   **Active Life Expectancy at Age 65 by Education and Race**

Source: From "Reflections on Present and Future Research on Bio-Behavioral Risk Factors" by G. Kaplan, in
New Research Frontiers in Behavioral Medicine: Proceedings of the National Conference by S. Blumenthal,
K. Matthews, and S. Weiss (Eds.), 1994, Washington, DC: NIH Publications.

as well as those in power are likely to accept this approach to change rather than more radical
approaches. Finally, this may be one of the least expensive forms of social change for community activists to pursue if they use certain vehicles such as public media for dissemination. A picture may indeed be worth a thousand words. Similarly, a research report written
in lay terminology can easily be distributed to many individuals at once.

There are disadvantages, however. Closed minds are not easily opened, no matter how
much information is presented. Also, the vehicle for dissemination may have to be custom
designed for the audience. For instance, consciousness-raising groups worked well to disseminate information about feminism in the women's movement (Levine & Perkins, 1987).
However, for physicians' groups, professional journals may be the best vehicle. Another
disadvantage, especially of using the mass media for large-scale intervention, is that media
advertising sometimes promotes the very behavior the educational intervention is designed
to reduce or prevent (Jason, 1998). An example would be televised advertisements for beer
juxtaposed with an educational campaign designed to lessen or prevent drunk driving.

PUBLIC POLICY AS A MEANS OF SOCIAL CHANGE

Suppose that the Marvins and the other homeowners first went to their local newspaper with
their story, then went to their state legislator who had read the story in the paper. Out of

concern, after some additional persuasion from the homeowners, the legislator agreed to work with them to introduce legislation designed to govern regulation of replacement cost insurance. Had this happened, the Marvins and their legislator would have affected public policy, the topic of this chapter.

Did you vote in the last election? It is often surprising how many citizens, college students in particular, do not vote. Voting, drafting legislation, lobbying for particular interests, and so on comprise actions that change, and often change dramatically, our national and local social agendas. For citizens and community psychologists alike, participating in public policy endeavors opens a "window of opportunity" (Nikelly, 1990) for what can often be sweeping social changes.

Just what is **public policy?** The aim of public policy is to improve the quality of life for community members. Although the term is often used for government-mandated legislation, it can refer to policy at a specific agency or at the local community and state governmental levels. Public policy can also influence to what issues various resources are allocated (Levine & Perkins, 1997).

A concept relevant to public policy is **policy science,** which is the science of making findings from science (and in the case of community psychology, findings from social science) relevant to governmental and organizational policy (Oskamp, 1984). A well-known example of this is the use of actual scientific studies on desegregation of schools to shape policies on integration (Oskamp, 1984; Perkins, 1988).

At this point in your reading, you have learned about the variety of techniques that can be utilized to create social change. Any reliable change agent knows that a multifaceted approach is best. That is, a single change strategy by itself may be weak. Utilizing several change techniques is more likely to result in the desired outcomes. Case in Point 4.3 describes the evolution of rape crisis centers, which generally take this multifaceted strategy of social change.

Issues Related to the Use of Public Policy

Politics and community psychology are deeply intertwined (Vogelman, 1990), although changing social policy is a relatively unexplored extension of community psychology (Phillips, 2000). There is general agreement among community psychologists that their science and politics are inseparable. However, community psychologists do not agree on how much science should impinge on policy and how much public policy should pervade science. Some argue that good policies are those based solely on scientific evidence. In other words, one should not attempt to influence any public policy until one has solid scientific evidence. Others argue that pressing social problems such as AIDS and homelessness do not afford one the luxury of time for conducting research. Society is not likely to have solutions to this complex situation for some time to come.

Most community psychologists do agree that the development of public policy should be a collaborative effort between researchers, affected populations, and the decision or policy makers. The idea of collaboration leads psychologists to avoid "colonial" relationships with the affected community members (Chavis et al., 1983). In fact, collaboration with appropriate community members, particularly those affected by policy research and/or policy decisions, is not only strategically sound, it is good ethics (Robinson, 1990).

■ ■ ■ ■ ■ ▬▬▬

CASE IN POINT 4.3

RAPE CRISIS CENTERS: A NATIONAL EXAMINATION

Campbell, Baker, and Mazurek (1998) hypothe-sized that many rape crisis centers have undergone significant changes since their early beginnings during the feminist movement of the 1970s. The researchers used interviews with center directors to examine the current structure and functions of 168 randomly selected rape crisis centers across the nation.

First, the study demonstrates that there are many avenues to social change. An early goal of rape crisis services was the provision of services to survivors of sexual assault. Ancillary to this was the provision of 24-hour crisis intervention hotlines as well as counseling and assistance in negotiating the legal and medical systems. Many, but not all, centers also eventually sought to raise public awareness about sexual assault in the community. Some centers additionally became active in public demonstrations such as Take Back the Night marches. Finally, some centers also sought to con-duct large-scale change by lobbying state legisla-tures for reform. In response, most states did alter their rape statutes in the late 1970s and early 1980s.

Second, although the average center studied was 16 years old, there were many that were older

or younger than this. The older, free-standing, col-lective centers had larger budgets and staffs as well as a change orientation when interacting with other social services agencies. These centers utilized par-ticipatory decision making for deciding internal issues. Older centers were also more likely to par-ticipate in public demonstrations such as Take Back the Night marches and in prevention pro-gramming. The younger centers, especially those that were affiliated with larger service agencies and which therefore followed a hierarchical organiza-tional structure, were more likely to engage in political lobbying rather than preventive education and public demonstrations as their forms of social activism.

Both types of centers, then, engaged in social activism or social change but the types of activities differed by organizational structure and age. In addition, this study also demonstrates that rape cri-sis organizations and perhaps other service-ori-ented organizations often need to adapt to the changing political climate in order to continue to provide quality services to their communities.

Americans like to think that the public policy that guides social change is predicated on science, humanism, and logical thinking, but often what happens in Washington and else-where occurs whether or not rational thought enters the process (Johnson, 1991). The polit-ical climate, lobbying groups with cross-purposes, and other vicissitudes can often influence the end product in public policy as much or more than science and other logical factors. Phe-nomena such as a more sophisticated electorate than that of yesteryear (Greenberg, 1999) and shifting public concern (e.g., from national defense issues to social problems) (Johnson, 1991) can sway the direction of public policy. Likewise, funding created for various policy changes will remain a heated issue in the foreseeable future, and behavioral and social sci-entists unfortunately are often the underdogs for social change funding (American Psycho-logical Society, 1991). The media also set an important emotional tone that shapes public policy in this country (Schmolling, Youkeles, & Burger, 1989) and influences what people think about. This is called **agenda setting.** And recently, scandals associated with government leaders have reduced public trust in the government (Chanley, Rudolph, & Rahn, 2000).

Policy science serves several functions: instrumental, conceptual, and persuasive (Shadish, 1990). The authors personally feel that research can and should also serve a predictive purpose. When research shapes the direction of change or of public policy, then it serves an **instrumental purpose.** Research can also be aimed at changing the way people think or conceptualize social problems and solutions. Research with this function serves a **conceptual purpose.** When research persuades policy makers to support a particular position or solution to a social problem, it then functions in the **persuasive** mode. Finally, when research is designed to forecast what change will occur in the future or to predict whether change will be accepted, the function is **predictive.**

Is there any evidence that social science research influences legislators as they develop public policy? Yes, one can see the impact of researchers, in part, by what type of research is funded by the federal government. Except for economists, psychologists perhaps receive the largest amount of funding of all social scientists (Oskamp, 1984). Furthermore, public officials have reported utilizing social science in the drafting of policies with psychological research cited as the most influential of all these sciences (Caplan, Morrison, & Stambaugh, 1975). While on the staff of the United States Senate, Trudy Vincent (1990) reported that the activities in which members of Congress engage are very similar to those of ecologically minded community psychologists. That is, legislators also need to pay careful attention to the people, settings, events, and history of their districts before establishing policy. Directly and indirectly, then, psychology can influence public policy.

No matter what the role of research in policy development or in the community, it should always be "returned" to the community for application (Chavis et al., 1983) and not kept solely in the scientific journals for consumption by scientists. Remember, though, that when research is given away to the community, it can also be used for political ammunition, manipulation, and self-serving purposes (Oskamp, 1984).

Research in the service of public policy is not the only way to address social change. Community psychologists and community members can also **lobby** to change policy. To lobby means to direct pressure at public officials to promote the passage of a particular piece of legislation or policy. Individuals wishing to influence policy can also disseminate appropriate pieces of information, such as public opinion polls and results of field research, to policy makers in an attempt to educate them (Perkins, 1988). Education and information dissemination as a means of social change have already been discussed.

The average citizen hoping to influence legislation may find the process bewildering, whether it is at the local, state, or federal level. Fortunately, there are materials available to the average citizen that will take the mystery out of the legislative process (Alderson & Sentman, 1979; Ebert-Flattau, 1980; Zigler & Goodman, 1982). The American Psychological Association (APA) has created a Public Interest Directorate, the mission of which is to advance the scientific and professional aspects of psychology as applied to human welfare. The directorate disseminates reports and other written materials to state and federal governments and legislators. Similarly, APA also developed a guide to advocacy in the public interest that includes sections on the legislative process and on effective means of communications with congressional staff.

A community psychologist or community member could also seek an elected office, work on the campaign of a particular candidate, or vote for a particular candidate supporting a favored social change program. While holding an important elected office may seem alien to some, it is often the ideal role for a scientist. Why? The community scientist's training places him or her in the position to be able to demand evidence for proposed programs. Scientists also best know the importance of evaluating change mechanisms such as new or experimental programs (Fairweather & Davidson, 1986).

Another role for politically active scientists is to act as expert witnesses and *amicus curiae* (friend of the court). A case of the *amicus curiae* role for psychologists in the courts was the use of sex stereotyping research by Susan Fiske in the *Price Waterhouse* v. *Hopkins* case heard and cited in the local, appellate, and Supreme Courts. The American Psychological Association also filed an *amicus curiae* brief in the case. The testimony about the psychology of stereotyping played a crucial role at each court level as well as in the eventual vindication of the wronged female employee (Fiske, Bersoff, Borgida, Deaux, & Heilman, 1991). Community psychologists in these endeavors play a role in shaping case law and setting precedents on which other cases may be based (Jacobs, 1980; Perkins, 1988).

Advantages and Disadvantages of Public Policy Changes

The advantage of using public policy efforts—including research, lobbying for or sponsoring a particular policy, and elections—is that sweeping social changes can often be induced, especially if the efforts of broad alliances are all aimed in the same direction. Another advantage is that the average U.S. citizen is known to have considerable respect for the law (Kohlburg, 1984; Lempert & Sanders, 1986), and some people may accept the change because it is the law.

Often, the real issues underlying social problems are economic and political rather than psychological, so the policy solution might be the most appropriate anyway (Nikelly, 1990). Finally, policy makers often, but not always, have a broad perspective on the community that elected or appointed them, so are likely to understand the interrelationships between seemingly segregated groups and isolated social problems. Therefore, solutions in the form of policy can take a broadbrush and long-term approach rather than a narrow or short-term focus, which is more likely to fail.

No method of social change is without problems, however, and policy science and public policy are not without theirs. For instance, much social science research is completed by academics operating in a "publish or perish" mode (Phares, 1991) to impress colleagues; the research is often not returned to the community for social change. Similarly, community researchers are often perceived as agents of a traditional system that has historically been oppressive and are consequently not perceived as guests or collaborators in the community (Robinson, 1990). Therefore, research participation, results, and dissemination efforts are shunned, rendering the research useless.

Another serious problem with using public policy avenues to create social change is the electorate. Bond issues, school budgets, referenda, and other elections are participated in by a select few. Most voters are disproportionately well educated and older than the average citizen. Hence, the voices of the poor, the young, and the minorities are not heard via voting. This means that those who may most benefit from prosocial change are not partici- pating in the direction of these changes (Hess et al., 1991).

Perhaps the greatest disadvantage to using public policy efforts to create social change is that policy shaping can be a slow, cumbersome, politicized process. For instance, the aver- age time span from initial writing to passage of a bill in Congress is about a year. However, less controversial policies pass more quickly. More complex or controversial issues take much longer. In the meantime, the needs of the affected groups may have changed; indeed, the group, itself, may have evaporated, or its needs may have become more severe so that the original policy solution is insufficient.

SUMMARY

Many methods for creating and sustaining social change exist. Each has its own advantages and disadvantages. Activists hoping to fashion social change need to consider what strate- gies will work best for the issues they hope to address. Some combination of strategies will probably work better than a single strategy, and what worked once might not work again or in a different community or for a different issue.

Planned change, such as grass-roots activism and information dissemination, inten- tionally addresses and prepares the community for changes. The primary purpose of planned change should always be to improve the community. Each method of planned change has its disadvantages and advantages. Methods available for induced change include citizen par- ticipation, networking with other community resources, the use of professional consultants, education or knowledge dissemination, and participation in public policy efforts by citizens and scientists.

In citizen participation, citizens produce the changes they desire by mechanisms such as grass-roots activism, which is a type of bottom-up rather than top-down change. Such change results in empowerment, in which individuals feel they have power or control over their own lives.

When community agencies come together to aid one another, they are networking. Networking has been shown to directly assist in the longevity of community organizations. Sometimes umbrella organizations, such as United Way, also provide services to commu- nity agencies or enhance their functioning, thus again ensuring their success.

Professional change agents or consultants can also help communities evolve. Com- munity consultants need to be careful not to overtake the community but rather empower the community to create its own changes.

Education and information dissemination are yet other means of producing social change. Although these methods sometimes produce vast changes, care must be taken to utilize the most appropriate information with sensitivity to the cultural diversity of the com- munity.

Passing new legislation and policies or revamping existing laws and policies are other means of creating social change and are known collectively as public policy. Public policy changes can create sweeping social change but often such policy is fraught with the politics of competing groups and can take much time to fashion and implement.

CHAPTER 5

STRESS, COPING, AND SOCIAL SUPPORT
Toward Community Mental Health

The renown which riches or beauty confer is fleeting and frail;
mental excellence is a splendid lasting possession.
—Gaius Sallustius Crispus, 86–34 B.C.

Arthur, or Art to his friends, is filled with anxiety. He is a first-semester freshman and his midsemester grades are poor; in fact, Art is afraid that he will flunk out between semesters. He feels that the main reason for his poor grades is that his roommates have interfered with his studying. Most freshmen are in double rooms; Art had the misfortune of ending up in a triple room. He hopes to have a different rooming situation next semester, but for now he has to cope with the living habits of not one but two other people—difficult people in Art's opinion. One roommate is moody and unpredictable. The other is out until all hours of the night and comes home and wakes up the whole floor of residents.

Adjusting to the rigors of academic life at college has been hard for Art, too. He breezed through high school, where little studying and homework were required. At college, Art sometimes has to read 30 pages a night per subject, and the crush of examinations and papers all due at the same time is overwhelming him.

To make matters worse, Art spent this past weekend at home. He was so happy to get off campus and get away for a few days. However, when Art arrived home, his parents sat him in the living room and broke the distressing news to him that they were divorcing after 25 years of marriage.

The depressed and dejected Art sat in his residence hall on the Sunday night after his visit home and wondered how he would manage all the stress. Maybe he should just drop out of school? Would working for a year ease the tension between his mother and father by contributing needed income? Perhaps his being home would make his parents understand how important a family is.

In everyday life there are many factors to which people must adjust. Personal relationships, changes in work schedules and living habits, and major happenings such as a war, a poor economy, or a natural disaster are some of the events that require good coping skills from almost everyone, no matter how healthy or disabled. This chapter will examine what mental health is and what individuals and communities can do to optimize (primary and secondary prevention) an individual's mental health. First, three classic theories (and therapies) for promoting mental health and treating mental disorders will be discussed. You can contrast them with more contemporary interventions from the field of community psychology, which are delineated in the last half of the chapter. The three major forces or theories in psychology are psychoanalysis, behaviorism, and humanism.

HISTORICAL NOTES ON MENTAL HEALTH AND MENTAL DISORDER

The Medical Model: Psychoanalysis

For those of you who are psychology majors or have taken a course in abnormal, child, or personality psychology (or are fans of Woody Allen movies), Sigmund Freud (1856–1939) will be no stranger. Freud is the father of psychoanalysis. Although many people today disagree with his theories, it cannot be denied that Freud's influence is felt in psychology as well as in psychiatry. Although Freud believed that biology played an important role in the development of psyches, he argued that most psychological disorders are treatable or curable with the use of free association or verbal therapy. Psychoanalytic treatment takes the form of individual verbal therapy up to five times a week over several years.

Somewhat later, the psychoanalytic approach began to split into two paths: traditional psychoanalytic individual verbal therapy versus biological psychiatry, or the **medical model.** A German contemporary of Freud's, Adolf Meyer (1866–1950), argued for the importance of the interplay between biology, psychology, and environment, but many others preferred only biology as an explanation for mental disorders, after a strict medical model. The traditional psychoanalytic individual verbal therapy model has consistently shown to be ineffective with the severely mentally ill (Wilson, O'Leary, & Nathan, 1992). Therefore, given the strength of the biological, or medical, model, the two authoritative references about mental illness (*The Diagnostic and Statistical Manual of Mental Disorders [DSM]* and the *International Code of Diagnosis [ICD]*) were developed. The medical model left at least two important legacies in traditional psychology. One is the reliance on diagnostic labels, as found in the DSM. The other legacy is the assumption of authority and power by the professional over the patient. Both of these legacies, though, are eschewed by community psychologists.

The Behavioral Model: The Social-Learning Approach

As you may recall from your introductory psychology course, by using dogs as subjects, the Russian physiologist Ivan Pavlov (1849–1936) was able to demonstrate that behavior could be formed as a result of **classical conditioning.** This is the process by which a response comes to be elicited by a stimulus, an object, or a situation other than that which is the natural or normal stimulus. That is, Pavlov repeatedly exposed his dogs to a **conditioned stimulus** in the form of a bell whenever the **unconditioned stimulus** in the form of meat powder was present. Although the **unconditioned response** or natural response for meat powder was salivation, eventually these dogs learned to display a **conditioned response** or learned response in the form of salivation *in the absence of* meat powder. A more human example is necessary here. Returning to the opening vignette in this chapter, you might predict that if Art isolated himself in his room each time he felt depressed (the unconditioned stimulus or unlearned stimulus), he would soon perceive his room (conditioned stimulus or learned stimulus) as depressing. In fact, you might predict that the room itself would eventually trigger depression in Art (the conditioned response or learned response).

Dissatisfied with the psychoanalytic approach and rejecting the method of **introspection** or self-examination (a method advocated by Wilhelm Wundt, the father of experimental psychology), two U.S. psychologists, John B. Watson (1878–1985) and B. F. Skinner (1904–1990), further developed Pavlov's theory by using humans as subjects. Instead of pairing a conditioned stimulus with an unconditioned stimulus, Skinner developed and preferred the use of **operant conditioning,** in which behavior is more likely to be engaged in when it is **reinforced** or rewarded. Often, the reinforcers and the conditioned and unconditioned stimuli are provided by something external to the organism. Thus, in part, behavioral tradition provides one with a sense that ecology is important. For example, Art would more likely be nice to his roommates if they returned in-kind behavior.

Extending the principles of learning theory, or the **behavioral model,** Martin Seligman (1975) argued that depression can be explained as a form of **learned helplessness,** or a lack of perceived control due to uncontrollable events in the environment. In the case of Art, the social-learning approach would argue that the reason he felt depressed was due to the fact that he had experienced many life events over which he had little control. For example, he had little control over his parents' divorce. In other words, lack of control reinforced Art's feelings of depression or helplessness. Other advocates of the social-learning approach, such as British psychiatrist Han Eysenck, Sr., and U.S. psychologist Joseph Wolpe, have developed techniques such as **desensitization** or step-by-step relaxation training to change phobic or fearful behavior.

Generally speaking, the social-learning model is an effective treatment with many forms of mental distress. However, it is labor intensive, because each behavioral treatment must be tailored to match the individual's needs. Moreover, to many critics, the social-learning approach appears to deal with the symptoms rather than the cause of mental distress. Finally, most community psychologists would note that this model treats one individual at a time—not a very efficient way to manage change.

The Humanistic Model

The 1960s witnessed the growth and emphasis of the movement of human rights, such as the introduction of the Civil Rights Act in 1969. This had a profound impact on how mental health and mental disorders were perceived or defined. That is, to some mental health care experts and professionals, such as U.S. psychologists Abraham Maslow (1908–1970) and British psychiatrist R. D. Laing, maladjustment had more to do with **labeling,** or an individual being told he or she is not healthy or is "sick," than with innate determinants. In other words, people sometimes behave in accord with what they are told. Thus, treatments should be designed to assist these people to understand and reflect on their unique feelings. In conjunction with this notion, U.S. psychologist Carl Rogers (1902–1987) developed **client-centered therapy,** in which the role of the therapist is to facilitate the client's reflection on his or her experiences. Note the word **client** in the previous sentence. To humanistic psychologists, clients are not "sick" and thus are not labeled **patients.** If Art were to visit a counselor and the counselor diagnosed him as depressed, Art might indeed come to think of himself as a very depressed individual according to this labeling hypothesis.

Similar to the psychoanalytic model, the **humanistic model** emphasizes the use of verbal therapy. Unlike the psychoanalytic model, both individual and group verbal therapy are common to the humanistic model. However, the humanistic model suffers from some of the same criticisms as does the psychoanalysis theory. Faith, Wong, and Carpenter (1995) found that the effectiveness of a sensitivity training group (a form of humanistic group therapy) is not so much due to the fact that people gain a sense of self-worth but due to improved mental health as a function of social skills learned during therapy.

Case in Point 5.1 provides information about the various mental health providers. Table 5.1 briefly summarizes the characteristics of the three major theories just discussed.

There are, however, at least two more major ideas derived from humanistic psychology that have been transplanted to the field of community psychology. One is that all people are worthy individuals and have the right to fulfill and discover this worth. The second is that the individual best knows himself or herself and thus needs to provide input on solutions to problematic issues. To that end, the next topic in this chapter is how people handle a pervasive problem of today: stress.

TABLE 5.1   Characteristics of the Medical, Behavioral, and Humanistic Models for Studying Mental Illness/Health

	MEDICAL	BEHAVIORAL	HUMANISTIC
Philosophy	Unconscious sexual energy shapes human behaviors	Human behaviors can be molded or conditioned	Humans are innately striving for actualization or positive self-regard
Method of Investigation	Case study	Experimental	Case study and correlational experiment
Treatment	Psychoanalysis (may include medication)	Various behavioral techniques (e.g., biofeedback)	Individual and group psychotherapy

■ ■ ■ ■ ■

CASE IN POINT 5.1

MENTAL HEALTH CARE PROFESSIONALS

Various professional services are available to help people cope with stress. Many of the mental health care services are delivered by individuals from four major professional disciplines. **Psychiatrists** are medical doctors (M.D.s). who specialize in psychiatry. They can be employed in either the public (governmental) or private sector (such as private practice). In addition to their training, psychiatrists must pass a licensing examination before they can practice the discipline. Within the field, there are subspecialties such as biological psychiatry and community psychiatry. Nonetheless, the role of psychiatry is usually medication maintenance, although mental health patients who are financially capable can often receive some form of therapy such as psychoanalytic therapy up to five times a week.

Many individuals who hold advanced degrees in any subfields of psychology consider themselves psychologists. **Clinical psychologists** are mental health care professionals who have advanced training (usually a doctoral degree) in clinical psychology and hold licenses from the states in which they practice. Similar to psychiatrists, clinical psychologists can be employed in either the public or private sector. Unlike psychiatrists, clinical psychologists cannot prescribe medication.

The long-standing professional conflict between the fields of psychiatry and clinical psychology has created many interesting twists as to who is qualified to be called a *psychologist.* One outcome is that, in many instances, the government (state and federal) recognizes as psychologists only those individuals with advanced training in clinical psychology or related areas such as counseling or industrial psychology and who have passed some licensing examination.

Furthermore, these scenarios are complicated by several other factors. Sometimes, the term **therapist** is used interchangeably with the terms *clinician* and *psychologist,* although not all clinicians and therapists (such as those in social work and psychiatric nursing) have training in clinical psychology. Also, many doctoral-level psychologists receive their training in nonclinical areas such as community psychology.

There are also disagreements within the subfield of clinical psychology. Traditionally, clinical psychologists were trained using the **scientist-practitioner model** or trained to be both scientists and practitioners. These psychologists hold a Doctor of Philosophy (Ph.D.), the highest degree in any scientific discipline. Now, there is a growing trend in the subfield of clinical psychology to train people as clinicians or *practitioners.* A degree known as Doctor in Psychology (Psy.D.) has been created.

A third group of mental health care professionals who deliver services and treatments are **social workers,** who generally hold a degree called a Master of Social Work (M.S.W.). Unlike psychiatrists, they cannot prescribe medication. Similar to psychiatrists and clinical psychologists, social workers can be employed in either the public or private sector. The primary role of a social worker is as a practitioner. Similar to clinical psychologists, social workers also sometime pose a professional threat to psychiatrists. Again, some of this controversy has to do with licensing.

What psychiatrists, clinical psychologists, and social workers have in common, though, is that they treat *individuals* who are experiencing stress. That is, they do little to promote the mental health of large groups of people or the whole community. Another common feature is that all of these caregivers are usually construed as authority figures in the lives of the individuals they treat. Rarely do the individuals feel empowered to do something about their own situation.

A final and important issue related to these mental health care providers is the one of health insurance or third-party payments. Health insurance companies act as third parties who pay the mental health care provider, whether that professional is a psychiatrist or social worker, for the treatment of the client or person covered by the insurance. Many individuals in the United States have no insurance coverage. For those who do, there appears to be a somewhat disconcerting trend for insurance companies to reduce their payment costs such that those providers who charge less (for example, the psychiatric nurses and social workers) are the ones impaneled or covered by insurance. Community activists need to stay on top of this issue—for example, by conducting research to ascertain whether there is a relationship between the success of treatment and the cost of the treatment. The issue of health insurance is addressed in more detail in Chapter 10.

Interestingly, community psychologists, who sit outside most of these territorial disputes, believe that an ounce of prevention is by far the most cost-effective intervention of all. Mental health education could go a long way toward preventing the need for treatment and health insurance coverage all together.

STRESS

A Definition

Stress is a complex concept but it can be briefly defined as "a call for action when one's capabilities are perceived as falling short of the needed personal resources" (Sarason, 1980, p. 74). Stress responses vary from physiological reactions, such as ulcers or high blood pressure, to psychological reactions, such as avoidance of a stressful event in the future, to the serious psychological condition called *learned helplessness.*

Physical Responses to Stress

The typical reactions to stress have been described in the classic work of Hans Selye (1956, 1974) on the **general adaptation syndrome (GAS).** This syndrome includes a set of physical responses to stress in three different stages. The first stage is **alarm,** in which the sympathetic nervous system is activated so heart rate, respiration, and other physiological responses increase. The second stage of the GAS is **resistance,** where the body tries to resist the stress if it persists. Although the individual might appear fine, the bodily defenses are actually eroding, according to Selye. Finally, if the stress continues long term, the final stage of **exhaustion** will be reached. Exhaustion can lead to death.

Does stress lead to actual physical illness or ruin the immune system? The popular press likes to relate stories that this is indeed true. However, a review of the scientific literature shows two things. First, many of the studies are poorly designed. For instance, many are retrospective studies—that is, people are asked to remember backward in time, a technique that is susceptible to memory problems and other errors. Second, the literature as a whole shows a weak but positive correlation between stress and illness. The correlations usually range from .20 to .30, with the highest correlation possible being 1.0 (Lippa, 1990).

A sample study about stress, health, and college examinations ties in with the opening vignette about Art. Jemmet and Magloire (1988) followed students' physical well-being over the course of a semester. The researchers found more immunoglobin in the saliva of healthy college students during nonexamination periods than during periods of examination, such as finals week. Immunoglobin protects people from illness. Thus, students are more prone to colds and other ailments during examination periods (Dorian, Keystone, Garfinkel, & Brown, 1982) and thus may need additional support from the college (academic and medical) during exams.

Psychological Responses to Stress

Psychological reactions to stress are quite varied. Individuals can respond to stress by personal growth, by a decrease in psychological well-being (even psychopathology), or without any noticeable psychological change (Dohrenwend, 1978). What determines, in part, how an individual responds are **moderating factors** such as one's personal characteristics and one's social resources. A moderating factor is considered to be operative when, if in its presence, the relationship of stress to illness (mental or physical) is weaker than in its absence (Bloom, 1988). For example, if a person is hardy, then the effects of stress are less deleterious than for an individual who is less hardy but who experiences the same amount of stress. Moreover, hardy individuals perceive minor events such as everyday hassles as less stressful than individuals who are not hardy (Banks & Gannon, 1988). **Hardiness** is typified by a sense of personal control, a sense of commitment to work and self, and a tendency to perceive change as a challenge rather than as a threat (Kobasa, 1979).

Other personal characteristics may also moderate the effects of stress. Chan (1977) and Baum, Singer, and Baum (1981) postulated that locus of control (internal or external, as discussed in Chapter 4), a sense of helplessness (described earlier in this chapter), chronic anxiety, and low self-esteem are central personality determinants of stress reactions. Other research (Nelson & Cohen, 1983), however, has sometimes failed to support that certain of these constructs actually do moderate the effects of stress.

Social resources can also moderate the effects of stress and include, when under stress, one's sense of social support in the community. In fact, the concept of social support has received enormous attention in the literature of community psychology.

FACTORS THAT INFLUENCE ADJUSTMENT
AND COPING

Life Events as Sources of Stress

Holmes and Rahe (1967) asked individuals to assign 0 to 100 points to life events according to the degree of readjustment these people required, with 100 points indicating much readjustment. Topping off the eventual list of stressful events was the death of a spouse (100 points), followed by divorce (73 points) and marital separation (65 points). Other events high on the list of stressors were a jail term (63 points), personal injury or illness (53 points), and being fired from a job (47 points). Interestingly, some positive life events were also construed as stressful or requiring adjustment. For example, marriage (50 points), pregnancy (40 points), retirement (45 points), and holidays such as Christmas (12 points) were considered to be stressful, as well. In other words, both positive and negative life changes probably produce stress because they require people to make adjustments. In fact, research (Kofkin & Repucci, 1991) has found that a single event can also be construed as both positive and negative at the same time. Those changes that are uncontrollable or unpredictable seem to be most stressful (Baron & Byrne, 1994; Vinokur & Caplan, 1986).

Horowitz, Schaefer, Hiroto, Wilner, and Levin (1977) have developed the **Life Events Questionnaire** in line with Holmes and Rahe's work. The questionnaire, however, takes into account the kind of life event and the time since the event occurred. Other research (Kale & Stenmark, 1983) has indicated that this particular questionnaire is a significantly good predictor of psychological adjustment compared to other available scales.

The research on stressful life events did not end there, however. Holmes and Masuda (1974) found that the more stress points (points accumulated by summing together the "score" for each stressor) an individual accumulated over the course of a year, the more likely that individual was to experience a major physical illness. In fact, individuals with over 300 points showed a high incidence of illness over the next nine months. One might predict that with Art's problematic adjustment to college life, the rigors of his studies, his roommate problems, and his parents' divorce, he might soon become seriously ill.

Hassles of Daily Life as Stressors

Major life events such as those already mentioned are relatively rare. What is more common are everyday hassles such as being caught in traffic or in long lines, losing money, forgetting phone numbers, having too much to do, and fearing confrontations with friends. Art, the freshman in the opening vignette, seems to be experiencing some of these hassles, too. Lazarus and Folkman (1984) developed a **Hassles Scale** for individuals; the researchers found that the more hassled an individual feels, the greater the reported stress. Scores on this scale are also related to an individual's psychological symptoms. That is, the more the minor irritants in a person's life, the poorer the individual's psychological well-being. Other research using the Hassles Scale and other measures of daily irritants has demonstrated that the presence of numerous or accumulated daily annoyances rather than exposure to a single life trauma may result in poorer health (Lazarus, 1984). For example, studies in industry show that daily hassles on the job or mismatches between one's personal characteristics and one's job demands are especially good predictors of major illnesses (Chemers, Hays, Rhodewalt, & Wysocki, 1985).

Chronic versus Acute Stress

Life events and daily hassles create **acute stress,** but what about long-term or chronic stress? McGonagle and Kessler (1990) suggested that emphasis would be better placed on chronic or continuous stress from continual financial or marital problems, prolonged illnesses, and other stressors that have no endpoint. Their research with nearly 2,000 men and women indeed demonstrates that chronic stresses are more strongly related to depressive symptoms than acute stress. Interestingly, by not aggregating the effects of chronic and acute stress in their sample, the researchers also discovered that depression created by acute stress is less pronounced among people who have preexisting chronic difficulties than those without such difficulties. One might logically expect something different—for example, that chronic stress is exacerbated by acute episodes of stress. It is not clear why this curious finding exists. McGonagle and Kessler suggested that chronic adversity facilitates the development of coping resources associated with resiliency to subsequent stress. A second possibility is that enmeshment in an ongoing stressful situation marshals more rapid mobilization of coping resources for subsequent stress. Perhaps acute stress might lead to resolution of chronic stress, as when a poor marriage (chronic stress) ends in divorce (acute stress).

Meanwhile, other studies suggest that the "timing" of a stressor(s) may be an important dimension of how people react to or cope with stress. Most studies focus on stressors that lead to major life events; there is a growing interest to examine how stressors occurring during an extended follow-up interval or during the treatment/posttreatment interval predict long-term outcomes (Belsher & Costell, 1988; Cronkite, Moos, Twohey, Cohen, & Swindle, 1998; Lloyd, Zisook, Click, & Jaffe, 1981; Monroe, Roberts, Kupfer, & Frank, 1996; Murphy, 1983). In one study, Monroe and associates (1996) found that severe stressors at intake predicted a lower likelihood of recurrent depression over a three-year interval, whereas severe events that occurred during the follow-up period predicted a higher likelihood of a recurrent course of depression. Yet, in order to fully understand the dynamic of stress and coping, future studies need to examine how *chronicity* (acute versus chronic) and *intensity* (degree of severity) of stress interact with the *timing* of stress in the context(s) of people's lives.

The Environment

The Physical Environment

Sometimes environmental phenomena are distressing or demand adjustment. For example, noise, pollution, and other environmental stressors can cause adjustment problems. Prisons and schools are prime examples of how the effects of a physical environment can create stress. Art's rooming situation certainly was creating stress in his life. Likewise, inmates in overcrowded prisons have been shown to have higher blood pressure than inmates in less crowded prisons (Paulus, McCain, & Cox, 1978) as well as more complaints of illness (Wener & Keys, 1988).

Similarly, noise can be distressing. Cohen and colleagues (Cohen, Evans, Stokols, & Krantz, 1986) examined the health and performance of schoolchildren who lived in the flight paths of the Los Angeles airport. The researchers found that these children had higher blood pressure, had lower mathematics scores, and were less persistent at problem solving than children from similar backgrounds who did not live near a major airport. Other research (Bronzaft, 1981) has confirmed that students on the noisy side of school buildings perform less well than children on the quiet side of the same school building, but performance improves when the children are moved to the quiet side of the building.

On the other hand, there are factors that one might intuitively predict would play a role in emotional well-being, but research indicates otherwise. For example, Adams (1992) examined urban versus suburban neighborhoods and their impact on psychological health. Classic urban theory would suggest that living in highly urbanized areas of a city results in social isolation, disorganization, and psychological problems. However, Adams's research found that people living in the suburbs were no more likely to express satisfaction with their neighborhood or with the quality of their lives than those living in cities.

The Psychosocial Environment
No other factor related to sources of distress has received more attention in the field of community psychology than the psychosocial environment. Specifically, community psychologists are concerned about the fit of the person to the psychosocial environment. If the fit is not good, then the consequence may be distress. Likewise, community psychologists acknowledge that the person and environment interact such that both the person and the environment make demands on each other (Tracey, Sherry, & Keitel, 1986).

One psychological element of a person's social settings is social integration. **Social integration** is defined as people's involvement with community institutions as well as their participation in the community's informal social life (Gottlieb, 1987). (See Chapter 10 for related concepts and their impact on health status.) Holahan and colleagues (Holahan, Betak, Spearly, & Chance, 1983) examined the relationship of social integration and mental health in a biracial community. They were attempting to move the literature away from relying on intrapsychic dynamics, as seen in psychoanalytic and other traditional theories of mental disorder. The research resulted in complex but interesting findings. African Americans reported significantly more psychological symptoms than Whites. Perhaps prejudice against African Americans in mainstream society created this difference. However, some African Americans were less socially integrated into their communities than were Whites, thus providing another explanation for the first finding. In fact, African Americans low in social integration showed more symptoms than either Whites or other African Americans with high levels of social integration. In other words, social integration seems to contribute to one's sense of well-being. Quite possibly, the converse is true, too; one's lack of well-being keeps a person from being better integrated socially.

Culture or subculture is also another factor relevant to adjustment. Poverty surely is a factor that results in distress (e.g., depression). However, cultural values that differ from mainstream or traditional U.S. values can also create distress. For example, Aldwin and Greenberger (1987) found that Korean youths overall were more depressed than Caucasians. However, different models accounted for or predicted depression in the two groups. For Koreans, perceived parental traditionalism was a strong predictor of depression, whereas for Caucasians, academic stress was a significant predictor of depression. These findings argue for greater attention to the importance of cultural values in studying adaptation to stress.

PRIMARY PREVENTION: COPING STRATEGIES

Rather than utilize highly individualized methods such as client-centered therapy, psycho-analysis, or behavioral techniques (see Case in Point 5.1), community psychologists take several different approaches to promoting mental health (i.e., primary prevention) and managing stress (i.e., secondary prevention). This section will first examine some of the latest debates and issues pertaining to primary prevention, followed by a review of a few of these approaches, including social support, information and education, as well as sports, recreation, and exercise.

Primary Prevention as Science or Pseudoscience

Recently, an entire issue (April 1997) of the *American Journal of Community Psychology* was dedicated to the examination of the concept of and empirical evidence pertaining to primary prevention. In particular, a group of community psychologists and like-minded researchers commented on a meta-analytic study about the effect of primary prevention programs on children and adolescents (Durlak & Wells, 1997). Collectively, these articles addressed two broad issues and their correlates: (1) What is primary prevention? and (2) Who is the target audience? Being able to define or articulate the component(s) of primary prevention implies that strategy(ies) of such prevention can be postulated and operationalized. Identification of the target population allows for the specification of the outcome(s) of interest.

There have been a lot of debates concerning the definition of primary prevention in the last 30 years. In his historical review of the field, Cowen (1997) noted that "the Joint Commission on Mental Illness and Health of 1961 [described primary prevention] as an article of faith rather than an 'applicable scientific truth'" (p. 153). Although progress (i.e., empirical evidence) has been made and observed in the past 30 years, there is still no consensus on what constitutes primary prevention. To say a primary prevention program is efficacious or effective implies that something (i.e., negative behavior) has been averted. In other words, a certain at-risk or high-risk group has been identified and benefited from the primary prevention program. According to Durlak and Wells (1997), due to the low base rates of many disorders, "there is difficulty in demonstrating that a negative outcome has *not* occurred" (p. 116). Meanwhile, the Institute of Medicine (IOM, 1994) suggested renaming primary prevention for high-risk groups as "selective intervention." In addition, the IOM recommended the exclusion of mental health promotion as a primary strategy.

It appears that the IOM is using a conservative definition of primary prevention. Koretz and Moscicki (1997, p. 191) noted the following:

> The relationship between prevention and promotion . . . stems from a confusion between promotion as a strategy (enhancement of competencies) and promotion as a goal (enhancement of mental health). Intervention studies often use promotive strategies that enhance competencies while assessing the prevention of mental disorders and related negative outcome as a goal. The distinction between prevention and promotion is therefore more apparent than real at the level of strategy for inducing change. As a goal, promotion is often skirted because of the absence of psychometrically sound, independent, consensually agreed upon measures of mental health.

Mindful of these issues, Durlak and Wells (1997) utilized a more inclusive definition: "Primary prevention was defined as an intervention designed specifically to reduce the future incidence of adjustment problems in currently normal populations, including efforts directed at the promotion of mental health" (p. 120). Moreover, a purpose of the meta-analysis was to validate the conceptual utility of a typology: the type of prevention (i.e., person- vs. environment-centered intervention) and the types of target populations (i.e, universal, high-risk, and transitional). For person-centered prevention, there were three broad categories: (1) affective education, (2) interpersonal problem solving, and (3) other person-centered programs (e.g., behavioral approach). Environment-centered intervention included two broad categories: (1) school-based and (2) parent training. An example of a universal population is all children in first grade.

Findings of the meta-analysis revealed that most categories of programs not only reduce problem behaviors but also increase competencies. "In practical terms, the average participant in a primary prevention program surpasses the performance of between 59% to 82% of those in the control group, and outcomes reflect an 8% to 46% difference in success rates favoring prevention groups" (Durlak & Wells, 1997, p. 115). Primary prevention programs not only exert positive effects on specific outcomes (i.e., reducing problem behavior) but they also enhance or strengthen protective factors (e.g., coping skills) to promote people's general well-being (i.e., mental health). These findings suggest that "the Institute of Medicine's (1994) decision to exclude health promotion as a preventive intervention is premature" (Durlak & Wells, 1997, p. 141).

Social Support

Anyone who has experienced divorce of their parents, as Art is experiencing, knows the stress and sadness that divorce creates. Had a friend referred Art to a support group of others who had experienced parental divorce, Art might have benefited. The friend would be providing social support by caring enough to make a referral for help with coping. The support group recommended by the friend would provide added support by providing Art with peers who have common emotional ground and therefore useful coping techniques to deal with their distress. Art might have learned some of these techniques from them.

In groups such as Alcoholics Anonymous and Overeaters Anonymous, individuals with common issues come together to assist and support one another. The groups are usually comprised of individuals who are searching for useful coping strategies, such as better ways to provide parenting or to maintain sobriety, or who have special problems such as overeating, gambling, or reentering the community after a stay in a psychiatric institution. These **self-help groups** are sometimes led by a professional but more often they are simply comprised of laypeople whose experiences and common situations act as motivators and guides for others in the group. Hence, another name for these groups is **mutual help groups** (Levine, 1988).

Individuals need not belong to formal or organized groups to come to the assistance of each other. Friends, families, and coworkers often come to one another's aid in times of crisis or stress. Whether the support comes from an established mutual help group or from a caring friend, social support has become an important construct in the field of community psychology. **Social support** can be defined as an exchange of resources between two individuals perceived by the provider or the recipient to be intended to enhance the well-being of the recipient (Shumaker & Brownell, 1984).

The concept of social support was first identified by physician John Cassel (1974) and later elaborated upon by Gerald Caplan (1974). Interest in the definition, measurement, and effects of social support quickly grew. Within the two years that *Psychological Abstracts* first contained the term *social support* in its index, over 450 studies appeared (Brownell & Shumaker, 1984). A comprehensive discussion of this vast literature cannot be attempted here, but its main points will be highlighted.

Most studies of social support examine support between adults, but a few have also studied support among children (Barrera, 1986). Interest in the effects of social support has also expanded worldwide (Gidron, Chesler, & Chesney, 1991), but no one is exactly sure how social support functions. In fact, there is no one accepted definition in the literature but the one just given generally captures the typically accepted elements of social support.

A matter related to the confusion over the definition is that social support has been criticized as too broad a concept (Barrera, 1986; Brownell & Shumaker, 1984). More concise and definitive terminology might be useful. Three other terms have been offered as composing the more generic concept of social support. Social embeddedness seems to be one aspect of the broader concept of social support. **Social embeddedness** is the number or quantity of connections an individual has to significant others who might offer assistance. In that regard, it is the opposite of social isolation. A socially embedded individual has many friends, family members, and associates upon whom he or she can draw when seeking social support. **Enacted support,** or the availability of actual support, refers to the very real actions others perform when they render assistance. In other words, an individual may have a large network of friends or be socially embedded, but the friends might not actually give support. The number of available supportive friends, then, is less than the number who actually support the needy individual. Finally, **perceived social support,** the most frequently examined construct in the literature, refers to the cognitive appraisal of being reliably connected to others. In other words, it is the perception of *how available* and *how adequate* social support is. For example, an individual might have many friends who offer support, but the support is useless or not consistently given. Both Barrera (1986) and Brownell and Shumaker (1984) suggested the field would be better served if researchers made these three distinctions before they commence their work.

Issues Related to Social Support

Perhaps the most important issue related to social support is its effect. The bulk of the research (cf. Brownell & Shumaker, 1984) shows that social support has beneficial effects. Early research (Brownell & Shumaker, 1984) has demonstrated beneficial effects of support groups for cancer patients, first-time parents, the bereaved, and rape victims. More recent research has shown positive effects for social support among early adolescents (Cauce, 1986), those suffering from chronic stress (Cummins, 1988), those who attempt suicide (Veiel, Brill, Hafner, & Welz, 1988), the elderly (Chapman & Pancoast, 1985; Heller & Mansbach, 1984), parents of children with cancer (Chesler & Barbarin, 1984), adolescent mothers (Unger & Wandersman, 1985b), low-income mothers (Green & Rodgers, 2001), rural welfare recipients (Taylor, 2001), scoliosis patients (Hinrichsen, Revenson, & Shinn,

1985), divorcing mothers (Tetzloff & Barrera, 1987), children with disabilities (Wallander & Varni, 1989), mothers charged with child abuse (Richey, Lovell, & Reid, 1991), caregivers to the elderly (Greene & Monahan, 1989), gamblers (Turner & Saunders, 1990), and the homeless (Rivlin & Imbimbo, 1989), among other groups. However, social support is *not always beneficial* (Barrera, 1986; Shinn, Lehmann, & Wong, 1984). The reasons why will be discussed shortly, under the topic of disadvantages of social support.

Related to the issue of whether social support is effective is the issue of *how* it is effective. The literature is replete with explanations, but three seem to stand out: the direct, indirect, and interactive effects of social support (Brownell & Shumaker, 1984). The **direct effects** of social support mean that interpersonal contact and assistance directly facilitate healthier behaviors. For instance, when friends encourage an ill individual to stick to his or her medical regime and eat a healthy diet, they are directly supporting and aiding the unhealthy individual.

The **indirect effects** of social support mean that social support influences an individual's well-being by decreasing the perceived severity of stressful events. For example, when parents convince a child that a difficult math class is a challenge rather than a stressful event, the parents are providing indirect support to that child. Another way to provide indirect support is to redefine the scale of a larger problem into a smaller, more controllable one or to help resolve a small problem before it becomes a bigger one (Brownell & Shumaker, 1984).

The largest portion of the research on social support, though, focuses on its **interactive effects** or its **buffering effects.** In this case, social support is interpreted to mitigate or ameliorate the adverse effects of stressful events by influencing the recognition, quality, and quantity of coping resources. An example of this would be that a friend points out that the distressed individual is coping as well as or better than others in the situation or that the distressed individual has many caring friends. Another possible indirect effect has been identified also, a **boostering effect** (Okun, Sandler, & Bauman, 1988) in which social support actually enhances the beneficial effects of positive life events. In this case, the social supporter points out the life-enhancing effects of some positive experience.

Research on exactly how social support works has not yet established a firm understanding of its functions in our literature. For example, Cohen and colleagues (1986) found a direct effect but no buffering effect for social support on psychological symptoms in an inner-city elderly population. On the other hand, Bowers and Gesten (1986) did find buffering effects in an experiment using college students who waited alone, with a friend, or with a stranger for an interview in which the students thought they would have to answer highly personal questions while being videotaped. Of course, the group of students waiting with friends reported the lowest anxiety of the three groups. Research continues to tease out the main mechanism by which social support functions.

One explanation for these differing research results could be the different methodologies and statistical techniques utilized. The first study primarily used correlational techniques (with surveys and network analysis, for example), whereas the second utilized an experimental paradigm with active manipulations. Depner, Wethington, and Ingersoll-Dayton (1984) and Tebes and Kraemer (1991) more fully address these and other complex methodological and research issues in studies of social support.

Related to the issue of how social support functions is the **transactional nature of social support** (Shinn et al., 1984). This transactional feature of social support has also been called the *exchange process* (Shumaker & Brownell, 1984). By *transactional* is meant that support is a two-way phenomenon. Social support affects how individuals function, and how individuals function influences the amount and kind of social support they receive. In times of distress, for example, individuals often seek social support to assist in their coping. Divorcing women sometimes turn to their friends for help in managing the emotional burden of divorce. On the other hand, in times of distress, social support can be disrupted by the individual's behavior. The woman who turns to her friends may find that her married friends shun her for fear she will disrupt their own marriages. Hence, social support is both a cause and an effect.

Another issue in the social support literature is its measurement—not a surprising circumstance given the disagreement over the construct's definition. A variety of measures have been developed, but the psychometric properties and soundness of these measures are still being examined (Fiore, Coppel, Becker, & Cox, 1986; Shinn et al., 1984). Three such measures are the Inventory of Socially Supportive Behaviors (Barrera, Sandler, & Ramsay, 1981), the Social Support Behaviors Scale (Vaux, Riedel, & Stewart, 1987), and the Social Support Questionnaire (Sarason, 1983). Discussion of each of these scales is beyond the scope of this chapter, however.

Who the supporter is comprises another important issue in social support. For example, Dunkel-Schetter (1984) found that cancer patients reported that advice from health care professionals was helpful but that the same type of advice from friends and families was not beneficial. Research has also demonstrated that not all helpers or social supporters are equally adept. Toro (1986) coded and analyzed audiotapes of natural and professional helpers. He found that although there were many similarities between professionals and layhelpers, the type of advice offered, the amount of information given, and other similar dimensions varied as a function of the type of interpersonal interaction and who the helper was. For instance, of the professional helpers, lawyers did the most talking and showed the greatest proportion of information giving and closed questions—circumstances not beneficial in all crises.

Classic research on the **bystander effect** has curiously but clearly demonstrated that the larger the number of available helpers, the less likely it is that any of them will step forward to offer help (Latane & Darley, 1970). Psychologists assume that one of the main reasons for this phenomenon is **responsibility diffusion** (Baron & Byrne, 1994), in which one feels less responsible for another's fate when others present could also accept responsibility. When people are alone, they feel 100 percent responsible for another in need of help.

You might be curious to know what the profile of the typical natural helper is. Gottlieb and Peters (1991) completed a large-scale survey of Canadian mutual help group participants and found that the typical participant is a middle-class woman between the ages of 25 and 44. This does not mean that men or lower-income individuals do not participate; they simply did not dominate the sample of helpers. The ratio of men to women who reported participating in social support programs, for example, was four to six.

You should be cautioned that Canadian data probably do not hold for other cultures. For example, Gidron and colleagues (1991) examined support groups in Israel and found that Israeli groups differed from those in North America. For instance, in Israel, groups are often facilitated by government professionals, which means that the groups do not always function as autonomously in Israel as they do in the United States.

Of course, who the recipient is also matters. When an individual in need of help is perceived as responsible for his or her problem, then that person is less likely to receive aid than one whose situation is attributed to uncontrollable or external causes (Schmidt & Weiner, 1988). In other words, if people blame the victim for his or her dilemma, they are far less likely to offer support. People are also more likely to aid others whom they perceive as similar to themselves (Dovidio, 1984) or whom they like (Schoenrade, Batson, Brandt, & Toud, 1986).

Much of the discussion on who the helper and recipient are reveals that the social support literature has focused on the individual level of analysis. Although that offers a beginning, experts in the field of community psychology are calling for psychologists to move beyond the individual to extra-individual levels. Psychologists need to expand notions of social support to examine the role of groups and networks and to explore the functional and structural characteristics of these social networks (Felton & Shinn, 1992).

Advantages and Disadvantages of Support Groups and Social Support

Shumaker and Brownell (1984) provided an excellent review of the beneficial effects of social support from which this section is based. Of course, the main advantage of social support as a coping strategy is that it often has beneficial effects—that is, it enhances the well-being of the individual who receives the support. This general function can be reduced to several more specific functions.

Social support seems to gratify basic affiliative needs. In other words, through social support, individuals make contact with others and find companionship. When people perceive that others care for them, these people feel a sense of belonging.

Social support also seems to enhance self-identity and therefore self-esteem, which is part of one's identity. For instance, Thoits (1983) argued that it is through interactions with others that one's personality develops. Stated another way, through social exchanges, people acquire an awareness of who they are and where they fit in the social hierarchy. Here's a simple example. Suppose a professor returns an essay examination to you and at the top is a grade of 45. "Yikes," you think. "That's not a very good grade." You turn to a friend and see that she has a 35, while another classmate received a 28 and yet another a 17. "A-hah!" you say, "Now my 45 doesn't look so bad; I must be one of the smarter people in this class." By comparing yourself to appropriate others, you come to know yourself better.

Social support, as Shumaker and Brownell (1984) argued, also serves a stress-reducing function, so in that respect, support is beneficial. How does social support do this? First, social support at the prestress stage probably broadens an individual's cognitive appraisal of the stressful event. Hence, a clearer understanding of the stress is obtained. Second, social support from others can often assist individuals in finding a number of techniques for responding to the stress. For example, a trusted friend of Art's might have known to which professional agencies he could turn for counseling or might model appropriate emotions for Art because the friend had also been through a recent parental divorce. Social support might come in the form of direct aid, too. For instance, Art might have friends who take him out to dinner to get his mind off his problems. As mentioned earlier, a final advantage of social support is that it seems to work not just for individuals who have experienced losses but for all types of individuals experiencing life changes. Its possible applications seem endless.

Although the advantages of social support and self-help groups seem fairly obvious, the disadvantages are less so. First, as already mentioned, not everyone wants to be an involved citizen or participant. Some individuals are not natural caregivers nor feel comfortable with or motivated to help others. And some individuals who are continuous caregivers experience burnout (Brownell & Shumaker, 1984).

Second, research (Brownell & Shumaker, 1984) has uncovered that social support in some instances can be harmful. For example, Shinn and associates (1984) reported that aid sometimes threatens the recipient's self-esteem, especially if aid implies superiority-inferiority positions of the giver and recipient, respectively. Likewise, if the giver-recipient relationship requires the recipient to admit impairment, social support can be detrimental. Similarly, recipients often want to reciprocate the aid. In fact, in U.S. society there exists a **norm of reciprocity** (Baron & Byrne, 1994) in which people expect to reciprocate with those who do something for them. Often, there is no opportunity to repay a lay caregiver, thus embarrassing or humiliating the recipient. In this case, the professional caregiver, such as a client-centered therapist, where no expectation for reciprocity exists, is perhaps advantageous (Shinn et al., 1984). These and other situations mean that social support does not always benefit and can, in fact, harm the receiver. The Test of Negative Social Exchange by Ruehlman and Karoly (1991) is a scale designed to test these negative social exchanges.

A related notion is that the timing of social support is also important. Support given at the wrong time can perhaps be detrimental. For instance, Shinn and colleagues (1984) reviewed research on bereavement and reported that in early stages of grieving, empathy and emotional support are valuable. In the later stages, support that aids reintegration into normal social life is more valuable.

These and other factors related to social support indicate that support is not always beneficial, especially when it is not timely nor well introduced. As with any method of coping, social support is not without its drawbacks. Shinn and colleagues (1984) cautioned that in each support situation, the person-environment fit must be carefully examined. That is, one must consider the caregiver's intent and the recipient's perception of the assistance as well as the timing, amount, source, and function of the social support. See Case in Point 5.2 for further discussion of this issue.

Information and Education about Mental Health

Besides social support, there are other avenues for promoting emotional and physical well-being. An earlier chapter of this book discussed education and information dissemination as a means of social change. Education can also pave the way toward better mental health. When education assists people in acquiring knowledge, skills, and attitudes that directly contribute to their mental health and to their effect on the mental health of others, it is known as **mental health education.** Moreover, Cowen (1980) argued that the goal of prevention (including mental health education) should emphasize teaching people *how* to think instead of *what* to think, thus enabling them to make reasonable choices and decisions as well as to have a sense of responsibility. In other words, the "ability to think straight paves the way for emotional relief, prevents dysfunction, and promotes health" (Shure & Spivack, 1988, p. 69).

Morrison (1980) asserted that mental health education is particularly valuable in "demythologizing" the public's perception of mental illness. Education can change public

---

CASE IN POINT 5.2
CAREGIVING: THE COST OF HEALING

There is a body of literature indicating that caregivers (of people living with severe mental illness and AIDS as well as other chronic illnesses) have a higher risk of experiencing psychological difficulties or problems compared to the general population (Oldridge & Hughes, 1992; Turner & Catania, 1997). These difficulties or problems might be due, in part or whole, to the caregivers' constant exposure to stressful situations or stimuli. Although this side effect or "dark side" of social support has been known to community psychologists for a long time, its underlying mechanism has yet to be fully elucidated.

In one study, St. Onge and Lavoie (1997) examined the effect of burden and social support on a cohort of women caregivers in Montreal, Canada, who had adult children with mental illness. Specifically, *burden* was defined as "subjective perceptions of the experience of taking responsibility for the care . . . burden related to residual psychiatric disabilities, burden related to the daily and social life of the respondents, the perception of the support for daily living given to the relative, and finally, concern for the relative's well-being" (p. 76). *Social support* was defined as the degree of congruence per the child's condition between the view of the woman and her spouse or important confidant. The outcome of interest was perceived distress

among the women. Also examined was the effect of the women's general health on perceived distress.

Results indicated that both burden and social support were significantly related to self-reported distress among these women. More importantly, negative interactions between these women and their spouses or most important confidants were more predictive of self-reported distress than the quality of the relationship. Women who had poor health tended to have higher self-reported distress.

This pattern of findings suggests that caregiving can exert its toll on caretakers. The positive side is that those who have supportive spouses tend to fair better psychologically than those with less supportive spouses. However, this general perceived social support does not override the negative effect of specific negative social interactions with family member(s). In other words, a woman might perceive her spouse as supportive but might not agree in how to deal with a specific condition of the child's mental illness—this disagreement is more detrimental to the woman's mental health. This inference has significant implications for prevention targeting the caregiver. That is, having social support is not enough; in addition, how the relationship is manifested or handled by the caregiver and her support system must be an integral part to prevention.

---

opinion away from the concept of mental illness as a disease to one of mental illness as having a psychosocial nature. Morrison reasoned that if community members view a person with mental disorders as less dangerous and more in need of skills to cope with problems in living, then the public is more likely to accept this person as a neighbor. The concept of educating the public about mental disorder and mental health is important to the present discussion as well as to the next chapter on deinstitutionalization of people with serious mental disorders.

Ketterer (1981) suggested that mental health education is of two types: (1) improving the coping skills and competencies of normal and at-risk populations and (2) public information strategies that inform the public about mental health problems and preventive or treatment services. To accomplish these goals, mental health educators generally use three main techniques: the mass media, lectures and/or demonstrations, and small-group discussions.

Muñoz, Glish, Soo-Hoo, and Robertson (1982) provided an example of the first type of mental health education. They attempted to improve the knowledge of and competency of a community population by broadcasting a series of televised segments about depression, self-control, and social learning on a local televised news program. Citizens in the San Francisco area were selected at random from the telephone directory. They participated in pre- and postprogram interviews. The interviews contained behavioral questions as well as a measure of depression. The postprogram interview also contained questions about which segments the viewers had seen. Between the two interviews, the educators showed nine four-minute segments on a local news program three times daily. Each segment modeled a mentally healthy approach to daily life, such as telling oneself to stop thinking upsetting thoughts.

The results showed that two specific behaviors increased significantly as a consequence of the televised segments: stopping thinking about upsetting events and taking time to relax. A more general result was that individuals who had high initial levels of depression and who had viewed the segments showed a significant reduction in depressed mood in comparison to individuals who were depressed and who did not view the televised segments.

An example of the second type of mental health education again involves using the media but this time to inform the public about general mental health resources in the community. Sundel and Schanie (1978) investigated 21 television and radio announcements for use in the Louisville, Kentucky, area over a 60-week period. In the messages, the phone number of the local crisis intervention and information center was also provided. The results demonstrated that both well-educated and uneducated audiences benefited from these messages, with uneducated audiences benefiting the most. Calls to the crisis and information center also increased as a result of the broadcast announcements. There was also a significant increase in knowledge about local community mental health resources, as indicated by pre- and postbroadcast interviews conducted every few weeks during the broadcasts with community members selected by random sampling.

A third example of use of the media in mental health education is Taylor, Lam, Roppel, and Barter's (1984) multimedia campaign entitled "Friends Can Be Good Medicine." This mental health campaign was conducted statewide in California. The program goals were to (1) encourage the development of supportive ties to others and (2) educate people about the relationship between social support and lower rates of psychopathology and health. Those who participated in the program reported greater gains in knowledge, attitudes, and intentions to socialize with others than those in the control group. These differences were maintained at one-year follow-up. Once again, the use of the mass media is an effective means for heightening community awareness and perhaps changing behaviors.

A follow-up study after one-year indicated that the gains in knowledge, attitudes, and intentions to seek social support were maintained (Hersey, Klibanoff, Lam, & Taylor, 1984). The authors noted that the campaign was most effective when it used *multiple channels of communication*. This is a most important point about education and information dissemination. Multiple approaches ordinarily result in stronger gains than narrowly focused efforts. For example, when a campaign uses both print and broadcast media, it is more likely to be successful than a print-only campaign.

Sports, Recreation, and Excercise

In his presidential address to the Division of Community Psychology of the American Psychological Association, Steve Danish (1983) encouraged community psychologists to involve themselves in the study of sports as related to the development of personal competence. He contended that sports have become cultural phenomena that permeate all of society; sports are a social institution comparable to other social institutions such as religion, law, government, neighborhoods, medicine, and human services systems. Danish also concluded that sports, when not ultra-competitive, help build character and heighten concern for others, as well as develop a sense of community, especially team sports.

There is also evidence that exercise and physical fitness help buffer the effects of stress (Brown, 1991). Brown measured the physical fitness of college undergraduates by observing them on a piece of exercise equipment. He also obtained self-reports of illnesses as well as measures of students' health from university health records. In addition, Brown obtained measures of the students' self-reported stressful life events. For students who were physically fit, high stress did not produce deterioration in their health, whereas high stress did lead to more illnesses and thus unfit students had more visits to the infirmary. In other studies, avid exercisers report improved quality of life, increased sense of accomplishment and well-being, and more feelings of relaxation (Sime, 1984).

Providing sufficient space for fitness and exercise is also related to a community's crime rate. In neighborhoods that provide adequate parks and recreational facilities, there is a lower crime rate than in neighborhoods that do not contain sufficient facilities for its residents, especially its youthful residents. Unfortunately, it is likely to be the affluent neighborhoods that house more recreational facilities per capita. In Chicago, for example, near the more affluent lakefront neighborhoods, there are 41 acres of park land per 1,000 residents. On the less advantaged west side of Chicago, there is only 0.5 acre per 1,000 residents (Grace, I-Chin Tu, Rochman, & Woodbury, 1994).

There are several problems with sports and physical fitness as answers to promotion of better mental and physical health, however. Danish (1983) reported that one problem is that when athletic participation takes on a physical fitness rationale, it feels like an obligation and loses some of its intrinsically motivating properties. This may be why adherence to physical fitness programs is so low despite the fact that physical fitness is so beneficial. As many as half of the people who start a physical fitness or exercise program drop out within the first few months; a year later, the number drops dramatically again (Bloom, 1988).

To improve adherence to sport or physical fitness programs, some authorities recommend that exercise occur in group settings such as at school, at work, or with the whole family (Bloom, 1988). Group or communal participation seems to sustain adherence, thus reinforcing the idea that ecology is important. In fact, worksite physical fitness programs have increased in popularity (Falkenberg, 1987). These worksite programs reduce absenteeism, enhance productivity, and contribute to commitment toward the work organization (Shephard, Cox, & Corey, 1981). On the other hand, schools, where physical fitness can be introduced at early ages, *do not* seem to actively promote physical fitness as a means for developing a sense of mastery or for promoting better physical and mental health. Only about a third of the young people between the ages of 10 and 17 participate in daily physical education programs in schools (Iverson, Fielding, Crow, & Christenson, 1985). Nonetheless, the benefit of physical activities for mental health deserves closer examination. Physical activity benefits children. For example, in their meta-analytic review, Allison, Faith, and Franklin (1995) found that children with a diagnosis of disruptive behavior or related problems who engaged in some form of a physical activity regiment were significantly less likely to display disruptive behaviors than those who did not.

SUMMARY

The traditional models of mental health and mental disorder are derived from clinical psychology; therefore, they emphasize individualized forms of treatment such as psychotherapy. Freud's psychoanalytic theory, based on a medical model, is one of the older theories. The behavioral model also offers individualized treatment. In behaviorism, maladjustment is caused by faulty learning. Behavioral treatments involve the modification of learned responses or relearning of more appropriate responses. The humanistic model is another approach to individualized treatment based on the premise that people can be assisted to better understand their own unique feelings. Individuals might not be "sick" per se but rather are behaving in accord with labels that others have applied to them. One other theme of humanistic theory is that all individuals have worth and that worthiness should be promoted and enhanced perhaps through psychotherapy.

Today, people recognize that life events and daily hassles create stress in individuals and that many individuals need to adjust and cope with these problems. Both positive and negative changes as well as minor and major life events can trigger stress reactions. Adjusting to physical stressors in the environment or not being socially integrated into the community or social environment can also create the need to adjust.

Community psychologists have moved away from individual psychotherapy to interventions that promote mental health on a wider scale. Community psychologists also empower individuals to help themselves. Encouraging social support or developing self-help or mutual help groups is one such intervention. Another involves mental health education by which communities are educated about means for coping and about general mental health issues often via the mass media. One other suggested intervention involves noncompetitive group sports and physical fitness programs.

CHAPTER 6

THE MENTALLY DISORDERED
A Place in the Community

In individuals insanity is rare, but in groups, parties, nations and epochs it is the rule.

—Friedrich Wilhelm Nietzsche,
Beyond Good and Evil, 1955 translation

Min, age 25, was of Chinese descent and lived in the United States. Not only was she convinced that her psychiatrists did not understand her illness but she was also convinced that they did not understand her Chinese values.

Min had drifted in and out of a large state hospital because of what her doctors called her schizophrenia. Each time Min entered the hospital, she was given medication that eased her symptoms, particularly her hallucinations and the imaginary voices talking to her. When medicated, Min would develop better contact with those around her, take better care of her daily needs, and then be released from the hospital to her family's care. However, her two parents worked hard to support themselves, her brother, her sister, and Min. Her siblings were in school. Therefore, Min was alone much of the time. Because her family was not available to supervise her medications, Min often forgot to take them. Eventually, she would become "out of control," which would prompt the family to call their psychiatrist, who, after some pleading from the family for intervention, would tell them to return Min to the hospital.

Such was Min's state. She would leave the hospital only to return. She would take her medication and momentarily be liberated from her symptoms only to forget the medication later. Min is one of the country's chronically mentally ill who seem to be in desperate need of long-term, coordinated intervention but who are not necessarily receiving it.

This chapter will examine the plight of Min and others like her. It will begin with some historical highlights and move next to the issue of deinstitutionalizing the mentally ill. While examining deinstitutionalization, discussions will focus on how to measure the success of moving individuals out of institutions as well as the common alternatives to institutionalization. Interestingly, many contemporary alternatives are tantamount to reinstitutionalization.

HISTORICAL NOTES ABOUT MENTAL DISORDERS

Although the ancient world has always been portrayed as less than civilized, some older cultures gave more emphasis to the study of mental health than others. For example, to most Chinese (ancient and modern), physical and psychological well-being is thought to depend on a balance of two natural forces: **Yin,** the female force, and **Yang,** the male force. Furthermore, these two forces are thought to regulate the five elements—gold, wood, water, fire, and earth—that are responsible for people's daily health. Among other things, the concentration of each element is thought to vary with the type of food group. Thus, a proper diet and regular exercise are important to maintain a balance between these elements.

According to Chinese folklore, a wise king named Sun Lone Tse, whose name meant "to cultivate," in ancient times (circa 600–700 B.C.) was thought to be responsible for the first classification system of herbs used in medicine. Also, Chinese historical texts mention a doctor named Wah Torr as the father of Chinese medicine. On one occasion, he performed minor surgery on a general's arm, using **acupuncture** as anesthetic. That is, needles were used to stick into the **meridians** (pressure points) to facilitate the release of **endorphins** (natural pain relievers) in the brain. Also, Wah Torr wrote many medical texts. These concepts relating mind and body are important to the fields of clinical psychology and behavioral medicine, sister disciplines to the field of community psychology. If Min were in ancient China or even modern-day China, the treatments for her disorder might indeed be different from what they are in the United States.

As one moves through history, the ancient Greeks are also important. Hippocrates (circa 460–377 B.C.), who was known as the father of Western medicine, spoke about four natural **humors,** or fluids, that were thought to regulate people's mental health. Specifically, great fluctuations in mood were thought to be caused by an excess of blood. Fatigue was considered to be caused by an excess of phlegm or thick mucous. Anxiety was thought to be caused by an excess of yellow bile or liver fluid, and depression by an excess of black bile.

Whatever medical and psychological advancements achieved by the ancient Chinese and Greeks, the majority of their contemporaries relied on the supernatural to explain mental illness. After the collapse of the Roman Empire in Europe (circa 500 A.D.), supernatural or religious beliefs became the norms for explaining mental illness in Western society. For example, according to the church and those in power in many Western societies, the mentally ill and other disenfranchised people were thought to be sinners. Religious zealotry reached its peak in 1484, when Pope Innocent VIII officially sanctioned the persecution of witches, some of whom were actually suffering from mental illness; many others were just dissenters of the mainstream cultures. This period of almost 900 years in Western societies has come to be associated with the infamous name, the Dark Ages.

In many Western societies during the Renaissance (revival) period (circa 1400–1700), the idea of **humanism** finally developed. Thus, the mentally ill gained indirect benefits from the notion that all people had certain inalienable rights and should be treated with dignity. Furthermore, some doctors began to challenge the concept that mental illness was a defect of moral character. By the middle of the 1600s, institutions known as **asylums,** or madhouses, were established to contain the mentally ill. Perhaps the most famous was London's Bethlehem Hospital, nicknamed "Bedlam," which is now a word meaning chaos and confusion. The first asylum in the United States was established in the late 1700s. Nonetheless, **asylums** were places where the socially undesirable or misfits were kept. More often than not, residents of the asylums were chained.

The further development of humanism during the American (1776) and French (1789) Revolutions provided more incentives to the mental health care reform movement throughout the European continent and in the United States. For example, two pioneers were instrumental in the movement in this country. Benjamin Rush (1745–1813), known as the father of American psychiatry, wrote the first treatise on psychiatry and established its first academic course. The second person was Dorothea Dix (1802–1887), whose experience with mental health care was derived from her teaching of women inmates. During her day, it was not unusual for the mentally ill to be kept in prisons. Dix traveled extensively in the country to raise money to build mental hospitals.

The mental health care reform movement further benefited from the pioneer work of several doctors who devoted their lives to the development of scientific **nomenclatures,** or classifications, of mental illness. These classifications eventually led to the study of **etiology,** or the cause of mental illness. It was probably a French doctor named Phillipe Pinel (1745–1826) who first used the term **dementia** to describe a form of psychosis that was characterized by deterioration of judgment, memory loss, and personality change. A German doctor, Emil Kraepelin (1956–1926), further studied this condition and described it using the term **dementia praecox** (premature dementia). Subsequently, Swiss doctor Eugen Bleuler (1857–1930) gave the same disorder the name **schizophrenia,** which has become a household name in today's psychiatric practice. Also, Bleuler extended previous work by describing several subtypes of this illness.

Meanwhile, the **germ theory,** as advocated by Frenchman Louis Pasteur, had gained unprecedented recognition in the medical and scientific community. That is, many illnesses were thought to be caused by germ infections. Thus, the development of psychiatry as a field was destined to take on a medical, or biological, tone. In other words, under the influence of germ theory, mental illness was conceptualized as a *disease* rather than a *disorder* or psychological dysfunction.

At about the same time, the American Psychiatric Association and the American Psychological Association were formed in 1844 and 1892, respectively. Although the original mission of the American Psychological Association was not specifically concerned with issues relating to mental health and mental illness, as the subdiscipline of clinical psychology became more dominant, these issues became a priority. This emphasis no doubt does not sit well with the American Psychiatric Association, which sees itself as the sole guide in the field of mental health and mental illness since its inception. Over the years, these professional conflicts have been further complicated by a number of other factors, including the emergence of social work as a professional field.

After the work of Benjamin Rush and Dorothea Dix, the mental health care reform in this country can be roughly divided into three more eras: 1875–1940, 1940–1970 (Grob, 1991), and 1970 to the present (Shadish, Lurigio, & Lewis, 1989a). During the period from 1875 to 1940, the government assumed the major responsibility in caring for the mentally ill. Two-thirds of all the patients were living in state-run psychiatric hospitals. In many ways, this system was an extension of Dorothea Dix's thesis of moral management. More often than not, these patients received little treatment.

Meanwhile, there were a small number of privately owned psychiatric hospitals, such as the Menninger Foundation and the Institute of Living, providing services or treatments to those who could afford the costs. Although these services or treatments may be crude by today's standards, they contributed to the development of **community psychiatry,** a subdiscipline of psychiatry that argues that mental patients should be treated using the least restrictive method and in the least restrictive environment. Many of these private mental patients lived in small comfortable units, and they were encouraged to take lessons in cooking, sewing, and other self-improvement courses.

However, the initial optimism associated with moral management began diminishing in society. In almost all instances, psychiatric hospitals were no more than human warehouses. If treatments were provided, they tended to be **electroconvulsive therapy,** or electric shock to the brain, and **lobotomy,** or brain surgery. Furthermore, the cost associated with these hospitals had become a major strain on society, especially during the Great Depression and the Second World War.

Beginning in the 1960s, the **zeitgeist,** or atmosphere, of the society began to change. For example, the introduction of **psychotropic drugs** (mood-altering drugs) such as Thorazine rekindled the idea that the mentally ill could be treated with dignity. Coupled with the ideology of community psychiatry, the use of medication allowed for the discharge of many mentally ill back into the community.

In this chapter's opening vignette, medications successfully allowed Min to return to her family. When she went off medication, her problems resurfaced. A consequence was the development of **outpatient treatment,** or nonhospitalized treatment (e.g., community mental health centers), as opposed to **inpatient treatment,** or hospitalized treatment. Also, to accommodate these newly released inpatients, alternative housing such as **community residences,** or group homes, were established but not without controversy.

Meanwhile, the fields of psychiatry and psychology began to recognize that not all the mentally ill could be treated the same way, such as those who had committed a crime due to their mental illness. **Forensic psychology,** or the study of crime and mental illness, started to emerge as a specialty (also see Chapter 9). The definition of treatment expanded to include issues such as vocational training. The rights of the clients have increasingly become a central issue. That is, clients who demonstrate competence have the right to decide on their treatment. Thus, organizations such as the National Alliance for the Mentally Ill were established to address or monitor client rights.

As the fields of psychiatry and psychology continue to expand, many have quickly learned that without systematic planning, many people who have mental disorders are likely to end up using the "revolving door" of an institution. That is, individuals who receive treatment are released, readmitted, and treated again in an unending cycle, as with Min, the woman in the opening vignette. Although former First Lady Rosalyn Carter was instrumental in reforming the mental health care system, many of her efforts have been repealed. Meanwhile, as the national budget deficit continues to increase, less and less money is available for treatments and rehabilitation services. In the 1990s, many urban cities such as Los Angles and New York have witnessed a growing population of homeless mentally ill (Levine & Huebner, 1991; Susser, Moore, & Link, 1993).

DEINSTITUTIONALIZATION

Deinstitutionalization is usually defined as sending mental patients back into the community. Recall that Min was institutionalized and sent back to her community—in fact, she was repeatedly institutionalized and returned to the community. This definition, however, is too simplistic. A casual review of the field of mental disorders indicates that there is a great deal of controversy about what exactly *deinstitutionalization* is (Grob, 1991; Shadish et al., 1989a). A deeper examination of some of these definitions and related issues is in order.

John Talbott (1975), a renowned psychiatrist, argued that the term *deinstitutionalization* is a misnomer. Instead, a better term is **transinstitutionalization** to describe "the chronically mentally ill patient who has his or her locus of living and care transferred from a single lousy institution to multiple wretched ones" (p. 530). The individual in the opening vignette, Min, presents a picture of this phenomenon. Min was in and out of institutions, living with her family between institutionalizations. On a related note, Mathew Dumont (1982), another psychiatrist, argued that "deinstitutionalization is nothing more or less than a polite term for the cutting of mental health budgets" (p. 368).

The popular literature, such as the *New York Times,* defined *deinstitutionalization* as "moving mental patients from enormous, remote hospitals into small community residences" ("Willowbrook Plan Worked," 1982). Another *New York Times* editorial stated that deinstitutionalization is "dumping mental patients out of state hospitals onto local communities, with promises of community treatment that never came true." Also, the *New York Times* claimed that *deinstitutionalization* is synonymous with *homelessness* ("Redeinstitutionalization," 1986, p. A24).

Indeed, these definitions illustrate the many different aspects of deinstitutionalization. Reconciling these differences, some mental health care experts (Bachrach, 1989; Rein & Schon, 1977; Shadish et al., 1989a) proposed that the term *deinstitutionalization* should be understood as a semantic mechanism to frame the complex, often conflicting, and seemingly unrelated sets of issues associated with ongoing mental health care reform. In other words, *deinstitutionalization,* like any term, has its concrete (explicit) and implied (implicit) meaning. More often than not, the concrete aspects of deinstitutionalization, such as budget constraints, are the impetus for the driving forces behind mental health care reform. Policy is likely to be the product of practical concern or ideology (Grob, 1991; Kiesler, 1992; Warner, 1989). However, a growing number of mental health care professionals are arguing that society must look beyond the immediate practical concern, to develop plans that can anticipate *long-term* consequences. For example, one concern is the growing number of the homeless mentally ill who also have the human immunodeficiency virus (HIV) or have acquired immunodeficiency syndrome (AIDS). According to a survey conducted in a New York City shelter that housed homeless men, Susser and colleagues (1993) found that 12 out of 62, or 19.4 percent, of the homeless mentally ill men tested positive for HIV. These men need all three issues (mental disorder, homelessness, and AIDS) addressed over the long run.

How and what can a society do to anticipate some of these long-term mental health care consequences? To that end, Bachrach (1989) provided a more heuristic or meaningful definition of *deinstitutionalization* as

> the shunning or avoidance of traditional institutional settings, particularly state mental hospitals, for chronic mentally ill individuals, and the concurrent development of community-based alternatives for the care of this population. *This definition assumes three primary processes:* depopulation—*the shrinking of state hospital censuses through release, transfer, or death;* diversion—*the deflection of potential institutional admissions to community-based service settings;* and decentralization—*the broadening of responsibility for patient care from a single physically discrete service entity to multiple and diverse entities, with an attendant fragmentation of authority.* (p. 165)

According to Bachrach (1989), this definition of *deinstitutionalization* underscores three related elements: facts, process, and philosophy. That is, sound mental health care policy must be based on credible research or evidence (the facts). In order to plan for long-term goals, one must know the characteristics of the mentally ill and the resources or systems where they receive their services (process). Also, sound policy is often the result of a thorough study of historical and philosophical precedents. That is, historical events and philosophical ideology often determine the direction of mental health care movement (philosophy).

The Many Aspects of Deinstitutionalization

What were some of the issues U.S. society (especially mental health care professionals and policy makers) did and did not anticipate about the "watershed effect" of deinstitutionalization beginning in the late 1960s? Although it is beyond the scope of this chapter to give a full account, these complex issues can be understood from several related perspectives: philosophical, biomedical, economic, sociological, and psychological.

If Sir Thomas More were alive in the 1960s, he probably would have felt the optimism in the United States that Americans were on their way to Utopia. Indeed, President John F. Kennedy was asking middle-class Americans to give to the less fortunate. Programs such as Project Head Start (e.g., including free meals for schoolchildren from low-income families) and the Peace Corps (e.g., teaching people in Third World countries about family planning, including the practice of prenatal care as well as abortion as an option of family planning) were established. The notion or philosophy of humanism appeared to reach its peak. The field of mental health benefited from these effects. Meanwhile, the advancement in medical technology also allowed people with mental disorders who were once unmanageable now to be "controllable" by using psychotropic drugs such as Elavil and Thorazine. Thus, professionals had one more reason to treat the mentally ill using the least restrictive method.

This optimism was fused by both professional (Thomas Szasz's *The Myth of Mental Illness*) and popular writing (Ken Kesey's *One Flew Over the Cuckoo's Nest*). People in the legal profession also took up the cause—for example, the American Civil Liberty Union initiated the "Mental Health Law Project" and the Church of Scientology initiated the "Citizens Commission on Human Rights." A common theme in these legal efforts was an opposition to involuntary hospitalization (Torrey, 1997).

However, some mental health care experts (Kiernan, Toro, Rappaport, & Seidman, 1989; Warner, 1989) have argued that however admirable and persuasive the notion or philosophy of humanism is, a more heuristic explanation to account for the occurrence of deinstitutionalization is economics. Investigating deinstitutionalization in different Western countries in the past 30 years, Warner (1989) found that

> the process was stimulated by the opportunity for cost savings created by the introduction of disability pensions and, in some countries, by postwar demand for labor. Where labor was in short supply, genuinely rehabilitative programs were developed. Where cost saving was the principal motivation, community treatment efforts were weak. (p. 17)

Also, Kiernan and colleagues (1989) found that manufacturing employment was negatively related to both first admissions in state hospitals and case openings in community outpatient facilities. That is, when the economy was good, fewer people were admitted into state psychiatric hospitals.

Since World War II, the world economy had been relatively good until the 1970s. The argument that deinstitutionalization is associated with economic stability appears to be consistent with the number of psychiatric hospital beds per 10,000 individuals in the Western industrialized countries. That is, as long as there was a demand for a labor force, more people were deinstitutionalized.

Whether one agrees with this interpretation or not, deinstitutionalization has significant economic impact. The federal budget for care of the mentally ill has increased from 2 percent in 1963 to 62 percent by 1994, and is rising. States have little financial incentive to provide comparable assistance since significant sources of these care are in the form of Supplemental Security Income, food stamps, Medicaid, Medicare, and so on. This imbalance between federal and state resources directed to the care of the mentally ill has created havoc (Torrey, 1997). Indeed, in a critical analysis of factors associated with deinstitutionalization, Brooks, Zuniga, and Penn (1995) found that financial burden is the principal determinant in this process. These researchers argued that "faced with the increasing costs associated with replacing or upgrading an aging system . . . most changes in services have been the outcome of budget, not medical, decisions, with medical or legal rationalizations applied post hoc or in parallel" (pp. 55–56).

Use of mental health facilities is related to personal poverty. Banziger and Foos (1983) found that unemployment and welfare factors were strong predictors of utilization of mental health centers. Bruce, Takeuchi, and Leaf (1991) also demonstrated a causal link between mental disorder and poverty. They examined the patterns of new disorders that developed over a six-month period in an epidemiologic study. Their sample included African Americans, Hispanics, and Whites. The researchers found that a significant proportion of new episodes of mental disorder could be attributed to poverty. In addition, Bruce and associates found that the risk for developing disorders was equal for men and women and for African Americans and Whites—in other words, poverty does not discriminate on the basis of race or gender.

Although these findings appear to explain the reasoning behind deinstitutionalization, they do not adequately account for its falling short of its goal to enhance the quality of life of the mentally disordered. Community psychologists and mental health care experts (Cheung, 1988; Earls & Nelson, 1988; Lovell, 1990; Mowbray, 1990; Mowbray, Herman, & Hazel, 1992; Struening & Padgett, 1990) have argued that sociological factors (such as adequate housing) and psychological factors (such as stigmatization) often hinder the progress of deinstitutionalization. Case in Point 6.1 discusses interesting research on stigmatization—research in which institutionalized patients faked their disorders.

In a case study, Cheung (1988) argued that the successful reintegration of the mentally disordered into the community to a large extent is dependent on public relations. That is, community members who are not familiar with mental illness are likely to be concerned with or resistant to having a halfway house built in their neighborhood. Earls and Nelson (1988) found that housing concern was positively correlated with negative affect. That is, former patients who had to worry about basic shelter were likely to have poor mental health. These two findings indicate the difficulty of balancing the seemingly incompatible forces of "public good" and "private want."

Also, many people with mental disorders are discharged from hospitals into the community without adequate planning or support systems. For example, Mowbray (1990) argued that many of them do not have adequate living or social skills (e.g., cooking and paying bills) to survive in an unstructured environment. In order for deinstitutionalization to be effective, adequate and appropriate treatments must be in place. Struening and Padgett (1990) found that homeless adults in New York City had high rates of alcohol and other drug abuse as well as mental illness. It is not unlikely that a large portion of these people were mental patients who were discharged from hospitals without adequate planning. Thus, they became homeless and had alcohol and other drug-abuse problems (Levine & Huebner, 1991; Susser et al., 1993). Meanwhile, a majority of the mentally disordered are continuously being discharged from hospitals into nursing homes or in board-and-care homes that are ill prepared to provide the services these patients need. Another consequence is a high burnout rate among staff at these agencies (Shadish et al., 1989b).

Deinstitutionalization of people with mental disorders is also viewed as one of the major reasons (Pogrebin & Poole, 1987; Pogrebin & Regoli, 1985) for the increasing number of former mental health patients in prisons (Jemelka, Trupin, & Chiles, 1989). Some view prisons as the new dumping grounds for the mentally disordered. Because prisons are secure places, judges perhaps believe that prisons will keep disturbed offenders from dis-

■ ■ ■ ■ ■ ■

CASE IN POINT 6.1
ROSENHAN'S EXPERIMENT ABOUT STIGMATIZATION

Researcher D. L. Rosenhan was especially interested in whether mental health professionals (particularly psychiatrists) could detect genuine mental disorders or problems from fake ones. He decided to conduct an experiment. First, Rosenhan (1973) trained his graduate students and others in how to fake symptoms of psychiatric disorders. For example, he instructed the pseudopatients (fake patients) to tell hospital staff that they heard a thudding sound or a voice saying "thud." Rosenhan then sent his pseudopatients to a psychiatric emergency facility.

To Rosenhan's amazement, the students were admitted. Soon after their admission to the psychiatric ward, the pseudopatients were each given diagnoses. All of them but one were labeled *schizophrenic*. The pseudopatients were kept in the hospital from 7 to 52 days, with the average stay being 19 days.

Not long after their admission, the pseudopatients began to act "normal." Curiously, many of the other patients realized that the pseudopatients were normal. The staff did not recognize this normal behavior when they saw it, which, according to Rosenhan, was not often, as the staff did not spend much time with the patients.

The pseudopatients began to request to be released from the psychiatric ward. However, the staff consistently told the students that they were not well enough to be released. Eventually, Rosenhan had to intervene so that some of the pseudopatients could be released. When the pseudopatients were released, many were labeled *schizophrenia in remission.*

Without minimizing the agony associated with mental disorders, Rosenhan demonstrated that many perceived disorders are due to the process of labeling. Although some mental health professionals might argue otherwise, Rosenhan demonstrated that, at times, diagnosing a patient is more of an art than a science, and that once labeled, it is difficult to overcome the label.

rupting society (Toch & Adams, 1987). Prisons, however, offer little by way of treatment for these individuals.

In an interesting study of what happens to the chronically mentally disordered, Diamond and Schnee (1990) tracked 21 men who were perceived to be most at risk for potential violence and were also high users of jails. The men were tracked for two and a half years through various service systems. The men used up to 11 different systems, including the mental health, criminal justice, health care, and social services systems. Criminal justice services were the most frequently used ones, and mental health services were usually only short-term, crisis care services, although some of the men had been hospitalized for long-term psychiatric care. Diamond and Schnee believe that their figure is an *underestimate* but calculated that the cost of care of the 21 men in all service systems totaled $694,291. That figure does not include costs to victims nor property damaged in the men's violent episodes. The researchers called for a more coordinated effort of the various systems to better assist the men and to reduce costs.

Belcher (1988) suggested that when people with mental disorders are released from hospitals or institutions, they are often unable or unwilling to follow through on their own aftercare. This situation increases the likelihood of these individuals being involved in the criminal justice system. In addition, because the legal system and the mental health systems view mental disorders differently (Freeman & Roesch, 1989), the mentally disordered are not afforded the same level of therapeutic services for their disorder when they are incarcerated. The legal system narrowly deals with mental illness only as incompetence to testify in one's own behalf or as insanity, which is a defense against guilt. Hochstedler's (1986) research demonstrates that individuals with a history of mental disorder elicit more lenient penal sanctions and that the court uses its authority in these cases to impose mental health treatment. However, such coercive treatment of the mentally ill can violate both ethical standards of the professionals and patients' rights (Geller, 1986).

Treatment for the mentally disordered while in jail is rare because jail and prison personnel are not trained in mental health issues. Corrections staff are more concerned with custodial matters (Pogrebin & Regoli, 1985). The solution may be that mental health, criminal justice, and other professionals *need to collaborate in innovative and integrative ways to prevent* the mentally ill from being incarcerated in a correctional facility and to treat their disorders when they are incarcerated (Diamond & Schnee, 1990; Pogrebin & Regoli, 1985).

Common Alternatives to Institutionalization

The ideal setting for the institutionalized individual would be one that enhances his or her well-being because of the optimal fit between the individual's competencies and the support provided in the environment. However, this may be but a pipe dream. In reality, many community placements are based as much on what is available and on economics as on the individual's competencies.

If not in institutions, where are the people who have mental disorders? Ironically, today most chronic mental patients are still cared for either in institutions such as nursing homes or in other community settings often characterized by poverty, stigma, social isolation, and poor care that depict large psychiatric hospitals (Shadish et al., 1989a). About 1.15 million mentally disordered individuals reside in nursing homes; in fact, the nursing home industry is the largest system of long-term care for the severely and persistently mentally disordered (Bootzin, Shadish, & McSweeney, 1989). Research suggests that nursing homes do not return patients to mental hospitals as often as other forms of mental health care that is provided to deinstitutionalized persons (Bootzin et al., 1989). The reason, however, is not that the patients improve. Research demonstrates that symptomatology does not change; in fact, it might become slightly worse. The reason that nursing homes do not return patients to mental hospitals might be related to economics. More mental health dollars go to nursing home care than to any other mental health program (Kiesler, 1980). It behooves nursing homes to keep their clients!

Another type of community placement is **board-and-care homes.** These are typically community-based shelter-care facilities that include group homes and family care homes. The Public Health Service (1980) estimates that 400,000 people with chronic mental disorders may reside in these settings. This particular industry, compared to nursing homes, is relatively unregulated and more decentralized. The individuals in these settings tend to be younger and need less intensive care than those in nursing homes. Their care is typically paid for by Supplemental Security Income (disability checks), which they turn over to the shelter owners (Shadish et al., 1989a).

Segal, Silverman, and Baumohl (1989) examined these care facilities in the state of California and concluded that there are several types. The *family care home* is small, has a family-oriented atmosphere, and often is owner occupied. These homes typically shelter a couple of older, more emotionally stable residents. The homes are not medically oriented in that the residents are not treated like patients, but neither are any programs provided that are designed to make the residents more independent or to move them out of the shelter. The *small group home* has a typical bed capacity of 30 residents. These homes also serve an older population and do not emphasize control over the residents like the family homes. That is, there are no curfews or many rules or schedules for the residents to follow. However, the smaller group homes, unlike the family homes, use extramural staff for medical, social, and psychological services. The *larger group homes* offer some programs designed to enhance social skills and rehabilitation for their residents. Also, in the larger group homes there is more control over the residents' lives compared to the other two types of facilities.

The remainder of the deinstitutionalized individuals are scattered across many settings. About 250,000 remain in mental hospitals. Another 150,000 to 170,000 live with their families, and the rest are either homeless or live elsewhere, such as in jails (Shadish et al., 1989a).

This fragmentation of care and the supposed economization of services implies that society has essentially moved from a mental health system to a welfare system (Kennedy, 1989). It is time to look at the success (or failure) of these changes in care for the mentally disordered.

Measuring "Success" of Deinstitutionalized Persons

Many in the mental health field would quickly jump to the conclusion that deinstitutionalization has not been successful. We have reviewed here some of the myriad problems that deinstitutionalization has created, including but not limited to transinstitutionalization, homelessness, and jail terms. How is successful integration into the community measured? The answer depends on whom you ask and what issues you discuss.

Society needs to take a closer look at the measurement of success of deinstitutionalization. Table 6.1 shows the names of famous individuals who at one time or another experienced mental impairment but who were also able to integrate successfully into society.

The typical measures of success are social integration and recidivism. **Social integration** was defined in the last chapter as people's involvement with community institutions as well as their participation in the community's informal social life (Gottlieb, 1981). **Recidivism** means relapse or return to the institution or to care—in this case, return to the psychiatric hospital. However, both of these terms imply limited criteria. Recent efforts in the literature of the field of community psychology indicate that measurement of success is a more complex issue.

For example, Shadish, Thomas, and Bootzin (1982) found that different groups use different criteria for success. Residents, staff, and family members of community care facilities often express that the quality of life (e.g., a clean place to live and something to do) ought to serve as a measure of success. On the other hand, federal officials and academicians cite psychosocial functioning (e.g., social integration and reduction of symptomatology) as good measures of success of community placement.

TABLE 6.1   Some Famous Individuals with Some Form of Mental Disorder

PERSON	FIELD	MENTAL DISORDER
Dick Cavett	Contemporary American entertainment celebrity	Depression
Connie Francis	American 1950s singer	Manic-depressive disorder
Ernest Hemingway	American Nobel Prize writer	Depression
Abraham Lincoln	Sixteenth American president	Depression
Vincent Van Gogh	Late-nineteenth-century Dutch painter	Psychosis
Virginia Woolf	Early-twentieth-century British writer	Depression

Clinicians (psychologists and psychiatrists) also use different criteria for different groups. Stack, Lannon, and Miley (1983) queried clinicians about their prognostic judgments for 269 patients in a state community mental health center. Specifically, the clinicians were asked to judge their expectations that the patients would be readmitted within the next two years. Clinicians' judgments were biased in regard to the patients' ethnicity; that is, they judged African American patients as more likely to be rehospitalized than White patients. The same clinicians were unduly influenced by their perceptions of the severity of the patients' disorder instead of other favorable factors such as lack of prior hospitalization, youthfulness, lack of severe impairment, and living in a residentially stable neighborhood.

Despite suspected clinician bias, do client characteristics help clinicians make accurate judgments about whether particular clients will be more successful once released from an institution? Mitchell's (1982) work seems to suggest this is so. Mitchell recruited 35 clients from outpatient psychiatric clinics, as well as their family members. The ability of the client to solve problems and to be independent positively related to the number of intimates or friends and the degree of support received from peers that the clients reported.

However, environmental factors also moderate the amount of success each deinstitutionalized individual will experience. Kruzich (1985) found that cities of 10,000 to 100,000 do have sufficient community resources for clients, but cities over 100,000 are so large that problems of distance and safety preclude high levels of involvement in community life or in accessing resources. Small towns and rural areas ranked in the middle of these other two sizes. Kruzich also found that depersonalizing care practices of the community facilities also predict the clients' level of integration into the community. **Depersonalization of services** means that the clients' individual needs are not attended to; that is, they do not have their own personal possessions, birthdays are not celebrated, and so on. When depersonalization is high, integration is low.

Another environmental factor related to whether former patients from psychiatric institutions will successfully integrate into the community is the attitude of the community citizens (Link & Cullen, 1983). There is a wealth of research indicating that Americans have negative and rejecting attitudes toward people with mental disabilities (Scott, Balch, &

Flynn, 1983). Although the literature is somewhat inconsistent, various demographic variables have been suggested as related to attitudes toward the mentally disabled. Education is thought to increase tolerance of these individuals (Halpert, 1985) and low socioeconomic class is thought to decrease tolerance (Scott et al., 1983).

A few in the field of community integration of the chronically mentally disordered feel that the criteria for judging community competence of people with mental disabilities are amorphous and ambiguous. These professionals feel that a psychometric scale should be used to optimize the fit between the client and the community placement. Searight, Oliver, and Grisso (1986) suggested using the Community Competence Scale, which is a multiscale instrument of an individual's problem-solving skills, appropriateness of social judgment, and other factors related to social competence. In their research, Searight and associates found that the scale discriminated effectively between client groups requiring differing levels of guidance in the community.

BEYOND DEINSTITUTIONALIZATION

Certainly, the preceding scenarios do not reflect the optimism when deinstitutionalization began in the late 1960s. It was thought then that the introduction of the **Community Mental Health Act** could "reduce the census of state hospitals and to provide treatment to maintain psychiatric patients in the community" (Levine, Toro, & Perkins, 1993, p. 526). Now, with 20/20 hindsight, it seems obvious that one reason for the existing "patchwork" system is the lack of systematic planning, or poor coordination. However, some mental health care experts (Rein & Schon, 1977) argued that "the villain . . . is not poor coordination but the poor quality of services" (p. 244). Responding to this challenge, the National Institute of Mental Health (NIMH) and some state agencies have begun to collect data about the characteristics of the mentally disabled, including people who are not part of the mainstream population. That is, quality of services are dependent on professionals' knowledge about people who have mental disorders.

In the early 1980s, the NIMH surveyed the psychiatric status of more than 20,000 people in five cities. This study, known as the **Epidemiologic Catchment Area Study (ECA),** attempted to estimate and describe the incidence and prevalence of psychiatric disorders meeting the criteria of the *Diagnostic and Statistical Manual of Mental Disorders,* 3rd edition *(DSM-III).* For example, in a comparison of three communities, Robins and colleagues (1984) estimated that lifetime prevalence rate of a given DIS/*DSM-III* disorder was 28.8 percent, 38.8 percent, and 31.0 percent, respectively, in New Haven, Baltimore, and St. Louis. Moreover, substance abuse (15 percent in New Haven, 17 percent in Baltimore, and 18.1 percent in St. Louis) and anxiety (10.4 percent in New Haven, 25.1 percent in Baltimore, and 11.1 percent in St. Louis) were the two most common disorders. Men and women were equally likely to be afflicted with psychiatric disorders. Myers and colleagues (1984), in a comparison of three communities, estimated that six-month prevalence of psychiatric disorders among both sexes was 16.9 percent, 22.5 percent, and 14.8 percent, respectively, in New Haven, Baltimore, and St. Louis. A significant number of people had **comorbidity** diagnoses or two or more disorders. Men were more likely to be afflicted with substance disorder than women. A higher rate of mental illness was observed in younger adults compared to older adults.

Findings from the ECA are consistent with the **Midtown Manhattan Study,** a longitudinal study investigating the prevalence of psychopathology from 1952 to 1960. A more recent 1994 national study of 8,000 adults again confirms these findings (Human Capital Initiative, 1996). Thus, contrary to popular belief, some form of mental disorder is probably present in 1 of 10 American adults.

Changing Profiles and Populations

The multifacet of deinstitutionalization and efforts such as the ECA has stimulated mental health professionals to seriously consider the magnitude of mental illness—for example, who are these individuals? What are they suffering from? What are some of the correlates (e.g., substance abuse, sexual abuse, and so forth.) of their condition(s)? Several major themes emerge in the research literature: comorbidities or co-occurring conditions, mental health among inmates and probationers, the homeless mentally ill (including many veterans), and children and youth (including young adults) with mental illness.

According to the ECA, individuals with mental illness have a lifetime prevalence for alcohol abuse of 22.3 percent and for drug abuse of 14.7 percent (also see Table 6.2). For the general population with no mental illness, the rates are 13.5 percent and 6.1 percent, respectively. The ECA did not find a significant difference in the type of drugs abused among different psychiatric diagnoses. Reasons for use include attempts to alleviate anxiety and depression, increase social interactions, and feel "high." Although these reasons are similar to those of individuals without mental disorders, drug abuse has a more deleterious effect on the mentally ill, possibly due to biological or genetic predisposition.

Comorbidities or co-occurring conditions pose tremendous challenge in treating the mental ill. A major issue is compliance or adherence to treatment. Studies indicate that mentally ill individuals who have a history of substance abuse or who currently are abusing substances often fail to be compliant with psychiatric medication. These individuals are also likely to have a history of violence (Dixon & DeVeau, 1999).

Research and surveys consistently indicate that many of these individuals have encountered the legal system at one time or another (see Figure 6.1). An estimated 283,800 (over a quarter million) mentally ill offenders were incarcerated in prisons and jails in 1998.

TABLE 6.2   Mental Illness and Comorbidity

MENTAL ILLNESS	ANY SUBSTANCE ABUSE	ALCOHOL ABUSE
Schizophrenia	47.0%	33.7%
Bi-polar Disorder	56.1%	46.2%
Major Depression	27.2%	16.5%

FIGURE 6.1   Some Facts about Mentally Ill Inmates and Probationers

- 283,800 mentally ill in prison or jail; 547,800 on probation
- White inmates more likely than blacks or Hispanics to report a mental illness
- Offender mental illness highest among the middle-aged
- Mentally ill more likely than other offenders to have committed a violent crime
- Half of mentally ill inmates reported 3 or more prior sentences
- Mentally ill more likely than other inmates to be violent recidivists
- Homelessness more prevalent among mentally ill offenders
- About 4 out of 10 inmates with a mental condition unemployed before arrest
- Family history of incarceration and alcohol and drug use prevalent among mentally ill
- Mentally ill report high rates of past physical and sexual abuse
- A third of mentally ill offenders alcohol dependent
- Mentally ill offenders report negative life experience related to drinking
- Mentally ill expected to serve 15 months longer than other inmates in prison
- Disciplinary problems common among mentally ill inmates
- 6 out of 10 mentally ill received treatment while incarcerated
- Female mentally ill more likely than males to report treatment

Source: Adapted from P. M. Ditton (1999). Mental health and treatment of inmates and probationers. *Bureau of Justice Statistics (Special Report).* Office of Justice Program, U.S. Department of Justice.

According to a recent survey, 16 percent of state prison inmates, 7 percent of federal inmates, and 16 percent of inmates in local jails reported either a mental condition or an overnight stay in a mental hospital. About 16 percent (an estimated 547,800) of probationers self-reported a mental condition or had stayed overnight in a mental health hospital at some point in their lifetime. Although a majority of mentally ill prisoners have a history of substance abuse, they are less likely to be incarcerated for a drug-related offense. They are more likely to be incarcerated for a violent offense; however, they are more likely to be under the influence of alcohol or drugs at the time of the crime. Also, many have a history of physical or sexual trauma (Ditton, 1999).

Many also reported living on the street or in a shelter in the 12 months prior to arrest. A sizeable number of these individuals are veterans (for example, Hoff, Beam-Goulet, & Rosenheck, 1997), who may be suffering from posttraumatic stress disorder, exacerbated by alcohol and drug abuse, which places them at risk for multiple problems including sexually transmitted diseases, such as HIV (e.g., Sullivan, Koegel, Kanouse et al., 1999). (See Chapter 11 for more discussion on HIV.)

A subpopulation of the mentally ill who are incarcerated are youths (including young adults). Unfortunately, there is a paucity of research on the prevalence and types of mental disorders among youths in the juvenile justice system. Acknowledging this limitation, Cocozza and Skowya (2000) observed that

1. Youths in the juvenile justice system experience substantially higher rates of mental health disorders than youths in the general population (based on a review of 34 studies conducted by Otto, Greenstein, Johnson, & Friedman, 1992).

2. A high percentage of these youths have a diagnosable mental health disorder.
3. It is estimated that at least one out of five of these youths has a serious mental health problem.
4. Many of these youths also have co-occurring conditions, such as substance abuse.

The period of adolescence (young adulthood) can be a stressful time for individuals who are different or bucking against peer or societal norms. A growing body of research (e.g., Falkner & Cranston, 1998; Garofalo, Wolf, Kessel, Palfrey, & DuRant, 1998; Garofalo, Wolf, Wissow, Woods, & Goodman, 1999; Remafedi, French, Story, Resnick, & Blum, 1998; Rotheram-Borus & Fernandez, 1995; Rotheram-Borus, Hunter, & Rosario, 1994; and Russell & Joyner, 2001) documents that sexual minority youths (i.e., gay, lesbian, bisexual, or transgendered) have a high rate of suicide attempt, among other mental health conditions, compared to their self-identified heterosexual counterparts. In one study of 9th through 12th grade students in Massachusetts, Faulkner and Cranston (1998) found that self-identified gay, lesbian, or bisexual youths were three times more likely than their heterosexual counterparts to have attempted suicide in the past year. Using data from the National Longitudinal Study of Adolescent Health, Russell and Joyner (2001) noted that "regardless of age and family background, males and females who reported same-sex romantic attraction or relationships were more likely than their peers to report suicidal thoughts" (p. 1278).

This increased interest in the mental health of children and youths is evidenced in a recent conference (September, 2000) held under the leadership of the U.S. Surgeon General, Dr. David Satcher. A report was issued on January 3rd, 2001 (see http://www.surgeon-general.gov/cmh/childreport.htm). Key issues addressed in the report include stigma and related factors of mental illness and treatment options (including medication) in a population that is still going through tremendous physical and psychological development.

The Privatization of Public Mental Health Delivery

The Surgeon General's report barely scratches the complexities of the issue at hand: a place for the mentally ill in the community. Mental health professionals, such as Brooks and others (1995) and Ross (2000), argued that while the intentions of the Mental Health Care Act and other related federal, socially engineered programs (including Medicaid and Medicare) in the 1960s are admirable, these programs have significant unanticipated negative consequences. Although the original goal of these programs aimed to deliver necessary health care to underserved or vulnerable populations (including most mentally ill patients who were discharged from state and federal facilities), the unanticipated effect "of this large pool of public money devoted to health care was an inflationary increase in the costs of health care overall" (Brooks et al., 1995, 52). The federal government then began to take action with what is now known as "cost containment" strategies. An agency (formerly known as the Health Care Financing Administration, but as of 2001 known as the Center for Medicaid and Medicare Financing) has been created for the purpose of determining how health care should be financed. The agency has devised elaborate health care delivery reimbursement systems (see Chapters 2 & 3 of Pol & Thomas, 2001). These systems (how a condition—disease or illness—should be treated and paid for) are more or less based on a medical model (that is, biological). In the case of mental illness, biological determinants are often less clear; nonetheless, a Diagnostic Related Groups (DRGs) system of reimbursement has been developed. Mental health professionals (especially psychiatrists) are now required to use this for their practices. Many quickly learn that there is little incentive to treat the underinsured, uninsured, or poor. In other words, what is not billable or reimbursable, one should *not* treat. Adequate or high quality mental health care has become a luxury for many, especially the large number of people who have been discharged from state and federal facilities and are now living in the community. This phenomenon is known as "privatization of public mental health care" (Brooks et al., 1995)—an irony contrary to the intent of the Mental Health Care Act and contrary to the spirit of federal programs, such as Medicaid and Medicare. Sadly, Ross (2000) stated that "The linkage between Medicaid and public mental health has not occurred. Adequate services to persons with serious mental illness do not exist in many parts of the country and are more an exception than the norm" (p. 20).

One significant impact of these developments often results in less than optimal or culturally inappropriate or incompetent care. For example, family members may be used for language interpretation because language interpretation is not a billable service. Even when it is billable, there are often not enough qualified (e.g., licensed) interpreters. Meanwhile, other factors contribute to the debate about culturally appropriate or competent care. For example, some mental health experts argue that ethnic minorities are likely to be underrepresented in the ECA and Midtown study due to certain cultural norms (cf. Wilson, O'Leary, & Nathan, 1992). Sue, Fujino, Hu, Takeuchi, and Zane (1991) and Bui and Takeuchi (1992) found that Asian and Hispanic Americans tended to underutilize mental health care services, whereas African Americans tended to overutilize such services. Indeed, to many Chinese people, such as Min in the opening vignette, seeking mental health care services is not only a "loss of face" but also a disgrace to the extended family. Many Chinese believe the body and the mind are one and the same thing: the "body-mind duality" of Western society is alien to most Chinese (Cheung, 1986).

According to Sue and colleagues (1991), even when ethnic minorities do seek mental health care services, they tend to have a higher attrition rate than Whites. However, ethnic minorities are less likely to terminate treatments when the mental health care providers are of similar ethnic background. In addition to good planning and coordination, this finding illustrates the important thesis that for mental health care services to be efficient and effective, treatment models must be culturally sensitive (Mock, 1999)—something often incongruent with a "cost containment model."

Model Programs for Individuals with Mental Disorders

It is sad to note that community psychologists and mental health care experts know more about what does *not* work rather than what *does* work with people who are mentally disordered. However, coupled with the knowledge gained from pioneer programs such as the **Lodge Society** (Fairweather, Sanders, Maynard, & Cressler, 1969) and epidemiological investigations, some innovative psychosocial rehabilitation models (Bond, Miller, & Krumweid, 1988; Bond, Witheridge, Dincin, & Wasmer, 1991; Bond, Witheridge, Dincin, Wasmer, Webb, & DeGraaf-Kaser, 1990; Olfson, 1990) have been developed for treating people with mental disorders. Fairweather's concept of Lodge Societies encompassed structured halfway houses or group homes for the mentally disabled that emphasized skill building and shared responsibility as well as decision making.

Common to the newer models is the use of **case management,** or intensive case support, including instruction in daily living skills (e.g., cooking and paying bills). Service delivery linking both the monitoring and brokering of delivery of a variety of services performed by the case manager is also advocated (Snowden, 1992). In other words, a case manager (usually a social worker) works *closely* with former mental patients, possibly being on call 24 hours a day for any emergency that might arise. Also, case management can easily be integrated into **residential** or outpatient treatments.

It is thought that intensive social support in the form of case management should mitigate recidivism or relapse. This approach is consistent with the philosophy of the field of community psychology: **empowerment.** Compared to traditional treatments (e.g., outpatient), case management is labor intensive. However, research indicates that case management "repeatedly has been shown to reduce both hospital use and costs across a number of different studies performed in different communities . . . , although other desirable effects (e.g., symptom reduction, improved social relationships, . . .) have been less than robust (Levine, Toro, & Perkins, 1993, p. 529). These findings are understandable, given the complex nature of mental disorder. As you may recall, even when housing is not a problem, improved social relationships are contingent on many different people—the patient being just one of the many.

One model case management program will be examined here. **Assertive community treatment (ACT),** known variously as *mobile treatment teams* and *assertive case management,* is designed "to improve the community functioning of clients with serious and persistent mental illness, thereby diminishing their dependence on inpatient care while improving the quality of life" (Bond et al., 1990, p. 866). Assertive community treatment focuses on teaching practical living skills such as how to shop for groceries and maintain finances. More than that, in a single or team case manager (professional staff), ACT ensures attention to medications, service planning and coordination, as well as assessment and evaluations. Assertive community treatment usually also means a fairly low staff-client ratio—for example, 10:1. Moreover, clients do not visit staff offices but rather staff visit clients *in vivo*—that is, in their own environments.

Stein and Test (1985) developed one of the first ACT programs in this country in Madison, Wisconsin. Wanting more research on ACTs, Bond and colleagues (1990) compared ACT clients to clients at a drop-in center. Drop-in centers usually provide an informal meeting place for clients who typically are formerly institutionalized mental patients. These centers offer a range of social and recreational programs in a self-help atmosphere. In sharp contrast to ACT, drop-in centers have a central meeting place, a higher client-staff ratio, and no requirement for frequent staff contact.

Bond and associates (1990) found overall that after one year, 76 percent of the ACT clients were still involved in ACT, whereas only 7 percent of the drop-in clients were involved in their program. The ACT staff team averaged only two home and community visits per week per client but their clients averaged significantly fewer state hospital admissions and fewer days per hospital stay. The researchers estimated that ACT saved over $1,500 per client per year. The ACT clients themselves reported greater satisfaction with their program, fewer contacts with the police, and more stable community housing than clients from the drop-in center.

"Wraparound Milwaukee," a multiyear program targeting juvenile delinquents and their families, "sustains itself by pooling dollars with its system partners and taking an integrated, multiservice approach...based on the Wraparound philosophy and the managed care model, offers care that is tailored to each youth" (Kamradt, 2000, p. 14). The key approaches of the program are (1) strength-based strategy to children and families, (2) family involvement in the treatment process, (3) needs-based services planning and delivery (see Figure 6.2), (4) individualized service plan, and (5) outcome-focused approach. These approaches are structurally integrated into and implemented by four components: (1) care coordination, (2) the child and family team, (3) a mobile crisis team, and (4) a provider network. An innovative feature is the blending of funding (Medicaid, Supplemental Security Income, and other insurances) in order to maximize quality of care based on a case management model. It is estimated that "child welfare and juvenile justice systems fund Wraparound at $3,000 per month per child. Prior to Wraparound, these funds were used entirely

FIGURE 6.2   Services in the Wraparound Milwaukee Benefit Plan

Care coordination	Crisis home care
In-home therapy	Treatment foster care
Medication management	Residential treatment
Outpatient —individual family therapy	Foster care
Alcohol/substance abuse counseling	Day treatment/alternative school
Psychiatric assessment	Nursing assessment/management
Psychological evaluation	Job development/placement
Housing assistance	Kinship care
Mental health assessment/evaluation	Transportation services
Mentoring	Supervision/observation in home
Parent aide	Afterschool programming
Group home care	Recreation/child-oriented
Respite care	Discretionary funds/flexible funds
Child care for parent	Housekeeping/chore services
Tutor	Independent living support
Specialized camps	Psychiatric inpatient hospital
Emergency food pantry	

Source: Adapted from B. Kamradt (2000). Wraparound Milwaukee: Aiding youth with mental health needs. *Juvenile Justice, 7,* 14–23.

for residential treatment care systems [that] paid $5,000 or more per month per child" (Kamradt, 2000, p. 18).

Preliminary results of the program indicated that use of residential treatment has decreased by 60 percent (from an average daily census of 364 placements to fewer than 140) since the inception of Wraparound Milwaukee. Inpatient psychiatric hospitalization has dropped by 80 percent (also see Table 6.3).

Assertive community treatment takes an ecological (in vivo) approach to clients. The staff is assertive in offering assistance to clients and in capitalizing on client strengths, the latter of which meets the tenets of community psychology. Assertive community treatment prevents further client deterioration and provides a strong community alternative to hospitalization. Finally, ACT utilizes a holistic approach with each client as well as integration of services (Mowbray, 1990), all within the philosophies of the field of community psychology introduced at the beginning of this book.

These studies are, however, not without criticism, although other reviewers (Mowbray, 1990) have questioned why community psychologists have not been *more* involved in research on ACT and the seriously mentally disordered. Toro (1990), for example, suggested that the study had differential and therefore biasing drop-in ratios in the two groups. Toro also argued that such research on ACT indicates that even though ACT prevents rehospitalization, more research is needed on its impact in other domains such as employment and social relationships. Salem (1990) concluded that a more thorough investigation of consumer- or client-run programs is needed, as well as more diversity among interventions for people with mental disabilities.

TABLE 6.3   **Recidivism Rates of Delinquent Youth Enrolled in Wraparound Milwaukee (n = 134)**

OFFENSE	1 YEAR PRIOR TO ENROLLMENT	1 YEAR POST ENROLLMENT*
Sex offense	11%	1%
Assaults	14%	7%
Weapons offenses	15%	4%
Property offenses	34%	17%
Drug offenses	6%	3%
Other offenses (primarily disorderly conduct without a weapon)	31%	15%

*Data collected and analyzed as of September 1999.

Source: Adapted from B. Kamradt (2000). Wraparound Milwaukee: Aiding youth with mental health needs. *Juvenile Justice, 7,* 14–23.

The Battle Continues: Where Do We Go from Here?

Although having a mental disorder is still a stigma in society, the general public has become more familiar with mental health and mental illness. This awareness is responsible, in part, for the formation of the National Alliance for the Mentally Ill (NAMI). The NAMI functions as more than a self-help group; it also functions as a political lobbying body. It is estimated that the NAMI has about 1,050 affiliates in the country with a membership of about 130,000. The NAMI is a key player in the ongoing mental health care reform. At the local level, individual chapter members provide support to each other as well as educate the public via educational activities, including education about medication and rehabilitative services.

Some psychosocial models based on the concept of case management and political efforts such as those engaged by the NAMI appear to be hopeful for the mentally disabled. However, mental health care reform is at a critical juncture. That is, although community psychologists and mental health care professionals can empower the mentally ill using appropriate and culturally sensitive treatment models, mental health care reform must *not* be carried out in isolation from other health agendas. Mental health care needs to be framed within a *unified* health care agenda. Research (D'Ercole, Skodol, Struening, Curtis, & Millman, 1991; Levine & Huebner, 1991; Susser et al., 1993) indicates that physical health and mental health are interdependent, such as is the case of drug abuse among many homeless mentally disordered. D'Ercole and colleagues found that physical illnesses among psychiatric patients tended to be underdiagnosed when using the traditional psychiatric diagnostic tools of the DSM-IV. This was especially true for older and female patients. These findings suggest that poor physical health is likely to exacerbate existing poor mental health, which can become a vicious cycle.

Knowledge that community psychologists have gained in the past 30-plus years about health issues (mental health and mental illness in particular) strongly argues for the fact that we, as a nation, must not fall prey to the same false optimism of the 1960s. Also, no one should be denied mental health care services simply because she or he cannot afford to pay for such services; quality of services must *not* be contingent on amount of payment.

Meanwhile, the barometer is rising. According to Torrey (1997), approximately 150,000 people with mental illness are homeless on a given day, and another 150,000 are in jails and prisoners. The aging baby boomers pose another challenge for caring for the older or elderly mentally ill (Hatfield, 1997). Each of these scenarios demands a somewhat different response or strategy, although the populations are not mutually exclusive. People with mental illness probably have multiple problems, thus no single solution is likely to be adequate or meet their needs. For example, a homeless elderly person with mental illness needs housing, preferably a nursing home instead of emergency shelter or single residence occupancy (SRO). A nursing home environment is likely to provide more stability for this elderly person than a SRO, which requires a certain level of independence or social skills. Yet, if the person's mental illness is related to violence, his or her condition might pose a danger to himself or herself as well as those living in the nursing home. The goal here is to provide the best care to promote the quality of life among the mentally ill.

Proponents such as Breakey (1996) have argued that the pressure of managed care on psychiatry and clinical psychology is likely to limit the role of these clinicians. That is, the type of care that is not reimbursable is not allowed. Although evidence (e.g., ACT) reviewed in this chapter suggests that people with mental illness who receive *integrated services* tend to fair better than those who do not receive such services, yet integrated care comes with a big price tag (real dollar and other human capitals and resources). (Sharstein, 2000).

On the other end of the continuum, influential psychiatrists such as Torrey (1997) have argued that recent discoveries in biological psychiatry indicate that "severe psychiatric disorders are no more linked to minor mental perturbations than are multiple sclerosis, Parkinson's disease.... Their proper treatment demands expertise in brain physiology and pharmacology, rather than human relationships" (p. B5). Torrey argued for a formal separation or "divorce" of mental health (in this case, including community psychology) from psychiatry. Resources should be redirected to allow psychiatry to merge with neurology

> to produce researchers and clinicians who possess expertise on the full spectrum of brain diseases. This would place neuropsychiatry as a single entity exactly where it was 100 years ago, before the Freudian revolution and the mental-hygiene movement led it to focus on general mental health rather than the most severe mental disorders. (p. B5)

This is both a provocative and ominous statement! Given the rapid advancement in medical technology, it is all too easy to lose sight of the human side of feelings and behaviors. The atmosphere of managed care certainly aids in this process. These issues no doubt fuse the debate whether clinical psychologists should have the right to prescribe psychotropic medications. Currently, a small number of clinical psychologists who have gone through a pilot training program are allowed to prescribe psychotropic medications. This issue is more than just "identity politics"—the reality is that being able to prescribe such medications translates to another revenue for reimbursable services.

In the foreseeable future, people in community psychiatry and community mental health have an unenviable task: to argue that integrated care (e.g., case management) is the "norm." Meanwhile, this shift to an emphasis in biological psychiatry will likely hinder work already under study in areas such as the severe mentally ill in rural settings. Maybe some of the effort should be used to apply the concept of integrated care in rural settings—an argument of external validity.

SUMMARY

A casual review of the field of mental health and illness indicates that there is a great deal of controversy about exactly what deinstitutionalization is. Some have argued that a better term is *transinstitutionalization* to describe the "dumping" of patients from one setting to another. Also, the characteristics of the mentally disabled have changed in the past 30-plus years. Now, ethnic minorities constitute a sizable sample of the mentally disordered, and they are likely to be undetected by the existing systems.

The most common placement for a deinstitutionalized individual is, interestingly, another institution, usually a nursing home. The functioning of a person who is mentally disordered in the community usually includes social integration and recidivism, or rate of return to the psychiatric hospital. Most analyses of success focus on problems of the individual; however, the environment, such as depersonalization of services, can also account for problems deinstitutionalized individuals face.

The ideal that led to the enactment of the Community Mental Health Act in the 1960s has not been fully realized. Now, it seems obvious that one reason for the existing "patch-work" system is the lack of systematic planning, or poor coordination. On the other hand, some mental health care experts argue that the villain is poor quality of services. Responding to this challenge, the National Institute of Mental Health and some state agencies have begun to collect data about the characteristics of the mentally disabled, including people who are not part of the mainstream population. That is, quality of services is dependent on knowl-edge about people who have mental disorders.

Coupled with the knowledge gained from epidemiological investigations such as the Epidemiologic Catchment Area Study and the Midtown Manhattan Study, some innovative psychosocial rehabilitation models have been developed for treating the mentally disor-dered. Common to these models is the use of case management or intensive social support (e.g., assertive community treatment), including some form of daily living skill training. Also, case management can be easily integrated into residential or outpatient treatments. It is thought that intensive social support in the form of case management should mitigate recidivism or relapse. However, research evidence is equivocal.

Mental health care reform is at a critical juncture. Although community psychologists and mental health care professionals can empower the mentally ill by using appropriate and culturally sensitive intervention models, mental health care reform must *not* be carried out in isolation from other health agendas. That is, mental health care needs to be framed within a *unified* health care agenda..

SOCIAL AND HUMAN
SERVICES IN THE COMMUNITY

> *This nation, this people, this generation, has man's first chance
> to create a Great Society; a society of success without squalor, beauty
> without barrenness, works of genius without the wretchedness of poverty.*
>
> —Lyndon B. Johnson

Rock was a high school junior. His girlfriend, Monique, was a sophomore in the same school. Both teenagers lived in middle-class suburban homes. Rock was bored with his humdrum life in the suburbs and liked to "live on the edge." It was his unpredictability and careless living that attracted Monique to Rock, although neither set of parents was thrilled with their child's choice of dating partner.

Rock and Monique were caught smoking marijuana in school. (Both also had a history of cutting classes and running away from home.) Because both were minors, the judge ordered Rock and Monique to enroll in a drug-treatment program.

The drug-treatment program was one of a dozen funded by a federal agency in collaboration with two state agencies. The goal was to *prevent* (not intervene or treat) youths from using alcohol and other drugs. Past research has shown that youths who have risk factors (e.g., cutting class and stealing) are more likely to use or abuse drugs than those who do not. Thus, youths who have risk factors are supposedly identified by the child and family welfare division and are referred to the drug-treatment programs at the other state agencies.

In the case of Rock, he was ordered by the court (rather than identified by the child and family welfare agency) to enroll in a drug-treatment program. After intake, Rock was immediately placed into one of the programs. He was to participate in both individual and group counseling. Family counseling with Rock's parents was provided on a limited basis, because the program was mainly designed for drug treatment.

Monique's placement was still pending. Incidentally, during intake, it was discovered that she was pregnant. The state agency responsible for the drug-treatment programs did not accept pregnant clients. Meanwhile, staff at both state agencies did not know what to do with Monique. Also, both agencies were experiencing some difficulty in complying with the requirements of the federal agency that funded the drug-treatment programs.

This incident reflected one more symptom of the already strained relationship between the two state agencies. The road that led to the collaboration between the two agencies was shaky, at best. The original proposal to seek federal funds to establish drug-treatment programs for youths was largely engineered by the state agency that was responsible for drug-treatment services. Although its executive director had agreed in principle with the proposal, the state agency responsible for child and family welfare was more an observer than a player in the process.

Since the inception of the drug-treatment programs, several major political changes at the state level had led to a leadership vacuum at the two state agencies. For example, the two executive directors of the respective state agencies resigned after the governor announced that he would not seek reelection. A consequence was the lack of coordination of the patient referral process.

Meanwhile, direct-care staff felt strongly that alcohol and other drug abuse in youths was likely to be symptomatic of other issues, including parent-child and school problems. Moreover, most of these youths were already using or abusing some form of drug; therefore, to talk about "prevention" was a misnomer. However, since the federal funding agency focused on prevention, the staff were obligated to comply by educating about preventing the use of drugs.

The preceding true story illustrates that, more often than not, social problems do not have a single cause or do not develop in isolation. In the case of Rock and Monique, direct-care staff appeared to be correct in stating that drug treatment for both was merely treating the symptom (drug habit) but not the cause(s) (e.g., school climate). Moreover, Monique needed a treatment program that specialized in drug rehabilitation for pregnant women. However, staff at the drug-treatment program were limited by their resources and expertise. Here is a good example of the inappropriate depletion of limited and sometimes scarce social and human resources. Effective social and human services delivery is contingent on good organizational infrastructure and management.

This chapter will begin with a review of what poverty is and how social welfare emerged in Western society. In particular, selected social and human services will be discussed, as well as affected groups.

BRIEF HISTORICAL NOTES ABOUT SOCIAL WELFARE IN WESTERN SOCIETY

What is **poverty?** Does poverty merely mean the lack of (sufficient) money to acquire essential things, such as food, in order to survive? Or does poverty mean being born and living in a ghetto or slum, which might lead to attending a school that is ill equipped (e.g., lack of funds to attract good teachers) and which might further lead to a vicious cycle for future generations? Probably, the latter notion is what President Lyndon B. Johnson had in mind when he made his 1964 State of the Union address about the War on Poverty. Poverty can be a cause or an effect; it is multidimensional. Case in Point 7.1 provides some compelling and alarming statistics about poverty in the United States. Poverty is not just about lacking money; it is also about hopelessness, prejudice, and discrimination. For example, without a good education, one is likely to be discriminated against and unable to find a decent-paying job. Also, poorly educated people are less likely to be well-informed citizens

■ ■ ■ ■ ■

CASE IN POINT 7.1

POVERTY IN AMERICA

Community psychologists and other experts consider poverty the number one social problem in the United States as well as the root cause of many other social problems, such as delinquency, substance abuse, school problems, crime, and homelessness (U.S. Bureau of the Census, 1997). Here are some startling statistics about poverty both in the United States and worldwide:

- Every 3.6 seconds, someone in the world dies of hunger.
- Seventy-five percent of these starving individuals are children under 5.
- One in 10 U.S. families (12 million children and 19 million adults) cannot afford to buy the food they need.

- During 1995, 21 percent of American children under age 18 lived in families with incomes below the poverty level. This is a significantly higher number than the 15 percent whose families were poor in 1970.
- In the United States in 1998, the states expended $15.6 billion on child welfare services alone.
- Little funding in the United States is targeted for prevention services. Less than $1.5 billion is expended on prevention and related services compared to $9.4 billion for maintenance (welfare) services.
- Ninety percent of all welfare recipients are women.

compared to those who are educated, especially about their basic rights or entitlement. With these premises in mind, you are now ready to examine the effectiveness of public assistance, or welfare, one objective of which is to lift people from their misery so that they can move on to a better life. Case in Point 7.2 further discusses the issues of poverty and wealth, whereby the rich indeed get richer (Conger, Conger, Matthews, & Elder, 1999).

According to Handel (1982), **social welfare** is "a set of ideas and a set of activities and organizations for carrying those ideas, all of which have taken shape over many centuries, to provide people with income and other social benefits in ways that safeguard their dignity" (p. 31). Without sounding simplistic, this seemingly innocuous statement describes the complex nature of social welfare. Social welfare serves both ideological (e.g., political and religious) and practical (e.g., unable to provide for oneself) concerns. Some of the issues associated with these two broad categories of concern will be discussed.

Until modern times, the three major forms of social welfare were charity/philanthropy, public welfare, and mutual aid. **Charity/philanthropy** refers to social welfare in which a **donor** (giver) assists a **recipient** (taker). **Public welfare** is basically an extension of charity/philanthropy, in which the government assumes the responsibility for the poor.

Both charity/philanthropy and public welfare involve some form of religious ideologue (e.g., Christian love). They can be further understood from the perspectives of both the donor and the recipient. Specifically, to those who are in the position to assist the less fortunate, honor or salvation may be the driving force behind their generosity. On the other hand, the recipients must demonstrate their need (practical concern) for assistance (e.g., income or maintenance in the form of food). An indicator of need is the **standard of living** or the economic means of subsistence of an individual. For example, people who are not able to adequately provide for themselves or their families or both are often considered in need of assistance. However, the notion of "needs" may be more elusive than people think. For instance, how does one classify people who live in poverty not because they cannot work but because they are not motivated. Interestingly, research demonstrates that most welfare recipients would like to work (Allen, 2000); Scott, London, & Edin, 2000). Also, notions of standards of living may vary. For example, everyone could live without televisions, but most don't want to. However, even many of the poorest people (likely to be recipients of some form of social welfare) in this country have televisions. In other words, does possessing a television mean that these people should not be entitled to social welfare?

Meanwhile, the processes inherent in charity/philanthropy and public welfare are likely to create social stigma. Handel (1982) argued that recipients of social welfare

> are widely believed to be lazy and immoral. . . . Although recipients must prove their need, their claims are often thought to be fraudulent. . . . These people receive less social honor than other members of society. Such methods of providing income are therefore regarded as demeaning, as impairing the dignity of the people who depend upon them. (pp. 8–9)

Even recipients of social welfare are likely to have a negative view of other recipients (Coley, Kuta, & Chase-Lansdale, 2000).

As noted earlier, the nature of social welfare is largely a function of the ideology of the period. For example, research indicates that during religious seasons (e.g., Christmas and Easter), people are more likely to be charitable than during nonreligious seasons. Fur-

CASE IN POINT 7.2
ARE THE RICH GETTING RICHER?

The U.S. Census Bureau has been studying the distribution of income since the late 1940s. The first income inequality statistics for families were published and came from the annual demographic supplement to the Current Population Survey (CPS). The most commonly used measure of income inequality, the *Gini index* (also known as the *index of income concentration*),[1] indicated a *decline* in family income *inequality* of 7.4 percent from 1947 to 1968. Since 1968, there has been an *increase* in income inequality, reaching its 1947 level in 1982 and increasing further since then. The increase was 16.1 percent from 1968 to 1992 and 22.4 percent from 1968 to 1994 (see Figure 7.1).

Living conditions of Americans have changed considerably since the late 1940s. In particular, a smaller fraction of people live in families (two or more people living together related by blood or marriage). Therefore, starting in 1967, the Census Bureau began reporting on the income distribution of households in addition to families. By coincidence, 1968 was the year in which measured postwar income was at its most equal for families. The Gini index for households indicates that there has been growing income inequality over the past quarter-century. Inequality grew slowly in the 1970s and rapidly during the early 1980s. From about 1987 through 1992, the growth in measured ine-

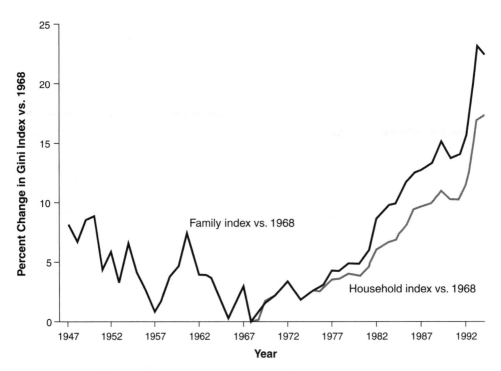

FIGURE 7.1   Change in Income Inequality

Source: From "A Brief Look at Postwar U.S. Income Equality" by D. H. Weinberg, June 1996, *Current Population Reports,* Washington, DC: U.S. Bureau of the Census.

quality seemed to taper off, reaching 11.9 percent above its 1968 level. This was followed by a large jump in 1993, partly due to a change in survey methodology. The Gini index for households in 1994 was 17.5 percent above its 1968 level.

The long-run increase in income inequality is related to changes in the nation's labor market and its household composition. One factor is the shift in employment from those goods-producing industries that have disproportionately provided high-wage opportunities for low-skilled workers, toward services that disproportionately employ college graduates, and toward low-wage sectors such as retail trade. But within-industry shifts in labor demand away from less-educated workers are perhaps a more important explanation of eroding wages than the shift out of manufacturing. Also cited as factors putting downward pressure on the wages of less-educated workers are intensifying global competition and immigration, the decline of the proportion of workers belonging to unions, the decline in the real value of the minimum wage, the increasing need for computer skills, and the increasing use of temporary workers.

At the same time, changes in living arrangements have taken place that tend to exacerbate differences in household incomes. For example, divorces and separations, births out of wedlock, and the increasing age at first marriage have led to a shift away from married-couple households and toward single-parent and nonfamily households, which typically have lower incomes. Also, the increasing tendency for men with higher-than-average earnings to marry women with higher-than-average earnings has contributed to widening the gap between high-income and low-income households.

Another way to look at shifts in income distribution is to examine the changes in family size, or the change in the ratio of family income to its poverty threshold. Poverty thresholds vary by family size and composition, reflecting consumption efficiencies achieved through economies of scale (i.e., families of two or more people can share certain goods such as housing). A ratio of 1.00 indicates that the family has an income equal to the poverty threshold for its size and composition. The average ratio in the bottom quintile in 1968 was 1.04, while the average in the top quintile was 6.13. By 1994, these ratios were 0.92 and 9.22, respectively (and 0.89 and 8.39 in 1992), also indicating a widening income gap (see Figure 7.2). The ratio for the middle quintile also rose, from 2.80 in 1968 to 3.26 in

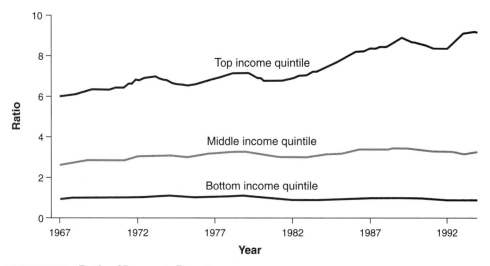

FIGURE 7.2   Ratio of Income to Poverty

Source: From "A Brief Look at Postwar U.S. Income Equality" by D. H. Weinberg, June 1996, *Current Population Reports,* Washington, DC: U.S. Bureau of the Census.

(continued)

CASE IN POINT 7.2   CONTINUED

both 1992 and 1994. In sum, when money income is examined, each of these indicators shows increasing income inequality over the 1968 to 1994 period. But are there other perspectives that change this story?

Since 1979, the Census Bureau has examined several experimental measures of income. These measures add the value of noncash benefits (e.g., food stamps and employer contributions to health insurance) to, and subtract taxes from, the official money income measure. The Census Bureau's research in this area has shown that the distribution of income is more equal under a broadened defini-

tion of income that takes into account the effects of taxes and noncash benefits. Further, government transfer benefits play a much more equalizing role on income than do taxes. Nonetheless, although the levels of inequality are lower, this alternative perspective does not change the picture of increasing income inequality over the 1979 to 1994 period.

[1]The Gini index ranges from 0.0, indicating that every family (household) has the same income, to 1.0, indicating that one family (household) has all the income. It is therefore one way to measure how far a given income distribution is from equality.

Source: From "A Brief Look at Postwar U.S. Income Equality" by D. H. Weinberg, June 1996, *Current Population Reports,* Washington, DC: U.S. Bureau of the Census.

thermore, people who have been described as "poor" are considered to be more worthy of assistance than those who have been described as "welfare recipients" (Baron & Byrne, 1994). Although people might want to think of themselves as honorable and noble people, evidence suggests otherwise. In fact, these beliefs and perceptions (including the political climate) often shape how individuals think social and human services should be conducted and delivered.

Moving beyond these so-called traditional forms of social welfare, discussion now turns to two modern forms of social welfare: social insurance and social service. **Social insurance,** or **public assistance,** has its origin in the nineteenth century, around the time of the Industrial Revolution. Similar to public welfare, the basic premise of social insurance is that the government assumes responsibility for the poor. The funds for this derive from taxes. In other words, the *difference* between public welfare and social insurance (a consequence of the Industrial Revolution) is that "the recipients of social insurance are receiving benefits that have been earned by work, either their own, or work by someone else on their behalf" (Handel, 1982, p. 15), and recipients of public welfare do not contribute to this process. Some well-known programs of social insurance in this country include Temporary Assistance for Needy Families (TANF), food stamps, Medicaid (for the poor), Medicare (for the elderly), Social Security (unemployment benefits or old-age pensions), and veterans' benefits. Eligibility guidelines (e.g., poverty index as a function of household income) are established by the government, although they are often very cumbersome and lengthy.

Social services, or public charity (nonmaterialistic benefits that often overlap with social insurance), is an offshoot of charity/philanthropy. Derived from the nineteenth century or the Industrial Revolution, the government uses taxes to provide services. A major goal of social services is to ensure and maintain a productive workforce via prevention or intervention of social ills (Handel, 1982). Rock and Monique, the two teenagers in the opening vignette, were the recipients of social services from the child and family welfare agency and the substance-abuse agency in the state where they resided. It is hoped that these services can prevent (or intervene with) both youths from becoming more dependent on marijuana or other drugs without becoming a major burden to society in the years to come.

A seemingly more enlightened view of public assistance is emerging in the United States among the public and some government officials. First, there is growing concern that people should be less dependent on public assistance. Such assistance is seen as degrading and stigmatizing. Second, recipients should be encouraged to work; that is, incentives to encourage work should be more available than incentives to encourage dependence on public assistance. This appears to be the underlying philosophy of the Personal Responsibility and Work Opportunity Reconciliation Act of 1996 (Scott, London, & Edin, 2000). Third, there is growing recognition that if employment participation is made mandatory, employment should make families better off by working rather than by not working. Finally, critics of public assistance acknowledge that if recipients are to become self-sufficient, employment and training services will not necessarily reduce poverty if such work pays low wages. In fact, a recent study found that women who leave welfare to work are no better off than low-income women never on welfare (Loprest, 1999-2000). For an interesting alternative to welfare for reducing poverty, see Case in Point 7.3.

Although newer programs that exchange work for assistance seem to have either neutral or even some positive results (Green, Fender, Leos-Urbel, & Markowitz, 2001), such programs are not without their critics. Piven and Cloward (1996) noted that proponents claim miraculous social and cultural transformations that are unrealistic, such as increased family cohesion and lower crime rates. Piven and Cloward viewed such welfare-to-work programs as nothing more than a class war between the haves and the have-nots. Opulente and Mattaini (1997) suggested that sanction-based programs are likely to be ineffective and

■ ■ ■ ■ ■ ▬▬▬▬▬▬▬▬▬▬▬▬▬▬▬▬▬▬▬▬▬▬▬▬▬▬▬▬▬▬▬▬

CASE IN POINT 7.3
THE GRAMEEN BANK

Can a small loan (microcredit) of $25 to $50 "cure" poverty? An interesting experiment is under way worldwide. The experiment in microcredit is known as the Grameen Bank. Founder Muhammad Yunus was struck by the extreme poverty, especially of women, in Bangladesh. In 1976 with some difficulty, he took out a loan from a bank and distributed the money to poor women in Bangladesh. In fact, the loans go to the poorest of the poor. The small loans were generally used by the women to begin their own cottage-type industries, such as raising farm animals and produce or creating crafts to sell. The Grameen Bank, then, views microcredit as a cost-effective weapon to fight poverty. Yunus

found that the repay rate for the loans was very, very high. He could not, however, convince any traditional banks to continue loaning money to the poor, so he started his own bank, the Grameen Bank.

The Grameen Bank uses principles that run counter to traditional banking wisdom. Yunus's bank seeks out the poorest borrowers. No collateral is necessary for a loan. Instead, the system is based on trust, accountability, participation, and creativity. Borrowers are required to join the bank in groups of five; the group members provide each other with support and advice. The Grameen Bank is now the largest rural financial institution in

(continued)

CASE IN POINT 7.3 CONTINUED

Bangladesh with more than 2.3 million borrowers in almost 39,000 villages. Furthermore, the bank brings the loans to the people rather than the other way around. Another 4,000 people have completed Grameen Bank training so as to create 223 replication programs in 58 different countries. Does this sound like community psychology in action?

Another cogent question is this: Does the Grameen Bank have a positive effect on these impoverished individuals? The answer is a resounding "yes." First, over 95 percent of the loans are repaid, indicating that people are not always looking for a free handout. Second, the bank has a positive effect on both the women and their children. Independent research demonstrates

that the women's economic security and status within the family are elevated. The children of the women are better schooled and healthier than other children in the community. And best of all, extreme poverty (as defined by the United Nations) declines by more than 70 percent within five years of the borrowers' joining the bank.

Would such a program work in the United States? Yunus thinks not. Costs in the United States are such that the operations would be more expensive. The Grameen Bank model, however, has now successfully spread to 40 countries with about 22 million poor people having access to microcredit. Muhammad Yunus, by the way, has a degree in economics, not in community psychology.

Adapted from "The Grameen Bank," Muhammad Yunus, *Scientific American,* November 1999, 114–119 and from www.grameen-info.org.

to produce undesirable side effects. Wilson, Ellwood, and Brooks-Gunn (1996) have offered the criticism that the best research methods are not being used to examine the outcomes and processes of such programs. Finally, Aber, Brooks-Gunn, and Maynard (1995) concluded that welfare-to-work programs do little to enhance children of poor parents.

SPECIFIC SOCIAL ISSUES AND SOCIAL SERVICES

Many groups access social and human services for a variety of reasons. To evaluate and judge the effectiveness or impact of these services, a consensus of standards is essential. According to Price, Cowen, Lorion, and Ramos-McKay (1988), model programs possess one or more of five characteristics:

1. These programs have a specific target audience.
2. The goal of these programs is to make a long-term and significant impact on the target groups, thus enhancing their well-being.
3. The programs provide the necessary skills for the recipients to achieve their objectives.
4. The programs strengthen the natural support from family, community, or school settings.
5. The programs have evaluative mechanisms to document their success.

Using these criteria as standards, discussion now turns to four groups to examine the problems, the people, and approaches to addressing concerns within social and human services systems. These groups have been for several reasons. First, these groups are large or growing in number, such as the elderly and the homeless. Second, some of these groups are currently receiving much media attention, including maltreated children and pregnant teens. Third, all four groups have received significant attention in the field of community psychology.

Child Maltreatment

Scope of the Issue

It is estimated that over one million children a year are subject to maltreatment and that 2,000 children a year die due to maltreatment (Cecchetti & Lynch, 1993; Children's Bureau, 2001). Boys and girls are equally affected by abuse, which can include physical and emotional abuse and neglect. Many of the victims are under the age of four years. The toll of child abuse on the victim is often enormous and varied—from neurodevelopmental and cognitive impairment and emotional and behavior dysregulation to school failure, antisocial behavior, and substance abuse (Olds, Hill, & Rumsey, 1998). The costs to society are also monumental. Child abuse costs the United States upward of $94 billion *every year* or $258 million *a day* in investigative and hospitalization costs, mental health care, welfare, delinquency, and adult criminality (Levine, 2001), especially violent criminal behavior (Widom, 1998). Abused children, as well as the abusers, are often the focus of intensive efforts from various social and human services specialists. Suspected cases of maltreatment are often investigated by the Department of Social Services. Abused children and their parents are often referred by judges and other professionals to mental health care providers for treatment.

Causes of Maltreatment

Levine and Perkins (1997) have discussed several risk factors related to child maltreatment. They noted that the vast majority of children who die because of maltreatment are under the age of 5 and that many of these children live in low-income homes and are abused by a male. Hamilton (1989) noted that there is widespread agreement among family violence experts that there are multiple factors responsible for child maltreatment such as stressors in the parents' lives, poverty, social isolation, and unrealistic expectations of children. Recent studies have also identified poor prenatal care, dysfunctional caregiving, closely spaced unplanned pregnancies, dependence on welfare, and parental substance abuse as causes (Olds, Hill, & Rumsey, 1998). Researchers, therefore, need to look at several levels including but not limited to societal, institutional, and interpersonal factors as providing the explanatory framework for child maltreatment and other forms of family violence such as partner violence. Societal factors, for example, can contribute to child maltreatment in the following way: Poverty and economic downturn diminish the capacity for consistent and involved parenting. Paternal job loss might produce pessimism and irritability in the father. The father might then become less nurturing and more arbitrary in his interactions with his children (McLoyd, 1989).

Community psychologists would be quick to point out that other ecological factors contribute to child maltreatment. Indeed, child maltreatment may represent one of the greatest failures of the environment to offer opportunities for fostering wellness (Cicchetti, Toth, & Rogosch, 2000). Garbarino (Garbarino & Kostelny, 1992; Garbarino, 1994) investigated community dimensions in child maltreatment. He examined two predominantly African American and two predominantly Hispanic areas of Chicago. Some 60,000 child maltreatment cases were plotted for location for the years 1980, 1983, and 1986. Garbarino found that there were significant location differences in maltreatment. As part of this same research, community leaders from social services agencies were also interviewed. The interviews revealed that high-risk locations were characterized by a lack of community identity, whereas low-risk areas were characterized by a sense of community or greater community cohesiveness. Garbarino concluded that abuse is not necessarily a sign of an individual or a family in trouble but rather a sign of a community in trouble. Coulton, Korbin, and Su (1999) agreed that neighborhood factors, such as impoverishment, affect child maltreatment as much as or more than individual risk factors.

Korbin and Coulton's (1996) research in which they conducted in-depth interviews with residents in 13 high-, medium-, and low-risk census tracts in Cleveland, Ohio, also demonstrates that intervention efforts can be reoriented to the neighborhood level. They found that such neighborhood conditions as distrust of neighbors and of social agencies as well as the dangers and incivilities of daily life limit the abilities of neighbors to help one another to act in the best interests of neighborhood children. Neighbors *do* feel that they should be able to help each other; in fact, many participants reported being optimistic that they could help prevent child maltreatment. However, neighborhood conditions often inhibited their willingness to do so. The researchers concluded that because economic and social conditions are inextricably bound together, child maltreatment prevention programs must be embedded within comprehensive efforts to strengthen communities.

Traditional efforts at intervention occur at the individual clinical level where maltreated children and their parents are given counseling to help them overcome their personal problems and understand the abuse. Although these methods are laudable, they do little to prevent the abuse in the first place. This method of treatment is also difficult and expensive to implement on a wide scale. These methods focus only on the family and not on some systems that might also share responsibility.

Some people have argued that the best way to improve the caregiving system for abusers and their victims is through national policies aimed at creating jobs, reducing unemployment and other stressors, and income maintenance such as welfare or public assistance. Better and more realistic strategies, however, might be aimed at high-risk groups *before* the abuse commences (Olds, Henderson, Chamberlin, & Tatelbaum, 1986).

Prevention Programs

Perhaps one of the best known and highly acclaimed preventive programs is one designed by David Olds and his research team (Olds et al., 1986 Olds, Hill, & Rumsey, 1998). Their project, known as the Prenatal/Early Infancy Project, provides nurse home visitation to prevent a wide range of maternal and child health problems associated with poverty, one of which is child abuse. One of the aspects of this program that makes it outstanding is that research is well designed; that is, randomly assigned experimental and control groups are used.

Primiparous mothers (women having their first child) who are less than 19 years old, of single-parent status, or who are from the lower socioeconomic class are welcomed into the studies. The researchers want to avoid the appearance of being a program only for potential child abusers. By recruiting a heterogeneous group, the interventionists are better able to compare those who are not at risk for abuse with those who are at risk for abuse.

Nurses visit the homes during the prenatal (before birth) and the perinatal (after birth) periods every other week for 60 to 90 minutes. The mother's primary support person (perhaps her own mother, a friend, or the baby's father) is also invited to attend.

Social support from the nurses and significant others is a vital component of this program. Even when abuse has already occurred, social support is also important. Research (Goleman, 1989) has demonstrated that abused children who have someone they can turn to who is truly nurturing—a relative, teacher, minister, or friend, for example—fare better than those children who have no or little social support.

The nurses carry out three major activities during their home visits: educating parents about fetal and infant development, promoting the involvement of family members and friends in support of the mother and care of the child, and developing linkages between family members and other formal health and human services in the community. In the education component, mothers and family members are encouraged to complete their own educations and to make decisions about employment and bearing additional children. Before birth, the nurses concentrate on educating the women to improve their diets and to eliminate the use of cigarettes, drugs, and alcohol; recognize pregnancy complications; and prepare the parents for labor, delivery, and care of the newborn. After the baby is born, the nurses concentrate on improving parents' understanding of the infants' temperaments and promoting the infants' socioemotional, cognitive, and physical development. The nurses also provide for the families to be linked to other formal services, such as health providers, mental health counselors, nutritional supplement programs for mother and infants (Women, Infants, and Children [WIC] programs), as well as others.

One of the most important results of the program is on verified cases of child abuse and neglect. For women with all three risk characteristics (poor, unmarried, and adolescent) of abuse, there is usually a remarkable 75 percent reduction in the incidence of verified cases of child abuse and neglect over the comparison group. The mothers in the nurse-visited group also report that their infants are easier to care for. The interviewers of the mothers often observed less punishment and restriction of the mothers toward their children and a greater number of growth-promoting playthings in the homes of the nurse-visited mothers. The medical records of the nurse-visited families show there are fewer visits to emergency rooms for illnesses and childhood accidents. This is true even for the women who report little sense of control over their lives when they first registered for the program. The results also hint at improved developmental life courses for the nurse-visited mothers, as well. For example, once these mothers become older and more employable, they work at their jobs more than their counterparts in the comparison group. Olds (1997; Olds, Hill, & Rumsey, 1998) has replicated this program in several communities across the United States with equally impressive results. The newest research, however, has unveiled at least one limitation of nurse home visit programs designed to reduce child maltreatment: In homes where other forms of domestic violence are occurring, nurse home visitation is less effective at reducing child maltreatment (Eckenrode, Ganzel, Henderson, Smith, Olds, Powers, Cole, Kitzman, & Sidora, 2000; Gomby, 2000). Further research has also shown that other, more long-term programs, such as ones based in schools where children are taught to identify abuse, especially sexual abuse, may be as effective as nurse home visitation (Davis & Gidycz, 2000).

The causes of child maltreatment are many. Cases of abuse keep large numbers of social workers and mental health professionals busy with their aftermath. However, Olds's work demonstrates that child abuse can be prevented. Expenditure of human and social services efforts at the outset may be more productive, less destructive, and more cost effective than efforts after the fact.

Teen Pregnancy

Scope of the Issue

Adolescent pregnancy has long been a concern, but the issue has recently become one of the most frequently cited examples of perceived social decay in the United States. About one million teenagers become pregnant each year with 95 percent of the pregnancies unintended. Although the rate of teen pregnancy is lower than it was in the 1980s, adolescent birth rates in the United States still remain higher than those in other industrialized countries (Coley & Chase-Lansdale, 1998; Centers for Disease Control, 1999). Even though U.S. teenagers do not exhibit different patterns of sexual activity as compared with teens from other countries, they use contraception less consistently and less effectively, thereby giving the United States a much higher birth rate (Coley & Chase-Landsdale, 1998).

There has been a recent decline in teen pregnancies (Clinton, 2000), in some cases as dramatic as 20 percent, so quite possibly some prevention programs are beginning to work. Teen pregnancy, nevertheless, remains an important issue because these mothers' babies are often low in birth weight and have a disproportionately high mortality rate. The young mothers themselves have a high rate of dropout from school and often live in poverty (U.S. Department of Health & Human Services, 2001). The Centers for Disease Control estimates that between 1985 and 1990, teen pregnancies cost $120 billion in health care, welfare funding, lost wages, and the like (Centers for Disease Control, 1999).

Causes of Teen Pregnancy

Some critics argue that the social welfare system in the United States may, in fact, be responsible for the nation's high pregnancy rate among teens. That is, they believe that public assistance as a source of income support actually promotes teen pregnancy and the growth of female-headed households. However, this assumption is not supported by research. Other industrialized countries, such as Sweden and the United Kingdom, that have more comprehensive welfare programs than the United States have lower teenage pregnancy rates (Kotch, Blakely, Brown, & Wong, 1992). Similarly, Darity and Myers (1988) stated:

> Statistical inquiry does not indicate that the teens' decisions about childbearing are a response to the amounts [of money] made available. Their [teenagers'] decisions are not primarily pecuniary in character, anyway; the decisions are primarily affectional. The existence of welfare may facilitate black teen motherhood and increased female-headship, but it is not the fundamental cause. In fact, the decade of the 1970s was one in which the real value of AFDC and food stamps fell while black female-headship grew at an accelerating pace. (p. 285)

Therefore, public assistance does not cause young women to become or want to become pregnant. Limiting access to such assistance might, in fact, be harmful (Wilcox, Robbennolt, O'Keeffe, & Pynchon, 1996).

In terms of absolute numbers of pregnancies, the concern that teen pregnancy is an African American problem may in fact be misplaced. African American teenage pregnancies do not represent the majority of teen pregnancies. Although it is true that in the United States the rate of African American adolescent childbirth is significantly greater than the rate of Whites, in absolute numbers the incidence of White adolescent childbirth is much greater than that of African American adolescents (Meyer, 1991). In her article on teen pregnancy, Meyer chided researchers and the media for misplacing public opinion about teen pregnancy. Not only did Meyer feel that teen pregnancy is not just an African American issue, neither is it solely a female issue. She said that males, especially White males, are invisible in the literature on research and intervention strategies. Another group of concern, but which is often ignored, is Latina teens who recently have experienced only a small drop in teen pregnancy rates (USA Today, 2001).

Besides focusing mainly on females, mainstream psychological literature on adolescent pregnancy focuses on the individual and individual deficients. Reasons often cited for teen pregnancy include lack of self-esteem (Foster, Greene, & Smith, 1990), low expectancies (Scales, 1990), and psychopathology (Reppucci, 1987). Thus, the typical solution offered for lowering the pregnancy rate is counseling (Hofferth, 1991). Another usual approach to preventing adolescent pregnancy is sex education (Fielding & Williams, 1991). However, no one really knows the true effects of sex education (Reppucci, 1987). Other efforts involve assertiveness training ("Just Say No"), but these efforts often seem futile and misguided (Scales, 1987).

Community psychologists typically examine contextual causes for adolescent pregnancy. School alienation that produces low educational aspirations, a childhood spent in poverty, perceptions of limited life options as well as the mass media and peer pressure (Schinke, 1998) also correlate with the likelihood that an adolescent girl will become pregnant (Coley & Chase-Landsdale, 1998). Whatever the causes of adolescent pregnancy, the issue needs to be addressed, for early pregnancy often results in lower rates of school completion, lower levels of marital stability, lower employment security, and higher rates of poverty for adolescent mothers and their children as compared to peers who postpone childbearing (Coley & Chase-Landsdale, 1998).

Prevention Programs

The overly rationalistic perspective that prevention efforts simply need to expose adolescents to more information or provide them with contraceptives is too narrow (Reppucci, 1987) and often disappointing. For example, Zabin, Hirsch, Smith, Streett, and Hardy (1986) offered inner-city adolescent girls sex education as well as an in-school clinic at which contraceptives were available. These researchers found that in senior high school, 72.3 percent of the girls and 91 percent of the boys were sexually active. Before the program, 26 percent of the girls and 37 percent of the boys did not use contraceptives. The program seemed somewhat to have reduced unprotected intercourse: 18.1 percent of the girls and 32.2 percent of the boys reported not using contraception. Although these data show decreases, you must remember that the data indicate that large numbers of adolescents continued to have sexual experiences that were likely to result in pregnancy or abortion.

Many similar prevention programs for adolescent pregnancy have been disappointing. As Reppucci (1987) reiterated, "The limited effects of these changes are evident in the concomitant high rates of pregnancy, clinic dropouts, and contraceptive nonuse" (p. 7).

What is perhaps needed is less focus on the individual level of analysis (Patterson, 1990) and more focus on an ecological or transactional approach to teen pregnancy (Allen-Meares & Shore, 1986). The ecological approach suggests that there are ways of enhancing already existing environmental resources (such as the teens' parents) that might be effective (Reppucci, 1987). The ecological approach takes into account the environment surrounding the adolescent who is sexually active or about to be sexually active. However, the ecological perspective is complicated. It is complex because the adolescent may be confronted by differing viewpoints on sexuality by peers, family members, and the community. For example, up to three generations of family members may influence a teen's sexual decisions (Johnson, Lay, & Wilbrandt, 1988). Furthermore, the media to which the adolescent is exposed flagrantly exploit sexuality yet prohibit contraceptives from being advertised (Reppucci, 1987).

Finally, the issue of the status of women in the United States needs to be addressed (Bond, Hill, Mulvey, & Terenzio, 2000). Early motherhood may be an attractive alternative to low-paying, dead-end jobs available to adolescent women (Lawson & Rhode, 1993).

One successful prevention program for teen pregnancy and school dropout is reported by Allen, Philliber, and Hoggson (1990). They attempted to assess which groups of participants and under what conditions a school-based prevention program was most effective. The program was the Teen Outreach Program of the Association of Junior Leagues. It used a curriculum that provided information on human development, information on skills for making life-option decisions, and supportive group decisions. The program also emphasized volunteer service to the community. The 632 participants in the program varied in terms of age, race, parents' educational level, and other factors. In other words, the study was not focused just on inner-city, African American youths. Program participants were compared to 855 similar others who did not participate. Results indicated that the Teen Outreach participants had lower levels of suspension, school dropout, and pregnancy. Moreover, the program worked best overall for older students *and* when the volunteer experience was emphasized. For younger students, the program worked best when the classroom component was intense. This study showed that there was no one best way to prevent school dropout, teen pregnancy, and other problems. More recently, Allen and colleagues were able to replicate the Teen Outreach Program at 25 sites nationwide where they obtained similar results (Allen, Philliber, Herring, & Kupermine, 1997).

Many other programs are beginning to appear. A second sample program is not school based but instead utilizes the mass media—Campaign for Our Children. This program is designed to promote abstinence among 9 to 14 year olds, an age group not yet likely to have experienced sexual intercourse. In this way, the program practices primary prevention. The program is engulfing in that it utilizes many forms of media—print, television, radio, billboard, and even mass transit media. The research-based materials developed by Campaign for Our Children can be used in schools, by communities, and by parents and other individuals or groups. There is also an interactive website available where individuals can join chat groups and where teens, parents, public officials, health professionals, and others can look up relevant information. Teachers can access lesson plans, and researchers can locate much data. The queries teens ask at the "Ask the Expert" portion of the website reveal a lack of understanding of human reproduction, a lack of access to health care providers, and mistrust in these same providers. Such data could help inform sex education professionals and policy makers about what needs to be emphasized in order to help young people protect themselves from unwanted pregnancies and sexually transmitted diseases (Campaign for Our Children, 2001; Flowers-Coulson, Kushner, & Bankowski, 2000). Research on Campaign for Our Children in the state of Maryland, which was the first state to was the first state to institute it, shows a dramatic decline in teen pregnancy rates. Maryland ranked fourth highest in the nation in 1987, but had dropped to thirtieth by 1996. Campaign for Our Children has now spread in varying degrees to all 50 states (Campaign for Our Children, 2001).

Franklin and her associates (1997) analyzed 32 different outcome studies on the primary prevention of adolescent pregnancy. In their meta-analysis, they probed for three different outcomes: a decrease in sexual activity, an increase in contraceptive use, and a reduction in pregnancy rates. The results indicated that pregnancy prevention programs had little to no impact on frequency of sexual activity, a finding that favors the theory that abstinence programs alone do not work. There was support for the efficacy of prevention programs via increased contraceptive use and moderate support for program effectiveness in reducing pregnancy rates.

Secondary Prevention: Working with Pregnant Teens

Because many prevention programs have failed, teenage pregnancy rates remain higher than desired. As mentioned earlier, the United States leads all industrialized countries in teenage pregnancy, abortion, and childbearing. Data indicate that there is a trend for teens to become pregnant at younger ages (Coley & Chase-Landsdale, 1998; Thomas, Rickel, Butler, & Montgomery, 1990).

For those teens who beome pregnant, primary prevention is too late. Programs are needed that will encourage them to continue their education and give them parenting skills. Seitz, Apfel, and Rosenbaum (1991) reported a successful school-based intervention program with inner-city African American, low-income school-aged mothers. The young mothers-to-be were placed in the Polly T. McCabe Center, a separate school for pregnant teens, yet fully a part of the New Haven (Connecticut) School System. The program was comprised of health care, education, and social services. Specifically, the program consisted of small academic classes augmented with counseling and prenatal health care services, as well as special classes to prepare the girls for parenthood. The parents of the pregnant girls were also invited to be involved in school events.

The primary concern of the researchers was what effect the program had on academic achievement, especially for those girls who had been poor students before becoming pregnant. Overall, 51 percent of the girls at two years postpartum were academically successful. What was most striking was that students who had never received grades as high as Cs were now successful. In fact, the poorer students became indistinguishable from the better students in terms of academic success. The results confirm that adolescents who appear to have minimal academic promise prior to their pregnancies are nevertheless very responsive to school-based intervention.

The Elderly

Scope of the Issue

The population of the United States is aging. As the swell of baby boomers moves through time, the ranks of the aged are increasing. Medical advances allow people to live longer, with most women outliving men. At the beginning of the twentieth century, only 4.1 percent of the total U.S. population was elderly (Blakemore, Washington, & McNeely, 1995). Today, approximately 35 million Americans, or about 13 percent, are 65 years or older (Federal Interagency Forum on Aging-Related Statistics, 2001; Steffen, 1996). By the year 2030, that percent is expected to increase to 21.2 (Harper, 1995). The stereotype of the elderly in the United States is that of a wrinkled, incoherent person rocking in a chair in a nursing home. Obviously, this stereotype is incorrect. Most elderly, in fact, live in their own homes (Steffen, 1996) and die in their homes rather than in hospitals or in nursing homes.

This is not to say that the aging population is not without problems, however. For example, two frequent and particularly important transitions of aging are loss of health and loss of spouse (Finch, Okun, Barrera, Zautra, & Reich, 1989). Loss of spouse and significant others in an elderly person's life can cause depression and stress (Siegel & Kuykendall, 1990). In addition, declining health is exacerbated by perceived lack of control over health matters, personal barriers such as memory deficients, and societal barriers such as lack of transportation and high cost of health care (Chipperfield, 1993). Families of the elderly who provide caregiving can also find themselves under stress (Singleton, 2000), especially employed family members (Gignac, Kelloway, & Gottlieb, 1996).

The ecological situation in which the elderly find themselves also has a bearing on them. For example, married elderly are more likely to report wanting energetic lifestyles (Rapkin & Fischer, 1992). A second environmental factor involves the actual setting in which the elderly find themselves; some are relocated in terms of their living arrangements. Many elderly who have to relocate often use various strategies such as reminiscence to preserve their sense of self despite their new surroundings.

The elderly, unfortunately, have been largely ignored in the community psychology literature. Steffen (1996) reviewed articles in the *American Journal of Community Psychology* from 1988 to 1994 and found a weak emphasis on aging. Over the seven-year period, only 13 articles focused specifically on older adults.

We will concentrate here on two issues that have received much play in the literature—personal control and social support . Both are postulated to enhance the well-being of the elderly. Note, however, that there may well be many other factors that affect the well-being of the elderly (Lehr, Seiler, & Thomae, 2000).

Prevention Programs

Social Support.   A myriad of programs exist for the elderly that focus on enhancing the quality of their lives. Only a few are mentioned here. One well-examined approach to preserving the emotional well-being and sense of security of the elderly is to provide them with social support. Social support by means of informal networks of family (Tice, 1991), confidants (Lowenthal & Haven, 1968), or other social supports (Abrahams & Patterson, 1978–1979) has been reputed to increase morale, buffer the effects of loss of loved ones, and slow deterioration of health (Choi & Wodarski, 1996).

In a well-scrutinized study, Heller, Thompson, Trueba, Hogg, and Vlachos-Weber, (1991) set up telephone dyads first among professional staff people and an elderly phone companion and then between pairs of elderly. Interestingly, there were no significant differences in well-being between the phone dyads and a no-contact group. There are several explanations as to why this was so.

One postulated reason was that the lonely elderly in this study did not see their phone companions as *reliable* sources of social support. In other words, the phone companion was not deemed as necessarily being available in a time of need (Willis, 1991) nor as an enduring source of support (Schiaffino, 1991). Another reason could have been that this was too new a relationship for the phone companion to be a true confidant (Vaux, 1991). Heller and associates also used random assignment—a strange mechanism by which to find a "friend"; similarly, the phone is a peculiar context in which to make a good friend (Vaux, 1991). Given some of these criticisms, perhaps phone dyads with family members would have been more successful (Roak, 1991). Social support, therefore, does not offer a panacea for the loneliness and isolation that some elderly experience.

Enhancing the self-esteem of the elderly has been another approach in the literature. A favored approach is to encourage the elderly to feel productive. Various projects (Becker & Zarit, 1978; Blonsky, 1973; Priddy & Knisely, 1982; Ruffini & Todd, 1979) employing senior citizens as voluntary helpers, senior companions, or peer counselors report positive effects (e.g., Oman, Thoresen, & McMahon, 1999). However, most of these intervention studies used either uncontrolled demonstration projects or preselected participants who are likely to be more motivated or of higher economic and educational backgrounds than the typical senior citizen (Heller et al., 1991).

Sense of Personal Control.   Every facet of aging, such as health and cognitive functioning, involves the issue of personal control (Baltes & Baltes, 1986). Increasing the **sense of personal control** of the elderly is also a technique that has proven to produce positive results (Thompson & Spacespan, 1991), such as better mental health (Reich & Zautra, 1991). An enhanced sense of control leads to feelings of empowerment, a coveted principle of community psychology.

Langer and Rodin (1976) matched two groups of elderly in a nursing home on age, health, and other important considerations. One group was shown in detail how much control they had over their lives. They decided how to arrange their rooms, when to greet visitors, and how to spend spare time. Each of these residents was also given a plant to care for. The second group was told that their lives were mainly under staff control. For example, these elderly were also given a plant but were told the staff would take of it. Pre- and postintervention questionnaires about feelings of personal control, happiness, and activity were administered to the elderly and also completed by the staff about the elderly participants.

Almost all before-after comparisons favored the intervention group—the one with higher perceived control. Eighteen months later, Rodin and Langer (1977) conducted a follow-up. Half as many experimental participants had died as had control participants. This study demonstrates that the quality of life for the elderly can indeed be enhanced when they perceive they have control over it (Schultz & Heckhausen, 1996).

Finally, health education has the potential to have sweeping preventive effects on future generations as they age.

If it were possible to help our citizens more thoughtfully direct the course of their lives, prepare in advance for retirement, maintain appropriate health habits, develop satisfying avoca-
tional interests, and maintain a healthy self-esteem, the despair of millions of Americans
could be drastically reduced. (Lombana, 1976, p. 144)

Homelessness

The topic of homelessness was introduced in Chapter 1 when discussing the concept of
blaming the victim. Very often, when people see homeless individuals on the street, they
believe that these individuals caused their own problems (Phelan, Link, Moore, & Stueven,
1997). For example, many stereotype the homeless as drunk or mentally disabled old men
who deserve what they get—a life of misery on the streets. Marybeth Shinn's research,
which was reviewed in Chapter 1, clearly demonstrates that many of today's homeless are
victims of problems they, themselves, did *not* create, such as lack of affordable housing
(Lindsey, 1998) and other structural (societal) problems (Yeich, 1996). The issue of homelessness is further discussed here because the homeless often interface with a variety of
social and human services systems.

Scope of the Issue

The extent of the problem of homelessness is difficult to determine. For example, depending
on the method of study, the U.S. government estimates that the number of homeless ranges
anywhere from four to eight million (Department of Health and Human Services, 1998),
whereas the National Law Center on Homelessness and Poverty estimates that over 2 million men, women, and children are homeless (National Law Center on Homelessness and
Poverty, 1998). One reason for the difficulty in making accurate estimates is that the homeless are a heterogeneous group; the group includes people of all races, families with or without children, single individuals, individuals who move from temporary shelters to
homelessness and back to some type of shelter, as well as many others (National Coalition
for the Homeless, 1999). Second, estimates vary depending on the motives of the groups
doing the estimating. Dowell and Farmer (1992) contended that because the image of homelessness in a community is not good for business, community officials often underestimate
or minimize the problem. Varying estimates of homelessness can cause policy gridlock, too.
If some people view the problem as insignificant, then they will also view the problem as
not necessitating immediate nor extensive attention. However, others might urgently press
for sweeping solutions.

Who are today's homeless? The answer to this question varies, depending on which
study one examines. Morse, Calsyn, and Burger (1992) found four types of homeless individuals: an economically disadvantaged group, an alcoholic group, a mentally disordered
group (perhaps the deinstitutionalized individuals described in the preceding chapter), and
a somewhat advantaged group who nonetheless remain homeless. Mowbray, Bybee, and
Cohen (1993) also found four clusters of homeless whom they call the depressed group, the
substance abusers, the hostile-psychotics (perhaps approximating the mentally disordered
group just mentioned), and the best-functioning group (perhaps approximating the advantaged group).

Rossi (1990) has devised yet another way of classifying the homeless. He suggested that there are old homeless and new homeless. The **old homeless** are the individuals who are generally stereotyped as homeless. These are older, alcoholic men who sleep in cheap flophouses or skid-row hotels. They are "old" because they are the type of homeless who were seen on city streets after World War II. The **new homeless** are indeed truly homeless. They do not sleep in cheap hotels but rather sleep on the streets or find public buildings to escape into during inclement weather. Other typologies for classifying the homeless exist, as well (see Kuhn & Culhane, 1998).

The new homeless include many women and children. Rossi (1990) estimated that among the old homeless, women made up fewer than 5 percent of that population; today, women comprise 25 percent of the homeless population. Likewise, there are age differences between the new and old homeless, with the new homeless being much younger. The National Coalition for the Homeless (1999) estimated that children under the age of 18 accounted for 25 percent of the urban homeless population. In general, fewer elderly homeless are seen on the streets today. Rossi also suggested that today's homeless suffer a much more profound degree of economic destitution than the old homeless. Indeed, even if individuals and families receive assistance and food stamps (food vouchers), the total is still *under* the poverty level as defined by the federal government (National Coalition for the Homeless, 1999). One final difference between the old homeless and the new homeless is that the ethnic and racial composition has changed over the years. Today's homeless are more likely to be from minority groups rather than White, as was true of the old homeless.

Homeless children suffer a number of compounding problems, largely due to their homelessness. Studies have consistently shown that homeless children have elevated levels of acute and chronic health problems compared to housed children (Wright, 1987), as well as poorer nutrition (Molnar, Rath, & Klein, 1990). Homeless children are also more likely to experience developmental delays such as short attention spans, speech delays, inappropriate social interactions (Molnar, 1988), and psychological problems in the areas of anxiety, behavioral problems, and depression (Bassuk & Rosenberg, 1988). Also, achievement scores on standardized tests for homeless children are well below those of housed children (Rafferty, 1990). These children often move from school to school when they are lucky enough to be enrolled in school.

Causes of Homelessness

Studies show that homelessness is episodic, or at least is not a chronic condition for most individuals (National Coalition for the Homeless, 1999; Shinn, 1997; Sosin, Piliavin, & Westerfelt, 1990); thus, environmental situations may account for much homelessness. For instance, the rate of psychiatric hospitalization for today's homeless is as low as 4 percent when the whole family is homeless (Shinn & Weitzman, 1990; Weitzman, Knickman, & Shinn, 1990). As for the homeless mentally ill, a lack of housing may be more critical to the likelihood of their rehospitalization than is the quality of their psychiatric care (Rosenfeld, 1991). Unemployment is also a major consideration (McBride, Calsyn, Morse, Klinkenberg, & Allen, 1998). Koegel, Burnam, and Farr (1990) found that 33 percent of the homeless had been employed within the last month, and 59 percent had been employed in the last six months. Person-centered approaches such as mental disorders and unemployment are only partially useful for explaining homelessness regardless of how popular these explanations are in the mass media. Poverty is probably a better explanation than unemployment. A minimum wage worker typically needs to work 87 hours a week (two full-time jobs) to afford a two-bedroom apartment (National Coalition for the Homeless, 1999).

Shinn (1992) conducted research to expand the understanding of whether structural or person-centered variables explain homelessness. In her study, a sample of 700 randomly selected homeless families requesting shelter were compared to 524 families selected randomly from the public assistance caseload. The first group represented "the homeless" and the second "the housed poor." Only 4 percent—a small percentage—of the homeless in the sample had been previously hospitalized for mental illness. Only 8 percent of the homeless and 2 percent of the housed poor had been in a detoxification center for substance abuse. The researcher concluded that individual deficits were relatively unimportant in differentiating the homeless from the housed poor. Corroborating this finding, Morse and colleagues (1992) identified various subgroups of homeless, including an economically disadvantaged group, an alcoholic group, a mentally disabled group, and a somewhat advantaged group of homeless. They searched for differences between these four groups and found few. They concluded that many policies and services should cut across these subgroups because many of their needs are the same.

To return to Shinn's (1992) research, she found that only 37 percent of the homeless, compared to 86 percent of the poor housed families, had broken into the housing market (i.e., had been primary tenants in a place they stayed a long time). In addition, 45 percent of the homeless versus 26 percent of the housed poor reported having three or more persons per bedroom in the place they had stayed the longest. The researcher regards poor housing opportunities and crowding to be better explanations for homelessness than personal deficits. (See also Shinn & Tsemberis, 1998.)

In a five-year follow-up on homelessness, Shinn and her colleagues (1998) more recently identified that "subsidized housing is the only predictor of residential stability after shelter" (p. 1655). In other words, the research team found that once a family entered a shelter, five years later many were able to have their own residences but only with financial assistance. Thus, with newer time limits on welfare and fewer new subsidized housing units available, future homeless families may not fare as well. Zlotnick, Robertson, and Lahiff (1999), in a 15-month prospective study, also reported that subsidized housing is one of the most important factors associated with exits from homelessness.

No social problem in the United States seems to originate from a single cause. Beyond the scarcity of low-income housing and the deinstitutionalization of the mentally disabled, what else makes some families more vulnerable than others to this crisis? Weitzman and associates (1990) studied the same families as those included in Shinn (1992) and who were new entrants to homelessness during a six-month period. These researchers compared the newly homeless who were receiving public assistance with another group of individuals who had housing but were also receiving public assistance. These families were interviewed about their housing histories, social support networks, welfare and work experiences, and physical and mental health. The results indicated that homeless families do not comprise a homogeneous population; instead, there are three distinct pathways to the door of the homeless shelter.

One group of families had relatively stable housing situations but something had gone awry; for example, they had recently been evicted from housing. These families made a rapid descent into homelessness. Weitzman and colleagues suggested eviction-prevention programs and more realistic public assistance allowances to assist these families.

Other families had a slow, painful slide into homelessness. These families had typically resided with others, moved around, and experienced some of the same problems (e.g., evictions, landlord harassment, and crowding) as the families whose descent to homelessness was more rapid. However, some of these families were experiencing multiple problems such as substance abuse and domestic violence. Weitzman and colleagues (1990) recommended some counseling programs for these homeless as well as a more adequate housing supply.

A third large group of families had never had the benefit of a primary residence. For these young families, doubling up with others in an overcrowded housing situation had been an ongoing way of life. This group contained a large number of young mothers whose own parents had themselves received public assistance. These women had few resources beyond public assistance and their own families. However, the women and their small families had never really become stable, independent, or self-reliant units. These individuals lack the search skills to cope with the dramatic scarcity of low-income housing units. Weitzman and colleagues suggested giving them priority in receiving permanent housing. The researchers further suggested providing these families with day care and job training.

Many other causes of homelessness have been identified (National Coalition for the Homeless, 1999). The National Coalition for the Homeless also identifies lack of affordable health care and disability as causes of homelessness. Individuals who are struggling to pay the rent and who also have a serious illness or disability can start a downward spiral into homelessness when payment of medical bills results in lack of funds to pay rent. Domestic violence also results in homelessness. Women who have to choose between abuse and homelessness often choose homelessness. These factors do not exhaust the list of causes but help identify the myriad pathways by which individuals and families descend into homelessness. Clearly, solutions to the problem of homelessness are not simple.

Prevention Programs

A suggestion for addressing homelessness has already been reviewed—increasing the amount of affordable housing. Given that this approach takes much time and money, what else is available to address homelessness?

Providing job skills and job-relevant knowledge (e.g., the importance of meeting deadlines and respecting lines of authority) to those who want them can and does result in employment opportunities (Winch, McCarthy, & Reese, 1993).

For example, Ferrari, Billows, Jason, and Grill (1997) assessed an ingenious program that provided the homeless with job skills; not only did these skills supply the homeless with employment experience but other individuals may have benefited, as well. Specifically, 29 homeless individuals, through the Needs Foundation in Chicago, were trained as nonmedical caregivers to elderly clients with physical challenges. The researchers utilized psychometric scales to assess outcomes of the caregiving experience. Both men and women caregivers enjoyed providing care to the disabled *and* received much needed on-the-job experience. The caregivers also reported that they experienced more satisfaction than stress, which is important because caregivers can often experience burnout. Finally, the caregivers also reported that they would recommend the experience to others. Unfortunately, Ferrari and colleagues have not yet published data on the perceptions and experiences of the disabled recipients of such care.

Wenzel (1992) conducted research that demonstrates that job training and employment alone do not "cure" homelessness. She found that for persons with low levels of social support and prolonged homelessness, poor employment outcomes resulted. The combined results of all of these studies imply that multiple solutions are most appropriate; simply providing adequate and affordable housing is not the only answer to homelessness (Sosin et al., 1990).

The ultimate solutions to homelessness do not lie in the provision of temporary shelter. However, perhaps in the short run, society can improve the shelters or at least understand which shelters offer the best quality of life. Shinn, Knickman, Ward, Petrovi, and Muth (1990) examined various types of shelters for the homeless in New York City. In New York, shelters consist of "welfare hotels" (private hotels where the city rents rooms), congregate shelters (large barrack-type rooms), and shelters run by nonprofit organizations (such as churches). How was shelter quality judged in this study? The researchers determined that, first, shelters should not be expensive (i.e., they should not divert needed money from the development or construction of permanent housing). Second, shelters should provide services to help the homeless manage the trauma of homelessness and prepare to resume a normal life. Third, shelters should promote normative behavior by creating culturally normative conditions such that the shelters look like and feel like homes. Shelters should help residents preserve their dignity. In other words, they should not be filthy, regimented, and promote invasion of privacy. Shinn and colleagues found that the nonprofit organizations were doing an admirable job of enhancing the life of the homeless and that the city should continue to phase out the congregate and welfare hotel shelters.

Another solution to homelessness has been the American Psychological Association's (APA) *pro bono* program for the homeless that is being piloted in the Washington, DC, area. There are two objectives to this program. The APA wanted to provide psychologists with the opportunity to volunteer their services, and the APA wanted to provide psychologists and other professionals with a *pro bono* or volunteer service delivery model.

Shelter staff in the Washington, DC, area were contacted to determine whether they perceived a need for psychological services. Of course, they did. Volunteers were recruited to serve as consultants in the development of the project, to assist in screening processes with the homeless, and to provide peer consultation to other volunteers. The APA also developed an orientation program for the volunteer psychologists, who provide life-skills training, assessment of the mental health problems of the homeless, and psychotherapy to those who need it.

The best solution to the homeless problem in the United States, though, may be a concerted and organized federal public policy program. Charities and local governments alone cannot meet the growing needs of the homeless (Gore, 1990). One piece of legislation aimed at grappling with the homeless problem on a national level is the McKinney Act. It established an Interagency Council on Homelessness to coordinate, monitor, and improve the federal response to the problems of homelessness—in other words, to reduce duplication of effort. The act also established an Emergency Food Shelter Program National Board as well as local boards across the country to determine how program funds could best be used. Grants and demonstration programs—for example, for drug and alcohol-abuse treatment—were authorized by the act, and the Temporary Emergency Food Assistance Program was reauthorized by the act (Barak, 1991). A coherent policy of federal legislation needs to continue to pursue increased low-income housing, treatments for the mentally disabled and substance-abusing homeless, and education and job training for homeless individuals (Gore, 1990).

What have we learned by examining child maltreatment, teen pregnancy, the elderly, and the homeless? Messages for community psychologists and others cut across these groups:

- The types of individuals affected by these problems are diverse.
- There are multiple causes for each of these social problems, few of which are created by the individuals affected by the issue.
- Single solutions for these problems probably will not work; multipronged, coordinated efforts will yield better results.
- When various social service agencies are involved in interventions—whether the interventions be primary or secondary in nature—efforts need to be coordinated in order to be effective.
- Affected individuals need to participate in designing and implementing the interventions.
- Government officials, affected individuals, and social service agencies need to work together to coordinate their efforts in order to address these social issues.

SUMMARY

Social welfare or ideas and activities to promote social good have a long history in Western society. Until modern times, the three major forms of social welfare were charity/philanthropy (private assistance), public welfare (public assistance), and mutual aid (self-help). During the nineteenth century (around the time of the Industrial Revolution), two other forms of social welfare were born: social insurance (public assistance derived from taxation) and social service (public nonmaterialistic human services derived from taxation). With the exception of mutual aid, in order to receive social welfare, people must demonstrate their need, usually in the form of a low standard of living or poor economic means.

It is generally believed (i.e., stereotyped) that recipients of social welfare are lazy, despite the fact that these people might genuinely need such assistance. On the other hand, donors are perceived to be honorable people, although research indicates that willingness to help often is a function of environmental factors (e.g., people are more generous during religious seasons). These scenarios suggest that the nature of social welfare is largely a function of the ideology of the period. Social welfare in this country is no exception to the rule.

Four groups that interface regularly with human services in U.S. communities are maltreated children and their families, pregnant teens, the elderly, and the homeless.

Teen parents and others—such as people who themselves were abused children—are predicted to be at risk for committing child abuse. Providing social support, parenting and prenatal education, and links between the parents and services in the community can sometimes prevent child abuse.

The problem of pregnant adolescents is a major one; the United States leads other countries in this statistic. Many Americans, however, view this as an African American problem as well as a female problem. It is not. Programs to reach teenagers before they become sexually active include sex education. The prevailing culture does not provide good role models, however; thus, the problem persists. Community programs to provide teen parents with further education, job training, and day care can better ensure that they will not be stuck in the welfare quagmire.

The elderly sometimes interface with services in the community, too. Declining health, loss of mobility, death of loved ones, and loss of control are problems for the elderly. As is true with other groups, not all community interventions are effective. However, encouraging the elderly to volunteer as companions or peer counselors and increasing their sense of control and personal responsibility can maintain the self-esteem of the elderly and perhaps maintain their health for longer periods.

Homelessness is an increasing problem in the United States. Stereotypically, the homeless are drunk or mentally disabled old men. The new homeless, however, include many children and women, as well as previously employed and previously housed individuals. Providing more affordable housing, *pro bono* services from professionals, and better and coordinated public policies will go a long way toward solving this problem.

What has been learned from the examination of abused children, pregnant teens, the elderly, and the homeless? For one, not all interventions work equally well and no single intervention works for all groups. Not all interventions require professional help, however. Many social support and mutual help groups are organized and run by laypeople and often are free and effective. Finally, interventions need to be multifaceted; that is, they must address multiple issues and utilize multiple approaches. For example, when professionals are involved, their efforts should be combined with peer or family efforts as well as take into account ecological factors. Efforts also need to be well coordinated so as to avoid duplication or "cracks" in the system.

SCHOOLS, CHILDREN, AND COMMUNITIES

> *I touch the future. I teach.*
> —Christa McAuliffe (teacher, astronaut)

Mi nombre es Roberto. Nací en Mexico y me mude a los Estados Unidos cuando era un niño. En mi casa, solamente se hablaba español. Un día, cuando estaba en el séptimo grado, mi maestra me pidió que leyera en frente de la clase. Yo trate de leer, pero no pude reconocer algunas de las palabras en inglés. La maestra me interrumpió y me dijo que yo no sabía leer muy bien y que debía sentarome. Después, ella llamó a un niño Americano, quien leía mejor que yo. Yo me senti bastante avergonzado.

How many of you could read this passage? Imagine how frustrating textbooks, television programs, and public announcements are to individuals for whom English is a second or third language. We will restart, this time in English.

My name is Roberto. I was born in Mexico and I moved to the United States when I was a child. In my house, only Spanish was spoken. One day, when I was in the second grade, my teacher asked that I read in front of the class. I tried to read, but I was not able to recognize some of the English words. The teacher interrupted me and told me that I did not know how to read very well and to sit down. After that, she called on an American child who read better than I. I was quite embarrassed.

I had to repeat the second grade but this time with a different teacher, Miss Martinez. She had experienced much the same embarrassment when she was a child, so she was sympathetic to my situation. Her extra help inspired me to do my best. In no time, I was speaking and reading English well, almost as well as my classmates. By high school, I was a very good student. My good grades and my ability to play soccer well had endeared me to my fellow classmates enough so that they liked me. Unlike some of the other Hispanic students, I was quite popular, which made my life easier than theirs.

Today, I am in college; I am studying to be a lawyer. Actually, I don't want to be a lawyer; I want to be a legislator. I view law as the avenue to a political career. One of my goals as a legislator is to reform American schools so that all children will feel welcome and comfortable in them.

Consider for a moment how it feels to be a child whom others view as different, either because of a different skin color, a foreign-sounding name, an accent or language other than English, or the use of a wheelchair. This chapter will explore the world of schools as they relate to children and families. In a special issue about human capital, the National Behavioral Science research agenda committee of the American Psychological Society (1992) remarked, "There is no better way to invest in human capital than to improve our schools" (p. 17). The schools themselves are small communities as well as integral parts of the communities they serve. Every issue cannot possibly be covered here, but this chapter will touch on some of the more salient ones: child care, diversity in the classroom, and stressful events, such as school violence and parental divorce.

THE EARLY CHILDHOOD ENVIRONMENT

Urie Bronfenbrenner (1979, 1999) presented what he considered an unorthodox approach to child development. Bronfenbrenner formulated the ecological perspective of human development. **Development,** to Bronfenbrenner and other psychologists, usually means "a lasting change in the way in which the individual perceives and deals with the environment" (p. 3). The **ecological setting** refers to a set of nested structures, or settings, one inside the other. At the innermost level is the immediate setting in which the individual finds himself or herself, such as the home or a classroom. The next layer consists of the interrelationship between these settings, as in the links between the child's home and the school. The third level, interestingly, is the environment that the child or individual is not in but that has an effect anyway, such as the policies of the parents' places of employment that have an impact on the child (e.g., day care). All levels are interconnected rather than independent of one another. The way the individual transacts with these settings and how the individual perceives them is important in influencing the course of the individual's development. As you may already know, the ecological perspective and the transactional nature of the individual's encounters with various elements in the environment is of utmost importance in community psychology.

A concrete example might further your understanding. Suppose Johnnie is having trouble focusing his attention on his studies in the third grade. Using the individual level of analysis, his teacher might believe that Johnnie needs extra tutoring and additional assistance with his math and spelling or that Johnnie needs medication for his attention-deficit disorder. An ecological perspective would take into account other contexts, such as Johnnie's home and neighborhood or even the playground at the school. The reality might be that Johnnie's home life is distressing because his parents are divorcing. Furthermore, his father might be unemployed, which is contributing to his parents' discord and Johnnie's inattention. Perhaps what would most assist Johnnie is some social support from other children whose parents' have divorced, not extra tutoring from the teacher.

As Bronfenbrenner suggested, then, advances in understanding development require investigation in the actual environments, both immediate and remote, in which human beings live. This chapter will examine settings in which children develop, especially educational ones such as day-care centers and schools. Although some of the topics presented will be discrete for the sake of parsimony, it is important to remember that children do not enter each situation in a vacuum; they bring connections and experiences from a myriad of other contexts, regardless of their stage of development. For example, immediately following this paragraph, the topic of day care will be discussed. Research has demonstrated that the tripod of family structure (one versus two parents), the day-care structure (in-home care or day-care center), and the day-care process (content of the activities) influence a child's language development in very complex ways (DeHart, in press; Goelman, 1988). Research has demonstrated that other ecological factors such as the family environment and teacher perceptions of students predict future academic success (Seyfried, 1998). Studies generally show that in-school prevention programs have significant positive impacts on children (Durlak, 1995). Because the organization in this chapter is chronological (i.e., human developmental), early childhood care will be discussed first.

Day Care

Day care in the United States is not without controversy. Some individuals believe that day care, which means separation in early life from the parents, can be harmful to young children. Others argue that it is not *whether* care is provided but *the type and quality of care* that is provided that make a difference in the children's lives. Yet others comment that availability of *good* care at a reasonable cost is this nation's biggest problem. These and other issues will be explored here in more detail.

Necessity for Day Care

Child day care can be defined as all the ways children are cared for when they are not being cared for by the mother or guardian (NICHD, 2001). In the opening vignette, Roberto did not reveal whether his parents worked and what his early life at home was like. However, if his parents worked and he was left with a neighbor, he would have been in child day care. Child-care or day-care providers can include licensed and unlicensed centers, family members or relatives other than the parents, neighbors, or in-home sitters.

Effects of Day Care

In the 1970s, a popular question asked by parents and researchers was: "How much damage is done to infants and young children by working mothers?" (Scarr & Eisenberg, 1993). What was really being asked was whether nonmaternal care was a threat to the child. For example, if Roberto was left with a neighbor, would that affect his development differently than if his mother cared for him at home? In a summary of research on maternal employment and children's adjustment, Gottfried and Gottfried (1988) concluded that whether mothers and fathers work has no impact on their children's adjustment. Jackson (1997), however, found that child-care arrangements (or the lack thereof) affect the psychological functioning and employment success of mothers.

A second important issue, however, is what effect nonmaternal care has on the rest of the child's development: social, cognitive, language, and other abilities. Scarr and Eisenberg (1993) have warned that there is no simple answer. For example, child care includes for-profit (such as the large national chains) and not-for-profit centers (such as church-sponsored centers, family-based care, and other permutations of child care). Not only are there different types of care but there are also differences in the *quality* of care within the same category of care.

Quality is often measured by such factors as health and safety of the children, responsiveness and warmth between the staff and children, and staff turnover, among other variables (Scarr, 1998). Well-designed studies, however, can control these factors so that useful conclusions can be drawn about the effects of early child care on child development. It is also important to control for the variables of family and socioeconomic backgrounds of the children, as these alone can often explain developmental differences among children (Scarr & Eisenberg, 1993).

Scarr (1998) states that there are three reasons for the necessity of child day care. One is that the mother or both parents work. This trend is historically increasing, as demonstrated in Figure 8.1. Second, high-quality child care can enhance children's development. Third, child care has been used to intervene with economically disadvantaged and ethnic minority children to socialize them to the cultural mainstream.

High-quality care is very important to child development, but not all children in day care receive quality care. Zigler and Gilman (1998) estimated that about one-third of present U.S. child-care settings (which affect about 3 million children) are so poor as to be potentially damaging to children's development. Quality of care has been linked to cognitive and social development (Wasik, Ramey, Bryant, & Sparling, 1990; Zigler & Gilman, 1998), with high-quality care enhancing development.

What constitutes high-quality child care? Scarr (1998) has defined *high-quality care* as care by "warm, supportive adults in a safe, healthy, and stimulating environment where

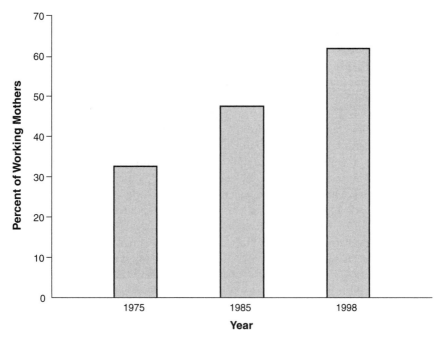

FIGURE 8.1   Percent of Working Mothers of Children under Age 6

Source: U.S. Bureau of the Census, 1999.

early education and trusting relationships combine to support individual children's physical, emotional, social and intellectual development" (p. 102). There are several other dimensions of good care. One is that the caregiver provides developmentally appropriate materials for the children; another dimension is that the child-to-staff ratio be low. Scarr has also identified other factors, including appropriate space and adequate staff training with low staff turnover.

Regulations such as the Federal Interagency Day Care Requirements (FIDCR), adopted in 1968, were intended to prevent poor child care, but experts view these regulations as inadequate. For example, these regulations do not include provisions for noncenter care (such as private family day-care homes) or children under age two or children who have disabilities. Neither do the regulations clearly delineate the responsibilities of the centers (Zigler & Goodman, 1982).

Does regulation or licensing guarantee higher-quality care? Phillips, Howes, and Whitebook (1992) examined this issue. They assessed 227 different child-care centers in five metropolitan areas in several states. The states in which the centers were located varied in terms of how stringent their child-care regulations were; however, all were subject to the FIDCR regulations. In general, the results demonstrated that centers in more stringently regulated states tended to have better staff-child ratios, staff with more child-related training, and lower staff turnover rates. Centers that complied with the regulations had significantly more age-appropriate classroom activities, less harsh, more sensitive teachers, and teachers who possessed specialized training. Interestingly, the researchers also found that nonprofit centers, such as those affiliated with churches, offered better-quality care than for-profit centers, such as the national chains. In fact, some authors believe that churches are ideal day-care facilities because they are in prime locations in most communities and have space that is not normally utilized during the week (Klein, 1992).

Fiene, Lutcovich, Johnson, and Koppel (1998) also examined the link between quality of care and professional development opportunities of the day-care center's staff. In a two-year study of 120 child day-care centers, a clear association was seen between opportunities for staff training and development and the quality of care. Centers where staff reported more opportunities for professional growth provided higher quality care.

Fortunately, there is an important study of child day care that may address multiple concerns; this study is known as the NICHD Study of Early Child Care. NICHD stands for the National Institute of Child Health and Human Development. In Phase I, this study followed the development of over 1,300 children from birth through age three at ten different sites in the United States. Phase II followed their development through first grade, while Phase III is currently studying their development in middle childhood (NICHD, 2001).

The primary purpose of the NICHD study is to examine how variations in nonmaternal care are related to children's social adjustment and cognitive and physical development. The life course approach of this study helps focus attention on the timing of events and transitions in the lives of the young children and their families. The network of researchers has attempted to obtain a sample of children that includes families from diverse geographic, economic, and ethnic backgrounds with parents who have diverse work issues. The parents, however, come from higher educational and income levels than the census data indicate are typical, and Whites are overrepresented. However, on many other variables the sample is quite representative of the U.S. population (NICHD, 2001).

The study involves observations in the home and various measures of social-emotional as well as linguistic and cognitive development. Several indices of quality of day care, such as training of the staff and child-to-staff ratios, were also utilized. Because of the study's design, the psychologists are able to follow children through a wide range of child-care experiences and to assess combinations and changes in child-care arrangements over time. For example, some infants are cared for at home in the first few months of life, then are turned over to a relative (perhaps a grandmother or an aunt) until the parents decide the child can attend day care or preschool at the age of two.

In the NICHD study, by age 36 months, 92 percent of the children had experienced some form of regular nonmaternal care. Thus, we can assume that the study of day care is a very important issue. Family and maternal income accounted for every aspect of the child's care experience, such as the age at which the child entered care, the number of hours spent in care, and type of care received. Families with the lowest income were the most likely to place infants in care before age three months (NICHD, 2001).

In early childhood, quality of nonmaternal care was best when the children were in small groups; child-to-adult ratios were low; caregivers had less authoritarian beliefs about child rearing; and the physical environments were safe, clean, and stimulating. By the time the children were older (ages 6 to 36 months), though, most care did not meet the guidelines of the American Public Health Association and the American Academy of Pediatrics. Quality, then, is an important variable in this study.

Quality of observed care was positively related to children's performance on measures of cognitive and linguistic abilities. It was also directly related to children's behavior problems, with quality care producing fewer problems. On the other hand, poor quality care was related to increased incidence of insecure infant-mother attachment, especially when the mother was relatively low in sensitivity and responsiveness to her child. Similarly, children in group care had more illnesses. Preliminary results from the second phase of the study demonstrated that quality of care continues to be associated with developmental outcomes throughout the preschool years.

Other factors also appear to play a role in outcomes. Children in *group* care demonstrated more cooperation and fewer negative interactions with their mothers than children not in group care *but* only after the second year of life. On the other hand, the number of times children changed care arrangements had little impact on outcomes for the children. In the end, despite these interesting results, total child-care arrangements had less impact on social-emotional and cognitive development than family characteristics. This last finding makes clear that early child care cannot be adequately assessed without taking into account the children's experiences in their own families. These findings, as ever, hold important implications for public policy and for families making decisions about child care.

Possible Remedies to the Day-Care Dilemma

"The question is not whether there is a child care problem but rather what can be done about it" (Winget, 1982, p. 351). The child-care literature has suggested solutions to the problem of *affordable, available, high-quality* child care for U.S. parents. Most experts call for policy changes (Phillips et al., 1992; Scarr & Eisenberg, 1993; Winget, 1982). Based on their research, Phillips and associates (1992) favor more federal intervention because state policies vary from good regulations to nonexistent or unenforced ones. However, this might be easier said than done. Despite the lobbying efforts of women's groups and child advocates, very little progress has been made in terms of policy.

What other ideas does the literature hold for improved child care? Some early childhood experts have suggested parental involvement in the child-care centers (Zigler & Turner, 1982). However, research has documented that parents actually spend a minuscule amount of time in centers, even when the centers promote parental involvement (Zigler & Turner, 1982). On the other hand, parent education about the key ingredients of quality care might help replace the weak policy and regulation system now in existence (Phillips et al., 1992). After all, parents are the consumers of the child-care delivery system in the United States; perhaps the centers, especially the for-profit ones, might be responsive to consumer demands.

Zigler and Goodman (1982) also suggested training high school students and senior citizens in child development; they would be good regular or emergency child-care workers. Switzerland has a law that no institution for the elderly can be established unless it is adjacent to and shares facilities with a day-care center, school, or some other kind of institution serving children (Bronfenbrenner, 1986).

Private industry also holds great potential for child-care improvement. Zigler and Goodman (1982) have suggested that companies can offer on-premise day care or reimbursements to employees for child-care costs. Extended maternity leave as well as paternity leave are other corporate possibilities. Such benefits are regularly provided in the European community (Scarr & Eisenberg, 1992). Finally, corporations could donate some of their profits to charitable causes such as nonprofit day-care centers (Zigler & Goodman, 1982). Abella (1991) also detailed information about **satellite learning centers** that link businesses with schools. The pupils are the children of employees and are students in kindergarten through second grade. They are taught on the grounds of private companies that share the costs with the public school systems. Chapter 12 discusses other accommodations modern organizations can make for employees and their family members.

Compensatory Education and Early Intervention

Several major historical controversies in the psychological and educational literature have focused on economically disadvantaged children or children from various ethnic or racial groups. In 1961, J. McVicker Hunt published a book, *Intelligence and Experience,* in which he likened a child's mind to a field waiting to be cultivated; the key to an IQ (intelligence quotient) harvest was proper stimulation. Hunt believed that by governing the encounters that children had with their early environments—that is, by providing children with adequate stimulus enrichment—their intellectual development could be enhanced. This "naive environmentalism" (Zigler & Muenchow, 1992) promoted a belief in the importance of early childhood education. Programs designed to assist disadvantaged children—those believed to be living in impoverished environments—came to be known as **compensatory education** or **early intervention** programs. The children most targeted for these programs were primarily from the lower socioeconomic class and included many African American, Hispanic, and other minority children.

Are compensatory education programs really beneficial to these children? For example, if Roberto had attended a preschool designed especially for Hispanic children about to enter mainstream public schools, would his early elementary education have been easier and more productive? To address this question, we will explore the best-known compensatory education program: **Head Start.**

The Economic Opportunity Act of 1964 established a variety of ways that children might benefit from social programs, one of which was Project Head Start. The goal of Head Start is to reach children between the ages of three and five from low-income families through a comprehensive preschool program. It is a total program in that it attempts to meet the children's mental, emotional, health, and educational needs.

Head Start is now the largest program providing comprehensive educational, health, and social services to young children and their families living in poverty; thus, it is an important player in the early childhood service delivery system (Buscemi, Bennett, Thomas, & DeLuca, 1996). Head Start now boasts over 16 million graduates from 1,400 or more different sites (Administration for Children and Families, 1998). Despite the impressiveness of these figures, Head Start today reaches only one in five of the eligible children (Kozol, 1990). The federal government picks up much of the cost, although under various administrations the program has fared better or worse (Zigler, 1994; Zigler & Muenchow, 1992). Although the federal government is facing major economic problems, Project Head Start has recently received some of its largest budget increases ever.

Head Start is somewhat unique among compensatory education programs. Because of some of these unique features, it approximates community psychology philosophy as outlined in Chapter 1. First, it is a nationwide program; others are local demonstration projects or at least not as broadly based. Second, Head Start was one of the first programs to demonstrate that a single approach or a single intervention is insufficient. For example, Project

Head Start is not just a preschool program. One of the revolutionary ideas of this program is to involve parents as decision makers and learners (Zigler & Muenchow, 1992). Many Head Start parents have become certified Head Start teachers; over 800,000 parents volunteer in local programs (Department of Health and Human Services, 2001). In fact, parental involvement is now fairly standard in most intervention programs for young children (Honing, 1988).

Although not meant to substitute for regular health care, Head Start was also designed to ensure that the children received health screening and follow-up treatment. Many other programs simply develop educational programs in a vacuum or provide one or two services (Zigler & Muenchow, 1992). Researchers have discovered that full-service programs result in more gains for children than partial-service programs (King & Kirschenbaum, 1990). Moreover, Project Head Start was not designed simply to enrich children's environments so as to enhance IQ. Rather, the program was developed so that children would be motivated to make the most of their lives (Zigler & Muenchow, 1992).

In terms of cost effectiveness, early intervention programs pay their way. Cost effectiveness is a measure of interest to taxpayers and legislators. Several studies indicate that society can save $4.00 to $7.00 in costs for remediation, welfare, and crime for every dollar spent on early intervention (Zigler & Muenchow, 1992). Despite all this good news, some early childhood experts believe that for very high-risk children, good preschool intervention is still not sufficient for success (Halpern, 1991).

Has Head Start been successful in achieving its lofty goals? Zigler (1994) concluded:

> The literature shows beyond a doubt that Head Start's basic concept, methodology, and goals are sound. That is, when young children receive comprehensive services, including physical and mental heath care, nutrition, and a developmentally appropriate educational program, when their parents are involved in their activities, and when their families receive needed services and support, they do become more competent socially and academically. (p. 38)

Zigler (1994), however, offered some criticisms and needed changes in the program. He admitted that the quality of service is not the same across local programs; some programs provide poor experiences for the children and their families. He also noted that most programs allow opportunities only for poor children and thus lack integration of wealthier children, a situation that does not prepare children for the real world and also results in stereotyping of the poor children. Head Start programs also need funding for children of parents who work, so that there are no gaps in the care provided (e.g., in the summer). Zigler also commented that Head Start needs to start earlier and end later such that children are given a true head start and are also assisted with the transition to public schools.

Head Start is not the only early intervention program available, but it probably is the best-known one. The High/Scope Perry Preschool program was also designed to alter the causal chain that leads from childhood poverty to school failure to subsequent adult poverty and related social problems. This program incorporates into its design developmentally appropriate learning materials based on psychological principles of development, small class sizes, staff trained in early childhood development, in-service training for staff, parental involvement, and sensitivity to the noneducational needs of the child and family. What is fairly unique about this program is that it views the child as an active, self-initiating learner. The child selects his or her own activities from among a variety of learning areas the teacher prepares (Weikart & Schweinhart, 1987).

Longitudinal research on the High/Scope Perry Preschool Project is also impressive. Follow-up research on participants in the High/Scope Perry program showed that later in life they had fewer arrests, lower overall scores for total misconduct, lower incidences of fighting and other violent behaviors, lower incidences of property damage, and fewer police contacts than controls. The participants also had better academic performance in high school and more socioeconomic success as measured by lower welfare rates and higher monthly and household earnings. A recent cost-benefit analysis of the High/Scope Perry Preschool Project indicates a savings to the public of more than seven times the initial investment per child. The savings occurred in lowered welfare assistance, fewer special education and justice system costs, savings to crime victims, and increased tax revenues from higher earnings by the participants (Parks, 2000). Therefore, the adult graduates of the program and the public both benefited from the program.

THE PUBLIC SCHOOLS

Although education law varies state by state, at the age of five or six, most children in the United States are attending public schools: elementary school first and then high school. These schools are remarkable social institutions shaped by political and social events (Sarason & Klaber, 1985), some of which are exemplified by the Civil Rights movement, the introduction of computers into schools, and the changing demographic trends such as the current high divorce rates. A few events of importance—either historical or contemporary—will be reviewed in the following passages.

Read Case in Point 8.1 on school readiness to understand the difficult transition children make from early childhood to public school. Times of transition or milestones help community psychologists predict who is at risk for developing adjustment problems (Koizumi, 2000; Warren-Sohlberg, Jason, Orosan-Weine, Lantz, & Reyes, 1998).

Desegregation, Ethnicity, and Prejudice in the Schools

Because Roberto, the young man in the opening vignette, is about 20 years old, he has probably benefited from the Civil Rights movement of the 1950s and 1960s. Or has he? It is necessary to examine the complex effects of societal prejudice as well as public policy designed to confront prejudice, discrimination, and segregation of families—in particular, the children and the schools. In fact, Seymour Sarason (1997), a leading expert on U.S. schools, called the nation's schools our "Achilles heel." He argued that the near total failure of our education reform movement has had and will continue to have consequences beyond the educational arena, one of these being racism.

The Historical Context
Perhaps in the arena of desegregation, psychologists have possibly had their greatest public influence (Oskamp, 1984). Despite the fact that amendments to the Constitution had long ago given equal protection of the laws and the right to vote to all citizens, it was not until the

CASE IN POINT 8.1
READINESS FOR SCHOOL

The concept of *readiness* has recently captured the attention of educators, the media, and policy makers (Graue, 1992). Although each school district and various teachers define *readiness* differently (Graue, 1992), it generally means that a child's developmental level is mature enough for the experience the child is about to have in school. Readiness usually means that a child about to enter kindergarten is developmentally prepared to enter kindergarten, or it can sometimes mean that when children are going to learn to read, they are ready to read. Readiness is important and has been tied to U.S. child-care issues by certain authors (Kagan, 1990).

Much of the effort to determine whether a child is developmentally ready and to assist children who do not appear to be ready has been targeted at the individual level of analysis. For example, there are many developmental tests available to detect readiness (Ellwein, Walsh, Eades, & Miller, 1991). Districts expend much money administering these tests to predict who is and is not ready for certain academic experiences (Tramontana, Hooper, & Selzer, 1988). Unfortunately, these tests have very poor predictive validity and probably should not be used to make decisions that change the whole life course of a child (Graue, 1992).

When a child does not appear to be ready, some experts suggest inducing readiness for kindergarten in the child by sending him or her to pre-kindergarten (Reynolds, 1991) or retaining the child in the same grade before promoting him or her to the next grade (Smith & Shepard, 1988). Teachers who view readiness as an individual difference, as a trait, are most likely to subscribe to retention as a solution for lack of preparedness (Smith & Shepard, 1988).

Different patterns of retention among schools suggest that each school has its own view of what

readiness is (Shepard, Graue, & Catto, 1989). In ethnographic research, Graue (1992) discovered that each community seems to adopt its own definitions and standards for readiness. Graue was a participant observer in three different classrooms in three different schools within the same school district. She also interviewed teachers and parents and examined school records to determine how each constituency and each school construed readiness. Each school community had different notions of what readiness entailed. Thus, readiness is context specific rather than specific to the child. Complicating this is that national associations attempt to define readiness and set national standards of readiness (National Association of State Boards of Education, 1988).

It seldom occurs to many educators to change the schools rather than the children and the standards for the children (Graue, 1992). Changing the schools might be just the solution to the readiness controversy because it may be that the schools are not ready for the diversity of children attending them.

Graue (1992) maintained that schools can be altered to accommodate children. For example, rather than being keepers of arbitrary curriculum standards, teachers could plan curricula that span a variety of age levels. Schools also need to engender more cooperation and collaboration between teachers of various grade levels within a school, which would make sorting children by readiness level less likely. Finally, Graue proposed comprehensive community plans for the transition between home and school, which could tie together the concerns of the home, the preschool, and the elementary school. Schools need to collaborate more with parents. Graue's participant observer study showed that not all parents have an equal opportunity to be heard about the issue of readiness.

1950s that events took place that today have had a lasting and sweeping effect on our schools.

In 1954, the Supreme Court of the United States decided the case of *Brown* v. *Board of Education of Topeka, Kansas.* In fashioning their decision, the Supreme Court justices heard major testimony from social scientists about the detrimental effects of segregation on African American pupils (see, for example, Clark & Clark, 1947). In the official rendering, the unanimous judges cited social science research as being influential in their deliberations (Levine & Perkins, 1987). The consequence of the decision was that there would no longer be a place for segregation in schools, not even for separate but equal educational facilities. Interestingly, the judges were not initially concerned with implementing their decision nor in the precise effects of desegregation on children once it was instituted.

Some school authorities scrambled to come into compliance with the ruling. The chosen method for desegregation was often "one-way busing" (Oskamp, 1984), where inner-city children were bused to the suburbs and to all-White districts. Some school systems dragged their heels and some openly defied the ruling; subsequent court-ordered desegregation plans were imposed on them. Public policy changed some discriminatory behaviors, voluntarily or involuntarily, but did it change all related behaviors? An equally important matter was whether the children were better off with this policy. Social scientists quickly became concerned with these and other issues of desegregation. How far has the United States come since the 1954 decision on the *Brown* v. *Board of Education* case?

Prejudice and Its Companions

In the opening vignette, Roberto revealed to us that he thought the other children believed he was dumb. Is this a form of prejudice?

Prejudice is an attitude (usually negative) toward the members of some group, based solely on their group membership (Baron & Byrne, 1997). If Roberto's classmates thought he was dumb because he was Hispanic, then they indeed were prejudiced. A companion to prejudice is discrimination. **Discrimination** involves what are often prejudiced actions toward particular groups based almost solely on group membership (Baron & Byrne, 1997). If Roberto's classmates refused to play with him on the playground because of his ethnic background, they would have been discriminating against him. Interestingly, studies in social psychology have demonstrated that people can be prejudiced without discriminating or can discriminate without harboring prejudices (e.g., La Piere, 1934). **Stereotypes,** a highly related concept, are beliefs that all members of certain groups share the same or common traits or characteristics (Baron & Byrne, 1997). In keeping with the same example, if Roberto's classmates classified all Hispanics as dumb, then they would have held a stereotype.

Important historical research on stereotyping in classrooms was conducted by Rosenthal and Jacobson (1968). In their study, teachers were told that perfectly normal children were either "bloomers" or "normal." Teachers were *not* told to treat these two groups differently. By the end of the study, the so-called bloomers showed dramatic improvements in classroom performance and IQ scores, probably because they had been the beneficiaries of positive prejudice. It is important to remember that all children were *randomly* assigned to the conditions of "normal" or "bloomer." This study demonstrates that teachers' labels and stereotypes of children somehow fulfill the teachers' prophecies. This phenomenon where a labeled individual fulfills someone else's forecast is called the **self-fulfilling**

prophecy. Studies have shown that teachers' expectations in a variety of classroom settings do influence student achievement and motivation (Weinstein, Soule, Collins, Cone, Mehlhorn, & Simontacchi, 1991).

Research on contemporary society indicates that people's prejudices and labels may be quite different from those of the cohort groups previous to the Civil Rights movement. Before 1950, there was more *overt* racism with open name calling, different laws for certain groups ("Negroes ride in the back of the bus"), and, in fact, mob actions against and lynchings of certain groups. In **modern prejudice** (Dovidio & Gaertner, 1998; Duffy, Olczak, & Grosch, 1993), people's attitudes are more *covert* and subtle. In other words, these subtle forms of prejudice and discrimination allow their users to conceal the hidden, negative views they really hold.

Pettigrew and Meertens (1995) offered an interesting demonstration of the existence of blatant as well as more modern forms of prejudice. They administered prejudice scales and found people who were high in blatant or overt prejudice, high in subtle or modern prejudice, or low on both types of prejudice. As predicted, participants' attitudes toward immigrants could be forecast by their scores on the prejudice scales. Those high in blatant or old-fashioned prejudice wanted to send immigrants back to their own countries. Those low in all types of prejudice wanted to take actions that would help immigrants remain in their new country and improve the rights of the immigrants. But most interestingly, those who scored high on the modern racism scale tended to reject immigrants in subtle and covert ways—for example, they were not willing to do anything to improve immigrant rights nor their own relations with the immigrants.

Prejudice, then, has not disappeared because the courts have ruled that desegregation and equal opportunity must prevail. Prejudice has just taken on a different appearance—a more subtle hue. Given that prejudice probably still pervades society, the question becomes: When children from different backgrounds are intermingled in school classrooms, what can adults do to lessen the effects of any prejudices they bring from home? Psychologists have some innovative responses to this question.

Fostering Acceptance of Diversity in the Classroom

In a famous demonstration with children called "The Eye of the Storm," teacher Jane Elliot told the dark-eyed children that they were inferior to the light-eyed children. In fact, she said they were so inferior that the light-eyed children were not to play or have contact with the dark-eyed children. The light-eyed children soon segregated, taunted, and mistreated the dark-eyed children. Elliot then reversed the roles; the light-eyed children were now the inferior ones. When Elliot debriefed the children and they discussed their feelings, the children talked about how horrible it felt to be the victims of such intense prejudice. This demonstration reveals but one means by which children in schools can be familiarized with what prejudice feels like. What other techniques are in the psychological arsenal for fostering acceptance of diversity in classrooms?

One approach to reduce prejudice is to *actively* involve children with one another. **Intergroup contact** is when two conflicting groups come together, and the contact enables them to better understand and appreciate one another (Brewer, 1999). Research demonstrates that only certain intergroup contacts enhance people's understanding and acceptance of each other (Marcus-Newhall, & Heindl, 1998).

Stuart Cook has been a leading proponent of the **contact hypothesis** for reducing prejudice. The contact hypothesis states that personal contact between people from disliked groups works to decrease the negative attitudes *but only under certain conditions*. The five conditions are:

1. The groups or individuals must be of equal status.
2. The attributes of the disliked group that become apparent during the contact must be such as to disconfirm the prevailing stereotyped beliefs about the group.
3. The contact situation must encourage, or perhaps require, a mutually independent relationship or cooperation to achieve a joint goal.
4. The contact situation must promote association of the sort that will reveal enough details about members of the disliked group to encourage seeing them as individuals rather than as persons with stereotyped group characteristics.
5. The social norms of contact must favor the concept of group equality and egalitarian intergroup association (Allport, 1954; Cook, 1985).

Several quasi-experimental and laboratory experimental studies of the intergroup contact hypothesis have been conducted and support the hypothesis (Pettigrew, 1998). Only one set of studies will be reviewed here. Wright, Aron, McLaughlin-Volpe, and Ropp (1997) examined the hypothesis that if it is known that an in-group member has a close relationship with an out-group member more positive intergroup attitudes will result. The **in-group** is the group with which one identifies, whereas the **out-group** is the group one perceives as being different from one's own group, as in racial groups to which one does *not* belong (Duffy & Atwater, 2002).

In one study, Wright and colleagues (1997) found that participants who knew an in-group member who had a friendship with an out-group member held less negative attitudes toward the out-group. In another study, competition and conflict were induced to create in- and out-groups. When in-group members discovered that their own group members had across-group friendships (that in-group members were friends with some members of the out-group), negative attitudes toward the out-group were reduced.

Elliot Aronson and his colleagues pioneered another technique called the **jigsaw classroom.** In this classroom, students initially work on a project in mastery groups. In this first type of group, students all learn the same general material, but each group learns different details about that material. The mastery groups then break into jigsaw groups such that one student from each mastery group comprises the jigsaw group. For example, if students were learning about prejudice, one mastery group would learn the definitions and examples for *prejudice, discrimination,* and *stereotypes.* A second mastery group would learn about the detrimental effects of prejudice. A third might learn about ways to reduce prejudice, and so on. In the jigsaw groups, one student from the definition group, one student from the detrimental effects group, and one from the how-to-reduce-prejudice group would come together and teach the others the appropriate module. In this way, isolated students become more central to the group, and competitive students learn to cooperate. Without everyone's interdependence and cooperation in the jigsaw group, the group cannot achieve its learning goals. Students who trip over English words are prompted and assisted by the other children; otherwise, no one can learn (Aronson, Blaney, Stephan, Sikes, & Snapp, 1978; Walker & Crogan, 1998).

In one of the first major experiments on the jigsaw technique, Blaney, Stephan, Rosenfield, Aronson, and Sikes (1977) found that liking for classmates and the school environment, self-esteem, learning from others, and school performance all improved over control students in standard classrooms. Of course, competitiveness also declined. Other research has documented that peer teaching, as utilized in the jigsaw method, improves peer liking, learning, and perceptions of the classroom climate (Slavin, 1985; Wright & Cowen, 1985). Exciting news is that positive results from cooperative strategies such as peer teaching seem to generalize to other minority children not in the immediate school environment (Miller, Brewer, & Edwards, 1985).

Since the jigsaw technique was introduced, other similar cooperative learning techniques have been developed (e.g., Slavin, 1996). What is important is that the positive results of these forms of cooperative learning have been replicated in thousands of classrooms, thus making cooperative learning "a major force within the field of public education.... [Cooperative learning] is generally accepted as one of the most effective ways of improving race relations and instruction in desegregated schools" (Aronson, Wilson, & Akert, 1999, p. 544).

Some states have experimented with **magnet schools** to reduce prejudice, where students from a variety of school districts attend because the school specializes in a particular discipline such as music or foreign languages. Interested students are thus attracted to the schools like steel to a magnet. These schools create a natural experiment on intergroup contact because students of many backgrounds can attend. Rossell (1988) compared the effectiveness of *voluntary* plans at magnet schools to *mandatory* reassignment desegregation plans. She found that magnet schools produce greater long-term interracial exposure than mandatory reassignment, probably because of what she and others have called "White flight" from the reassigned districts.

One can conclude that once classrooms are desegregated, by court order or by voluntary design, there are researched means by which the children can become more accepting and helpful to one another. But what happens to the academic performance of these students? If the courts determined that separate education was not only unequal but inferior for many economically disadvantaged students, did desegregation accelerate the academic achievement of the targeted children?

Effects of Desegregation

Some early studies of the effects of desegregation on academic achievement of minority students showed that desegregation did not improve the academic achievement of any of the affected students. For instance, Gerard and Miller's (1975) large study of the Riverside, California, system showed that minority students' marks generally fell because teachers who were initially lenient made an effort to move to a more uniform standard of grading for all students. The data showed a trend for the minority children's being less adjusted than the White children. Furthermore, sociometric ratings showed that few minority students were selected as workmates or friends. Not surprisingly, the teachers' attitudes also influenced some of these measures. The students in the classrooms of the more biased teachers showed the greatest drops in verbal achievement scores. You will recognize this as the self-fulfilling prophecy.

Other studies produced mixed results with some gains and declines in achievement, whereas still others showed only positive effects or no effects at all of desegregation. What conclusions can be made from these mixed results? First, consider that most studies are not well done. That is, many studies are not longitudinal; they do not track the long-term effects of desegregation from before the desegregation to afterward. Second, many studies are correlational in nature, thus cause and effect cannot adequately be determined. Another important element is that few of the conditions for intergroup contact, as described earlier, are met in most desegregated school settings (Cook, 1984). Finally, and very importantly, all of the studies are *reactive.* That is, the researchers wait for desegregation to occur and then examine it to declare it a success or failure. Cook (1985) suggested that this approach is bound not to support desegregation. Researchers ought to be *proactive,* according to Cook. They should be looking for innovative means to carry out school desegregation *before* it occurs so as to enhance the academic achievement of all involved students (Cook, 1985).

Because desegregation has been part of mainstream America for more than four decades now, one is able to study its long-term effects, those beyond the classroom. In a review of research on desegregated versus segregated schools and their long-term effects on assimilation of African Americans into adult life, Braddock (1985) revealed that African Americans who attended desegregated schools were more likely than those attending segregated schools to attend desegregated colleges, have more White friends and work associates, earn higher incomes, and hold higher-status jobs. Desegregation alone might not explain these results. Other processes—such as access to social networks, reduced social inertia, avoidance of stereotypical behavior, being shunned by employers, and other factors—might also account for the apparent advantages of desegregation. Furthermore, some African Americans might argue that their assimilation into mainstream U.S. culture is a disaster; it diminishes the preservation of their own, rich cultures. Regardless of the reasons, school desegregation may be the most significant example of a national-policy innovation (Braddock, 1985) with far-reaching, long-term effects.

In the fall of 1994, minority students in elementary and secondary schools totaled almost 32 percent of all enrollments (Association for Educational Communications and Technology, 1998). The number of Hispanic students historically has increased at a greater rate than any other group. Society must continue its efforts to understand the effects of diversity in the schools and to foster its acceptance. In conclusion, school desegregation and diversity in the classroom are controversial issues, but they are not going away.

The Schools and Adolescents

Despite nationwide efforts to desegregate U.S. schools and despite the best-laid plans to provide early intervention programs for targeted children, it remains true that many children isolated in the inner city continue to be economically disadvantaged. These children are usually from a racial or ethnic minority, yet they have never benefited from these programs. Inner-city children mature to adolescence still trapped in poverty. Psychologists consider inner-city adolescents most at risk for academic failure, dropping out of school, teen pregnancy, drug use, and myriad other problems that interfere with obtaining an education so that the cycle of poverty can be broken (Children's Defense Fund, 1991). As adults, they are more likely to experience life's stresses and strains (Golding, Potts, & Aneshensel, 1991).

In the interest of space, two issues will be examined here: dropping out of school and school violence. First, however, will be a discussion of the role of the school in creating some of the problems found there (Branson, 1998).

The School Climate

It is not just inner-city and minority children who have problems in school. There are a multitude of reasons middle-class students drop out, get pregnant, fail, or underachieve in school. Some of the reasons are the same as for the inner-city students. Remember also that not all minorities live in the inner city. Those in the suburbs need to be tapped for research, as well (Milburn, Gary, Booth, & Brown, 1991). A student need not be failing nor be an underachiever to experience school problems. Gifted children often become bored with or disinterested in school, too (Feldheusen, 1989; Meade, 1991).

Earlier discussion alluded to the construct of **alienation from school.** According to Bronfenbrenner (1986), *alienation* means lacking a sense of belonging, feeling cut off. *School alienation* means lacking a sense of belonging in school. This phenomenon has received much attention in the community psychology literature.

It would be easy to blame students for being alienated, for having some personality flaw that makes them young and restless. However, developmental and educational specialists have also focused on the circumstances in which the alienated child finds himself or herself. In 1983, Seymour Sarason authored *Schooling in America: Scapegoat and Salvation* in which he suggested that schools are relatively uninteresting places for both children and teachers. Sarason contended that children often exhibit more intellectual curiosity and learn faster outside of school (Sarason, 1983; Weinstein, 1990). Bronfenbrenner (1986) suggested that children under stress at home can easily feel distracted and alienated at school.

My own (Duffy) research with students in two community psychology classes reveals another interesting feature of schools. I asked two different classes of students six years apart (1985 and 1991) to record their most memorable experience from school. Out of 40 students, only 1 reported a positive academic experience, 4 reported positive nonacademic experiences, and 34 reported negative nonacademic experiences. The students mostly remembered sad or frightening incidents involving fights between students or students and teachers, fires, bombs, child abuse, and other unfortunate events. The 4 positive nonacademic experiences all pertained to championship sports teams. In other words, at least retrospectively, the salient features of schools seem to be negative and unrelated to learning. Some of the students' experiences are revealed in Case in Point 8.2.

There is little doubt that the school environment itself serves as a risk factor to children (Branson, 1998; Weinstein et al., 1991). Understanding the school and its environment is therefore important. Several scales are available to measure school climate; one well-known one is the Classroom Environment Scale by Moos (1979). The scale measures dimensions such as task orientation, order, organization, and relationships. There are discernible individual differences in student perception and behavior based on different climates (Harpin & Sandler, 1985). For example, in classes where relationships are emphasized, students report higher levels of satisfaction and friendship. In an atmosphere of order and organization, student achievement is higher (Moos, 1979).

Educational planners in the United States have turned to **alternative education** as the answer to poor school climate. Alternative education or alternate schools have components that differ from traditional schools. For example, in traditional schools, the curriculum and requirements are designed by teachers and administrators. In alternative settings, the students and perhaps their parents in consultation with teachers design the curriculum or select classes in which the student will enroll. In alternative education, the classes might be smaller

■ ■ ■ ■ ■

CASE IN POINT 8.2

STUDENTS' MEMORIES OF PUBLIC SCHOOL

As described in your reading, I (Duffy) asked students in my community psychology classes to record their most memorable experience in school. No other instructions were given. For example, I did not tell them to think of a positive or negative experience. Most incidents recalled by the students were negative and almost all pertained to nonacademic events such as fights, disagreements between teachers and students, bombs, and so on. Here are some randomly selected ones:

In tenth grade I had a chemistry teacher who enjoyed belittling students. One girl was the brunt of almost every joke. She was overweight and he called her a whale and would make comments like "Nuke the whales!" Not surprisingly, she dropped out of the class, but the joking didn't stop. One day, disgusted with my teacher, I raised my hand in the middle of one of his rampages. When he called on me, I proceeded to tell him that I thought he was the most immature, cruel, vindictive, and irresponsible teacher I'd ever met... He told me that since I felt I had to come to [this overweight girl's] rescue that he'd just pick on me. From then on, his teasing of me became nastier than it had been before.

Four honor students planted a bomb in my high school one night, attempting to blow up the school. They were all caught, tried, and sentenced. One culprit would have probably been salutato-

rian. The administration hush-hushed the incident, so I don't know why they did it or how long their sentences were.

It was the last day of school and my teacher was in the process of distributing our report cards. After he had done about three-fourths of the class, he announced that anyone he hadn't given one to had to line up at his desk and get their birthday spanking from him before they got the report card (their birthdays were in the summer, so everyone else had gotten their [spanking] during the course of the school year).... Three years later my teacher was convicted of over 100 counts of child molestation involving his step-daughter. I guess these spankings meant a lot more to him than we could have ever known.

I had a [Black] friend who got into an argument with a White kid. The White kid called [him] a Nigger at one point (big mistake). [My friend] punched the kid once, square in the nose. The kid wobbled around for a second or two before he fell unconscious on the floor. His nose had a metal plate on it for about a month. [My friend] had to pay medical expenses.... A day without a physical fight was very rare.

Schools are indeed places of learning but not just of reading, writing, and arithmetic. The whole school environment is a learning experience that can sometimes place the students at risk.

(Boyd-Zaharias, 1999; Muir, 2000–2001), and learning sometimes occurs outside a traditional classroom setting (Coffee & Pestridge, 2001).

One promising intervention currently receiving much attention in the literature is the use of mentors to assist children with their social, interpersonal, and other skills both inside and outside the school (Novotney, Mertinko, Lange, & Baker, 2000; Phillip & Hendry, 2000). A **mentor** is a caring and responsible adult role model who can make a positive and lasting impression on a child.

Solomon, Watson, Battisch, Schaps, and Delucchi (1996) designed another alternative program to provide students with the environment and experiences essential to the development of a sense of community in their schools. Students in this alternative program were compared to nonparticipating students in order to evaluate the program. Specifically, the program included cooperative rather than individual learning, interpersonal helping and other prosocial activities, active promotion of discussions about prosocial values (such as fairness), and empathy and interpersonal understanding. Results indicated that the program was successful in heightening the sense of community in the classrooms. Moreover, sense of community related positively to a number of student outcomes such as ability to manage conflicts and likelihood of helping others.

Other studies indicate that alternative education is successful in creating higher student and teacher satisfaction with the schools and often better student achievement (Arnold, Ortiz, Curry, Stowe, Goldstein, Fisher, Zelio, & Yershova, 1999; Catterall & Stern, 1986; Coffee & Pestridge, 2001; Gray & Chanoff, 1986; Trickett, McConahay, Phillips, & Ginter, 1985). What are the mechanisms by which alternative education creates these effects? Studies have identified the elements of student participation, self-direction, and empowerment (Gray & Chanoff, 1986; Matthews, 1991); innovative and relaxed atmospheres (Fraser, Williamson, & Tobin, 1987; Matthews, 1991); and empathic teachers (Taylor, 1986–1987). All of these factors are *outside* the student; they are not personality attributes of the students in the alternate settings but rather factors related to the ecology of the alternate setting.

Other Factors Related to School Adjustment

The school climate is not the only school-related risk factor for children. For example, students who transfer from one school to another and those who are moving from elementary to junior high or junior high to high school (Compas, Wagner, Slavin, & Vannatta, 1986; Koizumi 2000; Reyes, Gillock, Kobus, & Sanchez, 2000; Reyes & Jason, 1991) are also considered at risk for problems. These and a host of other factors require attention from educators if children are to adjust to various processes within the schools. Also important is the finding that poor marks in school, absence of positive coping behaviors, presence of negative coping behavior and other indicators in the early grades predict later mental health problems some 15 years later (Ialongo, Werthamer, Kellam, Brown, Wang, & Lin, 1999; Spivack & Marcus, 1987).

One of the most promising approaches to ensure healthy adjustment—not just in school but throughout life—is **cognitive problem solving** (Cowen, 1980) or other programs that teach social skills (Magee Quinn, Kavale, Mathur, Rutherford, & Forness, 1999). This type of problem solving involves generating alternative strategies to reach one's goal as well as consideration of the consequences of each alternative. Cognitive problem solving also generally includes developing specific ideas for carrying out one's chosen solution (Elias, Gara, Ubriaco, Rothbaum, Clabby, & Schuyler, 1986).

Cognitive problem solving can be used for interpersonal problems such as conflicts, school-related problems, and many other areas of concern. When used for interpersonal problems, it is called **interpersonal cognitive problem solving** (Rixon & Erwin, 1999; Shure, 1997, 1999; Shure & Spivack, 1988). Research has uncovered the fact that a significant difference between well-adjusted and maladjusted children is that the maladjusted children fail to generate and evaluate a variety of solutions for coping with a personal problem. Although this method is not without controversy (Gillespie, Durlak, & Sherman, 1982; Rickel & Burgio, 1982), training in cognitive problem solving has been used successfully as an intervention to assist children with coping with stressors. Both teachers and parents can be trained to teach children to use cognitive problem solving.

Using a pre-post design, Elias and colleagues (1986) taught elementary children inter-personal cognitive problem-solving skills and compared them to a no-treatment group upon entry into middle school. The intervention group's curriculum included training in interpersonal sensitivity, generating alternative methods to reach goals, discovering obstacles for solving problems, and creating in the children expectancies that their initiatives could result in positive resolution of their problems. The training was significantly related to reductions in the severity of a variety of middle-school stressors, such as finding one's way around a new school, establishing new peer relations, and resisting pressure to engage in certain behaviors (e.g., smoking). Work and Olsen's (1990) research also demonstrated that training in problem solving improves adjustment in children and is probably effective because of increases in empathy in the trained children. Elias and associates (1986) suggested that the reason some studies show equivocal results for cognitive problem-solving training is that they are conducted simultaneously in too many different and varied settings.

There have been well over 50 child and adolescent interventions conducted based on the premise that cognitive problem-solving skills mediate adjustment (Denham & Almeida, 1987; Shure, 1999). Although many of the studies support this strategy as competency enhancing, cognitive problem solving is not without its critics. Durlak (1983), for example, advocates task-specific rather than generic problem-solving training.

Dropping Out of School

In the opening vignette, Roberto wisely chose to stay in his school despite his early feelings of alienation from the school and from the other children. Some students, however, do not choose to stay in school; they drop out. The nationwide school dropout rate is estimated to be about 20 percent overall, but the dropout rate for minorities is different from that of Whites. Hispanics have the highest dropout rates followed by African Americans (National Center for Education Statistics, 2001). Interestingly, the overall rate of young people failing to complete high school has declined dramatically; in 1940, the dropout rate was a whopping 60 percent. The government claims that the data on declining dropout rates are solid, but others contest these findings (Fossey, 1996), claiming the government rates are artificially low.

The costs of dropping out of school are high. High school dropouts experience more unemployment during their work careers and have lower earnings than those students who complete high school or college. Young women who drop out of school are more likely to become pregnant at young ages and more likely to become single parents living in poverty (Cantelon & LeBoeuf, 1997).

Why do students drop out? Many factors have been identified besides alienation from school. School failure and behavior problems in school are two other school-related elements. Family factors such as low income or socioeconomic class (Orthner & Randolph, 1999; Pong & Ju, 2000), English as a second language, and the absence of learning materials in the home have been implicated. Students who have friends who drop out are likely to drop out, too. Some young people drop out because they would rather work and earn money. Finally, personality variables such as low self-esteem, loss of a sense of control (Reyes & Jason, 1991), and shyness (Ialongo, Westhamer, Kellam, Brown, Wang, & Lin, 1999) predict dropping out.

What can be done about the dropout problem in the United States? Many school programs are rightly aimed at preventing dropping out and are assisted by the fact that it can now be predicted who is at risk (Evans & DiBenedetto, 1990; O'Sullivan, 1990). Many of the efforts are focused on the individual student and include counseling (Baker, 1991; Downing & Harrison, 1990; Rose-Gold, 1992) or improvement of self-image or self-esteem (Muha & Cole, 1990).

Because there are *multiple causes* of dropping out (Ialongo et al., 1999; McNeal, 1997; Svec, 1987), a more ecological approach is desirable (Oxley, 2000). An ecological approach would take into account the environment (such as the characteristics of the school) as well as of the individual who is about to drop out. A more sophisticated approach is also desirable because there are so many differences among individuals in their reasons for dropping out of school. For example, Streeter and Franklin (1991) have identified differences for dropping out between middle- and lower-socioeconomic-class students. Middle-class students tend to drop out because of family problems or behavioral problems; lower-class students are more likely to drop out for academic and economic reasons. Similarly, there are school environment and school structure factors that probably influence the decisions of some adolescents to drop out. Patrikakou and Weissberg's (2000) research determined that teachers' outreach toward students who might drop out and their parents is just as important as any characteristic of the student or the family. Likewise, Vartonian and Gleason (1999) identified neighborhood variables, such as social isolation and impoverishment, that also affect students' decisions to leave school.

One of the more successful, better-known prevention programs for students at risk for dropping out is one designed by Felner (Felner, 2000; Felner, Gintner, & Primavera, 1982). The program was designed to address multiple issues, but it will be discussed here as a model program to address school dropouts. Felner and associates redefined the role of the home-room teacher to provide counseling and guidance to incoming freshmen making the transition from junior to senior high school. The homerooms were also comprised solely of program participants. The program's other component was aimed at reducing the complexity of the school; participants were in several classes together in only one wing of a large school. With these ecological changes, the program resulted in better attendance, higher grade-point averages, and more stable self-concepts compared to a nonparticipating control group.

Another program, HUGS (Help Us Guarantee Success), has been reported by Fortune, Bruce, Williams, and Jones (1991). Students who had dropped out were interviewed to assess their reasons for dropping out. Students reported dropping out because they (1) felt they were being ignored, helpless, or unwanted in school; (2) were new parents; or (3) were having academic difficulties. These three primary reasons for dropping out were addressed in the program that was designed after the interviews. The HUGS program therefore included a one-day weekly after-school teacher-student interaction period, a weekly tutor program, and a student options program with provisions for work release and child care. The program resulted in significant declines in dropout rates. In the year before HUGS was implemented, the dropout rate was 107 students out of 2,500; after implementation, only 64 of 2,500 dropped out. Notice that the HUGS program did not stop all dropping out because, as the researchers noted, there were more than the three cited reasons for dropping out. One issue related to this intervention is important to community psychologists. It appears that students did *not* participate in the design of the HUGS program; perhaps if they had been empowered and consulted, dropout rates would have been further reduced.

Although some programs were successful, others have been less successful for a variety of reasons, such as larger school size (Reyes & Jason, 1991). Other ideas are therefore needed. Organized youth sports, for example, offer untapped potential for diverting youths from all sorts of problems, including dropping out of school (Danish & Gullotta, 2000).

School Violence

In one recent year, students ages 12 through 18 were victims of about 255,000 incidents of serious violent crimes in schools. Such violence in one year resulted in the death of 105 individuals, 76 of whom were students. Some 5 percent of all twelfth-graders reported that while they were at school they had been injured with a weapon such as a knife, gun, or club during the past 12 months. Teachers of adolescent students reported 619,000 violent crimes against them (such as rape, robbery, or assault) in another recent five-year period (National Center for Education Statistics, 1998). It seems that the nation's middle and high schools are experiencing an epidemic of violence.

The United States Department of Education (1998), out of concern for this epidemic of violence, issued A Guide for Safe Schools. Other authors have echoed these same concerns (e.g., Garbarino, 2001). The guide offers warning signs for parents and teachers of potentially violent students:

- Social withdrawal
- Excessive feelings of isolation and rejection
- Low school interest and poor performance
- History of discipline problems, including aggressive behavior
- Intolerance for differences and prejudicial attitudes
- Access to drugs, alcohol, and/or firearms

Many of these warning signs appear to blame the individual student and do not address issues of student-school fit or school climate, which may inadvertently present challenges to violence-prone children (Baker, 1998a); nor do they directly address prevention. Just what can be done in the schools to reduce or prevent violence and aggression among students? Are the schools waiting for violence to occur or are the schools working with younger children (students not yet in middle or high schools) to prevent violence altogether? The national data seem to demonstrate that we are waiting too long to introduce nonviolent methods into the schools. Adolescence may be too late. At best, many high schools offer counseling after a particularly violent incident. We perhaps need to dip earlier into children's academic careers to abate this epidemic of violence. (Howard, Flora, & Griffin, 1999).

Farrell and Meyer (1997) acknowledged that violence prevention in the schools should be comprehensive in focus. They designed a school-based intervention for children in middle school to reduce violence among urban youths. Using six different middle schools, the researchers collected preintervention data on over 1,000 students. A curriculum was then implemented that was designed to prevent violence rather than just resolve conflict or treat the aftermath of violence once it occurred. The curriculum was comprised of 18 sessions focusing on building trust and respect for others, the nature of violence and various risk factors for it (such as carrying a weapon to school), anger management, values clarification, consequences of fighting, and nonviolent alternatives to fighting. Most topics were taught in health classes.

Farrell and Meyer collected a number of measures from pre- to postintervention—for example, the frequency of self-reported violent behaviors before and after the intervention. The participants were also asked to answer questions such as: "How much did you like the program?" "How important was it to you?" "How helpful would it be to your friends?" and How much fun was it?" Their results showed that participating in the program at the onset of the school year resulted in lower scores for committing violent behaviors, especially for boys. For girls, who are less likely to commit violence, and for students who came into the program late, the effects were not as substantial. The results also demonstrated a lower frequency of being threatened with a weapon by someone else. In other words, the intervention reduced the risk of a child being either a perpetrator or a victim of violence in middle school. Data still need to be gathered about the long-term effects of this program. For example, do these middle-school children carry with them their newly found skills and knowledge about nonviolence to high school?

Are there any secondary preventive interventions designed to reduce violence once it has appeared? Aber, Jones, Brown, Chaudry, and Samples (1998) utilized a program that is rapidly becoming popular across the United States: the Resolving Conflict Creatively Program (RCCP). This program incorporates several modalities of managing conflict into a single design. The overall objective of RCCP is to help young people see that they have many choices for managing interpersonal differences besides aggression and to help them develop skills to make those choices real in their own lives. The multiple components of this program are as follows:

■ The recruitment and training of teachers in a curriculum promoting conflict-resolution skills and intergroup understanding
■ The classroom instruction of children by these trained teachers in conflict resolution and intergroup understanding
■ The recruitment, training, and supervision of children as peer mediators who facilitate resolution of conflicts and understanding of differences in the classroom and elsewhere in the school

You will read more about mediators and mediation in the next chapter. For now, you should be familiar with the definition of *mediation.* Mediation utilizes a neutral third party to assist disputants in mutually resolving their conflict.

The researchers tracked developmental changes over time. Consistent with other research, they found that especially without the program, children reported significantly higher levels of hostile attributional biases, aggressive negotiation strategies, aggressive fantasies, and conduct problems over the course of the school year. Thus, the mere presence of children in our schools places them at risk for increased aggression and violence. The results of the study indicated that in classrooms where teachers took more initiative with RCCP (e.g., taught more lessons about nonviolence), the developmental trajectories of the children were different—that is, RCCP appeared to be effective for reducing fantasized and actual aggression among the children in these classrooms. The researchers have suggested, however, that future research also needs to examine classroom normative beliefs about whether aggression is acceptable. In other words, the culture of the classroom is important in that not all teachers "bought into" the RCCP concepts and thus their children showed trajectories of aggression rather than nonviolence. The children in this study were enrolled in the second to sixth grades; they were not adolescents. By adolescence, it may be too late for primary or even secondary intervention. We must reach further down into the schools to teach nonviolent strategies to resolving conflicts. Two other programs designed to reduce school violence include Safe Harbor (Nadel, Spellmann, Alvarez-Canino, Lausell-Bryant, & Landsberg, 1996) and PeaceBuilders (Embry, Flannery, Vazsonyi, Powell, & Atha, 1996).

Other ideas for reducing school violence and victimization are appearing in the literature. For example, the violence surrounding children in their own neighborhoods (Raviv, Erel, Fox, Leavitt, Raviv, Dar, Shahinfar, & Greenbaum, 2001) and in the media (Jason, Kennedy, & Brackshaw, 1999) needs to be reduced, perhaps by public policy or other changes. Likewise, when teachers make salient to their students the norms against aggression, aggressive behavior diminishes (Henry, Guerra, Huesmann, Tolan, VanAcker, & Eron, 2000).

Similarly, good after-school programs are being developed to address school violence and other problems (Danish & Gullotta, 2000). Interestingly, juveniles are at the highest risk of being victims of violence at the *end* of the school day rather than during school. In fact, after-school programs offer more promise of reducing youth violence than other proposed solutions, such as curfews (Bilchik, 1999b). Taulé-Lunblad, Galbavy, and Dowrick (2000) reported on one after-school program that puts the "cool" back into the after-school hours. The psychologists essentially turned the schools into community centers when the school day was over; the centers offer supervised activities, such as drama, art, computer technology, academic tutoring, karate, and other activities, in a safe, drug-free, healthy environment. While complete evaluative data are not yet available, preliminary results indicate an increase in students' grades for core academic subjects.

Case in Point 8.3 discusses an additional problem U.S. children face when they attend school. The high divorce rate in the United States produces many children of divorce. These children do not leave their angst at home when they cross the threshold at the school's door.

■ ■ ■ ■ ■ ▒▒

CASE IN POINT 8.3
CHILDREN OF DIVORCE

Studies of divorce have indicated that in the child's natural environment there are several factors that can moderate the effects of stress from parental divorce, such as the availability of support from other family members (Farber, Felner, & Primavera, 1985), and, to a lesser extent, peer support (Lustig, Wolchik, & Braver, 1992). In fact, there is a consistent and fairly strong negative correlation between the child's adjustment to divorce and the availability of social support, especially from other adults (Wolchik, Ruehlman, Braver, & Sandler, 1989). However, in this same research, it was discovered that social support is a complex issue. The effectiveness of support depends on the level of stress and the source of support. For example, children under high levels of stress with support from both nonfamily and family adults report fewer adjustment problems than children with no support. However, children under low levels of stress with high support from nonfamily adults were significantly more poorly adjusted than were children with no or low support.

Some interventionists prefer not to take a passive role by waiting to see whether there are tools available in the child's natural environment that can help the child cope. The schools can build and participate in interventions for children of divorce. Cowen (1996) and his colleagues at the Primary Mental Health Project, a comprehensive school-based program that promotes overall mental health in children, did just that. One aspect of the multi-faceted Primary Mental Health Project is the Children of Divorce Intervention Program (CODIP). CODIP is based on the premise that timely preventive intervention for children of divorce can offer both important short- and long-term benefits. CODIP's goals, simply stated, are to provide social support and to teach coping skills to children of divorce.

The program was initially designed for fourth- to sixth-graders. Newer versions have been tailored to younger children. CODIP is conducted in groups because children who have gone through common stressful experiences are more credible to peers than those who have not had these experiences. Developmental factors shape the group size as well as the methods used. For example, younger children have shorter attention spans and are more prone to want concrete activities than older children.

In a typical group, both a man and woman (selected from school personnel) act as leaders. They are selected because they are interested, skilled, and sensitive to the needs of the children of divorce and are trained in the CODIP program

techniques. Modules for a typical fourth- to sixth-grade group might include the following:

- Fostering a supportive group environment (e.g., the importance of confidentiality)
- Understanding changes in the family (e.g., a group discussion stimulates children to express their feelings about changes)
- Coping with change (e.g., discussing adaptive ways to cope with divorce, such as losing one's temper is not adaptive)
- Introducing a six-step procedure for solving interpersonal problems (similar to interpersonal cognitive problem-solving discussed earlier)
- Understanding and dealing with anger (e.g., how to use "I"-statements)
- Focusing on families (e.g., understanding that there are diverse family forms)

Results of program evaluations of CODIP demonstrate that the program results in gains for children's school-related competencies and their ability to ask for help when needed. Likewise, the program appears to decrease school-related problem behaviors in children of divorce. Parents also report positive improvements in their children's home adjustment; for example, parents reported that the children were less moody and anxious (Cowen, Hightower, Pedro-Carroll, Work, Wyman, & Haffey, 1996; Pedro-Carroll, 1997).

SUMMARY

The world of schools, children, families, and communities is a fascinating and complex one. Some children enter school at risk for a variety of problems, but innovative programs are available to prevent or treat the children and their families. Traditional interventions have focused mostly on deficits of the child or the family, but the more effective programs usually take into account the setting, such as the school's climate, as well as the actors in it.

Psychologists recognize how important the early childhood environment is. Children who are advantaged economically or otherwise in early childhood often have fewer problems in later life than disadvantaged children. Intervention programs for young children at risk include quality child day care and compensatory education programs, such as Project

Head Start. Research has demonstrated that children of working mothers are not disadvantaged. However, these mothers need day care if they are to stay employed. On the other hand, inner-city and some minority children are at risk for a variety of problems day care cannot adequately address. Programs designed to give them the early push they need to later succeed in school are often successful. Project Head Start is one such example. Although early research demonstrated that Head Start was not successful in increasing IQ, its proponents argue that Head Start was not designed for that purpose. Head Start programs are all-encompassing programs; for example, they include parental involvement. Studies demonstrate that children who have attended Head Start have an easier transition into elementary school, achieve at higher levels, and have had their health problems attended to as compared to children who do not enroll in such programs.

Desegregation has had an interesting effect on U.S. schools. Desegregation touches children of all ages and races. When the courts ordered the schools to desegregate, the Supreme Court justices did not envision the effects of desegregation on children nor formulate methods for fostering acceptance of diversity in schools. Those jobs fell to psychologists, who have demonstrated that desegregation often has positive effects for minority as well as White children. Various active methods for decreasing prejudice include intergroup contact—for example, the jigsaw classroom. The more passive means seem to fail.

Young children are not the only ones facing problems in this country. Adolescents often use drugs, drop out of school, or become pregnant. Most of the programs that are successful in preventing school dropout do not just try to change the at-risk individual but also make adjustments in the school environment to better accommodate the individual learner.

School violence is another concern with older students who are more at risk for committing violence. Again, appropriate programs and student involvement can enhance school safety. Children of divorce are often considered at risk for a variety of school-related as well as other problems. Once again, intervention programs for children of divorce have proven successful when they provide for appropriate changes and needed social support.

LAW, CRIME, AND THE COMMUNITY

Two men look out through the same bars;
one sees the mud, and one the stars.
—Frederick Langbridge

Mike was only 4 months old when he was adopted by a middle-class, older couple, Edna and Walt Farnsworth, who had always wanted children but were unable to bear their own. Mike's childhood was uneventful, although Mike's father, Walt, felt that his wife "doted on the boy a bit too much."

During his childhood, Mike was an average student in school. By junior high school, he seemed more interested in sports and cars than in his studies. When Mike reached puberty, he grew quickly, and by the time he was 16, he soared to 6 feet 2 inches, 210 pounds. His imposing size and apparent boredom with school inspired consternation in his teachers who were unsure how to manage Mike.

It was at this point that trouble came to the Farnsworth home. Mike realized that his father, who was a slender man of slight frame, was intimidated by him. Mike would yell at his mother and disrespect his father. Mike called his father "old man" as often as he could to embarrass Walt. Mike reasoned that his parents were older than his friends' parents.

When Mike was old enough to drive, he wanted nothing but to take his parents' car after school and drive around his small town, showing off to his friends or assessing what "action was going down" on Main Street. The town had few organized activities for its youths. He and his father argued often about the car, Mike's coming home late, and Mike's school grades.

One night, Mike had been drinking beer despite knowing that he was under age. His father was particularly angry when he smelled his son's breath. When Walt yelled at Mike, "You could have killed somebody with *my* car!" Mike struck out at his father. Walt went crashing through the drywall of their small home. Mike fled into the night, which left his poor mother, Edna, with immense worry as to what Mike would do next and great sorrow that her husband had been injured in the fracas.

This scenario was repeated again and again between Mike and Walt, who raged at both his wife and his son that he "didn't want this kid around any more." Edna tried to referee these fights between Mike and Walt but to little avail. As the conflicts escalated, Mike asserted his size and independence more and more.

Taking matters into his own hands and without consulting Edna, Walt went to the local police department to have his son arrested for "anything you can arrest him for— just get him out of my house." The police were used to such domestic squabbles and didn't feel an arrest was in order. Instead, they referred Walt Farnsworth to the probation department so that he could have Mike declared PINS (Person in Need of Supervision). The Probation Department was not surprised to see Walt; they had interviewed many parents just like him, all making the same request.

Was Mike really headed for a life of crime? Was the family at fault for the turmoil in their home? Were any community systems also to blame? For example, was the school environment so alienating that Mike's disenchantment with school was displaced onto his family? How would the justice system ordinarily manage this family dispute?

This chapter will examine the criminal justice system in the United States. We will again look at the traditional system and how it manages those individuals who interact with it. We will also address some alternative and innovative programs designed to humanize this same system. As community psychologists, we will also examine how the environment or context contributes to crime, fear of victimization, and other justice system processes.

THE TRADITIONAL JUSTICE SYSTEM

Criminal Justice Processess

Pick up any newspaper from a major city in the United States and you see splashed across its pages reports of crime—crime in the streets, conflict in homes, corruption in business and government, crime just about everywhere. Community psychologists share the average citizen's concern about "the grim reality" (Thompson & Norris, 1992) of interpersonal violence and crime in our communities. Citizens and psychologists want to know what can be done to prevent crime and how to treat the offenders so that they will not return to a life of crime. Community psychologists also share the concern that victims be assisted in their recovery from crime.

In a special edition of the *American Journal of Community Psychology,* Roesch (1988) called for increased involvement by community psychologists in criminal justice proceedings by going beyond the individual level of analysis to the examination of situational and environmental factors that contribute to criminal behavior. He called for community psychologists to help predict problematic behavior and adopt preventive measures for at-risk individuals. Yet, today, there is still little involvement by community psychologists in justice system processes or research. In fact, Biglan and Taylor (2000) argued that we have made more progress on reducing tobacco use than we have on reducing violent crime. Why? We lack both a clear, cogent, empirically based analysis and a set of organizations that effectively advocate policies and programs with regard to crime. Melton (2000) added to this emphasis by suggesting that law should be a major focus of study for those who wish to understand community life.

The justice and enforcement systems in society are multilayered. They involve the various courts (municipal, state and federal, civil and criminal, and higher and lower) as well as the judges, juries, lawyers, plaintiffs, and defendants; the prisons, jails, and corrections officers; the police, sheriffs, and other enforcement agencies; the departments of parole and probation; and the multitude of ancillary services such as legal aid societies and neighborhood justice centers.

Crime and Criminals

Did Mike commit a crime because he hit his father? Some would argue he did. Others would suggest that Mike was simply a confused or frustrated adolescent—a person in need of some counseling, but certainly not a criminal.

Just what is a crime? It is beyond the scope of this book to argue about definitions of the term *crime.* Just as laws are never perfect, definitions are never perfect. Laws that determine and therefore define *crime* change from society to society and from one historical era to the next (Hess, Markson, & Stein, 1991), making the definition of the term difficult. Nonetheless, a rudimentary definition of crime might assist you in understanding its complexity. A **crime** is an intentional act that violates the prescriptions or proscriptions of the criminal law under conditions in which no legal excuse applies and where there is a state with power to codify such laws and to enforce penalties in response to their breach (Nettler, 1980). As a means of further clarification, consider the following:

- There is no crime without laws and without a state to punish the breach of the law, the implication being that laws are political.
- There is no crime where an act that would otherwise be offensive is justified by law (such as killing another person in self-defense).
- There is no crime without intention (prosecutors must establish the purpose of the crime).
- There is no crime where the offender is deemed incompetent (as in "insanity") (Nettler, 1980).

Thus, self-defense, mental illness, the absence of a law, and so on can "save" a person from breaking the law and being labeled a criminal or offender.

Given the daily headlines about crimes and violence, just how frequent is crime in the United States? And what are the causes of crime? These difficult questions require one to venture into the area of **forensic psychology**, the study of the impact of legal phenomena on individual behavior. Inciardi (1980) reviewed the history and issues related to crime statistics. *The Uniform Crime Reports*, the first national effort at crime data collection, have been collected by the Federal Bureau of Investigation (FBI) since 1930. These statistics are based on the compilations of reported crimes of local law enforcement agencies such as city police and county sheriffs departments throughout the nation. The data, however, include only crimes *known* to the police. There is often little correspondence between the crimes that are committed in a community and the crimes that are reported. Research suggests that often the committed crimes, especially violent ones, are about twice the reported crimes in number (U.S. Department of Justice, 1991). An example of an unreported crime would be a store-keeper who catches his neighbor's son shoplifting but who admonishes the boy not to shoplift rather than face the boy's parents with the news that the son is a thief who will be prosecuted. A more extreme and unfortunate example is the case of rape; slightly more than half of the rapes that occur go unreported (Bureau of Justice Statistics, 1993). On the other hand, homicide is almost always reported to the police.

What type of crimes are occurring in the United States? Approximately 28.8 million violent and property crimes were experienced by Americans age 12 or older during 1999, according to the National Crime Victimization Survey. Overall, victimization included about 21.2 million property crimes, such as household theft; 7.4 million violent crimes, such as rape or assault; and approximately 0.2 million personal thefts, such as purse snatching (Rennison, 2000).

Gun violence represents a major threat to the health and safety of all Americans. Every day in the United States, more than 90 people die from gunshot wounds, and another 240 sustain gunshot injuries. This fatality rate is roughly equivalent to that associated with HIV/AIDS (Bilchik, 1999b). The impact of gun violence is especially pronounced for juveniles and adolescents. The firearm homicide rate for children underage 15 is 16 times higher in the United States than in 25 other industrialized countries *combined*. Incredibly, a teenager in the United States is more likely to die of a gunshot wound than from the total of all natural causes of death. Young African American males have the most elevated homicide victimization rate of any racial group. Homicides involving firearms have been the leading cause of death for them since 1969 (Bilchik, 1999b). Although there appears to have been a recent lessening of violent victimization (Maltz & Zawitz, 1998; Rennison, 2000), it is the sheer volume of violent crimes and their effects on victims and communities that have concerned government officials, citizens, and psychologists.

Perhaps the number of guns available in the United States explains part of this country's crime rate. Similar countries, such as Canada, have much lower handgun homicide rates and much tougher laws regarding handguns. Cross-national comparisons, however, can be sticky business. Unlike Canadians, Americans believe they have a constitutional right to bear arms. American gun control advocates suggest this is a misinterpretation of the Constitution (Spitzer, 1999). In the United States, it is known that guns are used far more often to commit crimes than for self-defense (Hemenway & Azrael, 2000).

Often, in a particular country, other types of homicide rates (e.g., with a knife) are high, yet one would not readily say that high rates of knife ownership caused the killing (Kleck, 1991). One needs to know more about a nation's cultural and ethnic homogeneity, history of racial conflict, rigidity and obedience to authority, subjective sense of unjust deprivation, and so on before one can make claims that gun control within a nation causes fewer handgun deaths (Kleck, 1991; Spitzer, 1999).

Many cross-national studies of gun control are also correlational (e.g., Killias, 1993), meaning that conclusions cannot be drawn about causality. If a positive correlation is found between the number of guns held by citizens and the number of homicides, it might be that (1) gun ownership levels are a *response* to already existing high violence rates or (2) gun ownership levels may serve as indicators of the population's willingness to inflict lethal violence on others (Kleck, 1991).

In the United States, Jung and Jason (1988) did find that U.S. gun control legislation has some impact, if only temporary, on firearm assaults. On the other hand, Lester and Murrell (1986) discovered that states with stricter handgun control statutes have lower suicide rates but not lower homicide rates than states with no such statues. In a similar vein, studies of owners of registered handguns reveal that gun owners are White, middle-class males, yet they are not the ones likely to die in nor cause homicides (Cook & Ludwig, 1997; Hess et al., 1991).

As concerned citizens, Americans need to understand the reasons for Black-on-Black violence. One postulated reason is the low income or poverty level of African Americans. Poverty, however, cannot be the only explanation, because other minorities (e.g., Hispanic Americans) also have low incomes, yet their homicide rates are significantly lower than that for African Americans (Stone, 1999).

Inciardi (1980) offered another explanation. He suggested that violence was not part of the cultural heritage African Americans carried from Africa; hence, violence was learned in the United States. Inciardi argued that African Americans are the only minority group that came to U.S. shores involuntarily as slaves. Additionally, they are the group that is most salient in terms of racial features. Because of this, perhaps Whites harbor more prejudice against them than any other group. Of all the minorities and powerless peoples, African Americans seem to be the most frustrated by historical circumstances and present conditions. Frustration and blocked opportunities perhaps cause Black-on-Black violence (Hess et al., 1991) as much as or more than handguns or poverty. Wheeler, Cartwright, Kagan, and

Friedman (1987) have confirmed, in part, the role played by social power in the United States. By analyzing court case data from as early as the 1870s, they concluded that the "haves" (Whites) have been coming out ahead of the "have nots" (minorities) in this country's justice system for a long time.

Community conditions have also been postulated to be the reason crime falls so heavily on some groups. In today's research, there is increasing focus on neighborhoods and communities. Differences in victimization and crimes among the various races typically disappear when researchers compare similar neighborhoods of different races. Regardless of race, when people live in neighborhoods of concentrated disadvantage or social disorder, victimization and crime rates are high (Stone, 1999). Race is also a major predictor of outcomes in the justice system. African Americans, for example, are more likely to be profiled using stereotypes, searched by police, and convicted of the alleged crime (Stone, 1999). Race is also pertinent to jury verdicts and sentences. Minorities are more likely to receive guilty verdicts and more severe sentences than Whites. As a result, 28 percent of African American men will enter state or federal prison during their lifetimes, compared to 16 percent of Hispanic males and 4.4 percent of White males (Bureau of Justice Statistics, 1998b). There are also more minorities on death row, their numbers being disproportionate to their numbers in the general population (Snell, 1996). Prejudice may indeed be the underlying cause of much criminal behavior, as well as the vehicle that drives outcome in the justice system. (Prevention of prejudiced thinking was discussed in Chapter 8.)

The Prisons

The traditional means to address violent crime is to arrest, prosecute, convict, and imprison, or **incarcerate,** the guilty individual. When Walt Farnsworth approached his local police department in the opening vignette, he had this process in mind. He wanted his son arrested, taken out of the home, and removed from him and the rest of society. At the least, Walt wanted Mike declared as a **person in need of supervision (PINS).** Do these procedures remedy the crime situation in the country? The skewed results of these processes for African Americans have already been presented; the focus now will be broader data to answer this question.

Of the total adult population in the United States, 1 in every 150 (or 1.8 million) was incarcerated at midyear 1998 (Community Policing Consortium, 1999b). The incarceration rate has more than tripled since 1980 largely because of drug-related crimes, such as use of illicit drugs (Bureau of Justice Statistics, 2001). An even larger number (6.3 million or 3.1 percent of all adults) is under some other type of justice system supervision in the community (Bureau of Justice Statistics, 2001). One community alternative in which the individual is supervised by the justice system in lieu of incarceration is **probation**; another alternative is **parole**, which is the early release of an inmate before the sentence expires. Figure 9.1 depicts the increase in the number of adults under the care or custody of a corrections agency.

The philosophy of incarceration and legal supervision is generally retribution, not rehabilitation. **Retribution** in the legal system is supposed to mean repayment for the crime, but it translates in reality to punishment for the crime. If anyone is repaid, it is usually not the victim. Indeed, the victim is the only person who has no official role in the process; the victim need not even appear at the trial (Forer, 1980). The "state" is the entity that adminis-

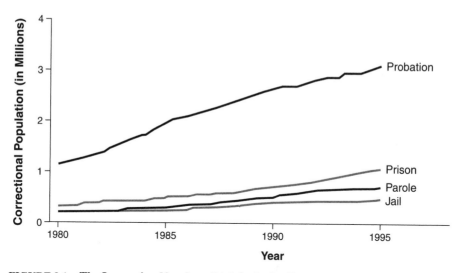

FIGURE 9.1   The Increasing Number of Adults in the Correctional Population

Source: Bureau of Justice Statistics Correctional Surveys (The National Probation Data Survey, National Prisoner Statistics, Survey of Jails, and The National Parole Data Survey) as presented in *Correctional Populations in the United States, 1996* and *Prisoners in 1999.*

ters the punishment and receives the remuneration, if any. For instance, if an individual is found guilty and is fined, the fine does not go to the victim but rather to the state. If the guilty party is sent to prison, the state decides the sentence and the type of prison. In the past, the victim rarely got to speak out about any of these issues.

Does this retributional approach work? That is, is the convicted person reformed? Does he or she return to a better life or **recidivate** (return to) a life of crime? Of the 108,580 persons released from prisons in 11 states in 1993, an estimated 62.5 percent were rearrested for a felony or serious misdemeanor within three years, 46.8 percent were reconvicted, and 41.4 percent returned to prison or jail (Bureau of Justice Statistics, 1998b). According to these statistics, retribution does not seem to work.

A classic study in psychology highlights what occurs in prisons that makes reform unlikely. Philip Zimbardo and colleagues (Haney, Banks, & Zimbardo, 1973) obtained volunteers to act either as prisoners or guards in a mock prison. Subjects were all mentally healthy before the study began and were randomly assigned to their roles. The researchers told the guards to do only what was necessary to keep order. The prisoners were all "arrested" unexpectedly at their homes and driven to the mock prison by real police officers. The prisoners were stripped, searched, dressed in hospital-style gowns, and given identification numbers by the guards. Within a few days of assuming their roles, the guards became abusive of the prisoners. They harassed the prisoners, forced them into crowded cells, awakened them in the night, forced them into frequent countdowns, and subjected them to hard labor and solitary confinement. Conditions in the mock prison became so brutal, the prisoners so depressed, and the guards so involved in their roles that Zimbardo and his colleagues prematurely ended the study. The prison experience, even for these "normal" men, proved overwhelming.

Inmates today often live in overcrowded conditions. This overcrowding has led to more and more individuals living under community supervision, which may be unsettling to community citizens (see Figure 9.1). Additionally, HIV is present in our prisons and the rates of this virus and hepatitis care growing rapidly (Community Policy Consortium, 1999b).

Furthermore inmate-to-inmate violence and a prison culture not conducive to successful and productive return to mainstream society are problems with the prison and jail system. In fact, one set of justice experts wrote that local jails serve only to brutalize and embitter men, further preventing them from returning to a useful role in society (Allen & Simonsen, 1992). Perhaps had Walter Farnsworth known the state of the corrections system, he would not have jumped so quickly at the notion of having his adopted son arrested.

Courts have ruled that the prison system must be restructured (*Ruiz* v. *Estelle*), but this restructuring has sometimes escalated inmate-inmate and inmate-guard violence (Marquart & Crouch, 1985). Similarly, inmate lawsuits over the crowded conditions in prisons have led to many inmates' early release, which sometimes results in higher recidivism rates and return to the crowded prisons (Kelly & Ekland-Olson, 1991). Although legal decrees to change total institutions (loosely called *institutional laws*) do exist, there is concern that the decrees will not translate readily into *real* institutional change (Haney & Pettigrew, 1986). In the meantime, the growth in the number of prisoners continues to exceed the growth in prison space, which leads only to more overcrowding.

Victims and Fear of Being Victimized

Recall that in 1999, U.S. citizens experienced approximately 28.8 million crimes (Rennison, 2000). Of households surveyed in 1995 that reported crime as a neighborhood problem, 44 percent said the problem was so objectionable that they wished to move (DeFrances & Smith, 1998). This latter statistic demonstrates that crime is not just the police's or the victims' problem, but it is a problem belonging to the community, as well. Case in Point 9.1 offers an example of what a community can do about crime.

Community psychologists are interested both in fear of crime and in actual victimization (Thompson & Norris, 1992). Those who are the most fearful are sometimes the least likely to be victimized—a phenomenon called the **fear-victimization paradox.** Not all research supports the inverse relationship between fear and actual victimization (Mawby, 1986; Taylor & Shumaker, 1990; Thompson & Norris, 1992), but the phenomenon is an interesting one. Discussed here are data that support the paradox.

Young men are the most likely to be victimized yet the least afraid of violent crime. Conversely, elderly women are most fearful yet least likely to be victimized (Mawby, 1986; Perkins & Taylor, 1996; Rountree, 1998; U.S. Department of Justice, 1988). Young women also fear crime more than young men but are less likely to be victimized than young men (Perkins, 1997; Roll & Habemeier, 1991). Actual victim or not, the cost of fear and suffering to potential or real victims is enormous. Thompson and Norris (1992) found that victims of violent crimes, especially those of low status, suffer pervasive consequences of the crime, including alienation, fear of crime, avoidance, and other behaviors.

Why do some individuals fear crime even if they are not likely to be victimized? For one, people often perceive urban environments as dangerous (Glaberson, 1990; Wanders-

CASE IN POINT 9.1
THE DEXTER HOUSE

The Dexter House project was initiated in Bend, Oregon, to improve a local apartment complex that was being visited frequently by law enforcement, children's services, and other social service agencies.

The Bend Police Department provided training so the landlord and tenants could recognize and reduce criminal activity in the complex. Community-service crews built a playground on the property for the tenants' children. Several community agencies combined financial resources to rent space in the building for a community resource center. The center is used as an outpost for Bend police and various social service agencies. The center also contains a classroom for parenting classes and for a homework club.

The tenants formed a cooperative day-care center to allow unemployed tenants to attend job search/job skills classes and to provide day care for the tenants.

By the end of the first year, police calls to this complex were reduced by over 50 percent. The majority of calls are now *from* the tenants themselves rather than *about* the tenants (Community Policing Consortium, 1999a).

man & Nation, 1998). City residents with the greatest fear are usually dissatisfied with their neighborhoods or are mistrusting of other residents. When an area contains abandoned buildings, vandalism, graffiti, litter, idle teenagers, and other signs of "incivilities" (Taylor & Shumaker, 1990), its residents are more fearful because these signs suggest deterioration of the social controls (Lewis & Salem, 1981) or social disorder (Ross & Jang, 2000) on which their safety depends. Other research demonstrates that adverse neighborhood conditions, such as poverty, also increase the risk of children's emotional and behavioral problems above and beyond genetic predispositions (Caspi, Taylor, Moffitt, & Plomin, 2000). Other factors, such as population size of the city, (Baron & Byrne, 1994) and desirability of the city as a place of residence (Levine, Miyake, & Lee, 1989), are not necessarily related to true crime rates.

Perkins and Taylor (1996) developed three methods for assessing community disorder and found them to be equally valid. One method simply used content analysis of newspaper articles on crime. Another method was to survey residents of various neighborhoods about their perceptions of crime. The third method utilized the Block Environmental Inventory (Perkins, Meeks, & Taylor, 1992), which employs raters who walk the neighborhood and inventory various physical and social characteristics such as abandoned cars, activities of the residents, litter, and so on. Using these techniques, Perkins and Taylor found that such assessors can be used to predict fear of crime. They were also able to demonstrate the importance of community context. For example, the researchers found that women with more men as neighbors reported higher—not lower—fear of crime. They also discovered that physical disorder—such as the presence of litter, graffiti, and dilapidation—may more likely induce feelings of vulnerability than presence of social disorder such as teenagers "hanging out."

As already mentioned, the fear of victimization and actual victimization is not always supported by empirical research. Taylor and Shumaker (1990) offered an interesting explanation for why there is only a marginal link between fear and likelihood of being victimized in a crime. They suggested that individuals in high-crime areas become desensitized to the probability of crime. This desensitization is adaptive in that losing the fear of crime perhaps lowers one's stress level. Actual victims of crime also respond adaptively to fear of further crime; they sometimes express less fear than nonvictims, much as if the original crime experience inoculates them from more fear. Taylor and Shumaker offered data from research on natural disaster victims that support their contentions that a disaster inoculates and desensitizes the victims in the future.

Taylor and Shumaker (1990) suggested that their heuristic of crime as a natural disaster holds important policy ramifications. For one, in high-crime areas, individualized crime-prevention strategies may merely serve to continually resensitize and therefore distress the residents. A better approach, they have advised, might be to adopt a social problems orientation. That is, treat high-risk neighborhoods by finding global solutions to social problems such as unemployment and lack of recreational facilities for youth that might otherwise contribute to crime. On the other hand, in low-crime communities where individuals need to be somewhat sensitized to crime, an individualized orientation to crime prevention (adding security systems or learning self-defense) might be more appropriate. In sum, Taylor and Shumaker recommended that not all crime-prevention programs are equally good for all neighborhoods. They and other community psychologists (Norris & Kaniasty, 1992) have recommended policies that create a "fit" between the neighborhoods, the residents, and the programs. This is especially true because citizen-initiated preventions on their own appear highly inadequate, according to Taylor and Shumaker.

Aside from fear of crime, there are other concerns about victims. Victims often do not know their rights; because of this, many victims' assistance programs have opened in the United States. There are nearly 3,000 such organizations today (U.S. Department of Justice, 1995), but today only a fraction of crime victims receive much needed services (Turman, 2001). Victim assistance can include crisis intervention, counseling, emergency transportation to court, and support and advocacy during the justice process. Because of fairly new public policy, victims in most states now have the right of notification of all court proceedings; the right to participate in proceedings; the right to be reasonably protected from the accused, the right to have input at sentencing; and the right to information about the conviction, imprisonment, and release of the offender (U.S. Department of Justice, 1995).

Enforcement Agencies

Some see the police as peace officers, keeping communities harmonious and free of crime. Perhaps this attitude led Walt Farnsworth to the police when the conflict with his son, Mike, escalated. Others see the police as dishonest and unethical, especially if the perceiver is a member of a minority (Ackerman, Anderson, Jensen, Ludwig, Montero, Plante, & Yanez, 2001). Regardless of one's views of the police, interesting research has demonstrated how difficult the job of policing communities can be. In fact, there is mounting interest in police burnout and stress (Anshel, 2000; Goodman, 1990).

Why is the career of an enforcement officer so difficult? One reason is that the police force and the community's citizens hold different views of the role of the officers. New police recruits often maintain a serve-and-protect orientation toward the community, but after training, their attitudes often shift toward one of remoteness from the community. In fact, police officers increasingly see themselves as hampered by community attitudes and constraints (Ellis, 1991) and as holding differing views from the community as to which policing style is effective (Alpert & Dunham, 1986).

The police force and citizens also hold different views as to which community incidents ought to involve the police. Police are often called by citizens for public nuisance offenses (e.g., loud noise or drunkenness), traffic accidents, illegally parked vehicles, and investigation of suspicious persons (Nishimura & Suzuki, 1986)—not very glamorous tasks and surely not the exciting roles portrayed in televised, fictional dramas about the police. The police are also likely to be called to intervene in family conflicts—a role for which they need more training—which can sometimes lead to assault on the officer if managed ineffectively (Buchanon & Chasnoff, 1986). Another frequent role of the police is to intervene in psychiatric crises; that is, the police are asked to intercede in a mental health crisis, make a quick evaluation, and decide whether to utilize placement in a hospital or jail if the person is a danger to self or others. Police officers do not relish this job and are often required to make quick mental health decisions without much training in mental health issues (Borum, 2000; Cordner, 2000).

A primary question about policing is whether active enforcement and a police presence in a community affect the crime rate. Sampson and Cohen (1988) examined effects of proactive policing in 171 U.S. cities. The overall results suggest that there is an inverse effect of policing on robbery rates. In other words, the larger the police presence, the lower the robbery rates. In another study, Watson (1986) examined the effects of awareness of increased police enforcement as a general deterrent in noncompliance with seat belt laws. Using a field experiment and media campaign, Watson found that the increased threat of legal punishment reduced by one-half the number of noncompliers. Salmi, Voeten, and Keskinen (2000) found that seeing police on foot patrol rather than in cars increases police visibility as well as improving the relationship between the police and the public. The threat of police enforcement, then, is sometimes effective in reducing crime, but is it the only way or the best way?

Community psychologists, of course, believe that crime prevention is better than arrest and prosecution after the fact. The following section will examine programs designed by community psychologists and others interested in addressing the diverse needs of the citizens, victims, offenders, and professionals involved in the criminal justice system.

ADDRESSING DIVERSE JUSTICE SYSTEM NEEDS WITH COMMUNITY PSYCHOLOGY

Preventive Measures

Predicting At-Risk Behavior

Was there anything in Mike Farnsworth's background that would have helped someone predict that he would turn into an irascible and difficult adolescent? Perhaps his adoption, being placed with older parents, his large size, school alienation, and other factors contributed to his family difficulties. This section will examine predictors of criminal and violent behavior.

Can psychologists and other professionals in the justice system predict *better* than lay persons which individuals are at risk for breaking the law or committing violence? If psychologists are good forecasters, then they ought to be able to prevent at-risk individuals from fulfilling their prophecies. Is it possible to predict who those individuals at risk are? The answer is "yes" to some extent, although no prediction is ever 100 percent accurate.

Summarizing research results, the federal Office of Juvenile Justice and Delinquency Prevention (Morley, Rossman, Kopczynski, Buck, & Gouvis, 2000; Office of Juvenile Justice and Delinquency Prevention, 2001; Wilson, 2000) has provided the following list of risk factors. Keep in mind that there are multiple pathways to delinquency and crime. Not all children with these risk factors become criminals nor do all offenders experience these risks. Likewise, while multiple risk factors increase the likelihood of problem behavior, no one individual is likely to be exposed to all of these:

COMMUNITY RISK FACTORS
- Availability of drugs and firearms
- Community laws/norms favorable to drug use, firearms, gangs, street violence, and crimes
- Media portrayals of violence
- Life transitions and mobility (e.g., the family moving several times)
- Low attachment to neighborhoods
- Community disorganization
- Extreme economic deprivation or poverty

FAMILY RISK FACTORS
- Family history of problem behaviors
- Family management problems (e.g., failure to set rules; severe punishment)
- Family conflict and violence
- Favorable parental attitudes toward and involvement in the problem behavior

SCHOOL-RELATED RISK FACTORS
- Early and persistent antisocial behavior
- Academic failure beginning in elementary school
- Lack of commitment to school

INDIVIDUAL RISK FACTORS
- Alienation and rebelliousness
- Friends who engage in a problem behavior
- Favorable attitudes toward the problem behavior
- Early initiation of the problem behavior
- Constitutional factors (e.g., attention deficit disorder)
- Cruelty to animals
- Inability to get along with others
- Repeated victimization (e.g., peer bullying or child abuse)

Let us examine one of these factors—exposure to violence—in more detail for a better understanding of the complexity of these issues. In another chapter, we discuss the frequency and causes of child maltreatment. But what are the consequences? Child maltreatment, especially physical or sexual abuse, is linked to risk for delinquency, crime, and violence. In fact, being abused or neglected as a child increases the likelihood of arrest as a juvenile by 53 percent and of arrest for a violent crime as an adult by 38 percent. On average, abused and neglected children begin committing crimes at younger ages. They also commit nearly twice as many offenses as nonabused children and are arrested more frequently (Wilson, 2000).

Children are exposed to violence in other ways besides direct maltreatment. Millions of children witness other violence. Police around the country report that in domestic violence situations as many as half a million children are probably exposed to the violence against their caretakers each year. There is also an overlap of 30 to 60 percent between violence against children and violence against women in the same families (Wilson, 2000).

In one study at a Boston hospital, one out of every ten children treated at a primary care clinic had witnessed a shooting or stabbing before the age of six. Almost all of the children had been exposed to multiple forms of violence, and half had been exposed to violence in the past month. Half of the children witnessed the violence elsewhere in the community rather than at home (Taylor, Zuckerman, Harik, & Groves, 1994).

Additionally, a 1992 study (Huston, Donnerstine, Fairchild, Feshbach, Katz, Murray, Rubinstein, Wilcox, & Zuckerman, 1992) indicates that before a child turns 18, he or she will have witnessed more than 200,000 acts of violence on television, including 16,000 murders. It is highly likely that the numbers have increased since then (Wilson, 2000). The media can be used, however, for promoting prosocial behavior; in that respect, prosocial messages may indeed have greater effects on behavior than antisocial messages (Friedlander, 1993).

While young people (especially teenagers) make up about 18 percent of all those arrested, they represent about 25 percent of all crime victims. Thus, children are more likely to be subjected to violence than to create it. Certain children are particularly likely to be crime victims, including the shy, lonely, compliant, or emotionally disturbed children or those with disabilities (Wilson, 2000).

The consequences of these statistics for children often are mental health problems, educational difficulties, substance abuse, employment problems, and delinquency. In fact, delinquency is likely to co-occur with other problem behaviors, such as substance abuse (Huizinga, Loeber, Thornberry, & Cothern, 2000). Posttraumatic stress disorder also affects about 2 million adolescents; this condition is characterized by depression, anxiety, flashbacks, nightmares, and other psychological and behavioral symptoms (Wilson, 2000). Some children fortunately have protective factors, such as application of consistent standards for prosocial behavior within both the community and the family, strong bonds with their families or other adults, family stability, low-risk peers, opportunities for some meaningful involvement in prosocial activities, and rewards for positive behaviors (Browning & Huizinga, 1999; Morley, Rossman, Kopczynski, Buck, & Gouvis, 2000).

Although the emphasis on prediction of delinquency is on males, females can also be delinquent. In fact, the number of female delinquents sadly has increased (Bilchik, 1999a;

Scahill, 2000). Research shows that most female delinquents have experienced some type of childhood trauma, such as sexual abuse. Female delinquency might really be a sign of disclosure that victimization (e.g., sexual molestation) is occurring (Bowers, 1990). All of these studies bring one to the conclusion that people *can* forecast who is at risk for breaking the law. Community psychologists also need to try to be able to predict group behavior better, too. In the meantime, the next question logically becomes: Once these at-risk individuals have been discovered, what can one do to intercede in their lives to prevent misconduct?

Prevention with At-Risk Individuals

Given the list of risk factors above, you can probably guess some of the suggested methods for reducing risk for violence and crime. Removing violence from the media might go a long way toward changing the cultural norms for violence. Similarly, the nurse home visitation program developed by David Olds and his colleagues (see Chapter 7) is also helpful. Let us here examine two other programs designed to intervene with at-risk youths.

Early studies on resiliency in children suggest that at-risk youth who are involved with at least one caring adult are more likely to withstand a range of negative influences, such as poverty, family conflict, impoverished neighborhoods, and so forth. **Resiliency** can be defined as the capacity of those who are at risk to overcome those risks and avoid long-term negative outcomes (Bilchik, 1998). One factor frequently cited as a predictor of a child's resilience is a close bond with a caregiver or other adult, such as a coach, teacher, neighbor, or clergy—in other words, a **mentor**. Mentoring can be informal, such as when a neighbor has frequent, unstructured contacts with a child over a period of time; or mentoring can be formalized in a mentoring program. For children who do not have a naturally occurring mentoring network, a formal mentor can supply the extra attention, affection, supervision, and prosocial role modeling that is not always available in other environments (Bilchik, 1998). Mentors play various roles, such as tutoring for school subjects, attending or participating in recreational activities with the child, and talking to the child about various issues.

One of the best-known and oldest mentoring programs is Big Brother/Big Sister. This program primarily connects middle-class adults with disadvantaged youths. Another federally sponsored program is **JUMP** (or Juvenile Mentoring Program). In both programs, mentors are selected, trained, and matched to children (often by race and/or gender). The mission of such mentoring programs is usually to prevent delinquency and/or improve school performance by providing a caring adult role model. JUMP also involves coordination of community resources (referrals to human service agencies in the community), the schools, and the families, although there is variation from program to program (Bilchik, 1998).

While there is little research on mentoring, the early data are promising. Tierney, Grossman, and Resch (1995) compared data from mentored youths in the Big Brother/Big Sister Program to youths on a waiting list. At the end of the 18-month study period, several positive results were documented for the mentored youths. Mentored youth were less likely to use drugs and alcohol or initiate use, more likely to attend school (missing half as many days as the wait-list group), and less likely to report hitting someone.

Some preliminary data are also available for JUMP (Bilchik, 1998). Both youths and mentors responded positively on a survey about the mentoring experience with youths being more positive than their mentors. When mentors and youths were asked whether mentoring improved or prevented problems, they generally responded "yes" to varying degrees. Adults and children reported that the mentored child was getting better grades; attending classes; staying away from alcohol, drugs, gangs, knives, or guns; avoiding friends who start trouble; and getting along better with their families. Mentoring, then, holds great promise for reducing the risk of delinquent behavior.

A very different program is SHIELD, or Strategic Home Intervention and Early Leadership Development program (Wyrick, 2000). SHIELD uses seasoned police officers trained to recognize at-risk youths. The unique position of law enforcement personnel allows them to have much contact with at-risk youths. Examples of such youths are those who have witnessed domestic violence, who are involved in families committing crimes, or who themselves are crime victims. During routine calls, the officer fills out a report that contains a notation for a SHIELD referral. A trained resource person, using a standardized rating form as well as other information, such as the incident report, then assesses whether the youth is indeed at risk. If the child is deemed at risk, the officer refers the case to the Youth and Family Resource Team, comprised of school personnel, a specialist in substance abuse, counseling staff, a social worker, a recreation specialist, and others. This multidisciplinary team develops and recommends an intervention plan for the youth. SHIELD relies on community programs already in place. When the plan is in place, the team monitors the child's progress every three weeks. In the early stages of the SHIELD program, cracks in community services were discovered and addressed. Early data on the outcome of SHIELD demonstrate that it is an effective referral program. Data are still needed on whether the program definitively reduces delinquency.

Designing the Environment to Prevent Crime

The issue of how the environment contributes to perceptions that an individual is likely to be the victim of crime needs to be examined further. **Environmental psychologists**—those who study the effect of the environment on behavior—have much to offer community psychologists in terms of recommendations for arranging the environment so that crime is less likely to occur.

Do characteristics of the environment influence crime? Research suggests the answer is yes (Robinson, 2000). Traditional approaches to crime deterrence in various environments would include installing burglar alarms, motion sensors, and other devices designed to catch someone in the act of breaking the law. However, research on environments proposes that built environments can incorporate safety features that deter or prevent crime. For example, D'Alessio and Stolzenberg (1990) found that the location in the neighborhood, the parking lot size, and the number of hours convenience stores were open determined whether the stores were robbed. The researchers suggested that changes along these dimensions might prevent robberies at stores built in the future. For example, stores with large parking lots were robbed more often. Smaller lots for future stores might deter robbers.

Levine, Wachs, and Shirazi (1986) studied high- and low-crime bus stops and found that the particularly dangerous stops shared common environmental features. For example, crime was higher at bus stops where those waiting mingled with passersby. Levine and associates recommended that locational and environmental information should be used when planning the development of future bus stops in order to reduce crime. For instance, plexiglass shelters that shield those waiting for the bus from passersby might reduce certain crimes.

With regard to residences, MacDonald and Gifford (1989) asked 43 individuals arrested for breaking and entering what cues various homes possessed that would prohibit them from being burglarized. Houses that were easily surveillable were rated as least vulnerable, whereas houses with frequent *symbolic* barriers (e.g., door decorations) increased vulnerability because the barriers communicate both the value of and the availability of high-quality care for the house. Similarly, Riga and Morganti (1992) found that owner-occupied homes, compared to rental homes, had more *actual* barriers (e.g., fences) that help prevent crime as well as signify an effort to exert control over the environment (Altman, Wohlwill, & Werner, 1985). Finally, Schweitzer, Kim, and Mackin (1999) found that crime is higher when residents have front porches and shared driveways.

In summary, violence and crime tend to be magnified in certain environments. Individual characteristics alone do not always account for crime. Attending to environments and reducing problematic environmental characteristics could perhaps reduce crime and violence in society.

Reducing the Fear of Crime

We have already discussed that many individuals harbor fear about being victimized by crime, whether they are potential or actual victims. These fears create stress in the individuals. Community and other psychologists have developed methods by which these sometimes unrealistic fears can be addressed.

Taylor and Shumaker (1990) stated that responses to hazards, real or imagined, include protection of the self or property, avoidance of dangerous situations, and joining collective anticrime efforts. Although private security measures such as burglar alarms have increased in number, these devices are not affordable by everyone and perhaps only serve to remind people of crime potential. Thus, community citizens must turn to other strategies. One such example is the development of **neighborhood crime watches** (National Crime Prevention Council, 1989). In neighborhood crime watches, neighbors are on active alert for suspicious activity or actual break-ins to each other's homes (Bennett, 1989). Fear of crime is one of the factors that seems to differentiate neighbors who do or do not join watches. Certain environmental factors also predict who will and will not join neighborhood watches as well as other neighborhood associations (Perkins, Florin, Rich, Wandersman, & Chavis, 1990; Sampson, Raudenbush, & Earls, 1997). Crime watches as collaborative activities among neighbors help build a sense of community (Levine, 1986), and conversely, a sense of community is the most important variable related to lower fear of crime (Schweitzer, Kim, & Mackin, 1999).

Other community scientists have also recommended actual fear-reduction programs. A police presence is often used to reduce fear of crime as well as actual crime in neighborhoods, but such actions have not been shown to actually reduce fear (Bennett, 1991). On the other hand, programs that empower citizens to take control of preventive and intervention measures do seem to reduce fear. In one program, Burke and Hayes (1986) taught "senior security" to elderly citizens. Participants learned practical self-protection methods and awareness strategies by means of films, lectures, and discussions. In a related program, Burke and Hayes taught seniors to counsel other senior citizens who had been victimized by crime. Participants in these programs reported better knowledge of community services as well as an increase in problem-solving abilities designed to reduce their fear of victimization.

Citizen Involvement in Police Matters

The discrepancies between police attitudes and community attitudes about how the police should serve their communities has already been reviewed. Programs that reduce these discrepancies might give citizens more confidence in their police, reduce citizens' fears, and allow the police to better serve their communities.

Walker and Walker (1990) have described a **Community Police Station Program** in which citizens play a major role in the determination, design, and delivery of crime-prevention programs. Citizens from the community see to the daily operation of the station and to the delivery of specific programs such as "Seniors Calling Seniors," a program designed to give shut-in or isolated seniors a sense of contact with others. The program also includes a citizens advisory board that helps identify the crime-prevention needs of each area of the city and sees that programs are developed to address those needs. In the Community Police Station Program, the police and citizens collaborate to make police services more acceptable and effective. In other communities, citizens and community members have been used to help recruit and select new police officers, again allowing collaboration and building a sense of community among citizens and enforcement personnel (Ellison, 1985).

Secondary Prevention: Early Intervention Efforts

This section will explore exemplary measures designed to intercede as early as possible after an individual has started down a path of crime. Primary prevention at this point is too late. The strategy thus becomes early detection and intervention. In the case of Mike Farnsworth in the chapter opening vignette, when Mike first argued with his father, stayed out beyond the agreed-upon curfew, or missed school, someone should have or could have intervened before the situation deteriorated. This is *secondary prevention*. Efforts in secondary prevention have focused primarily on juvenile delinquents, so it is this emphasis that will be addressed first.

Reducing Recidivism in Juvenile Delinquents

Community psychologists and others involved with the criminal justice system are concerned about recidivism rates for youthful offenders, and not without good cause. Unfortunately, for many youths, arrest and justice system processing do little to affect future delinquency and sometimes make it more likely (Browning & Huizinga, 1999). Before addressing recidivism, though, the following is a brief description of how the process through which juveniles pass differs from that of adults (described earlier).

The **juvenile court system** was designed to prevent children and adolescents from undergoing the stress of adult court procedures. The juvenile system is therefore less formal than the adult one, although the U.S. Supreme Court has reduced informality to safeguard due process rights of youths (Hess et al., 1991). One result of the informality is that in juvenile court, professional decisions can be quite disparate. One youth guilty of larceny might be incarcerated; another youth facing the same charge might receive rehabilitative treatment; and a third might receive probation. Furthermore, many youths in this system are from marginalized groups or from single-parent families. For these and other reasons, judges often adopt a protectionist attitude toward youthful offenders. Judges' treatment decisions may be colored by their tendency toward protectionism, especially for girls. Girls usually receive less care, but often it is more gender specific or stereotyped (Morley, Rossman, Kopczynski, Buck, & Govis, 2000).

With that discussion in mind, a community-based program developed by Tolan, Perry, and Jones (1987) will be discussed. The program involved multiagency consultation developed through the family court by a representative from the local mental health center. All juveniles appearing before the court for the first time were required to attend program sessions with at least one parent, because, as noted earlier, family characteristics have been found to be important in determining delinquency (Tolan & Lorion, 1988). The program sessions were presented by appropriate community agencies (e.g., police, judges, probation, and the schools). Each youth was required to attend two four-hour sessions a month. Sessions consisted of information on the juvenile justice process, the consequences of repeat offenses, attitudes of others toward repeat offenders, strategies the youth could try to decrease involvement in illegal activities, and local agencies available to support prosocial behavior. Family relations, parenting skills, the relationship between drug or alcohol use and delinquency, and a tour of the local juvenile facility were also included.

Treatment and no-treatment groups were tracked for seven months and compared for recidivism rates, time between first and second offenses, if any, and other relevant dependent measures. The most significant finding was that the program participants had a recidivism rate that was only one-fourth that of their no-treatment cohorts. Results are attributable to the program's success in managing juvenile offenders. This program also provides **intermediate treatment** by allowing the youth to stay in his or her own home but bringing the youth into contact with environments other than just his or her home (Smith, 1986). Such in-home treatment programs are, of course, much less expensive and are more humanistic than institutionalization (Rosenthal & Glass, 1990). Case in Point 9.2 discusses some of the issues related to working with at-risk youth.

Since the implementation of the Tolan, Perry, and Jones program, the number of models and theories about the best intervention for delinquents has grown. In a review of the literature on reintegration and aftercare of repeat juvenile offenders, MacKenzie (1999) concluded with some interesting and cogent comments on these newer theories and models:

- Treatment in juvenile facilities or within the juvenile justice system is less effective than other alternatives; treatment provided in community settings (e.g., halfway houses) may be more effective.
- Some combination of treatment, with or without surveillance in the community (e.g., drug testing), is effective in reducing juvenile recidivism.
- The research on juvenile aftercare needs to be improved. Often the research emphasizes surveillance rather than treatment aspects, and the program design has little internal validity.
- Clearly, however, treatment must be well matched to the juvenile to be effective (e.g., substance abuse counseling for drug users).

Early Assistance for Victims
Victims, too, need their concerns addressed as early as possible after the victimization. Some immediate steps can be taken.

Victims may experience a wide variety of emotions, ranging from fright, rage, a sense

CASE IN POINT 9.2
WORKING WITH AT-RISK YOUTH

Working with youths at risk for health-related problems, delinquency, running away from home, and dropping out of school can be challenging. Community psychologists, though, are learning how to work better and smarter with such street youth, who sometimes can be resistant to the most well-intentioned efforts. Two interesting projects that explored how best to work with at-risk youths are reviewed here.

Harper and Carver (1999) recognized that members of target populations, especially high-risk youth, often have minimal input into intervention programs. They targeted chronically truant, dropout, homeless, and runaway youth in an HIV prevention program. The researchers wanted to know about the risk behaviors and other life experiences of the youth and what strategies would work to involve and retain high-risk youth in HIV prevention programs. They recognized that any program designed for the youth would be better if the youth had a hand in designing the program and its evaluation. The youth eventually helped in all phases of the program. For example, the youth assisted in developing an ethnographic map of the community to help recruit participants as well as facilitated access to peers who were particularly suspicious of adults. Youth participants also developed population-specific educational materials and assisted with data collection. Harper and Carver concluded, "Giving high-risk youth a voice in prevention programs and evaluations through collaborative partnerships improves both science and service and makes for more credible and acceptable youth prevention programs" (p. 13).

In a second and interesting project, Hackerman (1996) recognized that just as a country has its own language, so, too, do street youth. Street gangs, in particular, such as the Crips and Bloods, use their own symbols and words to communicate. Psychologists and others (such as ministers, school officials, and youth probation officers) need to be able to speak the unique street language of these young people if they are to work with and design programs for such youth. Over a two-year period, Hackerman put together a much-needed glossary of terms for individuals working with this target group. She noted that not all terms were used by all youth. Hispanic youth in Los Angeles often speak a language different from African American youth in New York City. Hackerman's work demonstrates the importance of ethnography in community psychology. Following are some of the terms from her glossary. Cover the right column and see how many terms in the left column you know. Based on your awareness of terminology, how successful do you think you would be in working with street youth?

Street Terminology	Meaning of Term
Blue light	Order someone killed
Bo	A marijuana cigarette, a joint
Flying colors	Wearing gang colors
Jack up	Rob someone
Strap	A gun
Jankin'	Teasing

of violation, and vengefulness to sorrow, depression, despair, and shock. Victims also experience an array of health consequences after the crime (Britt, 2000). The justice system, though, does little for the victim, who does not even have an official role to play in the trial, if there is one (Forer, 1980). The National Victims Resource Center is a national clearinghouse that provides victims with educational materials, funds victim-related studies, makes referrals to assistance programs, and provides information on compensation programs. Some state governments have also developed victim assistance programs (Woolpert, 1991) where victims are compensated for their injuries or awarded money from the offender's selling his or her story to the media or where victims can participate in parole decisions related to their offenders (Educational Conference on Psychiatry, Psychology and the Law, 1990). However, victim compensation programs are rare because an offender in prison does not earn much money toward restitution (Forer, 1980).

Financial compensation alone, though, cannot take away the psychological pain of being victimized nor assist the victim in reducing vengeful or angry thoughts about being victimized. Even with a trial, victims may have to wait months or years before their side of the story is aired in court. There are three types of programs available to victims that afford them early and substantially successful interventions for their victimization: crisis intervention, neighborhood justice centers, and problem-focused and emotion-focused coping.

Crisis Intervention.   The first type of program available to victims is very much psychological in nature. **Crisis intervention** is developed as a set of procedures to help individuals recover from the effects of temporary or time-limited but extreme stress. Early efforts at crisis intervention were focused on potential suicides and victims of extreme violence, unpredictable or dangerous situations, and natural disasters (Caplan, 1989).

Crisis intervention is usually a face-to-face or phone (hot line) intervention that utilizes immediate intercession in the form of social support and focused problem solving to assist a victim in a state of elevated crisis or trauma. The immediate purpose of crisis intervention is to avert catastrophe. Crisis intervention centers can be staffed by professionals or trained volunteers and are often open 24 hours a day.

Since its early days, crisis intervention has expanded to assisting victims of major school incidents (Blom, 1986; Eaves, 2001; Weinberg, 1990), military disasters (McCaughey, 1987), sexual assaults (Kitchen, 1991), the chronically mentally ill (Dobmeyer, McKee, Miller, & Westcott, 1990; Holcomb & Ahr, 1986), students in a disciplinary crisis (Hagborg, 1988), and even victims of international terrorism (Lanza, 1986). Its potential uses seem limitless.

A pertinent question about crisis intervention is whether it is an effective means of providing help at the onset of the crisis and thus of preventing future problems. Echterling and Hartsough (1989) randomly selected evenings on which crisis telephone calls were sampled. Some 59 calls were monitored by the trained crisis intervention volunteers using a standardized monitoring form. In particular, the volunteer helpers' statements to the callers were recorded and coded to determine the sequence and usefulness of the steps in the process. The outcome of the call, whether it successfully averted the crisis, was also tracked. The researchers found that there are three important phases of short-term crisis intervention: assessment, emotional integration or responding to the caller's feelings, and problem solving or focusing on the specific actions to be taken after the call. These three phases, in this order, were most likely to result in a successful outcome for the caller.

More recently, Mishara (1997) examined the effects of different telephone styles used with suicidal callers. Using calls from 617 callers, nearly 70,000 responses by crisis counselors were categorized and then evaluated for success of the crisis intervention. Mishara found that Rogerian, or nondirective (rather than directive), interaction with the caller resulted in better outcomes—that is, in a decreased depressive mood and contractual behavior as to how to manage the crisis. Crisis counseling is even being conducted electronically (Wilson & Lester, 1998), but whether this is as effective as phone contact remains to be determined. Campfield and Hills (2001) found that the closer the crisis intervention occurs in time to the actual crime, the lower the number and severity of symptoms for the victim over the long run.

How else has successful crisis intervention been used? Baumann, Schultz, Brown, Paredes, and Hepeworth (1987) recognized that the police are often called on to do crisis intervention work, but this is not a good use of police time. Police work is designed to collect information related to the commission of a crime rather than to attend to the emotional state of a victim. In an innovative program, the Baumann group trained lay community citizens on police safety procedures and crisis intervention techniques. After the training, two-person lay teams could be called by any police officer to assist in a crisis. The program resulted in less police time spent on each crisis call except in cases of domestic disputes. In some crises, the police were able to depart the scene even while the crisis was in progress, as long as the trained citizen participants were available to assist. As for family disturbances, the researchers explained that these calls seemed to have a higher degree of danger of physical violence than other calls. Hence, police presence was required throughout the disturbance. The study demonstrates that trained citizens can assist the police in performing some of their duties, which include crisis intervention. Both of these studies suggest that crisis intervention is an effective and immediate means for assisting victims.

Neighborhood Justice Centers.   **Neighborhood justice centers or community mediation centers** comprise the secondary category of early intervention programs. These centers are established in the local community and are designed to handle cases from criminal and civil courts or from other community agencies, such as community mental health centers, probation departments, and family courts. The centers dispense with cases in a more timely fashion than is provided by the court system (Duffy, Grosch, & Olczak, 1991). One state reports a 15-day turn-around time from intake to resolution at its mediation centers (Crosson & Christian, 1990; Duffy, 1991).

At these neighborhood justice centers, a trained person hears the case as presented by both the victim (or claimant) and the respondent (the person responding to the charge). This trained neutral, the **mediator,** assists the two parties in understanding their conflict and in fashioning a resolution that is satisfactory to each. The resolutions in most programs are legally binding, do not require decisions about guilt or innocence (thus can "clear" an arrest record), and must be mutually agreeable (Duffy, 1991).

Most victims or claimants are highly satisfied with the process of mediation (Carnevale & Pruitt, 1992; Duffy, 1991; McGillis, 1997) because they get to tell their version of the story soon after their victimization. They are also allowed to ventilate their emotions (something usually prohibited in court) and they are availed of the opportunity to address the person they believe caused their distress. Respondents or defendants appreciate the process because they typically do not come out of it with a guilty verdict or a criminal record. Likewise, they are afforded the opportunity to provide evidence that the victim sometimes plays a role in the "crime" (as in harassment, where both parties have actually harassed each other).

Mediators utilize a variety of strategies to facilitate discussion and guide the two parties toward solutions (Carnevale & Pruitt, 1992; Ostermeyer, 1991). Mediators use reality testing (a process in which one person is asked to "get in the other person's shoes"), a futuristic (rather than retrospective) orientation, turn taking, compromise, reciprocity in concession making, and active listening, among other skills. In some respects, mediation and psychotherapy are parallel processes, but mediation focuses more on problems and issues rather than emotions or relationships (Forlenza, 1991; Milne, 1985; Weaver, 1986). The end result in about 85 to 90 percent of the cases is an agreement or contract between the parties (Duffy, 1991; McGillis, 1997). What is equally important is that 80 to 90 percent of victims and defendants emerge from the process satisfied (Duffy, 1991; McGillis, 1997). The agreements can contain anything from restitution and apologies to guidelines as to how in the future the parties will interact. Just about anything that both parties agree to that is legal can be part of the mediated settlement. Mediation has been successfully utilized in landlord-tenant and consumer-merchant disputes; neighborhood conflicts; crimes such as assault, harassment, and larceny; family dysfunction; racial conflict; environmental disputes (Duffy et al., 1991); and a host of other areas where individuals disagree or infract on each other's rights.

In fact, the opening vignette of Mike Farnsworth is a true story; Mike and his parents were referred to a mediation center by the probation department. Although the hearing was a long one, Mike and his parents eventually agreed on rules for Mike (e.g., curfews) and a reward system for Mike (which had been missing before the mediation). A punishment system had long been in place. The reward system would be used when Mike's grades were good or when his behavior was positive. During the hearing, Mike and his father finally listened to one another (rather than bellowed) and began to better understand each other's perspective. Mike's mother, Edna, learned some valuable skills from the mediator, such as compromise and reciprocity of concessions, for use in refereeing future disagreements between Mike and his father should they arise. The Farnsworths (whose name we changed to protect their anonymity) have lived much more harmoniously since their mediation.

Neighborhood justice centers have experienced tremendous growth in the last two decades (Duffy, 1991; Emery & Wyer, 1987; Meehan, 1986) but are not without their critics (e.g., Greatbatch & Dingwall, 1989; Vidmar, 1992). The phenomenal growth of mediation centers can be seen in Figure 9.2. The centers and the process of mediation embody many of the values of community psychology, too. The centers are generally available to the parties in or near their own communities. The centers provide an *alternative* to the sometimes oppressive, bureaucratic, and almost always adversarial court system (Duffy, 1991). Mediation *empowers* the parties to play a major and active role in determining their own solutions. Research on compliance with the contracts suggests that they usually *prevent* conflicts from recurring in the future (Duffy, 1991). Similarly, the centers are generally available to every community citizen regardless of income, race, or creed (Crosson & Christian, 1990; Duffy, 1991; Harrington, 1985), and the mediators are trained to *respect the unique perspective* and *diversity* of the parties (Duffy, 1991). Empirical research has demonstrated that mediation is a humanistic process because it enhances the functioning of both participants as measured by Maslow's hierarchy of needs (Duffy & Thompson, 1992). Research has also demonstrated that individuals who utilize mediation instead of court trials are respected and admired by others because they are seen as flexible and conciliatory (Duffy & Olczak, 1989).

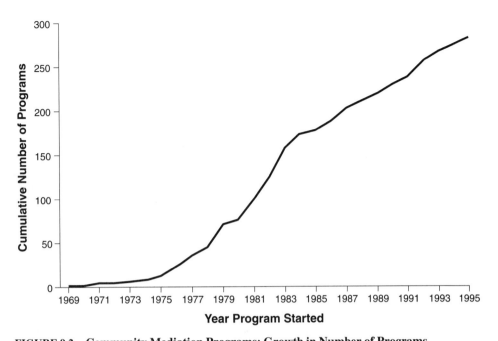

FIGURE 9.2   Community Mediation Programs: Growth in Number of Programs

Source: Community Mediation Programs: Developments and Challenges by D. McGillis, 1997, Washington, DC:
U.S. Department of Justice.

Problem-Focused and Emotion-Focused Coping.   There are two immediate problems of
victims. One is coping with the emotional watershed of being victimized; the other is developing problem-focused skills to deal with the reality of revictimization, which is perhaps
unlikely in reality but prominent in the victim's mind. Winkel and Vrij (1993) developed a
program designed to help victims cope in both ways soon after the crime. A police crisis
intervention program was developed in which the police conducted a criminal investigation
of the burglary victim's home, provided oral and written crime prevention information, and
performed a security check. Later measures of coping found that this program instilled in the
victims enhanced perceptions that the police were protecting them, reduced fear of future
crime, and increased preventive awareness and responsibility on the part of the victim.

Tertiary Programs: After-the-Fact Interventions for Chronic Justice System Problems

You know now that Mike Farnsworth's story had a fairly happy ending. The outcomes for
others involved in criminal justice processes, both victims and offenders, is not always so
happy. This section will review the role of and treatment of chronicity. Specifically, programs designed primarily for individuals who are involved long term in the turmoil of criminality will be reviewed.

Innovative Programs for Chronic Offenders

Despite the development of primary and secondary prevention programs, the approach of the traditional justice system tends to be punishment and use of restrictive institutional settings. Research has traditionally focused on two areas: efficacy of incarceration (imprisonment) compared to alternative programs and the effectiveness of prerelease programs during incarceration on recidivism rates.

Incarceration remains controversial in community psychology and is not a simple issue to examine. Many research projects that attempt to compare forms of incarceration to alternative community programs have sampling problems. For instance, judges are reluctant to divert dangerous or chronic offenders to community programs. Researchers therefore find different populations in each setting, thus creating differences at the outset of the study. Furthermore, community programs differ as much from each other as do prisons; program idiosyncrasies therefore become an issue and prevent drawing generalizations from one program to the next. We will therefore examine only a few sample programs and research findings.

Incarceration and Its Alternatives. The problems of incarceration have been well documented. They include but are not limited to reduced social status; isolation from family and community; feelings of guilt and self-rejection; lack of employment opportunities upon release, racial divisions, cliques, and gangs within the prison walls; drugs; and the spread of AIDS among the prison population. Some of these problems are severe. Ortmann (2000), based on his own longitudinal research, contended that prisons are extremely unfavorable places for the positive correction of people. Because of these and other problems caused by incarceration, the preference in community psychology seems to be to avoid incarceration and coercive punishment.

Mounting evidence suggests that alternative forms of punishment outside of the traditional prison system are not good alternatives either. Several studies have demonstrated that shock incarceration camps or **boot camps** that are run by corrections personnel but resemble intensive army training camps fall short of their goals (MacKenzie, Wilson, Armstrong, & Gover, 2001; Palmer & Wedge, 1989; Sechrest, 1989). A report of work of the Office of Juvenile Justice and Delinquency Prevention (U.S. Department of Justice, 1997) revealed that "reoffending youth in the experimental groups (boot camps) committed new offenses more quickly—that is, had shorter survival periods—than reoffending youth in the control group" (p. 23). In programs described in the report, youth in some of the boot camps actually recidivated at rates higher than those for youth not in boot camps (control groups). Figure 9.3 depicts the comparative recidivism rates following release from confinement of various youth from boot camps (experimental groups) or other means of confinement (control groups) such as youth correctional facilities.

Untangling the effects of incarceration versus alternative programs is sticky. Using parole violations and parole maladjustment measures, Fendrich (1991) found that the use of alternative programs was inversely associated with both measures. In other words, on both measures, the alternative programs came out better. However, in Fendrich's study, nonprogram variables, such as family problems, were *more* useful predictors of parole behavior. Thus, the alternative programs themselves are not always solely responsible for postrelease behavior.

Some studies compare incarceration to community alternatives and, as noted on several other occasions, the studies are replete with design problems. In one fairly well-

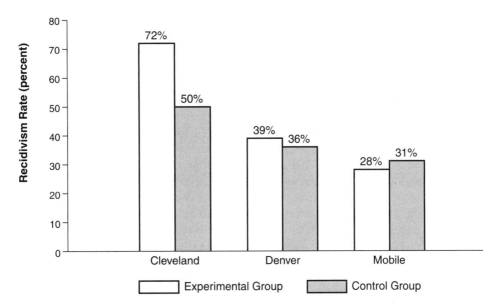

FIGURE 9.3   Comparative Rates of Recidivism Following Release from Confinement

Source: Boot Camps for Juvenile Offenders, Washington, DC: U.S. Department of Justice.

designed study (Chamberlain, 1990), juveniles remanded to a correctional facility were matched on age, sex, and date of commitment with two other groups of youths. One group was diverted to alternative but specialized foster care in the community and another group received traditional community placements. All youths were considered to be seriously delinquent. The results indicated that the youths in the specialized foster care were more likely to succeed in their diversionary programs than those placed in traditional community settings such as group homes. At one and two years posttreatment, the group receiving specialized foster care was less likely to be reincarcerated or incarcerated for as long as the two other groups of youths. Again, one must be cautioned that not all research demonstrates that alternative community programs are this successful (Coates, 1981).

Prerelease Programs.   Imagine how Mike Farnsworth would feel upon release had he been imprisoned for, say, five years because of his repeated assaults on his father. Mike would have learned much in prison, most of it counterproductive. He may have learned how to make weapons out of ordinary household implements, such as mirrors and cigarette lighters. He may have learned how to intimidate others merely by staring at them in a certain way, and he may have learned how to commit more heinous crimes than the assault on his father. But, even though prison may have hardened Mike, he might also have felt intimidated about his reentry into society and felt insecure about his newly acquired freedom. Where would he find a job? How would he feel about going to see his parole officer? Would his parents allow him to come home? What would his neighbors think? **Prerelease programs** that ease entry back into the community can perhaps prevent stress and future problems for inmates.

There is probably no other inmate for whom release is more problematic than forensic patients. These are the mentally disordered, incarcerated individuals discussed earlier in the book. These individuals suffer not only the social stigma of incarceration but of mental disorder, as well. They are probably less well received upon return to their communities than any other individual. Maier, Morrow, and Miller (1989) described a highly successful prerelease program for forensic patients that eases them back into the community rather than abruptly casts them out of the forensic unit. The participants had been hospitalized in a forensic unit for 2 to 10 years. The program contained modules that reoriented the participants to the community and to community living skills as well as contained provisions for release planning groups, buddy systems, debriefings upon visits to the community, and meetings with community leaders. In other words, the researchers encouraged the participants to take "small steps at a time" before release to the community. Over a 24-month period, only one crime was committed in the institution (but it was a fairly serious one of sexual assault) and none in the community in more than 11,000 excursions to it. Although this program did not guarantee that the community would be more accepting of the participants, it did assist the participants in successfully controlling behaviors in the community that otherwise would result in their return to the forensic unit.

Postrelease Programs. Once an individual is released from an adult or juvenile correctional facility, recidivism can be high. It is therefore important to have postrelease programs in place that support the individual in various ways to prevent recidivism. The Multisystemic Therapy (MST) approach offers new hope that recidivism can be decreased. The goal of MST is to provide an integrative, cost-effective, family-based treatment that results in positive outcomes for adolescents who have demonstrated serious antisocial and criminal behavior. MST also focuses on the peer context, school/vocational performance, and neighborhood/community supports.

In MST, sessions are typically held in the home, with up to 60 hours of contact between a counselor and the youth and the family over four months. The staff member monitors barriers to effective parental and family interactions, such as parental drug dependency or low social support. The youth is also assisted in developing more positive peer interactions. The school is utilized to enhance the youth's capacity for future employment and financial success. The staff member typically also acts as an advocate, or a broker of services, for the family and the youth.

One MST program in Simpsonville, South Carolina, has been flagged as being especially successful (Henggeler, 1997). In a rigorous, controlled evaluation, youth were either randomly assigned to MST or to usual youth services such as incarceration. In this study, MST reduced long-term rates of criminal behavior, increased family warmth and cohesion, and decreased youth aggression with peers. MST was also less expensive than traditional methods. Figure 9.4 depicts some of these comparative results.

Interventions for Victims

In other chapters of this book, long-term treatment for victims of a variety of abuses, such as child abuse, have been addressed. Here, the research by Kaniasty and Norris (1992) will address the role of social support in long-term, crime victim assistance. Social support, as you already have learned from Chapter 4, often has beneficial buffering effects for distressed individuals.

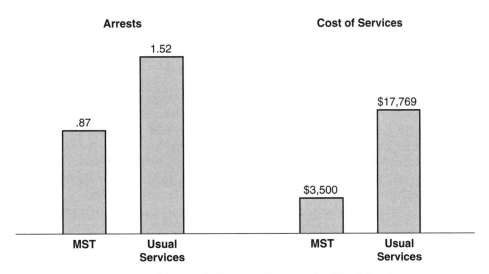

FIGURE 9.4   Results of Multisystemic Therapy Compared to Usual Services

Source: Treating Serious Anti-Social Behavior in Youth: The MST Approach by S. W. Henggeler, 1997, Washington, DC: U.S. Department of Justice.

Kaniasty and Norris have pointed out that criminal victimization results in depression, anxiety, fear, and hostility. Especially in the instance of violent crime, these feelings can persist for months. The more the perceived seriousness of the crime, the more vulnerable and wronged the victim feels (Beach, Greenberg, & Yee, 1992). Kaniasty and Norris wondered what role **social support**—support from significant others such as friends and family—played in the victims' coping with these diverse emotions.

Kaniasty and Norris took measures of several types of *perceived* support as well as several types of support *actually received* by victims of property and violent crimes. Analyses revealed that the positive or buffering effects of *perceived* support were more pervasive than those of *actual* or received support for victims of both types of crimes. On the other hand, received support in the form of information and material goods seemed to assist only victims of violent crimes and then more by way of reducing their fear of future victimization. Social support tends to be sought frequently from friends and family but often professional support is more helpful, especially in certain crimes such as sexual assault where rape crisis centers have been reported by victims as highly useful (Golding, Siegel, Sorenson, Burnam, & Stein, 1989). In other words, the victim, the crime, and the type of social support need to be carefully matched. Formal victim support programs tend to focus mainly on emotional support when what the victim may need is advice and material support. Kaniasty and Norris concluded that "providing support to crime victims is a very complex, involving, and delicate process. What is needed is a more proactive approach of educating the public about the role of social support, both perceived and received, in coping with criminal victimization" (1992, p. 236).

A second approach to assisting victims after their victimization is **victim-offender mediation (VOM).** There are nearly 300 such programs in the United States (Umbreit & Greenwood, 2000a, & 2000b). In VOM programs, the victim and offender are brought together to explore their impact on and feelings about each other. Their meeting is facilitated by a mediator. As in other community mediation, the two parties are usually empowered to develop plans for restitution (Woolpert, 1991) or restorative justice. **Restorative justice** is victim centered and allows both the victim and the offender to address the harm caused by the crime (Umbreit, 2000a, 2000b). Restoration, or restitution, is not the only strategy. If both parties agree, the offender can provide service to the community or offer the victim an apology. The victim can also request that the offender seeks counseling, and, if the offender agrees, therapy becomes part of the agreement. VOM is not appropriate for all victims, but it has been applied in property offenses, robbery, assault, rape, and even murder. Program evaluation of VOM has found that the parties leave with a high level of satisfaction and perceived fairness (Umbreit, Coates, & Roberts, 2000). Perpetrators are also less likely to return to crime (Nugent, Umbreit, Wiinamaki, & Paddock, 2001).

In conclusion, the criminal justice system is a complex one comprised of many different players with a variety of motives and functions. Community psychologists are collaborating with individuals involved in the justice system and together they are making headway on preventing crime and assisting those involved in the crime once it occurs.

SUMMARY

The traditional justice system includes enforcement agencies such as the police, the courts, the prisons, and related programs. Such programs allow a small role, if any, for the victim and tend to seek retribution or punishment for the offender.

Psychologists who have tried to parcel out the causes of crime know that guns, gun control, and related factors are not the only predictors of crime. Certain ecological settings and certain groups of individuals are likely to be involved in crime. Young African American men are most likely to be victimized by crime and most likely to be convicted of and incarcerated (imprisoned) for crime. Societal prejudice and the history of African Americans in the United States may, in part, be what underlie some of the statistics.

Prisons are bleak, overcrowded institutions often fraught with problems such as violence, AIDS, and illegal substances. Prisons do not tend to rehabilitate nor treat offenders.

Victims and those who fear crime have been neglected populations in the traditional criminal justice system. An interesting phenomenon, the crime-victimization paradox, which has limited support in the literature, suggests that those who fear crime the most are often least likely to be victimized. An example would be an elderly woman who fears crime but is very unlikely to be victimized.

Police are asked to play a variety of roles in a community. Some are roles for which they are ill prepared, such as intervention in domestic disputes. Police officers often report that they feel alienated from the communities they serve and feel that their superiors offer little understanding for street life.

Community psychologists believe that criminal behavior can be predicted. Some studies have successfully predicted delinquent behavior in at-risk youths. Environments can also be altered to reduce the probability of crime. An example is removing violent cues from the media, which usually tend to bias its reports of crime any way.

Community programs such as a neighborhood crime watch are also successfully reducing the fear of crime. Other innovative programs involve citizens in collaborative efforts with officers at enforcement agencies.

In terms of secondary prevention, community-based programs show much promise for intervening in the cycle of delinquency. There also exist programs for early assistance to actual crime victims. Two such programs include crisis intervention and neighborhood justice centers or community mediation centers.

Programs comparing incarceration to alternative community services are difficult to assess with research due to research confounds, but many community programs offer hope that even chronic offenders can be assisted. An especially important type of program is a multisystem prerelease program that is designed to ease adjustment of an incarcerated person into the community.

Victims may also need follow-up services long after the crime. One new and interesting program is the victim-offender mediation program in which the victim and offender meet face to face and discuss their impact on one another as well as plans for restitution to the victim.

HEALTH CARE

It is probable that, before medicine becomes truly preventive, there must be a radical alteration in the basis of payment for medical service. It is extremely unlikely that the average individual will ever resort to his physician until he experiences compelling symptoms of disease if the incurring of an immediate financial obligation is specifically involved.

—Charles-Edward Amory Winslow, 1923

Erika placed a single red rose on Tom's casket and then turned toward their children, Jessica and Scott. Grasping each other's hands, the three walked slowly away from Tom's grave.

Upon returning home, Erika weighed the events of the past 20 years. Erika met Tom at college in Michigan. She graduated with a teaching certificate in music; he earned his diploma in accounting. In August of their graduation year, they were married. Life seemed good during their early married life. Erika and Tom were both employed and making plans for their first child, Scott, who was born two years later. In another three years, Jessica was born.

While Erika taught music at the junior high, Tom's work for a large, successful accounting firm sent him all through the Midwest. Both of them were pleased that their lives were relatively carefree. Each had a good-paying job, the children never gave them trouble, and the family was able to afford a beautiful home in a respected neighborhood.

Everything changed suddenly in the twenty-fifth year of their marriage. Tom was not feeling well. He complained of a fever, night sweats, and swollen glands. Erika was stunned to learn that Tom had immune deficiency syndrome (AIDS). On his business trips and at the urging of his accounting buddies who were traveling with him, Tom had engaged prostitutes for "a few hours of fun." That fun eventually turned into a fatal illness: AIDS.

Erika could hardly forgive Tom for his indiscretion, but she was relieved that she, herself, had tested negative for AIDS. Her busy life and his travels ironically saved her from the illness. Erika felt guilty for the anger she held for Tom while he was dying. The day of his funeral, the guilt gave way to anguish. During the last half year of Tom's illness, he was unable to work, which forced Erika to teach private music lessons. She worked night and day. Erika's saving graces were that Scott and Jessica were old enough to care for themselves and that Tom's sister and Jessica were able to look after Tom's needs as his frailness progressed.

What frustrated Erika the most, though, were the mounting medical bills. Tom owned an excellent health insurance policy while he was with the accounting firm. When he resigned due to his illness, the family was covered by her insurance through the school. However, this insurance plan did not cover some of the major expenses, experimental drugs, and frequent doctor visits.

Erika sat alone in her house after the funeral and pondered the unpaid expenses. Tom's funeral alone had cost over $8,000, but the medical bills were the monumental cost. Erika wondered how she would ever pay the hundreds of thousands of dollars she owed the doctors and the hospitals. All the private music lessons in the world would never help her tackle those bills.

Despite the pioneer public health work of Charles-Edward Amory Winslow in the 1920s and those who followed him, Erika and Tom's story is tragic and, unfortunately, told all too often. Whether the catastrophic illness is AIDS, cancer, Alzheimer's disease, emphysema, or another disease, many Americans today are still faced with major health problems and have no way to cover all the expenses. The pain of the illness is magnified by the despair over the state of health care in this country. The health-related issues that face Erika and other Americans are the crucial ones explored in this chapter.

Americans pride themselves on living in one of the freest, richest, and most technologically advanced countries. Given this wealth of technology, Americans should be able to choose the types of health care services (e.g., outpatient mental health counseling or therapy) that best fit their needs. Unfortunately, people cannot agree on which health care model is best nor how health care should be funded.

At this writing, the "Patients' Bill of Rights"—an effort to empower consumers—is being hotly discussed in the U.S. Congress. There are three versions to the bill: (1) The McCain-Kennedy-Edwards Bill, (2) The Ganske-Dingell-Norwood Bill, and (3) The Fletcher Bill—all named for the senators or congressmen sponsoring them). The first is probably the most ambitious; this proposed bill would allow patients to seek a range of health care services without prior approval from health maintenance organizations (HMOs). In addition, patients would have the right to challenge through an independent, external review panel decisions by their HMOs. That is, patients could bring legal challenges of their HMOs in both state and federal courts. There would be no limits on economic and noneconomic (e.g., pain and suffering) damages in federal courts, plus up to $5 million in punitive damages. The second version is essentially the same as the first with the exception that it would allow the self-insured to deduct the cost of health insurance. The last version is the one supported by President George W. Bush. It has many elements of as the first two but would limit "noneconomic" costs in federal suits to $500,000.

The nuances in the debate are often confusing to educated laypersons, as well as to those in the health-related disciplines. A bill of rights for patients is long overdue. However, the "adversarial" framework (in the form of lawsuits) in the proposed bill addresses only one aspect of consumer empowerment; that is, only individuals with insurance in the first place are empowered. Millions of people have *no* health insurance. Moreover, the "insurance or financial" model used does not address psychosocial issues, such as practices of preventive measures to promote healthy lifestyles—the ultimate consumer empowerment!

In the not too distant past, access to health care more or less depended on one's purse string. The establishment of federally funded programs, such as Medicaid and Medicare, in the 1960s, as well as the institutionalization of employment-based health care, has been a significant step forward for a healthy nation. However, HMOs place restrictions on doctor-patient discourse. This overly simplistic description points to at least four sets of interrelated, multifaceted elements and players, if we as a country are to engage in a meaningful discourse in health care reform. So far, virtually all proposed efforts tend to focus on one or two elements. The first element is financing the mechanism; the second is legislation; the third is the health care providers; and the fourth is the consumers or patients. The first and second ones certainly have the most exposure in people's daily life. Often, the first dictates ability to access health care. Until this barrier is removed, there will always be less than optimal health among some segments of the population. However, research by Maloy, Darnell, Nolan, Kenney, and Cyprien (2000) argued that ability to access is a necessary, but not sufficient condition to promote healthy lifestyles. People's "willingness" to access is important for engagement and retention in care. This speaks to the traditional domain of doctor-patient discourse—that is your doctor "understands" you. This feeling of being "informed" illustrates consumer or patient empowerment.

Although all three versions of the Patients' Bill of Rights address some aspects of the four elements and players, the Bill of Rights is more or less grounded in a financial model. People who do not have health insurance are still persona-non grata. In addition, it is unclear whether the proposed Patients' Bill of Rights would integrate issues raised in "Healthy People 2010," which was designed to eliminate health disparity and promote a generation of healthy people. It seems that the Patients' Bill of Rights and Healthy People 2010—two strategies for a healthy nation— are working on independent, parallel trajectories.

IN SICKNESS AND IN HEALTH: SOCIAL INEQUITY

The issue of health care reform in the United States has gone through a frenetic period. Media coverage and public hearings, as well as scholarly writings, have dominated the country. Currently, *health care reform* has subtly become *managed care* and is likely to be the standard practice of medicine for a while. It is estimated that more than 40 million people are without health care coverage. Meanwhile, Dr. David Ho and colleagues have injected new hope to many people living with AIDS or HIV with the cocktail therapy. Not all people living with AIDS or HIV have access to the cocktail therapy, however, especially among the poor and disfranchised.

So, you might ask, what is the temperature of health care in this country today? What is the prognosis? What are the remedies for the current state of health? Kawachi, Kennedy, and Lochner (1997) have argued that **social cohesion,** or social trust, is a key ingredient to the health or well-being of the public. Reviewing empirical and historical findings as well as conducting their own research (correlational in nature), Kawachi and colleagues demonstrated that income inequity, or the **Robin Hood Index,** is negatively related to one's level of trust of other people. In addition, social trust is positively related to one's **quality of life.** In other words, increases in the income gap might impair social trust, which, in turn, affect health outcomes or status.

> Despite having one of the highest living standards in the world (the real gross domestic product [GDP] per capita was $24,680 in 1993), [the United States] has a lower life expectancy (76.1 years in 1993) than less affluent but more egalitarian countries like the Netherlands (GDP, $17,340; life expectancy, 77.5 years); Israel ($15,130; life expectancy, 77.7 years). In fact, societies with the smallest income differences between rich and poor, such as Sweden and Japan, tend to enjoy the highest life expectancy (78.3 and 79.6 years, respectively). An egalitarian distribution of wealth and income seems to imply a more cohesive, harmonious society. The quality of social relations . . . is the prime determinant of a country's human welfare and quality of life. (Kawachi et al., 1997, p. 59)

Kawachi and associates' (1997) thesis appears to have some validity. For example, the annual death rates were much higher in Pine Bluff, Arkansas, and Mobile, Alabama (some of the most economically divided regions), than the national average of 850 per 100,000 (Nemecek, 1999). More than half of the AIDS cases are among African Americans and Hispanic Americans, many of whom are economically disenfranchised (Centers for Disease Control and Prevention [CDC], 1998). The list goes on. Hence, an implication for any health care reform is that one needs to address broader social issues—such as access to quality health care and parity of services (distributions of resources)—to go beyond just having health care coverage. At its core, good health is about social justice (see Case in Point 10.1), a priciple consistent with the philosphy of community psychology.

CASE IN POINT 10.1

THE TIDE DIDN'T LIFT OUR BOAT: THE INTERSECTION OF PUBLIC MORALITY AND THE PUBLIC HEALTH RESPONSE TO IMMIGRANTS AND REFUGEES WITH HIV/AIDS IN THE UNITED STATES

Susan Sontag (1993) argued that the most feared diseases, such as HIV/AIDS, are those that transform the body into something alienating and often carry "negative moral" dimensions—unclean, repulsive, and the result of vice. Initially, the HIV/AIDS epidemic in this country was culturally associated with homosexuality and illicit drug use, which served as a "magnet for powerful moral formulations about disease, sexuality, drug use, and responsibility.... These very 'constructions' of AIDS are deeply held moral convictions about the nature of risk and responsibility for disease. Cultural beliefs and practices about disease are revelatory of a society's most basic moral beliefs and practices. These meanings and moral configurations, in turn, have a dramatic impact on both the care of those who are sick and on broader social and political policies" (Brandt & Rozin, 1997, pp. 4–5).

While all otherwise eligible immigrants must test HIV-negative to be allowed entry into the United States, the Immigration and Naturalization Services (INS) does have the authority to waive this requirement for certain classes of refugees. These refugees are automatically eligible for health care services (including HIV/AIDS), whereas many legal immigrants who subsequently become infected by the virus face major obstacles in securing the services and care they need—a dilemma exacerbated by the 1996 Welfare Reform (i.e., Medicaid eligibility). Moreover, health disparity in "Healthy People 2010" is couched more or less in racial/ethnic terms, a paradigm ill equipped to address the cultural and linguistic diversity of immigrants and refugees. Compared to other developed countries (e.g., Canada, Sweden), the United States has only begun to address the issues of immigration and HIV/AIDS in a semi-systematic way. For example, as of 1999, six cities (Boston, New York City, Chicago, San Diego, Minneapolis, and San Francisco) had been selected to host a limited number of HIV-positive refugees due to their advanced HIV prevention and care infrastructures. However, these "band-aid approaches" create confusions, such as who is eligible (refugees versus legal immigrants) for what services (e.g., cocktail therapy). Meanwhile, most mainstream programs are ill equipped to deal with the cultural and linguistic needs of most HIV-positive immigrants and refugees. For example, a sizeable number of Asians and Pacific Islanders (APIs) living with HIV/AIDS in the metropolitan New York City Area (about 13 percent of the API AIDS cases in the United States) have limited English-speaking ability. Many of their needs—a result of cultural and linguistic barriers—were not met until the founding of The Asian and Pacific Islander Coalition Against HIV, Inc. (APICAH), the largest community-based AIDS service organization in the East Coast targeting APIs, in 1989. In fact, via a national demonstration study funded by the Health Resources and Services Administration, APICHA serves 100 plus HIV-positive API clients with limited or no English-speaking ability (Chin & Wong, in press).

This country has a checkered history on immigration policy (e.g., The Chinese Exclusion Act); the argument of "moral character" often plays a significant role in crafting policies that determine the admission or exclusion of potential immigrants. The argument of "weak moral character" (e.g., disease prone) was used not too long ago to describe Eastern Europeans who migrated to this country. Although public health efforts targeting immigrants are not new, HIV/AIDS probably poses the hottest debate in this "moral immigration" drama. Thus, any meaningful discourse on these issues needs to address the intersection of public morality and the public health response to immigrants and refugees with HIV/AIDS.

PUBLIC VERSUS PRIVATE SECTOR:
MANAGED CARE

The demise of so-called health-care reform to the present state of managed care addresses only two versions of the story: **public versus private secto**r. Without being simplistic, the public or governmental health care strategy often assumes the form of subsidized or **socialized medicine.** Examples include but are not limited to Medicaid for the indigent or poor people and **Medicare** for the elderly. On the other hand, some people believe that health care delivery should be determined or driven by free market economy forces: a supply and demand principle. The enactment of the **Health Maintenance Organization (HMO) Act** of 1973 has more or less signaled the birth of **managed care** as we know it today. Consumers can enroll in a plan of their choice and change providers of their own choosing. There are various forms to this concept, including the idea of **medical saving accounts (MSAs),** which allow for a greater latitude among consumers to switch to low-priced providers.

In practice, the two pure forms of health care strategy do not exist. Instead, we now live in a hybrid world. At times, this hybrid world creates complications. For example, Medicaid and Medicare can be administered by HMOs or managed care providers. Legal immigrants (many are U.S. taxpayers) living with HIV are not eligible for emergency Medicaid; only those living with AIDS are eligible. Although this might be a legal maneuver, it is not humane and goes against recommendations for early intervention by the medical community. Meanwhile, the incomes of many U.S. citizens who are working poor do not qualify them for Medicaid. Many are self-employed or employed as part-time workers and lack the financial resources to purchase health care insurance on their own or via their employers. If they work in organizations with less than five people, their employers are not required by law to provide health care insurance.

Managed care providers or HMOs often place restrictions on consumers, such as exclusion for coverage on existing conditions, financial capitation on mental health services, and so on. One of many examples is the **Mental Health Parity Act** of 1996. The act is designed to ensure that services are available for mental illness comparable to that for physical illness. The act dictates that "group health plans may not set annual or lifetime dollar limits on a member's mental health care that are less than any such limits for general medical and surgical services" (Pear, 1998). Responding to this new demand, many group plans have simply replaced the dollar amounts with numerical limits (i.e., number of visits).

In other words, the public or governmental health care strategy is not *truly* free or available to those who need it. Meanwhile, more and more states are experimenting with the concept of managed care with Medicaid and Medicare. For example, a state may set up additional or new criteria for what it considers as reimbursable services. Many services once reimbursable may become nonreimbursable overnight. The private sector may make it difficult (e.g., higher copayment, second and third opinions, etc.) for consumers to use elective services or to change plans.

People's Power: The Missing Link

A missing piece in the discourse of the health care reform is the voice of the consumers (Rodwin, 1997). The implicit assumption of the discourse is that the only option consumers have in dealing with managed care providers or HMOs is to **exit** (e.g., change provider). Rodwin has argued that consumers can be empowered to create systematic change. Change is most effective when coming from a **"horizontal voice** (organized discussions and activities of consumers or employees)" (p. 48–49) than a **vertical voice** (individual effort). One such horizontal voice can be in the form of **consumer governance.** Rodwin has acknowledged the challenges in maintaining involvement among consumers. Consumer governance might be an ambitious goal, but it is attainable—small achievements have been observed in some areas. An example is the Group Health Cooperative of Pugent Sound (founded in 1947), which is jointly owned by the physician and the consumers. Another example can be found in the field of HIV/AIDS. In the early spread of the epidemic, the gay community began challenging the medical community and federal officials (e.g., Food and Drug Administration) about how drug and vaccine trials should be conducted. Not long ago, the CDC expanded the definitions of AIDS to include conditions specific to women. This change was the result of consumer advocacy. Today, the inclusion of consumer advisory boards is a common practice in how drug and vaccine trials are conducted. In some cases, consumers also advise in the review of proposals for funding.

COMMUNITY PSYCHOLOGY AND PUBLIC HEALTH

On a more microlevel, people's power can promote individuals' health. Some health care experts turn to the **public health model,** which emphasizes the importance of **preventive medicine** and **health education.** That is, people who practice healthy lifestyles are less likely to develop illnesses and thus lessen the burden (money) to the health care service delivery system. If Tom, the husband in the opening vignette, had been educated about safe sex, perhaps he could have avoided contracting the virus that led to the development of his AIDS.

The public health model has been around for more than 125 years. The American Public Health Association was established in 1872 and included Margaret Sanger's pioneering work on the establishment of maternity clinics for low-income women in the often hostile, early nineteenth-century New York City. However, not until the leadership of Julian Richmond, M.D., former U.S. Surgeon General, was public health given its long-overdue credit.

Specifically, based on scientific data as well as consultation with health care experts, Dr. Richmond outlined a set of goals and objectives (e.g., reduce the number of people who smoke) to improve the health of Americans within a 10-year period. Not all goals and objectives have been achieved, and some objectives and goals are less than optimal. For example, infant mortality rates had sharply decreased until the onset of the Reagan and Bush Administrations, whose many social agendas were not completely congruent with the philosophy of the public health model. Dr. Richmond's work established the public health and prevention foundations by challenging the American people to rethink what they *must* do in order to be healthy. Today, another set of goals and objectives entitled *Healthy People 2010: National Health Promotion and Disease Prevention Objectives* have been established.

For both the public health model and the field of community psychology, an important goal is to **empower** individuals by having them practice preventive medicine, although **intervention** and **treatment** must be available when needed. For instance, the model is noted for its relative success in preventing or reducing cigarette use, which has been linked to various forms of cardiovascular disease and cancer in later life (LeFebvre, Lasater, Carleton, & Peterson, 1987). Prevention or intervention programs against cigarette smoking generally use the mass media (e.g., Dr. Louis Sullivan, former Secretary of the Health and Human Services openly criticized the tobacco industry on national television) in conjunction with laws. For example, warning labels on cigarette packages and a ban on smoking on all domestic flights and in most restaurants have been legislated. Other successful smoking prevention programs are school based and usually involve teaching school-aged children assertiveness skills (Botvin & Wills, 1987).

Moreover, the public health model argues that health care service delivery should be sensitive to cultural and individual differences. For example, although research indicates that among Mexican Americans alcohol abuse tends to increase with acculturation, acculturated Mexican American females reported more alcohol abuse than their male counterparts (Gilbert & Cervantes, 1986). Therefore, these differences would need to be taken into account when designing an alcohol intervention program with Mexican Americans.

The use of certain traditional treatment modalities (e.g., psychotherapy) may be appropriate for some ethnic minorities and inappropriate for others. For example, "In traditional Chinese Medicine, . . . the state of mind and the state of health are considered simultaneously" (Cheung, 1986, p. 207). That is, the use of medicine cannot be separated from the use of psychological treatment in the Chinese culture.

These scenarios are further complicated by the fact that U.S. medicine is derived from a male-biased model. For example, dependent behavior (relying on others) in males is less likely to be associated with histrionic or dependent personality disorders than in females (Kaplan, 1983). In other words, it is possible that when women seek relief from male physicians, the physicians interpret distress due to social problems or dependency as symptomatic of psychological disorders rather than of women's station in life (Muller, 1990).

The public health model is not without controversy. Some advocates argue that preventive care should *not* be equated with **health promotion,** which may consist of governmental interventions or **socialized medicine.** That is, in countries such as Canada and Singapore, governments not only educate their citizens about preventive care but also those who do not adhere to governmental health standards (e.g., no more than two children per family in Singapore) can be penalized. Americans who value their freedom of choice often find health promotion intrusive (Terris & Terris, 1990). As Erika and Tom, the couple in the opening vignette, might have believed, many Americans think that the government should not legislate morality. For example, although many Americans acknowledge that smoking is associated with a higher chance of developing cancer, they also perceive a smoking ban as an infringement on personal freedom. Nonetheless, in a critical analysis on drug prevention and intervention research, Pentz (2000) found that regulatory policies (including all formal laws, regulations, and ordinances) have the most immediate effect on youth tobacco and alcohol use, although programmatic policies have the most potential for longer-term effects. However, Pentz identified several barriers to institutionalizing community or public health prevention efforts. These include (1) perceived lack of empowerment by community leaders in prevention work; (2) lack of cross-fertilization between evidence-based work and practice; (3) disincentive to explore new approach(es) due to existing investment; and (4) perceived uniqueness of problems within each community. In brief, these arguments demonstrate the intertwining relationship between health care service delivery and practice, personal attitudes and culture, and governmental regulation. The following section on seat belt use illustrates the complexity of health care prevention—a mix of policy and individual and community empowerment.

Seat Belt Use: Road Warriors

Figure 10.1 presents a set of questions addressing an activity people frequently do not practice on a consistent basis: highway safety.

Extent of the Issue

The laws related to highway safety were designed to keep you and other citizens safe on the nation's highway. Yet, each day, thousands of motorists ignore these precautions, which is probably why there are 125 traffic deaths *each day* in the United States. Consider this staggering fact: More Americans die in vehicle crashes in one and one-half years than soldiers were killed *in all 10 years* of the Vietnam War (Geller, 1991). Given these statistics, why do intelligent adults put their lives at risk when simple actions on the nation's roads could prevent such tragedy?

Interventions Designed to Increase Safety

Because the average citizen is so resistant to common safety needs, psychologists have begun to experiment with means to increase highway safety. Berry and Geller (1991) tinkered with reminder systems in automobiles to "buckle up." The systems were visual (e.g., lights) or auditory (e.g., chimes) reminders to buckle seat belts. Some drivers were given two consecutive rather than one reminder. The results indicated that these prompts increased safety belt use for some but not all drivers.

FIGURE 10.1   War Against War on the Highways

Many Americans do not practice automobile safety although the behaviors are quite simple. How many safe practices do you follow?

1. Do you always wear your seat belt when you are a driver or passenger in a car?
2. Do you make sure that you do not exceed the speed limit when driving a car?
3. Do you carefully signal your intentions when you change lanes on a highway or intend to turn?
4. Do you come to a complete stop at stop signs?
5. Do you refrain from disposing of litter on the highways?
6. Do you play your car radio at a low enough volume so that you can hear oncoming sirens?
7. Do you pass only on the left?
8. Do you thoroughly clean snow and other debris that could disrupt your vision from your windshield before starting out in the morning?
9. Do you frequently inspect your windshield wipers, lights, and tires to make sure that they are in good working order?
10. Do you drive only when sober?

In a second study, Ludwig and Geller (1991) used group meetings of pizza deliverers who made a personal commitment to utilize their seat belts. Again, there was an increase above baseline in seat belt (143 percent increase) and turn signal (25 percent) use among some but not all of the drivers.

In yet a third study, Nimmer and Geller (1988) attempted to improve seat belt use of employees at a community hospital. Employees signed a pledge card, displayed a signed pledge in their vehicles, and had to wear their seat belts in order to receive an extra $5.00 in their paychecks at the week's end. Seat belt use increased overall, especially for the card signers, from 29.4 percent to 75.1 percent during the period in which they received extra pay for improved safety. Although there was some decrease in safety belt use when the reinforcer was removed, use was higher than the initial baseline measures for those individuals who had been reinforced with the extra pay.

Other research has demonstrated that these programs are effective with children, as well. Roberts, Fanurik, and Wilson (1988) developed a seat belt program at 25 schools. Children who buckled up received a reward (stickers, bumper strips, and chances on pizza dinners). The rewards increased compliance from 18.1 to 62.4 percent in the children.

As you can see from these studies, a variety of methods must be utilized to improve seat belt use (Geller, 1988). It is also apparent that not all methods are 100 percent effective. Some individuals are resistant, no matter how beneficial the behavior might be!

One last study demonstrates the importance of cultural context, too. Hayden (1989) examined the effects of laws in Illinois and then Yugoslavia. The laws mandated seat belt use in both geographic areas. Interestingly, in Illinois, there was marked public opposition to the laws, whereas in Yugoslavia, there was little open opposition to the laws (when the study was conducted, Yugoslavia was under Communist control). Curiously, compliance to the laws was greater in Illinois than in Yugoslavia. The results raise larger questions about the importance of cultural context, especially the cultural differences in receptivity and response to public policy changes.

URBAN VERSUS RURAL HEALTH

The interface between public and private sectors and community involvement (people's power) is likely to have different meanings in urban settings than in rural settings. Community psychologists know more about **urban health** than **rural health.** A common myth is that people living in rural settings (e.g., in the country) enjoy better health than those living in urban areas (e.g., with increased susceptibility to social ills such as infectious diseases, including HIV). Evidence does not substantiate this postulation. For example, according to CDC (unpublished data between 1994 and 1997), "The percent of total AIDS cases in nonmetropolitan areas has been rising, whereas it has been decreasing overall in metropolitan statistical areas (MSAs) with populations greater than 500,000 and holding fairly steady in those between 50,000 and 500,000" (NASTAD HIV Prevention Community Planning Bulletin, 1998).

A major challenge for studying rural health and its correlates (e.g., prevention) is what constitutes a *rural* setting (cf. Spoth, 1997). Population density is one criterion. How does one classify a low-density setting in close proximity to a metropolitan area—is it rural or suburban? What sort of public health system or policy should be adopted in such a setting? How does one engage people in such a disperse setting in coalition building?

In an exploratory study investigating rural HIV service delivery networks, Berry, McKinney, and Marconi (1997) provided some blueprints. Using a case-study methodology, the researchers identified three typologies: (1) degree of rurality, (2) AIDS prevalence, and (3) risk categories. The first typology included "population size, population density, [and] adjacency to MSAs as a proxies for access to HIV-related services" (p. 219). Prevalence of AIDS, the second typology, and risk categories (i.e., modes of transmission), the third typology, were based on standards set by the CDC. At a minimum, Berry and colleagues argued that "when a rural area is located in close proximity to an MSA, many HIV services can be provided through urban outreach programs" (p. 221). No doubt, more isolated areas (frontier and core rural areas) hinder the effectiveness of such programs. More importantly, these researchers stated that contextual factors need to be integral to the application and interpretation of these typologies. Given HIV and AIDS have extreme social stigma, rural areas with little history in providing public health services witnessed greater resistance in coalition building (e.g., mythologizing that AIDS is a "big-city problem"). People infected with the virus would travel outside their areas so as not to risk exposure of their identities (including being gay or bisexual), or they exclusively utilized private services. Advocates in these areas also spent more time on raising awareness and consciousness of the disease than providing services. In brief, these analyses suggest that effective rural health prevention and intervention need to be mindful of how a health issue (e.g., HIV) is being manifested (prevalence and risk category) and handled by its community (degree of rurality, such as public versus private sector and proximity to other resources).

SUMMARY

Health care is a multidimensional entity. At its core, good health is about social justice. At a macro level, social cohesion might have an effect on people's perceived quality of life—an important aspect of public health. In order to promote social cohesion, the discourse between the public and the private sectors needs to be complimented with the voice of the consumers or people's power. This power is most advantageous when the voice is a horizontal voice, as opposed to a vertical voice. At a micro level, people's power can be used to promote the health of individuals.

COMMUNITY HEALTH AND PREVENTIVE MEDICINE

Food and sex are human nature.
—Analect—Confucius, c. 550–478 B.C.

Anthony, age 65, and Danielle, age 63, have been married for more than 30 years and have three grown children. Anthony had been suffering from impotency the past 15 years. He and Danielle had no sexual relationship during these years. Recently, his doctor prescribed to him the drug Viagra; Anthony said he felt like a new man. Nine months into the treatment, Anthony tested positive for gonorrhea, a curable sexually transmitted disease (STD). Fortunately he tested negative for the human immunodeficiency virus (HIV) (also sexually transmittable) and other STDs. Danielle also tested positive for gonorrhea. Anthony was extremely embarrassed and admitted to Danielle that he had sex with prostitutes on several occasions. Anthony and Danielle agreed to a separation, to allow each other time to sort things out. Meanwhile, the children are disgusted with their father's behavior.

Biological and natural sciences have gained tremendous progress in the past several decades, ranging from the first open heart surgery to the recently cloned sheep named Dolly to the so-called miracle drug Viagra. Meanwhile, Americans still die from preventable diseases related to smoking and tobacco use (Center for Disease Control and Prevention, 2000). Each year more than one million Americans are injured in alcohol-related traffic accidents (National Highway Traffic Safety Administration, 1997). Infectious diseases (including STDs) are on the rise, coupled with the emergence of drug-resistant bacteria and viruses (Morbidity and Mortality Weekly Report [MMWR], 1998a). Collectively, these scenarios speak to the importance of community health or preventive medicine as an integral component of a healthy lifestyle. Perhaps Anthony's condition might have been preventable had he used condoms during his sexual escapades.

To that end, this chapter will examine five health issues from the perspectives of community psychology and preventive medicine; policy-based prevention targeting society in general or a community will also be discussed. These health issues were chosen for two main reasons. First, they have each received enormous attention in the media. Second, each is highly preventable if certain activities are practiced. In addition, a large number of people are affected or have the potential to be affected if prevention does not occur.

Statistics used to describe each of the health issues are drawn from various agencies in the U.S. Department of Health and Human Services (US DHHS) (e.g., CDC) and other federal (e.g., National Highway Traffic Safety Administration); state (e.g., Massachusetts Department of Public Health); national (e.g., American Public Health Association); and local (e.g., Asian and Pacific Islander Coalition on HIV/AIDS, Inc.), as well as international (e.g., the United Nations Programme on HIV/AIDS) entities. Each agency or source has its own approach and method in estimating the extent of a health issue (e.g., substance abuse). For example, the Substance Abuse and Mental Health Services Administration (SAMHSA), an agency within US DHHS whose mission is provision of substance-abuse treatment and services, conducts the National Household Survey on Drug Abuse targeting noninstitutionalized individuals age 12 and above nationwide. Another US DHHS agency, CDC, whose mission is public health epidemiology and surveillance, conducts the **Youth Risk Behavior Surveillance System (YRBSS)**—a school-based survey—and also yields estimates of alcohol use. Given this variability and the lag time in reporting the latest findings, you are encouraged to check these various resources for their methodologies and updated information (see Table 11.1 for some examples).

TOBACCO

Extent of the Problem

The **National Household Survey on Drug Abuse (NHSDA)** is the primary source of information on the prevalence, patterns, and consequences of drug and alcohol use and abuse in the general U.S. civilian noninstitutionalized population (including shelters, rooming houses, dormitories, and civilians living in military bases), age 12 and older. Results indicated that during the period between 1988 and 1996, among persons aged 12 to 17, the incidence of initiation of first **tobacco use,** or **smoking,** increased by 30 percent; first daily use

TABLE 11.1   Some Resources for Health-Related Statistics and Information

AGENCY	SOURCE	INTERNET ADDRESS
American Psychological Association	APA Monitor (June 2001 for special issue on substance abuse)	www.apa.org
American Public Health Association	The Nation's Health	www.apha.org
Asian and Pacific Islander Coalition on HIV/AIDS, Inc.		www.apicha.org
Asian and Pacific Islander Wellness Center		www.apiwellness.org
Centers for Disease Control and Prevention (including National Center for Health Statistics, Office on Smoking and Health)	Morbidity and Mortality Weekly Report Behavior Risk Factor Surveillance (adults only) Youth Risk Behavior Surveillance System	www.cdc.gov
Food and Drug Administration		www.fda.gov
The Legacy Foundation		www.americanlegacy.org
National Institutes of Health (including National Cancer Institute, National Institute on Drug Abuse)		www.nih.gov
Office of National Drug Control Policy		www.whitehousedrugpolicy.gov
Substance Abuse and Mental Health Services Administration	National Household Survey on Drug Abuse	www.samhsa.gov
United Nations Programme on HIV/ AIDS	AIDS epidemic update Declaration of Commitment on HIV/AIDS	www.unaids.org

increased by 59 percent; and in 1996, 1,226,000 persons aged 18 and above became daily smokers in 1996. Among persons aged 12 to 17, the incidence of first cigarette use decreased from 1974 (132.2 percent) to 1987 (98.6 percent) but increased from 1988 (107.0 percent) to 1995 (139.1 percent). For persons aged 18 to 25, first use decreased from the late 1960s through the late 1980s but increased during the 1990s (MMWR, 1998b).

The Youth Risk Behavior Surveillance System (YRBSS), the health-related survey funded by CDC, is nationwide, including 33 states, 3 territories, and 17 local schools grades

9 through 12. Findings indicated that, in 1999, 34.8 percent of adolescents reported smoking cigarettes on at least one day in the preceding 30 days ("current cigarette use"), up from 27.5 percent in 1991. Since 1995, rates have remained relatively stable. However, the rate of "frequent smokers" (those who reported smoking cigarettes on 20 of the preceding 30 days) rose from 12.7 percent in 1991 to 16.8 percent in 1999. White and Hispanic students were more likely (38.6 percent and 32.7 percent, respectively) than Black students (19.7 percent) to report current smoking. However, smoking among Black youths, which had been consistently declining, increased in the past decade.

Older students were more likely to smoke than younger students. Forty and one-half percent of twelfth grade females reported current cigarette use, compared to 29.2 percent of ninth grade females. The same was true for males; 45.2 percent of twelfth grade males reported being current smokers, compared to 26.1 percent of ninth grade males. It is estimated that each day 6,000 adolescents will try smoking, and 3,000 persons under age 18 will become daily smokers.

One of every six deaths in the United States is attributable to tobacco use, or smoking. These terms are often used interchangeably; note, however, that tobacco use also includes smokeless tobacco (see Figure 11.1), which is linked to various oral cancers. Regular tobacco use increases the risk for developing a number of serious diseases, including heart and blood problems, chronic bronchitis and emphysema, and cancer of the lung, just to name a few. Smoking alone is responsible for 21 percent of all coronary heart disease deaths (40 percent of those under age 65), 87 percent of lung cancer deaths, and 30 percent of all cancer deaths (Office on Smoking and Health, 1989).

Smoking during pregnancy is a major risk for giving birth to **low-weight infants** (less than 2,500 grams or 5.5 pounds), which accounts for 20 to 30 percent of these infants (Kleinman & Madanas, 1985). Birth weight is directly correlated with chances of survival. Also, 14 percent of **preterm births** (usually less than 37 weeks of gestation) are attributable to smoking, as are 10 percent of all infant deaths (Office on Smoking and Health, 1989). Mean-

FIGURE 11.1   Some Ingredients in Smokeless Tobacco

Acetaldehyde (irritant)

Benzopyrene (cancer-causing agent)

Cadmium (used in car batteries)

Formaldehyde (embalming fluid)

Lead (nerve poison)

Nicotine (addictive drug)

N-Nitrosamines (cancer-causing agents)

Polonium 210 (nuclear waste)

Uranium 235 (used in nuclear weapons)

while, 25 percent of pregnant women continue to smoke throughout their pregnancies (National Center for Health Statistics, 1989).

Another way to appreciate the negative consequences of smoking is to calculate or estimate the money needed to provide medical and health-related services to people who are suffering or dying from smoking-related diseases or illnesses. These services include but are not limited to ambulatory care, prescription drugs, hospital care, home health services, and nursing-home care. These services are used to calculate **state medical expenditures (SAEs)**—the financial cost to the state in providing medical and health-related services to people suffering from smoking-attributable diseases or illnesses (CDC, 1996). In a comprehensive analysis, Miller, Zhang, Rice, and Max (1998) found that in 1993, "the estimated proportion of total medical expenditures attributable to smoking for the United States as a whole was 11.8%. . . . Total U.S. medical expenditures attributable to smoking amounted to an estimated $72.7 billion in 1993" (p. 447). In short, these dollar figures are staggering! Holding the tobacco industry financially and legally liable has become an increasingly popular strategy among state officials in their antitobacco efforts.

Although some progress has been made in the reduction of tobacco use in the past 35 years (e.g., 40 percent of adults smoked in 1965 versus 23.6 percent of adults in 1996; MMWR, 1997), the fight for a smoke-free society is far from over. The fight was never more vivid and clear than when First Lady Hillary Rodham Clinton declared the White House a smoke-free environment. Mrs. Clinton's effort is substantiated with scientific evidence gathered by the Environmental Protection Agency in classifying **environmental tobacco smoke (ETS),** better known as **secondhand smoke,** as a Group A (known human) carcinogen. Exposure to ETS is responsible for approximately 3,000 lung cancer deaths per year in nonsmoking adults. Also, an estimated 150,000 to 300,000 cases of lower respiratory tract infections (e.g., bronchitis and pneumonia) every year in infants and children up to 18 months of age alone are attributed to ETS (Massachusetts Department of Public Health, 1991).

Antitobacco Efforts

Antitobacco efforts include smoking bans by the Pentagon in all military facilities as well as proposed laws to regulate tobacco products by the federal Food and Drug Administration (FDA) due the addictive nature of nicotine. Also, the **National Cancer Institute** (NCI, 1991) funds longitudinal demonstration projects. In brief, the NCI emphasizes a tripartite model that uses (1) media (i.e., mass media), (2) policy (e.g., regulations or laws and taxation), and (3) services and programs (e.g., cessation programs) to target specific vulnerable groups, such as ethnic minorities, youth, and women, via multiple channels (e.g., hospitals and schools).

Based on these standards and funds from an increase in the tobacco excise tax, the states of California and Massachusetts are engaging in the most comprehensive tobacco prevention and control programs in the United States. In 1994, the Massachusetts Tobacco Control Program funded more than 300 programs ($96 million), ranging from media campaigns to smoking cessation programs in primary care settings, as well as school-based interventions. Other states, such as Arizona, are following suit with aggressive antitobacco campaigns. In fact, drawing from a tobacco excise tax, Arizona has spent $30 million a year since 1995 on tobacco prevention and control. Smoking among residents in Arizona decreased by 21 percent between 1996 and 1999, with substantial decreases among men, women, Blacks, and Hispanics in all age and education groups (The Nation's Health, 2001). The recent settlement by the tobacco industry on a lawsuit brought by the various state attorneys has resulted in the creation of The Legacy Foundation, a one-of-a-kind organization, the sole mission of which is to prevent tobacco use, especially among youths.

Despite these antitobacco efforts, every year the tobacco industry spends millions of dollars in advertising and promoting tobacco (e.g., free coupons, leather jackets with logos of the product, etc.). In addition, the industry is quick to use image-based propaganda, which has been demonstrated to be effective with youth as well as the less educated. For example, DiFranza and colleagues (1991) found that Joe Camel (a cartoon character smoking a Camel cigarette) was more readily recognized by children than Mickey Mouse. Meanwhile, the prevalence of smoking remains disproportionately high among African Americans, blue-collar workers, and the less educated (U.S. Department of Health and Human Services, 1991). Also, although the use of illicit drugs among youth actually *decreased* in the 1990s, smoking among adolescent females *appears to be on the rise* (Johnston, O'Malley, & Bachman, 1993).

In constant dollars, money spent by the tobacco industry on advertising and promotion has tripled since 1975. The total expenditure for cigarette advertising and promotion in 1988 was $3.3 billion, a 27 percent increase over 1987 expenditures (Centers for Disease Control, 1990). Also, there is evidence to indicate that the industry is focusing more attention on the use of indirect strategies, such as the use of "front groups" to conceal its own involvement in fighting local tobacco control ordinances (Traynor, Begay, & Glantz, 1993). In other words, those who engage in antitobacco efforts (including the NCI) are facing a Herculean task.

Community-Based Approaches

The fact that 66.7 percent of youth in a nationwide school-based survey (1997 Youth Risk Behavior Surveillance System) were able to purchase cigarettes without proof of age (MMWR, 1998b) suggests that health-related legal policy (e.g., "no sale to minors") is just the first step in the fight for a smoke-free environment (Jason, Berk, Schnopp-Wyatt, & Talbot, 1999). Biglan and associates (1996) argued that

> many law enforcement officers feel that there are more important crimes to deal with and that judges will be annoyed if such cases are brought before them. In addition, if the value of reducing such sales has not been adequately publicized, there is a risk that enforcement will produce a backlash against tobacco control efforts. (p. 626)

Implicit in these words are that members in a community must have a sense of ownership, including how they view and implement health-related legal policy. To test this premise, Biglan and colleagues designed a five-component intervention program to reduce youth access to tobacco products in two small Oregon communities. The outcome of interest was the proportion of tobacco outlets in the community that were willingly to sell tobacco products to youth.

Using a quasi-experimental design, Biglan and colleagues (1996) conducted their five-component intervention in the two selected Oregon communities; two other similar communities did not receive the intervention. Specifically, activities of *mobilization of community support* included a letter and signature campaign sought from members of various community sectors (e.g., school district, health care providers, and civic organizations) to produce a proclamation of no sale of tobacco to youth. *Merchant education* involved visits and distribution of the proclamation to all tobacco outlets. A modified sting operation was employed to *change consequences to clerks* for selling or not selling tobacco to those under age 18. That is, those who complied with the law were rewarded each time with a gift certificate worth $2 for use in a local business. Those who violated the law were given a reminder of the law and the community proclamation of no sale of tobacco to youth. These activities were described in public media (e.g., newspaper) as part of the *publicity intervention strategy*. Finally, *owners of tobacco outlets were personally informed* about these activities (identity of clerks were masked). In brief, the five components represented a range of macro level (e.g., mobilization of community) to micro level (e.g., feedback to store owners) intervention strategies. Results indicated that tobacco outlets' willingness to sell tobacco products to youth was significantly lower in the intervention group than those in the control group.

The research by Biglan and colleagues (1996) speaks to the importance of community-based involvement in augmenting health-related legal policy. Similar strategies were used by Lichtenstein, Lopez, Glasgow, Gilbert-McRae, and Hall (1996) to work with northwest Native American tribes to promote the tribes' involvement in tobacco control use policies. These researchers used a consultation model to build trust among community members (especially in light of the historical relationship between Native Americans and the mainstream U.S. society) in an intervention with a quasi-experimental design. The methodology used was the **wait-list design** in which both the intervention group and wait-list control group received the pretests, and the wait-list control group received the intervention after the completion of the posttest in the intervention group. The components of the intervention included (1) a tribal representative attending a kickoff orientation, (2) follow-up visits to the tribes, (3) distribution of tobacco policy workbooks, and (4) phone consultations. Integral to these components were active engagement with tribal members in the decision-making process. Results revealed greater tobacco policy stringency (i.e., for tobacco control) and enactment of new policies in the intervention group than in the control group.

ALCOHOL

Extent of the Problem

In addition to cigarette smoking, **alcohol** is a gateway drug to other drug use or abuse. According to the 1997 Youth Risk Behavior Surveillance System (Morbidity and Mortality Weekly Report, 1998c), 79.1 percent of all students had had at least one drink of alcohol during their lifetimes. Nearly one-third (31.1 percent) of all students had first used alcohol (more than a few sips) before 13 years of age. There were gender by racial/ethnic by grade differences in this behavior. For example, male students (35.7 percent) were significantly more likely than female students (25.7 percent) to use alcohol before 13 years of age.

State prevalence rates (current behavior) ranged from 24.3 to 61.1 percent (median was 50.5 percent); local school prevalence rates ranged from 59.2 to 78.2 percent (median was 72.5 percent). There were graded by gender by racial/ethnic differences in these rates. For example, students from grades 11 and 12 were significantly more likely to drink than students in grades 9 and 10, and male students were significantly more likely than female students to drink.

Alcohol use before or during sex is a major risk for unprotected sex (Leigh & Stall, 1993), which might result in unwanted pregnancy and acquisition of STDs (including HIV). One-fourth (24.7 percent) of all students had used alcohol or drugs at their most recent sexual intercourse. State prevalence rates (current behavior) ranged from 10.9 to 26.1 percent (median was 26.6 percent); local school prevalence rates ranged from 15.5 to 28.4 percent (median was 20.0 percent). Overall, male students (30.5 percent) were significantly more likely than female students (18.5 percent) to use alcohol or drugs during their most recent sexual intercourse. Overall, White students (26.0 percent) were significantly more likely than Black students (18.1 percent) to engage in this behavior.

Almost one-fourth (22.4 percent) of all students had had five or more drinks in a row on more than one occasion during the 30 days preceding the survey (i.e., episodic heavy drinking). There were gender by racial/ethnic by grade differences in this behavior. For example, male students (37.3 percent) were significantly more likely than female students (28.6 percent) to report episodic heavy drinking.

In a recent survey of 15,000 students at 116 universities and colleges in 36 states, Wechsler, Dowdall, Maenner, Gledhill-Hoyt, and Lee (1998) found that **binge drinking** (consumption of five or more drinks in a row for men or four or more drinks in a row for women) is on the rise. It is noted that many of these students were probably under age. Some of the key findings are:

■ The proportion of drinkers who "drank to get drunk" increased by one-third, from 39 percent in 1993 to 52 percent in 1997.

■ The proportion of drinkers who got drunk three or more times in the previous month increased by 22 percent.

■ More than one-third of the students surveyed reported driving after drinking, a 13 percent increase since 1993.

■ Four out of five fraternity and sorority members were binge drinkers.

However, Wechsler and associates noted that significantly more students abstained from drinking in 1997 (19 percent) than in 1993 (15.6 percent).

Other findings of the survey reveal that four out of five nonbinge drinkers living on campus had experienced at least one secondhand effect of binge drinking. That is, some of these nonbinge drinkers were victims of unwanted sexual advances, having property vandalized, or having sleep or studies disrupted.

Blood Alcohol Content (BAC) Laws

Misuse of alcohol is responsible for 1.4 million **DWI (driving while intoxicated)** citations annually (National Highway Traffic Safety Administration, 1996). Moreover, approximately one-third of these DWI cases are repeated offenders (National Highway Safety Administration, 1995). Annually, 1 million people are the victims of alcohol-related traffic accidents; approximately 17,000 died in these accidents (National Highway Traffic Safety Administration, 1997). The highest rate of drunken-driving fatalities occurred among young adults, ages 21 to 34 (49.8 percent) (The Nation's Health, 1998).

Despite these grim statistics, at the time of this writing, alcohol-related deaths have dropped to a historical low since recordkeeping began in 1975. Of the 41,967 traffic fatalities in 1997, 38.6 percent (16,189) were related to alcohol; the rate for 1996 was 40.9 percent. Policy makers and researchers alike attribute this decline to the tough law in lowering the **blood alcohol content (BAC)** to 0.08. Of the 15 states with this law, 10 continue to observe declines in alcohol-related fatalities. One state, Kansas, witnessed a drop from 40.2 percent in 1996 to 29.5 percent in 1997. Some policy makers argue for even tougher standards, such as the 0.02 BAC law in South Carolina (The Nation's Health, 1998). Using the state of Maine as a case study, Hingson, Hereen, and Winter (1998) demonstrated that "fatal crashes involving drivers with recorded prior DWI convictions declined by 25% following passage of the 0.05 DWI law, while the proportion rose in the rest of new England during the same year" (p. 440). Before the change, Maine had 0.10 BAC law.

In September 1998, Vice President Al Gore announced incentive grants (under the Transportation Equity Act for the 21st Century) totaling more than $71 million for states to help deter drinking and driving. About $49 million were dedicated to enforce the BAC 0.08 law (see Case in Point 11.1).

A Community Psychology Approach

As argued earlier, health-related legal policy is most appreciated or effective when people feel they are empowered to make informed choices and decisions, including why they should heed health advice by experts or government officials. A key component in this equation is that empowerment (and its effect on decision making) often begin at home (e.g., parents talk to their children about the good and bad of drinking, premarital sex, etc.) and at school (e.g., peers for prosocial behaviors). In other words, values and skills learned or derived from these two Oregon communities or environments are thought to be instrumental in health-related decision-making processes. Thus, next is a brief review of a study using parent-child involvement as a strategy to address alcohol use among youth.

Spoth, Redmond, Hockaday, and Yoo (1996) identified (1) affectional relationship with parents, (2) affiliation with prosocial peers, and (3) mastery esteem (being in control of the forces affecting one's destiny) as three key protective factors to reduce the risk of substance use among youth in an intervention study (Preparing Drug Free Years or [PDFY]) using a wait-list design. The basic format of PDFY consisted of a total of five 2-hour sessions involving at least one parent and the child. Each session was a mixture of family-

CASE IN POINT 11.1
ALCOHOL WARNING

Beginning in November 1989, Title VIII of Public Law 100-690 mandated the use of warning labels on all alcoholic beverage containers and warning signs posted in places where liquor is sold. Specifically, the message states:

> GOVERNMENT WARNING: 1. According to the Surgeon General, women should not drink alcoholic beverages during pregnancy because of the risk of birth defects. 2. Consumption of alcoholic beverages impairs your ability to drive a car or operate machinery and may cause health problems.

Some success has been observed with the use of warning labels on tobacco products and consumer goods (e.g., saccharin). Researchers Barrett, Wong, and McKay (1993) wanted to know if similar success was evident with alcohol warning labels and signs, especially among women of childbearing age (alcohol use during pregnancy is a major risk for fetal alcohol syndrome). The two main outcomes of interest were self-reported alcohol use and ability to recall information about pregnancy risk contained in the warning labels and signs.

As part of a population telephone survey conducted in Illinois during the spring and summer of 1990, Barrett and colleagues asked 1,515 women of childbearing age (18 to 45) the following questions:

1. Have you seen the warning labels that are printed on alcoholic beverage containers?
2. Have you seen the new government signs posted in places where liquor is sold?

For those who answered yes to these two questions, they were asked:

3. What do you remember about what the warning label/sign says?

It was found that pregnant women were significantly less likely than nonpregnant women to report using alcohol in the past 30 days. Approximately one-fourth of all women were able to recall information about pregnancy risk contained in the warning labels and signs. However, women who were African American, lived in urban areas other than Cook County (including Chicago), were classified as potential problem drinkers, reported using alcohol in the past 30 days and in the past year were less likely than women without these characteristics to recall such information. In other words, the impact or effectiveness of alcohol warning labels and signs among women of childbearing age is or might be moderated by socioeconomic factors such as education, income, and history of alcohol use.

focused competency training and skills building. It was hypothesized that positive parental involvement would increase the youth's tendency to select peers who have similar values as those of the youth's parents. This prosocial peer relationship would, in turn, lead to mastery esteem. Overall, results supported the claim of the protective effects of the three factors on self-reported behavioral tendency toward alcohol abstinence. That is, such effects were significantly more pronounced in the intervention group than in the control group.

ILLICIT DRUGS

Extent of the Problem

According to a report of the **Office of National Drug Control Policy** (1998), overall drug use remained stable in 1996. An estimate of 6.1 percent (13 million) of the U.S. household population age 12 and over were current drug users. This percentage was a significant improvement since 1979 (14.1 percent). However, 34.8 percent of youth and young adults continued to experience or use illicit drugs.

According to the 1997 Youth Risk Behavior Surveillance System (MMWR, 1998c), "ever used" of (1) **marijuana,** (2) **cocaine** (including powder, crack, and freebase), (3) **steroids,** (4) **intravenous drugs,** (5) **other illegal drugs** (including LSD [lysergic acid diethylamide], PCP [phencyclidine], ecstasy [methylenedioxymethamphetamine], mushrooms, speed [especially amphetamine], ice [methamphetamine], and heroin), and (6) **inhalants,** were reported by 47.1 percent, 8.2 percent, 3.1 percent, 2.1 percent, 17.0 percent, and 16.0 percent, respectively, of all students. About 1 in 10 of all students (9.7 percent) had tried marijuana before 13 years of age. There were gender by grade by race/ethnic differences in this behavior. For example, male students (12.2 percent) were significantly more likely than female students (6.7 percent) to have tried marijuana before age 13.

For marijuana, state prevalence rates (current behaviors) ranged from 12.3 to 35.3 percent (median was 25.3 percent); local school prevalence rates ranged from 15.7 to 29.3 percent. For cocaine, state prevalence rates ranged from 0.2 to 5.8 percent (median was 3.5 percent); local school prevalence rates ranged from 0.6 to 4.4 percent (median was 1.8 percent). For steroids, state lifetime (i.e., ever used) rates ranged from 0.5 to 6.7 percent (median was 4.2 percent); local school lifetime rates ranged from 1.8 to 4.6 percent (median was 3.4 percent). For intravenous drugs, state lifetime rates ranged from 0.3 to 4.2 percent (median was 2.5 percent); local school lifetime rates ranged from 0.8 to 3.5 percent (median was 2.0 percent). For other illegal drugs, state prevalence rates ranged from 0.9 to 26.4 percent (median was 16.4 percent); local school prevalence rates ranged from 2.6 to 15.9 percent (median was 7.6 percent). For inhalants, state prevalence rates ranged from 7.4 to 28.4 percent (median was 18.3 percent); local school prevalence rates ranged from 6.2 to 17.7 percent (median was 12.1 percent).

Marijuana was the most popular choice of drug—26.2 percent of all students had used marijuana one or more times during the 30 days preceding the survey. However, there is a great deal of variability in illegal drug use depending on such factors as gender, grade, and race/ethnicity. For example, male students were more likely then female students to use marijuana (50.7 vs. 42.9 percent), steroids (4.1 vs. 2.0 percent), and inhalants (17.6 vs. 14.15 percent). Hispanic and White female students (5.3 and 2.3 percent, respectively) were significantly more likely than Black female students (0.2 percent) to report current cocaine use.

There are many dire consequences due to illicit drug use, including but not limited to crime, domestic violence, illnesses, loss in productivity, and increases in sexually transmitted diseases (STDs) (including HIV). About 60 percent of federal prisoners in 1995 were sentenced for drug-related violations. In 1996, 1.5 million Americans were arrested for drug-related violations. The increase in drug offenders accounts for nearly three-quarters of the growth in the federal prison population between 1985 and 1995. In 1996, an estimate of 1.9 million illicit drug users worked part time; however, their drug habits were likely to make them less dependable. Research has consistently demonstrated that illicit drug use increases the transmission and acquisition of STDs (including HIV). It is estimated that 35 percent of new HIV cases are directly or indirectly linked to intravenous drug users (IVDUs). Finally, it is estimated that illicit drug use costs our society about $67 billion each year (Office of National Drug Control Policy, 1998).

Possible Solutions and Challenges

The report, **The National Drug Control Strategy, 1998,** of the Office of National Drug Control Policy outlines a 10-year plan. This report was prepared as a result of newly enacted law, The Drug-Free Communities Act of 1997, which amends the National Narcotics Leadership Act of 1988. The 10-year plan describes the federal approaches, in consultation with state and local as well as international governments, on the war against drugs. There are a total of five goals; each has multiple objectives:

1. Educate and enable America's youth to reject illegal drugs as well as alcohol and tobacco.
2. Increase the safety of America's citizens by substantially reducing drug-related crime and violence.
3. Reduce health and social costs to the public of illegal use.
4. Shield America's air, land, and sea frontiers from the drug threat.
5. Break foreign and domestic sources of supply.

   A total of 12 programs were highlighted in the report:

1. Youth Anti-Drug Media Campaign
2. School Drug Prevention Coordinators
3. Drug Treatment
4. Drug Research
5. Youth Tobacco Initiative
6. Criminal Justice System—Drug Intervention Program
7. Methamphetamine Initiative
8. Southwest Border—Border Patrol
9. Ports-of-Entry—U.S. Customs Service
10. Interdiction—U.S. Coast Guard
11. Interdiction Support—Defense
12. International Country Support

Of the 12 programs, 7 employ law-enforcement strategies on the war against drugs. Thus, they have disproportionately received more federal resources and support (in dollar amounts) than prevention programs. (The term **prevention** is used here in an inclusive sense to capture the overlap of primary, secondary, and tertiary modalities that occur in the illicit drug literature and in the implementation of the clinical programs.) One question comes to mind: What does community psychology or community-based research have to say about the war against drugs? In the late 1980s to the mid-1990s, federal agencies such as the Center for Substance Abuse Prevention and Centers for Substance Abuse Treatment funded a series of demonstration projects (community-based prevention strategies). Some of these initiatives are still in operation today. A review of articles published in the *American Journal of Community Psychology* and *Journal of Community Psychology,* as well as various monographs, such as those published by the National Institute on Drug Abuse from 1990 to 1998, revealed scant empirical community-based illicit drug-prevention studies (especially those delineating effective strategies). It is possible that lag time is needed for researchers to publish their findings. Meanwhile, the relative small role played by community-based perspectives (in the spirit of community psychology) in the national strategies on the war against drugs (excluding tobacco and to some extent alcohol) call for a more proactive role in advocating for such perspectives.

Available evidence strongly indicates the contribution of community psychology on the war against drugs. In an experimental study with pre- and postmeasures, Latkin, Mandell, Vlahov, Oziemkowska, and Celentano (1996) used social norms to influence drug-use habits among IVDUs. At baseline, all participants provided social norm information about their drug-use networks (known as *indexes' drug networks*) before being randomly assigned into an experimental group or a control group. Those enrolled in the experimental group were known as the *indexes.* They were asked to encourage their eligible IVDU friends to enroll in the study. During an 18-month period, all participants received HIV testing and risk-reduction information. In addition, experimental participants (including the indexes and their friends eligible for the study) were instructed to use "self-help, network-centered and psychoeducational approaches" for safer behavior maintenance. These self-help activities were designed for the experimental participants to reconceptualize HIV risks. Results indicated that the experimental group reported less needle sharing and injection of heroin and cocaine than the control group.

Evidence for community-based prevention strategies (e.g., school-based) targeting youths is also available. Using a meta-analytic technique as a tool to integrate 207 universal school-based drug prevention programs, Tobler, Ronna, Ochshorn, Marshall, Streke, and Stackpole (2000) found that interactive programs (e.g., development of interpersonal skills) were more effective than noninteractive programs (e.g., lecture). This finding suggests that youths need to feel "engaged"—not just be passive recipients—to reap the benefit of the prevention message.

SEXUALLY TRANSMITTED DISEASES

Extent of the Problem

The United States has the highest rates of **sexually transmitted diseases (STDs)** in the industrialized world. For example, although **gonorrhea** incidence in the United States declined nearly 60 percent during 1980 to 1996, the 1996 rate of 124 per 100,000 was 26 times greater than the rate in Germany (4.7 per 100,000) and 50 times the rate in Sweden (2.4 per 100,000). Furthermore, gonorrhea continues to grow among certain subpopulations, such as **men who have sex with men (MSM),** especially among young MSM, in the United States. Based solely on the 1996 routine disease-reporting system, the rate of gonorrhea among African American women ages 15 to 19 and African American men ages 20 to 24 alone was 3 percent. In 1996, the incidence rate for **syphilis** in the United States was 20.2 percent, 13 times higher than the rate in Germany (1.5 percent) and 33 times higher than the rate in Sweden (0.6 percent). In addition, rates of primary and secondary syphilis are about 50 times more prevalent among African Americans than Whites. In 1996, regardless of race or socioeconomic status, 5 to 10 percent (prevalence) of sexually active adolescents in the United States had **chlamydia** (MMWR, 1998a). Adolescents and young people are at greater risk for STDs due to their riskier behaviors, such as having multiple partners or engaging in unprotected sex. Female adolescents are at a particularly higher risk, as many STDs are more easily spread from male to female and often remain undetected in females. While it is difficult to know exactly the prevalence of STDs among young people, it is estimated that chlamydia, a common STD, infects

- 308.4 per 100,000 males aged 15–19
- 2,359 per 100,000 females aged 15–19
- 432.5 per 100,000 males aged 20–24
- 1,952.7 per 100,000 females aged 20–24 (CDC, 2000)

While many STDs are completely curable with antibiotics, some viral infections—such as Hepatitis, Human Papillomavirus (HPV), and HIV—can be treated but never cured. The effects of some STDs can last a lifetime; some forms of HPV are the precursor to cervical cancer and effects of chlamydia, if untreated, can lead to infertility. As in the case of HIV, the precursor to AIDS, the result may even be death.

The nature and impact of STDs are multifaceted. The Institute of Medicine (1997) estimated that in 1994, $10 billion was spent on STD treatments; another $6.7 billion was spend on HIV treatments. Although many people experience little to no symptoms (thus are never treated), diseases such as chlamydia might cause infertility in women. Other STDs such as **Hepatitis A** (sexually transmitted or food borne due to fecal contamination) and **Hepatitis C** tended to be more prevalent among MSM and **intravenous drug users (IVDUs),** respectively. Moreover, rates of STDs tend to be higher among drug users (both intravenous and nonintravenous [including alcohol and other drugs] drug users). Epidemiologic studies consistently demonstrate that concurrent STDs increase the transmission probability for HIV infection. The mutually reinforcing nature of these infectious processes has been termed **epidemiological synergy** (MMWR, 1998a).

Possible Solutions and Challenges

The Advisory Committee for HIV and STD Prevention made the following recommendations:

1. *Assess and ensure timely access to high quality STD clinical care for persons seeking medical services for symptoms of STDs in private and public medical-care setting.*

2. *Screen for asymptomatic or recognized STD infection in medical-care settings according to current guidelines, and expand screening as needed based on prevalence of infections detected in pilot screening efforts.*
3. *Establish or expand STD screening in nonmedical settings where persons at high risk for HIV infection and curable STDs are encouraged and can be treated efficiently, including jails and other correctional facilities, substance abuse treatment centers, and hospital emergency departments.*
4. *Provide cross-training to program and management staff including HIV prevention community planning groups, on the role of STD detection and treatment in HIV prevention. (MMWR, 1998a, p. 11)*

These recommendations are derived from an extensive review of the scientific and empirical literature on STD prevention and intervention. One successful prevention/intervention program was conducted in the Mwanza district of Tanzania. In this community-level trial, provision of STD treatments reduced the acquisition of HIV infection. The impact was independent of changes in sexual behaviors and condom use. Most of all, "the program's cost-effectiveness of $217 (U.S.) per HIV infection averted and $10 (U.S.) per disability-adjusted life-year (DALY) saved, compared favorably with other highly effective public health interventions (e.g., childhood vaccinations, which cost $12–$17 [U.S.] per DALY" (MMWR, 1998a, pp. 3–4).

This trial in Tanzania demonstrates that it is possible to prevent STDs (including HIV). However, can these results be replicated in the United States? In addition to access to care as well as early detection and screenings, implicit in the recommendations is that sex education as part of a healthy lifestyle must be integral to the community-focused or community-based prevention and intervention programs, which are echoed in the recent report, *The Surgeon General's Call to Action to Promote Sexual Health and Responsible Sexual Behavior,* by the U.S. Surgeon Dr. David Satcher (2001). The challenge for U.S. community-based researchers is how to integrate sex education into such programs without coming across as promoting certain sexual practices or lifestyles (e.g., bisexual) that a major segment of the society finds unacceptable. A review of studies published in the *American Journal of Community Psychology* and the *Journal of Community Psychology* from 1990 to 2001 presumes that community psychologists have done little or no work on STD (excluding HIV and AIDS) prevention and intervention. What are the reasons for the paucity or lack of research? Is it because sex is a taboo or an uncomfortable topic for discussion? Or are we too disease focused (e.g., HIV) instead of being promoters of a healthy lifestyle, which includes sexuality?

In the opening vignette, Anthony came from a generation in which sex education was not available. Morality aside, *safer sex* was not part of his vocabulary. Even if Anthony had wanted to use condoms with Danielle, his action would very likely have been perceived by her as a sign of infidelity. Nonetheless, if Anthony had used condoms during his sexual escapades, both he and Danielle would likely have been spared from acquiring gonorrhea. Meanwhile, many people in U.S. society are uncomfortable with the notion that individuals in Anthony's age category still enjoy and can have sex. In addition to changes in social or community norms and a longer life span, the explosion of medical advances are likely to affect people's sexual behaviors and practices. To have a drug such as Viagra without the appro-

■ ■ ■ ■ ■

CASE IN POINT 11.2

STDS TESTING AND EDUCATION IN A COMMUNITY SETTING

The Asian and Pacific Islander Wellness Center (APIWC), located in San Francisco, is the largest agency in the country providing HIV-related services to people of Asian and Pacific Islander (API) descent. The center is located in an area where there is a high concentration of commercial sex workers (many are undocumented APIs) and other high-risk and at-risk APIs (e.g., preoperative transgender individuals who occasionally trade sex for money to buy hormones).

In 1998, APIWC initiated an innovative pilot STD-prevention program targeting high-risk and at-risk Asian and Pacific Islanders. Working with the San Francisco Department of Public Health, an initial biweekly night clinic was set up for STD screening. As part of the screening, health-related

education materials (including sex education) were distributed to all clients. Also, APIWC staff worked with clients on health-related and social services referrals. The success of the program was almost immediate; by the third night, clinic staff at APIWC had to turn away clients.

The program is still in operation. The lesson here is that STD prevention and intervention, especially among vulnerable populations, must be an integral part of the promotion of a healthy lifestyle. To many of the clients, STD screening or treatment is one of many reasons they seek services at APIWC. Another important reason includes a social support system (e.g., health-related social services referrals).

priate social technology, such as how to engage in safer and enjoyable sex in later life, is to ask for disaster to happen. It was fortunate that Anthony got a curable STD—gonorrhea. Using the same logic, access to STD-related services is only the first step. Our society or communities need to seriously consider how to integrate sexuality into healthy lifestyle prevention and intervention strategies (see Case in Point 11.2).

HUMAN IMMUNODEFICIENCY VIRUS (HIV) AND ACQUIRED IMMUNODEFICIENCY DISEASES

Overview

At the time of this writing, more than 36.1 million people in the world have been infected with the **human immunodeficiency virus (HIV),** which is thought to be responsible for the **acquired immunodeficiency syndrome (AIDS),** an incurable disease. Some countries are more severely affected by the pandemic than others. For example, it is estimated that one out of five adults in Zimbabwe is infected with HIV and more than three million HIV-positive people live in India (United Nations Programme on HIV/AIDS [UNAIDS], 2000). With the disease in its third decade, the United Nations finally announced a formal "Declaration of Commitment on HIV/AIDS" on June 27, 2001(UNAIDS, 2001), although compromise was needed to pacify those who objected to inclusion of and targeting of sex workers, men who have sex with men, injection drug users, and so forth as vulnerable populations in the fight against the virus. Special languages were used to include such individuals without explicitly mentioning them.

FIGURE 11.2   Characteristics of People with HIV or AIDS

Brain lesions (advanced stage of AIDS)

Frequent diarrhea

Loss of appetite

Low-grade fever that will not go away

Low T-cell count (below 400; T-cells are involved in fighting infection)

Oral thrush (e.g., lesions inside the mouth)

Pneumonia

Skin lesions (e.g., Kaposi's sarcoma)

Swollen glands

Weight loss

It is noted that HIV is *not* the cause of AIDS. Rather, being HIV-positive weakens one's immune system, thus opening the door for opportunistic infections (OIs) that lead to AIDS (see Figure 11.2). However, there is a small group of dissenting scientists who do not believe HIV is responsible for AIDS; they are generally ignored by the mainstream scientific community.

In the late 1970s and early 1980s, the medical community in the United States began to notice a strange disease, mostly infecting homosexual men and IVDUs. Very soon, terms such as *HIV, AIDS,* and *ARC* (AIDS-related complex) became household words. Although HIV and AIDS were first recognized in homosexual men in this country, the disease has now been shown to infect all men, including heterosexual men, and women (see Table 11.2). Scientists and laypeople alike speculate about the origin of HIV and AIDS; theories range from the "green monkey theory" (a specie of African monkeys that is thought to be the genesis of the incurable disease) to biological warfare conducted by the U.S. Central Intelligence Agency. Still others (Eigen, 1993) have argued that HIV has been present in human beings for more than 120 years, just waiting for the right circumstances to attack the human immune system.

At the time of this writing, according to the Centers for Disease Control (CDC, 2000) AIDS is no longer one of the top nine leading causes of death for most people in the United States, although HIV infection continues to rise (especially among African Americans and Hispanic Americans as well as heterosexual women). The significant drop in AIDS' deaths first observed in 1997 is attributed to the new **cocktail or combination drug therapy** (including **protease inhibitors**). Where available, the combination drug therapy using protease inhibitors has dramatically reduced the morbidity and mortality related to AIDS. For example, several clinical studies have reported a 65 to 75 percent decrease in the death rate and incidence of **opportunistic infections (OIs)** between 1994 and 1997, the same time during which combination therapies became increasingly prescribed.

TABLE 11.2   Regional HIV Statistics and Features, End of 2000

REGION	EPIDEMIC STARTED	ADULTS & CHILDREN LIVING WITH HIV/AIDS	% OF HIV-POSITIVE ADULT FEMALES	MAIN MODE OF TRANSMISSION FOR ADULTS
Sub-Sahara Africa	Late 1970s–early 1980s	25.5 million	55%	Heterosexual sex
North Africa & Middle East	Late 1980s	400,000	40%	Heterosexual sex Injection drug use
South & Southeast Asia	Late 1980s	5.8 million	35%	Heterosexual sex Injection drug use
East Asia & Pacific	Late 1980s	640,000	13%	Injection drug use Heterosexual sex Men having sex with men
Latin America	Late 1970s–early 1980s	1.4 million	25%	Men having sex with men Injection drug use Heterosexual sex
Caribbean	Late 1970s–early 1980s	390,000	35%	Heterosexual sex Men having sex with men
Eastern Europe	Early 1990s	700,000	25%	Injection drug use
Western Europe	Late 1970s–early 1980s	540,000	25%	Men having sex with men Injection drug use
North America	Late 1970s–early 1980s	920,000	20%	Men having sex with men Injection drug use Heterosexual sex
Australia	Late 1970s–early 1980s	15,000	10%	Men having sex with men
Total		**36.1 million**	**47%**	

Source: Adapted from *AIDS epidemic update: December 2000* (UNAIDS, 2000).

Extent of the Problem

African Americans and Hispanic Americans (especially among heterosexual women) have been disproportionately infected by the virus and affected by the epidemic. For example, African Americans compose 12 percent of the population in the country, yet over one-third of HIV/AIDS cases and 43 percent of new cases occur in the African American community (CDC, 2000). Responding to the concerns and challenges raised by the Congressional Black Caucus and many of its public health allies, former President Clinton declared the situation a crisis, with an initiative providing additional financial support to fight the virus in racial/ethnic minorities, especially in the African American community. Meanwhile, CDC (2001) issued its five-year national strategic plan, with the overarching national goal to "reduce the number of new infections in the United States from an estimated 40,000 to 20,000 per year by 2005, focusing particularly on eliminating racial and ethnic disparities in new HIV infection." The impact of HIV and AIDS among the various racial/ethnic minority communities can be gleaned and understood from at least three interrelated perspectives: (1) **knowledge, attitudes, beliefs, and behaviors (KABB),** (2) **HIV testing,** and (3) **linkage to care.**

Although research on HIV/AIDS prevention and intervention indicates that knowledge, attitudes, and beliefs (KAB) alone are not sufficient for safer behavioral maintenance (staying HIV negative or practicing safer behaviors among HIV-positive individuals) or behavioral changes for safer behaviors (Choi & Coates, 1994), misconception or less than optimal KAB are likely to place people at risk. According to the 1997 Youth Risk Behavior Surveillance System (MMWR, 1998c), 91.5 percent of all students had been taught about HIV and AIDS in schools. However, White students (93.3 percent) were significantly more likely than Black (89.7 percent) and Hispanic (85.9 percent) students to have received HIV education. These racial/ethnic differences are consistent with other local surveys. For example, several studies (DiClemente, Zorn, Temoshok, 1987; Horan & DiClemente, 1993; Strunin, 1991) indicate that Asian and Pacific Islander youth (particularly) have less HIV/AIDS-related knowledge compared with youth of other racial/ethnic backgrounds. Figure 11.3 presents some statements about AIDS to test one's knowledge about this disease. In addition, with the exception of self-identified gay men, API adults (particularly immigrants and refugees) tend to view HIV/AIDS as a White or gay disease compared with adults of other racial/ethnic groups (Wong, Chng, & Choi, 1998).

Findings from the 1997 YRBSS (MMWR, 1998c) indicated that among all currently sexually active students, 56.8 percent reported that either they or their partners had used a condom during the last sexual intercourse. Overall, male students (62.5 percent) were significantly more likely than female students (50.8 percent) to report condom use. These rates of condom use are clearly less than optimal. Other than sexual abstinence, condom use is the most effective means of preventing acquisition of STDs (including HIV).

Once a person becomes HIV-positive, treatment is a critical issue for the infected individual. Using a dataset (with AIDS diagnosis) from the CDC in a secondary analysis, Eckholdt and Chin (1997) found that during the period from January 1984 through December 1994, Asian and Pacific Islanders were significantly more likely than other racial/ethnic groups (i.e., White, African American, Latino American, and Native American) to be diagnosed with **Pneumocystis carini pneumonia (PCP),** an opportunistic infection that is easily and readily treatable with prophylactic agents. These researchers remarked:

FIGURE 11.3   Test Your Knowledge of AIDS

Determine whether the following statements are True (T) or False (F):

1. Most infants born to mothers infected with HIV will test negative after 18 months.

2. The *window period* refers to the time between infection and the detection of antibodies in the blood.

3. Once you have tested positive for HIV, it is certain that you will develop AIDS.

4. *Confidential testing* means that you do not have to give your name when you get tested.

5. Latex condoms are an effective barrier to HIV.

6. You cannot get HIV if you are having sex with only one partner.

7. Oil-based lubricants should be used with latex condoms to prevent HIV.

8. In 1995, complications from AIDS was the leading cause of death for all Americans, ages 25 to 44.

Answers: 1. F; 2. T; 3. T; 4. F; 5. T; 6. F; 7. F; 8. T

The consistently high proportion of PCP diagnoses among Asians and Pacific Islanders with AIDS is thought, in part, to be the result of barriers to adequate care.... Barriers to proper care are the result of the lack of culturally and language-appropriate educational materials, denial, distrust of institutes, fear of being identified as a person with AIDS, poor knowledge of the disease and its sequelae." (p. 1266)

The number of presenting opportunistic infections was related to survival time as well as probability of death. Using the same dataset, Eckholdt, Chin, and Harris, and Kim (1998) found that groups at greatest risk for OIs were Asian and Pacific Islanders, Native Americans, male intravenous drug users who have sex with males, residents of central United States, and young age groups. These researchers indicated that "differences between Race groups and Regions of Residence may be indicative of systematic barriers to health care."

One such barrier is HIV testing, which serves as a critical entry point to ensure linkage to care. By the mid-1990s, over one-third of adults in the United States had been tested for HIV, including blood donation, the proportion having increased from 16 percent in 1987 to 40 percent in 1995 (Anderson, Carey, & Taveras, 2000). In the three national surveys of household-based probability samples on which these figures are based, rates of testing were much higher for persons at increased risk (e.g., multiple sexual partners, injection drug use) for HIV. Twice as many people received HIV tests in private locations (medical offices, hospitals and emergency rooms, employee clinics, nursing home, and at home via home testing kits) as in public locations (health departments, community clinics, HIV counseling and testing sites, family planning clinics, military and immigration sites, and STD clinics). Of those at increased risk for HIV, 70 percent had been tested for HIV.

These patterns of findings suggest that there are at least two aspects to HIV testing: ability to access services and willingness to access services (including how to access services). Just because service (HIV testing) is available does not mean that people (especially among disenfranchised populations, including immigrants and refugees as well as those with limited English-speaking ability and some segments of racial/ethnic and cultural groups) will use it. In fact, available data indicate disparity in HIV testing among certain racial/ethnic and cultural groups—for example, Asians and Pacific Islanders have one of the lowest testing rates. However, little is known about why people are unwilling to access HIV testing. Meanwhile, although the overall rates of HIV testing were high, more than half of the persons tested in public programs did not report that a health professional talked to them about HIV-related issues (KABB) when they were tested, indicating that many persons are not receiving counseling or are not recognizing their interaction with staff as counseling. The rate of counseling is even lower in private settings. These findings further underscore the complex relationship of KABB, HIV testing, and linkage to care, and most of all, their less than optimal effect in the fight against HIV.

Complexities and Controversies

For the thousands of people currently living with AIDS/HIV in the United States, the dramatic recoveries due to use of combination drug therapy represent a sort of resurrection or second life. This thinking, however, has opened the door to a whole host of new challenges for people living with AIDS/HIV, including reevaluation of personal goals and expectations, adherence to long-term treatment regimens, and maintenance of low-risk behaviors. In brief, are new prevention messages and strategies needed for these "temporarily recovered" individuals? If this is the case, we would also need a new baseline or types of KABB, including how these people appraise the positive effect of the combination drug therapy in relation to their "recovered" lifestyles (e.g., sexual activities and use of recreational drugs). Some of these issues will be briefly examined in the following sections.

The treatment regimen for combination drug therapy is extremely demanding. Moreover, many of the protease inhibitors cause adverse effects. This poses an enormous barrier to therapy for many, as can be seen in poor adherence rates. In a national survey (Gallent & Block, 1998), 43 percent of patients admitted to not taking medications as prescribed, and HIV-treatment physicians reported, on average, that 54 percent of their patients do not properly adhere to their regiments. The reason(s) for delaying, stopping, or rejecting treatment are varied and complicated. For example, Lo, Teresaki, Wong, and Mayer (1998) noted that a key reason for nonadherence among a cohort of HIV-positive men is the "if-it-ain't-broke-don't-fix-it" philosophy. Other reasons include distrust of doctors, no insurance and insufficient funds to pay for medication, and the belief that it is better to wait for more effective drugs to be developed.

Meanwhile, both scientists and clinicians are concerned with treatment nonadherence in that it may potentially build up resistance (to the drugs) in the virus, which may lead to a new strain(s). Anecdotal reports suggest that people with a history of substance abuse have a higher rate of treatment nonadherence than those who do not. Some segment of the medical and public health communities raise the issue of "ethics of treatment." For example, if a medical doctor suspects his or her client might not fully comply with treatment, should the doctor withhold treatment to prevent potential breeding of resistant strains of the virus?

Researchers and clinicians (Lo et al., 1998) have begun to notice that some segment of the people who are benefiting from the combination drug therapy are also engaging in more risky behaviors. That is, for the longest time many of these people have been too sick to engage in any risky behaviors. The combination drug therapy has now improved their **quality of life** (making them feel better). Some have begun to reexamine their lives (e.g., having a sex life again or returning to work). For others, feeling "fine" (often based on subjective assessments as having no overt physical symptoms) implies they may cut down or stop taking their medications. In other words, the advent of medical treatment might have inadvertently created a viscous cycle for some people: Feeling fine encourages more risky behaviors and less or no medications—less or no medications and more risky behaviors therefore must be okay.

Possible Solutions: Community-Based Approaches

The preceding issues only scratch the surface of a very complex—and often volatile—problem. The virus is more than a biological epidemic; it has its political and social valences, as well. It is beyond the scope of this chapter to review all solutions; however, an heuristic approach is to conceptualize solutions (with an emphasis on the principles of community psychology) along three interrelated dimensions: (1) **prevention (KABB)**, (2) **HIV Testing** (see Case in Point 11.2), and (3) **Linkage to care** (including psychosocial support) (see Case in Point 11.3). The term *prevention* is used here in an inclusive sense to capture the overlap of primary, secondary, and tertiary modalities that occur in the AIDS literature and in the implementation of the clinical programs.

AIDS education raises many controversial questions. As part of education, should condoms be distributed in schools to prevent the spread of AIDS? If so, at what grade level of education? Such controversy has almost torn apart school systems across the nation. People with AIDS are growing impatient with the Food and Drug Administration (FDA) in the regulation of experimental drugs and treatment criteria. In order to be treated, people must have more than 20 symptoms as defined by the Centers for Disease Control and Prevention (CDC), a federal agency that oversees most HIV and AIDS surveillance. However, it took a lot of political lobbying before the CDC added to its list symptoms specific to women with AIDS (e.g., cervical cancer). Meanwhile, many people with AIDS have died from taking illegal treatments (usually smuggled into this country). The American Foundation for AIDS Research (Honorable Chairperson Elizabeth Taylor) publishes a listing of all drugs for treating AIDS, including those that do not have FDA approval. The list is available free of charge.

Morality and politics aside, community psychologists and public health advocates have learned to use the public health model to slow down the spread of AIDS. After two decades of fighting the epidemic, it has been widely recognized that behavioral changes are paramount in *preventing* the transmission of HIV (National Commission on AIDS, 1993). Moreover, attitudinal variables are often viewed as determinants of compliance with HIV prevention recommendations (Fisher & Fisher, 1992). According to the **Health Belief Model** (Becker, 1974; Rosenstock, 1986), readiness to perform health-related behaviors is seen as a function of perceived vulnerability, perceived severity of disease, perceived barriers to health-protective action, and feelings of self-efficacy concerning ability to protect

CASE IN POINT 11.3

THE BILINGUAL PEER ADVOCATE (BPA) PROGRAM

Nationwide, a majority of the AIDS/HIV cases among Asian and Pacific Islanders are foreign-born individuals. In New York City, AIDS cases among APIs account for 95 percent of adult AIDS cases among APIs in the state and 13 percent of adult cases among APIs in the United States (Sy, Chng, Choi, & Wong, 1998).

Although they represent an expanding population (e.g., the highest growth rate from 1980 to 1990 in New York City) with increasing needs for HIV-related services, Asian and Pacific Islanders are prevented from adequately accessing such services because of a number of barriers, including the following:

- Lack of culturally competent, linguistically accessible, and HIV-sensitive providers
- Lack of health insurance
- Distrust of institutions
- Stigma in API communities surrounding sex, substance use, homosexuality, illness, and death
- Lack of coordinated primary care and case-management services

Ideally, any API immigrant living with AIDS/HIV in New York City would be able to access any needed HIV-related service in the language that he or she speaks. In this ideal situation, the service would also be provided in a way that recognizes the cultural practices and attitudes of the client or patient. But given a tight funding environment, a lack of prioritization of API issues, and the numerous API language, national, and cultural groups that exist, such an ideal is difficult to achieve. As part of a five-year national demonstration study (Chin & Wong, in press), the Bilingual Peer Advocate (BPA) program, with its reliance on part-time peer workers, was designed to allow the Asian and

Pacific Islander Coalition on HIV/AIDS, Inc. (APICHA) to hire a large team of workers to meet the diverse language and cultural needs of APIs living with AIDS, while also remaining within realistic cost parameters.

The BPA program trains and maintains a corps of paid, part-time BPAs to act as language interpreters, cultural guides, and advocates for clients as they negotiate New York City's service system. In addition to helping service providers understand the clients' culture, BPAs are able to explain the "culture" of the health and social services to clients. BPAs are provided clinical supervision by three full-time case managers, one speaking Mandarin Chinese and the other two speaking Japanese.

Bilingual Peer Advocates are paid because they commit more time to work and training than volunteers do. These individuals start with a three-day intensive training program and then receive a two- to three-hour follow-up training each month following. They are expected to be available on a regular basis, and some are on call and carry beepers. Bilingual Peer Advocates work only part time in order to retain a level of flexibility that full-time staff do not have, and more importantly, to allow APICHA to hire a broader range of individuals to represent more cultures and languages.

Currently, APICHA maintains a corps of 15 BPAs. Among them, they speak the following major languages: Bengali, Cantonese, English, Gujarati, Hindi, Japanese, Korean, Mandarin, Tagalog, Toisanese, and Urdu. Of APICHA's current 70-plus HIV-positive clients receiving comprehensive case management, 24 clients are being served by BPAs. Each month, BPAs spend about 8 to 12 hours working directly with clients, 3 to 5 hours conducting client outreach, 10 hours in travel, and 2 hours in training.

oneself from disease. This meta-model has since been adapted or modified to meet the challenges and needs of the specific populations participating in HIV prevention programs.

At the broadest level, HIV-prevention programs may include multifaceted components such as mass media educational campaigns, distribution of condoms, needle exchange, and safer sex outreach workshops. Many programs have utilized these approaches, with notable success with gay men in large urban areas (Coates, 1990) and IVDUs (Des Jarles et al., 1987).

Crawford and Jason (1990) provided a good model of a media program for AIDS prevention. For six consecutive days, 5- to 10-minute segments addressing AIDS and the family were broadcast during the noon and 9 P.M. newscasts of a major local TV station in the Midwest. The researchers randomly assigned 151 children and 94 parents to one of two conditions. In the experimental condition, the children were prompted (encouraged) to watch the broadcasts, and their families were given educational manuals. The printed material provided viewers with more in-depth coverage of the issues presented on television. In the other (control) condition, the children were not prompted nor provided the supplemental material. The children who were encouraged to watch the program viewed significantly more of the broadcasts, talked more about sexual issues with their families, and were more knowledgeable about AIDS than the control children (Crawford, Jason, Riordan, & Kaufman, 1990).

Other HIV-prevention programs have opted for more focused strategies. One mechanism to increase the synchronicity between attitudes and behavior is the use of **perceived social norms.** Social norms are those unwritten rules that society expects people to follow. Often, the majority of people in a community feel that they should be able to sanction those who fail to comply with the norms. Kelly and associates (1991) have demonstrated that peer influence or pressure is a significant predictor in the use of condoms by gay and bisexual men. The researchers first collected baseline data about attitudes and knowledge of HIV and AIDS in a gay community. Leaders were identified and recruited for a HIV communitywide prevention program. They were trained about communication skills and ways to prevent contracting HIV. Upon completion of the training, these leaders disseminated their knowledge in the community. People who were exposed to these leaders were significantly more likely to report an increase in knowledge about HIV and AIDS as well as to practice safe sex than those who were not.

Based on Kelly and colleagues' (1991) **diffusion model,** Miller and colleagues (1998) implemented an HIV-prevention program for hustlers in New York City. Opinion leaders were identified by bartenders and were recruited and trained about communication skills and ways to prevent contracting HIV. Results indicated that the intervention had direct effects on HIV-risk knowledge, norms, and behaviors. Knowledge of unsafe sexual practices for HIV transmission increased with time, and many important HIV-risk behaviors decreased following the intervention.

The diffusion model has also been demonstrated to be effective for HIV prevention targeting intravenous drug users. For example, Watters, Downing, Case, Lorvick, Cheng, and Fergusson (1990) identified community leaders who distributed one-ounce plastic vials of ordinary household bleach per IVDU along with a set of behavioral instructions (including instructions regarding safe sex). Results indicated that a significant percentage of IVDUs reported using bleach to decontaminate syringes and not sharing needles in the past year. Increased condom use was also reported.

Many of the studies and programs deriving from the premises of the diffusion model often have a peer-based component to their HIV-prevention messages. For example, peers are hired and trained as leaders to deliver the HIV-prevention messages. Research reviewed above and the literature in general argue for the utility and promise of the strategy. However, Luna and Rotheram-Borus (1999) cautioned that this strategy has its weakness, especially when the peer leaders involved are also coming from disenfranchised environments. These researchers found that professional boundaries are a major issue for a lot of youth peer leaders; a sizeable percentage (23 percent) of the youth peer leaders "engaged in substance use and sexual behaviors that placed themselves and uninfected youth in their peer education programs at risk" (p. 1). This important study illustrates a key principle of community psychology that "person-environment fit" is critical in gauging the adaptation of a strategy (cf. Hobfoll, 1998).

SUMMARY

This chapter has reviewed five health issues: tobacco, alcohol, illicit drugs, sexually transmitted diseases (STDs), and HIV/AIDS (human immunodeficiency virus/ acquired immunodeficiency syndromes). These issues were examined from the perspectives of community psychology and preventive medicine; policy-based prevention (targeting a community) was also discussed (see Table 11.3). These issues were chosen for two main reasons: They have each received enormous attention in the media and each is highly preventable if certain activities are practiced. In addition, a large number of people are affected or have the potential to be affected if prevention does not occur.

One of every five deaths in the United States is attributable to tobacco use. Moreover, according to one estimate, $72.7 billion was spent in health- and medical-related care attributable to tobacco-related illnesses in 1993. Consistent with the model of the National Cancer Institute, community-based researchers (Biglan et al., 1996) illustrated the use of information and public policy to change behavior (cigarette sales to minors) for the good of the community. Biglan's research also demonstrated how various community services such as the police, elected officials, merchants, and psychologists can collaborate on programs for the community.

Another major cause of premature death is alcohol-related traffic accidents. Research has cogently demonstrated that policy changes in lowering blood alcohol content can significantly reduce the number of fatalities. Other health policy-related research suggests that alcohol warning labels and signs may be a useful way to inform women of childbearing age about the danger of alcohol use during pregnancy.

Overall, illicit drug use has remained stable in this country. Yet, certain drugs continue to be used by some segments of the population. For example, marijuana is the most popular drug used among youth and young adults. Consequences of illicit drugs include crimes and domestic violence, among others (e.g., increased HIV transmission). According to one estimate, illicit drug use costs our nation $67 billion each year. Proportionately, this country spends more money on law enforcement-related activities than drug prevention, intervention, and treatment. Research has demonstrated the contribution of community psychology in preventing drug use; yet, community psychologists need to take a more proactive

TABLE 11.3 Five Issues of Community Health and Preventive Medicine: A Snapshot

ISSUE	EXTENT OF THE PROBLEM	CONSEQUENCE	POSSIBLE SOLUTION
Tobacco	■ 34.8% of all adoloscents smoked a cigarette at least once in past 30 days	■ 1 out of 6 deaths is tobacco related ■ An estimated $72.7 billion tobacco-related medical expenditures in 1993	■ Tobacco (sin) tax ■ Multistrategies (e.g., merchants education, sting operation, etc.) (Biglan et al., 1996)
Alcohol	■ 79.1% of all students have had at least one drink of alcohol during their lifetimes ■ 31% of all students have used alcohol before age 13	■ 1 million people a year are victims of alcohol-related accidents ■ Risk for contraction of HIV is increased	■ Government warning label ■ Parent–child skill building (Spoth et al., 1996)
Illicit Drugs	■ Marijuana—47.1% of students ever used ■ Cocaine—82% of students ever used ■ Steroids—3.1% of students ever used ■ Intravenous drugs—2.1% of students ever used ■ Other illegal drugs—17% of students ever used ■ Inhalants—16% of students ever used	■ About 60% of federal prisoners in 1995 were in prison for drug-related violations ■ 35% of new HIV cases are directly or indirectly linked to IVDUs ■ Illicit drug use costs the country an estimated $67 billion annually	■ National Drug Control Strategy, 1998 (Office of National Drug Control Policy, 1998) ■ Network intervention (Latkin et al., 1996)
STDs	■ Highest STD rates among the industrialized world	■ Risk for contraction of HIV is increased ■ $10 billion was spent on STD treatments in 1994 ■ $6.7 billion was spent on HIV treatment in 1994	■ Advisory Committee for HIV and STD Prevention (MMWR, 1998a) ■ Community intervention (e.g., Tanzania)
HIV/AIDS	■ African Americans compose 12% of the population in the country; they make up over one-third of HIV/AIDS and 43% of new cases ■ Racial/ethnic minority students have less exposure to HIV prevention education	■ Incurable disease with a long incubation period ■ Homophobia ■ Racism	■ KAAB prevention and intervention ■ Treatment choices (Lo et al., 1998) ■ HIV testing

role in advocating for more resources in prevention activities (i.e., other than law enforcement-related activities).

The United States has the highest rates of STDs in the industrialized world. In addition, epidemiologic studies consistently demonstrate that concurrent STDs increase the transmission probability for HIV infection. Unfortunately, community psychologists have done little or no work in this area. It is recommended that the field of community psychology needs to take a proactive role in heeding the recommendations of the Advisory Committee for HIV and STD Prevention, including promoting sexuality as a healthy lifestyle.

In the absence of a cure or vaccine, prevention and information dissemination and behavioral intervention (e.g., the diffusion model) appear to be the only hope to slow the spread of HIV, which is thought to be responsible for AIDS. Given that HIV/AIDS is also a political and social disease, coupled with the advent of medical technology, prevention takes on added dimensions and meanings beyond the traditional definition used in community health and community medicine.

COMMUNITY ORGANIZATIONAL PSYCHOLOGY

A business that makes nothing but business is a poor kind of business.

—Henry Ford

As Sarah Anderson walked out the door of Harmony House, she glanced back at the building that had been her home away from home for the last eight months. She felt a sense of relief and a paradoxical sense of sadness as she exited for the last time. "What went wrong?" she wondered. "How could my job have become such a sore point in my life when only a few short months ago I had accepted it so enthusiastically?"

Harmony House was run by a private nonprofit corporation that managed eight different group homes for at-risk adolescents in Sarah's city. The adolescents were sent to the homes, including Harmony House, by judges, probation officers, schools, and parents. The group homes boasted the ability to "turn kids around"—that is, get them off drugs, raise their school grades, and make them productive citizens again, in about six months.

A psychology major with a human services minor from a small liberal arts college, Sarah had been actively recruited by Harmony House after her summer volunteer work there. Her grades were very good, and the combination of training in college and her volunteer work plus her winning personality during interviews made her eagerly sought after by several community organizations. She had always wanted to be a case manager for one of them. Harmony House won her over because they offered the best salary and an excellent training program, and they had a good reputation. Harmony House seemed to be on the leading edge of innovations in treatment, which Sarah thought would give her the upper hand when she sought to move on to bigger and better agencies.

The idealistic and perhaps naive Sarah approached her first few days at Harmony House with immense enthusiasm. Her supervisor, Jan Hayes, mentored and coached her for the first few months. Sarah felt she was getting plenty of attention and good training under Jan. Sarah was slowly developing a sense of confidence in handling each new difficult youth as he or she entered Harmony House.

Six months into her service, Sarah's career took a downturn that mirrored the many changes occurring at corporate headquarters. Jan Hayes was moved from Harmony House to headquarters to become their chief trainer, and Sarah received a new supervisor, one who cared much less about mentoring Sarah and more about keeping costs low at Harmony House. Sarah explained to her new supervisor that she was fairly new to the job so would like to be mentored, but her new supervisor told her to stop complaining and start performing.

As the weeks passed, Sarah realized that not only was she without the tutelage and attention afforded her by Jan but that the budget cuts at the group home were taking their toll on the clients. The television broke, which left the youths with more free time than they needed. The furniture was in need of replacement, and the menu each day was much less appetizing. There were fewer field trips and fewer group therapy sessions, too. All these changes and others made the youths more discontented and harder to work with.

Sarah approached her supervisor and commented on these negative changes. His response was, "Sarah, these are tough times; I have to make these cuts and changes. I suggest that if you think things are better elsewhere, you find another job." Sarah worked another two months before she resigned. She did not have any active job prospects, but she was so utterly dismayed with the changes at Harmony House, she felt she had to quit.

Sarah's story is told to introduce this chapter on organizations, which, in a community psychology book, could be controversial. However, the authors and others (Keys & Frank, 1987; Klein & D'Aunno, 1986; Shinn & Perkins, 1994) feel that there is much that community psychologists can learn from organizational psychologists and just as much that organizational psychologists can learn from community psychologists. By now, both fields have built enough strength that neither will be overwhelmed by the other (Hirsch & David, 1983). Hence, this chapter weds community and organizational psychology.

WHAT DO ORGANIZATIONAL AND COMMUNITY PSYCHOLOGY SHARE?

As you now know, community psychology is the psychology that examines the effects of social and environmental factors on behavior as it occurs in various levels in communities, including the organizational level, in order to produce beneficial change. To understand the effects of environmental factors or settings on individuals, one must understand something about the setting—in this case, organizations, whether they be private sector businesses, mental health clinics, prisons, or any other community organization. In fact, it is futile to attempt to understand individuals apart from the settings to which they belong (Keys & Frank, 1987). This chapter will look at the effects of the organization on the individual and the effects of the individual on the organization with an eye toward the goals of community psychology. Specifically, discussions will attend to ways in which organizations adversely affect their members, both staff and clients, and means by which organizations can be improved to better serve their members and the community.

Organizational behavior and organizational psychology, which are the study of how groups and individuals interface with the organizations they are in, has much to offer community psychology. **Organizational psychology** approaches the examination of organizations from the perspective of the individual, whereas **organizational behavior** approaches the study of organizations from a systems perspective, or as if organizations are systems (Smither, 1998).

It is obvious what organizational psychology and organizational behavior have in common, but what do they share with community psychology? First, organizational specialists have developed paradigms, or models, as well as constructs and measurement techniques that go beyond the individual level of analysis (Riger, 1990; Shinn & Perkins, 2000). This is a goal of community psychology. For instance, from the study of organizations comes **organizational development (OD).** OD is a set of social science techniques designed to plan and implement long-term change in organizational settings for purposes of improving the effectiveness of organizational functioning and enhancing the individuals within the organizations (Baron & Greenberg, 1990; French & Bell, 1990). In other words, concern for the organization and the individual in the organization should be equal (Beer & Walton, 1990).

Another aspect of organizational psychology important to community psychology is the understanding that individuals and organizations have a dynamic relationship—that is, an ever-changing, transactional relationship over time (Keys & Frank, 1987). For instance, at one point, an individual might be highly motivated to stay in an organization, while at another time, he or she may be motivated to leave, as did Sarah. However, just when the disgruntled individual wants to leave the organization, the organization most needs that person. The cycle then continues. The study of such dynamic relationships is the domain of both community psychology and organizational psychology.

Organizational scientists as do community psychologists have a long tradition of conducting research from an ecological perspective as well as a systems perspective (Shinn & Perkins, 2000). They know how to include all organizational participants (e.g., managers and employees) as well as coordinating mechanisms and processes in their research endeavors as they attempt to study and change the overall organization. It is this multilevel or holistic type of research that community psychologists hope to achieve rather than endeavors focused merely on the individual.

Another aspect of similarity between organizational psychology and community psychology is that for most individuals, work is part of their self-concepts. Therefore, work has consequences for well-being, the promotion of which is a goal of community psychology (Price, 1985). Furthermore, there is "spillover" between work organizations and communities. Work influences how people feel; hence, if people emotionally withdraw from work, they might also feel alienated from their families and their communities. Likewise, feelings about community also "spill" into the work world. Working mothers, for example, probably experience more work stress than any other employee because they experience the most stress at home (Price, 1985). Another point of comparison is that both community and organizational specialists are concerned with diversity issues (Shinn & Perkins, 2000). That is, both sets of professionals are involved with accommodating people of different backgrounds and with promoting effective interaction among diverse populations.

Interestingly, there is a serious point at which the study of organizations and community psychology part company (Riger, 1990; Shinn & Perkins, 2000). In the field of organizational behavior, most efforts are aimed at improving organizational efficiency and profits, sometimes at the expense of the individuals in the organizations. If the organizational effort benefits individuals, it is often only incidental to the main task of improving the organization (Riger, 1990). For instance, if Sarah's new supervisor had taken into consideration Sarah's concerns about the budget cuts, he probably would have done so only if it affected Harmony House and not because it would have made Sarah happier. More specifically, suppose Sarah knew of a dangerous circumstance that might have resulted in Harmony House being sued, such as an elevator that was in disrepair. Sarah's new supervisor might likely have listened to her but not to please Sarah. Rather, he would have been concerned about the financial well-being of the organization.

On the other hand, the primary aim in community psychology is usually to enhance the functioning of individuals in organizations (Shinn & Perkins, 2000). The intent is to empower individuals within organizations to create innovative solutions to the problems facing them, to ensure that the innovations and changes are humanistic, and to promote a sense of community within the organization. From these values, organizational specialists can also learn. For instance, community psychologists feel that creating a sense of community within an organization or a sense of belonging to the organization can enhance human functioning. Organizational psychologists focusing less on the organization and more on the sense of community or cohesiveness are beginning to understand that work group cohesiveness and job satisfaction often go hand in hand (Burroughs & Eby, 1998). In fact, recent research has found that each organization develops its own unique sense of community (Hughey, Speer, & Peterson, 1999).

Managers of organizations have now come to understand that empowering those under them to participate in decision making in **quality of work life (QWL) programs** or programs of participatory decision making that create long-term change in organizations is a good idea (French & Bell, 1990). One example of a QWL program is a quality circle. **Quality circles** are small groups of volunteer employees (or volunteer clients of any community service) who meet regularly to identify and solve problems related to organizational conditions. Quality circles are considered to humanize organizational environments as well as to increase participants' satisfaction with the organization (Baron & Greenberg, 1990). If Sarah and other employees of Harmony House had participated in a quality circle, they might have realized that they were all discontented with the changes and so developed innovative solutions to the organization's problems *before* staff turnover became high.

A second example of the use of quality circles in organizations might be useful. In a rural mental health center, volunteer clients and staff might meet as a quality circle to discuss what to do about the lack of a public transportation system for clients without cars. Together, they could develop some innovative and workable solutions so that clients could more predictably obtain services as needed.

Those living with the issues best know how to address them, and quality circles and other participatory methods in organizations take advantage of this fact by empowering involved individuals to solve their own problems. In matters of empowerment, community psychologists lead the way for the organizational specialists.

EVERYDAY PROBLEMS IN COMMUNITY ORGANIZATIONS

Why this interest in organizations? People spend a great deal of their adult lives in organizations, particularly in their place of employment but also in volunteer, recreational, educational, and other organizations. One's organizational affiliations often bring economic well-being, emotional security, happiness, a sense of self-esteem and status, as well as the social rewards of belonging to a group and a sense of accomplishment (Schultz & Schultz, 1998). On the other hand, organizations can also frustrate and alienate people and cause much stress. With that in mind, we will turn to a sampling of the problems of today's organizations.

Stress

Stress was defined earlier in this book as a call for action when one's capabilities are perceived as falling short of the needed personal resources (Sarason, 1980). For instance, changes in the environment, especially unpredictable or uncontrollable ones (Vinokur & Caplan, 1986), can be stressful when they exceed one's coping resources. That means that even positive changes can bring stress. Receiving a promotion can be as stressful as being fired. But remember, these situations are construed as stressful *only* if the individual perceives them as taxing or exceeding his or her resources and endangering well-being (Lazarus & Folkman, 1984). Major readjustments, such as a new job (Holmes & Rahe, 1967), as well as everyday hassles (Kanner, Coyne, Schaefer, & Lazarus, 1981) like rising prices, too many things to do, and being late for work, can be stressful. Imagine with her relatively new job, dissatisfaction, and eventual unemployment how much stress Sarah must have experienced!

Stress can occur in any facet of people's lives, but the concern here is with causes of stress in organizations. Organizational causes of stress are varied and sometimes complex. Organizational members can be too busy *or* too bored, both of which can cause stress. Interpersonal conflicts between coworkers may exist, or the individual may not feel competent or sufficiently trained to do the work. Likewise, the individual may have a dangerous job, such as working on a ward with violent individuals, or be in a demanding environment where noise, fumes, poor lighting, or other environmental conditions produce stress. The person might also have a supervisor with whom he or she does not get along. There may be too many or too few rules or too much or too little structure. Or the individual might have problems at home that he or she brings to work or feel deprived when work detracts from family activities.

Burnout

A concept related to but slightly different from stress is burnout. **Burnout** is a feeling of overall exhaustion that is the result of too much pressure and not enough sources of satisfaction (Maslach, Schaufeli, & Leiter, 2000; Moss, 1981). Burnout has three components:

1. The feeling of being drained or exhausted
2. Depersonalization or insensitivity to others, including clients (which, in human services, certainly is counterproductive)
3. A sense of low personal accomplishment or the feeling that one's efforts are futile (Jackson, Schwab, & Schuler, 1986)

Symptoms of burnout include loss of interest in one's job, apathy, depression, irritability, and finding fault with others. The quality of the individual's work also deteriorates, and the individual often blindly and superficially follows rules and procedures (Schultz & Schultz, 1998), topics soon discussed in this chapter.

Burnout is most likely to affect those organizational members who are initially eager, motivated, and perhaps idealistic (Van Fleet, 1991). Because many community activists and human services professionals fit this description, burnout should be a major concern to community psychologists (Stevens & O'Neill, 1983). Research has demonstrated that many individuals in community service organizations—including police officers, Social Security employees, social workers, teachers, and nurses—indeed suffer from burnout (Pines & Guendelman, 1995). In fact, you may have realized that many of these occupations are primarily filled by women; it will not surprise you, then, to know that women suffer more from burnout than men (Pretty, McCarthy, & Catano, 1992). Perhaps this was part of Sarah's problem; she was simply too burned out and thus she resigned. Poor fit between the person and the organization can also result in burnout (Maslach & Goldberg, 1998). For example, Xie and Johns (1995) examined the roles of **job scope** or job-related activities performed by the employee and burnout. They found that individuals who perceived a misfit between their abilities and the demands or scope of the job experienced higher burnout and stress.

Workaholism

In other psychology courses you may have heard of the **Type-A/Type-B personalities** (Friedman & Rosenman, 1974). Type-A individuals, as opposed to the relaxed Type-Bs, have a chronic sense of time urgency, have a distaste for "down time" or idleness, are impatient, and are competitive. Type-As also work near maximum capacity, even when no deadlines are set, and are motivated by an intense desire to master their environments and to maintain control. Therefore, the Type-As of an organization tend to be the **workaholics.** Again, a mismatch between the person and the environment can be the basis for much stress in the workplace. A Type-A person working in a Type-B environment, or a Type-B person working in a Type-A environment can experience a great deal of stress (Smither, 1998) as can being the coworkers (Porter, 2001) or children of a workaholic (Robinson & Kelley, 1998).

The early literature on Type-A behavior linked the personality syndrome to heart disease and stroke. In fact, Type-A personality was previously called the *coronary-prone personality,* as it was thought that Type-As were twice as likely to have coronary heart disease than others (Schaubroeck, Ganster, & Kemmerer, 1994). However, research has found that not all Type-A traits induce heart disease. What most seems to link Type-A behavior to heart attacks is the hostility toward or cynicism about others held by many Type-As (Conte, Landy, & Mathieu, 1995).

Organizational Culture

Why is it that as individuals come and go from organizations, much as Sarah did, organizations do not seem to change much, even though their members do? The answer is organizational culture (Baron & Greenberg, 1990). Earlier in the history of its study, and as a narrower concept, organizational culture was referred to as *organizational climate.* Just as Type-A is related to an individual's style, organizational culture is related to the personality of the organization. **Organizational culture** consists of the beliefs, attitudes, values, and expectations shared by most members of the organization (Schein, 1985, 1990). Once these beliefs and values are established, they tend to persist over time as the organization shapes and molds its members in its image. For example, can you recall how different all of the freshmen looked in appearance and dress the first week of classes? By senior year, many of these same students looked more similar because other students pressured them to conform to the organization's image. Those students who most deviated from the norm of the campus often left rather than change.

Besides influencing conformity, the prevailing organizational culture guides the organization's structure. How decisions are made in the organization relates to its structure. For instance, whether decisions originate from the bottom, as when average organizational citizens participate in decisions, or from the top, when a centralized management makes the decisions, is part of the organization's structure.

The organizational structure, including the decision-making system, also determines class distinctions within organizations, such as status differences between executives and middle managers. The distribution of power in the organization is likely to be affected by the organization's culture, too. If lower-level members make decisions, they will have more power than if they are not allowed to participate in decision making. Finally, organizational culture affects the ideology of the organization. If the organization views human nature as good, it will tend to allow subordinate participation (Tosi, Rizzo, & Carroll, 1986). If the organizational culture emphasizes the development of human potential, then the members are more likely to be allowed to develop and create new ideas without much interference from the organization.

An **open culture,** one appreciative of human dignity and one that enhances human growth, is preferred by most organizational members and by most community psychologists. Open cultures foster a sense of community, better communication, and more empowerment, which can exist in an organization just as in neighborhoods (Klein & D'Aunno, 1986; Pretty & McCarthy, 1991). Such organizational cultures tend to foster employee commitment (Shadur, Kienzile, & Rodwell, 1999) among their other positive effects. However, when the culture is **repressive** in that it inhibits human growth or when there are huge gaps in what the organization professes to be (e.g., professing to have a positive culture that is negative in reality), then high levels of member cynicism develop, performance deteriorates (Baron & Greenberg, 1990), and cohesiveness drops. Perhaps this is what happened to Sarah as she felt the disregard of her new supervisor flood over her.

Community psychologists are studying a phenomenon related to organizational culture: the sense of community within an organization. Chapter 1 discussed sense of community in some detail. *Sense of community* pertains to an individual's feeling that he or she is similar to others and that the individual and the other individuals in the setting belong there. There is a sense of "we-ness" and belongingness coinciding with a sense of community.

Pretty and McCarthy (1991) explored the sense of community in men and women in corporations. They found that for different employees, the sense of community was predicted by different features of the organization. For instance, men and women differed, as did managers and nonmanagers, in the characteristics that determined a sense of community for them. Male managers' sense of community was predicted best by their perceptions of peer cohesion and involvement, whereas female managers' sense of community was predicted by their perceptions of supervisor support, involvement, and amount of work pressure.

Another aspect of organizational culture is the extent to which staff in the organization perceive a sense of empowerment; in fact, organizational culture provides an excellent framework for understanding and assessing the person-environment fit needed if empowerment is to succeed in organizations (Foster-Fishman & Keys, 1997). Empowerment in organizations has been found to be directly related to employee effectiveness (Spreitzer, 1995). What are those organizational characteristics that inspire empowerment? Using the case-study method, Maton and Salem (1995) found at least four:

- A belief system that inspires growth, is strengths based, and focuses beyond the individual
- An opportunity structure that is highly accessible

- A support system that is encompassing, is peer based, and provides a sense of community
- Leadership that is inspiring, talented, shared, and committed to both the setting and the members

This sounds very much like the open culture described earlier.

Other Ecological Conditions

Have you ever driven by an old factory that has weeds growing up around it and has had its windows smashed? When some of these factories were operating, the work conditions were dreadful. The factories were dark, polluted, noisy, and drafty. Today, people know that physical conditions in organizations affect what goes on in them, so the health of the national workforce has become one of the most significant issues of modern time (Ilgen, 1990). Temperature and humidity are known to affect performance, and excessive noise creates hearing loss (Smithers, 1998).

The size of organizations is important, too. Members of small organizations report more supportive environments, less discrimination, and more loyalty to the organization (MacDermid, Hertzog, Kensinger, & Zipp, 2001). On the other hand, large organizations often create negative conditions. For instance, Hellman, Greene, Morrison, and Abramowitz (1985) examined residential mental health treatment programs by measuring staff and client perceptions. Not surprisingly, the larger the program, the more the members experienced anxiety, held negative views of the psychosocial aspects of the organization, and perceived greater psychological distance from the organization. Beyond that, though, even the use of space in organizations affects comfort level; when the space is crowded, individuals in it feel most uncomfortable (Baron & Greenberg, 1990). Organizations that care about their members will create safe and comfortable environments for them.

It is not just the built environment that affects people at work. The social environment also plays a large role. The issue of prejudice was discussed earlier in this book (see Chapter 8). Recall that ethnic, race, and gender bias or **prejudice** is an attitude toward the members of some group, based solely on their group membership. Prejudice can probably most concretely be seen in the lower pay of minorities in the work place (Barnum, Liden, & Ditomaso, 1995).

Recent studies have examined prejudice in the work place. Hughes and Dodge (1997) studied both organizational as well as interpersonal racial bias in African American women. They found that bias was the most important predictor of job quality than any other stressors, such as low task variety, heavy workloads, and poor supervision. Racial bias was reported most often in predominantly White settings and in organizations requiring semiskilled and unskilled workers.

Other environmental factors can affect one's working life; these factors originate in the environment at large. Such factors as the economy, competition from other organizations, the introduction of new technologies, and so forth, can add to work-related stress. Case in Point 12.1 discusses one particular type of stressor—unemployment, which can result from a number of uncontrollable and unpredictable contextual factors.

CASE IN POINT 12.1
COMMUNITY PSYCHOLOGY AND UNEMPLOYMENT

Hard economic times bring unemployment and various strains and stresses. Unemployment affects nearly 10 million people in the United States every year (U.S. Bureau of Labor Statistics, 1992). The negative effects of unemployment are well documented and include anxiety, depression, and physical illness; in fact, the experience of unemployment has been documented to be severe enough so as to warrant intervention by a professional (Kessler, Turner, & House, 1988).

Studies searching for the causal link between unemployment and depression demonstrate that becoming unemployed doubles the risk of becoming depressed (Dooley, Catalano, & Wilson, 1994). In other words, being depressed does not lead to job loss; rather, job loss can lead to depression. Much of the distress is traceable directly or indirectly to financial hardship (Aubrey, Tefft, & Kingsbury, 1990; Broman, Hamilton, & Hoffman, 1990). The negative impact is not just on the unemployed individual. The families (Broman et al., 1990), and in particular the development of the children in those families (Liem & Liem, 1988), are adversely affected.

Traditional interventions for the unemployed focus on treating the individual by teaching stress reduction (Kessler et al., 1988) or by providing a job counselor armed with information about job openings and who assumes responsibility for the unemployed client's job placement (Gray & Braddy, 1988). Community psychologists would offer other alternatives. First, community psychologists would empower individuals to participate in client-centered job-seeking programs such as job clubs. **Job clubs** are self-help groups where job-search skills are shared and participants are encouraged to set job-seeking goals each week (Gray & Braddy, 1988). Such job clubs may well foster reemployment optimism, which is a predictor of psychological health and life satisfaction (Morrison, O'Connor, Morrison, & Hill, 2001).

Community psychologists would also focus on strengths and competencies of the unemployed rather than on their weaknesses. Following this line of thought, Turner, Kessler, and House (1991) wanted to identify the kinds of resources people use to cope with unemployment and the points in the stress process at which each resource exerts a positive influence. They wanted to assess both personal (e.g., self-esteem) and social (e.g., a supportive social network) resources. The participants they interviewed were selected from census tracts in Michigan, where there were high unemployment rates due to a recession that created plummeting car sales.

Turner and colleagues found that both personal and social resources can modify the effects of unemployment. More specifically, the researchers reported that integrating into a social network or having a confidant—someone to confide in—buffers the impact of financial strain on both physical health and emotional well-being. The researchers found that self-esteem is important, too. Self-esteem, or a feeling of self-worth, increases resistance to other stressors that might occur during unemployment. Self-esteem also motivates a person to seek reemployment, which has been shown in previous research to enhance well-being to the same level (or higher) found during prior employment. The researchers also admonished others to bear in mind that because reemployment is difficult in a poor economy, the unemployed need to be realistic—that is, flexible in their job searches.

The research by Turner and associates suggests that the unemployed need not suffer from as much stress as research suggests they do. Their research also has ramifications for intervention, particularly in making available a supportive network on which the unemployed can draw in times of stress.

Other scientists have developed alternative interventions for the unemployed. Caplan, Vinokur,

(continued)

■ ■ ■ ■ ■

CASE IN POINT 12.1 CONTINUED

Price, and van Ryn (1989) in a randomized field experiment followed over 900 unemployed individuals who either attended workshops on job seeking or who simply received a self-help pamphlet on job seeking. Not surprisingly, those who found employment were less anxious and depressed than those who remained unemployed. Those who attended the workshops found better jobs and higher job satisfaction than those who received only the pamphlets. Similarly, the workshop participants who did not find reemployment were more motivated to keep looking than those who received only the pamphlet. In a follow-up study on reemployment workshops, Vinokur and colleagues (2000) found that workshop participants still had higher reemployment rates and better mental health than nonparticipants.

Van Ryn and Vinokur (1992) discovered an important mechanism that underlies job-search behavior as provided for in such workshops. In other words, the researchers examined *how* pro-

grams on job-search training prompt the unemployed to seek work. Van Ryn and Vinokur found that self-efficacy seems initially to be responsible for job seeking in the unemployed who have been through job-search skills programs. **Self-efficacy** is the belief that one can successfully execute a behavior or course of action under possibly stressful or novel circumstances (Bandura, 1997). Self-efficacy generally affects the likelihood of initiating a behavior, persistence at the behavior, and quality of performance of the behavior. Van Ryn and Vinokur found that immediately after the job-search skills programs, self-efficacy directly and indirectly affected the participants' intentions to search for a job, actual job-seeking behaviors, and attitudes toward seeking a job (such as how hard it would be to find employment). Studies such as these indicate that interventions with the unemployed can be successful in abating the pain and poverty of unemployment. Research in this area continues.

TRADITIONAL TECHNIQUES FOR MANAGING ORGANIZATIONS

When Sarah left Harmony House, she was a discontented employee. Sarah was not the only one hurt by her decision to leave, though. The organization would suffer also. Harmony House would now have to recruit and select a replacement for Sarah as well as train and indoctrinate the new individual. Clients might perhaps feel disoriented when they came looking for Sarah but could not find her. What do organizations traditionally do to attract and retain good members and to manage poor members? Are these strategies helpful?

Compensation Packages

Many of the traditional attempts by organizations to treat employees well or to terminate them focus on the individual. An age-old method of motivating employees to work hard and work well is to manipulate compensation levels. In fact, setting compensation levels is often considered the primary function of many human resource management staffs (Milkovich & Boudreau, 1991). Interestingly, organizational members rarely mention pay as the job facet most related to their job satisfaction. Nonetheless, one of the common ways organizations

attempt to motivate their members is by tampering with compensation and benefits packages. One study showed that raising wage and salary levels was the most common response
to reducing quitting in organizations (Bureau of National Affairs, 1981). However, in reality, pay adjustments only partially increase job satisfaction (Schultz & Schultz, 1998). Interestingly, even when employees participate in their own performance reviews, which are
often tied to compensation levels, satisfaction with pay remains unaffected (Morgeson,
Campion, & Maertz. 2001).

Rules and Regulations

Organizations also attempt to control member behavior by means of policies and regulations. Policy manuals and codes of ethics for employees have become quite common
(Lewin, 1983). Some policies are specific: "No gambling on company property." Others are
less so: "Employees are expected to be loyal to the company." Add to this the multitude of
public policies or federal and state legislation intended to regulate organizations and the
individuals in them, and the total number of regulations is overwhelming. Federal Equal
Employment Opportunity Guidelines and the Occupational Safety and Health Regulations
alone would create a stack of policies higher than the average person is tall!

   The extent to which employees follow organizational policies is unclear, but some
classic studies of employee behavior indicate that not all organizational members appreciate
regulations. In the bank wiring room study of the classic Hawthorne research at the Western
Electric Plant in Hawthorne, Illinois, the men of the bank wiring room purposely worked
below the production standard set by their supervisors. Why? The men believed that if they
worked up to standard, their superiors would simply raise the standard (Roethlisberger &
Dickson, 1939), thereby forcing the men to work even harder. It is known today that in professional bureaucracies such as hospitals, universities, and other human services agencies,
the professionals prefer to operate according to their *own* codes rather than the formal policies of their organizations (Cheng, 1990; Mintzberg, 1979). Most organizational members
have little say in the policies or regulations of their organization; that may be the primary
reason they are discontented with the guidelines and violate the rules, as is often found in
studies of organizational rules. Additionally, rule violation can result in discipline, such as
termination, demotion, or leave without pay. Atwater and her associates (2001) found that
discipline is often perceived as unfair and that both recipients and observers consequently
lose respect for the person administering the discipline as well as for the organization.

   In summary, then, these traditional methods of regulating individuals in organizations
are typically the antithesis of what community psychologists would recommend. First, most
are aimed at the individual level of the organization. They do not address nor acknowledge
the role that the context or the organization itself plays in producing and influencing individual behavior. Second, most of these methods are not particularly humanizing. Community psychologists value strategies that benefit the individual and speak to the individual's
worthiness. On the contrary, in most of these traditional techniques, it is the organization
that benefits, if at all. Third, community psychologists emphasize prevention over treatment. In these solutions to organizational situations, the solution often comes *after,* not
before, the problem has occurred. Finally, community psychologists believe that individuals

should actively engage in—indeed, be empowered to—create their own environments and design the solutions to their problems. In none of these traditional approaches to organizational problems is there much room for that.

Our focus now turns to changes in organizations that encompass some of the values of community psychology. Although much of the progressive work in the fields of organizational behavior and organizational psychology has been conducted in and for industrial settings, you will see that what follows can also generally apply to most community organizations.

OVERVIEW OF ORGANIZATIONAL CHANGE

Reasons for Change

Organizations require change for a number of reasons, a few of which will be mentioned briefly here. Pressures for change may be internal or external. **Internal pressures to change** come from within and include pressures from clients, staff, supervisors, or all three. As in the case of Harmony House, internal budget pressures can force change. Organizations also sometimes change their focus or offer new or different services, which leads to further change.

Forces outside of the organization create **external pressures to change.** Government regulations, external competition, political and social trends, and other factors create the need for organizations to adapt. For example, the move to deinstitutionalize people who are mentally disabled has forced communities to provide alternative services such as group homes. Both the availability of homes and the conditions in the institutions have been affected by this trend.

Issues Related to Organizational Change

As already mentioned in Chapters 3 and 4, change is difficult. Organizational change is no different; it, too, is not easy. One reason organizational change is complex is because many organizational members resist change. They feel threatened by the changes, perhaps because they do not feel competent to handle the changes or they do not want to put forth the effort to adapt to them. Similarly, some organizations are more difficult to change than others—for example, public sector organizations, which are often bound by laws and civil service requirements (Shinn & Perkins, 2000).

There are other reasons change in organizations is complicated. Organizations are interdependent systems (Tosi et al., 1986). The people in the organization influence the organization and the organization influences the people. One cannot be changed without changes occurring in the other. For example, suppose in his budget cuts, the Harmony House supervisor decided also to cut staff to save money. Fewer staff means less attention to each youth; fewer staff also means more work for the remaining staff. Hence, the services of the organization may start to decline; therefore, its reputation might also decline, and it would perhaps attract fewer clients and fewer qualified job applicants because of the budget cuts.

Glidewell (1987) offered a second example of the interdependence of people and organizations from the community psychology literature. Glidewell worked with a group of citizens who hoped to change a school board, which desired instead to change the citizens' attitudes. Specifically, the citizens had voted down a tax referendum three times in one year; the board hoped the citizens would pass the referendum. Glidewell tracked the changes in the citizens and the school board over several years. His data clearly showed a mutually causative, sequential, yet circular system of influence. An increase in citizen negotiation skills was followed by changes in influence on board decisions as well as changes in self-esteem of the participants. Changes in self-esteem and changes in attendance at board meetings were followed by changes in risk taking. Changes in risk taking were followed by further changes in negotiation skills. Changes in negotiation skills attracted the attention of the board; thus, the board was more likely to listen to the citizens, whose esteem was further enhanced.

Another reason organizations are difficult to change lies in the fact that the intervention or change must fit the organizational paradigm (Cheng, 1990). What does this mean? Organizations are diverse in terms of their staffing, functions, structures, and other parameters. By using two dimensions from organizational theory, Schubert and Borkman (1991) found not one but five different types of self-help groups. The two dimensions were "dependence on external funds" and "extent of internal experiential authority" (or self-determination). Therefore, even in organizations with similar purposes—in this case, self-help groups—there are diverse types of organizations varying on several dimensions. Changing organizations requires customizing the intervention or fitting the change to the organizational model (Constantine, 1991) and to the organizational constituencies.

To ensure that change is indeed needed, change should commence with action research. The research can also address whether the organization is ready for change. Survey-guided feedback has been suggested as a viable method for monitoring organizational change (Shinn & Perkins, 2000). **Survey-guided feedback** involves the systematic collection of data from organizational members who also receive subsequent and repeated feedback about the changes.

Both need and readiness for change are generally prompted by dissatisfaction with the organization by its members (Baron & Greenberg, 1990). The age of the organization is also important, as there exist different stages of development of community organizations (Bartunek & Betters-Reed, 1987). Some preliminary plan for change should also be in place, although a long-range plan may be better (Taber, Cooke, & Walsh, 1990). Such planning should involve staff and perhaps clients in all phases. Staff participation has a significant effect on both job satisfaction and self-esteem (Roberts, 1991; Sarata, 1984).

Change in organizations can occur at the organizational level, the group level, or the individual level. Although some community psychologists might prefer to change the whole organization—the whole community, so to speak—often it is the subparts of the organization that are easiest to change. Next will be an examination of all levels of organizational change and a few techniques at each level. For a complete review of methods of organizational change, see Head and Sorenson (1988).

CHANGING THE WHOLE ORGANIZATION

Reorganization

Several techniques may be employed for changing the whole organization or system; two will be examined here. One change strategy is reorganization of the organization. **Reorganization** means that a structural change takes place; that is, the tasks, interpersonal relationships, reward system, or decision-making techniques are rearranged (Beer & Walton, 1990). For example, Hellman, Greene, Morrison, and Abramowitz (1985) studied residential mental health treatment programs and found that both staff and client perceptions of the program were more negative in the larger organizations. These researchers suggested that the change from three small homes to one large facility may have exacerbated the schizophrenic clients' fears about loss of self. Hellman and colleagues recommended careful review and related research by policy makers before commencing any other similar reorganizations.

Organizations can also be reorganized by becoming linked, affiliated with, or networked with other organizations. **Networks, enabling systems,** and **umbrella organizations** have been discussed in an earlier chapter. Suffice it to say here that these "master" organizations help ensure the survival and success of their member organizations. However, competition, lack of coordinating mechanisms, and other factors can diminish the effectiveness of such organizational federations.

Qualty of Work Life Programs

Another change that can be made throughout an organization is to introduce quality of work life (QWL) programs, mentioned earlier. Recall that these programs include **participatory decision making,** designed to encourage democracy and staff motivation, satisfaction, and commitment. Such programs also foster career development and leadership by empowering or fostering decision making in others besides the leaders or managers already designated on the organizational chart (Hollander & Offerman, 1990). In QWl programs, the staff and possibly the clients design programs and action plans that they think will be effective and that are well reasoned. The programs are then implemented and perhaps funded by higher levels in the organization. Such programs have been shown to be fairly effective in improving organizational productivity as well as employee satisfaction in various settings (Baron & Greenberg, 1990), although others (Labianca, Gray & Brass, 2000; Randolph, 2000) found that empowerment can be a particularly elusive and resisted concept in many organizations.

Bennis (1989) accused most of today's organizational leaders of being too self-absorbed and therefore causing some of the country's economic and social problems as well as organizational misery. He recommended that if managers do not allow participation by others within organizations, they should at least learn more humanistic leadership styles.

Hamilton, Basseches, and Richards (1985) suggested that the number of programs in communities that promote participatory decision making is steadily increasing, but several studies suggest that simply allowing participation in community organizations is hollow and therefore not beneficial. Prestby, Wandersman, Florin, Rich, and Chavis (1990) found that in order for individuals to continue to participate in block or neighborhood booster associations, benefits (such as getting to know one's neighbors better or learning a new skill like public speaking) have to exceed costs (such as feeling the association never gets anything done or finding less time to spend with friends and family). Community organizations need to manage their incentive efforts well so that participation by others results in satisfaction.

GROUP CHANGE WITHIN THE ORGANIZATION

In the Hawthorne studies mentioned earlier, one group of men in a bank wiring room developed their own group norms and standards that were well outside of those of the company. Groups in organizations often do that. You might have noticed this phenomenon in some of the groups to which you belong. For example, you may be taking classes outside of the psychology department. The psychology department perhaps has its own culture that is casual, personable, and informal. Students are called by their first names, class discussions are frequent, and students are allowed full representation and voting privileges within the department. On the other hand, a different department, say mathematics, might be more formal and less personable. Students are called Miss Smith or Mister Jones, there are few class discussions, and the department meetings are closed to students. Groups exist as mini-organizations within organizations, and groups in community organizations are no exception.

Several techniques for group change exist; two are mentioned here and have been targeted in the community psychology literature as important. Both team building and quality circles can result in better functioning of groups in community organizations and therefore result in better services to the community. In fact, multiple studies and literature reviews have revealed that within-group interventions in organizations result in positive changes in attitudes, group processes, productivity, and other employee behaviors (Shinn & Perkins, 2000). We should also note that group-to-group or intergroup interventions (such as conflict management) are also important in organizations and are possible.

Team Building

One technique for improving groups in organizations is team building. **Team building** is an ongoing group method in which group members are encouraged to work together in the spirit of cooperation that contributes to the group's sense of community. The purpose of team building is to *accomplish* goals and to analyze tasks, member relations, and processes such as decision making in the group. In other words, the group is simultaneously the object of and a participant in the process. Teams are proving to be such a powerful force for empowerment that they form the basic building block for any intelligent organization (Pinchot & Pinchot, 1993). Team building has been examined using a sophisticated technique called meta-analysis, which is utilized to statistically examine the literature on a particular process and to draw implications for policy and practice (Durlak & Lipsey, 1991). By means of meta-analysis, team building has been shown to be quite effective (Neuman, Edwards, & Raju, 1989; Svyantek, Goodman, Benz, & Gard, 1999).

Team building—or **team development,** as it is also known (Sundstrom, DeMeuse, & Futrell, 1990)—has been used to improve staff services to clients at mental health agencies (Bendicsen & Carlton, 1990; Cohen, Shore, & Mazda, 1991; Olson & Cohen, 1986) as well as to improve the performance of both the corrections officers and staff at forensic (psychi-atric) prisons (Miller, Maier, & Kaye, 1988), patients at methadone maintenance clinics (Magura, Goldsmith, Casriel, & Lipton, 1988), teachers (Thatcher & Howard, 1989), nurses at an eating disorders clinic (Sansone, Fine, & Chew, 1988), physicians (Bair & Greenspan, 1986), and staff at other types of service agencies (Davis & Luthans, 1988). Team building also has been successfully used to sensitize multiculturally staffed agencies to the needs of their diverse members (Ratiu, 1986). Some argue, though, that many employees resist teams primarily because of mistrust and low tolerance for change (Kirkman, Jones, & Shapiro, 2000).

Quality Circles

Quality circles as a change technique have also been mentioned earlier in this chapter. Qual-ity circles are small groups of volunteer employees who meet regularly to identify and solve problems related to organizational conditions. These solutions must be implemented if the quality circle's participants are to feel that their input has been useful. Implementation moti-vates the circle's members to continue their deliberations from meeting to meeting. These group solutions, when implemented, should result in higher member satisfaction and better service to clients. Quality circles function best when the members are well trained in prob-lem-solving skills, the leader is skilled at facilitating group communication, and participa-tion of the group's members is voluntary (Jewell, 1998). Research has shown that while quality circles can improve employee satisfaction and performance, these results are some-times short-lived (Klein, Ralls, Smith-Major, & Douglas, 2000).

HELPING INDIVIDUALS CHANGE WITHIN
THE ORGANIZATION

It has already been stated that community psychologists prefer the ecological approach where the whole system rather than the individual is examined and changed; however, the literature has emphasized the individual in community psychology. In line with this, the next section will discuss how individuals can change, especially in coping with everyday prob-lems instigated by their organizations. Note, however, that this particular level—the indi-vidual level—is the one most plagued by failed change efforts (Macy & Izumi, 1993; Shinn & Perkins, 2000).

Burnout and Stress

Burnout and stress are problems in contemporary organizations, as already noted. Today's organizations need to recognize that burnout and stress are related to organizational condi-tions rather than merely to an individual's makeup (McCulloch & O'Brien, 1986) or poor coping strategies (Shinn, Morch, Robinson, & Neuer, 1993). Some organizations, though, do little to help their staff cope with organizational stress (Shinn, Lehmann, & Wong, 1984). Organizations need to be involved in interventions, and community psychologists offer a growing literature on what can be done to alleviate these problems in organizations. Tradi-tional organizational interventions for stress in individuals include meditation and relaxation training as well as exercise programs (Ivancevich, Matteson, Freedman, & Phillips, 1990). Such interventions treat the individual and ignore the context in which that individual works. Community psychologists have developed alternative programs, which will be showcased next.

Social support from coworkers in the form of modeling various strategies for coping, showing empathy, and giving advice has been demonstrated to be useful in ameliorating the effects of stress and burnout in various community agencies (Bernier, 1998; Turnipseed, 1998). For instance, Kirmeyer and Dougherty (1988) demonstrated that social support for police dispatchers favorably reduces the officers' anxiety. Olson's (1991) research showed that appropriate support provides teachers with acculturation experiences and encourages them to make autonomous decisions. Hirsch and David (1983) and McIntosh (1991) found that social support from other nurses enables nurses to reduce general stress levels and cope better with patient death. Human services workers (Shinn et al., 1984), and more specifically social workers (Himle, Jayertne, & Thyness, 1991; Melamed, Kushnir, & Meir, 1991), also benefit from the social support of coworkers. Broman, Hamilton, and Hoffman (1990), Caplan and colleagues (1989), Turner and colleagues (1991), and Zippay (1990–1991) have shown that social support also alleviates the effects of unemployment for terminated employees.

Cautions are needed here, however. Social support often operates in complex ways in organizational settings (Schwarzer & Leppin, 1991), just as it does elsewhere; for example, group coping and support is often but not always better than individual coping strategies. And, in some instances, social support can actually worsen the individual's situation (Grossi & Berg, 1991). Similarly, regard must be given to each person's cultural background and what kind of support is most appropriate for that person (Jay & D'Augelli, 1991).

Finally, mass education programs on stress management can help employees and community citizens cope with stress. Jason and colleagues (1989) produced a series of television programs on stress and coping. Many viewers reported that they tried the coping methods. Measures of viewer adjustment and well-being showed significant improvement, especially among the most distressed viewers. Organizations can also provide mass education about stress and coping through newsletters, workshops, and trainings.

Other Issues

In modern society, personal problems also plague members of organizations. In human service settings, it is not just the clients who experience the myriad problems that the organization is designed to address. Chemical dependency, family strife, financial problems, mental health, and other issues also affect the staff and can lessen their enthusiasm and perhaps productivity while at work. People do not leave their personal problems outside the organization when they enter it each working day. Avant-garde organizations recognize that by assisting employees with personal problems, they are inspiring loyalty to the organization and thus helping the organization. Health insurance rates, turnover, and absenteeism are probably reduced when organizations help individuals cope with personal problems. Highlighted here are two different personal problems that can, but need not, interfere with an individual's working life: smoking and role conflict in working parents. Both of these issues have received recent attention in the community psychology literature.

Health: The Example of Smoking

Smoking by employees, even when not at the worksite, is troublesome for many reasons, among which are the health-related problems of the smokers, consequent health insurance costs to the organization, and complaints by others affected by secondhand smoke (Milkovich & Boudreau, 1991). In one study, psychologists hoping to reduce employee smoking enlisted participants from 43 different corporations. The smokers participated in a televised smoking cessation program combined with self-help abstinence groups. Compared to other smokers, those in the smoking cessation program reduced their smoking the most (Jason, Gruder, Martins, Flay, Warnecke, & Thomas, 1987). However, in this first study, **recidivism,** or return to the problem behavior—in this case, smoking—remained a dilemma. The conjectured reason for relapse was that worksites can be stressful and thus create the return to smoking.

In a second study, one group of employees received a self-help manual, another received the manual and an incentive to cease smoking, while a third group received the manual, the incentive, and social support. Social support in this study clearly had an effect both on quitting and on long-term cessation (McMahon & Jason, 2000). Therefore, when an organization provides assistance as simple as encouraging support groups, the organization also encourages the well-being of its members.

Family Issues

The second example of personal circumstance that can cause distress for employees of organizations is their family situation (Shinn & Perkins, 2000). There are more parents either from single- or dual-parent families who work today than in the past (Jacobs & Gerson, 2001). Finding child care, coordinating different family members' schedules, and so on can be a burden for these parents (Zedeck & Mosier, 1990). Some organizations remain unresponsive to the conflict created by work and family responsibilities, so there is a call for organizations to attend more to family/work balance (Hobson, Delunas, & Kesic, 2001). Day-care issues were already discussed in Chapter 8. In that chapter, Zigler's idea to link early childhood day care with public school systems was reviewed. This solution coupled with work-site day care might provide ample day care for children of harried parents. Here, the focus will turn to other possible solutions that are in line with community psychology's philosophies.

Adapting work schedules is one possibility. In **work schedule adaptations,** or job restructuring, employees' work-site time is not the standard 9-to-5 day. Instead, employees are usually given the freedom to select *when* and sometimes *where* they would like to work. One such system is flextime. In most **flextime** systems, there are core hours during which all employees must be present. However, the employee can often select the total number of hours worked, the length of the work week, or other variations. A wider variety of service hours might also be attractive to clients, too. While some studies demonstrate positive effects for flexible working hours (Shinn & Perkins, 2000), other research has not always demonstrated strong, positive effects of flextime and other work schedule adaptations. For example, in one study (Shinn, Wong, Simko, & Ortiz-Torres, 1989), perceived time flexibility was only weakly related to positive outcomes or had no effect on well-being. Other program dimensions, such as social support, were more strongly related.

Compressed workweeks offer another alternative. The compressed workweek is not the standard five-day, Monday-through-Friday week. In the typical scheme, all employees work four 10-hour days with either Friday or Monday off, which ensures a longer weekend and therefore more concentrated time with the family. Research generally has demonstrated that family-friendly work scheduling and other family-supportive work programs result in more commitment to the organization and in lower turnover (Aryee, Luk, & Stone, 1998; Baltes, Briggs, Huff, Wright, & Neuman, 1999).

Some organizations even allow **home work** in which the individual works at home for all or a portion of the week. These individuals are usually linked to their work site via computer or some other form of technology yet are also home with young children (Milkovich & Boudreau, 1991).

Some programs of work schedule alteration have been found to reduce organizational problems (Zedeck & Mosier, 1990) and perhaps improve family members' home and work lives. Greenberger, Goldberg, Hamill, O'Neill, and Payne (1989) found that organizational policies that are family responsive best assist women in coping with role strain, because it is women who still have greater responsibility than men for adjusting work life to meet the demands of their families.

Today, a variety of programs in organizations exist that are designed to help an individual cope with personal problems as well as financial, legal, emotional, drug, and other problems. **Employee assistance programs (EAPs)** are designed to assist employees with personal problems that may interfere with their organizational behaviors. EAPS in industrial settings have existed from as early as 1917 (New York State Employee Assistance Program Manual, 1990) and have grown rapidly in the last two decades (Bureau of National Affairs, 1986). Today over 90 percent of the Fortune 500 firms offer such programs (Sciegaj et al., 2001). When EAPs are designed and maintained by the employees themselves (rather than, say, managers), are on-site, and are voluntary rather than coercive, the programs fit the ideals of community psychology. Moreover, when EAPs are linked with **wellness programs** designed to prevent health problems before they begin and designed to change norms away from stress, substance abuse, and unproductive coping, then these programs certainly are aligned with the philosophy of community psychology (Shinn, 1987; Shinn & Perkins, 2000). Wellness programs include but are not limited to education about diet, weight loss, and exercise as well as lifestyle modification programs (Gebhardt & Crump, 1990). Although many employees do not equate EAPs with wellness nor with prevention (Mazloff, 1998), the presence of EAPs in an organization is associated with positive attitudes toward the organization's substance use policy and with employees' self-reported use of illicit substances (Bennett & Lehman, 1997).

CHANGING WHAT PEOPLE DO: ALTERING JOBS

As you now know from your reading, the context of work creates problems. The **job context**—that is, the jobs people do and how and where they do them—can also be a factor in organizational and individual well-being. There are a number of recently developed strategies for changing jobs that are important, a few of which are mentioned here.

Job Restructuring

Individuals can become frustrated by what they do in organizations. The jobs might be too demanding, too boring, too complex, or too difficult. Suppose that Sarah Anderson, the individual in the opening story, had become disenchanted with her job not because of budget cuts but because the job was not challenging enough. What could she and her supervisor have done about this? Two possible and seemingly similar strategies are job enlargement and job enrichment (Shinn & Perkins, 2000). **Job enlargement** involves adding more to the job, but what is added usually requires about the same level of responsibility and skill. Suppose that Sarah led therapy groups at Harmony House. If she did not find this challenging enough, perhaps she could have developed wellness, exercise and nutrition, or diet classes for interested youth, or perhaps she could have done outreach to other at-risk youth in the community.

Job enrichment involves adding higher-level responsibilities or more knowledge to an individual's repertoire. Perhaps Sarah felt she had accomplished all she could in her current position at Harmony House and was bored. She and her supervisor could have decided that Sarah had sufficient experience to train and mentor all new case managers who were hired. In this way, Sarah would have been further challenged by managerial responsibilities but also would have used all of the skills that she had already attained in supervising the new caseworkers.

Is there evidence to support the notion that job restructuring works? The answer is Yes. Shinn and Perkins (2000) recently examined several literature reviews of job restructuring, especially job enlargement and job enrichment. They found that changes in job structure generally result in constructive changes, sometimes strikingly positive changes. Shinn and Perkins cautioned, however, that job restructuring is not without pitfalls. For example, a change in the way one job is performed can result in unanticipated changes in adjacent or interrelated jobs.

One form of job enrichment for many Americans has been the addition of computers to their work. Computers may be the most profound technological change since the steam engine. Case in Point 12.2 further discusses the addition of technology to our work.

Management by Objectives

Altering staff perceptions of the job is also important, and there are at least two interesting methods for accomplishing this. In **management by objectives (MBO),** the staff person and his or her supervisor jointly discuss the tasks at hand and how goals related to them will be accomplished. The two then jointly set goals for the employee and, during a later review, decide whether the goals were accomplished or if not, were too over- or underambitious. MBO, therefore, is a sort of participative negotiation (Katzell & Thompson, 1990). Although the individual employee is not solely empowered to make his or her own decisions, the method is popular because some of the fear is taken out of traditional performance appraisal in that the employee knows in advance what is expected. The staff member is also motivated to accomplish the goals because he or she has had a role in designing them (Bandura, 1997).

CASE IN POINT 12.2
THE ROLE OF COMPUTERS IN SHAPING THE ORGANIZATIONAL COMMUNITY

In the last 20 years, there have been dramatic changes in the amount and nature of technology added to our working lives. Desktop computers, local area networks, voice mail, telecommuting, and the Internet have sparked the need for people to know more and more about technology. Technology indeed is changing the composition and distribution of the nation's workforce (McConnell, 1996).

What do we know about how technology shapes the sense of community inside an organization? Zack and McKenney (1995), utilizing a field study, examined electronic messaging by management groups. They studied the influence of the social context on the patterns of face-to-face communication compared to computerized communication. Results showed that different groups working in identical organizational structures and performing the same tasks used technology differently because of differing social contexts. Zack and McKenney suggested that researchers studying technology in organizations must *explicitly* take into account the social context. They also reminded managers that they, too, must *explicitly* manage the social context of the workplace prior to implementing technological change.

Following this advice about knowledge of the social context inside an organization, Hinds and Kiesler (1995) had technical and administrative employees keep logs of their communication patterns. Vertical and lateral communications both inside and outside of departments were tracked. Hinds and Kiesler explored what type of technology was utilized by whom and when. The researchers found that technical employees had more lateral or peer communication than did administrators and

that half of all employee communication was extradepartmental. Both types of communication seemed to occur by telephone, a synchronous form of communication. In other words, when communicating by phone, both parties communicate to each other at the same time. However, on occasions when asynchronous communication did occur, technical employees and administrators preferred different types of technologies. Administrators preferred voice mail; technical employees preferred electronic mail. Status within the organization or type of work performed may well influence our preference for how we communicate with other individuals when they are not physically available.

In another field study, Kanungo (1998) examined organizational climate and its effect on networked computer use. Kanungo hypothesized that particular types of organizational cultures foster computer-network effectiveness while other types hinder it. The results suggested that organizational culture interacts with the degree of use of technology that, in turn, affects user satisfaction. In task-oriented organizations, user satisfaction with technology was positively related to degree of use. In people-oriented organizations, a negative relationship existed between technology use and user satisfaction. In other words, in organizations that emphasize human interaction, the more employees have to utilize technology, the less they like it.

We might conclude, then, that not all employees or organizations benefit from nor are equally satisfied by the introduction of technology. Organizational specialists would be well served to follow the advice about person-environment fit from community psychology when they plan to introduce technological change into an organization.

Participation in goal setting and decision making in organizations has been shown to be highly effective. Using **meta-analysis,** which is a sophisticated statistical technique for reviewing relevant literature and deducing the overall utility of a practice, Rodgers and Hunter (1991) found MBO to be effective in 68 of 70 studies. Of the studies related to community services Rodgers and Hunter reviewed, MBO was used successfully to improve municipal governments (Poister & Streib, 1989), hospitals (Sloan & Schrieber, 1971; Stoelwinder & Clayton, 1978), the Equal Employment Opportunity Commission (Taylor & Tao, 1980), college faculty (Terpstra, Olson, & Lockeman, 1982), and a police diversion agency for youth (Williams, 1984).

Realistic Job Preview

Another method for altering perceptions of jobs is to provide a **realistic job preview (RJP)** to the individual *before* she or he takes the job. The discussion on burnout made clear that the most ideal or naive individual often burns out first. Why? The reason is simple. Idealistic individuals are not in touch with the realities of the job. Their expectations of the job are higher than reality, and thus they have the furthest to "fall." Providing a realistic sample of what the job entails, its glamorous as well as its gloomy side, enables individuals who are not appropriate for the job to remove themselves from the search. Perhaps Sarah was a little too idealistic for the realities of Harmony House. Had she been informed that budget problems were predicted and that some services had to be cut *before* she took the job, she might never have become so disillusioned.

Many human services workers heroically hope to "save the world." They frequently pin their high expectations on their clients' levels of progress. When they do, they burn out when the reality strikes that they are not going to "save" everyone. Case after case materializes and the workers do not see much progress. An *expectation shift* can help avoid this type of burnout. As noted earlier, if human services workers can shift their focus to other facets of their jobs, such as progress in their own learning or competence, then they are less likely to burn out (Stevens & O'Neill, 1983).

DOES ORGANIZATIONAL INTERVENTION WORK?

Many strategies for changing parts of or whole organizations have been reviewed in this chapter. At least one or two studies have been provided for each strategy that suggest that these techniques are viable. The field of organizational development is old enough at this point that several large-scale reviews of OD have been conducted in order to draw general conclusions about OD's efficacy.

Robertson, Roberts, and Porras (1993) compared almost 50 different OD studies conducted between 1975 and 1986. Many of the different techniques described in this chapter were utilized in the studies: MBO, quality circles, team building, and others. These outcome studies examined either individual, organizational, or both types of outcomes. Overall, the studies demonstrated that OD is beneficial. The results, however, were more beneficial to the organization than to the individual, and benefits were more likely to be obtained when a number of methods were used rather than just one. This last finding is not surprising in that most studies in community psychology show that multipronged efforts are more successful. One might conclude, then, that OD shows promise; however, it merits more research.

Anyone considering organizational change must also consider that changes need to be made in a coherent, systematic fashion. Hit-or-miss and one-shot approaches probably will not be productive in the long run. Bennis (1969) also suggested that organizations need to become **organic systems.** That is, organizations need to replace mechanistic methods (such as adherence to rules and regulations) with transactional methods such that *mutual* trust, *shared* control and responsibility, and *multigroup* membership are enhanced.

SUMMARY

Organizations are communities. Just like any community, organizations are comprised of various individuals and groups. Many of today's organizations need humanizing, as do many communities, if they are to enhance the well-being of the individuals in them.

By making today's community agencies and organizations better places in which to work for their staffs, organizations can deliver better services to their clients. The problems facing human services workers today include but are not limited to stress, burnout, workaholism or Type-A personality, repressive organizational cultures, poor environmental conditions, and human resources mismanagement.

Historically, organizations have considered individual employee's characteristics rather than anything organizational to be the root of the problems. Traditional techniques for managing problem individuals have been to alter compensation packages such as pay or to institute rules and regulations.

Community organizations need to undergo change if they are to continue to provide quality services and become more humane. That is, they need to adopt more avant-garde methods for coping with change and with problems inside the organizations. The whole organization can change or, within the organization, groups or individuals can change.

Methods for changing the whole organization include reorganization—for example, creating smaller, friendlier agencies from one large one. Another organizational strategy for change is to institute quality of work life (QWL) programs. These are programs where staff members and perhaps clients participate in planning and designing the changes the organization needs.

Groups within organizations can also change in order that they become more effective. Two methods for group change include team building, or ongoing team development, and quality circles, where small groups of volunteer organizational members meet to address problems within the organization.

Finally, individuals inside the organization bring with them an array of problems that can diminish the effectiveness of the organization. Burnout and stress are two examples. The use of social support from others within the organization is effective in assisting distressed individuals. Employee assistance programs (EAPs) and wellness programs are also useful for addressing a variety of personal problems individuals bring to work that decrease their ability to serve clients. These and other organizational development techniques have been proven effective according to recent research.

THE FUTURE OF
COMMUNITY PSYCHOLOGY

Yesterday is not ours to recover, but tomorrow is ours to win or lose.
—Lyndon B. Johnson, 1963

"So that's the face that goes with the voice I hear on the phone all the time," Rita said to John. John is in charge of a meal program for people living with acquired immune deficiency syndrome (AIDS). Rita is the head of the Meals on Wheels program for the elderly in the same semi-rural county. "Glad to finally meet you in person," replied John.

Rita and John had spoken to each other many times in the past but always by phone. Their conversations revolved around buying food in bulk at low cost, finding volunteers, and the toll rural roads and the weather take on getting clients the multiple services they need. The two agency heads had never met until an important conference was sponsored by the only college in the county.

In speaking to both John and Rita, as well as other agency heads, it became apparent to the volunteer coordinator at the college that volunteer services to these agencies was anything but coordinated. In fact, none of the services was coordinated with any other service. The volunteer coordinator, in consultation with the agency heads, planned a conference on the campus for all the agencies. Although they knew each other's names, and some had communicated with each other by phone and mail for years, many of the agency directors met each other for the first time at the conference.

The conference was successful in that agency directors could now better coordinate with each other in providing needed services. The directors also established formal communication channels (e.g., a conference every six months) and discussed mechanisms for moving service delivery forward (e.g., a part-time rural mass transit system so clients without cars could access services). The agency directors also discussed the problems with overlapping services, how to better utilize volunteers, and how they could share information about available grants and other funding sources. Some of the agency directors had never heard about private foundations and the grants they offered, and were excited to learn of them. The volunteer coordinator at the college agreed to make her office a clearinghouse for funding opportunities, communication, and other coordinated endeavors among the agencies.

Perhaps a paradoxical but good starting point for concluding this book would be to return to the beginning of the book. Chapter 1 reviewed some political and social history that influenced community psychology. Such ideologies are also used to frame and shape a sense of community (Humphreys & Rappaport, 1993; Linney, 1990). This chapter will commence by discussing the political and social agendas of the 1980s and 1990s.

RECENT SOCIAL AND POLITICAL AGENDAS
AFFECTING COMMUNITY PSYCHOLOGY

After the oil and hostage crises of the 1970s, Americans wanted a president such as Ronald Reagan who could tell them that "things are fine," a leader who was able to heal the wounded collective psyche. Reagan's charismatic leadership was also able to impress upon the American people that they have the determination to fix almost any problems that might arise. For example, Reagan did not hesitate to fire all the air traffic controllers as part of his deregulation of the airline industry. This action, however, indirectly sent a message to the U.S. public that "survival of the fitness" was the norm. Thus, people who were recipients of social programs or welfare tended to be viewed as nonproductive or lazy (i.e., victim blaming), and programs such as public assistance were often viewed as wasteful. As a consequence, more than $700 million was cut from various social programs during Ronald Reagan's first year in the presidency.

Meanwhile, AIDS, crack abuse, economic downturn, educational crisis and reform, homelessness, and urban violence and other social ills were looming, and many reached epidemic proportion. Reacting to these problems, George Bush, the successor to Ronald Reagan, plotted a course of action, the emphasis of which was on volunteerism, or Bush's "thousand points of light." Bush reasoned that rehabilitation of a community depended on volunteer and cooperative efforts, especially because of dwindling federal support. Certainly, this was not a new idea; similar ideology was evidenced during the administration of John F. Kennedy. However, unlike Kennedy, Bush was practicing the ideology of **individualism,** in which people are ultimately responsible for their *own* actions, rather than **collectivism,** where everyone in the community shares the responsibility for addressing social problems.

This redefinition of responsibility for the community became more evident with William Clinton. Clinton attempted to project himself and his administration as "new democrats," those who are socially conscious yet who are also fiscally conservative and responsible. Clinton wanted to "reinvent government," as he called it. For example, he proposed that college students who receive loans from the government pay back some of their money by performing community service. This concept is similar to the GI Bill of World War II; it has a similar flavor to the Peace Corps and the Job Training Partnership Act (JTPA).

Given the ideologies or slogans used by politicians, Linney (1990) argued that this country has observed a "shifting responsibility from federal to state government" (p. 4). That is, for one reason or another (and economics is an important one), "the federal government has reduced its level of involvement in many realms of service delivery" (p. 4). There are others who agree with Linney (Snowden, 1993), that major shifts in responsibility are taking place. Government commitment to services, especially preventive ones, and funding has never been very consistent nor very strong (Gesten & Jason, 1987).

The shifting of responsibility is both good news and bad news. The shifting responsibility has created an unprecedented opportunity for many state and local communities to be flexible and innovative in their approaches to handling social agendas or problems. Linney (1990) reviewed a number of innovative programs at the state and local levels, including such notable programs as the Citizens Clearinghouse for Hazardous Wastes and the National Alliance for the Mentally Ill. The Citizens Clearinghouse for Hazardous Wastes was founded by Lois Gibbs, President of the Homeowners Association at Love Canal. Love Canal (near Buffalo, New York) was a housing development built clandestinely on a hazardous waste dump. The residents became ill and their homes became relatively worthless because of seepage of waste into them. The Clearinghouse monitors illegal or irresponsible dumping of hazardous wastes.

Many similar programs have been inspired by citizen participation or grass-roots activism. Empowerment (including prevention and intervention) and social change can be achieved in local communities even under limited resources. The opening vignette about the agency heads and the volunteer coordinator is a good example. As governments slough off responsibility for social ills, more grass-roots citizens groups will evolve.

Perhaps another resource for community development in times of government cutbacks lies in disseminating information about possible funds available through private foundations. Money is sometimes available either for community research or community program development or both. Many community agencies do not know about these funding possibilities, as demonstrated in the opening vignette. Just as likely is that many agencies do not employ a grants writer. Community psychologists with grant-writing experience might enable and empower community programs to access this money by educating agency directors about such resources as well as about grant-writing skills.

So, what is the bad news as a result of this shifting responsibility from federal to state government? Social agendas and problems, such as AIDS, crack use, homelessness, and urban violence, are often construed and treated as separate and somewhat unrelated issues (cf. Final Report of Task Force on Homeless Women, Children, and Families, Society for Community Research and Action, 1994; Speer, Dey, Griggs, Gibson, Lubin, & Hughey, 1992).

Recall all that has been learned about interventions for those with mental disorders after deinstitutionalization. Studies have consistently demonstrated that some homeless mentally ill also have alcohol and other drug-abuse problems (e.g. Diamond & Schnee, 1990). Furthermore, many of these individuals are at risk for contracting HIV (Susser, Valencia, & Conover, 1993; Dennehy, Wong, Meyer, Colson, & Susser, 1994). However, funding agencies such as the National Institute on Drug Abuse and the National Institute of Mental Health often do not fund research that investigates those with mental disorders *who also have* alcohol and other substance-abuse problems. Instead, research dollars are often designated for mental disorders *or* alcohol and other drug abuse problems, *but not both.* Funding therefore is often fragmented, and the constant shifting of responsibility is likely to result in more fragmentation, because states and local governments have less money for funding large, multifocused programs.

In the opening vignette, it became apparent that some agencies in this rural county were providing overlapping services. Such overlap is wasteful of resources and money in tight economic times. Moreoever, fragmentation is an obstacle to effective service delivery (Snowden, 1993). Clients, for example, are likely to fall through service system "cracks" created by fragmentation. Coordination of funding and services rather than fragmentation of funding and services is crucial for the future. In fact, some see the integration and coordination of services possible only when there is interagency collaboration so that existing services can monitor the movement of clients between programs, thereby facilitating the delivery of services (Snowden, 1993). The conference described in the opening vignette was a good start to the integration and coordination of services in Jack and Rita's county.

Unfortunately, the perspective that social problems merit attention, intervention, and priority funding is not shared by all people, including the average community citizen. For example, more than 30 years ago, one of the first reports made by the surgeon general warned about the danger of tobacco use (including smokeless tobacco). One of every five deaths in the United States is still attributable to tobacco use, even though it is the single-most preventable cause of death. Many people continue to smoke and do not share the same social agenda as research scientists or government officials.

Furthermore, scientists and government officials can also have different motives and agendas. Andrea Solarz (2001) summarized some of these contrasts:

- The primary goal of scientists is to seek truth, to understand, and to explain while for politicians the goal is to decide and to act so as to advance public good.
- Most scientists believe their work should be value-free and based on standardized processes while policy makers see their work as adversarial and based on negotiation.
- Scientists take their time while for policy makers immediacy is critical.

- Expertise and knowledge are important to science while power and influence are important to policy making.
- Scientists are rewarded for experimenting while policy makers are rewarded for being "right" (i.e., pleasing their constituencies).

Private sector enterprises, on the other hand, do not necessarily share the same social agenda as the government or social scientists, which further complicates progressive social change. Not all companies and industries are socially conscious. For example, despite concerted antitobacco efforts, each year the tobacco industry spends millions of dollars advertising and promoting tobacco. In constant dollars, money spent by the tobacco industry on advertising and promotion has tripled since 1975. The tobacco industry spends over $6 billion a year on advertising (Vladeck, 1998).

In sum, government spending on social programs is declining. Given this situation and the fact that citizens are often indifferent to and private industry is sometimes hostile to scientists' agendas, social interventions and community research are needed more than ever. However, community experimenters will encounter more obstacles in the future. Social research and community intervention indeed require more resourcefulness, a special tenacity, and perhaps a larger research team than ever before (Gesten & Jason, 1987). At the expense of sounding trite, community psychologists have their future work cut out for them.

GENERAL RECOMMENDATIONS ABOUT
SOCIAL CHANGE AND COMMUNITY PSYCHOLOGY
FOR THE COMING YEARS

All the issues raised in previous chapters cannot be reviewed here, but a few important ones will be examined: dissemination of information, prevention, action research, diversity issues, cross-fertilization and linkages to other disciplines and organizations, and social policy. These issues were selected because they have been identified as especially important to the field by immediate past presidents of Division 27 of the American Psychological Association, the Society for Community Research and Action.

Dissemination of Information

Social change will be difficult to accomplish, but this is no reason for community activists to give up. Community intervention still holds more promise than individual intervention (e.g., face-to-face psychotherapy). One means by which community change can be accelerated is to avoid repeatedly reinventing change. Sorely needed in community psychology is more program replication and refinement for other settings (Gesten & Jason, 1987). Only when good ideas are disseminated through journals, conferences, and books will ideas be utilized by community activists elsewhere. Dissemination is also of utmost importance if citizen acceptance and practitioner utilization are to occur. Thus, research is also necessary to determine which factors facilitate dissemination and adoption (Heller, Wyman, & Allen, 2000). In the future, community psychologists may have to turn to the mass media as much as to their own literature. Interventions that have successfully utilized the mass media and newer technologies (e.g., the World Wide Web) for inducing social and individual change have been discussed elsewhere in this book. In so doing, community psychologists need to de-jargonize their work (Solarz, 2001).

In a similar vein, most community psychologists recognize that interventions are more easily implemented when they are consistent with community beliefs and values. It is important to recognize, though, that the more an intervention fits a community, the more minor it is likely to be and the less likely it is to produce substantial change (Heller, 1990; Wolf, 2001). Heller proposed an interesting social change solution that offers sensitivity to local concerns yet affords more power to individuals in local communities to influence public policy: **regionalization of community building** or coalition building. These coalitions are loose-knit, large-scale confederations of local groups with common interests, which, when called upon, can act in unison. This country is currently witnessing some very effective confederated associations at the national level that were built from local grass-roots groups. These coalitions of groups with similar interests provide the large-scale leverage to address important concerns. Heller offered MADD (Mothers Against Drunk Driving) as an example of a local group that developed national constituencies and therefore successfully influenced policy makers on a wide scale. All of this was done through regional and ultimately national coalition building and information dissemination. Case in Point 13.1 offers a second example of the success of coalition building. Coalition building is another vehicle for creating social change that needs more investigation and dissemination effort in community psychology.

In summary, planned social change is becoming more complicated and difficult. Communities would be well served if community psychologists would attend more to information dissemination outside of rather than within their own media.

■ ■ ■ ■ ■

CASE IN POINT 13.1

COALITION BUILDING: THE MASSACHUSETTS TOBACCO CONTROL PROGRAM

An example of local groups coming together to form a coalition is the establishment of the Massachusetts Tobacco Control Program (MTCP), now the largest tobacco control and prevention program in the world. Its funding was $96 million for fiscal year 1993–1994, which amounts to $10 per capita.

In 1992, the Massachusetts division of the American Cancer Society, which in the past had little political experience, successfully built a statewide, grass-roots network of over 200 organizations. Together they sought approval of a ballot question to raise the Massachusetts state cigarette excise tax 25 cents and to allocate these funds to tobacco control programs, comprehensive school health education, and health services. These organizations were able to convince state legislators to earmark these funds specifically for tobacco control and prevention activities, which is a rarity. The legislation and subsequent funding led to the MTCP.

The program is evidently successful. Since 1993, there has been a 10 percent decline in smoking, the largest single decline in the history of the Commonwealth of Massachusetts and three times higher than the U.S. average.

Prevention

Primary prevention is one of the guiding principals in community psychology. By 1985, Buckner and others found over 1,000 references on primary prevention alone. Recall that **primary prevention** attempts to block a problem from occurring altogether. Primary prevention refers most generally to activities that can be undertaken with a healthy population to maintain or enhance their physical or emotional health (Bloom & Hodges, 1988).

Modest but significant progress has been made in the understanding and implementation of primary preventive efforts (Heller, Wyman, & Allen, 2000), but no major disorder or social problem has thus far been eliminated or prevented altogether. For example, while teenage pregnancy remains an important social issue and the number of teen parents is still high, the overall rate of teenage births is slowing down, and more teens who are having babies are completing high school than at any earlier date (Levine, Toro, & Perkins, 1993). However, the truly disadvantaged still have high rates of out-of-wedlock births. It perhaps is to this group, the truly disadvantaged and those with multiple disorders that community psychology should give, that more attention and preventive efforts, and not just in the realm of teen pregnancy.

Both Durlak and Wells' (1997) and Cowen's (1997) publications on primary prevention contribute immensely to the field, but controversy still swirls around this concept. As Cowen has pointed out, the concept of prevention in its early days seemed to have nearly as many definitions as there were people writing about it. For example, is prevention the reduction of occurrences of new cases of mental disorder *or* the promotion of psychological wellness? Durlak and Wells have raised issues about where future research on prevention might lead. They have suggested, for example, that future researchers might attempt to clarify *how* participants' characteristics influence outcomes. Variables such as gender, family factors, and the specific presenting problem need to be examined and tracked. Similarly, researchers should continue to use multiple measures to assess how and whether prevention works. Likewise, Durlak and Wells have indicated that people change in different outcome domains (e.g., behaviors and cognitions). They also have recommended that psychologists develop better screening methods that can validly and efficiently identify individuals at risk for later problems so that programs can be better designed specially for these individuals. Durlak and Wells have expressed that community psychologists need to study long-term effects of preventive interventions as well as the effects of the intervention on significant others who surround the targeted individual. As you can see, much work remains to be done in the area of prevention.

Complicating *how* to intervene is the knowledge held by community psychologists that **comorbidity** usually exists. *Comorbidity* means that often an individual who manifests one disorder or problem behavior manifests other disorders or problem behaviors. Using an earlier example, you know that some individuals who have a mental disorder are also substance abusers. Many community psychologists would agree that multiple approaches are probably best if they can be offered, given funding and other problems. But how in prevention research can we intervene successfully with multiple problems and tease out the effects of which intervention components are most efficacious with what problems (Kessler & Price, 1993)? This is another very complex challenge for the future.

There are other issues related to *how* research on prevention is accomplished. If multiple preventive strategies are utilized, how can one tease out the effects of individual components of the prevention strategy? For example, through what processes are the components of the intervention achieving their effects and is each component contributing equally to success (West, Aiken, & Todd, 1993)?

Action Research

Chapter 2 discussed how community psychologists conduct research and how research in other areas of psychology often differs from research in community psychology. One consideration for the future involves community research participants. As Cook and Shadish (1994) and Jansen and Johnson (1993) noted, one is better able to draw causal inferences in experiments, field or laboratory, when one uses a random sample. A **random sample** was defined in Chapter 2 as a sample in which every member of a population has an equal chance of being selected. In much **action research** (research designed to resolve social problems), community participants from real community settings are under study. The participants commonly are volunteers *and thus have not been randomly assigned to conditions*. Random assignment, then, can be complicated at best and impossible at worst when evaluating social programs.

Causal inferences—such as about what interventions are most effective—are more difficult given the type of research usually conducted by community psychologists. It is incumbent on community psychologists in the future to find statistic analyses and other methods that will allow participants to volunteer for interventions, yet allow scientists to draw meaningful conclusions. For more discussion of this issue, see Cook and Shadish (1994), who dedicate a whole chapter to these and other issues related to community experimentation and action research.

A second solution to assessing action research and community interventions where studies vary in terms of samples and methods is meta-analysis, a method mentioned infrequently in this text. **Meta-analysis** emphasizes the robustness of a particular causal connection across a wide range of persons, settings, times, and cause-and-effect constructs (Heller, 1990). As studies accumulate about a particular concept, such as empowerment, or about a particular intervention, such as interpersonal cognitive problem solving, meta-analysis will allow community psychologists to make assessments that can guide the field in the future. Although not without its own drawbacks (Heller, Wyman, Allen, 2000), more meta-analytic research is needed in the future as the field matures and its potential scientific contributions unfold.

Another problem for action researchers is that their studies often demonstrate effectiveness or discover cause and effect in small samples only. Heller (1990) reminded us in his chapter in the *Annual Review of Psychology* that the effectiveness of a school intervention when administered to a sample of 100 students in a particular school may look effective on a large scale. However, at the group or community level, this is only a sample size of one. As stated earlier, replications in other samples and across other groups and communities are essential. This can happen only when dissemination of information occurs.

Yet another problem is that many research-related journal articles that concern community intervention are program evaluations. As a result, most of the data are outcome data. Because *the process by which an outcome is achieved is as important as the outcome,* more **process analysis** of underlying mechanisms by which change occurred is needed. The history of change is as important as the outcome of the change if other affected groups with similar or different histories are to benefit from the research by adapting it to their locales.

Community psychologists therefore need to extend the range and scope of the methods used to study community dynamics (Klein, 1995). Klein stated, "Despite efforts to promote approaches that are better suited to community phenomena, published research reflects lingering nostalgia for the paradigm of quantified, objective science" (p. 26). Klein recommended that community psychologists do more of the following:

- Qualitative research, such as participant observation
- Action-research and participatory designs that ground the inquiry process in the community groups' needs and perspectives
- Appreciative inquiry, which focuses on the positive life-giving forces rather than the deleterious effects of the phenomena being studied
- Gaming and simulation to explore complex community dynamics, which will help shed light on economic, political, social, and other ecological effects of community decision making

In his contribution to the special issue of the *American Journal of Community Psychology* on methodological issues in community research, Sechrest (1993) concluded that the problems of "research are not altogether intractable; they simply require the best of our thinking and the firmest of our commitments" (p. 665).

Diversity Issues

Community psychologists understand the richness of ideas and experiences that diverse ethnic, racial, and lifestyle groups can bring to a community. They understand well that studies of characteristics of specific cultures provide critical insights for understanding the role of culture in promoting social change and providing services. However, there is a potentially dangerous assumption that cultural differences are clear and recognizable—that they do not vary—and, therefore that they lend themselves easily to research and program development. This view, for example, tends to ignore the transitional nature of many cultures (Grotberg, 2001).

As more varied groups arrive in U.S. communities, are community psychologists, themselves, making progress in promoting diversity and examining diversity issues in their literature? Chapter 1 reviewed the research of Loo, Fong, and Iwamasca (1988), who reviewed the top journals in community psychology and found that about 11 percent of the articles pertain to ethnic minorities. They concluded that progress toward understanding this nation's diverse population is being made but more needs to be done.

Where is the field today, though, on this issue of diversity? For the purposes of writing this book, the authors examined the top U.S. journal in the field of community psychology for the publication year 1993, five years after Loo and his colleagues published their review of the percent of diversity issues in the community psychology literature. A somewhat generous definition of articles containing information related to diversity was used by the authors. The articles either pertained in the main to diverse ethnic, racial, or religious groups or at least reported the ethnic and racial background of participants. In the *American Journal of Community Psychology* from December 1992 to October 1993, the authors found that of the 45 articles published, 17 of them reported information about diverse groups in U.S. population. In other words, almost 38 percent of the articles pertained to groups other than White Americans. Given that most of the articles intensively studied diverse groups, this historic increase is substantial.

More recently (October 2000 to October 2001), the present authors examined the leading U.S. journal in the field. Of 11 empirical articles, 9 (over 80 percent) pertained to diverse groups. There were also two special volumes about feminism and community psychology. Clearly, the field is making great strides in sharing information about and examining issues relevant to our diverse population. However, community psychologists need to continue work with various groups so that interventions are sensitive to the needs and cultures of diverse groups. Various authors, for example, have called for increased input and information in the community psychology literature on other groups: individuals in rural settings (Hamby, 2000); gays, lesbians, and bisexuals (Hill, 1999; Maton, 1999); women (Bond, Hill, Mulvey, & Terenzio, 2000), children with disabilities (Solomon, Pistrang, & Barker 2001), and the elderly population (Heller, Wyman, & Allen, 2000). As we revise this edition of the book, there still exists a dearth of information about individuals involved with the justice system.

Cross-Fertilization and Linkages to Other Disciplines

Linking with other organizations that share the goals of community psychology is a priority for community psychologists (Ahlen-Widoe, 2000; Bond, 1998; Cherniss, 2000; Maton, 1999). According to Bond, to be effective, especially in the public policy arena or in designing prevention strategies, community psychologists need to coalesce with other groups. Until recently, there has been little systematic effort to document and understand the nature of the relationship community psychologists have to other disciplines and to deepen and broaden them (Maton, 1998). To this end, not only has Division 27 aligned itself with other divisions internal to the American Psychological Association (e.g., Division 37 for children, youth, and families) but it has also aligned with other national organizations, such as the Community Development Society, the National Prevention Coalition, the American Public Health Association, and the Society for Disability Studies.

Social Policy

Social policy is a defining area of concern for community psychologists (Bond, 1998). There is general agreement that community psychologists should do more in the policy area but it should be based on sound scientific research. By now you know that community psychologists can and do identify best practices and programs for communities, support individuals who are doing advocacy work, serve on task forces, and take part in congressional hearings related to policy matters. Bond has cautioned, though, that community psychologists must be clear about *why* they would want to take a stand on any issue and *how likely it is* that they can have an impact on any particular social issue. Maton (1998) added that, at present, community psychologists seem to lack the confidence, experience, clout, and unanimity of perspective to make a substantive impact on public policy. Division 27 now has a social policy committee to determine what specific policy activities should be pursued and to review procedures for establishing and approving official statements of the Division.

SUMMARY

The field of community psychology has grown in leaps and bounds since its founding at the Swampscott Conference in the 1960s. The growth has been witnessed in the number of journals, conferences, and graduate programs. There is also an ever-increasing interest in community psychology at the undergraduate level—hence, the need for this book. The field is only in its adolescence, however. Although community psychology perhaps does not have serious growing pains, it could use a few midcourse adjustments. The authors do believe, however, that the field can look forward to a healthy adulthood.

Abella, R. (1991). *Evaluation of the satellite learning centers program.* Paper presented at the Annual Convention of the American Psychological Association, San Francisco, CA.

Aber, J. L., Brooks-Gunn, J., & Maynard, R. A. (1995). Effects of welfare reform on teenage parents and their children. *Critical Issues for Children and Youths, 5,* 53–71.

Aber, J. L., Jones, S. M., Brown, J., Chaudry, N., & Samples, F. (1998). Resolving conflict creatively: Evaluating the developmental effects of a school-based violence prevention program in neighborhood and classroom context. *Development and Psychopathology, 10,* 187–213.

Abrahams, R. B., & Patterson, R. D. (1978–1979). Psychological distress among the community elderly: Prevalence, characteristics and implications for service. *International Journal of Aging and Human Development, 9,* 1–18.

Ackerman, G., Anderson, B., Jensen, S., Ludwig, R., Montero, D., Plante, N., & Yanez D. (2001). Crime rates and confidence in the police: America's changing attitudes toward crime and policy, 1972–1999. *Journal of Sociology & Social Welfare Special Issues, 28,* 43–54.

Adams, R. E. (1992). Is happiness a home in the suburbs? The influence of urban versus suburban neighborhoods on psychological health. *Journal of Community Psychology, 20,* 353–371.

Administration for Children and Families. (1998, December). *Head Start fact sheet.* www//fedstats.gov/index20.html

Ahlen-Widoe, R. (2000). Twenty cents and a new way of thinking. *Journal of Prevention & Intervention in the Community, 19,* 5–11.

Ajzen, I. (1985). From intensions to actions: A theory of planned behavior. In J. Kuhl & J. Beckman (Eds). *Action-control: From cognition to behavior* (pp. 11–39). Heidelberg, Germany: Springer.

Ajzen, I. (1991). The theory of planned behavior. *Organizational Behavior and Human Decision Processes, 50,* 179–211.

Ajzen, I., & Fishbein, M. (Eds.). (1980). *Understanding attitudes and predicting social behavior.* Englewood Cliffs, NJ: Prentice-Hall.

Albee, G. W. (1998). The politics of primary prevention. *Journal of Primary Prevention Special Issue: Politics of Primary Prevention, 19,* 117–127.

Alderson, G., & Sentman, E. (1979). *How you can influence Congress: The complete handbook for the citizen lobbyist.* New York: Dutton.

Aldwin, C., & Greenberger, E. (1987). Cultural differences in predictors of depression. *American Journal of Community Psychology,* 789–812.

Alinsky, S. (1971). *Rules for radicals: A practical primer for realistic radicals.* New York: Random House.

Allen, H., & Simonsen, C. E. (1992). *Corrections in America: An introduction.* New York: Macmillan.

Allen, J. P., Philliber, S., & Hoggson, N. (1990). School-based prevention of teen-age pregnancy and school dropout: Process evaluation of the national replication of the Teen Outreach Program. *American Journal of Community Psychology, 18,* 505–524.

Allen, J. P., Philliber, S., Herrling, S., & Kupermine, G. P. (1997). Preventing teen pregnancy and academic failure: Experimental evaluation of a developmentally based approach. *Child Development, 64,* 729–742.

Allen, L. (1990). A developmental perspective on multiple levels of analysis in community research. In P. Tolan, C. Keys, F. Chertok, & L. Jason (Eds.), *Researching community psychology: Issues of theory and methods.* Washington, DC: American Psychological Association.

Allen, N. (2000). Welfare reform and women's poverty: Exploring the need for broader social change. *The Community Psychologist, 33,* 11–13.

Allen-Meares, P., & Shore, D. A. (1986). A transactional framework for working with adolescents and their sexualities. Special issue: Adolescent sexualities: Overview and principles of intervention. *Journal of Social Work and Human Sexuality, 5,* 71–80.

Allison, D. B., Faith, M., & Franklin, R. D. (1995). The comparative efficacy of antecedent exercise in the treatment of disruptive behavior: A review and meta-analysis. *Clinical Psychology: Science and Practice, 2,* 279–303.

Allport, G. W. (1954). *The nature of prejudice.* Reading, MA: Addison-Wesley.

Alpert, G. P., & Dunham, R. G. (1986). Community policing. *Journal of Police Science and Administration, 14,* 212–222.

Altman, I. (1987). Community psychology twenty years later: Still another crisis in psychology? *American Journal of Community Psychology, 15,* 613–627.

Altman, I., Wohlwill, J. F., & Werner, C. (Eds.). (1985). *Home environments.* New York: Plenum.

American Anthropological Association response to OMB Directive 15: Race and ethnic standards for federal statistics and administrative reporting. www.aaa.org

American Association for Protecting Children. (1987, October 23). *National estimates of child abuse and neglect reports, 1976–1986.* Denver: American Humane Association.

American Psychological Association. (1985). *Standards for educational and psychological testing* (3rd ed.). Washington, DC: Author.

American Psychological Society. (1991). The importance of the citizen scientist in national science policy. *The APS Observer, 4,* 10, 12, 23.

American Psychological Society. (1992, February). Schooling and literacy. *APS Observer Special Issue: The Human Capital Initiative,* 17–20.

Anderson, J. E., Carey, J. W., & Taveras, S. (2000). HIV testing among the general US population and persons at increased risk: Information from national surveys, 1987–1996. *American Journal of Public Health, 90,* 1089–1095.

Annas, G. J., & Grodin, M. A. (1998). Human rights and maternal-fetal HIV transmission prevention trials in Africa. *American Journal of Public Health, 88,* 560–563.

Another round for the homeless. (1982, June 15). *The New York Times,* p. A28.

Anshel, M. H. (2000). A conceptual model and implications for coping with stressful events in police work. *Criminal Justice & Behavior, 27,* 375–400.

Arnold, D. A. Ortiz, C., Curry, J. C., Stowe, R. M., Goldstein, N. E., Fisher, P. H., Zelio, A., & Yershova, K. (1999). Promoting academic success and preventing disruptive behavior disorders through community partnership. *Journal of Community Psychology, 27,* 589–598.

Aronson, E., Blaney, N., Stephan, C., Sikes, J., & Snapp, M. (1978). *The jigsaw classroom.* Beverly Hills: Sage.

Aronson, E., Wilson, T. D., & Akert, R. M. (1999). *Social psychology.* New York: Longman.

Aryee, S., Luk, V., & Stone, R. (1998). Family-responsive variables and retention-relevant outcomes. *Human Relations, 51,* 73–87.

Association for Educational Communications and Technology. (1998, November). *Racial/ethnic enrollments.* www.aect.org/professdevel/racialethnicenrol l8494.html

Atwater, L. E., Waldman, D. A., Carey, J. A., & Cartier, P. (2001). Recipient and observer reactions to discipline: Are managers experiencing wishful thinking? *Journal of Organizational Behavior Special Issue, 22,* 249–270.

Aubrey, T., Tefft, B., & Kingsbury, N. (1990). Behavioral and psychological consequences of unemployment in blue-collar couples. *Journal of Community Psychology, 18,* 99–109.

Auerbach, J. D., Wypijewska, C., & Brodie, H. K. H. (Eds.). (1994). *AIDS and behavior: An integrated approach.* Washington, DC: National Academy Press.

Baba, Y., & Austin, D. M. (1989). Neighborhood environmental satisfaction, victimization, and social participation as determinants of perceived neighborhood safety. *Environment and Behavior, 21,* 763–780.

Bachrach, L. L. (1989). Deinstitutionalization: A semantic analysis. *Journal of Social Issues, 45,* 161–171.

Bagby, W. (1981). *Contemporary American social problems.* Chicago: Nelson-Hall.

Bair, J. P., & Greenspan, B. K. (1986). Teamwork training for interns, residents, and nurses. *Hospital and Community Psychiatry, 37,* 633–635.

Baker, J. (1998a). Are we missing the forest for the trees? Considering the social context of school violence. *Journal of School Psychology, 36,* 29–44.

Baker, J. (1998b). The social context of school satisfaction among urban, low-income, African-American students. *School Psychology Quarterly, 13,* 25–44.

Baker, R. A. (1991). Modeling the school dropout phenomenon: School policies and prevention program strategies. *High School Journal, 74,* 203–210.

Baltes, B. B., Briggs, T. E., Huff, J. W., Wright, J. A., & Neuman. G. A. (1999). Flexible and compressed workweek schedules on work-related criteria. *Journal of Applied Psychology, 84,* 496–513.

Baltes, M. M., & Baltes, P. B. (Eds.). (1986). *The psychology of control and aging.* Hillsdale, NJ: Erlbaum.

Bandura, A. (1977). Self-efficacy: Toward a unifying theory of behavior change. *Psychological Review, 84,* 191–215.

Bandura, A. (1986). *Social foundations of thought and action: A social cognitive theory.* Englewood Cliffs, NJ: Prentice-Hall.

Bandura, A. (1994). Social cognitive theory and exercise of control over HIV infection. In R. J. DiClemente and J. L. Peterson (Eds.), *Preventing AIDS: Theories and methods of behavioral interventions* (pp. 25–29.). New York: Plenum.

Bandura, A. (1997). *Self-efficacy: The exercise of control.* New York: Freeman.

Bank, L., Hicks, R., Marlowe, J., Reid, J. B., Patterson, G. R., & Weinrott, M. R. (1991). A comparative evaluation of parent-training interventions for families of chronic delinquents. *Journal of Abnormal Child Psychology, 19,* 15–33.

Banks, J. K., & Gannon, L. R. (1988). The influence of hardiness on the relationship between stressors and psychosomatic symptomology. *American Journal of Community Psychology, 16,* 25–37.

Banziger, G., & Foos, D. (1983). The relationship of personal financial status to the utilization of community mental health centers in rural Appalachia. *American Journal of Community Psychology, 11,* 543–552.

Barak, G. (1991). *Gimme Shelter: A social history of homelessness in contemporary America.* New York: Praeger.

Barnum, P., Liden, R. C., & Ditomaso, N. (1995). Double jeopardy for women and minorities: Pay differences with age. *Academy of Management Journal, 38,* 363–380.

Baron, R. A., & Byrne, D. (1994). Social psychology: *Understanding human interaction.* (7th ed.). Boston: Allyn and Bacon.

Barrera, M. (1986). Distinctions between social support concepts, measures, and models. *American Journal of Community Psychology, 14,* 413–445.

Barrera, M. (2000). Social support research in community psychology. In J. Rappaport & E. Seidman (Eds.), *Handbook of community psychology.* New York: Plenum.

Barrera, M., Sandler, I. N., & Ramsay, T. B. (1981). Preliminary development of a scale of social support: Studies on college students. *American Journal of Community Psychology, 9,* 435–448.

Barrett, M. E., Wong, F. Y., & McKay, D. R. R. (1993). Self-reported alcohol use among women of childbearing age and their knowledge of alcohol warning labels and signs. *Archives of Family Medicine, 2,* 1260–1264.

Barth, R. P. (1988). Social shell and social support among young mothers. *Journal of Community Psychology, 16,* 132–143.

Barth, R. P., Fetro, J. V., Leland, N., & Volkan, K. (1992). Preventing adolescent pregnancy with social and cognitive skills. *Journal of Adolescent Research, 7,* 208–232.

Bartunek, J. M., & Betters-Reed, B. L. (1987). The stages of organizational creation. Special issue: Organizational perspectives in community psychology. *American Journal of Community Psychology, 15,* 287–303.

Bassuk, E. L., & Rosenberg, L. (1988). Why does family homelessness occur? A case-control study. *American Journal of Public Health, 78,* 783–788.

Baum, A., Singer, J. E., & Baum, C. S. (1981). Stress and the environment. *Journal of Social Issues, 37,* 4–35.

Bauman, Z. (2000). The deficiencies of community. *The Responsive Community, 10,* 74–79.

Baumann, D. J., Schultz, D. F., Brown, C., Paredes, R., & Hepeworth, J. (1987). Citizen participation in police crisis intervention activities. *American Journal of Community Psychology, 15,* 459–472.

Bayer, R. (1998). The debate over maternal-fetal HIV transmission prevention trials in Africa, Asia, and the Caribbean: Racist exploitation or exploitation of racism. *American Journal of Public Health, 88,* 567–570.

Beach, S. R., Greenberg, M. S., & Yee, J. (1992, April). *Predicting the perceived seriousness of property crimes.* Paper presented at the annual meeting of the Eastern Psychological Association, Boston, MA.

Beacon Hill Institute for Public Policy Research. (1997, Winter). What charitable organizations have to say about volunteers. *NewsLink,* 1. Summary found at www.bhi.sclas.suffolk.edu/NewsLink/vln2volun.html

Beardon, L. J., Spencer, W. A., & Morroco, J. C. (1989). A study of high school dropouts. *School Counselor, 37,* 112–120.

Becker, F., & Zarit, S. H. (1978). Training older adults as peer counselors. *Educational Gerontologist, 3,* 241–250.

Becker, M. H. (1974). The health belief model and personal health behavior. *Health Education Monographs, 2,* 220–243.

Becker, M. H., & Maiman, L. A. (1980). Strategies for enhancing patient compliance. *Journal of Community Health, 6,* 113–115.

Beer, M., & Walton, E. (1990). Developing the competitive organization. *American Psychologist, 45,* 154–161.

Belcher, J. R. (1988). Are jails replacing the mental health care system for the homeless mentally ill? *Community Mental Health Journal, 24,* 185–195.

Belle, D. (Ed.). (1982). *Lives in stress: Women and depression.* Beverly Hills: Sage.

Belsher, G., & Costell, C. G. (1988). Relapse after recovery from unipolar depression: A critical review. *Psychological Bulletin, 104,* 84–96.

Bendicsen, H., & Carlton, S. (1990). Clinical team building: A neglected ingredient in the therapeutic milieu. *Residential Treatment for Children and Youth, 8,* 5–21.

Bennett, C. C., Anderson, L. S., Cooper, S., Hassol, L., Klein, D. C., & Rosenblum, G. (Eds.). (1966). *Community psychology: A report of the Boston conference of the education of psychologists for community mental health.* Boston: Boston University Press.

Bennett, J. B., & Lehman, W. E. K. (1997). Employee views of organizational wellness and the EAP: Influence on substance use, drinking climates, and policy attitudes. *Employee Assistance Quarterly, 13,* 55–71.

Bennett, T. (1989). Factors related to participation in neighborhood watch schemes. *British Journal of Criminology, 29,* 207–218.

Bennett, T. (1991). The effectiveness of a police-initiated fear-reducing strategy. *British Journal of Criminology, 31,* 1–14.

Bennis, W. G. (1989). *Why leaders can't lead: The unconscious conspiracy continues.* San Francisco: Jossey-Bass.

Benviente, G. (1989). *Mastering the politics of planning: Crafting credible plans and policies.* San Francisco: Jossey-Bass.

Bernier, D. (1998). A study of coping: Successful recovery from severe burnout and other reactions to severe work-related stress. *Work & Stress, 12,* 50–65.

Berry, D. E., McKinney, M. M., & Marconi, K. M. (1997, Summer). A typological approach to the study of rural HIV service delivery networks. *The Journal of Rural Health,* 216–225.

Berry, T. D., & Geller, E. S. (1991). A single-subject approach to evaluating vehicle safety belt reminders: Back to basics. *Journal of Applied Behavior Analysis, 24,* 13–22.

Biegel, D. (1984). Help seeking and receiving in urban ethnic neighborhoods: Strategies for improvement. In J. Rapport, C. Swift, & R. Hess (Eds.), *Studies in empowerment: Steps toward understanding and action.* New York: Haworth.

Biglan, A., & Taylor, T. K. (2000). Why have we been more successful in reducing tobacco use than violent crime? *American Journal of Community Psychology, 28,* 269–302.

Biglan, A., Ary, D., Koehn, V., Levings, D., Smith, S., Wright, Z., James, L., & Henderson, J. (1996). Mobilizing positive reinforcement in communities to reduce youth access to tobacco. *American Journal of Community Psychology, 24,* 625–638.

Bilchik, S. (1998). *1998 report to Congress: Juvenile mentoring program.* Washington, DC: Office of Juvenile Justice and Delinquency Prevention.

Bilchik, S. (1999a). *OJJDP research: Making a difference for juveniles.* Washington, DC: Office of Juvenile Justice and Delinquency Prevention.

Bilchik, S. (1999b). *Promising strategies to reduce gun violence.* Washington, DC: Office of Juvenile Justice and Delinquency Prevention.

Bingham, J., & Piotrowski, C. (1989). House arrest: A viable alternative for sex offenders. *Psychological Reports, 65,* 559–562.

Bishop, B., & Drew, N. (1998). The community psychologist as subtle change agent in the public policy arena. *The Community Psychologist, 31,* 20–23.

Blakely, C. H., Mayer, J. P., Gottschalk, R. G., Schmidt, N., Davidson, W. S., Roitman, D. B., & Emshoff, J. G. (1987). The fidelity-adaptation debate: Implications of the implementation of public sector social programs. *American Journal of Community Psychology, 15,* 253–268.

Blakemore, J. L., Washington, R. O., & McNeely, R. L. (1995). The demography of aging. In P. K. H. Kim (Ed.), *Services to the aging and aged: Public policies and programs.* New York: Garland.

Blaney, N. T., Stephan, C., Rosenfield, D., Aronson, E., & Sikes, J. (1977). Interdependence in the classroom: A field study. *Journal of Educational Psychology, 69,* 139–146.

Blom, G. E. (1986). A school disaster: Intervention and research aspects. *Journal of the American Academy of Child Psychiatry, 25,* 336–345.

Blonsksy, L. E. (1973). An innovative service for the elderly. *Gerontologist, 13,* 189–196.

Bloom, B. L. (1988). *Health psychology: A psychosocial perspective.* Englewood Cliffs, NJ: Prentice-Hall.

Bloom, B. L., & Hodges, W. F. (1988). The Colorado Separation and Divorce Program: A preventive intervention program for newly separated persons. In R. Price, E. W. Cowen, R. P. Lorion, & J. Ramos-McKay (Eds.), *14 ounces of prevention.* Washington, DC: American Psychological Association.

Bloom, M. (1987). Toward a technology in primary prevention: Educational strategies and tactics. *Journal of Primary Prevention, 8,* 25–48.

Boggiano, A. K., & Katz, P. (1991). Maladaptive patterns in students: The role of teachers' controlling strategies. *Journal of Social Issues, 47,* 35–52.

Bond, G. R., Miller, L. D., & Krumweid, R. D. (1988). Assertive case management in three CMHCs: A controlled study. *Hospital Community Psychiatry, 39,* 411–417.

Bond, G. R., Witheridge, T. F., Dincin, J., & Wasmer, D. (1991). Assertive community treatment: Correcting some misconceptions. *American Journal of Community Psychology, 19,* 41–51.

Bond, G. R., Witheridge, T. F., Dincin, J., Wasmer, D., Webb, J., & DeGraaf-Kaser, R. (1990). Assertive community treatment for frequent users of psychiatric hospitals in a large city: A controlled study. *American Journal of Community Psychology, 18,* 865–91.

Bond, M. A. (1990). Defining the research relationship: Maximizing participation in an unequal world. In P. Jolan, C. Keep, F. Chertok, & L. Jason (Eds.), *Research community psychology: Issues of theory and methods* (pp. 183–184). Washington, DC: American Psychological Association.

Bond, M. A. (1998). Social policy, prevention, and interorganizational linkages. *The Community Psychologist, 31,* 3–6.

Bond, M. A., Hill, J., Mulvey, A., & Terenzio, M. (2000). Weaving feminism and community psychology: An introduction to a special issue. *American Journal of Community Psychology, 28,* 585–597.

Booth, W. (July 22, 1991). Most elderly go gently. *Washington Post,* p. 3.

Bootzin, R. R., Shadish, W. R., & McSweeney, A. J. (1989). Longitudinal outcomes of nursing home care for severely mentally ill patients. *Journal of Social Issues, 45,* 31–48.

Borum, R. (2000). Improving high risk encounters between people with mental illness and the police. *Journal of the American Academy of Psychiatry & Law, 28,* 332–337.

Botvin, G. J., & Wills, T. A. (1985). Personal and social skills training: Cognitive-behavioral approaches to substance abuse prevention. In C. S. Bell & R. Battjes (Eds.), *Prevention research: Deterring drug abuse among children and adolescents.* National Institute on Drug Abuse Research Monograph Number 63. DHHS publication number (ADM) 87–1334. Washington, DC: Superintendent of Documents, U.S. Government Printing Office.

Bouey, P. D., Duran, B., Henrickson, M., Wong, F. Y., Haviland, L., Sember, R. E., & Lo, W. (1997). *A cultural competent model for HIV care: A conceptual framework for the collaborative evaluation of HIV services and care programs.* Unpublished document (originally prepared for Ryan White CARE Act's Special Projects of National Significance, National Multi-Site Evaluation Program).

Bowers, C. A., & Gesten, E. L. (1986). Social support as a buffer of anxiety: An experimental analog. *American Journal of Community Psychology, 14,* 447–451.

Bowers, L. B. (1990). Traumas precipitating female delinquency: Implications for assessment, practice, and policy. *Child and Adolescent Social Work Journal, 7,* 389–402.

Bowman, L. S., Stein, R. E. K., & Ireys, H. T. (1991). Reinventing fidelity: The transfer of social technology among settings. *American Journal of Community Psychology, 19,* 619–639.

Boyd-Zaharias, J. (Summer 1999). Project star. *American Educator,* 30–36.

Braddock, J. H., II. (1985). School desegregation and black assimilation. *Journal of Social Issues, 41,* 9–22.

Bradshaw, T. K. (1999). The community development society. *The Community Psychologist, 32,* 9–10.

Brandt, A. M., & Rozin, P. (Eds.). (1997). *Morality + health.* New York: Routledge.

Branson, R. K. (1998). Teaching centered schooling has reached its upper limit: It doesn't get any better than this. *Current Directions in Psychological Science, 7,* 126–135.

Bravo, M., Rubio-Stipec, M., Canino, G. J., Woodbury, M. A., & Ribera, J. C. (1990). The psychological sequelae of disaster stress prospectively and retrospectively evaluated. *American Journal of Community Psychology, 18,* 661–680.

Breakey, W. R. (Ed.). (1996). *Integrated mental health services: Modern community psychiatry.* New York: Oxford University Press.

Brenner, G. F., Norvell, N. K., & Limacher, M. (1989). Supportive and problematic social interactions: A social network analysis. *American Journal of Community Psychology, 17,* 831–836.

Brewer, M. B. (1999). The psychology of prejudice: Ingroup love or outgroup hate? *Journal of Social Issues Special Issue: Prejudice and Intergroup Relations, 55,* 429–444.

Britt, C. L. (2000). Health consequences of criminal victimization. *International Review of Victimology, 8,* 63–73.

Broman, C. L., Hamilton, V. L., & Hoffman, W. S. (1990). Unemployment and its effects on families: Evidence from a plant closing study. *American Journal of Community Psychology, 18,* 643–659.

Bronfenbrenner, U. (1979). *The ecology of human development: Experiments by nature and design.* Cambridge, MA: Harvard University Press.

Bronfenbrenner, U. (1986, February). Alienation and the four worlds of childhood. *Phi Delta Kappan,* 430–436.

Bronfenbrenner, W. (1999). Environments in developmental perspective: Theoretical and operational models. In S. L. Friedman & T. D. Wachs (Eds.), *Measuring environment across the life span: Emerging methods and concepts.* Washington, DC: American Psychological Association.

Bronzaft, A. L. (1981). The effect of a noise abatement program on reading ability. *Journal of Environmental Psychology, 1,* 215–222.

Brooks, E. R., Zuniga, M., & Penn, N. E. (1995) The decline of public mental health in the United States. In C. V. Willie, P. P. Rieker, B. M., Kramer, & B. S. Brown (Eds.), *Mental health, racism, and sexism* (pp.

51–117). Pittsburgh, PA: University of Pittsburgh Press.

Brown, J. D. (1991). Staying fit and staying well: Physical fitness as a moderator of life stress. *Journal of Personality and Social Psychology, 60,* 555–561.

Brownell, A., & Shumaker, S. A. (1984). Social support: An introduction to a complex phenomenon. *Journal of Social Issues, 40,* 1–9.

Browning, K., & Huizinga, D. (April 1999). Highlights of findings from the Denver youth survey. *OJJDP Fact Sheet,* 1–2.

Bruce, M. L., Takeuchi, D. T., & Leaf, P. J. (1991). Poverty and psychiatric status: Longitudinal evidence from the New Haven Epidemiologic Catchment Area Study. *Archives of General Psychiatry, 48,* 470–474.

Buchanon, D. R., & Chasnoff, P. (1986). Family crisis intervention programs: What works and what doesn't. *Journal of Police Science and Administration, 14,* 161–168.

Buckner, J. C. (1988). The development of an instrument to measure neighborhood cohesion. *American Journal of Community Psychology, 16,* 771–791.

Bui, K., & Takeuchi, D. T. (1992). Ethnic minority adolescents and the use of community mental health care services. *American Journal of Community Psychology, 20,* 403–417.

Burden, D. S., & Klerman, L. V. (1984). Teenage parenthood: Factors that lessen economic dependence. *Social Work, 29,* 11–16.

Bureau of Justice Statistics (2001). *Corrections statistics,* www.ojp.usdoj.gov/bjs/correct.htm

Bureau of Justice Statistics. (1993). *Highlights from 20 years of surveying crime victims.* Washington, DC: U.S. Department of Justice.

Bureau of Justice Statistics. (1998, November). *Criminal victimization, general.* www//ojp.usdoj.gov.bjs/cvictgen.htm

Bureau of National Affairs. (1981). Job absence and turnover control. *Personnel Forum Survey Number 132.* Washington, DC: Author.

Bureau of National Affairs. (1986). *Work and family: A changing dynamic.* Washington, DC: Author.

Burke, M. J., & Hayes, R. L. (1986). Peer counseling for elderly victims of crime and violence. Special issue: Support groups. *Journal for Specialists in Group Work, 11,* 107–113.

Burroughs, S. M., & Eby, L. T. (1998). Psychological sense of community at work: A measurement system and exploratory framework. *Journal of Community Psychology, 26,* 509–532.

Burtless, G. (1998). Can the labor market absorb three million welfare recipients? *Focus, 10,* 1–6.

Buscemi, L., Bennett, T., Thomas, D., & DeLuca, D. A. (1996). Head Start: Challenges and training needs. *Journal of Early Intervention, 20,* 1–13.

Campaign for Our Children. (2001). *About Campaign for Our Children.* www.cfoc.org

Campbell, R., Baker, C. K., & Mazurek, T. L. (1998). Remaining radical? Organizational predictors of rape crisis centers' social change initiatives. *American Journal of Community Psychology, 26,* 457–483.

Campfield, K. M., & Hills, A. M. (2001). Effect of timing of critical incident stress debriefing on posttraumatic symptoms. *Journal of Posttraumatic Stress Special Issue, 14,* 327–340.

Cantelon, S., & LeBoeuf, D. (1997, June). Keeping young people in school. Community programs that work. *Juvenile Justice Bulletin,* 1–9.

Caplan, G. (1964). *Principles of preventive psychiatry.* New York: Basic Books.

Caplan, G. (1974). *Support systems and community mental health.* New York: Behavioral Publications.

Caplan, G. (1989). Recent developments in crisis intervention and the promotion of support service. *Journal of Primary Prevention, 10,* 3–25.

Caplan, N., Morrison, A., & Stambaugh, R. J. (1975). *The use of social science knowledge in policy decisions at the national level: A report to respondents.* Ann Arbor: Institute for Social Research, University of Michigan.

Caplan, R. D., Vinokur, A. D., Price, R. H., & van Ryn, M. (1989). Job seeking, reemployment, and mental health. *Journal of Applied Psychology, 74,* 759–769.

Carnevale, P. J., & Pruitt, D. G. (1992). Negotiation and mediation. *Annual Review of Psychology, 43,* 531–582.

Caspi, A., Taylor, A., Moffitt, T. E., & Plomin, R. (2000). Neighborhood deprivation affects children's mental health: Environmental risks identified in a genetic design. *Psychological Science, 11,* 338–342.

Cassel, J. (1974). Psychosocial processes and "stress": Theoretical formulations. *International Journal of Health Services, 4,* 471–482.

Casswell, S. (2000). A decade of community action research. *Substance Use & Misuse Special Issue: Community Action and the Prevention of Alcohol-related Problems at the Local Level, 35,* 55–74.

Catterall, J. S., & Stern, D. (1986). The effects of alternative school programs on high school completions and labor market outcomes. *Educational Evaluation and Policy Analysis, 8,* 77–86.

Cauce, A. M. (1986). Social networks and social competence: Exploring the effects on early adolescent friendships. *American Journal of Community Psychology, 14,* 607–628.

CDC/IHS National Epidemiology Program. (2001). Centers for Disease Control and Prevention. Atlanta, GA: Author.

Cecchetti, D., & Lynch, M. (1993). Toward an ecological/transactional model of community violence and child maltreatment: Consequences for children's development. *Psychiatry, 56,* 96–118.

Centers for Disease Control and Prevention. (1996). *State behavioral risk factor surveillance system, 1993* [data tape]. Atlanta, GA: Author.

Centers for Disease Control and Prevention. (1998). *HIV surveillance report: U.S. HIV and AIDS cases reported through December 1997.* Year-end edition, Vol. 9, No. 2. Atlanta, GA: Author.

Centers for Disease Control and Prevention. (2000). *CDC fact book 2000/2001.* Atlanta, GA: Author.

Centers for Disease Control and Prevention. (2001). *HIV prevention strategic plan through 2005.* Atlanta, GA: Author.

Centers for Disease Control. (1990). Cigarette advertising—United States, 1988. *Morbidity and Mortality Weekly Report, 39,* 261–265.

Centers for Disease Control. (1997, September 19). AIDS deaths by year. *Morbidity and Mortality Weekly, 46,* 2.

Centers for Disease Control. (1999). *Teen pregnancy.* www.cdc.gov/nccdphp/teen.htm

Chamberlain, P. (1990). Comparative evaluation of specialized foster care for seriously delinquent youths: A first step. *Community Alternatives International Journal of Family Care, 2,* 21–36.

Chan, K. B. (1977). Individual differences in reactions to stress and their personality and situational determinants: Some implications for community mental health. *Social Science and Medicine, 11,* 89–103.

Chanley, V. A., Rudolph, T. J., & Rahn, W. M. (2000). The origins and consequences of public trust in government. *Public Opinion Quarterly, 54,* 239–256.

Chapman, N. J., & Pancoast, D. L. (1985). Working with the informal helping networks of the elderly: The experiences of three programs. *American Journal of Community Psychology, 41,* 47–63.

Chavis, D. M. (1993). A future for community psychology practice. *American Journal of Community Psychology, 21,* 171–183.

Chavis, D. M., & Wandersman, A. W. (1990). Sense of community in the urban environment: A catalyst for participation and community development. *American Journal of Community Psychology, 18,* 55–82.

Chavis, D. M., Florin, P., & Felix, M. R. J. (1992). Nurturing grass roots initiatives for community development: The role of enabling systems. In T. Mizrahi & J. Morrison (Eds.), *Community organization and social administration: Advances, trends, and emerging principles.* Binghamton, NY: Haworth.

Chavis, D. M., Stucky, P. E., & Wandersman, A. (1983). Returning research to the community: A relationship between scientist and citizen. *American Psychologist, 38,* 424–434.

Chemers, M. M., Hays, R. B., Rhodewalt, F., & Wysocki, J. (1985). A person-environment analysis of job stress: A contingency model explanation. *Journal of Personality and Social Psychology, 49,* 628–635.

Cheng, S. (1990). Change processes in the professional bureaucracy. *Journal of Community Psychology, 18,* 183–193.

Cherniss, C. (1999). Training in cultural competence: A survey of graduate programs in community research and action. *The Community Psychologist, 32,* 22–23.

Cherniss, C. (2000). President's column. *The Community Psychologist, 33,* 3–6.

Chesler, M. A., & Barbarin, O. A. (1984). Difficulties of providing help in a crisis: Relationships between parents of children with cancer and their friends. *American Journal of Community Psychology, 40,* 113–134.

Cheung, F. M. (1988). Surveys of community attitudes toward mental health facilities: Reflections or provocations? *American Journal of Community Psychology, 16,* 877–882.

Cheung, F. M. C. (1986). Psychopathology among Chinese people. In M. H. Bond (Ed.), *The psychology of the Chinese people.* New York: Oxford University Press.

Children's Bureau. (2001). *The scope and problem of child maltreatment.* www.acf.dhhs.gov/programs/publications/cb/ ncanprob.htm

Children's Defense Fund. (1991). *The state of American children.* Washington, DC: Author.

Chin, J. J., & Wong, F. Y. (in press). Bilingual Peer Advocates. In B. Peters, J. Erwin, D. Smith, & H. Myers (Eds.), *Ethnicity and HIV.* International Medical Press, in press.

Chin, J. J., Wong, F. Y., Bordador, N. E., & Rodgriguez, T. R. (1998, July). *Improving access to care for language/cultural/ racial minorities: The Bilingual Peer Advocate Program of the Asian & Pacific Islander Coalition on HIV/AIDS.* Poster presented at the 12th World AIDS Conference, Geneva, Switzerland.

Chipperfield, J. (1993). Perceived barriers in coping with health problems: A twelve-year longitudinal study of survival among elderly individuals. *Journal of Aging and Health, 5,* 123–139.

Choi, K-H., & Coates, T. J. (1994). Prevention of HIV infection. *AIDS, 8,* 1371–1389.

Choi, N. G., & Wodarski, J. S. (1996). The relationship between social support and health status of elderly people: Does social support slow down physical and functional deterioration? *Social Work Research, 20,* 52–63.

Christensen, J. A., & Robinson, J. W. (1989). *Community development in perspective.* Ames: Iowa State University Press.

Christensen, L. (1988). Deception in psychological research. *Personality and Social Psychology Bulletin, 14,* 664–675.

Christian, T. F. (1986). A resource for all seasons: A statewide network of community dispute resolution centers. In J. Palenski & H. Launer (Eds.), *Mediation: Contexts and challenges.* Springfield, IL: Thomas.

Cicchetti, D., Toth, S. C., & Rogosch, F. A. (2000). The development of psychological wellness in maltreated children. In D. Cicchetti & J. Rappaport (Eds.), *The promotion of wellness in maltreated children and adolescents.* Washington, DC: Child Welfare League of America.

Clark, K. B., & Clark, M. P. (1947). Racial identification and preference in Negro children. In T. M. Newcomb & E. L. Hartley (Eds.), *Readings in social psychology.* New York: Holt.

Clary, E. G., & Snyder, M. (1999). The motivations to volunteer: Theoretical and practical considerations. *Current Directions in Psychological Science, 8,* 156–160.

Clinton, W. (August 8, 2000). *Statement by the president press release.* www.hhs.gov/news/press/2000pres/20000808a.htm

Coates, T. J. (1990). Strategies for modifying sexual behavior for primary and secondary prevention of HIV disease. *Journal of Consulting and Clinical Psychology, 58,* 57–69.

Cocozza, J. J., & Skowya, K. R. (2000). Youth with mental health disorders: Issues and emerging responses. *Juvenile Justice, 7,* 3–13.

Coffee, J. N., & Pestridge, S. (May 2001). The career academy concept. *OJDP Fact Sheet,* 1–2.

Cohen, C. I., Teresi, J., & Holmes, D. (1986). Assessment of stress-buffering effects of social networks on psychological symptoms in an inner-city elderly population. *American Journal of Community Psychology, 14,* 75–91.

Cohen, M. D., Shore, M. F., & Mazda, N. A. (1991). Development of a management training program for state mental health program directors. Special issue: Education in mental health administration. *Administration and Policy in Mental Health, 18,* 247–256.

Cohen, S. A., Evans, G. W., Stokols, D., & Krantz, D. (1986). *Behavior, health, and environmental stress.* New York: Plenum.

Coley, R. L., & Chase-Lansdale, P. L. (1998). Adolescent pregnancy and parenthood. *American Psychologist, 53,* 152–166.

Coley, R. L., Kuta, A., & Chase-Lansdale, P. L. (2000). An insider view: Knowledge and opinions of welfare from African American girls in poverty. *Journal of Social Issues Special Issue: The Impact of Welfare Reform, 56,* 707–726.

Collins, C., & Coates, T. J. (2000). Science and health policy: Can they cohabit or should they divorce? *American Journal of Public Health, 90,* 1389–1390.

Comer, J. P., & Woodruff, D. W. (1998). Mental health in schools. *Child and Adolescent Psychiatric Clinics of North America, 7,* 499–513.

Community Policing Consortium. (1999a). Applying restorative principles for better communities. *Community Policing Exchange, VI,* 3.

Community Policing Consortium. (1999b). HIV and corrections professionals. *Community Policing Exchange, VI,* 3.

Compas, B. E., Wagner, B. M., Slavin, L. A., & Vannatta, K. (1986). A prospective study of life events, social support, and psychological symptomatology during the transition from high school to college. *American Journal of Community Psychology, 14,* 241–257.

Conger, R. D., Conger, K. J., Matthews, L. S., & Elder. (1999). Pathways of economic influence on adolescent adjustment. *American Journal of Community Psychology, 27,* 519–541.

Connors, M. M., & McGrath, J. W. (1997). The known, unknown, and unknowable in AIDS research in anthropology. *Anthropology Newsletter, 38,* 1–5.

Constantine, L. L. (1991). Fitting intervention to organizational paradigm. *Organization Development Journal, 9,* 41–50.

Conte, J. M., Landy, F. J., & Mathieu, J. E. (1995). Time urgency: Conceptual and construct development. *Journal of Applied Psychology, 80,* 178–185.

Cook, P. J., & Ludwig, J. (1997). *Guns in America: National survey on private ownership and use of firearms.* Washington, DC: U.S. Department of Justice.

Cook, S. W. (1984). The 1954 social science statement and school desegregation: A reply to Gerard. *American Psychologist, 39,* 819–832.

Cook, S. W. (1985). Experimenting on social issues: The case of school desegregation. *American Psychologist, 47,* 452–460.

Cook, T. D., & Shadish, W. R. (1994). Social experiments: Some developments over the past fifteen years. In L. W. Porter & M. R. Rosenzweig (Eds.), *Annual review of psychology.* Palo Alto, CA: Annual Reviews.

Cordner, G. W. (2000). A community policing approach to persons with mental illness. *Journal of the American Academy of Psychiatry & the Law, 28,* 326–331.

Coulton, C. J., Korbin, J. E., & Su, M. (1996). Measuring neighborhood context for young children in an urban area. *American Journal of Community Psychology, 24,* 5–32.

Coulton, C. J., Korbin, J., & Su, M. (1999). Neighborhoods and child maltreatment: A multi-level study. *Child Abuse & Neglect, 23,* 1019–1040.

Cowen, E. L. (1980). The wooing of primary prevention. *American Journal of Community Psychology, 8,* 258–284.

Cowen, E. L. (1996). The ontogenesis of primary prevention: Lengthy strides and stubbed toes. *American Journal of Community Psychology, 24,* 235–249.

Cowen, E. L. (1997a). The coming of age of primary prevention research: Comments on Durlak and Wells's meta-analysis. *American Journal of Community Psychology, 25,* 153–167.

Cowen, E. L. (1997b). On the semantics and operations of primary prevention and wellness enhancement (or will the real primary prevention please stand up?). *American Journal of Community Psychology, 25,* 245–255.

Cowen, E. L., Hightower, A. D., Pedro-Carroll, J. L., Work, W. C., Wyman, P. A., & Haffey, W. G. (1996). *School-based prevention for children at risk.* Washington, DC: American Psychological Association.

Crawford, I., & Jason, L. A. (1990). Strategies for implementing a media-based AIDS prevention program. *Professional Psychology Research and Practice, 21,* 219–221.

Crawford, I., Jason, L. A., Riordan, N., & Kaufman, J. (1990). A multimedia-based approach to increasing communication and the level of knowledge within families. Special issue: AIDS and the community. *Journal of Community Psychology, 18,* 361–373.

Crittenden, P. M., & Snell, M. E. (1983). Intervention to improve mother-infant interaction and infant development. *Infant Mental Health Journal, 4,* 23–31.

Cronkite, R. C., Moos, R. H., Twohey J., Cohen, C., & Swindle, Jr., R. (1998). Life circumstances and personal resources as predictors of the ten-year course of depression. *American Journal of Community Psychology, 26,* 255–280.

Crosson, M. T., & Christian, T. F. (1990). *The Community Dispute Resolution Centers Program annual report.* Albany, New York: Office of Court Administration.

Cummins, R. C. (1988). Perceptions of social support, receipt of supportive behaviors, and locus of control as moderators of the effects of chronic stress. *American Journal of Community Psychology, 16,* 685–700.

Cutrona, C. E., Russell, D. W., Hessling, R. M., Brown, P. A., & Murry, V. (2000). Direct and moderating effects of community context on the psychological well-being of African American women. *Journal of Personality & Social Psychology, 79,* 1088–1101.

D'Alessio, S., & Stolzenberg, L. (1990). A crime of convenience: The environment and convenience store robbery. *Environment and Behavior, 22,* 255–271.

D'Ercole, A., Skodol, A. E., Struening, E., Curtis, J., & Millman, J. (1991). Diagnosis of physical illness in psychiatric patients using Axis III and a standardized medical history. *Hospital and Community Psychiatry, 42,* 395–400.

Danish, S. J. (1983). Musings about personal competence: The contributions of sport, health, and fitness. *American Journal of Community Psychology, 11,* 221–240.

Danish, S. J., & Gullotta, T. P. (2000). *Developing competent youth and strong communities through after-school programming.* Washington, DC: Child Welfare League of America.

Darity, W., Jr., & Myers, S., Jr. (1987). *Transfer programs and the economic well-beings of minorities.* Mimeo.

Darity, W., Jr., & Myers, S., Jr. (1988). Distress versus dependency: Changing income support programs. In M. K. Brown (Ed.), *Remaking the welfare state: Retrenchment and social policy in America and Europe.* Philadelphia: Temple University Press.

Davidson, W. B., & Cotter, P. R. (1991). The relationship between sense of community and subjective well-being: A first look. *Journal of Community Psychology, 19,* 246–253.

Davidson, W. S., & Redner, R. (1988). The prevention of juvenile delinquency: Diversion from the juvenile justice system. In R. Price, E. L. Cowen, R. P. Lorion, & J. Ramos-McKay (Eds.), *14 ounces of prevention.* Washington, DC: American Psychological Association.

Davis, M. K., & Gidycz, C. A. (2000). Child sexual abuse prevention programs: A meta-analysis. *Journal of Clinical Child Psychology, 29,* 257–265.

Davis, T. R., & Luthans, F. (1988). Service OD: Techniques for improving the delivery of quality service. *Organization Development Journal, 6,* 76–80.

DeFrances, C. J., & Smith, S. K. (1998). *Special report: Perceptions of neighborhood crime, 1995.* Washington, DC: Bureau of Justice Statistics.

Delgado, G. (1986). *Organizing the movement: The roots and growth of ACORN.* Philadelphia: Temple University Press.

Denham, S. A., & Almeida, M. C. (1987). Children's social problem-solving skills, behavioral adjustment, and interventions: A meta-analysis evaluating theory and practice. *Journal of Applied Developmental Psychology, 8,* 391–409.

Department of Health and Human Services. (1998). *Profile of homelessness.* www/aspe.os.dhhs.gov/prog-sys/homeless/ profile.htm

Department of Health and Human Services. (2001). *Head Start factsheet 2001.* www2.acf.dhhs.gov/programs/hsb/about/ fact2001.htm

Depner, C., Wethington, E., & Ingersoll-Dayton, B. (1984). Social support: Methodological issues in design and measurement. *Journal of Social Issues, 40,* 37–54.

Des Jarles, C. D., Wish, F., Friedman, S. R., Stone-burner, R., Wildvan, D. E., El Sadr, W., Brady, E., & Cuadrado, M. (1987). Intravenous drug use and the heterosexual transmission of the human immunodeficiency virus: Current trends in New York City. *New York State Journal of Medicine, 20,* 283–296.

Deutsch, M., & Hornstein, H. A. (Eds.). (1975). *Applying social psychology: Implications for research, practice, and training.* Hillsdale, NJ: Erlbaum.

DeVita, C. J. (1997). *Viewing nonprofits across the states: Changing civil society.* www.urban.org/periodcl/cnp/ cnp_1.htm

Diamond, P. M., & Schnee, S. B. (1990, August). *Tracking the costs of chronicity: Towards a redirection of resources.* Presented to the Annual Meeting of the American Psychological Association, Boston, MA.

DiClemente, R., J., & Peterson, J. L. (Eds.). (1994). *Preventing AIDS: Theories and methods of behavioral interventions.* New York: Plenum.

DiClemente, R., Zorn, J., & Temoshok, L. (1987). The association of gender, ethnicity, and length of residence in the bay area to adolescents' knowledge and attitudes about acquired immunodeficiency syndrome. *Journal of Applied Social Psychology, 17,* 216–230.

DiFranza, J. R., et al. (1991). RJR Nabisco's cartoon camel promotes Camel cigarettes to children. *Journal of the American Medical Association, 266,* 3149–3154.

Directive 15. http://whitehouse.gov/omb/fedreg/ombdir15/html

Ditton, P. M. (July, 1999). Mental health and treatment of inmates and probationers. *Bureau of Justice Special Report.* Washington, DC: Office of Justice Program, U. S. Department of Justice.

Dixon, L. B., & DeVeau, J. M. (1999). Dual diagnosis: The double challenge. *NAMI: Advocate, 20,* 16–17.

Dobmeyer, T. W., McKee, P. A., Miller, R. D., & Wescott, J. S. (1990). The effect of enrollment in a prepaid health plan on utilization of a community crisis intervention center by chronically mentally ill individuals. *Community Mental Health Journal, 26,* 129–137.

Dohrenwend, B. S. (1978). Social stress and community

psychology. *American Journal of Community Psychology, 6,* 1– 14.

Dooley, D., Catalano, R., & Wilson, G. (1994). Depression and unemployment: Panel findings from epidemiologic catchment area study. *American Journal of Community Psychology, 22,* 745–765.

Dorian, B. J., Keystone, E., Garfinkel, P. E., & Brown, J. M. (1982). Aberrations in lymphocyte subpopulations and function during psychological stress. *Clinical and Experimental Immunology, 50,* 132–138.

Dovidio, J. F. (1984). Helping behavior and altruism: An empirical and conceptual overview. In L. Berkowitz (Ed.), *Advances in experimental social psychology* (Vol. 17). New York: Academic Press.

Dovidio, J. F., & Gaertner, S. L. (1998). On the nature of contemporary prejudice: The causes, consequences, and challenges of divisive racism. In J. L. Eberhardt & S. T. Fiske (Eds.), *Confronting racism: The problem and the response.* Thousand Oaks, CA: Sage.

Dowell, D. A., & Farmer, G. (1992). Community response to homelessness: Social change and constraint in local intervention. *Journal of Community Psychology, 20,* 72–83.

Downing, J., & Harrison, T. C. (1990). Dropout prevention: A practical approach. *School Counselor, 38,* 67–74.

Duffy, K. G. (1991). Introduction to community mediation programs: Past, present and future. In K. G. Duffy, J. W. Grosch, & P. V. Olczak (Eds.), *Community mediation: A handbook for practitioners and researchers.* New York: Guilford.

Duffy, K. G., & Atwater, E. (2001). *Psychology for living.* Upper Saddle River, NJ: Prentice-Hall.

Duffy, K. G., & Olczak, P. V. (1989). Perceptions of mediated disputes: Some characteristics affecting use. *Journal of Social Behavior and Personality, 4,* 541–554.

Duffy, K. G., & Thompson, J. (1992). Community mediation centers: Humanistic alternatives to the court system, a pilot study. *Journal of Humanistic Psychology, 32,* 101–114.

Duffy, K. G., Grosch, J. W., & Olczak, P. V. (1991). *Community mediation: A handbook for practitioners and researchers.* New York: Guilford.

Duffy, K. G., Olczak, P. V., & Grosch, J. W. (1993). *The influence of minority status on mediation outcome.* Paper presented to the International Association for Conflict Management, Henglehoef, Belgium.

Dumas, J. E., Rollock, D., Prinz, R. J., Hops, H., & Blechman, E. A. (1999). Cultural sensitivity: Problems and solutions in applied and preventive intervention. *Applied & Preventive Psychology, 8,* 175–196.

Dumont, M. P. (1982). Review of private lives/public spaces, by E. Baxter & K. Hopper, and shopping bag ladies, by A. M. Rousseau. *American Journal of Orthopsychiatry, 52,* 367–369.

Dunkel-Schetter, C. (1984). Social support and cancer: Findings based on patient interviews and their implications. *American Journal of Community Psychology, 40,* 77–98.

Durlak, J. A. (1983). Social problem-solving as a primary prevention strategy. In R. D. Felner, L. A. Jason, J. N. Moritsugu, & S. S. Farber (Eds.), *Prevention psychology: Theory, research, and practice.* New York: Pergamon.

Durlak, J. A. (1995). *School-based prevention programs for children and adolescents.* Thousand Oaks, CA: Sage.

Durlak, J. A., & Lipsey, M. W. (1991). A practitioner's guide to meta-analysis. *American Journal of Community Psychology, 19,* 291–332.

Durlak, J. A., & Wells, A. M. (1997). Primary prevention mental health programs for children and adolescents: A meta-analytic review. *American Journal of Community Psychology, 25,* 115–152.

Earls, M., & Nelson, G. (1988). The relationship between long-term psychiatric clients' psychological well-being and their perceptions of housing and social support. *American Journal of Community Psychology, 16,* 279–293.

Eaves, C. (2001). The development and implementation of a crisis response team in a school setting. *International Journal of Emergency Mental Health Special Issue, 3,* 35–46.

Eberhardt & S. T. Fiske (Eds.). *Confronting racism: The problem and the response.* Thousand Oaks, CA: Sage.

Ebert-Flattau, P. (1980). *A legislative guide.* Washington, DC: Association for the Advancement of Psychology.

Echterling, L. G., & Hartsough, D. M. (1989). Phases of helping in successful crisis telephone calls. *Journal of Community Psychology, 17,* 249–257.

Eckenrode, J., Ganzel, B., Henderson, C. R., Smith, E., Olds, D. L., Powers, J., Cole, R., Kitzman, H., & Sidora, K. (2000). Preventing child abuse and neglect with a program of nurse home visitation: The limiting effects of domestic violence. *Journal of the American Medical Association, 284,* 1385–1391.

Eckholdt, H., & Chin, J. (1997). Pneumocystis carinii pneumonia in Asians and Pacific Islanders. *Clinical Infectious Diseases, 24,* 1265–1267

Eckholdt, H., Chin, J., Harris, C., & Kim, D. (1998, June). *Opportunistic infections in the United States: Focus-*

ing health care and needs for people with AIDS. Poster presented at the 12th World AIDS Conference, Geneva, Switzerland.

Educational Conference on Psychiatry, Psychology and the Law. (1990). Dangerousness and discharge. *American Journal of Forensic Psychology, 8,* 19–58.

Edwards, R. W., Jumper-Thurman, P., Plested, B. A., Oetting, E. R., & Swanson, L. (2001). Community readiness. Research to practice. *Journal of Community Psychology, 28,* 291–307.

Egeland, B., Breitenbucher, M., & Rosenberg, D. (1980). Prospective study of the significance of life stress in the etiology of child abuse. *Journal of Consulting and Clinical Psychology, 48,* 195–205.

Eigen, M. (1993). Viral quasispecies. *Scientific American, 269,* 42–49.

Eisdorfer, C. (1983). Conceptual models of aging. *American Psychologist, 2,* 197–202.

Elias, M. J. (1987). Improving the continuity between undergraduate psychology and graduate community psychology: Analysis and case study. *Journal of Community Psychology, 15,* 376–386.

Elias, M. J., Gara, M., Ubriaco, M., Rothbaum, P. A., Clabby, J. F., & Schuyler, T. (1986). Impact of a preventative social problem solving intervention on children's coping with middle-school stressors. *American Journal of Community Psychology, 14,* 259–275.

Ellis, R. T. (1991). Perceptions, attitudes and beliefs of police recruits. *Canadian Police College Journal, 15,* 95–117.

Ellison, K. (1985). Community involvement in police selection. *Social Action and the Law, 11,* 77–78.

Ellwein, M. C., Walsh, D. J., Eades, G. M., & Miller, A. (1991). Using readiness tests to route kindergarten students: The snarled intersection of psychometrics, policy, and practice. *Educational Evaluation and Policy Analysis, 13,* 159–175.

Elvin, J. (July 21, 2000). Is mental illness all in your head? *Insight on the News, 16,* 35.

Embree, M. G., Avery, E., Dabrowski, J., Carpenter, S., Fryxell, D. R., Julian-Daws, P., Macken, J., & Valery, J. (1992). The practicum experience: Defining community psychology education. *The Community Psychologist, 26,* 11–13.

Embry, D. D., Flannery, D. J., Vazsonyi, A. T., Powell, K. E., & Atha, J. (1996). PeaceBuilders: A theoretically driven school based model for early violence prevention. *American Journal of Preventive Medicine, 12,* 91–100.

Emery, R. E., & Wyer, M. M. (1987). Divorce mediation. *American Psychologist, 42,* 472–480.

Evans, I. M., & DiBenedetto, A. (1990). Pathways to school dropout: A conceptual model for early prevention. *Special Services in the School, 6,* 63–80.

Eysenck, H. J. (1952). The effects of psychotherapy: An evaluation. *Journal of Consulting Psychology, 16,* 319–324.

Eysenck, H. J. (1961). The effects of psychotherapy. In H. J. Eysenck (Ed.), *Handbook of abnormal psychology.* New York: Basic Books.

Fairweather, G. W. (1986). The need for uniqueness. *American Journal of Community Psychology, 14,* 128–137.

Fairweather, G. W., & Davidson, W. S. (1986). *An introduction to community experimentation.* New York: McGraw-Hill.

Fairweather, G. W., Sanders, D. H., Maynard, H., & Cressler, D. L. (1969). *Community life for the mentally ill.* Chicago: Aldine.

Fairweather, G. W., & Tornatzky, L. G. (1977). *Experimental methods for social policy research.* New York: Pergamon.

Faith, M. S., Wong, F. Y., & Carpenter, K. M. (1995). Group sensitivity training: Update, meta-analysis, and recommendations. *Journal of Counseling Psychology, 42,* 390–399.

Falkenberg, I. E. (1987). Employee fitness programs: Their impact on the employee and the organization. *Academy of Management Review, 12,* 511–522.

Farber, S. S., Felner, R. D., & Primavera, J. (1985). Parental separation/divorce and adolescents: An examination of factors mediating adaptation. *American Journal of Community Psychology, 13,* 171–186.

Farrell, A. D., & Meyer, A. L. (1997). The effectiveness for a school-based curriculum for reducing violence among urban sixth-grade students. *American Journal of Public Health, 87,* 979–984.

Faulkner, A. H., & Cranston, K. (1998). Correlates of same-sex sexual behavior in a sample of Massachusetts high school students. *American Journal of Public Health, 88,* 262–266.

Fawcett, S. B. (1990). Some emerging standards for community research and action: Aid from a behavioral perspective. In P. Tolan, C. Kelp, F. Chertak, & L. Jason (Eds.), *Researching community psychology: Issues of theory and methods.* Washington, DC: American Psychology Association.

Federal Interagency Forum on Aging-Related Statistics. (2001). *Older Americans 2000: Key indicators of well-being.* www.agingstats.gov

Federal Mediation and Conciliation Service. (1984). *Thirty-sixth annual report, fiscal year 1983.* Washington, DC: U.S. Government Printing Office.

Feldheusen, J. F. (1989, March). Synthesis of research on gifted youth. *Educational Leadership,* 6–11.

Felner, R. D. (2000). Educational reform as ecologically-based prevention and promotion. The project on high performance learning communities. In D. Cicchetti & J. Rappaport (Eds.). *The promotion of wellness in children and adolescents.* Washington, DC: Child Welfare League of America.

Felner, R. D., Ginter, M., & Primavera, J. (1982). Primary prevention during school transitions: Social support and environmental structure. *American Journal of Community Psychology, 10,* 277–290.

Felton, B. J., & Shinn, M. (1992). Social integration and social support. Moving "social support" beyond the individual level. *Journal of Community Psychology, 20,* 103–115.

Fendrich, M. (1991). Institutionalization and parole behavior: Assessing the influence of individual and family characteristics. *Journal of Community Psychology, 19,* 109–122.

Ferrari, J. R., & Jason, L. A. (1996). Integrating research and community service: Incorporating research skills into service learning experiences. *College Student Journal, 30,* 444–451.

Ferrari, J. R., Billows, W., Jason, L. A., & Grill, G. J. (1997). Matching the needs of the homeless with those of the disabled: Empowerment through caregiving. *Journal of Prevention & Intervention in the Community, 15,* 83–92.

Fielding, J. C., & Williams, C. A. (1991). Adolescent pregnancy in the United States: A review and recommendations for clinicians and research needs. *American Journal of Preventative Medicine, 7,* 47–52.

Fiene, R., Lutcovich, J., Johnson, J., & Koppel, R. (1998). Child day care quality linked to opportunities for professional development: An applied community psychology example. *The Community Psychologist, 31,* 10–11.

Finch, J. F., Okun, M. A., Barrera, M., Zautra, A. J., & Reich, J. W. (1989). Positive and negative ties among older adults: Measurement modes and the prediction of psychological distress and well-being. *American Journal of Community Psychology, 17,* 585–605.

Fiore, J., Coppel, D. B., Becker, J., & Cox, G. B. (1986). Social support as a multifaceted concept: Examination of important dimensions for adjustment. *American Journal of Community Psychology, 14,* 93–111.

Fischer, C. S., Jackson, R. M., Stueve, C. A., Gerson, G., & McAllister-Jones, L. (1977). *Networks and places.* New York: Free Press.

Fisher, J. D., & Fisher, W. A. (1992). Changing AIDS-risk behavior. *Psychological Bulletin, 111,* 455–474.

Fiske, S. T., Bersoff, D. N., Borgida, E., Deaux, K., & Heilman, M. E. (1991). Social science research on trial: Use of sex stereotyping research in *Price Waterhouse v. Hopkins. American Psychologist, 46,* 1049–1060.

Flay, B. R., & Petraitis, J. (1991). Methodological issues in drug use prevention research: Theoretical foundation. In C. G. Leukefeld & W. J. Buoski (Eds.), *Drug abuse prevention intervention research methodology.* National Institute on Drug Abuse Research Monograph 107. DHHS publication number (ADM) 91–1761. Washington, DC: Superintendent of Documents, U.S. Government Printing Office.

Flick, L. H. (1986). Paths to adolescent parenthood: Implications for prevention. *Public Health Reports, 101,* 132–147.

Florin, P. (1989). *Nurturing the grassroots: Neighborhood volunteer organizations and American cities.* New York: Citizen's Committee for New York City.

Florin, P., & Wandersman, A. (1990). An introduction to citizen participation, voluntary organizations, and community development: Insights for improvement through research. *American Journal of Community Psychology, 18,* 41–54.

Flowers-Coulson, P. A., Kushner, M. A., & Bankowski, S. (2000). The information is out there, but is anyone getting it? Adolescent misconceptions about sexuality education and reproductive health and the use of the internet to get answers. *Journal of Sex Education & Therapy, 25,* 178–188.

Forer, L. G. (1980). *Criminals and victims: A trial judge reflects on crime and punishment.* New York: Norton.

Forlenza, S. G. (1991). Mediation and psychotherapy: Parallel processes. In K. G. Duffy, T. W. Grosch, & P. V. Olczak (Eds.), *Community mediation: A handbook for practitioners and researchers.* New York: Guilford.

Fortune, J. C., Bruce, A., Williams, J., & Jones, M. (1991). What does evaluation of your dropout prevention program show about its success?... Maybe not enough. *High School Journal, 74,* 225–231.

Fossey, R. (1996). School dropout rates: Are we sure they are going down? *Phi Delta Kappan, 78,* 140–144.

Foster, H. W., Greene, L. W., & Smith, M. S. (1990). A model for increasing access: Teenage pregnancy prevention. *Journal of Health Care for the Poor and Underserved, 1,* 136–146.

Foster-Fishman, P. G., & Keys, C. B. (1997). The person/environment dynamics of employee empowerment: An organizational culture analysis. *American Journal of Community Psychology, 25,* 345–369.

Foster-Fishman, P. G., Salem, D. A., Chibnall, S., Legler, R., & Yapchai, C. (1998). Empirical support for the critical assumptions of empowerment theory. *American Journal of Community Psychology, 26,* 507–536.

Fowler, R. (1990). Psychology: The core discipline. *American Psychologist, 45,* 1–6.

Frank, J. D. (1983). Galloping technology, a new social disease. *Journal of Social Issues, 39,* 193–206.

Franklin, C., Grant, D., Corcoran, J. Miller, P. O., & Bultan, L. (1997). Effectiveness of prevention programs for adolescent pregnancy: A meta-analysis. *Journal of Marriage & the Family, 59,* 551–567.

Fraser, B. J., Williamson, J. C., & Tobin, K. G. (1987). Use of classroom and school climate scales in evaluating alternative high schools. *Teaching and Teacher Education,* 219–231.

Freedman, A. M. (1989). Mental health programs in the United States: Idiosyncratic roots. *International Journal of Mental Health, 18,* 81–98.

Freedman, E. (1974). Their sisters' keepers: An historical perspective on female correctional institutions in the United States: 1870–1900. *Feminist Studies, 2,* 77–95.

Freeman, R. J., & Roesch, R. (1989). Mental disorder and the criminal justice system. *International Journal of Law and Psychiatry, 12,* 105–115.

French, W. L., & Bell, C. H. (1990). *Organizational development: Behavioral science interventions for organization improvement.* Englewood Cliffs, NJ: Prentice-Hall.

Friedlander, B. Z. (1993). Community violence, children's development, and mass media: In pursuit of new insights, new goals, and new strategies. *Psychiatry, 56,* 66–81.

Friedman, M., & Rosenman, R. (1974). *Type A behavior and your heart.* New York: Knopf.

Friedman, S. M., Neagius, A., Jose, B., Curtis, R., Goldstein, M., Ildefonso, G., Rothenberg, R., & DesJarlais, D. C. (1997). Network and sociohistorical approaches to the HIV epidemic among drug injectors. In L. Sherr, J. Catalan, & B. Hedge (Eds.), *The impacts of AIDS: Epidemiological and social aspects of HIV infection.* Chur, Switzerland: Harwood.

Frumkin, P. (2000). The face of the new philanthropy. *The Responsive Community, 10,* 41–48.

Gallent, J. E., & Block, D. S. (1998, May). Adherence to antiretroviral regimens in HIV-infected patients: Results of a survey among physicians and patients. *Journal of the International Association of Physicians in AIDS Care,* pp. 32–35.

Garbarino, J. (1999). *Lost boys: Why our sons turn violent and how we can save them.* New York: The Free Press.

Garbarino, J. (2001). *Making sense of school violence: Why do kids kill?* Washington, DC: American Psychiatric Press.

Garbarino, J., & Kostelny, K. (1992). Child maltreatment as a community problem. *Child Abuse and Neglect, 16,* 455–464.

Garbarino, J., & Kostelny, L. (1994). Neighborhood-based programs. In G. B. Melton & F. D. Barry (Eds.), *Protecting children from abuse and neglect: Foundations for a new strategy.* New York: Guilford.

Garn, S. M., & Petzold, A. S. (1983). Characteristics of the mother and child in teenage pregnancy. *American Journal of Diseases of Children, 137,* 365–368.

Garofalo, R., Wolf, C., Wissow, L. S., Woods, E. R., & Goodman, E. (1999). Sexual orientation and risk of suicide attempts among a representative sample of youths. *Archive of Pediatric Adolescent Medicine, 153,* 487–193.

Garofalo, R., Wolf, R. C., Kessel, S., Palfrey, J., & DuRant, R. H. (1998). The association between health risk behaviors and sexual orientation among a school-based sample of adolescents. *Pediatrics, 101,* 895–902.

Gebhardt, D. L., & Crump, E. (1990). Employee fitness and wellness programs in the workplace. *American Psychologist, 45,* 262–272.

Geen, R., Fender, L., Leos-Urbel, J., & Markowitz, T. (2001). *Welfare reform's effect on child welfare caseloads.* Washington, DC: The Urban Institute.

Geller, E. S. (1988). A behavioral science approach to transportation safety. *Bulletin of the New York Academy of Medicine, 64,* 632–661.

Geller, E. S. (1991). War on the highways: An international tragedy. *Journal of Applied Behavior Analysis, 24,* 3–7.

Geller, E. S., & Lehman, G. R. (1988). Drinking driving intervention strategies: A person situation-behavior framework. In M. D. Laurence, J. R. Snortum, & F. E. Zimring (Eds.), T*he social control of drinking and driving.* Chicago: University of Chicago Press.

Geller, E. S., Berry, T. D., Ludwig, T. D., Evans, R. E., Gilmore, M. R., & Clarke, S. W. (1990). A conceptual framework for developing and evaluating behavior change interventions for injury control. *Health Education Research, 5,* 125– 137.

Geller, J. L. (1986). Rights, wrongs, and the dilemma of coerced community treatment. *American Journal of Psychiatry, 143,* 1259–1264.

Gerard, H. B., & Miller, N. (1975). *School desegregation: A long-term study.* New York: Plenum.

Gesten, E. L., & Jason, L. A. (1987). Social and community interventions. In L. W. Porter & M. R. Rosenzweig (Eds.), *Annual review of psychology.* Palo Alto, CA: Annual Reviews.

Giamartino, G. A., & Wandersman, A. (1983). Organizational climate correlates of viable urban block organizations. *American Journal of Community Psychology, 11,* 529–542.

Gidron, B., Chesler, M. A., & Chesney, B. K. (1991). Cross-cultural perspectives on self-help groups: Comparisons between participants and nonparticipants in Israel and the United States. *American Journal of Community Psychology, 19,* 667–682.

Gignac, M. A. M., Kelloway, E. K., & Gottlieb, B. H. (1996). The impact of caregiving on employment: A mediational model of work-family conflict. *Canadian Journal of Aging, 15,* 525–542.

Gil, D. G. (Ed.). (1979). *Child abuse and violence.* New York: AMS Press.

Gilbert, M. J., & Cervantes, R. C. (1986). Patterns and practices of alcohol use among Mexican Americans: A comprehensive review. *Hispanic Journal of Behavioral Sciences, 8,* 1–87.

Gillespie, D. F., & Murty, S. A. (1994). Cracks in a postdisaster service delivery network. *American Journal of Community Psychology, 22,* 639–660.

Gillespie, J. F., Durlak, J., & Sherman, D. (1982). Relationship between kindergarten children's interpersonal problem solving skills and other indices of school adjustment: A cautionary note. *American Journal of Community Psychology, 10,* 149–153.

Ginexi, E. M., Weihs, K., & Simmens, S. J., & Hoyt, D. R. (2000). Natural disaster and depression: A prospective investigation of reactions to the 1993 Midwest floods. *American Journal of Community Psychology, 28,* 495–515.

Glaberson, W. (1990, February 19). Mean streets teach New Yorkers to just walk on by. *The New York Times,* pp. B1–B2.

Glenwick, D. S., Heller, K., Linney, J. A., & Pargament, K. I. (1990). Criteria of excellence I. Models for adventuresome research in community psychology: Commonalties, dilemmas, and future direction. In P. Tolan, C. Keys, F. Chertok, & L. Jason (Eds.), *Researching community psychology: Issues of theory and methods.* Washington, DC: American Psychological Association.

Glidewell, J. C. (1976). A theory of induced social change. *American Journal of Community Psychology, 4,* 227–239.

Glidewell, J. C. (1987). Induce change and stability in psychological and social systems. *American Journal of Community Psychology, 15,* 741–772.

Glynn, T. J. (1986). Neighborhood and sense of community. *Journal of Community Psychology, 14,* 341–352.

Goelman, H. (1988). The relationship between structure and process variables in home and day care settings on children's language development. In A. R. Pence (Ed.), *Ecological research with children and families*. New York: Teachers College Press.

Golding, J. M., Potts, M. K., & Aneshensel, C. S. (1991). Stress exposure among Mexican Americans and non-Hispanic whites. *Journal of Community Psychology, 19,* 37–59.

Golding, J. M., Siegel, J. M., Sorenson, S. B., Burnam, M. A., & Stein, J. A. (1989). Social support sources following sexual assault. *Journal of Community Psychology, 17,* 92–107.

Goleman, D. (1989, January 24). Sad legacy of abuse: The search for remedies. *The New York Times,* pp. C1, C6.

Gomby, D. S. (2000). Promise and limitations of home visitation. *Journal of the American Medical Association, 284,* 1430–1431.

Goodman, A. M. (1990). A model for police officer burnout. *Journal of Business and Psychology, 5,* 85–99.

Gore, A. (1990). Public policy and the homeless. *American Psychologist, 45,* 960–962.

Gottfried, A. E., & Gottfried, A. W. (1988). Maternal employment and children's development. In A. E. Gottfried & A. W. Gottfried (Eds.), *Maternal employment and children's development.* New York: Plenum.

Gottlieb, B. H. (1981). Social networks and social support in community mental health. In B. H. Gottlieb (Ed.), *Social networks and social support.* Beverly Hills: Sage.

Gottlieb, B. H. (1987). Using social support to protect and promote health. *Journal of Primary Prevention, 8,* 49–70.

Gottlieb, B. H., & Peters, L. (1991). A national demographic portrait of mutual aid group participants in Canada. *American Journal of Community Psychology, 19,* 651–666.

Gottschalk, B., & Gottschalk, P. (1988). The Reagan retrenchment in historical context. In M. K. Brown (Ed.), *Remaking the welfare state: Retrenchment and social policy in America and Europe.* Philadelphia, PA: Temple University Press.

Grace, J., I-Chin Tu, J., Rochman, B., & Woodbury, R. (1994, July 25). Out of the line of fire. *Time,* pp. 25–29.

Graue, M. E. (1992). Social interpretations of readiness for kindergarten. *Early Childhood Research Quarterly, 7,* 225–243.

Gray, D. O., & Braddy, B. A. (1988). Experimental social innovation and client-centered job seeking programs. *American Journal of Community Psychology, 16,* 325–343.

Gray, P., & Chanoff, D. (1986). Democratic schooling: What happens to young people who have charge of

their own education? *American Journal of Community Psychology, 94,* 182–213.

Greatbatch, D., & Dingwall, R. (1989). Selective facilitation: Some preliminary observations on a strategy used by divorce mediators. *Law and Society Review, 23,* 613–641.

Green, B. L., & Rodgers, A. (2001). Determinants of social support among low-income mothers: A longitudinal analysis. *American Journal of Community Health, 29,* 419–441.

Greenberg, A. (1999). Defending the "American people." *The Responsive Community, 9,* 52–58.

Greenberger, E., Goldberg, W. A., Hamill, S., O'Neill, R., & Payne, C. K. (1989). Contributions of a supportive work environment to parents' well-being and orientation to work. *American Journal of Community Psychology, 17,* 755–783.

Greene, V. L., & Monahan, D. J. (1989). The effect of a support and education program on stress and burden among family caregivers to frail elderly persons. *Gerontologist, 29,* 472–477.

Grob, G. N. (1991). *From asylum to community: Mental health policy in modern America.* Princeton, NJ: Princeton University Press.

Grossi, E. L., & Berg, B. L. (1991). Stress and job dissatisfaction among correctional officers: An unexpected finding. *International Journal of Offender Therapy and Comparative Criminology, 35,* 73–81.

Grotberg, E. H. (Spring 2001). Resilience and culture. *International Psychology Reporter,* 13–14.

Hackerman, A. E. (1996). Intervening with the adolescent gang member: Understanding the spoken language. *The Community Psychologist, 29,* 17–21.

Hadley-Ives, E., Stiffman, A. R., Elze, D., Johnson, S. D., & Dore, P. (2000). Measuring neighborhood and school environments: Perceptual and aggregate approaches. *Journal of Human Behavior in the Social Environment, 3,* 1–28.

Hagborg, W. J. (1988). A study of the intensity and frequency of crisis intervention for students enrolled in a school for the severely emotionally disturbed. *Adolescence, 23,* 825–836.

Halpern, R. (1991). Supportive services for families in poverty: Dilemmas of reforms. *Social Service Review, 65,* 131–151.

Halpert, H. P. (1985). Surveys of public opinions and attitudes about mental illness. *Public Health Report, 80,* 589–597.

Hambry, S. L. (2000). Rural residents: An at-risk and underserved group. *The Community Psychologist, 33,* 14–15.

Hamilton, S. F., Basseches, M., & Richards, F. A. (1985). Participatory-democratic work and adolescents' mental health. *American Journal of Community Psychology, 13,* 467–496.

Handel, G. (1982). *Social welfare in western society.* New York: Random House.

Haney, C., Banks, C., & Zimbardo, P. (1973). Interpersonal dynamics in a simulated prison. *International Journal of Criminology and Penology, 1,* 69–97.

Harper, G. W., & Carver, L. J. (in press). "Out-of-mainstream" youth as partners in collaborative research: Exploring the benefits and challenges. *Health Education and Behavior.*

Harper, M. S. (1995). Mental health and mental health services. In P. K. H. Kim (Ed.), *Services to the aging and aged: Public policies and programs.* New York: Garland.

Harpin, P., & Sandler, I. (1985). Relevance of social climate: An improved approach to assessing person-environment interactions in the classroom. *American Journal of Community Psychology, 13,* 329–352.

Harrington, C. (1985). *Shadow justice: The ideology and institutionalization of alternatives to court.* Westport, CT: Greenwood Press.

Hatfield, A. B. (1997, September/October). Elderly individuals with mental illnesses: The overlooked and underserved generation. *NAMI Advocate,* pp. 13–18.

Hayden, R. M. (1989). Cultural context and the impact of traffic safety legislation: The reception of mandatory seatbelt laws in Yugoslavia and Illinois. *Law and Society, 23,* 283–294.

Haynes, N. M., Emmons, C., & Ben-Avie, M. (1997). School climate as a factor in student adjustment and achievement. *Journal of Educational and Psychological Consultation, 8,* 321–329.

Head, T. C., & Sorenson, P. F. (1988). Contemporary trends in OD. *Organizational Development Journal, 7,* 13–24.

Hellem, D. M. (1990). Sixth grade transition groups: An approach to primary prevention. *Journal of Primary Prevention, 10,* 303–311.

Heller, K. (1989a). Ethical dilemmas in community intervention. *American Journal of Community Psychology, 17,* 367–378.

Heller, K. (1989b). Return to community. *American Journal of Community Psychology, 17,* 1–15.

Heller, K. (1990). Social and community intervention. In L. W. Porter & M. R. Rosenzweig (Eds.), *Annual review of psychology.* Palo Alto, CA: Annual Reviews.

Heller, K., & Mansbach, W. E. (1984). The multifaceted nature of social support in a community sample of elderly women. *American Journal of Community Psychology, 40,* 99–112.

Heller, K., Price, R. H., Reinharz, S., Riger, S., & Wander-

sman, A. (1984). *Psychology and community change.* Homewood, IL: Dorsey.

Heller, K., Thompson, M. G., Trueba, P. E., Hogg, J. R., & Vlachos-Weber, I. (1991). Peer support telephone dyads for elderly women: Was this the wrong intervention? *American Journal of Community Psychology, 19,* 53–74.

Heller, K., Wyman, M. F., & Allen, S. M. (2000). Future directions for prevention science; From research to adoption. In C. R. Snyder & R. E. Ingram (Eds.), *Handbook of psychological change: Psychotherapy processes and practices for the 21st century.* New York: John Wiley.

Hellman, I. D., Greene, L. R., Morrison, T. L., & Abramowitz, S. I. (1985). Organizational size and perceptions in a residential treatment program. *American Journal of Community Psychology, 13,* 99–110.

Hemenway, D., & Azrael, D. (2000). The relative frequency of offensive and defensive gun uses: Results from a national survey. *Violence Victims, 15,* 257–272.

Henggeler, S. W. (1997). *Treating serious anti-social behavior in youth: The MST approach.* Washington, DC: U.S. Department of Justice.

Henry, D., Guerra, N., Huesmann, R., Tolan, P., VanAcker, R., & Eron, L. (2000). Normative influences on aggression in urban elementary school classrooms. *American Journal of Community Psychology, 28,* 59–81.

Hersch, C. (1969). From mental health to social action: Clinical psychology in historical perspective. *American Psychologist, 24,* 906–916.

Hersey, J. C., Klibanoff, L. S., Lam, D. J., & Taylor, R. L. (1984). Promoting social support: The impact of California's "Friends Can Be Good Medicine" campaign. *Health Education Quarterly, 11,* 293–311.

Hess, B. B., Markson, E. W., & Stein, P. J. (1991). *Sociology.* New York: Macmillan.

Hill, J., Bond, M. A., Mulvey, A., & Terenzio, M. (2000). Methodological issues and challenges for a feminist community psychology: An introduction to a special issue. *American Journal of Community Psychology, 28,* 759–772.

Hill, R. J. (1999). An in-queery into theory and action. *The Community Psychologist, 32,* 15–17.

Himle, D. P., Jayertne, S., & Thyness, P. (1991). Buffering effects of four social support types on burnout among social workers. *Social Work Research and Abstracts, 27,* 22–27.

Hinds, P., & Kiesler, S. (1995). Communication across boundaries: Work, structure, and use of communication technologies in a large organization. *Organization Science, 6,* 373–393.

Hingson, R., Heeren, T., & Winter, M. (1998). Effects of

Maine's 0.05% legal blood alcohol level for drivers with DWI convictions. *Public Health Report, 113,* 440–446.

Hinrichsen, G. A., Revenson, T. A., & Shinn, M. (1985). Does self-help help? An empirical investigation of scoliosis peer support groups. *American Journal of Community Psychology, 41,* 65–87.

Hirsch, B. J., & David, T. G. (1983). Social networks and work/nonwork life: Action research with nurse managers. *American Journal of Community Psychology, 11,* 493–508.

Hobfoll, S. E. (1998). Ecology, community, and AIDS prevention. American *Journal of Community Health, 26,* 133–144.

Hobson, C. J., Delunas, L., & Kesic, D. (2001). Compelling evidence of the need for corporate work/life balance initiatives: Results from a national survey of stressful life-events. *Journal of Employment Counseling, 38,* 38–44.

Hochstedler, E. (1986). Criminal prosecution of the mentally disordered. *Law and Society Review, 20,* 279–292.

Hoff, R. A., Beam-Goulet, J., & Rosenheck, R. (1997). Mental disorder as a risk factor for human immunodeficiency virus infection in a sample of veterans. *The Journal of Nervous and mental Disorder, 185,* 556–560.

Hofferth, S. L. (1991). Programs for high risk adolescents: What works? Special issue: Service to teenage parents. *Evaluation and Program Planning, 14,* 3–16.

Holahan, C. J., Betak, J. F., Spearly, J. L., & Chance, B. J. (1983). Social integration and mental health in a biracial community. *American Journal of Community Psychology, 11,* 301–311.

Holcomb, W. B., & Ahr, P. R. (1986). Clinicians' assessments of the service needs of young adult patients in public mental health care. *Hospital and Community Psychiatry, 37,* 908–913.

Hollander, E. P., & Offerman, L. (1990). Power and leadership in organizations. *American Psychologist, 45,* 179–189.

Holmes, T. H., & Masuda, M. (1974). Life changes and illness susceptibility. In B. S. Dohrenwend & B. P. Dohrenwend (Eds.), *Stressful life events: Their nature and effects.* New York: Wiley.

Holmes, T. H., & Rahe, R. H. (1967). The social readjustment rating scale. *Journal of Psychosomatic Research, 11,* 213–218.

Honing, A. (1988). *Parent involvement in early childhood education.* Washington, DC: National Association for the Education of Young Children.

Horan, P. F., & DiClemente, R. J. (1993). HIV knowledge, communications, and risk behaviors among white, Chinese- and Filipino American adolescents in a high prevalence AIDS epicenter: A comparative analysis. *Ethnicity and Disease, 3,* 97–105.

Horowitz, M., Schaefer, C., Hiroto, D., Wilner, N., & Levin, B. (1977). Life event questionnaires for measuring presumptive stress. *Psychosomatic Medicine, 39,* 413–431.

Howard, K. A., Flora, J., & Griffin, M. (1999). Violence-prevention programs in schools: State of the science and implications for future research. *Applied & Preventive Psychology, 8,* 197–215.

Howard., J., Bouey, P. D., Greenwood, G., & Duran, B. (2001). *Sexual risk among seropositive Native American men and women in case management services.* Manuscript under review.

Hudiburg, R. A. (1990). Relating computer-associated stress to computerphobia. *Psychological Reports, 67,* 311–314.

Hudiburg, R. A., & Necessary, J. R. (1996). Coping with computer stress. *Journal of Educational Computing Research, 15,* 107–118.

Hughes, D., & Dodge, M. A. (1997). African American women in the workplace: Relationships between job conditions, racial bias at work, and perceived job quality. *American Journal of Community Psychology, 25,* 581–599.

Hughey, J., Speer, P., & Peterson, N. A. (1999). Sense of community in community organizations: Structure and evidence of validity. *Journal of Community Psychology, 27,* 97–113.

Huhn, R. P., & Zimpfer, D. G. (1988). Effects of a parent education program on parents and their preadolescent children. *Journal of Community Psychology, 17,* 311–318.

Huizinga, D., Leober, R., Thornberry, T. P., & Cothern, L. (November 2000). Co-occurrence of delinquency and other problem behaviors. *Juvenile Justice Bulletin, 1–7.*

Human Capital Initiative (Report 3). (1996, February). Reducing mental disorders:A behavioral science research plan for psychopathology. *APS Observer,* special issue.

Humphreys, K., & Rappaport, J. (1993). From the community mental health movement to war on drugs: A study in the definition of social problems. *American Psychologist, 48,* 892–901.

Hunt, J. M. (1961). *Intelligence and experience.* New York: Ronald Press.

Huston, A. C., Donnerstine, F., Fairchild, H., Feshbach, N. D., Katz, P. A., Murray, J. P., Rubinstein, E. A., Wilcox, B. L., & Zuckerman, D. (1992). *Big world, small screen: The role of television in American society.* Lincoln, NE: University of Nebraska Press.

Ialongo, N. S., Werthamer, L., Kellam, S. G., Brown, C. H., Wang, S., & Lin, Y. (1999). Proximal impact of two first-grade preventive interventions on early risk behaviors for later substance abuse, depression, and antisocial behavior. *American Journal of Community Psychology, 27,* 599–642.

Ilgen, D. R. (1990). Health issues at work. *American Psychologist, 45,* 273–283.

Inciardi, J. A. (1980). Problems in the measurement of criminal behavior. In D. H. Kelley (Ed.), *Criminal behavior: Readings in criminology.* New York: St. Martin's Press.

Institute of Medicine. (1994). *Reducing risks for mental disorder: Summary.* Washington, DC: National Academy Press.

Institute of Medicine. (1997). *The hidden epidemic: Confronting sexually transmitted diseases.* Washington, DC: National Academy Press.

Institute of Medicine. (2001). *No time to lose: Getting more from HIV prevention.* Washington, DC: Author.

Iscoe, I. (1994). The early years of community psychology. *The Community Psychologist, 28,* 22–23.

Ivancevich, J. M., Matteson, M. T., Freedman, J. M., & Phillips, J. S. (1990). Worksite stress management interventions. *American Psychologist, 45,* 252–261.

Iverson, D. C., Fielding, J. E., Crow, R. S., & Christenson, G. M. (1985). The promotion of physical activity in the United States population: The status of programs in medical, worksite, community, and school settings. *Public Health Reports, 100,* 212–224.

Jackson, A. P. (1997). Effects of concerns about child care among single, employed Black mothers with preschool children. *American Journal of Community Psychology, 25,* 657–673.

Jackson, S. E., Schwab, R. L., & Schuler, R. S. (1986). Toward an understanding of the burnout phenomenon. *Journal of Applied Psychology, 71,* 630–640.

Jacobs, J. A., & Gerson, K. (2001). Overworked individuals or overworked families? Explaining trends in work, leisure, and family time. *Work & Occupations, 28,* 40–63.

Jacobs, J. B. (1980). The prisoners' rights movement and its impacts, 1960–1980. In N. Morris & M. Tonry (Eds.), *Crime and justice: An annual review of research.* Chicago: University of Chicago Press.

Jansen, M. A., & Johnson, E. M. (1993). Methodological issues in prevention research: An introduction to the special issue. *American Journal of Community Psychology, 21,* 561–569.

Janz, N. K., & Becker, M. H. (1984). The health belief model: A decade later. *Health Education Quarterly, 11,* 1–47.

Jason, L. A. (1991). Participation in social change: A fundamental value of our discipline. *American Journal of Community Psychology, 19,* 1–16.

Jason, L. A. (1998). Tobacco, drug, and HIV preventive media. *American Journal of Community Psychology, 26,* 151–187.

Jason, L. A., Berk, M., Schnopp-Wyatt, D. L., & Talbot, B. (1999). Effects of enforcement of youth access laws on smoking prevalence. *American Journal of Community Health, 27,* 143–160.

Jason, L. A., Curran, T., Goodman, D., & Smith, M. (1989). A media-based stress management intervention. *Journal of Community Psychology, 17,* 155–165.

Jason, L. A., Gruder, C. L., Martins, S., Flay, B. R., Warnecke, R., & Thomas N. (1987). Work site group meeting and the effectiveness of a televised smoking cessation intervention. *American Journal of Community Psychology, 15,* 57–72.

Jason, L. A., Kennedy, H. L., & Brackshaw, E. (1999). Television violence and children: Problems and solutions. In T. P. Gulotta & S. J. McElhaney (Eds.), *Violence in homes and communities: Prevention, intervention, and treatment.* Thousand Oaks, CA: Sage.

Jason, L. A., La Pointe, P., & Bellingham, S. (1986). The media and self-help: A preventive community intervention. *Journal of Primary Prevention, 6,* 156–167.

Jay, G. M., & D'Augelli, A. R. (1991). Social support and adjustment to university life: A comparison of African-American and White freshman. *Journal of Community Psychology, 19,* 95–100.

Jemelka, R., Trupin, E., & Chiles, J. A. (1989). The mentally ill in prisons: A review. *Hospital and Community Psychiatry, 40,* 481–491.

Jemmett, J. B., III, & Magloire, K. (1988). Academic stress, social support, and secretory immuniglobin. *Journal of Personality and Social Psychology, 55,* 803–810.

Jemmott, J. B., & Jemmott, L. S. (1994). Intervention for adolescents in community settings. In R. J. DiClemente and J. L. Peterson (Eds.), *Preventing AIDS: Theories and methods of behavioral interventions* (pp. 141–174). New York: Plenum.

Jewell, L. N. (1998). *Contemporary industrial/organizational psychology.* Pacific Grove, CA: Brooks/Cole.

Johnson, D. (1991). Psychology in Washington: Why should government support science now that the Russians aren't competing? *Psychological Science, 2,* 133–134.

Johnson, F., Lay, P., & Wilbrandt, M. (1988). Teenage pregnancy: Issues, intervention, and direction. *Journal of the National Medical Association, 80,* 145–152.

Johnson, L. D. (1990, February 13). University of Michigan press release. Ann Arbor, MI: University of Michigan News Information Services.

Johnston, D. F. (1980). *The handbook of social indicators: Success, characteristics, and analysis.* New York: Garland STPM Press.

Johnston, L. D., O'Malley, P. M., & Bachman, J. G. (1993). *National survey results on drug use from monitoring the future study, 1975–1992.* Rockville, MD: National Institute on Drug Abuse.

Jones, E. E., & Nisbett, R. E. (1971). *The actor and the observer: Divergent perceptors of the causes of behavior.* Morristown, NJ: General Learning Press.

Joseph, M., & Ogletree, R. (1998). Community organizing and comprehensive community initiative. *Journal of Sociology and Social Welfare, 25,* 71–79.

Jung, R. S., & Jason, L. A. (1988). Firearm violence and the effects of gun control legislation. *American Journal of Community Psychology, 16,* 515–524.

Kagan, S. L. (1990). Readiness 2000: Rethinking rhetoric and responsibility. *Phi Delta Kappan, 71,* 272–279.

Kale, W. L., & Stenmark, D. E. (1983). A comparison of four life event scales. *American Journal of Community Psychology, 11,* 441–458.

Kamradt, B. (2000). Wraparound Milwaukee: Aiding youth with mental health needs. *Juvenile Justice, 7,* 14–23.

Kaniasty, K., & Norris, F. H. (1992). Social support and victims of crime: Matching event, support, and outcome. *American Journal of Community Psychology, 20,* 211–241.

Kanigsberg, J. S., & Levant, R. F. (1988). Parental attitudes and children's self-concept and behavior following parent's participation in training groups. *Journal of Community Psychology, 16,* 152–160.

Kanner, A. D., Coyne, J. C., Schaefer, C., & Lazarus, R. S. (1981). Comparison of two models of stress management: Daily hassles and uplifts versus major life events. *Journal of Behavioral Medicine, 4,* 1–39.

Kanungo, S. (1998). An empirical study of organizational culture and network-based computer use. *Computers in Human Behavior, 14,* 79–91.

Kaplan, G. (1994). Reflections on present and future research on bio-behavioral risk factors. In S. Blumenthal, K. Matthews, and S. Weiss (Eds.), *New research frontiers in behavioral medicine.* Proceedings of the National Conference. Washington, DC: NIH Publications.

Kaplan, M. (1983). A woman's view of DSM-III. *American Psychologist, 7,* 786–792.

Karim, Q. A., Karim, S. S. A., Coovadia, H. M., & Susser, M. (1998). Informed consent for HIV testing in a South African Hospital: Is it truly informed and truly voluntary? *American Journal of Public Health, 88,* 637–640.

Katz, D. (1983). Factors affecting social change: A social psychological interpretation. *Journal of Social Issues, 39,* 25–44.

Katzell, R. A., & Thompson, D. E. (1990). Work motivation. *American Psychologist, 45,* 144–153.

Kaufman, J., & Zigler, E. (1987). Do abused children become abusive parents? *American Journal of Orthopsychology, 57,* 186–192.

Kawachi, I., Kennedy, B. P., & Lochner, K. (1997). Long live community: Social capital as public health. *The American Prospect, 35,* 56–59.

Kazarean, S. S., & McCabe, S. B. (1991). Dimensions of social support in the MSPSS: Factorial structure, reliability, and theoretical implications. *Journal of Community Psychology, 19,* 150–160.

Kazden, A. E. (1980). *Research design in community psychology.* New York: Harper and Row.

Kelin, D. C. (1995). The future of community psychology: Towards building an agenda. *The Community Psychologist, 28,* 25–27.

Kellam, S. G., Koretz, D., & Moscicki, E. K. (Eds.). (1999a). Special issue: Prevention science, Part I. *American Journal of Community Psychology, 27,* 461–595.

Kellam, S. G., Koretz, D., & Moscicki, E. K. (Eds.). (1999b). Special issue: Prevention science, Part II. *American Journal of Community Psychology, 27,* 697–731.

Kelly, C., & Breinlinger, S. (1996). *The social psychology of collective action: Identity, injustice, and gender.* Washington, DC: Taylor & Francis.

Kelly, G. W. R., & Ekland-Olson, S. (1991). The response of the criminal justice system to prison overcrowding: Recidivism patterns among four successive parolee courts. *Law and Society Review, 25,* 601–620.

Kelly, H. H. (1973). The process of causal attribution. *American Psychologist, 28,* 107–128.

Kelly, J. A., Murphy, D. A., Sikkema, K. L., & Kalichman, S. C. (1993). Psychological intervention to prevent HIV infection are urgently needed: New priorities for behavioral research in the second decade of AIDS. *American Psychologist, 48,* 1023–1034.

Kelly, J. A., St. Lawrence, J. S., Diaz, Y. E., Stevenson, L. Y., Hauth, A. C., Brasfield, T. L., Kalichman, S. C., Smith, J. E., & Andrew, M. E. (1991). HIV risk behavior reduction following intervention with key opinion leaders of population: An experimental analysis. *American Journal of Public Health, 81,* 168–171.

Kelly, J. G. (1986a). An ecological paradigm: Defining mental health consultation as a preventative service. *Prevention in the Human Services, 4,* 1–36.

Kelly, J. G. (1986b). Context and process: An ecological view of the interdependence of practice and research. *American Journal of Community Psychology, 14,* 581–589.

Kelly, J. G. (1990). Changing contexts and the field of community psychology. *American Journal of Community Psychology, 18,* 769–792.

Kelsey, J. L., Thompson, W. D., & Evans, A. S. (1986). *Methods in observational epidemiology.* New York: Oxford University.

Kennedy, C. (1989). Community integration and well-being: Toward the goals of community care. *Journal of Social Issues, 45,* 65–78.

Kerlinger, F. N. (1973). *Foundations of behavioral research.* New York: Holt, Rinehart and Winston.

Kessler, R. C., & Price, R. H. (1993). Primary prevention of secondary disorders: A proposal and agenda. *American Journal of Community Psychology, 21,* 607–633.

Kessler, R. C., Turner, J. B., & House, R. H. (1988). Effects of unemployment on health in a community survey: Main, mediating, and modifying effects. *Journal of Social Issues, 44,* 69–86.

Kessler, R. C., Turner, J. B., & House, R. H. (1989). Unemployment, reemployment, and emotional functioning in a community sample. *American Sociological Review, 54,* 648–657.

Ketterer, R. E. (1981). *Consultation and education in mental health: Problems and prospects.* Beverly Hills: Sage.

Kettner, P. M., Daley, J. M., & Nichols, A. W. (1985). *Initiating change in organizations of communities: A macro practice model.* Monterey, CA: Brooks Cole.

Keys, C. B., & Frank, S. (1987). Organizational perspectives in community psychology (Special issue). *American Journal of Community Psychology, 15.*

Kiernan, M., Toro, P. A., Rappaport, J., & Seidman, E. (1989). Economic predictors of mental health service utilization: A time-series analysis. *American Journal of Community Psychology, 17,* 801–820.

Kiesler, C. A. (1980). Mental health policy as a field of inquiry for psychology. *American Psychologist, 35,* 1066–1080.

Kiesler, C. A. (1992). Mental health policy: Doomed to fail. *American Psychologist, 47,* 1077–1082.

Killias, M. (1993). Gun ownership, suicide, and homicide: An international perspective. In *Understanding crime: Experiences of crime and crime control.* Rome, Italy: United Nations Interregional Crime and Justice Research Institute.

Kilmann, P. (1984). *Human sexuality in contemporary life.* Boston: Allyn and Bacon.

King, C. A., & Kirschenbaum, D. S. (1990). An experimental evaluation of a school-based program for children at risk: Wisconsin early intervention. *American Journal of Community Psychology, 18,* 167–178.

Kirkman, B. L., Jones, R. G., & Shapiro, D. L. (2000). Why do employees resist teams? Examining the "resistance barrier" to work team effectiveness. *International Journal of Conflict Management, 11,* 74–92.

Kirmeyer, S. L., & Dougherty, T. W. (1988). Workload, tension, and coping: Moderating effects of supervisor support. *Personnel Psychology, 41,* 125–139.

Kitchen, C. D. (1991). Crisis intervention using reality therapy for adult sexual abuse victims. *Journal of Reality Therapy, 10,* 34–39.

Kleck, G. (1991). *Point blank: Guns and violence in America.* New York: De Gruyter.

Klein, A. G. (1992). *The debate over child care 1969–1990.* Albany, NY: SUNY Press.

Klein, D. C. (1995). The future of community psychology. *The Community Psychologist, 28,* 25–27.

Klein, K. J., & D'Aunno, T. A. (1986). Psychological sense of community in the workplace. *Journal of Community Psychology, 14,* 365–377.

Klein, K. J., Ralls, R. S., Smith Major, V., & Douglas, C. (2000). Power and participation in the workplace: Implications for empowerment theory, research, and practice. In J. Rappaport & E. Seidman (Eds.), *Handbook of community psychology.* New York: Plenum.

Klein, L., Luxenburg, J., & King, M. (1989). Perceived neighborhood crime and the impact of private security. Special issue: Controlling crime in the community: Citizen-based efforts and initiatives. *Crime and Delinquency, 35,* 365–377.

Kleinman, J. C., & Madanas, J. H. (1985). The effects of maternal smoking, physical stature, and educational attainment on the incidence of low birthweight. *American Journal of Epidemiology, 121,* 843–855.

Kling, R. (2000). Learning about information technologies and social change: The contribution of social informatics. *The Information Society, 16,* 217–232.

Kobasa, S. C. (1979). Stressful life events and health: An inquiry into hardiness. *Journal of Personality and Social Psychology, 37,* 1–11.

Koegel, P., Burnam, M. A., & Farr, R. K. (1990). Substance adaptation among homeless adults in the inner city of Los Angeles. *Journal of Social Issues, 46,* 83–107.

Kofkin, J. A., & Repucci, N. D. (1991). A reconceptualization of life events and its application to parental divorce. *American Journal of Community Psychology, 19,* 227–250.

Kohlberg, L. (1984). *Essays on moral development (Vol. 2). The nature and validity of moral stages.* San Francisco: Harper and Row.

Koizumi, R. (2000). Anchor points in transitions to a new school environment. *Journal of Primary Prevention, 20,* 175–187.

Korbin, J. E., & Coulton, C. J. (1996). The role of neighbors and the government in neighborhood-based child protection. *Journal of Social Issues, 52,* 163–176.

Koretz, D. P., & Moscicki, E. K. (1997). An ounce of prevention research: What is it worth? *American Journal of Community Psychology, 25,* 189–195.

Kozol, J. (1990, Winter/Spring). The new untouchables (Special edition). *Newsweek,* 48–49, 52–53.

Kreisler, A., Snider, A. B., & Kiernan, N. E. (1997). Using distance education to educate and empower community coalitions: A case study. *International Quarterly of Community Health Education, 17,* 161–178.

Kruzich, J. M. (1985). Community integration of the mentally ill in residential facilities. *American Journal of Community Psychology, 13,* 553–564.

Kuhn, R., & Culhane, R. (1998). Applying cluster analysis to test a typology of homelessness by pattern of shelter utilization: Results from the analysis of administrative data. *American Journal of Community Psychology, 26,* 207–232.

Kuhn, T. S. (1970). *The structure of scientific revolutions.* Chicago: University of Chicago Press.

Kuo, F. E., Sullivan, W. C., Coley, R. L., & Brunson, L. (1998). Fertile ground for community: Inner-city neighborhood common spaces. *American Journal of Community Psychology, 26,* 823–852.

La Piere, R. T. (1934). Attitudes and actions. *Social Forces, 13,* 230–237.

Lab, S. P., & Stanich, T. J. (1993). Crime prevention participation: An exploratory analysis. *American Journal of Community Psychology, 18,* 1–23.

Labianca, G., Gray, B., & Brass, D. J. (2000). A grounded model of organizational schema change during empowerment. *Organization Science, 11,* 235–257.

Laguna, K., & Babcock, R. L. (1997). Computer anxiety in young and older adults: Implications for human-computer interactions in older populations. *Computers in Human Behavior, 13,* 317–326.

Lamb, M. E., Hwang, C., Bookstein, F. L., Broberg, A., Hult, G., & Frodi, M. (1988). Determinants of social competence in Swedish preschoolers. *Developmental Psychology, 24,* 58–70.

Lambert, E. Y. (Ed.). (1990). The collection and interpretation of data from hidden populations. *NIDA Monograph 98.* Rockville, MD: NIDA.

Landers, S. (1989). Homeless children lose childhood. *The APA Monitor, 20* (12), 1, 33.

Langer, L. J., & Rodin, J. (1976). The effects of choice and enhanced personal responsibility for the aged: A field experiment in an institutional setting. *Journal of Personality and Social Psychology, 34,* 191–198.

Lanza, M. L. (1986). Victims of international terrorism. *Issues in Mental Health Nursing, 8,* 95–107.

Latane, B., & Darley, J., M. (1970). *The irresponsive bystander: Why doesn't he help?* New York: Appleton-Century-Crofts.

Latkin, C. A., Mandell, W., Vlahov, D., Oziemkowska, M., & Celentano, D. (1996). The long-term outcome of a personal network-oriented HIV prevention intervention for injection drug users: The SAFE study. *American Journal of Community Psychology, 24,* 341–364.

Lawson, A., & Rhode, D. L. (1993). *The politics of pregnancy: Adolescent sexuality and public policy.* New Haven, CT: Yale University Press.

Lazarus, R. S. (1984). Puzzles in the study of daily hassles. *Journal of Behavioral Medicine, 7,* 375–389.

Lazarus, R. S., & Folkman, S. (1984). *Stress, appraisal, and coping.* New York: Springer-Verlag.

LeFebvre, R. C., Lasater, T. M., Carleton, R. A., & Peterson, G. (1987). Theory and delivery health programming in the community: The Pawtuckett Heart Health Program. *Preventive Medicine, 16,* 80–95.

Lehr, U., Seiler, E., & Thomae, H. (2000). Aging in cross-cultural perspective. In L. Comunian & U. P. Gielen (Eds.), *International perspectives on human development.* Lengerich, Germany: Pabst Science Publishers.

Leigh, B. C., & Stall, R. (1993). Substance abuse and risky behavior for exposure to HIV: Issues in methodology, interpretation, and prevention. *American Psychologist, 48,* 1035–1045.

Leitenberg, H. (1987). Primary prevention of delinquency. In J. D. Burchard & S. N. Burchard (Eds.), *Prevention of delinquent behavior.* Newbury Park, CA: Sage.

Lempert, R., & Sanders, J. (1986). *An invitation to law and social science.* New York: Longman.

Leonard, P. A., Dolbeare, C. N., & Lazere, E. B. (1989). *A place to call home: The crisis in housing for the poor.* Washington, DC: Center on Budget and Policy Priorities and Low Income Housing Information Service.

Lester, D., & Murrell, M. E. (1986). The influence of gun control laws and personal violence. *Journal of Community Psychology, 14,* 315–318.

Lettieri, D. J., Sayers, M., & Pearson, H. W. (Eds.). (1984). *Theories on drug abuse: Selected contemporary perspectives.* National Institute on Drug Abuse Research

Monograph 30. Washington, DC: Superintendent of Documents, U.S. Government Printing Office.

Levi, Y., & Litwin, H. (1986). *Communities and cooperatives in participatory development.* Brookfield, VT: Gower Press.

Levin, M. (1985). Unwanted intercourse: The difficulty of saying no. *Psychology of Women Quarterly, 9,* 184–266.

Levin, T. (1983, December 11). Business ethics' new appeal. *The New York Times,* p. 4F.

Levine, I. S., & Huebner, R. D. (1991). Homeless persons with alcohol, drug, and mental disorders. *American Psychologist, 46,* 1113–1114.

Levine, M. (1988). An analysis of mutual assistance. *American Journal of Community Psychology, 16,* 167–188.

Levine, M. (1998). Prevention and community. *American Journal of Community Psychology, 26,* 189–206.

Levine, M. (Spring 1999). Prevention and progress. *The Community Psychologist, 32,* 11–14.

Levine, M. D. (1986). Working it out: A community re-creation approach to crime prevention. *Journal of Community Psychology, 14,* 378–390.

Levine, M., & Perkins, D. V. (1997). *Principles of community psychology: Perspectives and applications.* New York: Oxford University Press.

Levine, M., Toro, P. A., & Perkins, D. V. (1993). Social and community interventions. In L. W. Porter & M. R. Rosenzweig (Eds.), *Annual review of psychology.* Palo Alto, CA: Annual Reviews.

Levine, N., Wachs, M., & Shirazi, E. (1986). Crime at bus stops: A study of environmental factors. *Journal of Architectural and Planning Research, 3,* 339–361.

Levine, R. V., Miyake, K., & Lee, M. (1989). Places rated revisited: Psycho-social pathology in metropolitan areas. *Environment and Behavior, 21,* 531–553.

Levine, S. (April 9, 2001). The price of child abuse. *U.S. News & World Report,* p. 58.

Leviton, L. C. (1989). Theoretical foundations of AIDS prevention programs. In R. O. Valdiserri (Ed.), *Preventing AIDS: The design of effective programs* (pp. 42–90). New Brunswick, NJ: Rutgers University Press.

Levy, L. H. (2000). Self-help groups. In J. Rappaport & E. Seidman (Eds.), *Handbook of community psychology.* New York: Plenum.

Lewin, K. (1948). *Resolving social conflict.* New York: Harper.

Lewin, K. (1951). *Field theory in social science.* New York: Harper and Row.

Lewis, D. A., & Salem, G. (1981). Community crime prevention: An analysis of a development strategy. *Crime and Delinquency, 27,* 405–421.

Lichtenstein E., Lopez, K., Glasgow, R. E., Gilbert-McRae, S., & Hall, R. (1996). Effectiveness of a consultation intervention to promote tobacco control policies in northwest Indian tribes: Integrating experimental evaluation and services delivery. *American Journal of Community Psychology, 24,* 639–655.

Liem, R., & Liem, J. H. (1988). Psychological effects of unemployment on workers and their families. *Journal of Social Issues, 44,* 87–105.

Light, D., & Keller, S. (1985). *Sociology.* New York: Knopf.

Lindsey, E. W. (1998). Service providers; perception of factors that help or hinder homeless families. *Families in Society, 79,* 160–172.

Link, B. G., & Cullen, F. T. (1983). Reconsidering the social injection of ex-mental patients: Levels of attitudinal response. *American Journal of Community Psychology, 11,* 261–273.

Linney, J. A. (1990). Community psychology into the 1990's: Capitalizing opportunity and promoting innovation. *American Journal of Community Psychology, 18,* 1–17.

Lippa, R. A. (1990). *Introduction to social psychology.* Belmont, CA: Wadsworth.

Lippett, R., Watson, J., & Westley, B. (1958). *The dynamics of planned change.* New York: Harcourt, Brace, and World.

Lloyd, C., Zisook, S., Click, M., & Jaffe, K. E. (1981). Life events and response to antidepressants. *Journal of Human Stress, 7,* 2–15.

Lo, W., Teresaki, G., Wong, F. Y., & Mayer, K. H. (1998, July). *Model of illness and quality of life: Treatment choices among HIV infected men.* Paper presented at the Annual Meeting of the National Lesbian and Gay Health Association, San Francisco.

Lombana, J. H. (1976). Counseling the elderly: Remediation plus prevention. *Personnel and Guidance Journal, 55,* 143–144.

Long, B. B. (1992). Developing a constituency for prevention. *American Journal of Community Psychology, 20,* 169–178.

Loo, C., Fong, K. T., & Iwamasca, G. (1988). Ethnicity and cultural diversity: An analysis of work published in community psychology journals, 1965–1985. *Journal of Community Psychology, 16,* 332–349.

Loprest, P. (1999–2000). *Families who left welfare: Who are they and how are they doing? Assessing the new federalism.* Washington, DC: The Urban Institute.

Lorion, R. P. (1991). Targeting preventive interventions: Enhancing risk estimates through theory. *American Journal of Community Psychology, 19,* 859–865.

Lounsbury, J. W., Leader, D. S., Meares, E. P., & Cook, M. P. (1980). An analytic review of research in community psychology. *American Journal of Community Psychology, 8,* 415–441.

Lovell, A. M. (1990). Managed cases, drop-ins, drop-outs, and other by-products of mental health care. *American Journal of Community Psychology, 18,* 917–921.

Lowenthal, M. F., & Haven, C. (1968). Interaction and adaptation: Intimacy as a cultural variable. *American Sociological Review, 33,* 20–30.

Ludwig, T. D., & Geller, E. S. (1991). Improving the driving practices of pizza deliverers: Response generalization and moderating effects of driving history. *Journal of Applied Behavior Analysis, 24,* 31–44.

Luke, D. A., Rappaport, J., & Seidman, E. (1991). Setting phenotypes in a mutual help organization. Expanding behavior setting theory. *American Journal of Community Psychology, 19,* 147–167.

Luna, G. C., & Rotheram-Borus. (1999). Youth living with HIV as peer leaders. *American Journal of Community Health, 27,* 1–23.

Lustig, J. L., Wolchik, S. A., & Braver, S. L. (1992). Social support in chumships and adjustment in children of divorce. *American Journal of Community Psychology, 20,* 391–393.

MacDermid, S. M., Hertzog, J. L., Kensinger, K. B., & Zipp, J. F. (2001). The role of organizational size and industry in job quality and work-family relationships. *Journal of Family & Economic Issues Special Issue, 22,* 119–126.

MacDonald, J. E., & Gifford, R. (1989). Territorial cues and defensible spaces theory: The burglar's point of view. *Journal of Environmental Psychology, 9,* 193–205.

MacKenzie, D. L. (July 1999). Commentary: The effectiveness of aftercare programs—Examining evidence. *Juvenile Justice Bulletin,* 15–22.

MacKenzie, D. L., Wilson, D. B., Armstrong, G. S., & Gover, A. R. (2001). The impact of boot camps and traditional institutions on juvenile residents: Perceptions, adjustment, and change. *Journal of Research in Crime & Delinquency Special Issue, 38,* 279–313.

Macy, B. A., & Izumi, H. (1993). Organizational change, design, and work innovation: A meta-analysis of 131 North American field studies—1961–1991. In R. W. Woodman & W. A. Pasmore (Eds.). *Research in organizational change and development,* vol. 7. Greenwich, CT: JAI.

Madera, E. J. (1986). A comprehensive approach to promoting mutual AIDS self-help groups: The New Jersey Self-Help Clearinghouse model. *Journal of Voluntary Action Research, 15,* 57–63.

Magee Quinn, M., Kavale, K. A., Mathur, S. R., Rutherford, R. B., & Forness, S. R. (1999). A meta-analysis of social skill interventions for students with emo-

tional or behavioral disorders. *Journal of Emotional & Behavioral Disorders, 7,* 54–64.

Magura, S., Goldsmith, D. S., Casriel, C., & Lipton, D. S. (1988). Patient-staff governance in methadone maintenance treatment: A study in participative decision making. *Narcotic and Drug Research, 23,* 253–278.

Maier, G. J., Morrow, B. R., & Miller, R. (1989). Security safeguards in community rehabilitation of forensic patients. *Hospital and Community Psychiatry, 40,* 529–531.

Maloy, K. A., Darnell, J., Nolan, L., Kenney, K., & Cyprien, S. (2000). *Effect of the 1996 welfare and immigration reform laws on immigrants' ability and willingness to access Medicaid and health care services: Findings from four metropolitan sites* (Vol. I). Washington, DC: Center for Health Services Research and Policy, George Washington University School of Public Health and Health Services.

Maltz, M. D., & Zawitz, M. W. (1998). *Technical report: Displaying violent crime trends using estimates from the National Crime Victimization Survey.* Washington, DC: Bureau of Justice Statistics.

Mann, J., Tarantola, D., & Netter, T. (1992). *AIDS in the world.* Cambridge, MA: Harvard University Press.

Marcus-Newhall, A., & Heindl, T. R. (1998). Coping with interracial stress in ethnically diverse classrooms: How important are Allport's contact conditions. *Journal of Social Issues Special Issue: Understanding and Resolving National and International Group Conflic*t, 54, 813–830.

Marin, B. V., Marin, G., Perez-Stable, E. J., Otero-Sabogal, R., & Sabogal, F. (1990). Cultural differences in attitudes toward smoking: Developing messages using the theory of reasoned action. *Journal of Applied Social Psychology, 20,* 478–493.

Marin, G. (1993). Defining culturally appropriate community interventions: Hispanics as a case study. *Journal of Community Psychology, 21,* 149–161.

Marin, G., Marin, B. V., Perez-Stable, E. J., Sabogal, F., & Otero-Sabogal, R. (1990). Changes in information as a function of a culturally appropriate smoking cessation community intervention for Hispanics. *American Journal of Community Psychology, 18,* 847–864.

Marlatt, G. A., & Gordon, J. R. (1985). *Relapse prevention: Maintenance strategies in the treatment of addictive behaviors.* New York: Guilford.

Marlowe, L. (1971). *Social psychology: An interdisciplinary approach to human behavior.* Boston: Holbrook.

Maruschak, L. (1997). HIV in prisons and jails, 1995. *Bureau of Justice Statistics Bulletin.* Washington, DC: Bureau of Justice Statistics.

Maslach, C., & Goldberg, J. (1998). Prevention of burnout: New perspectives. *Applied and Preventive Psychology, 7,* 63–74.

Maslach, C., & Jackson, D. (1981). *Maslach burnout inventory manual.* Palo Alto, CA: Consulting Psychologist Press.

Maslach, C., Schaufeli, W. B., & Leiter, M. P. (2000). Job burnout. *Annual Review of Psychology, 52,* 397–422.

Massachusetts Department of Public Health. (1991). *Handbook on smoking laws and regulations for Massachusetts Communities.* Boston: Massachusetts Department of Public Health.

Maton, K. (1998). SCRA moving out: Beyond the disciplinary and organizational divides. *The Community Psychologist, 31,* 4–6.

Maton, K. (1999). SCRA moving onwards: Social policy, multidisciplinary linkages, diversity, and updates. *The Community Psychologist, 32,* 4–7.

Maton, K. (2000). Making a difference: The social ecology of social transformation. *American Journal of Community Psychology, 28,* 25–57.

Maton, K. I., Levanthal, G. S., Madera, E. J., & Julien, M. (1989). Factors affecting the birth and death of mutual help groups: The role of national affiliation, professional involvement, and member focal point. *American Journal of Community Psychology, 17,* 643–671.

Maton, K. I., Meissen, G. J., & O'Conner, P. (1993). The varying faces of graduate education in community psychology: Comparisons by program type and program level. *Community Psychologist, 26,* 19–21.

Maton, K. I. (1988). Social support, organizational characteristics, psychological well being, and group appraisal in three self-help group populations. *American Journal of Community Psychology, 16,* 53–78.

Maton, K. I., & Salem, D. A. (1995). Organizational characteristics of empowering community settings: A multiple case approach. *American Journal of Community Psychology, 23,* 631–656.

Maton, K. I., & Zimmerman, M. A. (1992). Psychosocial predictors of substance use among urban black male adolescents. In J. E. Trimble, C. S. Boleck, & S. J. Niemcryk (Eds.), Current perspectives in ethnic-minority drug abuse research. Special edition of *Drugs and Society, 6,* 79–113.

Matthews, D. B. (1991). The effects of school environment on intrinsic motivation of middle-school children. Journal of *Humanistic Education and Development, 30,* 30–38.

Mayer, J. P., & Davidson, W. S. (2000). Dissemination of innovation as social change. In J. Rappaport & E. Seidman (Eds.), *Handbook of community psychology.* New York: Plenum.

Mazloff, D. (1998). The importance of strategic worksite health promotion: A study of employee knowledge and employee assistance program promotion. *Employee Assistance Quarterly, 14,* 47–66.

McAlister, A. (2000). Action-oriented mass communication. In J. Rappaport & E. Seidman (Eds.). *Handbook of community psychology.* New York: Plenum.

McBride, T. D., Calsyn, R. J., Morse, G. A., Klinkenberg, W. D., & Allen, G. A. (1998). Duration of homeless spells among severely mentally ill individuals: A survival analysis. *Journal of Community Psychology, 26,* 473–490.

McCaughey, B. G. (1987). U.S. Navy special psychiatric rapid and intervention team (SPRINT). *Military Medicine, 152,* 133–135.

McConnell, S. (1996, August). The role of computers in reshaping the workforce. *Monthly Labor Review,* 3–5.

McCulloch, A., & O'Brien, L. (1986). The organizational determinants of worker burnout. *Children and Youth Services Review, 8,* 175–190.

McGillis, D. (1997). *Community mediation programs: Developments and challenges.* Washington, DC: U.S. Department of Justice.

McGonagle, K. A., & Kessler, R. C. (1990). Chronic stress, acute stress, and depressive symptoms. *American Journal of Community Psychology, 18,* 681–706.

McGrath, J. E. (1983). Looking ahead by looking backwards: Some recurrent themes about social change. *Journal of Social Issues, 39,* 225–239.

McIntosh, N. J. (1991). Identification of properties of social support. *Journal of Organizational Behavior, 12,* 201–217.

McKenna, M. W., & Rizzo, E. (1999). Student perceptions of the "learning" in service-learning courses. *Journal of Prevention & Intervention in the Community, 18,* 111–123.

McLoyd, V. (1989). Socialization and development in a changing economy: The effects of paternal job and income loss on children. Special issue: Children and their development: Knowledge base, research agenda, and social policy application. *American Psychologist, 44,* 293–302.

McLoyd, V. (1990). The impact of economic hardship on Black families and children: Psychological distress, parenting, and socioemotional development. Special issue: Minority children. *Child Development, 61,* 311–346.

McMahon, S. D., & Jason, L. A. (2000). Social support in a worksite smoking intervention: A test of theoretical modes. *Behavior Modification, 24,* 184–201.

McMillan, D. W., & Chavis, D. M. (1986). Sense of community: A definition and theory. *Journal of Community Psychology, 14,* 6–23.

McNeal, R. B. (1997). High school dropouts: A closer examination of school effects. *Social Science Quarterly, 78,* 209– 222.

Meade, J. (1991). Turning on the bright lights. *Teacher Magazine,* 36–42.

Medway, F. J. (1979). How effective is school consultation? A review of recent research. *Journal of School Psychology, 17,* 275–282.

Medway, F. J., & Updyke, J. F. (1985). Meta-analysis of consultation outcome studies. *American Journal of Community Psychology, 13,* 489–505.

Meehan, T. (1986). Alternatives to lawsuits. *Alternatives to Legal Reform, 6,* 9–12.

Meehl, P. E. (1954). *Clinical versus statistical prediction.* Minneapolis: University of Minnesota Press.

Meehl, P. E. (1960). The cognitive activity of the clinician. *American Psychologist, 15,* 19–27.

Melamed, S., Kushnir, T., & Meir, E. I. (1991). Attenuating the impact of job demands: Addictive and interactive effects of perceived control and social support. *Journal of Vocational Behavior, 39,* 40–53.

Melton, G. B. (2000). Community change, community stasis, and the law. In J. Rappaport & E. Seidman (Eds.). *Handbook of community psychology.* New York: Plenum.

Mental health among children. http://www.surgeon-general.gov/cmh/childreport.htm

Meyer, V. F. (1991). A critique of adolescent pregnancy prevention research: The invisible white male. *Adolescence, 26,* 217–222.

Milburn, N. G., Gary, L. E., Booth, J. A., & Brown, D. R. (1991). Conducting research in a minority community: Methodological considerations. *Journal of Community Psychology, 19,* 3–12.

Milkovich, G. T., & Boudreau, J. W. (1991). *Human resource management.* Homewood, IL: Irwin.

Miller, L. S., Zhang, X., Rice, D., & Max, W. (1998). State estimates of total medical expenditures attributable to cigarette smoking, 1993. *Public Health Report, 113,* 447–458.

Miller, N., Brewer, M. B., & Edwards, K. (1985). Cooperative interaction in desegregated settings: A laboratory analogue. *Journal of Social Issues, 41,* 63–79.

Miller, R. D., Maier, G. J., & Kaye, M. S. (1988). Orienting the staff of a new maximum security forensic facility. *Hospital and Community Psychiatry, 39,* 780–781.

Miller, R. L., & Klotz, D. (1993). HIV prevention with Latino hustlers. *The Community Psychologist, 27,* 43.

Miller, R. L., Klotz, D., & Eckholdt, H. (1998). HIV prevention with male prostitutes and patrons of hustler bars: Replication of an HIV prevention intervention. *American Journal of Community Psychology, 26,* 97–131.

Milne, A. (1985). Mediation or therapy—Which is it? In S. C. Grebe (Ed.), *Divorce and family mediation.* Rockville, MD: Aspen.

Mintzberg, H. (1979). *The structuring of organizations.* Englewood Cliffs, NJ: Prentice-Hall.

Mishara, B. L. (1997). Effects of different telephone intervention styles with suicidal callers at two suicide prevention centers: An empirical investigation. *American Journal of Community Psychology, 25,* 861–885.

Mitchell, R. E. (1982). Social networks and psychiatric clients: The personal and environmental context. *American Journal of Community Psychology, 10,* 387–402.

Mock, M. R. (1999). Cultural competency: Acts of justice in community mental health. *The Community Psychologist, 32,* 38–40.

Molnar, J. (1988). *Home is where the heart is: The crisis of homeless children and families in New York City.* New York: Bank Street College of Education.

Molnar, J. M., Rath, W. R., & Klein, T. P. (1990). Constantly compromised: The impact of homelessness on children. *Journal of Social Issues, 46,* 109–124.

Molnar, J. M., Rath, W. R., Klein, T. P., Lowe, C., & Hartmann, A. H. (1991). *Ill fares the land: The consequences of homelessness and chronic poverty for children and families in New York City.* New York: Bank Street College of Education.

Monroe, S. M., Roberts, J. E., Kupfer, D. J., & Frank, E. (1996). Life stress and treatment course of recurrent depression: Postrecovery associations with attrition, symptom course, and recurrence over 3 years. *Journal of Abnormal Psychology, 105,* 313–328.

Moos, R. H. (1979). *Evaluating educational environments.* San Francisco: Jossey-Bass.

Moos, R. H., Finney, J. W., & Cronkite, R. C. (1990). Alcoholism treatment: Context, process, and outcome. Oxford, England: Oxford University Press.

Morbidity and Mortality Weekly Report. (1997). *State-specific prevalence of cigarette smoking among adults, and children's and adolescents' exposure to environmental tobacco smoke—United States, 1996, 46,* 1038–1043. Atlanta, GA: Author.

Morbidity and Mortality Weekly Report. (1998a, September 11). *Preventing emerging infectious diseases: A strategy for the 21st century, 47* (No. RR-15). Atlanta, GA: Author.

Morbidity and Mortality Weekly Report. (1998b, October 9). *Incidence of initiation of cigarette smoking—United States, 47* (No. 39), 837–840. Atlanta, GA: Author.

Morbidity and Mortality Weekly Report. (1998c, August 14). *Youth Risk Behavior Surveillance—United States, 1997, 47* (No. SS-3). Atlanta, GA: Author.

Morgeson, F. P., Campion, M. A., & Maertz, C. P. (2001). Understanding pay satisfaction: The limits of a compensation system implementation. *Journal of Business & Psychology Special Issue, 16,* 133–149.

Morley, E., Rossman, S. B., Kopczynski, M., Buck, J., & Gouvis, C. (2000). Comprehensive responses to youth at risk: Interim findings from SafeFutures initiative. Washington, DC: Office of Juvenile Justice and Delinquency Prevention.

Morris, D. (2000). Devolution as if community matters. *The Responsive Community, 10,* 53–56.

Morrison, J. K. (1980). The public's current beliefs about mental illness: Serious obstacle to effective community psychology. *American Journal of Community Psychology, 8,* 697–707.

Morrison, T. G., O'Connor, W. E., Morrison, A., & Hill, S. A. (2001). Determinants of psychological well-being among unemployed women and men. *Psychology & Education: An Interdisciplinary Journal Special Issue, 38,* 34–41.

Morse, G. H., Calsyn, R. J., & Burger, G. K. (1992). Development and cross-validation of a system for classifying homeless persons. *Journal of Community Psychology, 20,* 228–242.

Moss, A. R. (2000). Epidemiology and the politics of needle exchange. *American Journal of Public Health, 90,* 1385–1387.

Moss, L. (1981). *Management stress.* Reading, MA: Addison-Wesley.

Mowbray, C. T. (1979). A study of patients treated as incompetent to stand trial. *Social Psychiatry, 14,* 31–39.

Mowbray, C. T. (1990). Community treatment for the seriously mentally ill: Is this community psychology? *American Journal of Community Psychology, 18,* 893–902.

Mowbray, C. T., Bybee, D., & Cohen, E. (1993). Describing the homeless mentally ill: Cluster analysis results. *American Journal of Community Psychology, 21,* 67–94.

Mowbray, C. T., Herman, S. E., & Hazel, K. (1992). Subgroups and differential treatment needs of young adults with long-term severe mental illness. *Psychosocial Rehabilitation Journal, 16,* 45–62.

Muha, D. G., & Cole, C. (1990). Dropout prevention and group counseling: A review of the literature. *High School Journal, 74,* 76–80.

Muir, E. (Winter 2000–2001). Smaller schools. *American Educator,* 40–46.

Muller, C. F. (1990). *Health care and gender.* New York: Russell Sage Foundation.

Muñoz, R. F., Glish, M., Soo-Hoo, T., & Robertson, J. (1982). The San Francisco Mood Survey project: Preliminary work toward the prevention of depression. *American Journal of Community Psychology, 10,* 317–329.

Murphy, E. (1983). The prognosis of depression in old age. *British Journal of Psychiatry, 142,* 111–119.

Myers, J. K., et al. (1984). Six month prevalence of psychiatric disorders in three communities. *Archives of General Psychiatry, 41,* 959–967.

Nadel, H., Spellmann, M., Alvarez-Canino, T., Lausell-Bryant, L., & Landsberg, G. (1996). The cycle of violence and victimization: A study of the school-based intervention of multidisciplinary youth violence-prevention program. *American Journal of Preventive Medicine, 12,* 109–119.

Naisbitt, J., & Aburdene, P. (1990). *Megatrends 2000.* New York: William Morrow.

NASTAD HIV Prevention Community Planning Bulletin. (1998, November). *Focus on HIV prevention in rural communities.* Washington, DC: Author.

Nation's Health, The. (1998, October). *DWI deaths reach historic low: Proportion falls below 40 percent of first time on record,.* Washington, DC: Author.

National Association of State Boards of Education. (1988). *Right from the start.* Alexandria, VA: Author.

National Behavioral Science Research Agenda Committee. (1992, February). Human capital initiative: Report of the National Behavior Science Research Agenda Committee: *APS Observer.* Special issue.

National Cancer Institute. (1991). *Strategies to control tobacco use in the United States: A blueprint for public health action in the 1990s.* NIH Publication Number 92–3316. Washington, DC: U.S. Department of Health and Human Services.

National Center for Education Statistics (2001). *Dropout rates in the United States: 1999.* http://nces.ed.gov/pubs2001/ dropout/execsumm2.asp

National Center for Education Statistics. (1998, November). *Indicators of school crime and safety, 1998: Highlights.* www/ /nces.ed.gov/pubs98/safety/highlights.html

National Center for Education Statistics. (2001). *Dropout rates in the United States: 1999.* http://nces.ed.gov/pubs 2001/ dropoutexecsumm2.asp

National Center for Health Statistics. (1989). *Smoking and other tobacco use: United States, 1987,* by C. A. Schoenborn & G. Boyd. Vital and health statistics. Series 10, No. 169. DHHS Publication Number (PHS) 89–1597. Hyattsville, MD: U.S. Department of Health and Human Services.

National Center on Addiction and Substance Abuse at Columbia University. (1998). *Behind bars: Substance abuse and America's prison population.* Columbia University. New York: Author.

National Coalition for the Homeless. (1999). *NCH Fact Sheets 1–3.* www.nationalhomeless.org

National Commission on AIDS. (1993). *Behavioral and social sciences and the HIV/AIDS epidemic.* Washington, DC: Author.

National Crime Prevention Council. (1989). The success of community crime prevention. *Canadian Journal of Criminology, 31,* 487–506.

National Crime Survey. (1991). *National crime survey preliminary press release.* March 24.

National Highway Traffic Safety Administration. (1995, February). *Repeat DWI offenders in the United States.* NHTSA Technology Series No. 85. Washington, DC: Author.

National Highway Traffic Safety Administration. (1996). *Traffic safety facts 1995: Alcohol.* Washington, DC: Author.

National Highway Traffic Safety Administration. (1997). *Setting limits, saving lives: The case for .08% BAC laws.* Pub. No. DOT HS 808 524. Washington, DC: Author.

National Household Survey on Drug Abuse. (1999). Rockville, MD: Substance Abuse and Services Administration.

National Law Center on Homelessness and Poverty. (1998). *Homelessness and poverty in America.* www.nlchp.org/ h&pusa.htm

Nation's Health, The. (1998, October). *DWI deaths reach historic low: Proportion falls below 40 percent of first time on record.* Washington, DC: Author.

Nelson, D. W., & Cohen, L. H. (1983). Locus of control and control perceptions and the relationship between life stress and psychological disorder. *American Journal of Community Psychology, 11,* 705–722.

Nelson, G. (1990). Women's life strains, social support, coping, and positive and negative affect: Cross-sectional and longitudinal tests of the two-factor theory of emotional well-being. *Journal of Community Psychology, 18,* 239–263.

Nelson, G., Ochocka, J., Griffin, K., & Lord, J. (1998). "Nothing about me, without me." Participatory action research with self-help/mutual aid organizations for psychiatric consumer survivors. *American Journal of Community Psychology, 26,* 881–912.

Nemecek, S. (1999). Unequal health. *Scientific American, 280,* 40–41.

Nemoto, T., Wong, F. Y., Ching, A., Chng, C. L., Bouey, P., Hendrickson, M., & Sember, R. E. (1998). HIV seroprevalence, risk behaviors, and cognitive factors among Asian and Pacific Islander American men who have sex with men: A summary and critique of empirical studies and methodological studies. *AIDS Education and Prevention, 10 (Supplement A),* 31–47.

Nettler, G. (1980). Definition of crime. In D. H. Kelly (Ed.), *Criminal behavior: Readings in criminology.* New York: St. Martin's Press.

Neuman, G. A., Edwards, J. E., & Raju, N. S. (1989). Organizational development interventions: A meta-analysis of their effects on satisfaction and other attitudes. *Personnel Psychology, 42,* 461–489.

New York State Department of Correctional Services (1992). *Characteristics of inmates under custody.* Albany, New York: Author.

New York State Employee Assistance Program Manual. (1990). Albany, NY: Governor's Office of Employee Relations.

Newbrough, J. R., & Chavis, D. M. (Eds.). (1986). Psychological sense of community, I: Forward. *American Journal of Community Psychology, 14,* 3–5.

NICHD Early Child Care Research Network. (2001). Nonmaternal care and family factors in early development: An overview of the NICHD Study of Early Child Care. *Journal of Applied Developmental Psychology, 22,* 457–492.

Nikelly, A. G. (1990, August). *Political activism: A new dimension for community psychology.* Paper presented to the Annual Convention of the American Psychological Association, Boston, MA.

Nimmer, J. G., & Geller, E. S. (1988). Motivating safety belt use at a community hospital: An effective integration of incentive and commitment strategies. *American Journal of Community Psychology, 16,* 381–394.

Nishimura, H., & Suzuki, S. (1986). Citizen-helping role of the police and inhabitants of the community. *Reports of National Research Institute of Police Science, 27,* 64–74.

Norris, F. H., & Kaniasty, K. (1992). A longitudinal study of the effects of various crime prevention strategies on criminal victimization, fear of crime, and psychological distress. *American Journal of Community Psychology, 20,* 625–648.

Novotney, L. C., Mertinko, E., Lange, J., & Baker, T. K. (September 2000). Juvenile mentoring program: A progress review. *Juvenile Justice Bulletin,* 1–8.

Nugent, W. R., Umbreit, M. S., Wiinamaki, L., & Paddock, J. (2001). Participation in victim-offender mediation and reoffense: Successful replications? *Research on Social Work Practice, 11,* 5–23.

O'Neill, P. (1989). Responsible to whom? Responsible for what? Some ethical issues in community intervention. *American Journal of Community Psychology, 17,* 379–383.

O'Neill, P., Duffy, C., Enman, M., Blackmer, E., & Goodwin, J. (1988). Cognition and citizen participation in social action. *Journal of Applied Sociology, 18,* 1067–1083.

O'Sullivan, R. G. (1990). Validating a method to identify at-risk middle school students for participation in a dropout prevention program. *Journal of Early Adolescence, 10,* 209–220.

Office of Juvenile Justice and Delinquency Prevention. (2001). *OJJDP research 2000.* Washington, DC: Author.

Office of National Drug Control Policy. (1998). *The national drug control strategy, 1998. A ten-year plan.* Washington, DC: Author.

Office on Smoking and Health. (1989). *Reducing the health consequences of smoking: 25 years of progress. A report of the Surgeon General.* DHHS Publication Number (CDC) 89–8411. Washington, DC: U.S. Department of Health and Human Services.

Okun, M. A., Sandler, I. N., & Bauman, D. J. (1988). Buffer and booster effects as event-support transactions. *American Journal of Community Psychology, 16,* 435–449.

Oldridge, M. L., & Hughes, I. C. T. (1992). Psychological well-being in families with a member suffering from schizophrenia. *British Journal of Psychiatry, 167,* 249–251.

Olds, D. (1997). The prenatal early infancy project: Preventing child abuse and neglect in the context of promoting maternal and child health. In D. A. Wolfe, R. J. McMahon, & R. D. Peters (Eds.), *Child abuse: New directions in prevention and treatment across the lifespan.* Thousand Oaks, CA: Sage.

Olds, D., Henderson, C., Chamberlin, R., & Tatelbaum, R. (1986). Preventing child abuse and neglect: A randomized trial of nurse home visitation. *Pediatrics, 78,* 65–78.

Olds, D., Hill, P., & Rumsey, E. (November 1998). Prenatal and early childhood nurse home visitation. *Juvenile Delinquency Bulletin,* 1–7.

Olfson, M. (1990). Assertive community treatment: An evaluation of experimental evidence. *Hospital Community Psychiatry, 41,* 634–641.

Olson, M. R. (1991). Supportive growth experiences of beginning teachers. *Alberta Journal of Educational Research, 37,* 19–30.

Olson, M., & Cohen, A. A. (1986). An alternative approach to the training of residential treatment. *Residential Group Care and Treatment, 3,* 65–88.

Oman, D., Thoresen, C. E., & McMahon, K. (1999). Volunteering and mortality among the community-dwelling elderly. *Journal of Health Psychology, 4,* 301–315.

Opulente, M., & Mattaini, M. A. (1997). Toward welfare that works. *Research on Social Work Practice, 7,* 115–135.

Orthner, D. K., & Randolph, K. A. (1999). Welfare reform and high school dropout patterns for children. *Children and Youth Services Review, 21,* 881–900.

Ortmann, R. (2000). The effectiveness of social therapy in prison—A randomized experiment. *Crime & Delinquency Special Issue: Advising Criminal Justice Policy Through Experimental Evaluations: International Views, 46,* 214–232.

Oskamp, S. (1984). *Applied social psychology.* Englewood Cliffs, NJ: Prentice-Hall.

Ostermeyer, M. (1991). Conducting the mediation. In K. G. Duffy, J. W. Grosch, & P. V. Oliczak (Eds.), *Community mediation: A handbook for practitioners and researchers.* New York: Guilford.

Otto, R. K., Greenstein, J. J., Johnson, M. K., & Friedman, R. M. (1992). Prevalence of mental disorders among youth in juvenile justice system. In J. J. Cocozza (Ed.), *Responding to the mental health needs of youth in the juvenile justice system* (pp. 7–48). Seattle, WA: The National Coalition for the Mentally Ill in the Criminal Justice System.

Oxley, D. (2000). The school reform movement. In J. Rappaport & E. Seidman (Eds.), *Handbook of community psychology.* New York: Plenum.

Palmer, T., & Wedge, R. (1989). California's juvenile probation camps: Findings and implications. *Crime and Delinquency, 35,* 234–253.

Pargament, K. I. (1986). Refining fit: Conceptual and methodological challenges. *American Journal of Community Psychology, 14,* 677–684.

Parks, G. (October 2000). The High/Scope Perry Preschool Project. *Juvenile Justice Bulletin,* 1–8.

Patrikakou, E., & Weissberg, R. P. (2000). Parents' perceptions of teacher outreach and parent involvement in children's education. *Journal of Prevention & Intervention in the Community, 20,* 103–119.

Patterson, D. (1990). Gaining access to community resources: Breaking the cycle of adolescent pregnancy. *Journal of Health Care for the Poor and Undeserved, 1,* 147–149.

Patteson, D. M., & Barnard, K. E. (1990). Parenting of low birth weight infants: A review of issues and interventions. *Infant Mental Health Journal, 11,* 37–56.

Paulus, P. B., McCain, G., & Cox, V. C. (1978). Death rates, psychiatric commitments, blood pressure, and perceived crowding as a function of institutional crowding. *Environmental Psychology and Nonverbal Behavior, 3,* 107–116.

Pear, R. (1998, November 26). *The New York Times,* p. A20.

Pedro-Carroll, J. (1997). The children of divorce intervention program: Fostering resilient outcomes for school-aged children. In G. W. Albee & T. P. Gullotta

(Eds.), *Primary prevention works*. Thousand Oaks, CA: Sage.

Pentz, M. A. (2000). Institutionalizing community-based prevention through policy change. *Journal of Community Psychology, 28,* 257–270.

Perkins, C. A. (1997). *Special report: Age patterns of victims of serious violent crimes*. Washington, DC: Bureau of Justice Statistics.

Perkins, D. D. (1988). The use of social science in public interest litigation: A role for community psychologists. *American Journal of Community Psychology, 16,* 465–485.

Perkins, D. D. (1995). Speaking truth to power: Empowerment ideology as social intervention and policy. *American Journal of Community Psychology, 23,* 765–794.

Perkins, D. D., Brown, B. B., & Taylor, R. B. (1996). The ecology of empowerment: Predicting participation in community organizations. *Journal of Social Issues, 52,* 85–110.

Perkins, D. D., Florin, P., Rich, R. C., Wandersman, A., & Chavis, D. M. (1990). Participation and the social and physical environment of residential blocks: Crime and community context. *American Journal of Community Psychology, 18,* 83–115.

Perkins, D. D., Meeks, J. W., & Taylor, R. B. (1992). The physical environment of street blocks and resident perceptions of crime and disorder: Implications for theory and measurement. *Journal of Environmental Psychology, 12,* 21–34.

Perkins, D. D., & Taylor, R. B. (1996). Ecological assessments of community disorder: Their relationship to fear of crime and theoretical implications. *American Journal of Community Psychology, 24,* 63–107.

Perkins, D. D., & Zimmerman, M. A. (1995). Empowerment theory, research, and application. *American Journal of Community Psychology, 23,* 569–579.

Peterson, J. L. (1998). Introduction to the special issue: HIV/AIDS prevention through community psychology. *American Journal of Community Psychology, 26,* 1–5.

Pettigrew, T. F. (1998). Intergroup contact theory. *Annual Review of Psychology, 49,* 65–85.

Pettigrew, T., & Meertens, R. W. (1995). Subtle and blatant prejudice in Western Europe. *European Journal of Social Psychology, 25,* 57–75.

Phares, J. E. (1991). *Introduction to personality*. New York: HarperCollins.

Phares, J. E., & Chaplin, W. F. (1997). *Introduction to personality*. New York: Longman.

Phelan, J. C., Link, B. G., Moore, R. E., & Steuven, A. (1997). The stigma of homelessness: The impact of the label "homeless" on attitudes toward poor persons. *Social Psychology Quarterly, 60,* 323–337.

Phillip, K., & Hendry, L. B. (2000). Making sense of mentoring or mentoring making sense? Reflections on the mentoring process by adult mentors with young people. *Journal of Community & Applied Social Psychology, 10,* 211–223.

Phillips, D. A. (2000). Social policy and community psychology. In J. Rappaport & E. Seidman (Eds.), *Handbook of community psychology*. New York: Plenum.

Phillips, D. A., Howes, C., & Whitebook, M. (1992). The social policy context of child care: Effects on quality. *Journal of Community Psychology, 20,* 25–50.

Pilisuk, M., & Acredolo, C. (1988). Fear of technological hazards: One concern or many? *Social Behavior, 3,* 17–24.

Pinchot, G., & Pinchot, E. (1993). *The end of bureaucracy and the rise of the intelligent organization*. San Francisco: Berrett-Koehler.

Pines, A., & Guendelman, S. (1995). Exploring the relevance of burnout to Mexican blue-collar women. *Journal of Vocational Behavior, 47,* 1–20.

Pittman, R. (1986). Importance of personal social factors as potential means for reducing high school dropout. *High School Journal, 70,* 7–13.

Piven, F. F., & Cloward, R. A. (1996). Welfare reform and the new class war. In M. B. Lykes, A. Banuazizi, R. Liem, & M. Morris (Eds.), *Myths about the powerless: Contesting social inequalities*. Philadelphia: Temple University Press.

Pogrebin, M. R., & Poole, E. D. (1987). Deinstitutionalization and increased arrest rates among the mentally disordered. *Journal of Psychiatry and Law, 15,* 117–127.

Pogrebin, M. R., & Regoli, R. M. (1985). Editorial. Mentally disordered persons in jail. *Journal of Community Psychology, 13,* 409–412.

Poister, T. H., & Streib, G. (1989). Management tools in municipal government: Trends over the past decade. *Public Administration Review, 49,* 240–248.

Pol, L.G., & Thomas, R. K. (2001). *The demography of health and health care (2nd ed.)*. New York: Kluwer Academic/ Plenum Publishers.

Pong, S. L., & Ju, D. B. (2000). The effects of change in family structure and income on dropping out of middle and high school. *Journal of Family Issues, 21,* 147–169.

Popper, K. R. (1968). *The logic of scientific discovery*. New York: Harper Torchbooks.

Porras, J. L., & Robertson, P. J. (1992). Organization development: Theory, practice, and research. In M. D. Dunnette & L. M. Hough (Eds.), *Handbook of industrial and organizational psychology* (2nd ed.). Palo Alto, CA: Consulting Psychologists Press.

Porter, B. E. (2001). Empowerment-based interventions are not useful. *The Community Psychologist, 34,* 22–23.

Porter, G. (2001). Workaholic tendencies and the high potential for stress among coworkers. *International Journal of Stress Management Special Issue: Workaholism in Organizations, 8,* 147–164.

Prestby, J., & Wandersman, A. (1985). An empirical exploration of a framework of organizational viability: Maintaining block organization. *Journal of Applied Behavioral Sciences, 21,* 287–305.

Prestby, J., Wandersman, A., Florin, P., Rich, R., & Chavis, D. (1990). Benefits, costs, incentive management and participation in volunteer organizations: A means to understanding and promoting empowerment. *American Journal of Community Psychology, 18,* 117–150.

Pretty, G. M., & McCarthy, M. (1991). Exploring the psychological sense of community among women and men of the corporation. *Journal of Community Psychology, 19,* 351–361.

Pretty, G. M., McCarthy, M. E., & Catano, V. M. (1992). Psychological environments and burnout: Gender considerations within the corporation. *Journal of Organizational Behavior, 13,* 701–711.

Prezza, M., M., Amici, M., Tiziana, R., & Tedeschi, G. (2001). Sense of community referred to the whole town: Its relations with neighboring, loneliness, life satisfaction, and area of residence. *Journal of Community Psychology, 29,* 29–52.

Price, R. H. (1985). Work and community. *American Journal of Community Psychology, 13,* 1–12.

Price, R. H. (1990). Wither participation and empowerment? *American Journal of Community Psychology, 18,* 163–167.

Price, R. H., Cowen, E. L., Lorion, R. P., & Ramos-McKay, J. (1988). *14 ounces of prevention.* Washington, DC: American Psychological Association.

Priddy, J. M., & Knisely, J. S. (1982). Older adults as peer counselors: Considerations in counselor training with the elderly. *Educational Gerontology, 8,* 53–62.

Primavera, J. (1999). The unintended consequences of volunteerism: Positive outcomes for those who serve. *Journal of Prevention & Intervention in the Community, 18,* 125–140.

Prince-Embury, S., & Rooney, J. F. (1995). Psychological adaptation among residents following restart of Three Mile Island. *Journal of Traumatic Stress, 8,* 47–59.

PsychInfo. (2002). Database at American Psychological Association, Washington, DC.

Public Health Service. (1980). *Toward a national plan for the chronic mentally ill.* Washington, DC: U.S. Department of Health and Human Services.

Putman, R. B. (1986). Important personal, social factors as potential means for reducing high school dropout rates. *High School Journal, 70,* 7–13.

Rabkin, J. G., & Ferrando, S. (1997). A "second life" agenda: Psychiatric research issues raised by protease inhibitor treatments for people with the human immunodeficiency virus or the acquired immunodeficiency syndrome. *Archives of General Psychiatry, 54,* 1049–1053.

Rafferty, Y. (1990). Testimony on behalf of Advocates for Children of New York and the American Psychological Association to the oversight hearings on homelessness. House of Representatives, Washington, DC.

Rafferty, Y., & Shinn, M. (1991). The impact of homelessness on children. *American Psychologist, 46,* 1170–1179.

Randolph, W. A. (2000). Re-thinking empowerment: Why is it so hard to achieve? *Organizational Dynamics, 29,* 94–107.

Rapkin, B. D., & Fischer, K. (1992). Personal goals of older adults: Issues in assessment and prediction. *Psychology and Aging, 7,* 127–137.

Rappaport, J. (1977). *Community psychology: Values, research, and action.* New York: Holt, Rinehart and Winston.

Rappaport, J. (1981). In praise of paradox: A social policy of empowerment over prevention. *American Journal of Community Psychology, 9,* 1–25.

Rappaport, J. (1987). Terms of empowerment/ Exemplars of prevention: Toward a theory for community psychology. *American Journal of Community Psychology, 15,* 121–148.

Rappaport, J. (1990). Research methods and the empowerment social agenda. In P. Tolan, C. Keys, F. Chertok, & L. Jason (Eds.), *Researching community psychology: Issues of theory and methods.* Washington, DC: American Psychological Association.

Rappaport, J. (2000). Community narratives: Tales of terror and joy. *American Journal of Community Psychology, 28,* 1– 24.

Rappaport, J., Seidman, E., Toro, P., McFadden, L. S., Reischl, T. M., Roberts, L. J., Salem, D. A., Stein, C. H., & Yimmerman, M. (1985). Collaborative research of a mutual help organization. *Social Policy, 15,* 12–24.

Rappaport, J., Swift, C., & Hess, P. (Eds.). (1984). *Studies in empowerment: Steps toward understanding and action.* New York: Haworth.

Ratiu, I. S. (1986). A workshop on managing in a multicultural environment. Special issue: International management and development. *Management Education and Development, 17,* 252–256.

Raviv, A., Erel, O., Fox, N. A., Leavitt, L. A., Raviv, A., Dar, I., Shahinfar, A., & Greenbaum, C. W. (2001). Individual measurement of exposure to everyday violence among elementary schoolchildren across various settings. *Journal of Community Psychology, 29,* 117–140.

Redeinstitutionalization. (1986, August 25). *The New York Times,* p. A18.

Redman, W. K., Cullari, S., & Farris, H. E. (1985). An analysis of some important tasks and phases in consultation. *Journal of Community Psychology, 13,* 375–386.

Reich, J. W., & Zautra, A. J. (1991). Experimental and measurement approaches to internal control in at-risk older adults. *Journal of Social Issues, 47,* 143–158.

Rein, M., & Schon, D. A. (1977). Problem setting in policy research. In C. H. Weiss (Ed.), *Using social research in public policy making.* Lexington, MA: Lexington Books.

Reissman, F. (1990). Restructuring help: A human services paradigm for the 1990s. *American Journal of Community Psychology, 18,* 221–230.

Remafedi, G., French, S., Story, M., Resnick, M. D., & Blum, R. (1998). The relationship between suicide risk and sexual orientation: Results of a population-based study. *American Journal of Public Health, 88,* 57–60.

Rennison, C. M. (August 2000). Criminal victimization 1999: Changes 1998–99 with trends 1993–1999. *National Crime Victimization Survey,* 1–15.

Reppucci, N. D. (1987). Prevention and ecology: Teen-age pregnancy, child sexual abuse, and organized youth sports. *American Journal of Community Psychology, 15,* 1–22.

Reyes, O., & Jason, L. A. (1991). An evaluation of a high school dropout prevention program. *Journal of Community Psychology, 19,* 221–230.

Reyes, O., Gillock, K. L., Kobus, K., & Sanchez, B. (2000). A longitudinal examination of the transition into senior high school for adolescents from urban, low-income status, and predominantly minority backgrounds. *American Journal of Community Psychology, 28,* 519–544.

Reynolds, A. J. (1991). Early schooling of children at risk. *American Educational Research Journal, 28,* 392–422.

Richey, C. A., Lovell, M. L., & Reid, K. (1991). Interpersonal skill training to enhance social support among women at risk for child maltreatment. *Children and Youth Services Review, 13,* 41–59.

Rickel, A. U. (1986). Prescriptions for a new generation: Early life interventions. *American Journal of Community Psychology, 14,* 1–15.

Rickel, A. U. (1989). *Teen pregnancy and parenting.* New York: Hemisphere/Taylor & Francis.

Rickel, A. U., & Burgio, J. C. (1982). Assessing social competencies in lower income preschool children. *American Journal of Community Psychology, 10,* 635–647.

Riga, J., & Morganti, J. B. (1992). *Rated differences in territorial barriers and exterior maintenance in owner-occupied vs. rental-only housing.* Paper presented at the meeting of the Eastern Psychological Association, Boston, MA.

Riger, S. (1985). Crime as an environmental stressor. *Journal of Community Psychology, 13,* 270–280.

Riger, S. (1989). The politics of community intervention. *American Journal of Community Psychology, 17,* 379–383.

Riger, S. (1990). Ways of knowing and organizational approaches to community psychology. In P. Tolan, C. Keys, F. Chertak, & L. Jason (Eds.), *Researching community psychology.* Washington, DC: American Psychological Association.

Riger, S. (1993). What's wrong with empowerment. *American Journal of Community Psychology, 21,* 279–292.

Rivlin, L. G., & Imbimbo, J. E. (1989). Self-help efforts in a squatter community. *American Journal of Community Psychology, 17,* 705–728.

Rixon, R., & Erwin, P. G. (1999). Measure of effectiveness in a short-term interpersonal cognitive problem-solving programme. *Counseling Psychology Quarterly, 12,* 87–93.

Roak, K. S. (1991). Facilitating friendship formation in late life: Puzzles and challenges. *American Journal of Community Psychology, 19,* 103–110.

Roberts, D. G. (1991). "I don't get no respect." *Organization Development Journal, 9,* 55–60.

Roberts, M. C., Fanurik, D., & Wilson, D. R. (1988). A community program to reward children's use of seat belts. *American Journal of Community Psychology, 16,* 395–407.

Robertson, P. J., Roberts, D. R., & Porras, J. I. (1993). Dynamics of planned organizational change: Assessing empirical support for a theoretical model. *Academy of Management Journal, 36,* 619–634.

Robins, L. N., et al. (1984). Lifetime prevalence rates of DIS/DSM-III disorders. *Archives of General Psychiatry, 41,* 952–958.

Robinson, B. E., & Kelley, L. (1998). Adult children of workaholics: Self-concept, anxiety, depression, and locus of control. *American Journal of Family Therapy, 26,* 223–238.

Robinson, M. B. (2000). From research to policy: Preventing residential burglary through a systems approach. *American Journal of Criminal Justice, 24,* 169–179.

Robinson, W. L. (1990). Data feedback and communication to the host setting. In P. Tolan, C. Keys, F. Chertak, & L. Jason (Eds.), *Researching community psychology: Issues of theory and methods.* Washington, DC: American Psychological Association.

Rodgers, R., & Hunter, J. E. (1991). Impact of management by objectives on organizational productivity. *Journal of Applied Psychology, 76,* 332–336.

Rodin, J., & Langer, E. J. (1977). Long-term effects of a control-relevant intervention with the institutionalized aged. *Journal of Personality and Social Psychology, 35,* 897–902.

Rodin, J., Timko, C., & Harris, S. (1986). The construct of control: Biological and psychological correlates. In C. Eisdorfer, M. P. Lawson, & G. I. Maddoy (Eds.), *Annual review of gerontology and geriatrics.* New York: Springer.

Rodwin, M. A. (1997). The neglected remedy: Strengthening consumer voice in managed care. *The American Prospect, 34,* 45–50.

Roesch, R. (1988). Community psychology and the law. *American Journal of Community Psychology, 14,* 451–463.

Roesch, R. (1995). Creating change in the legal system. *Law and Human Behavior, 19,* 325–343.

Roethlisberger, F. J., & Dickson, W. J. (1939). *Management and the worker: An account of a research program conducted by the Western Electric Company, Chicago.* Cambridge, MA: Harvard University Press.

Rogers, E. M. (1982). *Diffusion of innovations.* New York: Free Press.

Rogler, L. H., Cortes, D. E., & Malgady, R. G. (1991). Acculturation and mental health status among Hispanics. *American Psychology, 46,* 585–597.

Rokeach, M. (1960). *The open and closed mind.* New York: Basic Books.

Roll, J. M., & Habemeier, W. (1991, April). *Gender differences in coping with potential victimization.* Paper presented at the Annual Meeting of the Eastern Psychological Association, New York.

Rose-Gold, M. S. (1992). Intervention strategies for counseling at-risk adolescents in rural school districts. *School Counselor, 39,* 122–126.

Rosenfeld, S. (1991). Homelessness and rehospitalization: The importance of housing for the chronic mentally ill. *Journal of Community Psychology, 19,* 60–69.

Rosenhan, D. L. (1973). On being sane in insane places. *Science, 179,* 250–258.

Rosenthal, J. A., & Glass, G. V. (1990). Comparative impacts of alternatives to adolescent placement. *Journal of Social Services Research, 13,* 19–37.

Rosenthal, R., & Jacobson, L. V. (1968). *Pygmalion in the classroom: Teacher expectation and pupils' intellectual development.* New York: Holt.

Rosentock, I. M. (1986). Why people use health services. *Milburn Memorial Fund Quarterly, 44,* 94–127.

Rosenzweig, S. (1954). A trans-valuation of psychotherapy: A reply to Hans Eysenck. *Journal of Abnormal and Social Psychology, 49,* 298–304.

Ross, C. E., & Jang, S. J. (2000). Neighborhood disorder, fear, and mistrust: The buffering role of social ties with neighbors. *American Journal of Community Psychology, 28,* 401–420.

Ross, E. C. (2000). Will managed care ever deliver on its promises? Managed care, public policy, and consumers of mental health services. *Administrative Policy in Mental Health, 28,* 7–22.

Ross, R. R., Altmaier, E. M., & Russell, D. W. (1989). Job stress, social support, and burnout among counseling center staff. *Journal of Counseling Psychology, 36,* 464–470.

Rossell, C. H. (1988). How effective are voluntary plans with magnet schools? *Educational Evaluation and Policy Analysis, 10,* 325–342.

Rossi, P. H. (1989). *Down and out in America: The origins of homelessness.* Chicago: University of Chicago Press.

Rossi, P. H. (1990). The old homeless and the new homelessness in historical perspective. *American Psychologist, 45,* 954–959.

Rossi, P. H., Fisher, G. A., & Willis, G. (1987). The urban homeless: Estimating composition and size. *Science, 235,* 1336–1341.

Rotheram-Borus, M. J., & Fernandez, M. I. (1995). Sexual orientation and developmental challenges experienced by gay and lesbian youths. *Suicide Life Threat Behavior, 23 (Supplement),* 26–34.

Rotheram-Borus, M. J., Hunter, J., & Rosario, M. (1994). Suicidal behavior and gay-related stress among gay and bisexual male adolescents. *Journal of Adolescent Research, 9,* 498–508.

Rothman, J. (1974). Three models of community organization practice. In F. Cox, J. Erlich, J. Rothman, & J. Tropman (Eds.), *Strategies of community organization: A book of readings* (2nd ed.). Itasca, IL: Peacock.

Rotter, J. B. (1966). Generalized expectancies for internal versus external control of reinforcement. *Psychological Monographs, 80* (Whole No. 609).

Rountree, P. W. (1998). A reexamination of the crime-fear linkage. *Journal of Research in Crime and Delinquency, 35,* 341–372.

Ruehlman, L. S., & Karoly, P. (1991). With a little flak from my friends: Development and preliminary validation of the Test of Negative Social Exchange (TENSE). *Psychological Assessment, 3,* 97–104.

Ruffini, J. L., & Todd, H. F. (1979). A network model for leadership development among the elderly. *Gerontologist, 17,* 158–162.

Russell, S. T., & Joyner, K. (2001). Adolescent sexual orientation and suicide risk: Evidence from a national study. *American Journal of Public Health, 91,* 1276–1281.

Salazar, J. M. (1988, August). *Psychology and social change in Latin America.* Paper presented to the Annual Convention of the American Psychological Association, Atlanta, GA.

Salem, D. A. (1990). Community-based services and resources: The significance of choice and diversity. *American Journal of Community Psychology, 18,* 909–915.

Salmi, S., Voeten, M. J. M., & Keskinen, E. (2000). Relation between police image and police visibility. *Journal of Community and Applied Social Psychology, 10,* 433–447.

Sammons, M. T., Gorny, S. W., Zinner, E. S., & Allen, R. P. (2000). Prescriptive authority for psychologists: A consensus of support. *Professional Psychology: Research & Practice, 31,* 604–609.

Sampson, R. J., & Cohen, J. (1988). Deterrent effects of the police on crime: A replication and theoretical expansion. *Law and Society Review, 22,* 163–189.

Sampson, R. J., Raudenbush, S. W., & Earls, F. (1997). Neighborhoods and violent crime: A multilevel study of collective efficacy. *Science, 277,* 918–924.

Sandler, I. N., & Keller, P. A. (1984). Trends observed in community psychology training descriptions. *American Journal of Community Psychology, 12,* 157–164.

Sansone, R. A., Fine, M.A., & Chew, R. (1988). A longitudinal analysis of the experiences of nursing staff on an inpatient eating disorder unit. *International Journal of Eating Disorders, 7,* 125–131.

Sarason, I. G. (1980). Life stress, self-preoccupation and social supports. In I. G. Sarason & C. D. Speelberger (Eds.), *Stress and anxiety* (Vol. 7). Washington, DC: Halstead.

Sarason, S. B. (1972). *The creation of settings & the future societies.* San Francisco: Jossey-Bass.

Sarason, S. B. (1974). *The psychological sense of community: Prospects for a community psychology.* San Francisco: Jossey-Bass.

Sarason, S. B. (1976a). Community psychology and the anarchist insight. *American Journal of Community Psychology, 4,* 246–259.

Sarason, S. B. (1976b). Community psychology, networks, and Mr. Everyman. *American Journal of Community Psychology, 18,* 317–328.

Sarason, S. B. (1978). The nature of problem solving in social action. *American Psychologist, 33,* 370–380.

Sarason, S. B. (1983). *Schooling in America: Scapegoat and salvation.* New York: Free Press.

Sarason, S. B. (1997). The public schools: America's Achilles heel. American *Journal of Community Psychology, 25,* 771–786.

Sarason, S. B., Carroll, C. F., Maton, K., Cohen, S., & Lorentz, E. (1977). *Human services and resource networks.* San Francisco: Jossey-Bass.

Sarason, S. B., & Klaber, M. (1985). The school as a social situation. *Annual Review of Psychology, 36,* 115–140.

Sarata, B. P. V. (1984). Changes in staff satisfactions after increases in pay, autonomy, and participation. *American Journal of Community Psychology, 12,* 431–445.

Scahill, M. C. (November 2000). Female delinquency cases, 1997. *OJJDP Fact Sheet,* 1–2.

Scales, P. (1990). Developing capable young people: An alternative strategy for prevention programs. *American Journal of Community Psychology, 10,* 420–438.

Scales, P. C. (1987). How we can prevent teen pregnancy (and why it's not the real problem). *Journal of Sex Education and Therapy, 13,* 12–15.

Scarr, S. (1998). American child care today. *American Psychologist, 53,* 95–108.

Scarr, S., & Eisenberg, M. (1993). Child care research: Issues, perspectives, and results. *Annual Review of Psychology, 44,* 613–644.

Schaubroeck, J., Ganster, D. C., & Kemmerer, B. E. (1994). Job complexity, "type A" behavior, and cardiovascular disorder: A prospective study. *Academy of Management Journal, 37,* 426–439.

Schein, E. H. (1985). How culture, forms, develops and changes. In R. H. Kilmann, M. J. Saxton, & R. Serpa (Eds.), *Gaining control of the corporate culture.* San Francisco: Jossey-Bass.

Schein, E. H. (1990). Organizational culture. *American Psychologist, 45,* 109–119.

Schiaffino, K. M. (1991). Fine-tuning theory to the needs of the world: Responding to Heller et al. *American Journal of Community Psychology, 19,* 99–102.

Schilling, R. F., Ivanoff, A., El-Bassel, N., Soffa, F. (1997). HIV-related behaviors in transitional correctional settings. *Criminal Justice and Behavior, 24,* p. 261.

Schinke, S. P. (1998). Preventing teenage pregnancy: Translating research knowledge. *Journal of Human Behavior in the Social Environment, 1,* 53–66.

Schmidt, G., & Weiner, B. (1988). An attributional-affect-action theory of behavior. Replications of judgments of helping. *Personality and Social Psychology Bulletin, 14,* 610–621.

Schmolling, P., Jr., Youkeles, M., & Burger, W. R. (1989). *Human services in contemporary America.* Pacific Grove, CA: Brooks Cole.

Schneider, A. L. (1986). Restitution and recidivism rates of juvenile offenders: Results from four experimental studies. *Criminology, 24,* 533–552.

Schoenrade, P. A., Batson, C. D., Brandt, J. R., & Toud, R. E. (1986). Attachment, accountability, and maturation to benefit another not in distress. *Journal of Personality and Social Psychology, 51,* 557–563.

Schubert, M. A., & Borkman, T. J. (1991). An organizational typology for self-help groups. *American Journal of Community Psychology, 19,* 769–788.

Schultz, D., & Schultz, S. (1990). *Psychology and industry today.* New York: Macmillan.

Schultz, D., & Schultz, S. E. (1998). *Psychology and work today.* Upper Saddle River, NJ: Prentice-Hall.

Schulz, R., & Heckhausen, J. (1996). A life span model of successful aging. *American Psychologist, 51,* 702–714.

Schur, L. A., & Kruse, D. L. (2000). What determines voter turnout? Lessons from citizens with disabilities. *Social Science Quarterly, 81,* 571–587.

Schwarzer, R., & Leppin, A. (1991). Social support and health: A theoretical and empirical overview. *Journal of Social and Personal Relations, 8,* 99–127.

Schweitzer, J. H., Kim, J. W., & Mackin, J. R. (1999). The impact of the built environment on crime and fear of crime in urban neighborhoods. *Journal of Urban Technology, 6,* 59–74.

Sciegaj, M., Garnick, D. W., Horgan, C. M., Merrick, E. L., Goldin, D., Urato, M., & Hodgkin, D. (2001). Employee assistance programs among Fortune 500 firms. *Employee Assistance Quarterly Special Issue, 16,* 25–35.

Scileppi, J. A., Teed, E. L., & Torres, R. D. (2000). *Community psychology: A common sense approach to mental health.* Upper Saddle River, NJ: Prentice Hall.

Scott, E. K., London, A. S., & Edin, K. (2000). Looking to the future: Welfare- reliant women talk about their job aspirations in the context of welfare reform. *Journal of Social Issues Special Issue: The Impact of Welfare Reform, 56,* 727– 746.

Scott, R. R., Balch, P., & Flynn, T. C. (1983). A comparison of community attitudes toward CMHC services and clients with those of mental hospitals. *American Journal of Community Psychology, 11,* 741–749.

Searight, H. R., Oliver, J. M., & Grisso, J. T. (1986). The community competence scale in the placement of the deinstitutionalized mentally ill. *American Journal of Community Psychology, 14,* 291–301.

Sechrest, D. K. (1989). Prison "boot camps" do not measure up. *Federal Probation, 53,* 15–20.

Sechrest, L. (1993). Preventing problems in prevention research. *American Journal of Community Psychology, 21,* 665– 672.

Seekins, T., & Fawcett, S. B. (1987). Effects of a poverty-clients agenda on resource allocations by community decision-makers. *American Journal of Community Psychology, 15,* 305–322.

Segal, S. P., Silverman, C., & Baumohl, J. (1989). Seeking person-environment fit in community care placement. *Journal of Social Issues, 45,* 49–64.

Seidman, E. (1983). Unexamined premises of social problem solving. In E. Seidman (Ed.), *Handbook of social intervention.* Beverly Hills: Sage.

Seidman, E. (1990). Pursuing the meaning and utility of social regularities for community psychology. In P. Tolan, C. Keys, F. Chertak, & L. Jason (Eds.), *Researching community psychology: Issues of theory and methods.* Washington, DC.: American Psychological Association.

Seigel, J. M., & Kuykendall, D. H. (1990). Loss, widowhood, and psychological distress among the elderly. *Journal of Consulting and Clinical Psychology, 58,* 519–524.

Seitz, V., Apfel, N. H., & Rosenbaum, L. K. (1991). Effects of an intervention program for pregnant adolescents: Educational outcomes at two years postpartum. *American Journal of Community Psychology, 19,* 911–930.

Seitz, V., Apfel, N., & Efron, C. (1977). *Long-term effects of early intervention: A longitudinal investigation.* Paper presented at the Annual Meeting of the American Association for the Advancement of Science. Denver, CO.

Seligman, M. E. P. (1975). *Helplessness: On depression, development, and death.* San Francisco: W. H. Freeman.

Selye, H. (1956). *The stress of life.* New York: McGraw-Hill.

Selye, H. (1974). *Stress without distress.* Philadelphia: J. B. Lippincott.

Selznick, P. (2000). Reflections on responsibility: More than just following the rules. *The Responsive Community, 10,* 57– 61.

Serrano-Garcia, I. (1990). Implementing research: Putting our values to work. In P. Tolan, C. Keys, F. Chertak, & L. Jason (Eds.), *Researching community psychol-*

ogy: Issues of theory and methods. Washington, DC: American Psychology Association.

Serrano-Garcia, I. (1994). The ethics of the powerful and the power of ethics. *American Journal of Community Psychology, 22,* 1–20.

Serrano-Garcia, I., Lopez, M. M., & Rivera-Medena, E. (1987). Toward a social-community psychology. *Journal of Community Psychology, 15,* 431–446.

Seybold, J., Fretz, J., & MacPhee, D. (1991). Relationship of social support to the self-perception of mothers with delayed children. *Journal of Community Psychology, 19,* 29–36.

Seyfried, S. F. (1998). Academic achievement of African American preadolescents: The influence of teacher perceptions. *American Journal of Community Psychology, 26,* 381–402.

Shadish, W. R., Cook, T. D., & Leviton, L. C. (1991). *Foundations of program evaluation: Theories of practice.* Newbury Park, CA: Sage.

Shadish, W. R., Jr. (1990). Defining excellence criteria in community research. In P. Tolan, C. Keys, F. Chertak, & L. Jason (Eds.), *Researching community psychology: Issues of theory and methods.* Washington, DC: American Psychological Association.

Shadish, W. R., Lurigio, S. J., & Lewis, D. A. (1989a). After deinstitutionalization: The present and future of mental health long-term care policy. *Journal of Social Issues, 45,* 1–15.

Shadish, W. R., Lurigio, S. J., & Lewis, D. A. (Eds.). (1989b). After deinstitutionalization. *Journal of Social Issues, 45.*

Shadish, W. R., Thomas, S., & Bootzin, R. R. (1982). Criteria for success in deinstitutionalization: Perceptions of nursing homes by different interest groups. *American Journal of Community Psychology, 10,* 553–566.

Shadur, M. A., Kienzie, R., & Rodwell, J. J. (1999). The relationship between organizational climate and employee perceptions of involvement: The importance of support. *Group & Organization Management, 24,* 479–503.

Sharstein, S. (2000). Whatever happened to community mental health? *Psychiatric Services, 51,* 616–620.

Shealy, C. N. (1995). From Boys Town to Oliver Twist: Separating fact from fiction in welfare reform and out-of-home placement of children and youth. *American Psychologist, 50,* 565–580.

Shepard, L. A., Graue, M. E., & Catto, S. (1989). *Delayed entry into kindergarten and escalation of academic demands.* Paper presented at the annual meeting of the American Educational Research Association, San Francisco, CA.

Shephard, R. J., Cox, M., & Corey, P. (1981). Fitness program: Its effect on workers' performance. *Journal of Occupational Medicine, 23,* 359–363.

Shepherd, M. D., Schoenberg, M., Slavich, S., Wituk, S., Warren, M., & Meissen, G. (1999). Continuum of professional involvement in self-help groups. *Journal of Community Psychology, 27,* 39–53.

Shernock, S. K. (1988). An empirical examination of the relationship between police solidarity and community orientation. *Journal of Police Science and Administration, 16,* 182–194.

Shinn, M. (1990). Mixing and matching: Levels of conceptualization, measurement, and statistical analysis in community research. In P. Tolan, C. Keys, F. Chertok, & L. Jason (Eds.), *Research community psychology.* Washington, DC: American Psychological Association.

Shinn, M. (1992). Homelessness: What is a psychologist to do? *American Journal of Community Psychology, 20,* 1–24.

Shinn, M. (1997). Family homelessness: State or trait. *American Journal of Community Psychology, 25,* 755–769.

Shinn, M., & Gillespie, C. (1993). *Structural vs. individual explanation for homelessness: Implications for intervention.* Paper presented at the ninth annual Northeast Community Psychology Conference, New York.

Shinn, M., Knickman, J. R., Ward, D., Petrovi, N. L., & Muth, B. J. (1990). Alternative models for sheltering homeless families. *Journal of Social Issues, 46,* 175–190.

Shinn, M., Lehmann, S., & Wong, N. W. (1984). Social interaction and social support. *American Journal of Community Psychology, 40,* 55–76.

Shinn, M., Morch, H., Robinson, P. E., & Neuer, R. A. (1993). Individual, group, and agency strategies for coping with job stressors in residential child care programmes. *Journal of Community and Applied Social Psychology, 3,* 313–324.

Shinn, M., & Perkins, D. N. T. (2000). Contributions from organizational psychology. In J. Rappaport & E. Seidman (Eds.), *Handbook of community psychology.* New York: Plenum.

Shinn, M., Rosario, M., Morch, H., & Chestnut, D. E. (1984). Coping with job stress and burnout in the human services. *Journal of Personality and Social Psychology, 46,* 864–876.

Shinn, M., & Tsemberis, S. (1998). Is housing the cure for homelessness? In X. Arriaga & S. Oskamp (Eds.). *Addressing community problems: Psychological research and interventions.* Thousand Oaks, CA: Sage.

Shinn, M., & Weitzman, B. C. (1990). Research on homelessness: An introduction. *Journal of Social Issues, 46,* 1–11.

Shinn, M., Weitzman, B. C., Strojanovic, D., Knickman, J. R., Jimenez, L., Duchon, L., James, S., & Krantz, D. H. (1998). Predictors of homelessness among families in New York City: From shelter request to housing stability. *American Journal of Public Health, 88,* 1651–1657.

Shinn, M., Wong, N., Simko, P., & Ortiz-Torres, B. (1989). Promoting the well-being of working parents: Coping, social support, and flexible job schedules. *American Journal of Community Psychology, 17,* 31–55.

Shumaker, S. A., & Brownell, A. (1984). Toward a theory of social support: Closing conceptual gaps. *Journal of Social Issues, 40,* 11–36.

Shumaker, S. A., & Brownell, A. (1985). Introduction: Social support interventions. *Journal of Social Issues, 41,* 1–4.

Shure, M. B. (1997). Interpersonal cognitive problem-solving: Primary prevention of high-risk behaviors in the preschool and primary years. In G. W. Albee & T. P. Gullotta (Eds.), *Primary prevention works.* Thousand Oaks, CA: Sage.

Shure, M. B. (April 1999). Preventing violence the problem-solving way. *Juvenile Justice Bulletin,* 1–10.

Shure, M. B., & Spivack, G. (1988). Interpersonal cognitive problem solving. In R. H. Price, E. L. Cowan, R. P. Lorion, & J. Ramos-McKay (Eds.), 14 ounces of *prevention: A casebook for practitioners.* Washington, DC: American Psychological Association.

Siegel, J., & Kuykendall, D. A. (1990). Loss, widowhood, and psychological distress among the elderly. *Journal of Consulting and Clinical Psychology, 58,* 519–524.

Silberman, C. E. (1980). Race, culture, and crime. In B. H. Kelly (Ed.), *Criminal behavior: Readings in criminology.* New York: St. Martin's Press.

Sime, W. E. (1984). Psychological benefits of exercise training in the healthy individual. In J. D. Matarazzo, S. M. Weiss, J. A. Herd, N. E. Miller, & S. M. Weiss (Eds.), *Behavioral health: A handbook of health enhancement and disease prevention.* New York: Wiley.

Singer, M. (1994a). AIDS and the health crisis of the US urban poor: The perspective of critical medical anthropology. *Social Science and Medicine, 39,* 931–948.

Singer, M. (1994b). Implementing a community-based AIDS prevention program for ethnic minorities: The Comunidad y Responsibilidad Project. In J. P. Van Vugt (Ed.). *AIDS prevention and services: Commu-*
nity based research (pp. 59–92). Westport, CT: Gergin and Garvey.

Singer, M., & Borrero, M. (1984). Indigenous treatment for alcoholism: The evidence for Puerto Rican spiritism. *Medical Anthropology, 8,* 246–273.

Singer, M., Flores, C., Davison, L., Burke, G., Castillo, Z., Scaon, K., & Rivera, M. (1990). SIDA: The economic, social, and cultural context of AIDS among Latinos. *Medical Anthropology Quarterly, 4,* 73–117.

Singer, M., & Weeks, M. R. (1996). Preventing AIDS in communities of color: Anthropology and social prevention. *Human Organization, 55,* 488–492.

Singleton, J. (2000). Women caring for elderly family members: Shaping non-traditional work and family initiatives. *Journal of Comparative Family Studies, 31,* 367–375.

Siska, D. (1998, March/April). Boom time. *Foundation News and Commentary.* www.cof.org/fnc/28growth.htm#Growth

Slavin, R. (1996). Cooperative learning in middle and secondary schools. (Special section: young adolescents at risk). *Clearing House, 69,* 200–205.

Slavin, R. E. (1985). Cooperative learning: Applying contact theory in desegregated schools. *Journal of Social Issues, 41,* 45–62.

Sloan, H. A., & Schrieber, D. E. (1971). *Hospital management: An evaluation* (Monograph 4). Madison, WI: Bureau of Business.

Smith, D. B. (1986). The effect of intermediate treatment on a local juvenile criminal justice system. *Journal of Community Psychology, 14,* 278–288.

Smith, M. L., & Shepard, L. A. (1988). Kindergarten readiness and retention: A qualitative study of teachers' beliefs and practices. *American Education Research Journal, 25,* 307–333.

Smither, R. D. (1998). *The psychology of work and human performance.* New York: Longman.

Snell, T. L. (1996, December). Capital punishment, 1995. *Bureau of Justice Statistics Bulletin,* 1–16.

Snowden, L. R. (1987). The peculiar successes of community psychology: Service delivery to ethnic minorities and the poor. *American Journal of Community Psychology, 15,* 575–586.

Snowden, L. R. (1992). Community psychology and the "severely mentally ill." *The Community Psychologist, 25,* 3.

Snowden, L. R. (1993). Emerging trends in organizing and financing human services: Unexamined consequences for ethnic minority populations. *American Journal of Community Psychology, 21,* 1–13.

Snowden, L. R., Martinez, M., & Morris, A. (2000). Community psychology and ethnic minority populations.

In J. Rappaport & E. Seidman (Eds.), *Handbook of community psychology*. New York: Plenum.

Society for Community Research and Action. (1994). *Final report of the task force on homeless women, children, and families*. Washington, DC: American Psychological Associaton.

Solarz, A. (2000). Who are we? A little look at ourselves. *The Community Psychologist, 33*, 4–6.

Solarz, A. L. (2001). Investing in children, families, and communities: Challenges for an interdivisional public policy collaboration. *American Journal of Community Psychology, 29*, 1–14.

Solarz, A., & Bogat, G. A. (1990). When social support fails: The homeless. *Journal of Community Psychology, 18*, 79–96.

Solomon, D., Watson, M., Battisch, V., Schaps, E., & Delucchi, K. (1996). Creating classrooms that students experience as communities. *American Journal of Community Psychology, 24*, 719–748.

Solomon, M., Pistrang, N., & Barker, C. (2001). The benefits of mutual support groups for parents of children with disabilities. *American Journal of Community Psychology, 29*, 113–160.

Sontag, S. (1993*). Illness as metaphor; AIDS and its metaphors*. New York: Doubleday.

Sosin, M. R., Colson, P., & Grossman, S. (1990). *Homelessness in Chicago: Poverty and pathology, social institutions, and social change*. Chicago: University of Chicago, School of Social Service Administration.

Sosin, M., Piliavin, I., & Westerfelt, H. (1990). Toward a longitudinal analysis of homelessness. *Journal of Social Issues, 46*, 157–174.

Special Section: Papers from the CDC-ATSDR Workshop on the use of race and ethnicity in public health surveillance. (1994). *Public Health Reports, 109*, 4–52.

Speer, P. W., & Hughey, J. (1995). Community organizing: An ecological route to empowerment and power. *American Journal of Community Psychology, 23*, 729–748.

Speer, P., Dey, A., Griggs, P., Gibson, C., Lubin, B., & Hughey, J. (1992). In search of community: An analysis of community psychology research from 1984–1988. *American Journal of Community Psychology, 20*, 195–209.

Speigel, H. (1987). Coproduction in the context of neighborhood development. *Journal of Voluntary Research, 16*, 54–61.

Spillman, B. C., & Pezzin, L. E. (2000). Potential and active family caregivers: Changing networks and the "sandwich generation." *Millbank Quarterly, 78*, 347–374.

Spitzer, R. J. (Summer 1999). The gun dispute. *American Educator*, 10–17.

Spivack, G., & Marcus, J. (1987). Marks and classroom adjustment as early indicators of mental health at age twenty. *American Journal of Community Psychology, 15*, 35–56.

Spoth, R. (1997). Challenges in defining and developing the field of rural mental disorder preventive intervention research. *American Journal of Community Psychology, 25*, 425–448.

Spoth, R., Redmond, C., Hockaday, C., & Yoo, S. (1996). Protective factors and young adolescent tendency to abstain from alcohol use: A model using two waves of intervention study data. *American Journal of Community Psychology, 24*, 749–770.

Sprague, J., & Hayes, J. (2000). Self-determination and empowerment: A feminist standpoint analysis of talk about disability. *American Journal of Community Psychology, 28*, 671–695.

Spreitzer, G. M. (1995). An empirical test of a comprehensive model of intrapersonal empowerment in the workplace. *American Journal of Community Psychology, 23*, 601–629.

St. Onge, M., & Lavoie, F. (1997). The experience of caregiving among mothers of adults suffering from psychotic disorders: Factors associated with their psychological distress. *American Journal of Community Psychology, 25*, 73–94.

Stack, L. C., Lannon, P. B., & Miley, A. D. (1983). Accuracy of clinicians' expectancies for psychiatric rehospitalization. *American Journal of Community Psychology, 11*, 99–113.

Stein, L. I., & Test, M. A. (1980). An alternative to mental hospital treatment. I: Conceptual model, treatment program, and clinical evaluation. *Archives of General Psychiatry, 37*, 392–397.

Stein, L. I., & Test, M. A. (1985). The training in community living model: A decade of experience. In *New directions for mental health services* (Vol. 26). San Francisco: Jossey-Bass.

Stevens, G. B., & O'Neill, P. (1983). Expectation and burnout in the developmental disabilities field. *American Journal of Community Psychology, 11*, 615–628.

Stoelwinder, J. U., & Clayton, P. S. (1978). Hospital organization development: Changing the focus from "better management" to "better patient care." *Journal of Applied Behavioral Science, 14*, 400–414.

Stone, C. (April 1999). *Race, crime, and the administration of justice*. National Institute of Justice, pp. 26–32.

Streeter, C. L., & Franklin, C. (1991). Psychological and family differences between middle class and low income dropouts: A discriminant analysis. *High School Journal, 74*, 211–219.

Strother, C. R. (1987). Reflections on the Stanford Conference and Subsequent events. *American Journal of Community Journal, 15,* 519–522.

Struening, E. L., & Padgett, D. K. (1990). Physical health status, substance use and abuse, and mental disorders among homeless adults. *Journal of Social Issues, 46,* 65–81.

Strunin, L. (1991). Adolescents' perception of risk for HIV infection: Implications for future research. *Social Sciences Medicine, 32,* 221–228.

Suarez-Balcazar, Y., Durlak, J. A., & Smith, C. (1994). Multicultural training practices in community psychology programs, *American Journal of Community Psychology, 22,* 785–798.

Sue, S., Fujino, D., Hu, L., Takeuchi, D., & Zane, N. (1991). Community mental health services for ethnic minority groups: A test of the cultural responsiveness hypothesis. *Journal of Consulting and Clinical Psychology, 59,* 533–540.

Suffering in the streets. (1984, September 15). *The New York Times,* p. A20.

Sullivan, G., Koegel, P., Kanouse, D. E., Cournos, F., McKinnon, K., Young, A. S., & Bean D. (1999). HIV and people with serious mental illness: The public sector's role in reducing HIV risk and improving care. *Psychiatric Services, 50,* 648–652.

Sundberg, N. D. (1985). The use of future studies in training for prevention and promotion in mental health. Journal of Primary Prevention, 6, 98–114.

Sundel, M., & Schanie, C. E. (1978). Community mental health and mass media preventive education: The alternatives project. *Social Service Review, 52,* 297–306.

Sundstrom, E., DeMeuse, K. P., & Futrell, D. (1990). Work teams. *American Psychologist, 45,* 120–133.

Surgeon Generals Office. (2001). *The Surgeon General's call to action to promote sexual health and responsible sexual behavior.* Washington, DC: Author.

Susser, E., Moore, R., & Link, B. (1993). Risk factors for homelessness. In H. K. Armenian, L. Gordis, J. L. Kelsey, M. Levine, & S. B. Thacker (Eds.), *Epidemiologic reviews* (Vol. 15). Baltimore, MD: The Johns Hopkins University School of Hygiene and Public Health.

Susser, E., Valencia, E., & Conover, S. (1993). Prevalence of HIV infection among psychiatric patients in a New York City men's shelter. *American Journal of Public Health, 83,* 55–57.

Svec, H. (1987). Youth advocacy and high school dropout. *High School Journal, 70,* 185–192.

Svyantek, D. J., Goodman, S. A., Benz, L. L., & Gard, J. (1999). The relationship between organizational characteristics and team building success. *Journal of Business & Psychology, 14,* 265–283.

Swift, C., & Levin, G. (1987). Empowerment: An emerging mental health technology. *Journal of Primary Prevention, 8,* 71–94.

Sy, F. S., Chng, C. L., Choi, S. T., & Wong, F. Y. (1998). Epidemiology of HIV and AIDS among Asian and Pacific Islander Americans. *AIDS Education and Prevention, 10* (Supplement A), 4–18.

Szasz, T. S. (1961). *The myth of mental Illness.* New York: Dell.

Taber, T. D., Cooke, R. A., & Walsh, J. T. (1990). A joint business-community approach to improve problem solving by workers displaced in a plant shutdown. *Journal of Community Psychology, 18,* 19–33.

Talbott, J. A. (1975). Current cliches and platitudes in vogue in psychiatric vocabularies. *Hospital and Community Psychiatry, 26,* 530.

Tarantola, D., & Mann, J. (1993). Coming to terms with the AIDS epidemic. Issues: *In Science and Technology, 9,* 41–48.

Taulé-Lunblad, J., Galbavy, R., & Dowrick, P. (2000). Putting the cool into after school: Responsive after-school community learning centers. *The Community Psychologist, 33,* 33–34.

Tausig, M. (1987). Detecting "cracks" in mental health service systems: Application of Network Analytic Techniques. *American Journal of Community Psychology, 15,* 337–351.

Taylor, L. C. (2001). Work attitudes, employment barriers, and mental health symptoms in a sample of rural welfare recipients. *American Journal of Community Health, 105,* 443–463.

Taylor, L. W., & Tao, L. S. (1980). E.E.O.C.'s improved case management system. *Management, 1,* 14–16.

Taylor, L., Zuckerman, B., Harik, V., & Groves, B. M. (1994). Witnessing violence by young children and their mothers. *Journal of Developmental and Behavioral Pediatrics, 15,* 120–123.

Taylor, R. B., & Shumaker, S. A. (1990). Local crime as a natural disaster: Implications for understanding the relationship between disorder and fear of crime. *American Journal of Community Psychology, 18,* 619–641.

Taylor, R. L., Lam, D. J., Roppel, C. E., & Barter, J. J. (1984). Friends can be good medicine: An excursion into mental health promotion. *Community Mental Health Journal, 20,* 294–303.

Taylor, S. E. (1986–87). The impact of an alternative high school program on students labeled "deviant." *Educational Research Quarterly, 11,* 8–12.

Taylor, S. E., Helgeson, V. S., Reed, G. M., & Skokan, L. A. (1991). Self-generated feelings of control and adjustment to physical illness. *Journal of Social Issues, 47,* 91–110.

Tebes, J. K., & Kraemer, D. T. (1991). Quantitative and qualitative knowing in mutual support research: Some lessons from the recent history of scientific psychology. *American Journal of Community Psychology, 19,* 739–756.

Terpstra, D. E., Olson, P. D., & Lockeman, B. (1982). The effects of MBO on levels of performance and satisfaction among university faculty. *Group and Organization Studies, 7,* 356–366.

Terris, M., & Terris, L. D. (1990). Editorial. Confusion worse confounded: Health promotion and prevention. *Journal of Public Health Policy, 11,* 144–145.

Tetzloff, C. E., & Barrera, M. (1987). Divorcing mothers and social support: Testing the specificity of buffering effects. *American Journal of Community Psychology, 15,* 419–434.

Thatcher, J., & Howard, M. (1989). Enhancing professional effectiveness: Management training for the head teacher. *Educational and Child Psychology, 6,* 45–50.

The Center on Philanthropy. (April 18, 2001). *Report on the December 2000 Philanthropic Giving Index.* www.philanthropy.IUPUI.edu

The Nation's Health. (August 2001). *Arizona smoking rates decli*ne. Washington, DC: Author.

The White House. (1998, May 16). *Remarks by the President in apology for study done in Tuskegee* (press release). Washington, DC: Office of the Press Secretary.

Thoits, P. A. (1983). Multiple identities and psychological well-being: A reformulation and test of the social hypothesis. *American Sociological Review, 48,* 174–187.

Thomas, E., Rickel, A. U., Butler, C., & Montgomery, E. (1990). Adolescent pregnancy and parenting. *Journal of Primary Prevention, 10,* 195–206.

Thompson, M. P., & Norris, F. H. (1992). Crime, social status and alienation. *American Journal of Community Psychology, 20,* 97–119.

Thompson, S. C., & Spacespan, S. (1991). Perceptions of control in vulnerable populations. *Journal of Social Issues, 47,* 1–21.

Tice, C. H. (1991). Developing informal networks of caring through intergenerational connections in school settings. *Marriage and Family Review, 16,* 377–389.

Tierney, J. P, Grossman, J. B., & Resch, N. (1995). *Making a difference: An impact study of Big Brother/Big Sister.* Philadelphia Public/Private Ventures.

Tobin, S. S. (1988). Preservation of the self in old age. Special issue: Life transitions in the elderly. *Social Casework, 69,* 550–555.

Tobler, N. S., Ronna, M., Ochshorn, P., Marshall, D. G., Streke, A., & Stackpole, K. M. (2000). School-based adolescent drug prevention programs: 1998 meta-analysis. *The Journal of Primary Prevention, 20,* 275–336.

Toch, H., & Adams, K. (1987). The person as dumping ground: Mainlining disturbed offenders. *Journal of Psychiatry and Law, 15,* 539–553.

Tolan, P. H., & Lorion, R. P. (1988). Multivariate approaches to the identification of delinquency proneness in adolescent males. *American Journal of Community Psychology, 16,* 547–561.

Tolan, P. H., Perry, M. S., & Jones, T. (1987). Delinquency prevention: An example of consultation in rural community mental health. *Journal of Community Psychology, 15,* 43–50.

Tolan, P., Keys, C., Chertak, F., & Jason, L. (1990). *Researching community psychology.* Washington, DC: American Psychological Association.

Toro, P. A. (1986). A comparison of natural and professional help. *American Journal of Community Psychology, 14,* 147–159.

Toro, P. A. (1990). Evaluating professionally operated and self-help programs for the seriously mentally ill. *American Journal of Community Psychology, 18,* 903–907.

Torrey, E. F. (1997, June). The release of the mentally ill from institutions: A well-intentional disaster. *The Chronicle of Higher Education,* pp. B4–B5.

Tosi, H. L., Rizzo, J. R., & Carroll, S. J. (1986). *Managing organizational behavior.* Marshfield, MA: Pitman.

Tracey, T. J., Sherry, P., & Keitel, M. (1986). Distress and help-seeking as a function of person-environment fit and self-efficacy: A causal model. *American Journal of Community Psychology, 14,* 657–676.

Tramontana, M. G., Hooper, S. R., & Selzer, S. C. (1988). Research on the preschool prediction of later academic achievement: A review. *Developmental Review, 8,* 89–146.

Traynor, M. P., Begay, M. E., & Glantz, S. A. (1993). New tobacco industry strategy to prevent local tobacco control. *Journal of the American Medical Association, 270,* 479–486.

Trickett, E. J., McConahay, J. B., Phillips, D., & Ginter, M. A. (1985). Natural experiments and the educational context: The environment and effects of an alternative inner-city public school on adolescents. *American Journal of Community Psychology, 13,* 617–643.

Trimble, J. E., Bolek, C. S., & Niemcryk, S. J. (Eds.). (1992). *Ethnic and multicultural drug abuse: Perspectives on current research.* New York: Harrington Park Press.

Trotter, R. T. (1995). Drug use, AIDS, and ethnography: Advanced ethnographic research methods exploring the HIV epidemic. In R. H. Needle, S. G. Gesner, & R. T. Trotter (Eds.), *Social networks, drug abuse, and*

HIV transmission (pp. 38–53). Rockville, MD: National Institute on Drug Abuse.

Turman, K. M. (January/February 2001). Crime victims. *National Criminal Justice Reference Service Catalog*, p. 14.

Turner, D. N., & Saunders, D. (1990). Medical relabeling in gamblers anonymous: The construction of an ideal member. *Small Group Research: An International Journal of Theory, Investigation and Application, 21,* 59–78.

Turner, H. A., & Catania, J. A. (1997). Informal caregiving to persons with AIDS in the United States: Caregiver burden among central cities' residents eighteen to forty-nine years old. *American Journal of Community Psychology, 25,* 35– 59.

Turner, J. B., Kessler, R. C., & House, J. S. (1991). Factors facilitating adjustment to unemployment: Implications for intervention. *American Journal of Community Psychology, 19,* 521–524.

Turnipseed, D. L. (1998). Anxiety and burnout in the health care work environment. *Psychological Reports, 82,* 627–642.

U.S. Bureau of the Census. (1987). *Statistical abstract of the United States,* 1988 (108th ed.). Washington, DC: U.S. Department of Commerce.

U.S. Bureau of the Census. (1999). *Statistical abstract of the United States* (119th ed.). Washington, DC: U.S. Government Printing Office.

U.S. Bureau of the Census. (March 12, 2001). *Population change and distribution: Census 2000 brief.* www.census.gov/ population/cen2000/c2kbr012pdf

U.S. Bureau of the Census. (September 1997). America's children at risk. *Census Brief.* Washington, DC: Department of Commerce.

U.S. Bureau of the Census. (2001). *Older Americans 2000: Key indicators of well- being (Federal Interagency forum on aging-related statistics)* www.agingstats.govchartbook2001/population.html

U.S. Bureau of Justice Statistics. (1999, January). *Substance abuse and treatment of state and federal prisoners, 1997,* 1– 16.

U.S. Bureau of Labor Statistics. (1992, June). *Current labor statistics: Employment data. Monthly labor review.* Washington, DC: Author.

U.S. Department of Education. (1998). *Guide to safe schools.* Washington, DC: Author.

U.S. Department of Health and Human Services. (1991). *Healthy people 2000: National health promotion and disease prevention objectives.* DHHS publication number (PHS) 91–50212. Washington, DC: Superintendent of Documents, U.S. Government Printing Office.

U.S. Department of Health and Human Services. (2001). *A national strategy to prevent teen pregnancy.* www.Aspe.hhs.gov/ hsp/teenp/intro.lhtm

U.S. Department of Justice. (1988). *Criminal victimization in the United States, 1986. A national crime survey report.* Washington, DC: U.S. Department of Justice, Bureau of Justice Statistics.

U.S. Department of Justice. (1995). *State crime victim compensation and assistance grant programs.* Washington, DC: Author.

U.S. Department of Justice. (1997a). *Boot camps for juvenile offenders: Program summary.* Washington, DC: Author.

U.S. Department of Justice. (1997b). *What you can do if you are a victim of crime.* Washington, DC: Author.

Umbreit, M. S. (2000). *Family group conferencing: Implications for crime victims.* Washington, DC: Office for Victims of Crime.

Umbreit, M. S., & Bradshaw, W. (1997). Victim experience of meeting adult vs. juvenile offenders: A cross-national comparison. *Federal Probation, 61,* 33–39.

Umbreit, M. S., & Greenwood, J. (2000a). *Guidelines for victim-sensitive victim- offender mediation: Restorative justice through dialogue.* Washington, DC: Office for Victims of Crime.

Umbreit, M. S., & Greenwood, J. (2000b). *National survey of victim-offender mediation programs in the United States.* Washington, DC: Office for Victims of Crime.

Umbreit, M. S., Coates, R. B., & Roberts, A. W. (2000). The impact of victim- offender mediation: A cross-national perspective. *Mediation Quarterly, 17,* 215–229.

Unger, D. G., & Wandersman, A. (1985a). The importance of neighbors: The social, cognitive and affective components of neighboring. *American Journal of Community Psychology, 13,* 139–170.

Unger, D. G., & Wandersman, L. P. (1985b). Social support and adolescent mothers: Action research contributions to theory and application. *American Journal of Community Psychology, 41,* 29–45.

United Nations Programme on HIV/AIDS (UNAIDS). (2000). *AIDS epidemic update: December 2000.* Geneva, Switzerland: Author.

United Nations Programme on HIV/AIDS (UNAIDS). (June 27, 2001). *Declaration of commitment on HIV/ AIDS.* Geneva, Switzerland: Author.

United Way. (1996). *Measuring program outcomes: A practical approach.* Alexandria, VA: Author.

USA Today. (1993, March 9). Atlanta success story, p. 10A.

USA Today. (April 20, 2001). Bad news for Hispanic girls. *USA Today,* 14A.

Valdiserri, R. O., West, G., Moore, M., Darrow, W. W., & Hinman, A. R. (1992). Structuring HIV prevention services delivery systems on the basis of social science theory. *Journal of Community Health, 17,* 259–269.

Van Fleet, D. D. (1991). *Behavior in organizations.* Boston: Houghton Mifflin.

Van Ryn, M., & Vinokur, A. D. (1992). How did it work? An examination of the mechanisms through an intervention for the unemployed promoted job-search behavior. *American Journal of Community Psychology, 20,* 577–597.

Varmus, H., & Satcher, D. (1997). Ethical complexities of conducting research in developing countries. *New England Journal of Medicine, 337,* 1003–1005.

Vartonian, T. P., & Gleason, P. M. (1999). Do neighborhood conditions affect high school dropout and college graduation rates? *The Journal of Socio-Economics, 28,* 21–41.

Vaux, A. (1991). Let's hang up and try again: Lessons learned from a social support intervention. *American Journal of Community Psychology, 19,* 85–90.

Vaux, A., & Harrison, D. (1985). Support network characteristics associated with support satisfaction and perceived support. *American Journal of Community Psychology, 13,* 245–268.

Vaux, A., Riedel, S., & Stewart, D. (1987). Modes of social support: The Social Support Behaviors (SS-B) Scale. *American Journal of Community Psychology, 15,* 209–237.

Veiel, H. O. F., Brill, G., Hafner, H., & Welz, R. (1988). The social supports of suicide attempters. The different roles of family and friends. *American Journal of Community Psychology, 16,* 839–862.

Vidal, A. P. C., Howitt, A. M., & Foster, K. P. (1986). *Stimulating community report? An assessment of the local initiative support corporation.* Cambridge, MA: John F. Kennedy School of Government.

Vidmar, N. (1992). Procedural justice and alternative dispute resolution. *Psychological Science, 3,* 224–228.

Vincent, T. A. (1990). A view from the hill: The human element in policy making on capitol hill. *American Psychologist, 45,* 61–64.

Viney, L. L. (1985). They call you a Dole Bludger. *Journal of Community Psychology, 13,* 31–45.

Vinokur, A. D., Schul, Y., Vuori, J., & Price, R. H. (2000). Two years after job loss: Long-term impact of the JOBS program on reemployment and mental health. *Journal of Occupational Health Psychology, 5,* 32–47.

Vinokur, A., & Caplan, R. D. (1986). Cognitive and affective components of life events: Their relations and effects on well-being. *American Journal of Community Psychology, 14,* 351–370.

Vladeck, D. C. (1998). *Testimony before the Senate Judiciary Committee on first amendment implications of regulating the advertising and promotion of tobacco products to children and adolescents.* www.citizen.org/litigation/briefs/ dvtobac.htm

Vogelman, L. (1990). Psychology, mental health care and the future: Is appropriate transformation in post-Apartheid South Africa possible? *Social Science and Medicine, 31,* 501–505.

Wahl, O. F., & Lefkowits, J. Y. (1989). Impact of a television film on attitudes toward mental illness. *American Journal of Community Psychology, 17,* 521–528.

Walfish, S., Polifka, J. A., & Stenmark, D. E. (1986). The job search in community psychology: A survey of recent graduates. *American Journal of Community Psychology, 14,* 237–240.

Walker, B. S. (1992, December 8). Good-humored activist back to the fray. *USA Today,* pp. B1–B2.

Walker, C. R., & Walker, S. G. (1990). The citizen and the police: A partnership in crime prevention. *Canadian Journal of Criminology, 32,* 125–135.

Walker, I., & Crogan, M. (1998). Academic performance, prejudice, and the jigsaw classroom: New pieces to the puzzle. *Journal of Community & Applied Social Psychology, 8,* 381–393.

Wallander, J. L., & Varni, J. W. (1989). Social support and adjustment in chronically ill and handicapped children. *American Journal of Community Psychology, 17,* 185–202.

Wallerstein, N., & Bernstein, S.(1988). Empowerment education: Freire's idea adapted to health education. *Health Education Quarterly, 15,* 379–394.

Walsh, R. T. (1987). A social historical note on the formal emergence of community psychology. *American Journal of Community Psychology, 15,* 523–529.

Wandersman, A. (1990). Dissemination. In P. Tolan, C. Keys, F. Cherntak, & L. Jason (Eds.), *Researching community psychology: Issues of theory and methods.* Washington, DC: American Psychological Association.

Wandersman, A., & Florin, P. (2000). Citizen participation and community organizations. In J. Rappaport & E. Seidman (Eds.). *Handbook of community psychology.* New York: Plenum.

Wandersman, A., & Nation, M. (1998). Urban neighborhoods and mental health: Psychological contributions to understanding toxicity, resilience, and interventions. *American Psychologist, 53,* 647–656.

Wandersman, A., Hallman, W., & Berman, S. (1989). How residents cope with living near a hazardous waste landfill: An example of substantive theorizing. *American Journal of Community Psychology, 17,* 575–584.

Wandersman, A., Morrissey, E., Davino, K., Seybolt, D., Crusto, C., Nation, M., Goodman, R., & Imm, P. (1998). Comprehensive quality programming and accountability: Eight essential strategies for implementing successful prevention programs. *The Journal of Primary Prevention, 19,* 3–30.

Wardlaw, D. M. (2000). Persistent themes in the history of community psychology: A preliminary analysis of The Community Psychologist or do we have an identity after all? *The Community Psychologist, 33,* 15–18.

Warner, R. (1989). Deinstitutionalization: How did we get where we are? *Journal of Social Issues, 45,* 17–30.

Warren-Sohlberg, L., Jason, L. A., Orosan-Weine, A. M., Lantz, G. D., & Reyes, O. (1998). Implementing and evaluating preventive programs for high-risk transfer students. *Journal of Educational & Psychological Consultation, 9,* 309–324.

Wasik, B. H., Ramey, C. T., Bryant, D. M., & Sparling, J. J. (1990). A longitudinal study of two early intervention strategies: Project CARE. *Child Development, 61,* 1682–1696.

Watson, R. E. L. (1986). The effectiveness of increased police enforcement as a general deterrent. *Law and Society Review, 20,* 293–299.

Watters, J. K., Downing, M., Case, P., Lorvick, J., Cheng, Y., & Fergusson, B. (1990). AIDS prevention for intravenous drug users in the community: Street-based education and risk behavior. *American Journal of Community Psychology, 18,* 587–596.

Watters, J., & Biernacki, P. (1989). Targeted sampling options for the study of hidden populations. *Social Problems, 36,* 416–430.

Watts, R. J. (1992). Elements of a psychology of human diversity. *Journal of Community Psychology, 20,* 116–131.

Weaver, J. (1986). Therapeutic implications of divorce mediation. *Mediation Quarterly, 12,* 75–90.

Webb, D. H. (1989). PBB: An environment contaminant in Michigan. *Journal of Community Psychology, 17,* 30–46.

Weber, E. M. (1992). Alcohol- and drug-dependent pregnant women: Laws and public policies that promote and inhibit research and the delivery of services. In M. M. Kibey & K. Asghar (Eds.), *Methodological issues in epidemiological, prevention, and treatment research on drug-exposed women and their children.* National Institute on Drug Abuse Research Monograph 117. DHHS publication number (ADM) 92–1881. Washington, DC: Superintendent of Documents, U.S. Government Printing Office.

Wechsler, H., Dowdall, G. W., Maenner, G., Gledhill-Hoyt, L., & Lee, H. (1998). Changes in binge drinking and related problems among American college students between 1993 and 1997: Results of the Harvard School of Public Health College Alcohol Study. *American College Health, 47,* 51–55.

Weed, D. S. (1990, August). *Providing consultation to primary prevention programs: Applying the technology of community psychology.* Paper presented to the Annual Convention of the American Psychological Association, Boston, MA.

Weeks, M. R. (1990). *Community outreach prevention effort: Designs in culturally appropriate AIDS intervention.* Hartford, CT: Institute for Community Research.

Weeks, M. R., Schensul, J. J., Williams, S. S., Singer M., & Grier, M. (1995). AIDS prevention for African-American and Latina women: Building culturally and gender-appropriate intervention. *AIDS Education and Prevention, 7,* 251–263.

Weeks, M. R., Singer, M., Grier, M., Hunte-Marrow, J., & Haughton, C. (1991). *Project COPE: Preventing AIDS among injection drug users and their sex partners.* Hartford, CT: Institute for Community Research.

Weigel, R. H., Wiser, P. L., & Cook, S. W. (1975). The impact of cooperative learning experiments on cross-ethnic relations and attitudes. *Journal of Social Issues, 31,* 219–244.

Weikert, D. P., Bond, J. T., & McNeil, J. T. (1978). The *Ypsilanti Perry Preschool Project: Preschool years and longitudinal results through the fourth grade.* Ypsilanti, MI: High/Scope Press.

Weikart, D. P., & Schweinhart, L. J. (1997). High/Scope Perry Preschool Program. In G. W. Albee & T. P. Gullotta (Eds.). *Primary prevention works.* Thousand Oaks, CA: Sage.

Weinberg, D. H. (1996, June). A brief look at postwar U.S. income equality. *Current Population Reports.* Washington, DC: U.S. Bureau of the Census.

Weinberg, R. B. (1990). Serving large numbers of adolescent victim-survivors: Group interventions following trauma at school. *Professional Psychology Research and Practice, 21,* 271–278.

Weinstein, R. S. (1990). The universe of alternatives in schooling: The contributions of Seymour B. Sarason to education. *American Journal of Community Psychology, 18,* 359–369.

Weinstein, R. S., Soule, C. R., Collins, F., Cone, J., Mehlhorn, M., & Simontacchi, K. (1991). Expectations and high school change: Teacher-researcher collaboration to prevent school failure. *American Journal of Community Psychology, 19,* 333–362.

Weissberg, R. P. (1990). Fidelity and adaptation: Combining the best of both perspectives. In P. Tolan, C. Keys, F. Cherntak & L. Jason (Eds.), *Researching community psychology: Issues of theory and methods.* Washington, DC: American Psychological Association.

Weitzman, B. C., Knickman, J. R., & Shinn, M. (1990). Pathways to homelessness among New York City families. *Journal of Social Issues, 46,* 125–140.

Wells, B. L., & Conviser, R. (1998). Evaluating the elimination of disparities: Issues and approaches to health status and outcome assessment. *Journal of Health Education, 29,* 16–22.

Wener, R. E., & Keys, C. (1988). The effects of changes in jail population densities on crowding sick call, and spatial behavior. *Journal of Applied Psychology, 18,* 852–866.

Wenzel, S. L. (1992). Length of time spent homeless: Implications for employment of homeless persons. *Journal of Community Psychology, 20,* 57–71.

West, S. G., Aiken, L. S., & Todd, M. (1993). Probing the effects of individual components in multiple component prevention programs. *American Journal of Community Psychology, 5,* 571–605.

Wheeler, S., Cartwright, B., Kagan, R. A., & Friedman, L. M. (1987). Do the "haves" come out ahead? Winning and losing in state supreme courts, 1870–1970: *Law and Society Review, 21,* 403–445.

White, R. W. (1959). Motivation reconsidered: The concept of competence. *Psychological Review, 66,* 297–333.

Widom, C. S. (1998). Child victims: Searching for opportunities to break the cycle of violence. *Applied & Preventive Psychology, 7,* 225–234.

Wilcox, B. L., Robbennolt, J. K., O'Keeffe, J. E., & Pynchon, M. E. (1996). Teen nonmarital childbearing and welfare: The gap between research and political discourse. *Journal of Social Issues, 52,* 71–90.

Wilcox, W. B. (1983). An historian looks at social change. *Journal of Social Issues, 39,* 9–24.

Williams, L. (1984, February). A police diversion alternative for juvenile offenders. *Police Chief,* 54–56.

Willis, T. A. (1991). Comments on Heller, Thompson, Trueba, Hogg and Vlachos-Weber: Peer support telephone dyads for elderly women. *American Journal of Community Psychology, 19,* 75–83.

Willowbrook plan worked. (1982, September 4). *The New York Times,* p. 20.

Wilson, G. T., O'Leary, K. D., & Nathan, P. (1992). *Abnormal psychology.* Englewood Cliffs, NJ: Prentice-Hall.

Wilson, G., & Lester, D. (1998). Suicide prevention by e-mail. *Crisis Intervention and Time-Limited Treatment, 4,* 81–87.

Wilson, J. B., Ellwood, D. T., & Brooks-Gunn, J. (1996). Welfare-to-work through the eyes of children. In P. L. Chase-Lansdale & J. Brooks-Gunn (Eds.), *Escape from poverty: What makes a difference for children?* New York: Cambridge University Press.

Wilson, J. J. (2000). *Safe from the start: Taking action on children exposed to violence.* Washington, DC: Office of Juvenile Justice and Delinquency Prevention.

Wilson, W. J. (1987). *The truly disadvantaged: The inner city, the underclass, and public policy.* Chicago: University of Chicago Press.

Winch, C. L., McCarthy, P., & Reese, R. G. (1993). *Factors predicting successful completion of a welfare to work program.* Paper presented at the annual meeting of the American Psychological Association, Toronto, Canada.

Winget, W. G. (1982). The dilemma of affordable child care. In E. F. Zigler & E. W. Gordon (Eds.), *Day care: Scientific and social policy issues.* Boston: Auburn House.

Winkel, F. W., & Vrij, A. (1993). Facilitating problem- and emotion-focused coping in victims of burglary: Evaluating a police crisis intervention program. *Journal of Community Psychology, 21,* 97–122.

Winkler, A. E. (1998, April). Earnings of husbands and wives in dual-earner families. *Monthly Labor Review,* 42–48.

Wittig, M. A., & Schmitz, J. (1996). Electronic grassroots organizing. *Journal of Social Issues, 52,* 53–69.

Wolchik, S. A., Ruehlman, L. S., Braver, S. L., & Sandler, I. N. (1989). Social support of children of divorce: Direct and stress buffering effects. *American Journal of Community Psychology, 17,* 485–501.

Wolff, T. (1987). Community psychology and empowerment: An activist's insights. *American Journal of Community Psychology, 15,* 151–166.

Wolff, T. (2001). Introduction. *American Journal of Community Psychology Special Issue, 29,* 165–172.

Wollert, R. The Self-Help Research Team. (1987). The self-help clearinghouse concept: An evaluation of one program and its implications for policy and practice. *American Journal of Community Psychology, 15,* 491–508.

Wong, F. Y., & Bouey, P. D. (2001). *Substance use/HIV health among urban Native Indians.* Unpublished manuscript. Washington, DC: George Washington University School of Public Health and Health Services.

Wong, F. Y., Blakely, C. H., & Worsham, S. (1991). Techniques and pitfalls of applied behavioral science research: The case of community mediation. In K. G. Duffy, J. W. Grosch, & P. V. Olczak (Eds.), *Community mediation: A handbook for practitioners and researchers.* New York: Guilford.

Wong, F. Y., Chng, C. L., & Choi, K-H. (Eds.). (1998). HIV prevention among Asian and Pacific Islander American men who have sex with men: Theories, research, applications, and policies. *AIDS Education and Prevention, 10* (Supplement A).

Woolpert, S. (1991). Victim-offender reconciliation programs. In K. G. Duffy, J. W. Grosch, & P. V. Olczak (Eds.), *Community mediation: A handbook for practitioners and researchers.* New York: Guilford.

Worchel, S., & Lundgren, S. (1991). The nature of conflict and conflict resolution. In K. G. Duffy, J. W. Grosch, & P. V. Olczak (Eds.), *Community mediation: A handbook for practitioners and researchers.* New York: Guilford.

Worchel, S., Cooper, J., & Goethals, G. R. (1991). *Understanding social psychology.* Pacific Grove, CA: Brooks/Cole.

Work, W. C., & Olsen, K. H. (1990). Evaluation of a revised fourth grade social problem solving curriculum: Empathy as a moderator of adjustive gain. *Journal of Primary Prevention, 11,* 143–157.

Work, W. C., Cowen, E., Parker, G. R., & Wyman, P. A. (1990). Stress resilient children in an urban setting. *Journal of Primary Prevention, 11,* 3–17.

World Health Organization. (1997). *Weekly Epidemiological Record, 72,* 1–26.

Wright, J. D. (1987). Testimony presented before the U.S. House of Representatives Select Committee on Children, Youth, and Families. *The crisis in homelessness: Effect on children and families.* Washington, DC: U.S. Government Printing Office.

Wright, S. C., Aron, A., McLaughlin-Volpe, T., & Ropp, S. A. (1997). The extended contact effect: Knowledge of cross-group friendships and prejudice. *Journal of Personality and Social Psychology, 73,* 73–90.

Wright, S., & Cowen, E. L. (1985). The effects of peer teaching on student perceptions of class environment, adjustment, and academic performance. *American Journal of Community Psychology, 13,* 417–432.

Wurstein, A., & Sales B. (1988). Community psychology in state legislative decision making. *American Journal of Community Psychology, 16,* 487–502.

Wyrick, P. A. (November 2000). Law enforcement referral of at-risk youth: The SHIELD program. *Juvenile Justice Bulletin,* 1–7.

Xie, J. L., & Johns, G. (1995). Job scope and stress: Can job scope be too high? *Academy of Management Journal, 38,* 1288–1309.

Yates, M., & Youniss, J. (1998). Community service and political identity development in adolescence. *Journal of Social Issues Special Issue: Political Development: Youth Growing Up in a Global Community, 54,* 495–512.

Yeich, S. (1996). Grassroots organizing with homeless people: A participatory research approach. *Journal of Social Issues, 52,* 111–121.

Yoshikawa, H. (1995). Long-term effects of early childhood programs on social outcomes and delinquency. *Future of Children, 5,* 51–75.

Youngstram, N. (1991). Psychology helps curb cigarette smoking. *The American Psychological Association Monitor, 22,* 1.

Yunus, M. (November 1999). The Grameen Bank. *Scientific American,* 114–119.

Zabin, L. S., Hirsch, M. B., Smith, E. A., Streett, R., & Hardy, J. B. (1986). Adolescent pregnancy-prevention program: A model for research and evaluation. *Journal of Adolescent Health Care, 7,* 77–87.

Zack, M. H., & McKenney, J. L. (1995). Social context and interaction in ongoing computer-supported management groups. *Organization Science, 6,* 394–422.

Zander, A. (1990). *Social psychology as social action.* San Francisco: Jossey Bass.

Zax, M., & Specter, G. A. (1974). *An introduction to community psychology.* New York: Wiley.

Zedeck, S., & Mosier, K. L. (1990). Work in the family and employing organization. *American Psychologist, 45,* 240–251.

Zigler, E. (1990). Shaping child care policies and programs in America. *American Journal of Community Psychology, 18,* 183–216.

Zigler, E. (1994). Reshaping early childhood intervention to be a more effective weapon against poverty. *American Journal of Community Psychology, 22,* 37–48.

Zigler, E. F., & Gilman, E. D. (1998). Day care and early childhood settings: Fostering mental health in young children. *Child and Adolescent Psychiatric Clinics of North America, 7,* 483–498.

Zigler, E. F., & Goodman, J. (1982). The battle for day care in America: A view from the trenches. In E. F. Zigler & E. W. Gordon (Eds.), *Day care: Scientific and social policy issues.* Boston: Auburn House.

Zigler, E. F., & Muenchow, S. (1992). *Head start: The inside story of America's most successful educational experiment.* New York: Basic Books.

Zigler, E. F., & Stevenson, M. F. (1993). *Children in a changing world: Development and social issues.* Pacific Grove, CA: Brooks/Cole.

Zigler, E., Taussig, C., & Black, K. (1992). Early childhood intervention: A promising preventative for juvenile delinquency. *American Psychologist, 17,* 997–1006.

Zigler, E. F., & Turner, P. (1982). Parents, and day care workers: A failed partnership? In E. F. Zigler & E. W. Gordon (Eds.), *Day care: Scientific and social policy issues.* Boston: Auburn House.

Zimmerman, M. A. (1995). Psychological empowerment: Issues and illustrations. *American Journal of Community Psychology, 23,* 581–599.

Zimmerman, M. A., Ramírez-Valles, J., & Maton, K. L. (1999). Resilience among urban African American male adolescents: A study of the protective effects of sociopolitical control on their mental health. *American Journal of Community Psychology, 27,* 733–751.

Zimmerman, M. A., & Rappaport, J. (1988). Citizen participation, perceived control, and empowerment. *American Journal of Community Psychology, 16,* 725–750.

Zimmerman, M. A., Reischl, T. M., Seidman, E., Rappaport, J., Toro, P., & Salem, D. A. (1991). Expansion strategies of a mutual help organization. *American Journal of Community Psychology, 19,* 251–278.

Zippay, A. (1990–91). The limits of intimates: Social networks and economic status among industrial workers. Special issue: Applications of social support and social network interventions in direct practice. *Journal of Applied Social Sciences, 15,* 75–95.

Zlotnick, C., Robertson, M. J., & Lahiff, M. (1999). Getting off the streets: Economic resources and residential exits from homelessness. *Journal of Community Psychology, 27,* 209–224.

NAME INDEX

■ ■ ■ ■ ■